Watchdogs and Whistleblowers

watchdogs and Whistleblowers

A Reference Guide to Consumer Activism

STEPHEN BROBECK AND
ROBERT N. MAYER, EDITORS

*Foreword by Jim Guest, former
president and CEO, Consumer Reports*

 GREENWOOD™

An Imprint of ABC-CLIO, LLC
Santa Barbara, California • Denver, Colorado

Library of Congress Cataloging-in-Publication Data

Watchdogs and whistleblowers : a reference guide to consumer activism / Stephen Brobeck and Robert N. Mayer, editors ; foreword by Jim Guest, former president and CEO, Consumer Reports.
    pages cm
  Includes bibliographical references and index.
   ISBN 978-1-4408-2999-4 (print : alk. paper) — ISBN 978-1-4408-3000-6 (e-book)
1. Consumer protection—United States. 2. Consumers—United States. I. Brobeck, Stephen. II. Mayer, Robert N.
   HC110.C63W38 2015
   381.3'20973—dc23   2015003930

ISBN: 978-1-4408-2999-4
EISBN: 978-1-4408-3000-6

19 18 17 16 15   1 2 3 4 5

This book is also available on the World Wide Web as an eBook.
Visit www.abc-clio.com for details.

Greenwood
An Imprint of ABC-CLIO, LLC

ABC-CLIO, LLC
130 Cremona Drive, P.O. Box 1911
Santa Barbara, California 93116-1911

This book is printed on acid-free paper ∞

Manufactured in the United States of America

Contents

Foreword by Jim Guest, former president and CEO, Consumer Reports   vii

Preface   ix

Alphabetical List of Entries   xi

Subject Guide to Entries   xv

Timeline of U.S. Consumer Activism   xix

U.S. Consumer Activism: An Overview   xxiii

Global Consumer Activism: An Overview   xxxi

Select Books on Consumer Activism   xxxv

A–Z Entries   1

Contributors   509

About the Editors   517

Index   519

Foreword

Activism for consumer protections and reforms in the marketplace began in the early twentieth century, expanded in the latter part of the century, and has accelerated in recent years in the United States and other parts of the world. Along the way, extraordinary leaders emerged, advocacy organizations formed, and growing numbers of citizens mobilized to move the balance of power in the marketplace away from dominant commercial interests and toward the consumer interest.

Watchdogs and Whistleblowers: A Reference Guide to Consumer Activism tells the story of the expanding consumer influence, action, and achievements over this period—especially in more recent years, when the lessons of the past have been reflected in the mounting successes of the present. And it tells the story in the voices of nearly a hundred consumer activists who have been in the trenches day in and day out as individual leaders and heads of activist organizations and as trailblazers in the crusade to protect and empower consumers.

Consumer activists have had a huge and continuing influence on America society, from the early antitrust, food safety, and financial protection laws to reforms passed in just the past decade. Literally thousands of federal, state, and local consumer laws and regulations have been enacted. Hundreds of new institutions—nonprofit organizations, regulatory agencies, state and local consumer offices, and more—have been formed. There is a greater societal consciousness that consumers have interests and rights distinct from those of sellers—and not only that, but that they have the ability to assert those rights, as well as more avenues than ever for doing so.

The press has extensively covered the enactment of these laws and regulations, and during the heat of battle reporters have quoted activists and cited organizations that advocated for the reforms. But beyond that, those in the media have written or broadcast very little about the actual work of consumer activists and their organizations.

Watchdogs and Whistleblowers fills this void with inside information on and analysis of nearly four dozen consumer organizations in the United States alone, along with their efforts on dozens of issues. It includes articles on activities such as legislative advocacy, regulatory advocacy, litigation, policy research, grassroots organizing, Internet activism, referenda and ballot initiatives, and other creative ways to secure consumer rights. It also provides information about consumer movements in other parts of the world.

In addition, the co-editors of *Watchdogs and Whistleblowers*, Steve Brobeck and Rob Mayer, give us insightful overview essays that provide context and show linkages between the various consumer groups and issue activism. I can't think of two people more qualified to develop and edit this one-of-a-kind encyclopedic work.

Both are PhDs—Rob Mayer in sociology, Steve Brobeck in American studies—with numerous scholarly publications. Both have written extensively about the consumer movement. Their publications include *Encyclopedia of the Consumer Movement*, published by ABC-CLIO in 1997. And they are widely known and highly respected as consumer activists themselves. For the past thirty-five years, Brobeck has headed the Consumer Federation of America, comprising more than 250 U.S. consumer groups and related organizations. For many years, Mayer was a leader in the American Council of Consumer Interests, and he is an ongoing resource to consumer groups.

I've had the good fortune to work for nearly four decades as a consumer activist. Among other things, I served for many years as chair of the board of directors of Consumer Reports (formerly Consumers Union, which still advocates under that name) and as its president and CEO from 2001 to 2014. I've also been on the governing council of Consumers International, a federation of more than 250 consumer groups from 120 countries that serves as the global voice of consumers, and I currently serve as CI's volunteer president. So I'm doubly pleased that the passionate and influential work of consumer activists in the United States and abroad has been recorded and analyzed brilliantly in this new reference work. *Watchdogs and Whistleblowers* is a must-read.

Jim Guest, former president and CEO, Consumer Reports

Preface

Consumer activism has been a powerful force both in the United States and around the world. Particularly in the past half-century, consumer advocates have created influential organizations, mobilized public support for reforms, and persuaded public policymakers to make these reforms. Just in the past decade, these advocates have played an important role in the establishment of major new consumer protections in areas as diverse as financial services, privacy, and product safety.

This reference work represents the most comprehensive, up-to-date source of information about this activism. In a historical framework, it treats advocacy-related organizations, leaders, activities, and issues. Although the work focuses the most attention on U.S. activism, more than a quarter of the 141 entries discuss consumer movements in nations or regions outside the United States.

This work is related to the *Encyclopedia of the Consumer Movement*, released in 1997, in that it was prepared by the same editors and publisher and contains much of the same type of information. However, the current volume focuses most of its attention on the eighteen-year period after the publication of the first reference work. Furthermore, this book discusses issue activism in much greater detail than the earlier work. This discussion features accounts of this activism by leading consumer advocates.

The entries are arranged alphabetically. To facilitate their location, alternative titles for some entries are listed alphabetically. For example, the cross-reference listing of "Automobile Safety Advocacy" refers readers to the entry "Motor Vehicle Safety Advocacy." A detailed index is available to locate not only entries, but also specific information within entries.

Entries range in length from about 500 words to about 4,000 words. At the end of each article are cross-references to other related entries and sources for further reading. After the entries, and before the index, is a list of select books on consumer activism, some written by activists themselves, that represent important works about consumer advocacy in the United States. A timeline of important events—such as enactment of major federal legislation and establishment of national consumer organizations in the United States—introduces the articles, and two essays—on U.S. and worldwide activism—provide an integrative overview of the entries.

A unique feature of this reference work is that leading advocates have written many entries. In the dearth of scholarship about specific consumer organizations and issues, these contributions provide new and important information about consumer activism. Any bias of these activist authors is constrained by several factors. The authors are well educated—the large majority have advanced or professional degrees—and so are aware of scholarly norms of objectivity and balance. The editors instructed these authors to include certain types of information in their articles and to write about their topic as a detached third party. The editors then not only carefully reviewed, and sometimes rewrote, the articles, but also often sent them to others for review. To us, the risk of any remaining author bias is far outweighed by the benefit of first-hand author insight.

Many persons made important contributions to this book. We are most grateful to the authors for making time in their often hectic work lives to prepare their articles, as well as for working with us constructively to make any needed improvements. We are also indebted to two Consumer Federation of America staffers—Sara Cooper, who assisted in numerous ways, and Anna Marie Lowery, who worked with the publisher on its "author website" and facilitated author approvals of the publisher's contract. We also wish to thank ABC-CLIO. It was a pleasure to work with this well-established, high-quality publisher in the mid-1990s on our earlier encyclopedia. We have been just as pleased by our experience with ABC-CLIO on the current volume. Editor Stephen Gutierrez offered much useful advice as we developed the entries, and Senior Editor Hilary Claggett provided invaluable guidance as we completed the manuscript. Finally, we are grateful to our wives—Susan and Carol—for their patience and support.

Stephen Brobeck
Robert N. Mayer

Alphabetical List of Entries

AARP

Action for Children's Television

Advertising Advocacy

Advocates for Highway and Auto Safety

AFRICAN CONSUMER MOVEMENTS. *See* East African Consumer Movements; Kenyan Consumer Movement; West African Consumer Movements

Air Travel Advocacy

All-Terrain Vehicle Advocacy

American Council on Consumer Interests

Americans for Financial Reform

Antitrust Advocacy

Appliance Efficiency Advocacy

ATTORNEYS GENERAL. *See* State Attorneys General

Australian Consumer Movement

Austrian Consumer Movement

AUTOMOBILE INSURANCE ADVOCACY. *See* Insurance Advocacy

AUTOMOBILE SAFETY ADVOCACY. *See* Motor Vehicle Safety Advocacy

AVIATION SAFETY ADVOCACY. *See* Air Travel Advocacy

BALLOT PROPOSITIONS. *See* Initiatives and Referenda

Baltic Consumer Movements: Estonia, Lithuania, and Latvia

BANKRUPTCY REFORM ADVOCACY. *See* Credit Card Advocacy

BEUC: The European Consumer Organisation

Boycotts

Brazilian Consumer Movement

BRITISH CONSUMER MOVEMENT. *See* United Kingdom Consumer Movement

Cable Television Regulation

Canadian Consumer Movement

Caribbean Consumer Movements

Center for Auto Safety

Center for Digital Democracy

Center for Food Safety

Center for Responsible Lending

Center for Science in the Public Interest

Center for the Study of Services/Consumers' Checkbook

Central American Consumer Movements

Central and Eastern European Consumer Movements

CHECKBOOK MAGAZINE. *See* Center for the Study of Services/Consumers' Checkbook

Chinese Consumer Movement

COMMUNICATIONS ADVOCACY. *See* Cable Television Regulation; Digital Communications Advocacy; Internet Activism; Telephone Consumer Advocacy

Community Activism

Community Nutrition Institute

Complaint Resolution

Conference of Consumer Organizations

Congressional Consumer Advocacy

Consumer Action

Consumer Cooperatives

Consumer Education Advocacy

Consumer Federation of America

CONSUMER FINANCIAL PROTECTION BUREAU. *See* Americans for Financial Reform; Legislative Advocacy

CONSUMER JOURNALISM. *See* Journalism

Consumer Leagues

CONSUMER REPORTS. *See* Consumers Union/Consumer Reports

Consumer Representation in Government Agencies

Consumer Watchdog

Consumers for Auto Reliability and Safety

Consumers International

Consumers Union/Consumer Reports

Cosmetic Safety Advocacy

Credit Card Advocacy

Credit Report and Credit Score Advocacy

CREDIT SCORE ADVOCACY. *See* Credit Report and Credit Score Advocacy

Czech Consumer Movement

Danish Consumer Movement

Debt Collection Advocacy

Deceptive and Unfair Sales Practice Protections

Digital Communications Advocacy

Dutch Consumer Movement

East African Consumer Movements

Electricity Service Advocacy

Electronic Privacy Information Center

Energy Advocacy

Families USA

FINANCIAL EDUCATION ADVOCACY. *See* Consumer Education Advocacy

Finnish Consumer Movement

Food & Water Watch

FOOD COOPERATIVES. *See* Consumer Cooperatives

Food Safety Advocacy

French Consumer Movement

Front Groups

Funeral Consumer Advocacy

German Consumer Movement

Health Insurance Advocacy

Healthcare Advocacy

HOMEOWNERS INSURANCE ADVOCACY. *See* Insurance Advocacy

Hong Kong Consumer Movement

Household Product Safety Advocacy

HOUSING COOPERATIVES. *See* Consumer Cooperatives

Indian Consumer Movement

Indonesian Consumer Movement

Initiatives and Referenda

Installment Credit Advocacy

Insurance Advocacy

INTERNATIONAL ORGANIZATION OF CONSUMERS UNIONS. *See* Consumers International

Internet Activism

INTERNET GOVERNANCE. *See* Digital Communications Advocacy

Investor Protection Advocacy

Italian Consumer Movement

Japanese Consumer Movement

Journalism

Kenyan Consumer Movement

KOREAN CONSUMER MOVEMENT. *See* South Korean Consumer Movement

Labor Movement

LATIN AMERICAN CONSUMER MOVEMENTS. *See* Central American Consumer Movements; South American Consumer Movements

LEGAL ADVOCACY. *See* Litigation

Legislative Advocacy

LIFE INSURANCE ADVOCACY. *See* Insurance Advocacy

Litigation

LOBBYING. *See* Legislative Advocacy

Malaysian Consumer Movement

Middle Eastern Consumer Movements

Mortgage Lending Reform

Motor Vehicle Fuel Economy Advocacy

Motor Vehicle Safety Advocacy

Nader, Ralph

National Association of Consumer Advocates

National Consumer Law Center

National Consumers League

NATIONAL COOPERATIVE BANK. *See* Consumer Cooperatives

National Insurance Consumer Organization

National Low Income Housing Coalition

NETHERLANDS CONSUMER MOVEMENT. *See* Dutch Consumer Movement

NETWORK NEUTRALITY. *See* Digital Communications Advocacy

Norwegian Consumer Movement

Payday Loan Advocacy

Payment Protection Advocacy

Peterson, Esther

Pew Charitable Trusts

Philippine Consumer Movement

Polish Consumer Movement

Prescription Drug Advocacy

Privacy Advocacy

Privacy Rights Clearinghouse

PRODUCT SAFETY ADVOCACY. *See* Household Product Safety Advocacy

Product Safety "Victim" Activism

Public Citizen

Public Interest Research Groups

Public Power

Public Voice for Food and Health Policy

Real Estate Brokerage Advocacy

Regulators, Consumer Advocates as

Regulatory Advocacy

Research

RURAL ELECTRIC COOPERATIVES. *See* Consumer Cooperatives

Russian Consumer Movement

SAVINGS ADVOCACY. *See* Truth in Savings Advocacy

Serbian Consumer Movement

Slovenian Consumer Movement

SMOKING. *See* Tobacco Activism

South American Consumer Movements

South Korean Consumer Movement

Spanish Consumer Movement

State and Local Consumer Advocacy Groups

State and Local Consumer Affairs Offices

State Attorneys General

State Utility Advocacy

Swedish Consumer Movement

Telecommunications Research and Action Center

Telephone Consumer Advocacy

Tenant Activism

Tobacco Activism

Tort-Related Consumer Advocacy

TRADE UNIONS. *See* Labor Movement

Transatlantic Consumer Dialogue

Truth in Savings Advocacy

TURN

U.S. Consumer Protection Agency

U.S. PUBLIC INTEREST RESEARCH GROUP. *See* Public Interest Research Groups

United Kingdom Consumer Movement

United Nations Guidelines for Consumer Protection

UTILITY ADVOCACY. *See* Electricity Service Advocacy; Energy Advocacy; State Utility Advocacy; Telephone Consumer Advocacy

"VICTIM" ACTIVISM. *See* Product Safety "Victim" Activism

Virginia Citizens Consumer Council

Warne, Colston E.

Warranty Advocacy

Warren, Elizabeth

West African Consumer Movements

Whistleblowers

Woodstock Institute

Subject Guide to Entries

CONSUMER ADVOCATE ACTIVITIES

Boycotts
Complaint Resolution
Consumer Representation in Government Agencies
Initiatives and Referenda
Internet Activism
Journalism
Legislative Advocacy
Litigation
Regulators, Consumer Advocates as
Regulatory Advocacy
Research
Whistleblowers

U.S. CONSUMER ORGANIZATIONS

AARP
Action for Children's Television
Advocates for Highway and Auto Safety
American Council on Consumer Interests
Americans for Financial Reform
Center for Auto Safety
Center for Digital Democracy
Center for Food Safety
Center for Responsible Lending
Center for Science in the Public Interest
Center for the Study of Services/Consumers' Checkbook
Community Activism
Community Nutrition Institute
Conference of Consumer Organizations
Congressional Consumer Advocacy
Consumer Action
Consumer Cooperatives
Consumer Federation of America
Consumer Leagues
Consumer Watchdog
Consumers for Auto Reliability and Safety
Consumers Union/Consumer Reports
Electronic Privacy Information Center
Families USA
Food & Water Watch
Front Groups
Labor Movement
National Association of Consumer Advocates
National Consumer Law Center
National Consumers League
National Insurance Consumer Organization
National Low Income Housing Coalition
Pew Charitable Trusts
Privacy Rights Clearinghouse
Product Safety "Victim" Activism
Public Citizen
Public Interest Research Groups
Public Power
Public Voice for Food and Health Policy
State and Local Consumer Advocacy Groups
State and Local Consumer Affairs Offices
State Attorneys General
State Utility Advocacy
Telecommunications Research and Action Center
TURN
Virginia Citizens Consumer Council
Woodstock Institute

U.S. CONSUMER LEADERS

Nader, Ralph
Peterson, Esther

Warne, Colston E.
Warren, Elizabeth

U.S. ISSUE ADVOCACY

Advertising Advocacy
Air Travel Advocacy
All-Terrain Vehicle Advocacy
Antitrust Advocacy
Appliance Efficiency Advocacy
Cable Television Regulation
Consumer Education Advocacy
Cosmetic Safety Advocacy
Credit Card Advocacy
Credit Report and Credit Score Advocacy
Debt Collection Advocacy
Deceptive and Unfair Sales Practice
    Protections
Digital Communications Advocacy
Electricity Service Advocacy
Energy Advocacy
Food Safety Advocacy
Funeral Consumer Advocacy
Healthcare Advocacy
Health Insurance Advocacy

Household Product Safety Advocacy
Installment Credit Advocacy
Insurance Advocacy
Investor Protection Advocacy
Mortgage Lending Reform
Motor Vehicle Fuel Economy Advocacy
Motor Vehicle Safety Advocacy
Payday Loan Advocacy
Payment Protection Advocacy
Prescription Drug Advocacy
Privacy Advocacy
Real Estate Brokerage Advocacy
Telephone Consumer Advocacy
Tenant Activism
Tobacco Activism
Tort-Related Consumer Advocacy
Truth in Savings Advocacy
U.S. Consumer Protection Agency
Warranty Advocacy

INTERNATIONAL CONSUMER ADVOCACY

Australian Consumer Movement
Austrian Consumer Movement
Baltic Consumer Movements: Estonia, Lithu-
    ania, and Latvia
BEUC: The European Consumer Organisation
Brazilian Consumer Movement
Canadian Consumer Movement
Caribbean Consumer Movements
Central American Consumer Movements
Central and Eastern European Consumer
    Movements
Chinese Consumer Movement
Consumers International
Czech Consumer Movement
Danish Consumer Movement
Dutch Consumer Movement
East African Consumer Movements

Finnish Consumer Movement
French Consumer Movement
German Consumer Movement
Hong Kong Consumer Movement
Indian Consumer Movement
Indonesian Consumer Movement
Italian Consumer Movement
Japanese Consumer Movement
Kenyan Consumer Movement
Malaysian Consumer Movement
Middle Eastern Consumer Movements
Norwegian Consumer Movement
Philippine Consumer Movement
Polish Consumer Movement
Russian Consumer Movement
Serbian Consumer Movement
Slovenian Consumer Movement

South American Consumer Movements
South Korean Consumer Movement
Spanish Consumer Movement
Swedish Consumer Movement
Transatlantic Consumer Dialogue

United Kingdom Consumer Movement
United Nations Guidelines for Consumer
   Protection
West African Consumer Movements

Timeline of U.S. Consumer Activism

DATE	NATIONAL ORGANIZATIONS/ PUBLICATIONS	FEDERAL LEGISLATION
1890		Sherman Antitrust Act
1891	National Consumers League	
1903	Harvey Wiley's "Poison squad"	
1904	Ida Tarbell, *History of Standard Oil Co.*	
1906	Upton Sinclair, *The Jungle*	Pure Food and Drug Act
		Meat Inspection Act
1912	Better Business Bureau	
1914		Clayton Antitrust Act
		Federal Trade Commission Act
1933	Federal Consumer Advisory Board	Banking Act (FDIC)
	Arthur Kallet, F.J. Schlink, *100,000,000 Guinea Pigs*	
1934		Communications Act
1936	Consumers Union/Consumer Reports	Food, Drug and Cosmetic Act
		Wheeler-Lea Amendment (to FTC Act)
1953	American Council on Consumer Interests	
1958		Food Additives Amendment (to FDC Act)
1960	International Organization of Consumers Unions	
1962	President Kennedy's Consumer Bill of Rights	Kefauver-Harris Amendment (to FDC Act)
1964	First Presidential Assistant for Consumer Affairs	
1965	Ralph Nader, *Unsafe at Any Speed*	
1966		National Traffic and Motor Vehicle Safety Act
		Child Protection Act
		Fair Packaging and Labeling Act
1967	David Caplovitz, *The Poor Pay More*	Wholesome Meat Act
1968	Consumer Federation of America	Truth in Lending Act
		Poultry Inspection Act
1969	National Consumer Law Center	
1970	Center for Auto Safety	Poison Prevention Packaging Act
		Fair Credit Reporting Act
1971	Public Citizen	
	Center for Science in the Public Interest	
	Consumer Action	

(Continued)

DATE	NATIONAL ORGANIZATIONS/ PUBLICATIONS	FEDERAL LEGISLATION
1972		Consumer Product Safety Act
		Motor Vehicle Information and Cost Savings Act
		Drug Listing Act
1973	National Consumer Law Center	Toxic Substances Control Act
1974	Center for the Study of Services (*Consumers' Checkbook*)	Magnuson Moss Warranty Act
		Real Estate Settlement Procedures Act
		Equal Credit Opportunity Act
		Fair Credit Billing Act
1975		Energy Policy and Conservation Act
1977		Fair Debt Collection Practices Act
1978		National Consumer Cooperative Bank Act
		Electronic Funds Transfer Act
1980	National Insurance Consumer Organization Telecommunications Research and Action Center	
1982	Families USA	
1983	U.S. PIRG	
1987		Expedited Funds Availability Act
		Appliance Energy Efficiency Act
1988		Home Equity Loan Consumer Protection Act
		Fair Credit and Credit Card Disclosure Act
1989	Advocates for Highway and Auto Safety	
1990		Safe Medical Devices Act
		Children's Television Act
1991	Center for Digital Democracy	Truth in Savings Act
		Telephone Consumer Protection Act
1992	Privacy Rights Clearinghouse	Cable Act
1994	Electronic Privacy Information Center	Telemarketing and Consumer Fraud and Abuse Prevention Act
	National Association of Consumer Advocates	
1998	Transatlantic Consumer Dialogue	
2002	Center for Responsible Lending	
2003		Fair and Accurate Credit Transactions Act
2004	Pew Charitable Trusts	
2007		Energy Independence and Security Act (CAFÉ)
		Military Lending Act

2008		Consumer Product Safety Improvement Act
2009	Americans for Financial Reform	Credit CARD Act
2010		Affordable Care Act
		Food Safety and Modernization Act
		Wall Street Reform and Consumer Protection Act

U.S. Consumer Activism: An Overview

Consumer activism in the United States can be understood as the historic inter-action of individual activists, advocacy organizations, and public policy issues in a political environment. Knowing something about each and their relationships over time provides insight into how and why this activism developed and what influence it has had on consumers and the consumer marketplace. An overview of this subject provides context to help understand U.S. consumer activism in general and the role of U.S. organizations, leaders, activities, and issue advocacy—treated in some 100 encyclopedia entries—within this activism.

Advocates

The Progressive era of the late nineteenth and early twentieth centuries saw agitation for and enactment of many significant consumer reforms, including important drug and food safety legislation and establishment of the Federal Trade Commission. Yet the consumer activists of this period were not part of organized consumer groups. Although supportive of consumer reforms, the new National Consumers League (NCL) focused most of its efforts on improving the condition of women workers. The consumer reforms of the era resulted, in large measure, from the articles and books of muckraking journalists, the work of individual activists such as Harvey Wiley, and the support of reform-minded political leaders.

In the 1950s and early 1960s, many consumer leaders were academics who focused their efforts on informing consumers about products and achieving state consumer protections. They worked as volunteer leaders of small organizations with budgets that usually could not afford paid staff. Often trained as consumer economists, they associated with each other in the American Council on Consumer Interests, a professional organization supporting consumer research and education. In the late 1960s, they joined with national organizations to found the Consumer Federation of America but several years later split from this group to form the Conference of Consumer Organizations.

The most prominent consumer leader from the 1930s to the 1970s was Amherst College professor Colston Warne. As a longtime president and board member of Consumers Union/Consumer Reports, he was instrumental in the founding of both the American Council on Consumer Interests and the International Organization of Consumers Unions (now Consumers International).

The civil rights and antiwar movements of the 1960s spawned a new group of consumer activists. Many were lawyers who were often trained by elite law schools. Ralph Nader, for example, had a Harvard law degree, and longtime Consumers Union/Consumer Reports president Rhoda Karpatkin and congressional staff activist Michael Pertschuk had degrees from Yale Law School. The highest priority of many activists recruited by Nader was improved health and safety. Nader's early work included the publication of *Unsafe at Any Speed*, after which he helped found Public Citizen and inspired the founding of the Center for Auto Safety and the Center for Science in the Public Interest—also led by graduates of elite law, medical, or graduate schools—as well as other national organizations.

Nader, the highest profile and most influential of all U.S. consumer activists, also believed it important to encourage activism in young people. In the late 1960s, he persuaded hundreds of idealistic, reform-minded college, graduate, and professional school students to volunteer their time researching corporate and government abuses. "Nader's Raiders" were the forerunners of the thousands of students who since the early 1970s have participated in state public interest research groups.

Another group of lawyers, also often graduates of elite law schools, began their activism as Legal Aid attorneys. Influenced by books such as Michael Harrington's *The Other America* and by President Lyndon Johnson's War on Poverty, they worked not only to resolve the problems of low-income consumers but also to establish new consumer protections and promote their enforcement. Almost all the senior attorneys still at the National Consumer Law Center, founded in 1969, worked for a local Legal Aid group. The leader of the National Association of Consumer Advocates—organized in 1994 as an association of consumer attorneys and a support group for the law center—and many members of this group also got their professional start at Legal Aid. These two organizations have encouraged and helped thousands of other attorneys to make a career of representing consumers.

A separate group of activists, most of whom were not attorneys, focused on building consumer and citizen power through organizing. Many of these advocates were influenced by the New Left, especially Students for a Democratic Society (SDS), with its emphasis on empowerment, especially for the poor and people of color and for their communities. A couple of longtime consumer advocates, as students, even participated in SDS. If the New Left influenced the ideology of these activists, the community organizing centers in Chicago, particularly Saul Alinsky's Industrial Areas Foundation, provided the strategy—use a common enemy to mobilize communities to force change.

The Consumer Education and Protective Association (CEPA) in Philadelphia, led by Max Weiner, organized groups of consumers to resolve their individual grievances, using picketing as a last resort. This approach influenced organizers in Cleveland, Fort Wayne, Milwaukee, Dallas, San Francisco, and New York, among other cities. But CEPA's main long-term goal was building a Consumer Party that made public policy, in part by electing its members to public office.

Although these complaint-based groups have not survived, successors to the Citizen Action groups of the 1970s remain active. Influenced by the Alinsky-inspired

Midwest Academy led by 1960s activist Heather Booth, these state-based organizations mobilized citizens, often through door-to-door campaigning, to support progressive reforms that included consumer goals such as universal health care and low energy prices. They also often developed close ties with activist labor groups and involved themselves in electoral campaigns. In the past century, trade unions have provided critical political and financial support for consumer activism. Consumer leader Esther Peterson, who worked first in the labor movement, served as the first presidential advisor for consumer affairs.

A smaller number of activists were aroused by personal tragedy, usually a death to a family member caused by an unsafe product. A number of these individuals became advocates after they had lost loved ones to unsafe motor vehicles, hazardous household products, or contaminated food.

Although consumer activists can have varying views of the world and how to change it, they all share certain characteristics. They are idealistic, believing that people can work together to achieve fundamental change. They are progressive, emphasizing the importance of social justice and consumer/citizen empowerment. They are skeptical of business, ever mindful of corporate exploitation of consumers in a capitalist society. They are reformist, understanding that only reform, not revolution, is possible to begin achieving their idealistic goals. And they are pragmatic, usually willing to accept half, or sometimes even a quarter, of a loaf of actual reform while continuing to call for the whole loaf.

Organizations

These consumer activists created organizations that differ in important respects yet that also have similarities. For more than the past four decades, five national groups have worked on a broad array of consumer issues affecting all consumers. The National Consumers League (NCL) has made worker, as well as consumer, issues a high priority for more than a century. Consumers Union/Consumer Reports (CU/CR) was founded in 1936 as a product-testing organization and, in the 1970s, established advocacy offices in Washington, D.C., Texas, and California. In the late 1960s, CU/CR, state and local consumer groups, consumer cooperatives, and trade unions created the Consumer Federation of America, and today nearly 300 consumer and cooperative groups remain active in the federation. Ralph Nader's flagship organization, Public Citizen, was established in 1971 and since then has been the consumer movement's leader in health care and political reform, as well as its principal litigator. Nader also inspired the creation, in the 1970s and 1980s, of public interest research groups on college and university campuses that, today, are part of the U.S. Public Interest Research Group (U.S. PIRG).

Other national groups active for decades have worked on issues related to specific issue-areas—the Center for Auto Safety and Advocates for Highway and Auto Safety on motor vehicle safety, the Center for Science in the Public Interest on food and beverage safety and nutrition, the National Insurance Consumer Organization (now part of Consumer Federation of America) on insurance, the Center for Responsible Lending on financial services, Families USA on health care, and the Center for Digital Democracy, Privacy Rights Clearinghouse, and Electronic Privacy Information Center on communications and privacy. Still other national organizations have focused much attention on groups of vulnerable consumers—the National Consumer Law Center and National Association of Consumer Advocates on low-income Americans; Consumer Action on ethnic groups, especially recent immigrants; and AARP on the elderly.

Almost all the aforementioned organizations are incorporated as nonprofit groups with 501(c)(3) status, which limits the extent of their congressional lobbying and electoral activity. Although almost all the national groups lobby Congress, many very actively, the value of the time their employees spend on this legislative activity rarely exceeds the 20 percent permitted by federal law governing nonprofits. Groups, notably Public Citizen and the National Consumer Law Center, also litigate frequently. And some organizations have the ability to appeal effectively to groups outside Washington, D.C., for political support, for example: Consumers Union/Consumer Reports to its subscriber activists; Public Citizen to its contributors, often attorneys; the Center for Science in the Public Interest to its subscribers; the U.S. Public Interest Research Group to state PIRGS; and the Consumer Federation of America to its state and local consumer group members. Yet, for almost all consumer groups, their principal activity is researching and analyzing issues and then communicating their findings and policy recommendations to legislators or regulators as well as to the press and to other advocates.

The annual budgets of most major national consumer advocacy groups now total at least several million dollars. The initial support for these groups was often from individuals through memberships, subscriptions, or contributions or, in the case of the Consumer Federation of America, from other nonprofit organizations through dues payments and other contributions. Today, however, most of these groups also receive grants from national foundations, such as the Ford Foundation, and from *cy près* awards related to consumer litigation. Unlike many consumer groups in Europe, which depend heavily on government funding, few U.S. groups draw from this source. In fact, several major U.S. organizations will not accept government grants. That is also the case for corporate funding of consumer advocacy. In general, consumer groups will not accept business funding of their advocacy, though there has been one major exception—motor vehicle safety groups, such as Center for Auto Safety and Advocates for Highway and Auto Safety, accept contributions from automobile insurers, with whom they have strong congruent interests. Several consumer organizations—including the Consumer Federation of America, Consumer Action, and National Consumers League—will accept corporate support for some consumer research, education, and forums.

Though each has its own distinct identity, consumer groups work closely with each other. Their leaders serve on each other's boards of directors. For example, board members of Consumers Union/Consumer Reports have included leaders, in the past, from Public Citizen, the Center for Auto Safety, and Consumer Federation of America, and, at present, from the U.S. Public Interest Research Group and National Consumer Law Center. Moreover, the board of the Consumer Federation of America includes leaders of several dozen national and state consumer advocacy groups. From day to day, advocates from different organizations work closely together, chiefly in ad hoc coalitions related to specific issues, particularly when opportunities arise to influence legislation. Sometimes, these coalitions create separate organizations, such as Americans for Financial Reform or Advocates for Highway and Auto Safety, with their own budgets and staff.

Despite the separate institutional identities of these organizations, it is not surprising that these groups want to work closely together. As noted earlier, their leaders are all idealistic, progressive, skeptical of business, reformist, and pragmatic. This pragmatism includes recognizing that there is strength in numbers—advocacy groups can achieve policy reform most easily by working not separately, but together.

Issue Advocacy

Consumer organizations—notably, Consumers Union/Consumer Reports nationally and the Center for the Study of Services/Checkbook locally—provide consumers with information about the availability, performance, safety, and cost of goods and services. Moreover, a broad array of groups attempt to educate consumers how to select and shop for these products more intelligently. Another set of institutions seeks to resolve the grievances of individual consumers when they arise. The most active of these organizations are state and local consumer affairs offices, especially state attorneys general, though a few federal agencies, such as the Consumer Financial Protection Bureau, assist individuals with complaint resolution. Nonprofit groups, including Call for Action affiliates and local Better Business Bureaus, also offer services in this area. So have activist groups such as the Consumer Education and Protective Association, as well as the local groups it inspired, which used aggressive complaint resolution as a strategy not just to resolve individual grievances, but also to activate and organize consumers.

At both national and state levels, however, most consumer activism is directed at persuading governments to adopt, implement, and enforce new consumer protections (and, at times, to defend existing protections). Advocates convince legislators to approve new laws, persuade regulators to implement and enforce them, and petition the courts to ensure their implementation and enforcement. These protections—especially those related to advertising, deceptive and unconscionable sales, and warranties—can apply to all, or many, types of products—or they may relate to enforcement of the antitrust laws to promote competition among sellers. Yet most consumer activism over the past several decades has pursued one of two general goals—ensuring the safety of specific types of goods or the affordability of specific types of services.

Consumer advocates have focused great attention on the safety of motor vehicles, with a major goal of ensuring that manufacturers design passenger vehicles that protect the driver and passengers in crashes. These vehicles include all-terrain vehicles (ATVs). Also related to transport, activists have given some attention to improving the safety of air travel. In the area of home safety, advocates have sought to improve the safety of products, especially those used by infants and children.

Activists have given even greater attention to products that are ingested—food, alcoholic beverages, drugs, and tobacco. They have also campaigned to curb emergency room infections.

In the area of services, especially from the 1970s to the 1990s, many state advocates sought to restrain the cost of utilities—telephone service, cable television service, electric service, and natural gas—which were offered by monopolies that frequently sought to shift costs onto consumers. As these services were partly or entirely deregulated, and as the Internet rapidly broadened communications services, national groups gave increasing attention to federal regulation of these services and to attempts to limit mergers among companies providing the same or related services. The digital revolution also led to growing interest among advocates in consumer privacy issues.

Since the 1990s, an increasing number of national and state groups have made financial services reform their highest priority. Both national and state groups have joined together to curb high-cost lending, which until passage of the Wall Street Reform and Consumer Protection Act of 2010 was regulated only by the states. Both national and state groups have also worked to try persuading states and the federal government to curb predatory mortgage and installment loans. National groups, though, took the lead in convincing Congress in 2009 to approve consumer credit card protections that had the principal effect of significantly reducing fees paid by cardholders. National organizations also spearheaded efforts to persuade Congress to improve consumer disclosures on savings accounts (Truth in Savings) in 1991, reduce bank check holds in 1987, and strengthen consumer protections related to credit reports and scores in 1996 and 2003. And for the past couple decades, national groups have led advocacy to establish consumer protections for investors. In the area of automobile and home insurance, both national and state advocates have directed efforts at state insurance commissioners and other state officials because these products have been largely regulated by the states.

Consumer activists have addressed health insurance at both state and federal levels. Before state legislatures and the U.S. Congress, they have sought to expand affordable access to health care services. Though preferring a single-payer solution on this issue, consumer groups working on health care issues joined the broad-based coalition that in 2010 helped persuade Congress to approve the less radical Affordable Care Act ("Obamacare").

The effectiveness of consumer activism depends in part on the ability of advocates to implement their strategies in the face of well-funded opposition. Particularly important to their advocacy is undertaking and disseminating research that—largely through related press coverage—can help convince the public that a problem must be addressed by policymakers. That was the case in the early twentieth century, when the books and articles of Progressive-era muckrakers fueled advocacy which persuaded Congress to enact significant health, safety, and antitrust protections. That was also the case a half-century later, when Nader's *Unsafe at Any Speed*, and subsequent research inspired by Nader's work, helped convince federal policymakers to seriously address safety issues related to motor vehicles, household products, food, and drugs. And it was the case in the

1990s and 2000s when dozens of hard-hitting reports on financial services abuses, written by consumer advocates, helped make possible consumer lending reforms, as well as the creation of the Consumer Financial Protection Bureau.

The influence of this research, however, depends to a large extent on the ability of consumer advocates to persuade the press and policymakers to take it seriously. Most consumer advocacy involves communicating information about problems, and solutions to these problems, to these two influential groups. The effectiveness of this research and communications has been enhanced by the willingness of advocates from different organizations to work closely together. When they succeed in convincing the press and public that a serious problem exists, public policymakers are under some pressure to address the problem. Yet even when most Americans feel strongly that policymakers should act, these legislators and regulators frequently will not do so.

In examining the consumer reforms of the past half-century, it becomes evident that legislatures controlled by Democrats are the most likely to approve new consumer protections. In this period, virtually all major consumer legislation approved by Congress was enacted when Democrats held majorities in both the Senate and House. Much of this legislation was passed when a Republican was president—for example, the Consumer Product Safety Act and Magnuson Moss Warranty Act during the Nixon administration, and the Consumer Product Safety Improvement Act and Military Lending Act during the administration of George W. Bush. However, a Democratic Congress and president provide the best opportunity for enactment of path-breaking legislation. It is unlikely, for example, that both the Affordable Care Act and the Wall Street Reform and Consumer Protection Act, as approved by Congress, would have been signed into law by a Republican president.

By contrast, very little consumer legislation became law when one house was controlled by Republicans, even when the president was a Democrat. Faced with this political constraint, though, Democratic presidents have played an important role in ensuring that legislative reforms are responsibly implemented and enforced. These presidents have tended to appoint regulators who are far more pro-consumer than those selected by Republican presidents, some of whom have sought to thwart the mission of their agencies. Democratic presidents have sometimes even chosen consumer advocates as their regulators. These and other pro-consumer regulators most often institutionalize opportunities for consumer advocates to advise their agencies.

Stephen Brobeck

Global Consumer Activism:
An Overview

In 1960, the global consumer movement began its transformation from a few isolated organizations that focused primarily on product testing for affluent consumers into a geographically broad, socially and ethnically diverse, and mutually supportive network of organizations with a strong activist bent. In that year, the inelegantly named International Organization of Consumers Unions (IOCU) was conceived and founded by five organizations based in the United States, western Europe, and Australia. By the time IOCU renamed itself Consumers International (CI) in 1995, it had about 200 members in eight-five countries. Today, one would be hard pressed to arrive in a country without at least one consumer group. These consumer organizations not only learn from one another, but also collaborate to solve cross-border consumer problems that cannot be adequately addressed by national action alone.

From an initial focus on helping consumers make better informed decisions, IOCU quickly accepted the task of addressing a broader range of consumer issues and promoting consumer organizations in both more and less developed nations. Still, from the 1960s through the 1980s, the world's consumer movements traveled on somewhat parallel tracks. In more developed nations, consumer organizations tackled "problems of affluence," such as automobile safety defects, deceptive advertising, the absence of informative product labels, and inadequate product warranties. These relatively rich countries looked to each other for lessons on how to solve consumer problems. For example, the United States was the first country to require a warning on cigarette packages; other countries followed suit, often leapfrogging over the United States with more hard-hitting warnings. Conversely, New Zealand and Australia were the sites of the first mandatory seatbelt use laws— an idea that spread first to western Europe and later to the United States. The consumer organizations in these wealthy countries were generally well funded (often enjoying government subsidies), and their freedom of speech and assembly were guaranteed.

During the same period, consumer organizations in less developed nations were concerned with "problems of poverty." Citizens of these countries knew their primary consumer problem: poverty. Consumer information and education were nice, but food on the table and a roof overhead were necessities. Hence consumer organizations in less developed countries developed a different set of priorities, including clean water, adequate food, and safe pharmaceuticals. Consumer activists in these countries often viewed the western form of consumer activism as, at best, a luxury they could not afford. At worst, activists in less developed countries viewed the goals and strategies of their Western counterparts as irrelevant to a situation marked by economic deprivation and governments that were indifferent or hostile to consumer rights. For leaders such as Anwar Fazal of Malaysia, president of IOCU from 1978 to 1984, the consumer movement was about people, not products or markets, and it was part of a broader struggle for human dignity and social justice.

Consumer organizations in more developed countries, acting primarily through IOCU, tried to narrow the gap between the consumer movements of the more and less wealthy countries of the world. For example, IOCU opened regional offices in southeast Asia, South America, and, later, Africa to provide logistical and financial support for the budding consumer movements in these areas. IOCU, after a decade of campaigning, succeeded in 1985 in getting the United Nations to establish a set of principles for consumer protection to which all countries should adhere. Despite these efforts at unity within the global consumer movement, the differences between the priorities of groups in more and less developed countries were undeniable.

Recent decades have witnessed a growing convergence among the consumer movements in various areas of the world. Most fundamentally, consumer organizations exist today in part of the world where they were largely absent before the 1990s—most notably, central and eastern Europe, the Middle East, and Africa. In addition, the problems faced by consumers in more and less developed countries have become more similar as the latter have experienced economic gains. For instance, rates of obesity, especially among children, are just as alarming in Mexico, Saudi Arabia, and China as they are in the United States. As car ownership has exploded in countries such as Brazil, Russia, India, and China (the so-called "BRIC" countries), activism regarding the safety of drivers, passengers, and pedestrians has increased, too. Indeed, traffic deaths per capita and per mile driven are far higher in less developed countries than they are in more developed ones. Not very long ago, most consumers in less developed countries lacked access to any phone service—land-based or mobile. Today, the majority of households own mobile phones even in the poorest countries and therefore share with more affluent consumers the desire to establish clear rights, especially when making purchases with their phones. As a final example, concern regarding air and water pollution used to be regarded as a concern of consumers whose basic needs had already been met. Today, demands for clean air and water are heard loudly in countries such as China, India, Singapore, and Chile.

Beyond *similar* problems such as obesity, traffic fatalities, and pollution, countries at various stages of economic development are also experiencing *shared* consumer problems. These shared problems typically involve cross-border movement of goods and services and thus require international remedies. One example is fighting the scourge of counterfeit goods, whose use can be deadly when bogus pharmaceutical products and medical devices are involved. Another is cracking down on frauds and crimes perpetrated over the Internet. In debates regarding the protection of intellectual property such as scientific discoveries, films, music, book, and other creative works, more and less developed nations used to take sharply differing positions. Today, as less developed countries such as China create more intellectual property, they have more interest in enforceable international rules that balance property rights and consumer access. And, of course, climate change is a major consumer problem, and it can only be addressed through international cooperation.

The increasingly international nature of consumer activism is reflected in several trends. First, Consumers International continues to grow. As of 2014, it boasts about 240 members in 120 countries. Second, the themes of CI's campaigns address issues that are important to virtually all of its members. Each year, CI celebrates World Consumer Rights Day (March 15) by focusing on a single consumer issue. Recent campaigns have attempted to reduce marketing of unhealthy food to children, increase fairness in financial services, and establish rights for the users of mobile phones—objectives shared by consumers worldwide. Third, consumer organizations in less developed countries are turning with greater frequency to each other (rather than consumer groups in richer countries) for assistance and support. A key illustration is provided by Consumer Unity & Trust Society (CUTS). For two decades, CUTS confined its activities to its home country of India. Today, however, it operates programs in Zambia, Kenya, and Hanoi.

A 2013 report issued by CI reveals both the strength of consumer activism globally and the large task that remains for it. CI surveyed consumer organizations around the world, and seventy organizations from fifty-eight countries responded. Approximately 80 percent of the organizations reported that they are consulted by governments when consumer policies are being formulated. More than half of the organizations operate joint programs with the governments of their countries. Almost all consumer groups, including those in low-income countries, where funding for these groups is most challenging, are able to sustain multiple activities: consumer education, complaint handling, advocacy, and monitoring the implementation of consumer policies. Within this bright picture, though, the report revealed some dark spots. Among the eighteen low-income countries studied, many lack a general consumer protection law and most lack a coherent national policy on consumer protection. Even where laws exist, an absence of adequate enforcement often renders these laws moot.

Looking ahead to international consumer activism, two factors are noteworthy. The first is a challenge: Due to the budgetary problems of many national governments, financial support for consumer groups is on the decline. The effects of these budget cuts are especially visible in central and eastern Europe, where consumer groups are relatively young and have never faced the prospect of raising the bulk of their operating expenses. The other factor is a resource for consumer activism. Consumer organizations are among the most trusted actors in national politics, and this high level of trust applies across countries. According to the 2013 Consumer Markets Scoreboard, trust in independent consumer organizations in the countries of the European Union consistently exceeds trust in public authorities or businesses. Similarly, in the United States, consumer groups receive high ratings of trustworthiness with regard to their activities involving Internet security, health, energy efficiency, and new technologies. In the words of the 2013 CI report, consumer organizations around the world "have earned the right to be taken seriously" (p. 26).

Robert N. Mayer

Further Reading

Consumers International. 2013. *The State of Consumer Protection around the World.* www.consumersinternational.org/news-and-media/resource-zone/state-of-consumer-protection.
European Commission. 2013. *The 9th Consumer Conditions Scoreboard.* http://ec.europa.eu/consumers/consumer_evidence/consumer_scoreboards/index_en.htm.

Select Books on
Consumer Activism

Anderson, Oscar E. 1958. *The Health of a Nation: Harvey W. Wiley and the Fight for Pure Food.* Chicago, IL: University of Chicago Press.

Angevine, Erma, ed. 1982. *Consumer Activists: They Made a Difference.* Mt. Vernon, NY: Consumers Union Foundation.

Brobeck, Stephen. 1990. *The Modern Consumer Movement: References and Resources.* Boston, MA: G.K. Hall.

Brobeck, Stephen, Robert N. Mayer, and Robert O. Herrmann, eds. 1997. *Encyclopedia of the Consumer Movement.* Santa Barbara, CA: ABC-CLIO.

Caplovitz, David. 1967. *The Poor Pay More: Consumer Practices of Low-Income Families.* New York: Free Press.

Chase, Stuart, and F. J. Schlink. 1927. *Your Money's Worth.* New York: Macmillan.

Cohen, Lizabeth. 2003. *A Consumer's Republic: The Politics of Mass Consumption in Postwar America.* New York: Vintage.

Cox, Edward F., Robert C. Fellmeth, John E. Schulz. 1969. *The Nader Report on the Federal Trade Commission.* New York: Grove Press.

Glickman, Lawrence B. 2009. *Buying Power: A History of Consumer Activism in America.* Chicago, IL: University of Chicago Press.

Gorey, Hays. 1975. *Nader and the Power of Everyman.* New York: Grosset & Dunlap.

Green, Mark J., James M. Fallows, David R. Zwick. 1972. *Who Runs Congress?* New York: Bantam Books.

Griffin, Kelley. 1987. *More Action for Change.* New York: Dembner Books.

Hilton, Matthew. 2009. *Prosperity for All: Consumer Activism in an Era of Globalization.* Ithaca, NY: Cornell University Press.

Kallett, Arthur, and F. J. Schlink. 1933. *100,000,000 Guinea Pigs: Dangers in Everyday Foods, Drugs, and Cosmetics.* New York: Grosset & Dunlap.

Kirsch, Larry, and Robert N. Mayer. 2013. *Financial Justice: The People's Campaign to Stop Lender Abuse.* Santa Barbara, CA: Praeger.

Magnuson, Warren, and Jean Carper. 1968. *The Dark Side of the Marketplace: The Plight of the American Consumer.* Englewood Cliffs, NJ: Prentice-Hall.

Maney, Ardith, and Loree Bykerk. 1994. *Consumer Politics: Protecting Public Interests on Capitol Hill.* Westport, CT: Greenwood Press.

Mayer, Robert N. 1989. *The Consumer Movement: Guardians of the Marketplace.* Boston, MA: Twayne Publishers.

McCarry, Charles. 1972. *Citizen Nader.* New York: Saturday Review Press.

Mintz, Morton, and Jerry S. Cohen. 1971. *America, Inc.: Who Owns and Operates the United States.* New York: Dial Press.

Morse, Richard L. D., ed. 1993. *The Consumer Movement: Lectures by Colston E. Warne.* Manhattan, KS: Family Economic Trust.

Nadel, Mark V. 1971. *The Politics of Consumer Protection*. Indianapolis, IN: Bobbs-Merrill.

Nader, Ralph. 1965. *Unsafe at Any Speed: The Designed-in Dangers of the American Automobile*. New York: Grossman.

Nader, Ralph, and Donald K. Ross. 1971. *Action for a Change: A Student's Manual for Public Interest Organizing*. New York: Grossman.

Packard, Vance. 1957. *The Hidden Persuaders*. New York: David McKay Co.

Pertschuk, Michael. 1982. *Revolt against Regulation: The Rise and Pause of the Consumer Movement*. Berkeley: University of California Press.

Peterson, Esther, and Winifred Conkling. 1995. *Restless: The Memoirs of Labor and Consumer Activist Esther Peterson*. Washington, DC: Caring Publishing.

Silber, Norman I. 1983. *Test and Protest: The Influence of Consumers Union*. New York: Holmes & Meier.

Sinclair, Upton. 1906. *The Jungle*. New York: Doubleday.

Turner, James S. 1970. *The Chemical Feast: The Ralph Nader Study Group Report on Food Protection and the Food and Drug Administration*. New York: Grossman.

Warren, Elizabeth. 2014. *A Fighting Chance*. New York: Metropolitan Books.

AARP

AARP was founded in 1958 by Ethel Percy Andrus, a retired educator from California, as the American Association of Retired Persons, an organization serving older people through advocacy and services. Today, the organization seeks to meet consumer needs related to healthcare, retirement planning, affordable utilities, and protection from financial abuse, as well as income-related needs, including adequate Social Security benefits. With nearly 38 million members and an annual budget exceeding $1 billion, AARP is one of the nation's largest and most influential nonprofit organizations.

AARP and its affiliates are supported through membership contributions, royalties from the licensing of its intellectual property, advertisements in its publications, and government grants, among other sources. Some members join chiefly to receive discounts on rental cars, lodging, and vacation packages; other members highly value insurance products, such as Medigap policies, that are approved and endorsed by AARP but sold by insurance companies. Over the years, most independent evaluations have concluded that AARP's products offer good value.

Although AARP's first priority is serving the needs of its members and others in their age group, the organization's advocacy and services often benefit all consumers, especially those with lower incomes. In regard to advocacy, AARP has been particularly active at the state level in trying to help consumers save money on their utility bills and protect reliable utility services. In 2013 and early 2014, for example, AARP estimated that it saved consumers $3 billion on their electricity, gas, and phone bills:

- Communications from thousands of AARP members helped persuade the Arizona Corporation Commission not to deregulate electric services in that state.
- AARP advocacy helped convince the Colorado Public Service Commission not to deregulate telephone service.
- In Connecticut and Kentucky, AARP advocated successfully for the preservation of reliable landline phone service, on which older consumers are especially dependent.
- In Oklahoma, AARP advocacy was instrumental in persuading the public service commission to lower rates for residential gas and electric customers.
- In Missouri, AARP led opposition to legislation that would have raised electric, water, and gas rates.

AARP's advocacy for healthcare reform is more controversial but is also usually closely aligned with the advocacy of mainstream consumer groups, such as Consumers Union and Families USA. AARP's support for the Affordable Care Act ("Obamacare") was criticized by both some of its most conservative and most liberal members, yet the group's endorsement of the legislation, as well as its longtime advocacy for reforms that would provide coverage to the uninsured, helped win passage of the bill.

AARP federal advocacy has also helped preserve funding for food stamps, energy assistance, and housing to benefit lower-income Americans. The organization has supported better disclosure of fees on investment and banking services. Moreover, its litigation experts have fought against consumer and financial fraud and for stronger investor protections, better health and long-term care, and improved housing. (For several decades, the Legal Counsel for the Elderly, an AARP affiliate, has provided free legal and social services to vulnerable District of Columbia seniors faced with tax and mortgage foreclosures and evictions, among other problems.)

In 2013, AARP launched the Fraud Watch Network, which gives members access to resources and tools they can use to protect themselves and their families from fraud and identity theft. The network provides watchdog alerts about the latest scams and holds antifraud seminars ("scam jams") featuring local fraud experts who explain the tactics of fraudsters and how consumers can resist them.

Another AARP service benefiting consumers is AARP Foundation Tax-Aide, the largest free, volunteer-run tax assistance and preparation program in the United States. Founded in 1968 by four AARP volunteers, this program has benefited more than 2.5 million older adults annually in recent years, providing assistance through some 35,000 tax-aide volunteers who help older Americans prepare and file their tax returns.

The AARP Drive to End Hunger has worked for several years to focus attention on, and find solutions to, the problem of hunger among people aged 50 or older. Since 2011, it has leveraged the work of some 30,000 volunteers and raised $21 million through corporate partnerships and individual donations.

AARP provides extensive practical information to consumers about health, money, housing, entertainment, food, and travel. This information is included in two publications that are available only to members—"AARP Bulletin," published ten times each year, and *AARP: The Magazine*, published bimonthly.

However, much of this information is available to consumers who access AARP's free websites. AARP.org is a robust resource for health, financial security, and consumer protection, including 33 interactive tools to help people budget, save, invest, and plan for retirement. It also includes columns from prominent national experts, such as syndicated financial columnists Jane Bryant Quinn and Jean Chatzky. In 2013, the site logged 1.5 billion visits.

AARP is a 501(c)(4) nonprofit organization. Its affiliate, AARP Services Inc., functions as a for-profit that manages the products that AARP endorses and promotes. Another affiliate, the AARP Foundation, is a tax-exempt 501(c)(3) organization that focuses attention on poverty-related issues.

Many departments at AARP communicate and work with consumer groups. An AARP representative currently serves on the boards of the National Consumers League and the Consumer Federation of America.

Stephen Brobeck

See also: Electricity Service Advocacy; Healthcare Advocacy; Prescription Drug Advocacy; Telephone Consumer Advocacy

Further Reading

Morris, Charles R. 1996. *The AARP: America's Most Powerful Lobby and the Clash of Generations.* New York: Times Books.

Pear, Robert. 2007. "AARP Says It Will Become Major Medicare Insurer." *New York Times,* April 17.

Schurenberg, Eric, and Lani Luciano. 1988. "The Empire Called AARP." *Money,* 17 (October): 128–146.

ACTION FOR CHILDREN'S TELEVISION

Action for Children's Television (ACT) was a national nonprofit advocacy organization, in operation from 1968 to 1992, that worked to encourage diversity in children's television and to eliminate commercial abuses targeted at children. Founded and led by Peggy Charren, the organization increased public awareness of these issues and initiated several related reforms.

ACT was organized by Charren in her living room in suburban Boston. Distressed by commercialism in children's programming, she and three other mothers of preschoolers decided to form an organization to improve the quality and variety of such programming. Quickly, the group expanded to about thirty concerned parents. Its first target was sales pitches for products on *Romper Room.*

These activists, led by Charren, created a 501(c)(3) nonprofit organization whose budget ranged from about $150,000 to $450,000 annually. These funds supported a paid staff ranging from four to twenty persons. Many volunteers, 25,000 contributing members, and 150 national organizations also supported the organization.

ACT based its efforts to improve children's television on its interpretation of the Communications Act of 1934's public service requirement. The group understood this requirement to mean that broadcasters bear a legal responsibility to provide programming for youngsters that enlightens as well as entertains and to maintain practices that do not exploit the child audience. The organization opposed censorship, preferring instead to increase choice and diversity in programming. But it considered the overcommercialization of children's media "particularly offensive." Not surprisingly, it strongly supported the children's programming on public broadcasting stations, including such shows as *Mister Rogers' Neighborhood* and *Sesame Street.*

In 1970, ACT petitioned the Federal Communications Commission (FCC) to require daily programming for children. Four years later, in response to ACT's petition, the FCC established minimum guidelines on the amount of children's programming and set forth specific advertising policies. That same year, the National Association of Broadcasters incorporated into its television code guidelines to reduce the amount of commercial time on children's programs.

In 1984, the FCC reversed itself by eliminating all quantitative commercial guidelines for television broadcasting. Two years later, ACT petitioned the U.S. Court of Appeals, District of Columbia Circuit, for a judgment determining whether the FCC acted arbitrarily and without adequate explanation in eliminating its policy on commercialization of children's television programming. In 1987, the court ruled in favor of ACT, ordering the FCC to review its 1984 decision.

ACT waged its lengthiest campaign to persuade Congress to pass legislation increasing choices in children's programming. In 1985, Representative Timothy Wirth (D-CO) and Senator Frank Lautenberg (D-NJ) introduced legislation known as the Children's Television Education Act. This legislation failed to pass, as did similar bills introduced in the next Congress. In 1988, both the House and Senate passed similar legislation, but it was pocket-vetoed by President Ronald Reagan. Finally, after leadership by Representative Edward Markey (D-MA), the Children's Television Act was approved by both the House and Senate in 1990, becoming law without President George Bush's signature. This act requires each television station to air programs specifically designed to serve the educational needs of children, also requiring them to limit commercials on children's shows.

With the passage of this act, the leaders of ACT decided that the organization had served its function and should be disbanded. When ACT ceased to exist in early 1992, it left behind a legacy of congressional, regulatory, and court decisions that had improved the quality of television watched by children. Perhaps just as significant, by generating frequent news coverage of children's television issues, it had raised public awareness of the quality and effects of children's programs and their commercials.

Stephen Brobeck

See also: Cable Television Regulation; Center for Digital Democracy; Telecommunications Research and Action Center

Further Reading

"A Harsh Critic of Kids' TV." 1978. *Business Week* (May 29): 52.
Cole, Barry, and Mal Oettinger. 1978. *Reluctant Regulators: The FCC and the Broadcast Audience*. Reading, MA: Addison-Wesley Publishing Company.

ADVERTISING ADVOCACY

In the second decade of the twenty-first century, many advertising practitioners hate the lies and half-truths of political advertising, because these messages generate audience distrust of advertising in general that logically transfers to messages for products and services, making success more difficult for honest sales efforts. Thus a distinguishing feature of the history of advertising regulation is that it has often been supported by the advertising trade press and business leaders—maybe not universally, but strongly enough to be noteworthy—whereas other consumer protection activities found business resistance a primary obstacle to overcome. In a sense, advertising professionals sometimes played the role of self-critic, partially supplanting the role traditionally played in other domains by outside critics.

In addition, advertising's critics have not been confined to traditional activists—the individuals, social groups, book authors, or journalists who are critical of business practices. The consumer movement's success in controlling advertising has also required activist efforts by government officials. The officials did more than just react to public complaints. They often publicized problems as a positive political value and proposed policy solutions with little or no prompting.

Advertising has long been a heavily criticized business practice—arguably the most criticized—often serving as a focus for general consumerist disparagement. Even the Pontifical Council for Social Communications of the Catholic Church issued a report on the state of ethics in the advertising business in 1997. Most professionals would state that it is because advertising is so visible and intrusive that it has been denounced not only for its own sins of being offensive or for making inflated, potentially deceptive claims of product superiority, but also for being used to develop brand loyalty for products and services whose sale nonusers would wish to discourage or even ban.

For example, people who can't imagine why an adult would choose to purchase an addictive carcinogenic substance readily cite allegedly manipulative advertising appeals as a major reason that anyone still consumes the product. Similarly, certain target audiences are considered "vulnerable," inherently incapable of discerning advertising truth from fiction, and companies are accused of manipulating this vulnerability with the advertising appeals. Thus, through history, many activist efforts to regulate advertising practices were secondary effects of their efforts to protect vulnerable audiences or to attack any sales efforts of certain products the activists disliked. In blaming advertising for alcohol abuse, obesity, children's dental caries, or a public preference for the taste of junk food, the activism is often driven by presumptions of power over consumer thinking that advertising does not possess.

Finally, yet not distinct from the above social forces, advertising often has served as a scapegoat for those who inveigh against what they perceive to be the gross materialism and environmental destructiveness of modern lifestyles. In short, many attacks on advertising are really broadsides against something else, with advertising possibly being an easier target than broad social forces such as apposite changing lifestyles of the consumer culture. Common complaints about advertising echo Thorstein Veblen's nineteenth-century criticisms of consumption itself and an economic order that required the creation and development of widespread desires to purchase mass-produced products in ever greater amounts. For example, the often-repeated line from Chase and Schlink's 1927 book *Your Money's Worth*—"We are all Alices in a Wonderland of conflicting claims, bright promises, fancy packages, soaring words, and almost impenetrable ignorance"—blames mass communications for excessive shopping and apparent (to the critic) consumer irrationality in product selection. Into the modern era, these same antimaterialist perspectives on advertising are found in the writings of Vance Packard and Ralph Nader.

Foundation of Modern Advertising

The necessary first step to explain advertising regulation in the context of consumer movements requires a capsule summary of the foundations of modern advertising that began with the industrial revolution. And the summary requires correcting popular yet mistaken beliefs that advertising is virtually unchanged since 1776, or that advertising created the foundation for mass demand and mass distribution.

Advertising messages might have been found in the ruins of volcano-destroyed Pompeii in the very limited sense of signs such as "eat at Joe's." In the eighteenth century, advertising looked like modern classified advertising or the modern equivalent of Craigslist, listing items newly arrived in a general store or a shipment newly come into dock. However, the modern advertising of brands whereby manufacturers directly contact consumers with product messages—the concept of a brand image for a product, service or store—is a modern creation whose origins were concurrent with the forces that gave birth to the consumer movements.

The period of the first consumer movement was also the foundation era of modern advertising. In the late nineteenth century, mass distribution and consumer demand for manufactured products eventually led to the start of companies' branding products to provide a way to indicate how their product was a better buy, with the concurrent idea of selling those brands by directly to consumers by the use of mass-media advertising. The first consumer movement of that same period and into the early twentieth century retained a faith in the competitive marketplace, with consumer education and earliest business regulations focused on strengthening the core tenets of the economic presumptions of buyer–seller relations. Consumer education sought to help people be smart shoppers, yet consumers were still presumed to protect themselves.

During this turn-of-the-century period, honest businesses saw misleading advertising as a problem more readily than any consumerist critics. Just as modern advertising leaders dislike the prevarications of politicians, the most egregiously false advertising of the early twentieth century by patent medicines was felt to be causing harm to the credibility of messages for other products. In what has often been credited as one of the first acts of business self-regulation, the advertising business trade publication *Printers' Ink* proposed a model statute for the regulation of advertising deception—appropriately referenced to this day as "the *Printers' Ink* model statute of 1911"—which was quickly adopted in altered forms in laws passed in forty-five states that retained the basic concept of the original. To the positive benefit of businesses, the passage of laws did have a short-term effect of discouraging some of the more egregious problems of blatant deceptions while also serving a small assurance to the public that not all advertisers were dishonest shysters.

The seemingly modern idea that consumers might read paid advertising with a lower expectation of credibility and trust also had its foundation in that earlier period. Starting in 1912, access to low postage rates required magazines to make certain that their readers would not mistake advertising for editorial content. This distinction might have found its way into the law because of the pragmatic competitive desires of the magazine publishers, who, until a short time before that, had not been publishing any advertising content. The publishers supported the required distinction because it ensured inexpensive distribution for their publications but not for retail catalogs. Yet, regardless of motivations or rationale, when the broadcast media came into existence, the Radio Act of 1927 and Communications Act of 1934, the latter of which created the Federal Communications Commission, both drew on this postal law, including similar requirements on broadcasters today found in FCC rule 317.

In 1914, the Federal Trade Commission was created as a regulatory agency for the enforcement of then-new antitrust laws. Although advertising was not an explicit part of the FTC Act, the newly created agency's first enforcement cases, in 1915, dealt with allegations of deceptive advertising. Legislatively charged to regulate "unfair and deceptive acts and practices in commerce that tended to create a monopoly," the nascent agency pursued a legal theory that deceptive advertising could lead to increased market shares and, by driving out honest competition, potentially create monopoly power. This process of legal activism by the first commissioners and staff of a new regulatory agency initiated what is today the predominant force in government regulation of advertising veracity.

The consumer movement of the Great Depression era still retained a certain faith in market forces, but it came to recognize that consumers needed government assistance in stopping the sales of problem products or dealing with false information. Products were becoming far more complicated, with many features hidden from view; mass-produced food packaging meant potential dangers could be hidden beyond the ability of even the most cautious consumer to discern. Despite the founding of nonprofit product testing publications such as *Consumers' Research Bulletin*, and its offshoot organization Consumers' Union's publication *Consumer Reports*, corporate sources remained the predominant source of market information of which consumers might have been unable to discern the truth. During this period, the FTC Act was amended to directly empower the commission to regulate "unfair and deceptive acts and practices," removing the need for an explanatory legal theory connecting the deception to the potential creation of a monopoly.

During the 1930s, business and academic researchers took their first steps in assessing the effects of advertising communications. Academic mass communications research and related theory development also started in this period in a paranoid response to fear of the persuasive power that seemed to be commanded by Nazi propagandists. Yet, contrary to expectations, research quickly revealed that audiences are not passive tools manipulated by the power of the mass media—and that mass communications are rather weak influences on audience decisions. Advertising by itself is not able to create consumer desires; instead, effective messages must be based on the beliefs or desires an audience already holds. Nevertheless, consumer activists, as well as the public at large, retain an unshakeable belief that advertising is capable of molding and manipulating consumers to act against their own self-interests. However, these same communications research findings support the regulation of deceptive advertising by government, because it involves communication of information to a consumer audience that is at variance with the facts, regardless of what a message literally says or whether the information alone causes bad purchasing decisions.

Foundation of the Modern Reality

The consumer movement's vitality was renewed in the 1960s, aided by an act of corporate malfeasance involving General Motors, at the time the world's largest automobile company in both sales and market share. GM hired detectives to discredit Ralph Nader, author of *Unsafe at Any Speed*, which detailed allegations of indifference for motorist safety in product design. Nader's book also included a criticism of the U.S. automobile industry's emphasis on annual model changes, partially blaming advertising for creating consumers' belief that they needed a new car before it became functionally obsolete. Nader did not own a car himself, highlighting an important theme: criticisms of advertising made predominantly by people saying that they are not personally persuaded, influenced, or misled by advertising, but who seek to protect audiences unlike themselves—especially those whom they view as vulnerable, such as children, the mentally impaired, or people whose limited education results in an inability to fully comprehend the ramifications of their decisions.

After Richard Nixon's election to the presidency, for which he campaigned as the law and order candidate—ironic in the wake of his early exit from office—Nixon offered the position as chair of the Federal Trade Commission to Miles Kirkpatrick when Caspar Weinberger departed the position after six months. Previously, Kirkpatrick was chair of an American Bar Association study group that in September 1969 had issued an extremely critical review of the FTC, including its advertising regulation activities. Although not asserting that the report provided his blueprint as FTC leader, Kirkpatrick's time in that office starting in 1970 is generally considered a period of consumer protection activism by the FTC in both Trade Regulation Rules and case enforcement, including in attention to advertising and other purchase-relevant information provided to consumers. Advertising professionals were initially critical of the FTC, clearly disliking the added need for legal scrutiny of planned message strategies, but over time they came to value the resulting level playing field for honest behavior and improved consumer trust. For example, the FTC's Advertising Substantiation Program of 1971, which required advertisers to have on file a reasonable basis for claims for products involving consumer health and safety, was eventually accepted as a positive set of rules, endorsed by various business groups and revealed by studies of advertising content to have caused more concrete, consumer-useful information in the advertising of businesses covered by the rule.

Also starting in the 1970s, many states took the lead from the FTC and enacted their own "little FTC" laws, with state-level activist agencies mirroring the federal agency. At the same time, many state attorneys general were leaders in consumer protection efforts focused on advertising regulation. They didn't just act individually or in small groups, but the National Association of Attorneys General—commonly known by the unfortunate acronym NAAG—have frequently gone after advertisers, sometimes taking action before the FTC. Working as a national group in the successive decades, they were able to seek consumer redress for misleading price advertising on a national level from car rental firms and airlines or seek common remedies against practices that existed in multiple states, such as false claims of environmentally friendly "green" advertising, "free" credit report claims, and assertions of pills that can alter the size and shape of human anatomy without diet or exercise (especially the parts of the body not affected by diet or exercise).

The same antitrust laws that support a competitive marketplace, as well as provided a basis for the FTC's regulation of advertising deception, also limit the power of any effort of business self-regulation. A group of competitors that attempts to control how all companies in the same business sell their products or services would be a violation of antitrust laws in the United States, so a business group or trade association's only "enforcement" powers are limited to members' willing cooperation.

Since 1970, U.S. self-regulation of advertising has become synonymous with the activities of the Council of Better Business Bureau's National Advertising Division (NAD) and its appeals body, the National Advertising Review Board (NARB). No company is required to participate in the process, but very few have ever refused. Although they used to monitor advertising activity, new NAD cases today all come from complaints by consumers or competitors, helping it quietly settle disputes among its own professionals before the public or the FTC becomes aware of a possible problem. Although advertising regulation by government has faced fluctuations of funding or antagonism from antiregulation members of Congress in the past forty-five years, business support of CBBB's self-regulation has remained strong.

The Key Focus and Part of a Problem

As noted earlier, the activists' focus on advertising has mostly been reserved for the targeting of consumers paternalistically deemed vulnerable to particular sales messages: poor and poorly educated African Americans targeted for a new brand of cigarettes or high-alcohol-content beer; young people possessing limited financial literacy receiving messages for new credit cards on the day they first enroll in college; people facing expensive decisions on the burial of a recently deceased loved one; cancer patients sold faux cures; obese people offered pills to provide painless effortless weight loss; or, in the wake of the 2008 economic meltdown, lower-income people being offered too-good-to-be-true mortgage deals. The truly vulnerable, always a focus for protection from advertising, are children—though efforts to protect children eventually also provided the impetus for negative public reactions to government programs of consumer protection.

Through the 1970s, one of the most notable advertising-focused activists was the founder of Action for Children's Television, Peggy Charren. ACT made repeated petitions to the FCC to both ban all child-oriented television advertising and to require that broadcasters carry age-specific programming as part of public service obligations. Along with Michael Jacobson of the Center for Science in the Public Interest, ACT similarly sought to have the FTC ban television advertising targeted at children under the legal theory that the messages are inherently deceptive to audiences too young to understand the messages' selling intent. Related petitions to the agencies challenged child-oriented advertising for vitamins and high-sugar foods.

In response to ACT petitions, in 1973 the National Association of Broadcasters revised its code for member stations, whose audiences accounted for two-thirds of TV viewers, as well as the three major networks, reducing by one-fourth the acceptable commercial minutes per hour in children's programming. The leading toy and cereal manufacturers provided the funding through the Council of Better Business Bureaus and the NAD/NARB for a new Children's Advertising Review Unit, CARU, that in 1974 was created to direct the association's efforts of self-regulation of children-targeted advertising. By the final years of the decade, the FTC, Congress, and the FCC were all holding their own hearings on the content of child-oriented programs, each considering possible restrictions or bans on advertising that sold products to children. As more marketplace-focused commissioners who disregarded ACT arguments came into the leadership of regulatory agencies in the 1980s, ACT brought its argument in the courts and is credited with having eventually persuaded the FCC to enact the Children's Television Act of 1990, which included rules governing advertising during children's programming.

ACT's spur to potential regulatory actions also provided an impetus for numerous academic studies attempting to discover the age when children acquire perceptual skepticism as part of their reactions to marketing messages. Interestingly enough, neither ACT nor researchers could explain how children might experience consumer socialization to develop such abilities if the only advertising they see is aimed at their parents. This basic, yet never answered, question helped make the FTC's hearings a target of antiregulation politicians. Their perception of regulatory overreach contributed to what Michael Pertschuk called the "revolt against regulation," first revealed by the results of the congressional elections of 1978. With the *Washington Post* referring to the FTC as a "national nanny," and on the heels of technical legal questions about how child-oriented advertising bans could be narrowly defined to pass First Amendment muster and be enforced, all hearings ended in 1980 without any new rules imposed with regard to advertising directed at children.

During the three decades from 1978 to 2008, when many consumer protections were dismantled by government, the FTC and the CBBB did what they could to retain efforts at regulation of deceptive advertising. During the late 1990s, the FTC tried, mostly without success, to encourage mass media vehicles to increase (or, in some cases, start) efforts to spot and screen deceptive advertising, deciding which messages to publish or broadcast. After a workshop in 2002 with a thinly veiled threat that the commission could hold media vehicles liable for the dissemination of obviously false claims of worthless weight-loss pills and lotions, there was a short-run effect that saw a reduction in advertising by the sellers of these questionable dietary supplements in reputable large-audience media vehicles.

The recently created Consumer Financial Protection Bureau is the newest government entrant into the field of consumer information and advertising regulation. Its most important actions to date with respect to advertising involve mortgages include a nationwide sweep in 2012 of ads targeting older American and military veterans.

With today's highly fragmented media system, businesses are faced with an increasingly difficult job of getting through to consumers who are able to evade their messages. This is especially true of young audiences, which are most desirable to advertisers. In this realm, one of the oldest problems of advertising veracity has re-emerged today in the form of advertising messages that appear to be news or entertainment content. This "native advertising" (to use the newest term) is becoming a modern flashpoint for criticisms and, possibly, future advertising regulations. At one time, the blurring of advertising and media content was resisted by the media themselves, especially journalists, who were concerned that advertising-supported content would reduce the credibility of news reports. Yet as even the oldest and most venerable of news organizations, such as the *Wall Street Journal*, now admit to allowing the mixing of paid messages and other content, this first line of defense is breaking down. The regulatory question for the twenty-first century could become drafting an approach to advertising regulation that judges whether it matters whether news and editorial content enjoy corporate support. But therein resides a different tale regarding consumer activism, even now being written.

Herbert Jack Rotfeld

See also: Action for Children's Television; State Attorneys General

Further Reading

Pertschuk, Michael. 1982. *Revolt against Regulation: The Rise and Pause of the Consumer Movement.* Berkeley: University of California Press.

Preston, Ivan L. 1975. *The Great American Blow-Up: Puffery in Advertising and Selling.* Madison: University of Wisconsin Press, rev. 1996.

Rotfeld, Herbert Jack. 2001. *Adventures in Misplaced Marketing.* Westport, CT: Quorum Books.

Rotfeld, Herbert Jack. 2010. "A Pessimist's Simplistic Historical Perspective on the Fourth Wave of Consumer Protection," *Journal of Consumer Affairs*, 44 (summer): 423–429.

ADVOCATES FOR HIGHWAY AND AUTO SAFETY

Advocates for Highway and Auto Safety is a 501(c)(4) nonprofit organization that since its founding in 1989 has sought to advance public policy at federal and state levels to increase motor vehicle safety. It is supported and controlled by a unique coalition of insurer, consumer, medical, public health, and safety groups. The insurers fund the roughly $2 million annual budget and hold half the seats on the twenty-four-member board of directors. Nonprofit leaders hold the other dozen seats.

The organization was created in the wake of tough new regulations on property/casualty insurers imposed by California's Proposition 103, which voters approved in 1988 to restrain rising automobile insurance premiums. Some insurance leaders recognized that they needed to do more to reduce accident-related losses, which drive up insurance rates, and that they could do so most effectively in partnership with consumer and safety groups. At the same time, some consumer leaders also acknowledged that more effective loss control efforts, as well as regulation, were needed to restrain rates.

For a year, three CEOs—Gerald Maatman from Kemper National Insurance Companies, Robert Vagley from the American Insurance Association, and Stephen

Brobeck from the Consumer Federation of America (CFA)—worked together to build support for a new insurer–consumer alliance to address motor vehicle safety issues. With support from longtime safety advocates, including Herman Brandau of State Farm Insurance and Clarence Ditlow of the Center for Auto Safety (CAS), they created Advocates and hired Judith Stone as the organization's president and operating head. Since 1967, Stone had worked on safety issues in Congress, in the U.S. Department of Transportation, and as a leader in several nonprofit and safety organizations. One of her greatest contributions to the organization was maintaining the cohesion of strong-minded leaders from diverse organizations who had often fought on other issues.

The organization had a quick start, in part because its board selected Joan Claybrook as co-chair alongside Maatman. Claybrook was the longtime leader of Public Citizen but also had served as the administrator of the National Highway Traffic Safety Administration (NHTSA) during the presidency of Jimmy Carter. Working closely with Maatman and Stone, Claybrook helped give the organization high visibility and credibility among safety advocates in and outside Congress and NHTSA.

They were supported by senior staffers such as Jacqueline Gillan and Henry Jasny, who have been with the organization since its first days. Gillan, who had worked with Claybrook at NHTSA as well as in the U.S. Senate and at three state transportation agencies, served as vice president coordinating policy strategies until she was selected as the organization's president in 2011, a position she has held since then. Jasny, now vice president and general counsel, had worked with Ditlow at CAS after practicing law for several years as a litigation attorney. Another key staffer has been attorney Catherine Chase, governmental affairs vice president. To this day, Advocates enjoys strong support from a board that includes Claybrook, Ditlow, CFA auto expert Jack Gillis, and leaders from the American College of Emergency Physicians, the American Public Health Association, the American Trauma Foundation, the Emergency Nurses Association, KidsandCars.com, and many major automobile insurance companies.

One of the organization's strengths is that it works on a broad array of motor vehicle safety issues. Experts agree that this safety can be most effectively pursued if there is focus on the vehicle, the driver, and the roadway environment. Advocates prioritizes all three areas. To improve vehicles, it has worked on issues such as more effective occupant protection and vehicle crashworthiness, including air bag, rollover, and roof crush protections, and rear visibility improvements. To improve driving, it has sought reforms such as mandatory blood alcohol testing, enactment of optimal graduated driver licensing laws, and measures to reduce distracted driving. To improve the roadway environment, it has worked for improvements such as stronger highway, bridge, and geometric design standards. The organization also seeks improved information for consumers and more adequate funding for federal and state highway and auto safety programs.

The work of Advocates has been based on research and analysis of hazards and ways to mitigate them. It has included organizing broad coalitions, identifying victims and survivors to support legislation, testifying at committee hearings, drafting legislative language, seeking target appropriations and funding directives to federal safety agencies, lobbying members of Congress, and, if all else fails, litigating in federal and state courts. Since the organization's founding, it has submitted more than 500 rulemaking comments to major regulatory dockets. Also noteworthy among its efforts has been publishing an annual *Roadmap to State Highway Safety Laws* report, which evaluates and grades every state on passage of key traffic safety laws. This report is widely used by policymakers, safety advocates, and the press.

It is never easy to fully understand the precise role of all factors—including lobbying, congressional leadership, and public opinion—in the making of policy reforms. But no one would disagree about Advocates' playing a major role in the approval of numerous reforms related to motor vehicle safety. At the federal level, these reforms include driver and passenger-side air bags; rollover, ejection, and roof crush prevention standards; improved tire safety; truck and bus safety reforms; tougher drunk driving laws; and improved consumer information about new vehicles and child safety restraints. At the state level, improvements include retention and passage of state primary enforcement seat belt laws, all-rider motorcycle helmet use laws and child booster seat laws, novice teen or graduated driver licensing laws, and distracted driving laws.

Judith Stone, Stephen Brobeck

See also: Center for Auto Safety; Consumers for Auto Reliability and Safety; Motor Vehicle Safety Advocacy

Further Reading

Miller, Ted R., et al. 2011. "Fruits of 20 Years of Highway Safety Legislative Advocacy in the United States." *Annals of Advances in Automotive Medicine* 55 (October): 357–363.

AFRICAN CONSUMER MOVEMENTS

See East African Consumer Movements; Kenyan Consumer Movement; West African Consumer Movements

AIR TRAVEL ADVOCACY

Consumer advocacy related to air travel began in the 1970s, reflecting three main factors—increasing passenger travel, the deregulation of the airlines, and the rise of the modern consumer movement. As air travel and the industry both grew in the early decades of the twentieth century, there was mounting concern about the stability of carriers engaged in cutthroat competition. Accordingly, in the 1930s the federal government intervened, through the Civil Aeronautics Board (CAB), to begin controlling routes and prices. This regulation continued until the 1970s, when the CAB began loosening constraints and Congress passed the Airline Deregulation Act of 1978. (In 1958, Congress had approved the creation of an airline safety agency now known as the Federal Aviation Administration [FAA].)

In the decades before this deregulation, air passenger travel had grown significantly. From 1954 to 1978, the number of passenger enplanements increased more than sevenfold—from 35 million to 275 million. During the latter portion of this period, the modern consumer movement emerged. Its most visible and influential leader was Ralph Nader, who inspired and helped create new national and state consumer groups. One of these groups was the Aviation Consumer Action Project (ACAP).

ACAP was established in 1971 as a tax-exempt nonprofit organization to advocate the interests of air travelers, with a special focus on safety and customer service issues. But air traveler advocacy did not gain much public visibility until 1976, when Nader himself was bumped from an Allegheny Airlines flight and then sued the airline. Although Nader's claim for financial damages was rejected, the lawsuit led to the unearthing of anticonsumer practices that eventually persuaded the CAB to intervene by issuing a rule that required compensation for bumped passengers.

Cornish Hitchcock was a key ACAP leader during this period. From 1977 to 1981, he worked for ACAP, the last two years as executive director. For the next ten years, as an attorney with the Public Citizen Litigation Group, he served as ACAP's legal director. From 1984 to 1992, attorney Chris Witkowski directed ACAP, which focused most of its attention on safety issues. In this period, the organization raised safety concerns about President Reagan's firing of the air traffic controllers, FAA's underreporting of near-collisions, and inadequate crash and fire safety precautions in airline cabins. Since Witkowski left ACAP, he has worked for the Association of Flight Attendants union, where he has continued to address airline safety issues.

In 1995, attorney Paul Hudson joined the ACAP board of directors and, two years later, was appointed the organization's executive director, a position he continues to hold today. After Hudson lost a daughter in the 1988 terrorist bombing of a Pan Am flight, he created a Victims Family Organization that sought compensation for victims and new safety precautions. For the past two decades, Hudson has been the most active consumer advocate for air traveler protections. For example, in 1998, he sued the FAA to overturn the certification of the new Boeing 777-300 for failing to require traditional passenger evacuation testing.

In 2006, a new airline passenger advocacy group was organized by Kate Hanni, who was angered by being kept in an American Airlines plane for nine hours on the tarmac in Austin, Texas. Using her own personal resources, she created a FlyersRights organization that communicated with news media, lobbied Congress, and advocated before the Department of Transportation (DOT), which now was responsible for customer service issues. In 2013, Hanni stepped down as executive director of FlyersRights and supported its merger with ACAP. ACAP leader Hudson had represented Hanni in her lawsuit against American Airlines.

Although Hanni helped persuade members of Congress to propose legislation establishing new airline passenger rights, she and other advocates could not convince that body to approve the bills. However, they had greater success with DOT in the administration of a president, Barack Obama, who had voiced support for these passenger rights. In 2009, DOT issued a rule requiring airlines to give passengers, on domestic flights, the ability to leave planes stuck on the ground for more than three hours. In 2011, the department imposed a four-hour delay limit on international flights, required prominent posting of information about fees, and provided passengers greater flexibility to change tickets.

For several decades, mainstream consumer groups have, from time to time, addressed airline issues. During this period, Mark Cooper, Consumer Federation of America (CFA) research director, has analyzed and commented to the press and Congress about the consumer impacts of airline bankruptcies, mergers, and other competitive issues. Since 2008, the American Antitrust Institute has been active speaking out about mergers and competition. In 2011, CFA, Consumers Union, Consumer Action, and the National Consumers League filed comments in a DOT rulemaking on airline fees. Many consumer groups, and Ralph Nader, also have expressed concerns recently about airport security measures, such as the use of full-body scanners, that affect the privacy of travelers.

Stephen Brobeck

See also: Nader, Ralph; Public Citizen

Further Reading

Dickerson, Thomas A. 1982. "Travel Law: Securing Travelers' Rights and Remedies." *Trial* 18 (August): 44–47.

Morrison, Steven A., and Clifford Winston. 1988. "Air Safety, Deregulation and Public Policy." *Brookings Review* (winter): 10–15.

Subcommittee on Aviation of the Committee on Transportation and Infrastructure, House of Representatives. 2007. *Hearing on Airline Delays and Consumer Issues.* (April 9): v. 4.

ALL-TERRAIN VEHICLE ADVOCACY

All-terrain vehicles (ATVs) have been on the market for approximately forty years. ATVs are three- or four-wheel machines equipped with wide, knobby, or paddlelike tires and special suspension systems capable of handling rough terrain. These vehicles are specifically designed for off-road travel. Although the earliest three-wheel machines had little more power than large riding lawnmowers, the Consumer Product Safety Commission (CPSC) has found that the number of ATVs with large engines increased threefold between 1989 and 1997. Many ATVs can now be driven faster than 75 miles per hour.

By the mid 1980s, about 600,000 three- and four-wheel ATVs were sold annually in the United States. In 2001, according to the CPSC's "All-Terrain Vehicle 2001 Injury and Exposure Studies," about 5.6 million of these ATVs were in use. In 2010, according to the CPSC's most recent data, there were 10.6 million four-wheel ATVs in use.

Each year since 2004, nearly 800 Americans have died, and 140,000 have been injured, in ATV-related incidents. CPSC data indicate that in 2011, at least fifty-seven children lost their lives, and 29,000 children were injured seriously enough to require hospital treatment, in ATV incidents.

Concerned about increasing rates of injury and death to children in ATV incidents, in the 1980s a wide range of groups—Consumer Federation of America (CFA), U.S. Public Interest Research Group (USPIRG), Public Citizen, Consumers Union, American Academy of Pediatrics, and National Association for Attorneys General—urged the CPSC to take action. In 1985, the federal agency initiated rulemaking and, in 1987, filed a lawsuit against ATV manufacturers that asked the court to declare ATVs to be "imminently dangerous consumer products." The lawsuit sought to require that manufacturers end production of three-wheel ATVs, repurchase all three-wheel ATVs from dealer stocks, offer financial incentives to encourage owners of three-wheel ATVs to return them, and provide safety education to ATV users.

On the day it was filed, the lawsuit was settled by a negotiated consent decree. This decree, however, did not include important elements of the original CPSC lawsuit, including the requirement that manufacturers offer financial incentives to encourage owners of three-wheel ATVs to return them to dealers. Although manufacturers had opposed the lawsuit and the consent decree, they accepted the latter and reduced production of three-wheel ATVs.

When the consent decree expired in 1998—in 1991, the CPSC had terminated the rulemaking—the commission and major manufacturers entered into voluntary company-specific agreements, known generally as ATV Action Plans. However, these plans did not extend to new entrants into the market, which were selling an increasing number of vehicles. These companies were free to sell vehicles of any size to any individual, were not required to offer training to owners, and were exempt from the minimal oversight that major ATV makers exercised over their dealer networks.

In 2002, in response to the failure of the voluntary approach to ATV safety and the increasing death and injuries caused by ATVs, a coalition of advocacy groups filed a petition with the CPSC calling for the agency to ban the sale of adult-size ATVs for use by children. The coalition was led by CFA but also included AAP, the Natural Trails and Water Coalition, and Concerned Families for ATV Safety. In response to the petition, the agency, under the leadership of Chairman Hal Stratton, held numerous hearings across the country, denied the petition, and began a rulemaking process in 2005. Although the Senate held hearings on ATVs in 2006 and 2007, no significant legislative or regulatory activity occurred until the passage of the Consumer Product Safety Improvements Act (CPSIA) in 2008, which required that imported ATVs meet the same standards of ATVs manufactured domestically. Major manufacturers supported this new requirement.

The CPSIA included provisions that directed the CPSC to make the voluntary standard mandatory, required that all ATVs imported or sold in the United States be subject to an ATV Action Plan, required the CPSC to move forward with and complete its rulemaking, and banned three-wheel ATVs from being sold in or imported into the country. However, despite these reforms, the standard did not adequately respond to all safety concerns voiced by the consumer advocacy and medical communities, including changing the definition of an adult-size ATV from an engine size of greater than 90cc to a size-fit model whereby children of different ages could ride ATVs of certain speeds. The mandatory standard was published in late 2008 and became effective in April 2009. In August 2011, Congress passed legislation (H.R. 2715) that amended the CPSIA by directing the CPSC to complete the ATV rulemaking within a year of enactment. Yet by early 2015 the rule had not yet been completed.

In October 2012, the CPSC held an ATV Summit to inform its rulemaking activities. Physicians, academics, consumer advocates, parents whose children had died riding ATVs, ATV safety trainers, and ATV manufacturers, among others, participated in this meeting. Although advocates and "victims" called for tougher standards, industry representatives supported the size-fit transitional vehicle approach, objected to changing ATV designs to make ATVs safer, and objected to changing the legislative or regulatory status quo in any way.

Recently, ATV safety advocates have come together to work on the increasing problem of ATVs being driven on public roads. ATV labels indicate that the vehicles should not operate on public roads. Yet an increasing number of states and municipalities are passing laws allowing them to do so, increasing related injury and death on these roads.

Rachel Weintraub

See also: Household Product Safety Advocacy; Motor Vehicle Safety Advocacy

Further Reading

U.S. Consumer Product Safety Commission. 2013. *ATV Safety Summit: Keeping Families Safe on ATVs, Staff Report* (September).

Weintraub, Rachel, and Michael Best. 2014. *ATVs on Roadways: A Safety Crisis.* Consumer Federation of America (March).

AMERICAN COUNCIL ON CONSUMER INTERESTS

The American Council on Consumer Interests (ACCI) is a membership organization for academicians and other professionals involved in consumer and family economics. It promotes excellence in research and education as a means of enhancing the well-being of consumers and their households. The research conducted by ACCI members typically focuses on economic and financial issues facing households, and this research is often of practical use to individual consumers as well as to consumer policymakers. As a professional organization, ACCI also provides professional development activities for its members. These activities include publishing a peer-reviewed, multidisciplinary journal and convening an annual conference.

ACCI is one of the oldest consumer-oriented organizations in the United States. In 1952, Colston Warne, president of the board of directors of Consumers Union and economics professor at Amherst College, saw the need for a consumer education association. Warne's vision was shared by Henry Harap of the George Peabody College for Teachers and Ray Price of the University of Minnesota. Together, they convened a planning session at the University of Minnesota comprising approximately twenty prominent consumer educators. The session resulted, in 1953, in the establishment of the Council on Consumer Information. In 1969, the organization's name was changed to the American Council on Consumer Interests.

From its inception, ACCI embraced professionals from a variety of backgrounds. Its twenty-one charter members included nine from education, six from economics, three from home economics, and three from public policy. ACCI membership includes academics trained in economics, sociology, psychology, history, law, and a variety of applied fields.

In its early years, ACCI relied on financial subsidies from Consumers Union. By 1969, ACCI was self-supporting, but its relationship with Consumers Union has remained close. In particular, several of ACCI's leaders—including Gordon Bivens,

Robert Herrmann, Stewart Lee, Scott Maynes, Helen Nelson, and Norman Silber—have contributed their time and expertise to Consumers Union as members of its board of directors. ACCI is also a member of the Consumer Federation of America and Consumers International, two of the world's most important consumer advocacy organizations, but ACCI itself eschews any advocacy. ACCI defines its principal role in terms of promoting research and education that benefit consumers and society.

The most significant contribution of ACCI to the field of consumer affairs has been the organization's publications. For decades, the *ACCI Newsletter* provided timely information for consumer affairs professionals about publications, government consumer actions, organization activities, and other items of consumer interest. This publication was developed, and for three decades was edited, by Stewart Lee. In 1966, under the editorship of Gordon Bivens, ACCI launched the *Journal of Consumer Affairs (JCA)*, which continues to be the most important outlet for academic research articles on consumer topics. *JCA* has benefited from a series of visionary yet meticulous editors, including, most recently, Herb Rotfeld of Auburn University and the publication's current editor, Sharon Tennyson of Cornell University. *JCA* is currently published by Wiley Periodicals and is accessed frequently by scholars, students, and activists around the world.

At the conclusion of each annual conference, presented papers and speeches are circulated widely in the form of the *Consumer Interests Annual*. The proceedings of two special conferences served to summarize and advance research knowledge concerning consumer economics and consumer policy: *The Frontier of Research in the Consumer Interest* (1988), edited by E. Scott Maynes; and *Enhancing Consumer Choice* (1991), edited by Robert N. Mayer.

The commitment of ACCI's members to household economic well-being is reflected in the special lectures it sponsors and the honors ACCI bestows at its annual conference. The conferences feature two noteworthy addresses by leaders from the government, consumer organizations, and academia: the Colston Warne Lectureship and the Esther Peterson Consumer Policy Forum. Special awards presented at the annual conference have included the Applied Consumer Economics Award, the Friends of Consumers Award, the Stewart M. Lee Consumer Education Award, and the Rhoda Karpatkin International Consumer Fellows Lectureship. Additional awards for excellence in research reflect partnerships between ACCI and the National Endowment for Financial Education, the Certified Financial Planning Board, and the AARP Public Policy Institute. Individuals who have served ACCI for years, making special contributions, are honored by being named ACCI Distinguished Fellows. Forty members have received this special honor.

ACCI's budget and membership role are modest. The major sources of ACCI income are membership dues, royalties from the publication of the *Journal of Consumer Affairs*, and registration fees at the annual conference. Revenues for the 2013–2014 fiscal year were approximately $200,000; expenses were about $162,000. As of August 2014, there were 156 professional members, seven retiree members, forty-two student members, and five complimentary members. An additional 658 people receive communications about ACCI activities. Whereas ACCI's members are primarily drawn from the United States, about 10 percent of its active members are international members representing nine countries. ACCI is managed by a professional association management company with a part-time executive director. Its website is www.consumerinterests.org.

Robert N. Mayer

See also: Consumer Federation of America; Consumers International; Consumers Union/Consumer Reports

Further Reading

Mayer, Robert N., ed. 1991. *Enhancing Consumer Choice.* Columbia, MO: American Council on Consumer Interests.

Maynes, E. Scott, ed. 1988. *The Frontier of Research in the Consumer Interest.* Columbia, MO: American Council on Consumer Interests.

Merchant, Marjorie. M., ed. 1987. *The American Council on Consumer Interests: An Oral History.* Columbia, MO: American Council on Consumer Interests.

AMERICANS FOR FINANCIAL REFORM

Americans for Financial Reform (AFR) is a coalition of more than 200 consumer, civil rights labor, investor, business, faith-based, and community-based organizations working for reform of Wall Street and the financial sector. Formed in response to the financial and economic meltdown of 2008, it coordinated most of the public interest advocacy related to the Dodd–Frank financial reform legislation, with a particular focus on the establishment of the Consumer Financial Protection Bureau (CFPB). Since enactment of this legislation in 2010, AFR's top priority has been implementation of this new law.

In April 2009, representatives of the AFL–CIO, AFSCME, Service Employees International Union (SEIU), Center for Responsible Lending, Consumer Federation of America, Leadership Conference on Civil and Human Rights, U.S. PIRG, and several dozen other organizations met at AFL–CIO headquarters in Washington, D.C., with Elizabeth Warren as a featured speaker. They agreed to join forces in a new coalition to ensure that consumer and worker voices were heard as Congress debated responses to the financial crisis.

Beginning with $200,000 in seed money from the Arca Foundation and Panta Rhea Foundation, AFR leaders hired Heather Booth as director and Lisa Donner as deputy director. Booth has been a leading progressive activist since the 1960s. Her earlier activism had included founding and leading the Midwest Academy (which trained organizers), leading Citizen Action, and heading the AFL–CIO's advocacy in 2008 for health care reform. Donner had worked for SEIU and been a leader of the Center for Working Families and the Half in Ten Campaign.

Booth and Donner hired a small staff, built an infrastructure to connect its member groups and allow them to strategize and plan effectively together, formed task forces to coordinate plans in the major issue areas (including consumer financial products, investor protection, derivatives, and systemic risk), developed a network of local partners in key areas of the country, and began work helping to strengthen and secure passage of Dodd–Frank.

In the months before that law's enactment, AFR and its members held meetings and briefing sessions with administration officials and members of Congress; drafted policy papers, briefing materials, letters, and op-eds; and developed and disseminated policy and communications materials for advocates and the broader public. They held press conferences and briefings; organized grasstops outreach efforts, in-district events, and, in some cases, actions directly targeting Wall Street; organized online petitions and advocacy campaigns; and set up phone banks allowing people to contact members of the House and Senate.

The 2013 book *Financial Justice* analyzed AFR's role in Dodd–Frank and concluded that the coalition had a significant effect. Senator Warren was in agreement: "Dodd–Frank would have been a much weaker law if AFR had not been there. The AFR coalition played a critical role in pushing for a strong and independent Consumer Financial Protection Bureau and, after the law was passed, in defending the bureau against attack and helping it get started on the right path."

After passage of Dodd–Frank, Donner was made executive director of AFR. With an annual budget of under $1 million, provided mainly by foundations, she leads a small central staff that works closely with subject-specific task forces in which many of the members continue to participate. Policy decisions are overseen by a twenty-person executive committee and a six-person steering committee.

In the past three years, AFR has focused most of its efforts in three areas—defending the CFPB against attacks from the financial services industry and antiregulation members of Congress, supporting President Obama's nomination of Richard Cordray to become the first director of the bureau, and engaging in the making of dozens of rules by the CFPB and other agencies, such as the Securities and Exchange Commission. Cordray was confirmed by the Senate in July 2013, and to date, CFPB opponents have not succeeded in restructuring, and weakening, the agency.

Jim Lardner

See also: Legislative Advocacy

Further Reading

Kirsch, Larry, and Robert N. Mayer. 2013. *Financial Justice: the People's Campaign to Stop Lender Abuse.* Santa Barbara, CA: Praeger.
Warren, Elizabeth. 2014. *A Fighting Chance.* New York: Metropolitan Books.

ANTITRUST ADVOCACY

Numerous consumer groups have used antitrust laws to advocate for greater competition and consumer choice in the marketplace. These advocates have operated under the assumption that competition provides three important benefits to consumers—competitive prices, choice of whom to deal with and under what terms, and an innovative economy. This article describes longstanding antitrust protections, conservative challenges to these protections, and twenty-first-century consumer activism based on the traditional protections.

Antitrust Protections

The history of antitrust at the federal level commenced with passage of the Sherman Act in 1890, although several states had enacted antitrust laws earlier. In 1914, two additional federal laws were passed—the Clayton Act and the Federal Trade Commission (FTC) Act. Although there have been amendments, the basic framework they established has not changed since 1914. Private causes of action for anticompetitive harms are not only permitted, but are encouraged by the statutory trebling of damages and award of attorneys' fees. As a result, an estimated nine out of ten antitrust cases are private.

The Sherman Act has two key sections. Section 1 proscribes agreements in restraint of trade. The collective activity that is central to this provision can be between two or more competing sellers or buyers (horizontal) or a seller and purchaser (vertical).

In a landmark ruling in 1911, the U.S. Supreme Court held that Section 1 prohibited only restraints of trade that unreasonably restrict competition. Over the years, the concept of reasonableness has been analyzed in two ways: Some restraints are per se unreasonable, and others are subject to the so-called Rule of Reason. The former are restraints (such as horizontal price-fixing, bid-rigging, or the division of customers of markets among competitors) that are considered inherently anticompetitive and that do not require an elaborate examination of market context or effects.

For restraints that are not per se illegal, a detailed market study is necessary to decide whether the conduct is, on the whole, pro-competitive or anticompetitive. In recent years, the Rule of Reason, which has tended to favor defendants, has been applied to more forms of business conduct. The precise boundary between per se and Rule of Reason cases is often unclear.

Section 2 of the Sherman Act prohibits obtaining or preserving a monopoly by anticompetitive methods (monopolization). It does not consider great size or market share alone to be illegal.

The Sherman Act can be enforced as a civil law or as a criminal law, a judgment left to the Antitrust Division of the Department of Justice (DOJ). Typically, criminal prosecution is directed at the worst per se violations—primarily price fixing, bid rigging, and naked divisions of territories or customers. In recent years, corporations have often been heavily fined, and individuals sent to prison, with increasing frequency.

The early enforcement of the Sherman Act revealed weaknesses that were addressed in legislation in 1914. The Clayton Act outlaws specific types of conduct, such as tying arrangements, exclusive dealing, and anticompetitive mergers. Section 7 of this act is the principal tool for prohibiting anticompetitive concentrations related to mergers, acquisitions, and joint ventures.

Under the 1976 Hart–Scott–Rodino Act, mergers and acquisitions that exceed certain size thresholds must be reported to the DOJ and FTC in advance. The Robinson–Patman Act amended the Clayton Act in 1936 and prohibits price discrimination. Rarely enforced by federal agencies, it is, however, the basis for much private litigation.

In 1914, Congress also passed the Federal Trade Commission Act, which established the FTC as an independent regulatory agency. Section 5 of this act prohibits "unfair methods of competition" and "unfair or deceptive acts or practices." Each state has its own antitrust and consumer protection laws, often referred to as "Little FTC" or "Little Sherman" acts. In general, they are similar to federal law.

The FTC and DOJ's Antitrust Division have a similar antitrust jurisdiction. The FTC has no criminal jurisdiction but typically plays a larger role than DOJ in the issuance of reports and development of long-range policy. Whereas DOJ proceeds through the federal district courts, the FTC usually uses an administrative process. However, when it opposes a merger, the FTC also usually seeks an injunction in federal district courts.

As noted above, U.S. antitrust statutes encourage private enforcement. Private plaintiffs, who can recover reasonable attorneys' fees, are able to sue for treble damages and injunctions to remedy federal antitrust violations. They may use judgments or decrees entered against a defendant in a government antitrust suit as "prima facie evidence" against the defendant. Court-imposed restrictions on compensable injuries and limits on standing and recovers by indirect purchases have, to some extent, offset the statutory encouragements.

Attorneys for antitrust plaintiffs often are compensated on contingency, as a percentage of the recovery. Since many harms suffered by individual consumers are not large enough to justify expensive antitrust suits, consumers are usually represented in class actions. If consumers are indirect purchasers from the violator—e.g., the manufacturers collude to raise prices to the retailers who resell to consumers—they do not have standing in the federal courts under the Supreme Court's *Illinois Brick* opinion. However, many states have adopted *Illinois Brick* repealer statutes, which permit indirect purchaser class actions in states in which about half the U.S. population resides.

Conservative Redefinition of Antitrust

There is general agreement that the principal ultimate goal of antitrust laws and enforcement is the advancement of "consumer welfare." But this term has two very different meanings. Most people, and all consumer advocates, would define this welfare in terms of protection from unnecessarily high prices, the commercial peonage that results from the absence of choices, and economic stagnation. Yet, in the 1970s, conservative scholars, associated notably with the University of Chicago, defined consumer welfare in terms of maximizing economic output. These conservatives believed that large corporate size is probably necessary for efficiency, that high levels of concentration are not as important as competitive effects, that anticompetitive effects are usually found only when horizontal collusion occurs, that markets rarely fail but that government interference in markets often has anticompetitive side effects, and that government regulation, including antitrust enforcement, is more likely to worsen than to improve conditions.

These political and economic views were adopted by the Reagan administration, which substantially reduced antitrust enforcement budgets and appointed judges skeptical of antitrust. As a result, it became increasingly difficult for either the government or private plaintiffs to win cases. Predatory pricing was less likely to be treated as an illegal practice. The "essential facility" doctrine, which under some conditions required a monopolist to share certain assets with rivals, was undermined. And defendants found it easier to defend against antitrust challenges because of new procedural impediments.

In retrospect, it is evident that some decisions and doctrines in the 1960s and 1970s, which were rejected in the 1980s, promoted inefficiencies to the detriment of consumers. Moreover, the Reagan administration did bring cases against horizontal collusion, specifically price-fixing and similar anticonsumer practices. The breakup of AT&T, accomplished by Reagan's Antitrust Division, unleashed pro-consumer innovation. However, this deregulation also reduced government oversight without replacing it with aggressive antitrust, markets were allowed to become more concentrated, merger enforcement was reduced, monopolization was rarely challenged, and vertical restraints—such as resale price maintenance—were considered to promote efficiency.

During the 1990s, the Clinton administration practiced more traditional antitrust enforcement. For example, it brought a landmark case against Microsoft for monopolization of Internet browsers and another case against American Airlines for predatory pricing against budget rivals. The Bush administration scaled back enforcement against mergers and monopolization and applied a weak remedy in the Microsoft case. The Obama administration revived merger enforcement, for example, by dismantling a huge international cartel of auto parts. However, today federal enforcers are unwilling to challenge many problematic mergers and dominant firms, many judges hold conservative views of antitrust, and conservatives and business relentlessly attack class actions.

Consumer Advocacy

Until relatively recently, there was no consumer advocacy group focused exclusively on antitrust issues. Most multi-issue and single-issue consumer groups did, from time to time, make an antitrust issue a high priority. But this issue was usually only one of a number of priority issues they addressed. That is evident from a brief review of the recent work of some of the most active national organizations. This work included urging Congress or federal agencies to act, initiating lawsuits, and filing supporting amicus briefs in other lawsuits. For example, in 2012 Public Citizen filed an amicus brief asking for the ability to participate in a lawsuit that expanded antitrust immunity protecting business. In 2013, Consumers Union urged DOJ to require important concessions before approving the merger of American Airlines and U.S. Airways. In 2010, the National Consumers League and other groups urged DOJ to block a merger between Ticketmaster and Live Nation. In 2012, Food & Water Watch protested the merger of Conagra and Ralcorp and, in 2014, objected to the merger of Sysco and U.S. Foods. Especially during the past decade, both the Consumer Federation of America and Public Knowledge worked together against increasing media concentration, actively opposing mergers between Universal Music Group and EMI and between Comcast and Time Warner.

In 1998, however, Albert Foer created the American Antitrust Institute to promote competition, ensure that competition serves consumers, and challenge abuses of concentrated economic power. After earning a law degree from the University of Chicago, Foer worked for a large firm before joining the FTC's Bureau of Competition, where he dealt with antitrust issues for six years. Years later, after helping run the family jewelry business, he was encouraged by Ralph Nader to organize a new consumer group focused on antitrust issues. First with funding from businesses trying to protect themselves from anticompetitive practices, then increasingly with court *cy près* awards, Foer built an organization with a budget of just under $1 million, several staff, and more than 100 competition policy experts around the world.

Led by Foer, these staff and experts submitted amicus briefs in legal cases, published papers and book-length analyses of antitrust issues, and hosted symposiums on many antitrust topics. In the course of a typical year, AAI works on about two dozen separate antitrust issues, often with another consumer group. One of its most successful interventions was helping persuade the Obama administration to vigorously oppose AT&T's attempt to purchase T-Mobile USA, which the two companies abandoned. The work of AAI has continued until the present. In late 2013, Foer announced that he would retire as president in the coming year. In late 2014, Foer retired as president and was succeeded by Diana Moss, an economist who had worked for AAI since 2000.

Albert Foer, Stephen Brobeck

Further Reading

Lattman, Peter. 2011. "Finding Success in a Lifelong Passion for Fighting Monopolies." *New York Times* (December 21).

Peritz, Rudolph J. R. 2001. *Competition Policy in America: History, Rhetoric, Law.* New York: Oxford University Press.

APPLIANCE EFFICIENCY ADVOCACY

In large part because of the advocacy of environmental and consumer groups during the past forty years, the efficiency of home appliances has improved dramatically. Throughout the 1950s and 1960s, because appliances tended to become larger and more feature-laden (e.g., automatic defrost), energy use increased. But beginning in the early 1970s, interest in product efficiency increased considerably, driven both by rising energy prices (after the 1973 Arab oil embargo) and environmental concerns about power plant siting. Energy use peaked in 1974 and has declined since then, largely because of minimum efficiency standards for appliances. A striking example of this improvement has been the steep decline in average household refrigerator use—from more than 2,000 kilowatt-hours in 1974 to well under 500 kilowatt-hours by 2014.

Minimum efficiency standards are laws at state and federal levels requiring that products meet a specified minimum efficiency level in order to be legally sold or produced. For example, for refrigerators these laws specify maximum energy consumption, in kilowatt-hours per year, with the maximum varying by product size and features. Interest in standards in the United States emerged in the late 1960s, when standards were first mentioned as a policy tool following a major multistate electrical blackout in the Northeast in 1965.

In the early 1970s, environmental concerns about power plant siting on the West Coast led to a major analysis of energy policy options, including standards. This analysis spurred a policy debate that led, in 1974, to passage by the California legislature of the Warren–Alquist Act, which established the California Energy Commission with the authority to set appliance efficiency standards. The first standards of the commission took effect in 1976. The same year, New York began to adopt standards.

Activity at the state level, together with interest in reducing U.S. dependence on energy imports, led to consideration of standards at the federal level. At first, the chosen federal option was voluntary targets for appliance efficiency of 20 percent, on average, below current levels. These goals were formalized in an executive order by President Ford and then by congressional approval of the Energy Policy and Conservation Act of 1975. However, mandatory state standards began to take effect before the success of these voluntary targets could be assessed.

The Carter administration proposed mandatory federal standards, which, after extensive congressional debate, were approved with 1978 passage of the National Energy Conservation and Policy Act. This law included a provision directing the U.S. Department of Energy (DOE) to set mandatory minimum efficiency standards on appliances. DOE proceeded to develop new standards, but before they could be finalized, there was a change in presidents. The incoming Reagan administration was philosophically opposed to interventions in the marketplace and so rejected the appliance standards. However, in 1985, this decision was overturned by the federal courts.

In the early 1980s, states increased their standard-setting activity, and by 1986, six states had adopted standards for one or more products. The growing number of state standards and concerns about future federal standards persuaded appliance manufacturers to propose negotiations with energy efficiency advocates, including the Natural Resources Defense Council (NRDC), American Council for an Energy-Efficient Economy (ACEEE), state energy offices, and others. These discussions led to a consensus proposal that Congress adopt specific federal standards on many major appliances that would also preempt state standards. This agreement was approved by Congress and signed into law by President Reagan as the National Appliance Energy Conservation Act (NAECA) of 1987. The NAECA also included a provision calling on DOE to periodically review and revise minimum efficiency standards. To date, DOE has revised standards on several dozen products, including multiple revisions for some products.

Many steep drops in product energy use occurred right after new standards took effect. However, in recent years product efficiency has often been stagnant or improved slowly. A 2012 report by ACEEE estimates that taking into account products sold from the inception of each national standard through 2035, existing standards would net consumers and businesses more than $1.1 trillion in cumulative savings. Over the same period, cumulative energy savings would exceed 200 quadrillion Btus of energy, an amount equal to about two years of total U.S. energy consumption.

Work on appliance standards has included both environmental and consumer organizations. Efforts have often been led by energy efficiency and environmental groups—such as ACEEE, NRDC, and the Appliance Standards Awareness Project (ASAP)—but state energy offices, several major electric utilities wanting to reduce the need for new power plants, and consumer groups—such as Consumer Federation of America, Consumers Union, and National Consumer Law Center—have also played prominent roles. All these groups usually work together to develop common positions and advocate for them. Efforts to set new standards always involve some type of consumer life-cycle cost analysis in which the increased cost of more efficient products is compared to the energy bill savings consumers will realize. Standards are set only at levels where the benefits exceed the costs.

Although standards play a leading role in improving appliance efficiency, other policies contribute as well. Since the 1990s, the Energy Star program, run by DOE and the Environmental Protection Agency, has recognized products of above-average efficiency and helped consumers to easily identify these products. Typically, because Energy Star levels are intentionally set so that only about a quarter of units on the market qualify, the label induces manufacturers to develop more qualifying models—and consumers to purchase these models, thus increasing their market share. When this market share increases to roughly 50 percent, DOE and EPA raise the qualification levels so that, again, only about a quarter of products qualify. This process is supported by the rebates that many utilities have offered to customers who purchase Energy Star—or even more efficient—products.

Appliances are also labeled with "Energy Guide" labels, a program overseen by the Federal Trade Commission. Research to date has found that these labels have had minimum impacts on the efficiency of products in the U.S. marketplace. However, different types of labels used in other countries appear to have improved product efficiency.

Steven Nadel

See also: Electricity Service Advocacy; Motor Vehicle Fuel Economy Advocacy

Further Reading

Alliance to Save Energy. 2013. *The History of Energy Efficiency* (January).

Nadel, Steve, and David Goldstein. 1996. *Appliance and Efficiency Standards: History, Impacts, Current Status, and Future Directions*, Research Report A963. American Council for Energy Efficient Economy (January 1).

ATTORNEYS GENERAL
See State Attorneys General

AUSTRALIAN CONSUMER MOVEMENT

The first wave of consumer activism in Australia had its roots in early women's organizations that came to prominence in the first few decades of the 1900s such as the National Council of Women, the Country Women's Association, and the Federated Association of Australian Housewives. Considering the concerns that motivated them and the methods employed by these women's organizations, it's clear that some things have remained the same for almost a century. These women were troubled by issues related to health and nutrition, food safety, pricing, shopping hours, and inflation. Most of these issues remain concerns today. To ensure that their voices were heard, members of these organizations engaged in consumer boycotts and protest marches as well as in market-based interventions, such as by forming cooperatives and engaging in bulk buying.

The modern Australian consumer movement can be traced to the establishment of the Australian Consumers' Association (now known as Choice) in 1959. It was a product of the postwar boom, which saw an explosion in the availability of affordable household appliances and the consequent worldwide movement to establish independent consumer testing organizations to provide consumers with objective information. Choice was established by Ruby Hutchinson, the first woman to be elected to the Western Australia Legislative Council. Choice's main communications tool was its monthly magazine, also known as *Choice*, which disseminated the results of its laboratory tests. In the 1960s, members flocked to both the magazine and the organization, although most members now seek information via its digital products rather than the printed magazine. Successive Choice leaders have played important parts in Australia's consumer protection history, both from within Choice and from without. They include Philippa Smith, Alan Asher, Louise Sylvan, and Peter Kell.

Ruby Hutchinson is remembered and celebrated each year on March 15 (International Consumer Rights Day) by a lecture held in her name. The first such lecture was given in the 1980s by then Australian prime minister, Bob Hawke. He has been followed by a long list of passionate, articulate, and creative consumer advocates.

Choice is wholly self-funded by member subscriptions to its information products, revenue from its testing laboratories, and, more recently, member contributions. Choice does not take money from government, industry, or advertising, remaining fiercely independent.

Over the years, Choice's mandate has widened. Although Choice continues to test products, it also runs campaigns on issues of concern to its members. Some of the more prominent campaigns run by Choice in recent years have focused on excessive bank fees, food labeling, environmental marketing claims, and a number of issues associated with energy and telecommunications.

Choice was not the only consumer group to emerge in Australia during the postwar era. The organization's success, along with the influence of international initiatives such as Ralph Nader's 1965 pioneering work—*Unsafe at Any Speed*—led to the emergence of additional consumer organizations in the 1960s and early 1970s. Some of these groups specialized either in specific consumer issues or in particular regions or states. Governments, too, began to take notice, with the New South Wales (NSW) state government appointing the first consumer affairs minister in Australia in the 1960s and the Australian Commonwealth government passing the Trade Practices Act in 1974—landmark legislation that has been strengthened over the years. For example, Part V of the Trade Practices Act 1974—which dealt with consumer protection—was recently renamed the Australian Consumer Law and is now part of the Australian Competition and Consumer Act 2010.

Also in 1974, the Commonwealth government, under the prime ministership of Gough Whitlam, provided funding for the establishment of a body to provide a national voice for Australia's fledgling consumer movement. The body was originally known as the Australian Federation of Consumer Organizations (AFCO) but was renamed the Consumers Federation of Australia (CFA) in the early 1990s. Successive governments have provided core funding for the organization. At its peak, CFA had seven staff members devoted to training and coordinating the activities of 120 member groups around the country. CFA provided a means for grassroots organizations to have input into federal policymaking and representation on an array of committees and boards up until 1996, when government funding for the organization was abolished. CFA has continued since then thanks to the dedication of consumer advocates such as David Tenant, Carolyn Bond, Catriona Lowe, and Gordon Renouf, who volunteer their time and energy to ensure that it remains a strong voice advocating on behalf of Australian consumers.

The late 1970s also brought a radical edge to the consumer movement, with campaigns such as BUGA UP altering billboard advertising for cigarettes and alcohol to get a more health-oriented message across. Today, the radical side of Australian consumer policy can be seen with the recent plain packaging requirements for cigarettes, the first such in any nation. These requirements prohibit visual branding on cigarette packages and require packs to carry strong, graphic visual reminders of the health consequences of smoking.

Choice and CFA remain two of the preeminent independent generalist consumer entities in Australia. They have been joined by the Consumer Action Law Centre (CALC), which has reinvigorated grassroots campaigning. The center has seven paid staff members who provide dynamic leadership. Their funding comes from a combination of sources, including Legal Aid and Victorian state government funding. These three organizations have all developed tremendous advocacy skills and, though captive of neither, have worked closely with both governments and industry to achieve significant reforms over the years. Although they do from time to time use boycotts, picketing, and media stunts to draw attention to their issues, advocacy and engagement have become their core activism tools.

As to differences among Australia's three leading consumer organizations, CFA and CALC focus more on issues affecting vulnerable and disadvantaged consumers (e.g., payday lending, debt collection practices, and high pressure in-home sales), whereas Choice focuses on more mainstream consumer issues. There is, however, real crossover in the issues addressed by these three organizations, and all of them will usually have a seat at the table—as will Financial Counselling Australia, another key player in the Australian consumer protection policy landscape—whenever major consumer protection reforms are being considered.

The 1980s saw the emergence of additional, more specialized consumer groups, the professionalization of the sector, and the focus of activity shifting from products to services. It was in this decade that the Consumers Health Forum (1986), the Communications Law Centre (1988), and the Consumers' Telecommunications Network (1989) were established.

The 1980s also saw the deregulation of the financial sector in Australia. During this decade, interest rates were high and many households found themselves overextended and in financial crisis. This and other factors led to the formation of a range of free financial counseling services across Australia, as well as to the establishment of free consumer credit legal services in Victoria, NSW, and Western Australia. These two different types of services have become important to activists within the Australian consumer movement. The legal service centers receive government funding and draw upon university law students and legal professionals to provide *pro bono* help. The financial counseling sector receives additional funding from church and charity groups, but securing sufficient funding to meet demand is an ongoing concern for both groups. In addition to assisting individual clients, financial services activists have agitated to secure quality credit regulation for Australia (something that took decades of advocacy), sought reform of debt collection practices, and shone a light on unconscionable sales practices in remote indigenous communities.

Beginning in the 1980s, Australia established independent consumer ombudsmen in various industries (e.g., financial services, telecommunications, energy, water) to assist consumers. These programs, funded by industry, are overseen by boards made up of an independent chairperson and representatives composed equally of consumer and industry representatives. These alternative dispute schemes are now mostly required by legislation, and consumer advocates were vocal players in the development of the operating rules for these programs. They are free to consumers and have dealt with well over 1 million consumer complaints. In many cases, redress was provided in situations in which previously most complainants would have had no recourse to justice in light of the costs of legal actions in the courts.

A final important development during the 1980s was the establishment of the Federal Bureau of Consumer Affairs (FBCA) within the Commonwealth Government bureaucracy. This initiative was, in part, a result of lobbying by the consumer movement sector. The bureau was initially led by John Wood and located within the Attorney General's Department. Among other things, the FBCA led government initiatives in the fields of privacy, product safety, and promoting consumer protection in the South Pacific. The guiding philosophy of consumer policy moved from being primarily based on providing consumer justice to enhancing the role of consumers in markets. There were calls for the bureau to move to the central policymaking agency in the Department of Treasury, which happened in the 1990s.

The 1990s in Australia were characterized by an era of deregulation and governments seeking to work cooperatively with industry to resolve problems without legislation. The consumer sector was an important participant in the development of co-regulatory solutions such as codes of conduct and the aforementioned dispute resolution schemes. Although there was often disagreement between consumer representatives and other interested parties, it is fair to say that there tended to be widespread respect from both government and industry for the contribution consumer advocates made to discussions. That contribution was very much grounded in the work done by activist organizations in assisting individual consumers. Some of these co-regulatory initiatives, especially the ombudsman programs, have proven to be long-term successes. As for various industry codes of conduct developed back then, a few have stood the test of time and continue to deliver benefits to consumers (e.g., the Banking Code and the EFT code, recently renamed the e-payments code). The successful codes tend to be those that were developed against a background of real threat of legislation or serious industry lack of credibility. Other codes have withered, not delivering real benefits. The lessons from those times are now deemed relevant by consumer representatives whenever new co-regulatory initiatives are proposed.

During the 1990s, some organizations received significant financial awards as a result of litigation. For example, consumer champion Denis Nelthorpe negotiated a $2.5 million compensation payment by Household Financial Services to fund the establishment of the Consumer Law Centre of Victoria. This center existed from 1994 until 2006, when it merged with the Victorian Consumer Credit Legal Centre to form the Consumer Action Law Centre. In addition, the 1990s saw a change in the regulatory agencies that dealt with consumer issues. The Trade Practices Commission and the Prices Surveillance Authority merged to form the Australian Competition and Consumer Commission (ACCC). The commission remains the national consumer protection regulator for Australia. In addition, each state and territory has its own consumer protection agency, with these tending to focus more on local issues and the ACCC focusing on national and systemic issues causing significant consumer detriment. Also in the 1990s, the Wallis Inquiry into the Financial Services Sector led to the establishment of the Australian Securities and Investments Commission (ASIC) as the consumer protection regulator for financial services. Both the ACCC and ASIC have for many years had consumer advisory committees, made up of consumer advocates from a range of organizations, to advise them on their priorities and inform them about emerging issues.

Another initiative of the 1990s was the growing number of consumer protection professionals developing within businesses. A new organization, the Society of Consumer Affairs Professionals in Business (SOCAP), was established to support the work of consumer protection professionals. Close links were formed on some issues between SOCAP members and consumer protection advocates who often worked together to advance the interests of consumers.

The 2000s saw the emergence of additional sector-specific consumer organizations. Some of these organizations received government funding, usually raised via an industry tax. These include the Australian Communications Consumer Action Network (ACCAN) and energy groups including the Victoria-based Consumer Utilities Action Centre. The groups have become increasingly involved in regulatory issues that affect consumers, such as the design of the telecommunications network and pricing policies. One proposal that is yet to secure funding is an industry-specific legal center for superannuation (i.e., personal pensions). With Australia's compulsory superannuation system, and more than $3 trillion in superannuation savings, a legal center is greatly needed and remains a top priority for the consumer movement.

Consumer issues affecting Australia's indigenous people, many of whom are among the most vulnerable and disadvantaged of the country's populace, have been a focus for many of Australia's consumer groups and regulators. It was not, however, until around the beginning of the 2000s that the first indigenous group to focus primarily on consumer issues was formed. The Indigenous Consumer Action Network (ICAN) has played an invaluable role in bringing injustices to regulators' attention and working with agencies such as the ACCC, ASIC, and state and territory consumer bodies to bring to justice traders who engage in shoddy practices. Financial counselors have also made a significant contribution on a number of indigenous issues. One group of counselors from the Tangentyere Council, a service delivery agency located in Alice Springs, focuses on indigenous consumer issues.

One of the standout trends so far this century has been the use of behavioral economics (with its emphasis on how consumers think and act in real-world situations) by the consumer sector and others to better understand the root causes of consumer problems and design and lobby for smarter solutions. That lobbying is reflected in three of the major legislative reforms so far this century in the consumer protection space:

1. The Australian Consumer Law provides smarter regulatory responses to problems such as high-pressure door-to-door sales and unfair contract terms, along with significantly enhanced remedies and investigative tools. It was the product of a major inquiry into consumer protection regulation in Australia conducted by the Productivity Commission. The Consumer Action Legal Centre was particularly vocal and effective on this issue. Although many reforms advocated by consumer activists were created by the ACL, some remain to be taken up—including a funded independent consumer research body.
2. The national Consumer Credit Code emphasized responsible lending.
3. The Future of Financial Advice reforms sought to remove the distorting effect of commissions on quality advice by removing most of them and putting in place a range of other reforms to remove passive income and conflicts of interest.

As to what lies ahead, thanks to modern technology, the consumer sector is increasingly turning to solutions that don't necessarily require the involvement of government or industry to help consumers. Examples here include apps that help consumers make better choices (e.g., the FoodSwitch App), member/peer review services, and group buying initiatives (just like the early consumer pioneers at the beginning of the previous century). Concerns regarding environmentally sustainable consumption are increasingly overlapping on the priority lists of many consumer organizations with perennial issues such as access to services for disadvantaged consumers, confusion stemming from disclosure-based regulation in many sectors, challenges and opportunities brought by new technologies, and issues associated with an aging population.

New kinds of consumer-led campaigns are emerging. For example, "Vodafail" is a website that documents complaints about the telecommunications company Vodaphone. Adam Brimo, then 20 years old, created the site while sitting on hold waiting to resolve a complaint. More than 300,000 people subsequently logged on and expressed their frustration at Vodaphone's failed service promises, and the CEO apologized and invested significant sums into improving service quality. Thus an innovative generation of smart, articulate, and dedicated consumer advocates is emerging with new ideas and energy to help consumers face the challenges of tomorrow.

Delia Rickard, Jenni Mack

See also: Consumers International

Further Reading

Brown, Jane. 1995. *A History of the Australian Consumer Movement.* Melbourne: Consumers' Federation of Australia, 1995.

Hally-Burton, Stephen, Siddharth Shirodkar, Simon Winckler, and Simon Writer. 2008. *Harnessing the Demand Side: Australian Consumer Policy.* Canberra: Australian Department of the Treasury. http://archive.treasury.gov.au/documents/1451/PDF/07_Australian_Consumer_policy.pdf.

AUSTRIAN CONSUMER MOVEMENT

The consumer movement in Austria can be traced back to the second half of the nineteenth century, when the first consumer cooperatives were formed. The cooperatives supplied their members with good-quality foodstuffs and household goods at a cheap price, thereby supplementing the trade unions' struggle for better working conditions and higher pay.

It was not the idea of the consumer cooperative, however, that stimulated the development of Austria's present-day consumer movement. The cooperative movement, disrupted by the periods of the authoritarian state (1934–1938) and Nazi occupation (1938–1945), recuperated to become an important commercial force in post–World War II Austria but did not rise again to act as a "consumer voice." The task of representing consumer interests, both in the political arena and in giving individual advice and support to consumers, was taken up by labor organizations.

It is an Austrian peculiarity that labor is represented not only by trade unions, based on voluntary membership, but also by institutions established by law and encompassing almost all employees (except public servants and employees in the agrarian sector) as mandatory members. These "Arbeiterkammern" (literally "Chambers of Labor") were created in 1920 as a counterpart to the Chambers of Commerce, institutions that (also on the basis of mandatory membership) represent the interests of business and industry. Reestablished after the end of World War II, the chambers of labor became today's brain trust of the labor movement.

Though individual unions engage in collective bargaining and industrial action, the chambers of labor focus more on research, training, and general policy issues in connection with workers' interests. With this division of work between the two types of labor organizations, consumer issues were addressed mainly by the chambers of labor, which soon after World War II began to provide information for their members on key consumer questions.

The reason behind labor's strong interest in consumer issues was the same one that had inspired labor activists a hundred years earlier to form consumer cooperatives—namely, the principle that what is gained in collective bargaining on wages must not be lost in spending too much on overpriced or low-quality goods. This concept of the interconnectedness between labor and consumer interests is still crucial for an understanding of consumer policy and the consumer movement in Austria today.

In 1955, the Viennese chamber of labor began to fund the Association for Advice on Shopping (Verein für Einkaufsberatung), which established the first Austrian consumer advice center. In 1961, these efforts to provide consumer information were broadened. The Chambers of Labor (Arbeiterkammern)—together with the Austrian Trade Union Federation, the Federal Chamber of Commerce, and the main agricultural interest group—founded the Austrian Consumers Association (Verein für Konsumenteninformation, or VKI), which developed an Information Center in Vienna and still publishes the test magazine *Konsument* (Consumer).

Though the VKI started its magazine and its activities in comparative testing in 1961, it did not become an organization of nationwide prominence and importance until the 1970s. The 1970s in Austria was a decade of change and reform. The social democratic government, newly elected to office in 1970, pursued an active policy with respect to consumer issues that raised public awareness and led to better funding of consumer organizations. For example, in 1974 the federal government doubled the funds VKI received from its four founding members, thereby boosting the association's activities.

Austrian Consumers Association (VKI)

The VKI consists of just four regular voting members: two organizations representing labor, one representing business, and one representing farmers. The Republic of Austria, represented by the Federal Ministry of Labor's Division of Social Affairs and Consumer Protection, is a member without voting rights, except on budgetary matters.

To anyone not familiar with the Austrian political system, the logic behind this membership structure is hard to comprehend. It is a result of the special relationship between labor, industry, and agriculture known as Sozialpartnerschaft (social partnership), characterized by high involvement of the four major interest groups in government policy and by the lack of serious conflicts involving industrial relations.

Sozialpartnerschaft depends on consensus; the bylaws of the VKI, for instance, require a four-fifths majority for any decision, which in a four-member association means unanimity. Although formally the regular members hold equal rights in the association, it is generally understood that the VKI is considered the domain of the labor side, with the president traditionally coming from the chamber of labor. As a result, even though the membership structure is unusual, the VKI is generally accepted as Austria's leading consumer organization. As such, the VKI is a member of the two most important international consumer bodies: Consumers International and BEUC: The European Consumer Organisation.

The VKI is divided into four departments: counseling, legal, research, and publication. VKI does extensive comparative testing and publishes the monthly magazine *Konsument*, as well as a series of brochures and books. In 2012, the general circulation of *Konsument* reached 310,000 copies (approximately 60,000 going to subscribers). Research shows that *Konsument* reaches about 20 percent of the Austrian population. VKI also operates two information centers in Vienna and Innsbruck, with support of the European Consumer Centres Network (ECC-Net). Furthermore, VKI acts as a consumer voice in public policy decision making by using strategies such as press conferences or press releases to communicate opinions on planned legislation or to demand appropriate action by the authorities.

In the past few years, earnings from *Konsument* and the other publications rose to 40 percent of the organization's total budget, whereas membership dues declined to 30 percent. (The Federal Ministry of Labor's Division of Social Affairs and Consumer Protection pays half these dues.) The remaining 30 percent of the budget is earned by fulfilling contracts, mainly with public institutions. For example, VKI has developed criteria for environmental labeling and produced a comprehensive report on the status of consumer protection and law actions in Austria.

In recent years, the VKI has increased its activities in the judicial arena, especially with respect to class action lawsuits for violations of EU consumer protection laws. The VKI brings individual test cases of more widespread consumer problems on behalf of the Federal Ministry of Labor's Division of Social Affairs and Consumer Protection, and since the year 2000, class action lawsuits under Austrian law are generally transferred to the VKI. The system requires an active "opt-in" by consumers, and therefore the judgment is only effective for those consumers who took part in the joinder of claims. In contrast to the United States, there is no compensation for punitive damages. Austrian lawyers are not allowed to use a contingency system of payment whereby consumers share a predetermined percentage of any compensation. Instead, third-party companies may offer to finance a class action lawsuit in exchange for a share of any award. The VKI cooperates with such companies when filing a class action lawsuit. Therefore, aggrieved consumers can join the class action without the risks of the legal costs. The lawsuits of the VKI have become well known in Austria. In a poll taken by the daily newspaper *Der Standard* in February 2012, the interviewees ranked the VKI highest when asked, "Who in Austria stands for justice?"

Although the most important contribution of Austria's homogenous and comparatively strong trade union movement is its funding of VKI, it also takes additional actions in the field of consumer policy. The labor unions in every province, as well as the central organization in Vienna, have units specializing in consumer issues. These units work as a consumer lobby in the political process. They prepare new legislative measures for parliament, conduct research, and give advice to individual consumers.

In Austria, very little consumer activism is independent from labor organizations. However, specialized organizations of nationwide importance have developed in two areas: housing (especially tenant rights) and cars. In addition to these groups, there are smaller single-issue consumer groups—for instance, on data protection or specific environmental concerns.

Political Parties and Public Authorities

The Social Democratic Party has played an important role in consumer policy, especially between 1970 and 1983, when it formed a single-party government and gave consumer issues a prominent place on its political agenda. During the 1970s, Josef Staribacher, a popular minister of trade and industry, institutionalized consumer policy at the government level by appointing his onetime press secretary Fritz Koppe as state secretary for consumer protection. Koppe went on to become the best-known consumer leader in present-day Austria, heading the Viennese Arbeiterkammer's consumer policy unit while also serving as executive director of the VKI. (He retired from both jobs in 1994.) Since the 1990s, the vigor of the two major political parties has declined, and progress in the field of consumer protection has mainly been confined to the implementation of directives of the European Union.

In government, the Federal Ministry of Labor's Division of Social Affairs and Consumer Protection has the task of coordinating consumer policy. In that capacity, it works closely with the consumer organizations, especially the VKI and the Chambers of Labor. In addition, the ministry works as a consumer voice within government and supports consumer organizations, for instance, by offering training for employees of consumer organizations.

Recent Developments and Future Outlook

Austria is situated in the middle of Europe, has a highly export-oriented economy, and is increasingly interdependent with the economies of other European countries. A longstanding member of the European Free Trade Association, Austria became a member of the European Union in 1995. Thus the problems facing Austrian consumers do not differ much from those encountered by consumers in other countries of the European Union, and their rights are similar as well.

Several major developments currently affect Austrian consumers. One is the shift in purchasing from products to services and in decision making from questions of price to questions of quality. Deregulation and the gradual withdrawal of the state from business regulation is also a concern for consumers. Finally, the internationalization, even globalization, of markets creates both opportunities and problems for consumers. All these developments can be seen, for instance, in the domain of financial services, in which Austrian consumers have recently experienced an array of accentuated information problems in markets that are increasingly deregulated and international in scope.

Austria's successes in consumer policy are, to a large extent, a result of the culture of compromise and social partnership. Even when the country was ruled by single-party governments, major reforms were mostly undertaken only when the four major interest groups—who are also the regular members of the VKI—agreed. Thus advances in consumer policy have often been slow, but they have eventually been supported by all parties concerned. Another manifestation of this tradition of compromise and collaboration is participation of consumer representatives on numerous committees or advisory councils, where they establish working contacts on an equal level with business representatives.

Recently, the close cooperation between the major interest groups and their influence on government policy—the very core of the Sozialpartnerschaft—has come under attack. For various reasons, none directly related to consumer policy, the problem-solving capacity of the social partnership and its institutions has suffered greatly. In the future, it is likely that the major interest groups will focus more on issues of immediate importance to their membership, paying less attention to the consumer interest.

The readiness of business and consumer organizations to work collaboratively is decreasing markedly. This decline may result partly from the mounting pressure exerted by both constituencies not to be "too soft" with the other. It is also a consequence of the internationalization of commerce. The traditionally strong allegiance of Austrian entrepreneurs to their business organization has grown weaker as they have had to compete with foreign companies that are relatively unconcerned about their own reputation among Austrian business and consumer organizations.

If the social partnership continues to be strained, consumers may have to rely less on compromise and more on enforcement of consumer protection laws. Unfortunately, this enforcement is not always strong, especially in the courts. Consumer claims are usually low-value claims, and therefore consumers cannot afford—or do not want—to take the risk of costs of a trial. Therefore, in practice, enforcement is consumer law is often ineffective. This is why the Austrian population has little faith in the justice system. The class actions of the VKI are only a drop in the ocean. In the future, it will be the duty of the politicians to support stronger enforcement of consumer rights in the courts. This includes transposition of the EU directive on alternative dispute resolution into national law.

Hans-Peter Lehofer, Peter Kolba

See also: BEUC: The European Consumer Organisation; Consumers International

Further Reading

European Union. "Austria." http://ec.europa.eu/consumers/empowerment/cons_networks_en.htm.

VKI (Austrian Consumers' Association). www.konsument.at.

AUTOMOBILE INSURANCE ADVOCACY

See Insurance Advocacy

AUTOMOBILE SAFETY ADVOCACY

See Motor Vehicle Safety Advocacy

AVIATION SAFETY ADVOCACY

See Air Travel Advocacy

BALLOT PROPOSITIONS
See Initiatives and Referenda

BALTIC CONSUMER MOVEMENTS: ESTONIA, LITHUANIA, AND LATVIA

The consumer movement in the Baltic states of Estonia, Lithuania, and Latvia is strongly influenced by the socialist past of these countries. From the end of World War II until their independence in 1991, the Baltic states were republics of the Soviet Union, a country in which the concepts of consumer law and consumer activism had little relevance. In the Soviet socialist economy, where access to goods and services was limited and freedom of association in any form did not exist, the representation and protection of consumers' interests was organized and financed exclusively by government authorities. To this day, the consumer policies in all three Baltic states are mainly developed by the state. Nongovernmental consumer movements generally have had little influence, although some nongovernmental consumer organizations have over the years become more active and visible. The government consumer protection boards of the Baltic states and civil society consumer organizations participate in European Union (EU) and international consumer protection bodies such as BEUC: The European Consumer Organization, the European Association for the Co-ordination of Consumer Representation in Standardization (ANEC), and Consumers International. There is a special tradition in the Baltic states of seeking tighter connections to Scandinavian institutions. For example, on the issue of protecting consumer interests on the quick loan market, there is a close cooperation between the Baltic states and the Nordic consumer ombudsmen with respect to quick but very expensive small loans.

Estonia

In Estonia, it is first of all the governmental system of institutions that engages in consumer protection activities, but nongovernmental initiatives have considerably contributed to consumer protection. A first step was the establishment of the Estonian Consumers Union (ECU) in 1994, which plays the role of the national umbrella organization for seven regional consumer associations. Since 1996, the government has provided financial support to consumer organizations. In 2014 alone, the state budget provided 55,000 euros of support. The ECU engages in lobbying and campaigning on consumer issues, provides information and advice to consumers, manages an extensive website, and organizes and participates in seminars and workshops as set down in its strategy document for 2012–2016. The

ECU also has the right to take cases to court on behalf of consumers, but no such court cases have yet been brought. It is also member of European consumer federations and consultative structures, such as BEUC, ANEC, and the European Consumer Consultative Group. However, the level of Estonia's active contributions to these institutions has steadily decreased during the last few years. Even within its own borders, ECU's existing staff is generally unable to function effectively owing to a shortage of human resources.

Local consumer organizations in Estonia are very small and volunteer-based. Their main function is to provide information and general consultation in their region, but they have no capacity to provide professional, up-to-date, individualized advice to consumers. The most significant regional organizations devoted to consumer protection are those in Estonia's two largest cities, Tallinn and Tartu, but by European standards, these organizations are small and underfunded. The Consumer Protection Advisory Centre of Tallinn (CPAC) was developed with the support of the German government and at present receives no funding from the Estonian government. Through its advisory center, it provides advice to consumers on different issues by phone, e-mail, and its own website, and it keeps detailed records of the consumer complaints received. The Tartu Consumer Advice and Information Center (CAIC), founded in 2001, is an independent, volunteer-based association. It emphasizes consumer education for school-age children and participates in the EU's consortium for consumer education, the *Consumer Classroom.* It has also taken part in a project with consumer groups in Latvia, Lithuania, and Sweden to promote knowledge about energy efficiency among vulnerable groups such as the unemployed and retired.

The Ministry of Economic Affairs and Communications (MoEC) is generally responsible for setting consumer protection strategies and policy. Other important policy actors include the Ministry of Justice, the Ministry of Social Affairs, the Ministry of Agriculture, and the Financial Supervision Authority. (The latter organization runs an impressive consumer education website, www.minuraha.ee.) The Consumer Protection Board (CPB), which answers to the MoEC, is tasked with implementing, supervising, and enforcing consumer protection measures. The CPB administers the Consumer Complaints Committee (CCC) and takes targeted actions against abuses in specific markets such as used cars, pyramid schemes, quick loans, and telecommunication services. Still, the number of complaints solved by the CCC is remarkably low. The CPB is also a member of the Nordic–Estonian Consumer Education group, established in 2007 to promote consumer education on an informal and cooperative basis.

Activity by local governments is typically confined to providing consumers with advice and other forms of individual assistance. In some cases, governments appoint an officer who is authorized to deal with consumer protection issues; in other instances, local governments enter into cooperative contracts with local consumer organizations to provide these services.

Summing up the situation in Estonia, consumer protection activities generally have increased during recent years, but it remains a major problem that the nongovernmental consumer organizations are rather weak, small, and lacking in adequate resources to provide professional services to consumers. The main actors in this field remain public authorities.

Lithuania

The situation is quite different in Lithuania, where grassroots movements, a broad diversity of NGOs, and other forms of direct democracy have always been part of the nation's cultural identity. Lithuania developed independent nongovernmental entities whose aim was the protection of consumers' interests as early as 1989, when the Lithuanian Consumers Association was formed. In the NGO sector, about twenty consumer organizations have been registered in Lithuania within the last thirty years. Some of these, however, are run by a single person (often lawyers focusing on consumer law). Only a handful of the thirty are active on a permanent basis and have nationwide influence.

The oldest consumer organization is the Lithuanian Consumers Association (LCA). It is well known within the country, ranking in public awareness just below the State Consumer Rights Protection Authority. Still, the LCA is run mainly by a single (but very engaged and prominent) person and seeks to influence public discussions of consumer issues. It focuses on consumer rights, especially those of elderly people, and it cooperates closely with the State Consumer Rights Protection Authority. The LCA participates in various consumer-oriented projects that are either set up by international organizations or, less often, directly financed by Lithuanian public funds. The LCA is granted a certain transfer of value from the state budget at least insofar as the Vilnius city municipality provides free office space to LCA in central Vilnius.

The Lithuanian Consumer Institute, founded in 2000, is also quite prominent in discussions of consumer matters. It keeps consumers informed about products and services as well as recent developments in Lithuanian consumer policies; the institute has developed notable expertise in the field of nutrition.

Another important consumer organization, the Western Lithuania Consumer Federation, advocates for consumers based in Klaipeda (Lithuania's third-largest city) and the surrounding region, and the federation claims to represent a network of twenty member organizations from that region. The federation gives priority to issues involving advertising, food and health, and environmental protection. It announced ambitious plans to launch two new websites in 2014, as well as to offer a distance learning course and a manual for consumers.

In 2012, the Alliance of Lithuanian Consumer Organizations was established. It represents seven consumer associations: the Lithuanian Consumer Association, Lithuanian Consumer Union, Consumer Rights Protection Center, Lithuanian Association of Bank Customers, the Lithuanian Citizens Advice Union, National Association of Financial Services Consumers, and National Association of Financial Services Consumers. It remains to be seen what role the alliance plays among the consumer organizations of Lithuania.

Turning to government regulation of consumer issues, the Ministry of Justice is primarily responsible for developing consumer policy. Implementation and enforcement of ministry policies (as well as those of other ministries such as the Ministry of Economy and the Ministry of Education and Science) is the job of a specialized body established and operated by the Ministry of Justice—the State Consumer Rights Protection Authority. The authority also maintains a telephone hotline for consumer issues and an alternative dispute resolution system for business–consumer disputes.

Despite the number and variety of initiatives on behalf of consumers, the consumer movement in Lithuania still has had surprisingly difficulty in effecting large-scale results in the field of consumer protection. First of all, the cooperation among the organizations, as well as between the organizations and the state authorities, could be improved; consumer organizations in Lithuania do not speak with one voice, many projects are changed or cancelled before completion, and much of the restricted financial and human resources are consumed by the organizations' own management. Second, the overall state funding sum of approximately 17,500 euros (in 2011)—granted to all consumer organizations together—creates a rather tight financial framework and impedes essential progress.

Latvia

Latvia's institutional framework for consumer protection is quite similar to that of Lithuania. Still, no single central ministry in Latvia is explicitly responsible for consumer policy. Rather, the authority is shared among the Ministry of Economics, the Ministry of Justice, and several other ministries. The Consumer Rights Protection Center (SRPC), established in 1988, implements, supervises, and enforces the consumer protection measures set in place by the ministries.

In contrast to Lithuania, however, there is in Latvia one central umbrella consumer organization—the Latvian National Association for Consumer Protection (LPIAA in Latvian). The LPIAA, which was created in 1999, bundles a network of about a dozen of local organizations devoted to consumer protection. This arrangement makes cooperation among Latvian consumer organizations stronger than in Lithuania. Although the influence of LPIAA on consumer issues is quite extensive, Article 23 of the Latvian Consumer Protection Act allows for an even larger role for the LPIAA, but these potential competencies are at present not fully exhausted thanks to a lack of financial and human resources. The LPIAA does, however, have four full-time staff members who represent Latvia in BEUC, ANEC, and other European consumer organizations. Most regional Latvian consumer organizations, in contrast, are run by volunteers. Also, the cooperation between Latvian government authorities and NGOs is better than in Lithuania. Latvian consumer organizations are, for example, invited to participate in weekly meetings of government officials, and the LPIAA is regularly invited to speak at hearings in Parliament. In 2006, the Consumer Consultative Council was established, contributing as well to the smooth cooperation among the various stakeholders in consumer policy.

Still, the financial crisis in 2008 hit Latvia hard—and the state budget's share for consumer issues even harder. As a result, the central consumer policy document providing the main scheme for consumer protection measures expired in 2010 without being replaced. This had the effect of cutting all state funding to LPIAA, with the only remaining subsidy being free office spaces in the Ministry of Economics. (Currently, the ministry is preparing a new set of guidelines providing for consumer protection.) In general, the constitutional and policy framework for consumer protection is better developed and more effective in Latvia than in Lithuania, as is cooperation between state authorities and consumer organizations and among consumer organizations. But the influence of consumer activists on consumer protection policy is, for the moment, rather low owing to virtually nonexistent budgets for consumer organizations.

Surveying the three Baltic states as a group, there are many similarities in their consumer policy institutions at the government level. The membership of the three countries in the EU since 2004 will lead to further convergence in their specific consumer policies. But the civil society consumer organizations in the Baltic countries will have to use their limited public funding extremely efficiently if consumers there are to conceive and expect these associations to be at all comparable to those in other EU countries.

Thomas Hoffmann, Irene Kull

See also: BEUC: The European Consumer Organisation; Consumers International

Further Reading

BEUC: The European Consumer Organisation. 2012. *Analysis of the Consumer Movement in Central, Eastern, and South-Eastern Europe.* Brussels (October). http://ec.europa.eu/consumers/archive/reports/cesee2_2012_report_en.pdf.

Fielder, Anna. 2011. *The State of the Consumer Nation(s): An Evaluation of the Consumer Movement in Six Countries of Central, Eastern and South Eastern Europe.* Brussels: BEUC.

Kutin, Breda. 2011. "Consumer Movement in Central and Eastern Europe." *Consumatori, Diritti e Mercato,* no. 2: 102–110.

Petrauskas, Feliksas, and Aida Gasiūnaité. 2012. "Alternative Dispute Resolution in the Field of Consumer Financial Services." *Jurisprudence* 19, no. 1: 179–194.

Viitanen, Klaus. 2000. "The Baltic Model for the Settlement of Individual Consumer Disputes." *Journal of Consumer Policy* 23, no. 3: 315–339.

BANKRUPTCY REFORM ADVOCACY

See Credit Card Advocacy

BEUC: THE EUROPEAN CONSUMER ORGANISATION

BEUC: The European Consumer Organisation (Bureau Européen des Unions de Consommateurs) was created on March 6, 1962, by the consumer organizations of Belgium, Luxembourg, France, the Netherlands, Italy, and Germany. After working together for several years, these organizations decided to create a European association, based in Brussels, to influence policy at the level of the European Union (then known as the European Economic Community). BEUC was a pioneer in being one of the first lobbying organizations to set up a base in the seat of the European Union (EU) in a bid to influence the decision making process. Many other organizations followed, and the number of lobbyists rose exponentially to the present-day figure of more than 15,000. The intense pressure brought to bear on decision makers from this multitude of "lobbyists" working on behalf of commercial interests, regional and local authorities, trade unions and many others, highlights the need for BEUC to have a strong presence on the Brussels scene.

BEUC's fundamental philosophy is that consumers should be empowered by competitive markets, but complemented by health and safety safeguards. Only safe products and services that do not put at risk the health of consumers, future generations, and the natural environment should be available on the EU market. Where consumers cannot be empowered, regulatory measures must protect their economic and legal interests. This is especially essential for vulnerable consumers such as children, the elderly, and low-income people. The concept of environmental sustainability is also central to BEUC's campaigning. For example, in 2012, BEUC launched a cooperative project with the European Climate Foundation to lower carbon dioxide emissions from cars. It has also worked with AIM: The European Brands Association, a business association, to improve environmental labels and logos.

Today, BEUC has a membership of forty-one well-respected and independent national consumer organizations from thirty-one European countries (including some countries that are not members of the EU). BEUC membership was originally restricted to independent national consumer organizations in Europe working for consumers on a broad range of issues. More recently, however, BEUC's statutes have been changed to include other organizations that, while not having the status of independent national consumer organization, still work actively in the field of promotion of the consumer interests. Different types of member categories have been defined in order to cope with the variety of the consumer movement in its different expressions all over Europe and beyond. A distinction is made between full members (the independent and consumer-focused organizations) and affiliate members (organizations that comply in part but not on all points with the criteria for full membership). Full members have more rights related to the governance of BEUC, but both participate in our campaigning activities.

The BEUC statutes also provide for the conclusion of partnership agreements that allow for cooperation on specific policy issues in a particular sector. This arrangement brings added influence to BEUC's work by virtue of expanded expertise, research data, and political networks.

Taken as a whole, BEUC's membership is diversified. Some of its best-known members are large subscriber-based organizations publishing ad-free magazines, maintaining websites, or offering other kind of services to millions of consumers. Other members work with a small number of volunteers, providing small-scale advice or advocacy work and only very limited publishing activities. Also, whereas the activities of many member organizations are financed in large part by selling their publications and providing advice to consumers, others depend totally or in majority on public funding.

The leaders of BEUC are concerned that many of the consumer rights and protections that the organization has fought for and helped to establish are not being adhered to in practice. BEUC members report an acute lack of enforcement of consumer rights within the nations of the EU. Funding for national consumer protection authorities and subsidies for nonprofit consumer organizations has been scaled down, sometimes drastically, by their respective national governments. Consumers appear to be afraid or reluctant to go to court for minor litigation against big companies. Despite these obstacles, promoting consumer rights remains the guiding mission for BEUC, which, together with its members, will continue to encourage enforcement actions when consumer rights are violated.

More generally, promotion of consumer rights and interests is an ongoing challenge. Markets develop and European solutions are no longer enough to effectively protect consumers in a global, digital word. The threats linked to climate change and changing world demographics (population growth, aging, and urbanization), combined with new food technologies, also call for a different approach towards consumption patterns and strategies of consumer activism. It is BEUC's priority to raise awareness of EU decision makers to adapt policies and regulations to emerging market challenges and to maximize benefits for consumers.

Monique Goyens

See also: Austrian Consumer Movement; Baltic Consumer Movements; United Kingdom Consumer Movement; Central and Eastern European Consumer Movements; Danish Consumer Movement; Dutch Consumer Movement; Finnish Consumer Movement; French Consumer Movement; German Consumer Movement; Italian Consumer Movement; Norwegian Consumer Movement; Polish Consumer Movement; Serbian Consumer Movement; Slovenian Consumer Movement; Spanish Consumer Movement; Swedish Consumer Movement

Further Reading
BEUC. 2014. www.beuc.eu.

BOYCOTTS

Consumer boycotts have drawn upon a wide range of protest groups, target organizations, and social concerns in many regions of the United States. These boycotts have served not only economic objectives, such as lower prices, but also the political objectives of various special interest groups outside the consumer movement. These groups have included those representing animal welfare and environmental protection, as well as the rights of other groups, such as women, gays, African Americans, Mexican Americans, Chinese Americans, Jewish Americans, and various labor organizations. Since 1970, all these groups have, at one time or another, called for boycotts of consumer products or services in an effort to help realize their organizational objectives.

But consumer boycotts were also used by groups as far back as the American Revolution. The boycotts of British goods in Boston, New York, and Philadelphia after the passage of the Stamp Act in 1765 are described in many American history texts. More than a century later, in the early 1880s, the Knights of Labor resorted to boycotts, including those in Atlanta against the city newspaper and in Chicago against a streetcar company, to try to improve wages and gain union recognition. In the next century, during the 1930s and 1940s, the American Jewish community organized and led a boycott of German goods to protest Nazi treatment of Jews. Still later, from the 1960s through the 1990s, Cesar Chavez led United Farm Workers' boycotts of grapes and lettuce to gain union recognition and improved pay and working conditions. These historic boycott examples illustrate just a few of the various ways different groups have used consumer boycotts to promote and protect the rights of the powerless and disenfranchised segments of society.

Consumer boycotts are directed at individual consumers, not at organizational entities such as business firms or professional associations. In the history of the modern consumer movement, however, boycott organizers have varied their tactics. Some organizers have urged consumers to selectively withdraw participation in the marketplace directly and immediately—"marketplace boycotts"—whereas others have focused on creating dramatic demonstrations to attract the attention of the news media in the hopes that the resulting coverage will pressure boycott targets to make concessions—"media boycotts."

The early years of the modern consumer movement featured dozens of grassroots boycotts against supermarkets to protest rising food prices. A 1966 survey of the leaders of sixty-four boycott groups found that the leaders and most participants were housewives not working outside the home. In the next several decades, though, the availability of housewives for this type of protest diminished as increasing numbers entered the labor force.

At the same time, however, the increasing availability of mass communications to advocates created new opportunities for the use of consumer boycotts. In 1995, for example, the Rainforest Action Network (RAN), an activist ecology group, organized a media-based protest against a major corporation, Mitsubishi, for its extraction of tropical timber from third-world rainforests. RAN leaders knew that their group was too small, and its members too busy, to maintain pickets at the entrances of retail stores selling the company's products. Instead, these leaders decided to try to generate mass media coverage by unfurling a giant cloth sign, from the top of one San Francisco's tallest buildings, which read BOYCOTT MITSUBISHI. They succeeded in generating this coverage, which helped RAN in a continuing campaign that, three years later, resulted in Mitsubishi's pledge not to use wood from old-growth forests.

In the first years of the twenty-first century, the Internet, computers, and other personal communication devices have made possible new types of product-related protests that are just beginning to be explored. The recent series of vehicle recalls by General Motors reflects not just continuing media coverage, but also lasting viral communications through social media that threaten to permanently damage the huge company's reputation and sales. The new information and communication technologies, however, can be used to reward as well as punish corporate behavior. "Consumer buycotts" encourage purchase of certain products, and "carrotmobs" reward the environmentally beneficial actions of urban retailers.

Although some consumer boycotts have been successful, many more have not been. Two important factors have been lack of funding and the inexperience of leaders. It is not enough to simply call for a boycott. Leaders must have sufficient commitment and resources to organize and maintain boycott-related activities for months or even years. They must also understand and ensure that the "wrong" to be righted is emotionally compelling and that their demands are cognitively simple for consumers to understand. It is not sufficient for boycott leaders simply to gain media attention for a short time. For example, calling for a boycott of a movie theater chain for raising its prices is not likely to be successful without sustained picket-ing and other protests demanding lower prices. These requirements help explain why recently, despite the expansion of individual and group communications, there appear to have been fewer successful efforts to boycott consumer products and ser-vices. However, the increasing availability and low expense of social media, such as Facebook and Twitter, create new opportunities for entrepreneurial consumers and consumer groups to organize campaigns that influence corporate behavior.

Monroe Friedman

See also: State and Local Consumer Advocacy Groups

Further Reading

Friedman, Monroe. 1971. "The 1966 Consumer Protest as Seen By Its Leaders." *Journal of Consumer Affairs* 5: 1–23.

Friedman, Monroe. 1999. *Consumer Boycotts: Effecting Change through the Marketplace and the Media.* New York: Routledge.

Garrett, D. E. 1987. "The Effectiveness of Marketing Policy Boycotts: Environmental Oppo-sition to Marketing." *Journal of Marketing* 51: 46–57.

Hoffman, Stefan, and Katharina Hunter. 2011. "Carrotmob as a New Form of Ethical Con-sumption." *Journal of Consumer Policy.* doi:10.1007/s10603-011-9185-2.

Scott, James. 1985. *Weapons of the Weak: Everyday Forms of Peasant Resistance.* New Haven, CT: Yale University Press.

BRAZILIAN CONSUMER MOVEMENT

The movement for the defense of consumers emerged in Brazil in the mid-1970s. In order to understand the emergence and development of consumer activism in Brazil, it is necessary to take into consideration several factors. First, Brazil's con-sumer society was a latecomer compared to that in the United States and those in western Europe. Industrialization only began in earnest in Brazil at the end of the 1950s, and broad access to consumer goods by the urban middle classes began at the end of the 1960s. Second, Brazil experienced a military dictatorship from 1964 to 1985, which concentrated all political power in the hands of the state and created an environment not conducive to social movements. Third, Brazil experi-enced extreme inflation that began in the late 1970s, intensified in the 1980s (aver-age of 330% per year), and deepened even further from 1990 to 1994 (average of 764%). This environment of hyperinflation cut two ways in terms of consumer activism: On the one hand, it forced consumers to focus on issues of immediate affordability rather fundamental improvements in their rights, but on the other, it taught consumers the value of seeking their rights, even if only to protect their purchasing power.

The first organized manifestation of consumer activism in Brazil took place in 1976 with the foundation of two civil society bodies—the Porto Alegre Associa-tion for Consumer Protection (APC) and the Curitiba Association for Consumer Defense and Guidance (ADOC). But during the 1970s, Brazil was in the midst of two decades of military dictatorship and, as in the case of all civil associations during that era, consumer organizations were unable to grow in the shadow of an autocratic regime.

Nor were there any specific laws to protect consumers in the 1970s. For its part, the Brazil central government had only one department remotely relevant to consumers; it dealt with the subject of price control and supply and did not act effectively to protect consumers. It was thus only in 1976 that the first government agency emerged for the protection of consumers: PROCON, belonging to the state of Sao Paulo. Following this model, from 1976 to 1985, practically all the states of the Brazilian Federation created their own consumer agencies, or Procons.

In the absence of a centralized government body, the disjointed Procon system had obvious limitations. First, the defense of the consumer was being carried out by the government, not civil society itself. Second, damaging inflation dominated the national discussion of consumer problems. From 1986 to 1994, inflation led Brazil to adopt six economic plans and five currencies. For this reason, the Procons concentrated their efforts on protecting consumers from inflation, which reached approximately 2,500 percent in 1993. Subjects such as product safety and services became of secondary importance in the face of such an intractable reality. However, it is important to note that the Brazilian consumer became more aware of his or her rights and learned to fight for them, with the Procons acting in consumers' defense. This represented a critically important juncture for the creation of a culture defined by the protection of consumer interests.

The Movement Gains in Strength

The return of democracy to Brazil beginning in 1985 brought about important changes with regard to consumer protection during the next few years. In 1985, the federal government created the National Council for Consumer Defense, with the aim of using it as a basis for the crafting of public policies. The National Council was made up of a handful of consumer associations, two state-level Procons, the Brazilian Prosecution Service, federal departments such as the ministries of health and justice, and business associations. The council became a debating forum and formulator of types of consumer legislation, and it would leave its mark during the forthcoming decades.

During 1985 itself, the Law of Civic Public Action was enacted, which for the first time allowed for the judgment of class actions for the protection of various collective interests, among them, those of consumers. This law was the turning point in defense of Brazil's consumers. Furthermore, it was in the same context that 1987 witnessed the creation of the Brazilian Institute of Consumer Defense (IDEC), which became the most important civil entity for the defense of consumers.

In 1988, the new federal constitution was promulgated. It became known as the "Citizen's Constitution" for its overwhelming concern for protecting the rights of Brazilian citizens, both individually and collectively. This constitution concerned itself with the protection of consumers by expressly setting forth a requirement for the state to defend consumers. It singled out consumer defense as one of the principles of economic order and identified the need for a law to be passed that specifically dealt with consumer protection. As a result, consumer defense was to become public policy in the country.

In 1990, a further, crucially important event took place—the promulgation of the Consumer Defense Code. This general law brought forth a qualitative leap in the defense of the consumer. The code covered basic consumer rights, including the right to information. It also addressed responsibility for defective products and services, contained protections against abusive contract practices and clauses, and prohibited abusive and misleading advertising. The Consumer Defense Code did not only institutionalize basic rights; it also created instruments for the protection of these rights. It provided criminal and administrative sanctions to be applied by the public authority as well as the option for legal class actions filed, most notably, by IDEC and the Public Prosecutor Service. It is not too strong a statement to say that consumer defense in Brazil can be divided into two periods: before and after the Code of Consumer Defense.

Principal Actors

At present, there are three main categories of actors engaged in consumer protection: civil associations, public agencies, and academic institutes. The most important civil association continues to be the Brazilian Institute of Consumer Defense (IDEC). Among the six Brazilian organizations that participate in Consumers International (the umbrella organization for the world consumer movement), only IDEC is a full member. IDEC was founded and originally led by Marilena Lazzarini. (Lazzarini also served as president of Consumers International from 2004 until 2007.)

IDEC is a nonprofit association, and it acts independently of companies, governments, or political parties. Its operating costs are funded by contributions from its members (about 10,000) and by developing projects that are funded by public agencies and independent foundations. IDEC's main activities are providing information and guidance to consumers concerning their rights, testing products and conducting other types of research, representing the interests of consumers in various settings where public policy is formulated, and promoting class action lawsuits (against companies or state governments) in defense of the consumer. Its priority areas of interest are quality of public services, food safety, sustainable consumption, health protection, and financial services.

Existing alongside IDEC are other civil bodies (approximately twenty), all acting with some degree of coordination via the National Forum of Consumer Groups. Foremost among these entities are the highly active housewives' associations— notably the Housewives and Consumers of Minas Gerais Movement, founded in 1983. Another organization that deserves to be highlighted is the Association for Citizen and Consumer Defence (ADECON). Based in the Brazilian state of Pernambuco, ADECON exercises the right of duly constituted consumer associations to bring class action lawsuits to protect the collective but diffuse interests of consumers.

Turning from civil associations to government agencies, the Department for the Protection of Consumers was created in 1990 under the auspices of the federal government. In 2012, the National Secretary of the Consumer (SENACON) was established, falling under the Ministry of Justice. SENACON was devoted to setting up, coordinating, and executing National Policy for Consumer Relations, with the following objectives: (1) to guarantee the protection and exercising of consumer rights, (2) to promote harmonious relations between buyers and sellers, and (3) to promote the integration and joint action within Brazil's diverse national "system" of consumer protection. This system includes country-level bodies such as the National Consumer Secretariat, the Justice Ministry, and major consumer groups, but also the Procons, which exist in all Brazil's twenty-six states, as well as in nearly a thousand municipalities.

An actor that has stood out in the wake of the promulgation of the 1990 Consumer Defense Code has been the Public Prosecutor Service. This service has no strict equivalent in countries such as the United States, because the service is independent of the executive, legislative, and judicial branches of government. There are federal prosecutors, and each Brazilian state has its own prosecutor service. The great majority of class actions on behalf of consumers have been filed by the public prosecutors, and throughout Brazil there are prosecutors who are tasked exclusively with the protection of consumers. Recently, the Public Defender Service, whose goal is to provide full and free legal assistance to people who cannot afford it, has also added consumer protection to its priorities.

Since 1990, when the Consumer Defense Code was promulgated, a struggle began in Brazil to change the mindset of the judiciary, regulatory bodies, and companies. Here academic activities play an important role. The following should be highlighted in this regard: the introduction of the right of the consumer as a compulsory subject in the curricula of the most important law faculties; and the founding of institutes specializing in consumer law. Foremost among the institutes is the Brazilian Institute of Consumer Policy and Rights (Brasilcon), which was founded in 1992 and publishes the *Consumer Rights Journal*.

The Present

In recent years, Brazil has gained considerable importance on the world stage, and the globalization of its economy has seen all major world companies setting up shop there. As the economy has grown, Brazil's middle class has grown, but the opportunity to participate in the consumer market is just beginning for many of the country's citizens. According to the government-affiliated Institute of Applied Economic Research, 2012 saw 3.5 million people emerge from poverty (and an additional 1 million escape from extreme poverty) who then, in some form or another, went on to become part of consumer society.

The transition of Brazil from a less to a more developed country underlines the need for strengthening consumer protection. The challenge is immense. There have been clear improvements in government consumer protection activities at the federal, state, and municipal levels. In 2013, Brazil's president announced a national plan to improve consumer protection. The plan, called the National Consumption and Citizenship Plan, aims to promote marketplace transparency (especially for online purchases and banking services), improve dispute resolution, and increase sanctions against firms that break the law.

Government action represents only half of the consumer protection equation. In Brazil, consumers still lack incentives within civil society to organize themselves. The consumer associations belonging to the National Forum of Consumer Groups (a national umbrella organization comprising twenty members) have enormous difficulty, for example, standing up to the banking lobby and transnational companies. One of the main problems is the lack of financing that would enable civil bodies to act effectively and independently. Thus the consumer movement in Brazil remains a work in progress, but it is has an enormously important role to play for consumers.

Marcelo Gomes Sodré

See also: Consumers International; South American Consumer Movements

Further Reading

IDEC—Instituto Brasileiro de Defensa do Consumidor. www.idec.org.br.
Sodré, Marcelo Gomes. 2007. *Formação do Sistema Nacional de Defesa do Consumidor*. São Paulo, Brazil: Editora Revista dos Tribunais.

BRITISH CONSUMER MOVEMENT
See United Kingdom Consumer Movement

C

CABLE TELEVISION REGULATION

Cable television, originally named Community Antenna Television (CATV), originated in the late 1940s to provide television service to communities unable to receive traditional over-the-air broadcast signals either because of the surrounding terrain or because of the community's distance from a broadcast station. A community residing in a valley, for instance, might be unable to receive local broadcast signals thanks to interference created by mountains. For a fee, cable companies provided broadcast programming to such communities by carrying the content from a nearby antenna directly to the community through a coaxial cable.

At the time, subscribers could only receive retransmitted broadcast programming. Beginning in the late 1960s, cable companies started developing their own programming to attract subscribers, eventually developing well-known networks that included movie channels such as the Home Box Office (HBO), news channels such as the Cable News Network (CNN), and music channels such as Music Television (MTV). Cable television quickly became a viable competitor to traditional over-the-air broadcast television services. Once operating in select communities serving fewer than 15,000 households, cable television now services more than 90 million households across the United States in rural and urban communities alike.

To ensure the preservation of local broadcast service and to promote fair distribution of broadcast services throughout the country, the Supreme Court in 1968 affirmed the Federal Communications Commission's (FCC) authority to regulate cable operators in *United States v. Southwestern Cable*. Under this authority, the FCC developed rules addressing franchise standards, signal carriage, program carriage, cross-ownership, and technical standards.

Congress subsequently codified several of the FCC's rules through legislation that included the Communications Policy Act of 1984 (1984 Cable Act), the Cable Television Consumer Protection and Competition Act of 1992 (1992 Cable Act), and the Telecommunications Act of 1966 (1996 Act). The Cable Communications Policy Act of 1984 further clarified jurisdictional authority between federal and state and local entities in regulating cable. The law granted local municipalities the authority to issue and renew franchise licenses—a contractual relationship between the cable company and the municipality, where the cable company is permitted to construct, maintain, and operate its cable service within a specified geographic area in return for paying a negotiated franchise fee and remaining amenable to the interests of the community.

Before passage of the 1992 Cable Act, many cable operators negotiated exclusive franchises with communities, thereby preventing competition in the local market. These agreements could last anywhere from five to twenty years before renewal. In addition to negotiating a franchise fee, local authorities also typically negotiated public access, educational, and governmental channels (PEG channels) for the community, which the 1984 Cable Act subsequently mandated.

Although franchise agreements were regulated at the local level, the 1984 Cable Act preempted state and local authority to regulate rates associated with cable services. Through this distribution of power between federal and local authorities, the 1984 Cable Act sought to promote competition and deregulation in the cable industry. Though the law led to substantial growth in the cable industry, the industry remained largely controlled by local monopolies facing little to no competition. The federal government's preemption authority led to substantial deregulation, which resulted in cable service rate increases as high as three times the rate of inflation. The quality of service provided by cable companies simultaneously fell, and consumers increasingly complained of unanswered and unreturned phone calls, missed service calls, and poor signal quality.

In response to increasing rates and decreasing quality of service, Congress passed the Cable Television Consumer Protection and Competition Act of 1992. Gene Kimmelman, Consumer Federation of America's legislative director, played a leading role in drafting and promoting provisions that became law in 1992. The odds against enactment were daunting. In fact, the 1992 Cable Act was the only piece of legislation that then President George H.W. Bush vetoed but had overridden by a supermajority in Congress. Without consumer awareness and advocacy, the bill probably never would have become law.

The cable industry is widely considered a natural monopoly, because of the physical and economic limitations on the number of cable systems that can practicably operate in any given geographic area. Cable companies incur high up-front costs in building infrastructure, which are more difficult to defray when a competing cable company with a large number of subscribers already operates in the community. The cable industry also controlled the most popular programming, suppressing competition from competing operating systems, including satellite services. The 1992 Cable Act sought to increase consumer protections and promote competition in the cable television industry by addressing rate regulation, franchising terms, customer service, competitors' access to cable programming, and guaranteed carriage of over-the-air broadcast programming.

First, Congress instructed the FCC to regulate cable rates until effective competition was established within the market, existing when at least 50 percent of households in a franchise area have access to a comparable multichannel video service and at least 15 percent of those households subscribed to said service. The FCC has estimated that the 1992 Cable Act reduced consumer costs associated with cable service and equipment by more than $2 billion annually. Despite losing control over rate regulation, state and local municipalities retained authority under the 1992 Cable Act to negotiate franchise licenses and renewal agreements with cable companies, setting minimum customer service standards.

The law also provided program access rules, which required cable providers to offer their content to competing direct-broadcast satellite and other providers at reasonable rates, in order to promote competition and fair access to programming. The FCC, finding the rules antiquated, voted to sunset the program access rules' ban on exclusive distribution agreements in 2012 and today only regulates discriminatory carriage practices.

Finally, to ensure program diversity and the perpetuity of broadcast television, the 1992 Cable Act established a must-carry provision whereby cable operators are required to carry the content of locally licensed broadcast stations to its subscribers, even if the operator would prefer to carry its own cable programming exclusively.

The Telecommunications Act of 1996—the greatest transformation in telecommunications law since the Communications Act of 1934—significantly weakened regulations of cable television service. The purpose of the 1996 act is to promote competition and reduce regulation to secure lower prices, higher quality of service, and the rapid deployment of new and innovative technologies. To reach such ends, the 1996 act ended the market-based test for determining when a community reached a sufficient level of competition to remove federal rate regulation. Instead, small cable operators with annual revenues less than $250 million serving less than 1 percent of all cable subscribers nationwide were immediately exempt from rate regulation. For larger cable operators, the 1996 act provided that rate deregulation would occur within three years, regardless of whether competition existed in the local market. Although Congress approved substantial regulation of the cable industry in the 1984 and 1992 Cable Acts, the legislature endorsed deregulation as a means of promoting competition and spurring innovation in the 1996 Telecommunications Act.

At about the same time that Congress was passing the 1996 Telecommunications Act, DIRECTV and DISH Network launched their Direct Broadcast Satellite (DBS) service throughout the nation, presenting consumers nationwide with competitive options to the incumbent local cable operator. The two DBS companies eventually grew to be the second- and third-largest pay-television providers in the nation. Similarly, telephone companies introduced pay-television service (AT&T U-Verse, Verizon FiOS), as did so-called "overbuilders," or competitive cable operators, such as RCN. All this competition reduced the market share of cable but still left local cable operators in major markets with the largest market share of all pay-television providers.

Courts, like the FCC and Congress, similarly shape regulation of the cable television industry. Current copyright laws and retransmission agreements governing the industry today, for example, may be destabilized, pending decision by the U.S. Supreme Court. Under the 1992 Cable Act, cable companies are required to negotiate with content providers for retransmission consent—permission from the broadcaster to carry its programming in exchange for payment. Copyright laws simply prohibit the use or performance of copyrighted material across public airwaves without prior approval and compensation of its owner.

However, the law distinguishes "public" from "private" performances. Although public performances subject to copyright laws involve the showing of content to several people simultaneously, private performances showing content exclusively to one individual are exempt from any copyright licensing requirement. An individual homeowner, therefore, could place an antenna on his or her television to receive broadcast signals without violating copyright laws. By comparison, a cable company's act of retransmitting broadcast channels to its subscribers constitutes a public performance and is in violation of copyright law, unless it previously negotiated the broadcaster's consent for retransmission.

New and innovative technology companies, such as Aereo, Inc., have since emerged, providing broadcast television for a fee to subscribers on Internet-connected devices. Unlike cable companies, Aereo maintains that it need not obtain retransmission consent from the content providers, because its business model operates by leasing individual antennas to each of its customers and not by the showing of public performances. Aereo provides each subscriber with an individual antenna stored remotely at an Aereo facility. That antenna allows the Aereo subscriber to view broadcast programming over the Internet. Because Aereo leases an individual antenna for each of its subscribers, it considers the showing of content to be an individual and thus private, as opposed to public, performance exempt from retransmission consent obligations.

Broadcasters, concerned by the threat to their business model, brought suit against Aereo for copyright infringement, claiming that Aereo is, in fact, a cable operator providing pay-television service and therefore violating copyright law by not receiving a license from the broadcaster to retransmit local broadcast programming. Aereo's operation, the broadcasters further argued, not only reduces the size of the traditional broadcast audience, but also evades paying retransmission fees for distribution of its programming—fees typically constituting nearly 10 percent of a broadcaster's revenue. Despite Aereo's practice of providing individual antennas for each subscriber, broadcasters maintained that Aereo's service nonetheless constitutes a public performance. The broadcasters prevailed in June 2014, when the U.S. Supreme Court ruled that Aereo had violated copyright laws.

In addition to legal developments, structural changes through corporate mergers are poised to reconfigure the pay-television industry, assuming that federal and state government agencies do not block the transactions. At the time of this writing, Comcast, the largest cable operator in the U.S., and Time Warner Cable, the second largest cable operator, seek to merge, which would form the single largest pay-TV provider with roughly 30 percent market share. Also, AT&T and DIRECTV have agreed to merge, with the combined entity holding almost as many subscribers as the combined Comcast/Time Warner Cable. The impact on consumers of this consolidation could be profound.

David Goodfriend, Madeleine Lottenbach

See also: Digital Communications Advocacy; Telephone Consumer Advocacy

Further Reading

Crandall, Robert W., and Harold W. Furchgott-Roth. 1996. *Cable TV: Regulation or Competition?* Washington, DC: Brookings Institution.
Federal Communications Commission. "Evolution of Cable TV." www.fcc.gov/encyclopedia/evolution-cable-television.

Zarkin, Michael. 2010. *The FCC and the Politics of Cable TV Regulation, 1952–1980*. London, UK: Cambria Press.

CANADIAN CONSUMER MOVEMENT

The economies of Canada and the United States have been closely linked for more than a century, and Canadians have read about or seen media reports on many U.S. consumer problems ever since Upton Sinclair's 1906 exposé of meat-packing plants. Although many consumer problems in the two countries are similar, two factors help explain the different ways their respective consumer movements have developed. First, Canada is a confederation where fewer powers are exercised at the national level. Provincial powers include policymaking related to health care and most aspects of transportation, and as of 2014, there is still no national equivalent of the U.S. Securities and Exchange Commission. The second major influence stems from the fact that there is a "natural monopoly" in North America for comparative product testing in the form of the U.S.-based magazine *Consumer Reports*. Many identical products are sold in U.S. and Canadian markets, though Canadian labels must be in both English and French, and measurements are in metric. Tests published in *Consumer Reports* meet most English-language consumer information needs in both countries. As a result, no testing organization quite like Consumers Union has succeeded in Canada. Nevertheless, thousands of volunteers, through grassroots consumer activism, achieved many important improvements, particularly from 1940 to the 1990s.

Canada, like other countries, developed a market economy without the institutions required to ensure that exchanges were fair to consumers. In response, a confederation of Canadian women's groups founded the National Council of Women in 1897 to urge standards for honest weighing of goods and truthful grading. In addition, some cities had consumers' leagues composed primarily of housewives who monitored the quality of foods in shops.

A breakthrough for consumer protection came in December 1941, after Canada had been at war for two years. The Wartime Prices and Trade Board (WPTB) faced a crisis of shortages with sharp price increases. The minister of finance and the chairman of the WPTB called together many women's organizations to establish a consumer branch of the WPTB. Little did they know what they were creating. Thousands of women volunteered, founding active groups known as Women's Regional Advisory Committees (WRACs) in each province and in many cities. A year after the war ended, the WRACs were officially "terminated" by the government . . . or so the government thought. Many units, upset by rapid postwar price rises, refused to disband. In early 1947, volunteer Harriet Parsons, the economics convener of the National Council of Women, and its president, Blanche Marshall, formed a committee to study the creation of a national consumer organization. On September 29, 1947, seventy voting delegates from more than twenty women's organizations created the Canadian Association of Consumers (CAC)—cementing Canada's unique path to a consumer movement.

The CAC immediately provided a major challenge to seller control of the marketplace. The new organization's first victory came in 1948, when it fought successfully to have the ban on margarine lifted, resulting in lower butter prices. In

1949, the CAC also helped achieve labeling requirements for textiles. Immediately after that came a highly public consumer protest against the insulting and deceptive packaging of bacon. A marketing innovation in the 1950s was a package with a new cellophane window on which bacon marketers boldly printed red stripes to imitate lean meat. In 1951, consumers in central Canada were shocked to learn they had been eating meat from animals that were already dead when brought to meatpackers. With stunning skill, CAC volunteers Helen Morningstar, Therese Casgrain, and others led a campaign of outrage. Within a year, they had succeeded in establishing important food safety standards.

In the early 1960s, two important organizational changes were made to the Canadian Association of Consumers. In 1961, the women's organization agreed that men could meet membership standards. The next year, the organization renamed itself the Consumers Association of Canada (CAC). Subsequent consumer activism led to hundreds of other improvements at the provincial and national levels. CAC also helped persuade policymakers to create a list of safe food additives, pass the Hazardous Products Act (1970), mandate standardized packaging (1971), and in some provinces require elements of truth in lending.

One of CAC's greatest contributions was its key balancing role in the creation of Canada's Competition. Act. In 1889 (a year before the U.S. antitrust Sherman Act), Canada enacted antimonopoly prohibitions. The use of "toothless" to describe the law may be too favorable as it suggests that Canada's Act had jaws: In nearly 100 years, Canada never won a contested court case against a monopoly. In 1967 a national study recommended a new act. Lobbying by monopolists and by business groups was well-funded and pervasive. For the next sixteen years, the CAC led public support for legislation to promote competition. The Competition Act passed in two stages: 1976 for marketing practices, and 1986 for mergers. The law has been a major force for consumers in defining fair market practices and setting out the framework for a fairer market.

One major defeat suffered by the CAC was an industry campaign to overturn the 1969 pharmaceutical patent arrangement, which permitted generic drugs provided that they paid compulsory royalties to drug patent holders. It was a well-functioning example of sound patent policy for the world to see, and, that being the case, the international pharmaceutical industry was eager to see it ended. Consumers lost a highly public battle, but CAC action was the key reason for the creation of a Patented Medicines Prices Review Board. The board has had a small effect in restraining prices but little or no effect maintaining R&D spending in Canada. The loss of compulsory-licensing-with-royalties has cost Canadian consumers billions of dollars per year.

The consumer movement in Canada has campaigned for free trade, gaining two early victories on children's shoes and clothing. Most agreements—like the Canada–U.S. Free Trade Agreement or its sister, NAFTA—turn out to be "managed trade" deals that still contain nontariff barriers and special exemptions for powerful lobbyists. Despite highly public battles, CAC failed to block import restrictions introduced in 1974 for milk, eggs, chicken, and turkey products. The milk quota alone has cost Canadian consumers more than $1 billion every year since 1974.

A bilingual advocacy bulletin began in 1948 and was upgraded in 1963 when CAC published a plain-paper version of *Canadian Consumer*. The publication was rejuvenated as an attractive magazine in 1973, quickly finding success with consumers and the media and earning keen attention from politicians. (CAC intended to finance consumer advocacy through magazine revenues, but this never happened.) *Canadian Consumer* was most successful during the time CAC cooperated with Consumers Union. The first joint promotion took place right at the start. Canadians could, with one payment, acquire the product test results from *Consumer Reports* (consumer information) as well as reports on Canadian services and advocacy (collective action) from CAC and the *Canadian Consumer*. At its peak in 1982, sales of the Canadian publication were nearly 160,000 per month. An ill-advised price increase was one reason why subscriptions dropped to 63,000 by 1993, the year the magazine ceased publication. Since then, Consumers Union has published a Canadian insert in *Consumer Reports* for more than 200,000 Canadian subscribers. This works well for consumer information, but far less so for advocacy.

The striking success story of remarkable consumer leaders in Canada has not yet been fully appreciated. Coordination of campaigns in both English and French and over so many jurisdictions is a challenge and would be even without well-funded opposition. For fifty years after 1947, CAC policy operated with a broad-based set of provincial presidents who constituted a majority the organization's national board. Two longstanding CAC committees had stunning success. One, focusing on research and economics, was run for nearly twenty years to the mid-1980s by the "two Helens" (Morningstar and Anderson). The other was the food committee, run by the "two Ruths" (Jackson and Titheridge). These volunteer committees, working outside of Ottawa, recruited volunteer expertise of the highest order (sometimes even including the surreptitious participation of public-spirited industry leaders). In addition to contributions within Canada, some CAC leaders served at the international level with the International Organization of Consumers Unions (founded in 1960 and now named Consumers International), which CAC joined in 1963.

At its best, CAC had professional managers/researchers operating the national office; it had thriving provincial organizations in all ten provinces and the Yukon, as well as sixteen consumer associations in larger cities (Morningstar, 1977). As late as 1993, dedicated local volunteers were working on issues that included food quality, energy, environmental quality, telephone and cable rates and service, retirement plans, warrantees and redress, bus safety, personal finance, and education. One such volunteer, Margaret Stansfield from a local in Manitoba, single-handedly answered more than 35,000 calls for assistance. After her first 5,385 calls, she apologized that she "never had the physical strength to be active."

Three forces weakened the CAC. Progress with consumer legislation was a positive outcome, but success lowered the urgency of consumer issues. A second force of importance to volunteer organizations such as CAC was the shift of women into the formal labor force. Most of the local consumer activists who supplied Canada with effective national leaders from 1945 to the present have been women. Third, after the early 1980s, there was a gradual but steady decrease in federal government financial support for consumer research and advocacy, and this reduced the capability of the national CAC office. Importantly, the cutback was not matched by a comparable decline in support by the government in Quebec.

- Fortunately, the diminished vibrancy of CAC was accompanied by growth in organizations *not* based on the volunteer model of operation. The most prominent of these Canadian consumer organizations are members of Consumers International (CI):
- *Union des consommateurs*, or the Consumers Union of Quebec, is a not-for-profit umbrella association now grouping ten member organizations originating in the early 1970s into the Cooperative Association of Household Economy (ACEF). It operates mostly in French with a consumer focus, though it also orients some of its research projects to benefit the disadvantaged and for social justice purposes more generally. *Union* has provided support that resulted in policy action on privacy, food, and consumer law. It has been a participating member of CI since 1990.
- *Option consommateurs*, founded in 1983 and a CI member since 2003, is a bilingual not-for-profit consumer organization based in Montreal. *Option* has been highly visible in the media with class action suits in Quebec and as an independent voice for consumers throughout Canada, especially on energy, food safety, health, financial services wireless policies and market practices. *Option* represents Canadian consumers on more than twenty official committees and regulatory bodies.
- Also important is *Protégez-Vous*, a monthly French-language consumer magazine originating in 1973 with Québec government support. Re-formed in 2001, it is now an independent, self-financing, not-for-profit organization producing 100,000 magazines per month with test results. In fact, *Protégez-Vous* provides both consumer information and active consumer advocacy. Publishing in French provides a measure of insulation from competition from *Consumer Reports*. Insulation may not be needed, though, as *Protégez-Vous* can also be seen as a francophone invention well suited to Quebec's specific legal framework and to its cultural institutions. A CI member since 2013, *Protégez-Vous* operates three highly active websites that see more than 650,000 visitors per month.
- The Public Interest Advocacy Centre (PIAC), formed in 1976, is a not-for-profit advocacy organization with an operating model based on consumer-interest research funded primarily by governments. PIAC has produced research of lasting effect on telecommunications, e-commerce, privacy, broadcasting, and competition policy. It has been an affiliate member of CI since 2001.
- There are a number of other groups active in Canada. Perhaps the most visible is the Consumers Council of Canada (CCC). CCC provides consumer-interest research—most recently on Canada's wireless oligopolies—and funds its activity by its members and especially by its ability to locate public-interest funding. Several other consumer groups operate in Canada, but all are challenged by the famous "free rider problem": The market does not provide funds for "public goods" such as consumer protection laws or basic consumer science.

Quebec's Office de la protection du consommateur (OPC), founded in 1971, is another important government consumer organization. OPC was the original parent of *Protégez-Vous* and now provides consumer information, engages in consumer advocacy, and conducts research in support of consumer-interest legislation. OPC has been a supporting member of CI since 2001.

A distinct national ministry for consumers is long gone, but an important residual exists in the form of the Office of Consumer Affairs (OCA), located within

Industry Canada (a department within the Ministry of Industry). OCA makes available useful consumer material from its web site. The office was also a major force supporting the 2013 creation of Canada's national registry of academic consumer researchers (http://ccird.uwaterloo.ca). The registry is important because Canada—unlike many European countries—lacks a national consumer research institute with the ongoing capability of conducting research for the benefit of consumers, the consumer movement, and, indeed, for Canadian firms. OCA has been a government supporter of CI since 1987.

Measured against other countries, Canada has done relatively well in terms of supporting a variety of consumer organizations with a high degree of independence from both government and business funding. Consumer groups in the province of Quebec have achieved particular success. Still, much remains to be done in terms of fostering an environment that supports consumer organizations and provides consumers with information, competitive markets, and consumer protection.

Robert R. Kerton

See also: Consumers International; Consumers Union/Consumer Reports

Further Reading

Morningstar, Helen. 1977. "The Consumers Association of Canada—The History of an Effective Organization." *Canadian Business Review* 4 (autumn): 30–33.
Sadovnikova, Anna, Andrey Mikhailitchenko, and Stanley J. Shapiro. 2014. "Consumer Protection in Postwar Canada: Role and Contributions of the Consumers' Association of Canada to the Public Policy Process." *Journal of Consumer Affairs* 48, no. 2: 380–402.
Trebilcock, Michael J. 1991. "Taking Stock: Consumerism in the 1990s." *Canadian Business Law Journal* 19: 412–436.

CARIBBEAN CONSUMER MOVEMENTS

The Caribbean is a region, distinct from Central America and South America, that consists of thirteen sovereign nations as well as a similar number of semi-autonomous territories linked to France, the Netherlands, the United Kingdom, and the United States. (Some definitions of the Caribbean region include Guyana and Suriname, two countries on the northeastern coast of South America.) The richest country in the region, as measured by gross domestic product per capita, is the Bahamas, followed by Puerto Rico (a U.S. territory). The poorest country, by a wide margin, is Haiti.

The history of consumer activism in the Caribbean region can be traced back to 1966 and the founding of the National Consumers' League (NCL) in Jamaica. NCL is the oldest consumer association not only in the Caribbean, but in all Latin America. When NCL was established, Jamaica was one of the few politically independent countries in the region. Instead, the first stirrings of consumer protection activity in most of today's Caribbean countries and territories began under the auspices of western countries with longer traditions of consumer activism. Similarly, legal systems hospitable to consumer protection that existed when Caribbean countries were still colonies carried over after political independence. For this reason, consumer protection generally emerged earlier in the Caribbean islands than in mainland Latin America.

As mentioned, Jamaica was in the forefront of consumer protection in the Caribbean. In 1970, the government enacted the Trade Act, the main purpose of which was to regulate prices in the country. Furthermore, this legislation created the Price Commission in 1971. For the next twenty years, the main duty of the Price Commission was to control price inflation, but after many prices were deregulated, the Price Commission's mission shifted in 1992 to comprise all aspects of consumer affairs. With this shift, the Price Commission changed its name to the Consumers Affairs Commission. The commission has a board of directors appointed by the government and has a chief executive officer who oversees the commission's daily activities.

In 2005, a new Consumer Protection Act was approved in Jamaica. The act sets out criteria for determining the legitimacy of nonprofit organizations, and the act charges the Consumer Affairs Commission to promote the development of consumer organizations that meet these criteria. Nevertheless, the NCL remains Jamaica's primary civil society consumer organization, and it works in areas such as consumer education, food safety, and access to utilities. In 1967, NCL joined Consumers International (CI), the umbrella organization for the world consumer movement, and it remains an active member.

Saint Lucia's consumer protection history is similar to that of Jamaica. In 1970 a Price Control Commission was set up, an organism that later became the Consumer Affairs Department within the Ministry of Trade. There is not a comprehensive consumer law in the island, but, as happened with many of the Caribbean countries that follow the common law tradition, there are many more specific laws that deal with pricing, safety, measures and weights, and standards. An organization named the National Consumer Association was founded recently, is working on consumer issues, and has been accepted as a member of CI.

Trinidad and Tobago is the second wealthiest country in the Caribbean region (as measured by GDP per capita), and it gained independence from the United Kingdom in 1962, a few weeks after Jamaica did. Trinidad and Tobago established a consumer agency in 1985—the Consumer Affairs Division within the Ministry of Legal Affairs. A major law passed the same year established a Consumer Guidance Council made up of five representatives of government ministries and six representatives of consumer organizations, other nongovernmental organizations, and the general public. The tasks of the council are to monitor and make recommendations regarding consumer policy.

Cuba is the most populous nation in the Caribbean area. Like Trinidad and Tobago, Cuba does not have notable consumer organizations as part of civil society, but it does have consumer protection policies. In the 1980s, the Cuban Institute for Research and Orientation of Internal Demand (ICIODI) was created in the Ministry of Commerce to address issues related to consumer protection, such as prices, health, and safety. Although ICIODI is not a consumer protection agency that enforces consumer policies, Cuba has additional institutes and foundations—such as the Antonio Nuñez Jimenez Foundation—that work on consumer issues such as environmentally sustainable consumption.

After Cuba and Haiti, the Dominican Republic is the Caribbean country with the third largest population—almost 10 million people. The consumer protection movement began in the Dominican Republic in the late 1990s, with the formation of Fundación del Consumidor (FUNDECOM). FUNDECOM, which is a member of Consumers International, seeks to inform and educate consumers, and it has offices in various parts of the country. The work of FUNDECOM is complemented by a government consumer protection agency, Pro Consumidor. The agency has a strong presence in the media because of its actions on several issues, most notably financial services, public utilities, and food.

Countries and territories such as Antigua and Barbuda, Aruba, Barbados, Curaçao, Grenada, and Saint Vincent and the Grenadines have established government agencies to address consumer protection, but they often lack a comprehensive law on consumer protection. There are consumer associations in some of these countries and territories, including the Aruba Consumer Solidarity Group, the Barbados Consumer Research Organization, and the Curaçao Consumers Foundation.

Virtually all the countries and territories in the Caribbean region are affiliated—as members, associates, or observers—with the Caribbean Community (CARICOM). Established in 1973, the primary function of CARICOM is to promote economic integration and cooperation among its members, but it also serves as a forum for the discussion of consumer protection issues. For example, CARICOM has established an alert system through which information can be rapidly exchanged about potentially dangerous products (e.g., toys, jewelry, furniture, and motor vehicles) entering and trading within the region.

As an initiative of Consumers International, the Caribbean Consumer Council (CCC) was established in the 1990s. The CCC is composed of representatives of both consumer protection agencies and consumer associations and is itself registered as a nongovernmental organization in St. Lucia. Its main goals are to encourage the development of the consumer movement in the region and to influence CARICOM regarding consumer protection issues. After meeting regularly and participating in CARICOM policy discussions for several years, the CCC scaled back its activities due to lack of funding. However, the CCC was revitalized as a result of a three-year project—funded by the Inter-American Development Bank and coordinated by Consumers International—to strengthen the consumer movements of Barbados, Jamaica, and Trinidad and Tobago. The project conducted a baseline study of the status of consumer organizations in the region, conducted surveys on banking and credit use, provided training to consumer associations and government agencies, and conducted public service campaigns. The achievements of the project in a short time frame suggest that further investments in the consumer movements of the Caribbean countries are needed.

Antonino Serra Cambaceres

See also: Consumers International

Further Reading

Consumers International. 2013. "CI's Caribbean Project Has Concluded," *CI News*, March 1, www.consumersinternational.org/news-and-media/news/2013/03/carribean_project.

CENTER FOR AUTO SAFETY

The Center for Auto Safety (CAS) is a nonprofit 501(c)(3) research and advocacy organization that was founded in 1970 to provide consumers with a voice for automobile safety and quality and to provide information to consumers on how to purchase the best motor vehicle to meet their needs. Ralph Nader, who was a Consumers Union board member at the time, provided the inspiration, and Consumers Union provided the initial funding. In 1973, the CAS became independent of its founders when control was shifted to a five-member, self-perpetuating board of directors.

The CAS seeks to advance consumer rights in several ways. It petitions and participates in rulemaking before the federal agencies that regulate the auto industry, including the National Highway Traffic Safety Administration (NHTSA), the Federal Trade Commission (FTC), and the Environmental Protection Agency (EPA). It testifies before congressional committees on issues affecting the consumer and transportation. It publishes a wide range of self-help information for consumers, ranging from packets on defects in individual cars to books on lemon rights and auto warranties. And it seeks redress for groups of consumers with the same problem through actions such as public pressure on auto manufacturers and organizing class action lawsuits.

The center employs fewer than ten persons on an annual budget of around $600,000, which is supported by small contributions from some 15,000 members as well as by income from publications, grants, and other sources. However, over the past several decades, the organization has been an effective motor vehicle safety advocacy organization largely because of its leader, Clarence M. Ditlow, who has served as executive director since 1975. Ditlow holds a degree in chemical engineering from Lehigh University and law degrees from Georgetown and Harvard. Before becoming the executive director of the CAS, he was a patent examiner in the U.S. Patent Office from 1965 to 1970. From 1971 to 1975, he was an attorney and director with Ralph Nader's Public Interest Research Group.

The center's first director was Lowell Dodge, who earlier had participated in the civil rights movement and graduated from Yale Law School. Under his direction the organization's first action (in 1970) was to publish a book that developed new strategies for lemon purchasers and called for creation of new legal rights for lemon owners. Based on 5,000 consumer complaints received by Ralph Nader, the book became known as, and was eventually titled, *The Lemon Book*. It provided the foundation for lemon laws in all fifty states and the lemon provisions in the Magnuson–Moss Warranty Act of 1975.

In 1970, the center also began what became a twenty-year campaign to install airbags in all motor vehicles. The organization fought for airbags in the federal agencies, courts, Congress, and in the court of public opinion. The turning point in this campaign came when, in 1983, the U.S. Supreme Court overturned the Reagan administration's effort to revoke a rule that had been issued by NHTSA. In its early years, the center also issued a wide range of books, reports, and studies, including "Small—on Safety: The Designed-in Dangers of the Volkswagen."

With support from the State Farm Foundation, the CAS set up its Highway Safety Project in 1973 to try to improve the design of, and reduce construction hazards, in highways. This project wrote *The Yellow Brick Road*, which exposed hazards to policymakers and the public and also served as the basis for advocacy over the next decade. Because the Federal Highway Administration refused to address safety hazards in a timely fashion, the center sued the agency numerous times to comply with federal law and upgrade highway safety. The organization combined these interventions with such consumer actions as posting Highway Hazard Signs (with skull and crossbones) on a major Washington, D.C., road used by commuters.

During the 1970s, the CAS set up several branch offices and independent centers. Among the most successful were the Auto Safety Centers, headed up in Cleveland by Tom Vacar, who later became a consumer reporter, and in Hartford by Toby Moffett, who later served in Congress. Although these and other offices had success, they never established an independent financial basis and withered after their first leaders moved on.

In the 1970s and 1980s, the CAS helped start a number of independent consumer groups concerned with auto issues. One of these groups was Motor Voters (now known as Consumers for Auto Reliability and Safety or CARS), launched in San Diego by Rosemary Shahan to push for a state lemon law. Another group was the Automobile Protection Association in Canada, which was started by Phil Edmonston, who earlier had worked at the CAS for a year.

The center also helped single-issue consumer action groups and campaigns, which usually addressed a particular automotive problem for several years. Some of the most successful campaigns were organized around 1978–1985 General Motors (GM) cars with 350-cubic-inch diesel engines that had numerous defects. Other campaigns were built around Pontiac Fieros that caught fire, GM pickups with exploding sidesaddle gas tanks, Ford Cortinas lacking replacement parts, and Winnebagos with Renault diesel engines.

In 1978, the CAS became a membership organization. In the same year, it exposed the hazards of the Ford Pinto with exploding gas tanks, forcing a recall. In 1979, the CAS successfully called for the recall of 15 million Firestone 500 steel-belted radials for tread separation, the largest tire recall ever.

In 1980, the CAS published the second edition of its *Lemon Book* with Ralph Nader and called for passage of state lemon laws. Beginning in 1981, first with Connecticut and then with California, and concluding in 1992 with Arkansas, every state passed a lemon law. In recent years, CAS has evaluated every state's lemon law and made specific recommendations about how each could be strengthened.

CAS litigation was an especially important tool during the 1980s, when the Reagan administration tried to roll back automobile safety measures adopted during the 1970s. The center participated in and won lawsuits overturning the revocation of tire quality grading standards in 1982 and of the airbag rule in 1983. Other lawsuits restored the EPA's emission recall program in 1984, prohibited oversize trucks from operating on highways unless specific safety criteria were met in 1985, required the installation of gasoline vapor recovery canisters on cars in 1991, and required mandatory bridge inspections in 1992.

In 1990, the CAS published "Children at Risk," which was based on a study of NHTSA child seat standards and recall program that found that less than 7 percent of defective child seats were fixed under a recall. After Senate and House committee hearings, the agency adopted a child seat registration system so that owners of defective child seats could be notified of recalls. As a result of the CAS study, the agency also recalled 3.7 million Evenflo child seats for defective latches, the largest child seat recall ever.

In this decade, the center campaigned to expose secret warranties of auto companies. In 1994, the CAS wrote a book on the practice called *Little Secrets of the Auto Industry*, which revealed that, at any one time, there were more than 500 secret warranties covering more than $10 billion in defects. By 1995, four states— California, Connecticut, Virginia, and Wisconsin—had passed secret warranty disclosure laws to protect consumers from this abuse.

Recent CAS safety campaigns have focused on distracted driving, vehicle roof weakness, and sudden unintended acceleration. The organization used a Freedom of Information lawsuit to uncover a major Department of Transportation (DOT) study on the dangers of cell phone use while driving. This lawsuit led to a front-page *New York Times* article, a DOT distracted driving conference, and, eventually, passage by many states of laws against both texting and cell phone use while driving.

The results of CAS testing for roof crush on fifteen vehicles convinced NHTSA to issue improved roof crush standards and also to undertake dynamic testing to create front and side dynamic impact standards. As a result of the new roof crush standard, side impact bags, and an electronic stability control standard to reduce rollover crashes, thousands of deaths in rollover crashes each year are likely to be prevented.

Since the mid-1980s, CAS has worked to reduce the incidence of sudden unintended acceleration in vehicles. The center was one of the first to discover that Toyota's introduction of electronic throttle controls beginning with 2003 models led to the quadrupling of complaints about unintended acceleration in Toyota and Lexus vehicles. CAS pressure on NHTSA helped persuade the agency to recall 10 million vehicles for sticking gas pedals and jamming floor mats. From 2010 to 2013, CAS campaigned for the recall of 1993–1994 Jeep Grand Cherokees, whose fuel tanks could explode on impact, like those of the Ford Pinto many years earlier. Although Chrysler agreed to a safety defect recall, its remedy of a trailer hitch was called ineffective, even by an engineering official at the car company.

Over the years, CAS has worked on issues other than motor vehicle safety. Early on in the center's life it created the Mobile Home Task Force to focus on mobile home quality. Its report, "Mobile Homes—The Low Cost Housing Hoax," helped persuade Congress to pass the National Mobile Home Construction and Safety

Standards Act in 1974 and the creation of a division within the Department of Housing and Urban Development to oversee mobile home safety and construction. More recently, CAS has worked to win stronger fuel efficiency and emissions standards from the Obama administration. And for several decades, it has published *The Car Book*, prepared by Jack Gillis, to annually evaluate new car models.

Clarence M. Ditlow, Stephen Brobeck

See also: Advocates for Highway and Auto Safety; Consumers for Auto Reliability and Safety; Motor Vehicle Safety Advocacy

Further Reading

Jensen, Christopher. 1988. "This Man Gives the Auto Industry Nightmares." *Plain Dealer* (July 24): D-1.

Logan, Gary J. 1989. "Steering toward Safety." *Everyday Law* (February): 43–48.

CENTER FOR DIGITAL DEMOCRACY

Center for Digital Democracy, which calls itself CDD, is a 501(c)(3) nonprofit organization that uses research, public education, and advocacy to advance the public interest in the digital era. It focuses particular attention on holding digital and data industries accountable, especially on their commercial surveillance activities threatening privacy.

CDD's organizational roots date back to 1991, when Kathryn Montgomery and Jeff Chester founded the Center for Media Education (CME). Montgomery, currently a professor of communications at American University, has written two scholarly books and many articles on media and society. She served as president of CME, and then CDD, from 1991 until 2003. Chester is a former investigative journalist, author of *Digital Destiny: New Media and the Future of Democracy*, who has worked for CME and CDD since 1991. Since CME evolved into CDD in 1991, he has served as executive director of the organization, whose annual budget in recent years has ranged around $600,000.

CME was founded to help strengthen the public interest media movement during a period of change in the world of communications. Initially the organization focused on the implementation of the Children's Television Act of 1990. Its accomplishments included a 1992 report on children's programming practices, which together with subsequent research and public education, played an important role in the issuing of a 1996 rule, by the Federal Communications Commission (FCC), that required all television stations in the United States to air a minimum of three hours per week of educational programming for children.

In this period, CME also published the first documentation of "electronic redlining" in the new digital media. The study—released in 1994 by CME, Consumer Federation of America, National Council of La Raza, and the NAACP—helped launch a public debate over equitable access to new technologies.

In 1996, CME issued a report on Internet marketing and data collection practices targeting children that prompted the Federal Trade Commission (FTC) to conduct its own research into the area and eventually led to passage of the Children's

Online Privacy Protection Act (COPPA) of 1998. In 1997, the organization released a report on the prevalence of alcohol and tobacco websites targeting under-age youth that generated considerable press coverage, including a front-page story in the *New York Times*, and helped persuade the FTC to conduct an inquiry into alcohol marketing directed at young people. In 1998, CME organized a national conference, "Creating a Quality Media Culture for Children in the Digital Age."

In 2001, wanting to focus more exclusively on challenges raised by the rapidly evolving digital landscape, with the assistance of a Stern Family Fund grant, Chester launched the Center for Digital Democracy. Since then, CDD has been a public interest leader in promoting greater diversity of media ownership and expression (including minority ownership), in protecting the Internet's role as an open and nondiscriminatory medium, in expanding noncommercial space online and off, and in helping making the electronic media more accountable to the public.

Early on, CDD identified threats to "network neutrality" posed by the cable industry's business model for broadband. Its research, advocacy, and work with the press spurred creation of a movement supporting open online networks. CDD also tracked the growth of online financial marketing, documenting its role in the subprime crisis and financial debacle. As a member of Americans for Financial Reform, it drafted the section addressing online financial marketing for that coalition's white paper. CDD also publicly raised the issue of the consequences to civil liberties from the growing use of online ethnic and racial profiling, which led to legislative proposals with new safeguards.

By documenting new dangers to consumers and citizens from interactive data collection practices, CDD has generated considerable news coverage. And its advocacy using this information has helped persuade federal agencies to issue new safeguards. At the Food and Drug Administration (FDA), these safeguards related to public health risks from interactive and social media marketing of prescription drugs.

At the FTC, COPPA safeguards on children's online privacy were strengthened. Under revised rules, online behavioral advertising targeting children is prohibited unless a parent provides affirmative prior consent, geolocation and mobile information from and about a child cannot be collected or used without similar parental consent, and marketing techniques by social media companies and services such as "Like" buttons must also comply with these safeguards. CDD published a parent's primer explaining the new provisions and, in partnership with Georgetown University Law Center, produced a legal guide to help NGOs inform members and monitor compliance with the rules. Recently, CDD has filed several requests with the FTC calling for the agency to investigate and take enforcement action against companies that have violated the new rule.

Also recently, as part of a broader societal campaign to reduce youth obesity, CDD has helped expose the role of digital marketing of fast foods and beverages. The organization has written extensively on the subject, including providing regular updates through its own blog and through the Berkeley Media Studies Group/ CDD Digitalads.org website. CDD also organized a series of scholarly meetings on the issue for the Robert Wood Johnson Foundation held at the National Institutes of Health.

Jeff Chester

See also: Action for Children's Television; Digital Communications Advocacy; Privacy Advocacy; Telecommunications Research and Action Center

Further Reading

Chester, Jeff. 2007. *Digital Destiny: New Media and the Future of Democracy.* New York: New Press.

Montgomery, Kathryn. 2007. *Generation Digital: Politics, Commerce, and Childhood in the Age of the Internet.* Cambridge, MA: MIT Press.

CENTER FOR FOOD SAFETY

Center for Food Safety (CFS) is a U.S. nonprofit advocacy organization with two complementary goals: to protect human health and to protect the natural environment. CFS attempts to limit what it considers harmful aspects of food production technologies, especially pesticides and genetic engineering, while simultaneously promoting organic farming and other types of sustainable agriculture. (Opponents of genetic engineering prefer this term to the less scary-sounding genetic modification.) CFS employs the full panoply of advocacy methods, including public education, research, lobbying, litigation, boycotts, and the encouragement of citizen activism through its True Food Network.

From the establishment of CFS in 1997, opposition to genetically engineered food has been its signature policy position. In May 1998, it filed a lawsuit challenging the U.S. Food and Drug Administration's (FDA's) lack of regulation of genetically engineered food. Citing consumer health risks, the consumer's right to know the content of food, and even religious freedom, the suit sought greater safety testing and mandatory labeling of genetically engineered foods. Although the FDA has tightened its safety evaluation procedures over time, it remains opposed to mandatory labeling of genetically engineered food. In response, CFS and its allies have taken the fight for labeling to the state level. Their efforts have so far resulted in labeling legislation in Vermont, Maine, and Connecticut, although implementation in the latter two states requires action by additional states. Citizens in California and Washington have rejected labeling laws in statewide votes.

CFS has also devoted considerable resources to opposing concentrated animal feeding operations ("factory farming"). With respect to meat and poultry, it views overuse of antibiotics as both inhumane to animals (inasmuch as it allows them to survive crowded and unsanitary conditions) and dangerous to humans (inasmuch as it promotes antibiotic resistance). In 2012, CFS amassed more than a half million signatures on a petition urging Trader Joe's stores—a food chain that caters to well-educated and affluent consumers—to source and sell only meat and poultry raised without antibiotics. Although Trader Joe's continues to offer both conventional and antibiotic-free meat and poultry, CFS's efforts may have shifted the product mix offered to consumers.

CFS's priorities can be seen in combination in its work with respect to organic food. CFS supports a strict standard for what is to be considered "organic." It opposes that designation for any genetically engineered products. The organization also opposes the use of antibiotics in the production of organic apples and pears, and it promotes animal welfare regulations in organic poultry production. Other important issues to CFS are the survival of pollinating bees in the face of pesticide use, maintenance of seed diversity and thereby food security, and monitoring the effects of nanotechnology as it is rapidly introduced into food and food packaging.

CFS straddles the consumer and environmental movements in the United States. On the one hand, its commitment to food safety could not be more central to consumer welfare. On occasion, CFS acts in concert with mainstream consumer organizations, as it did in early 2014 in opposing cuts to the budget of the U.S. Department of Agriculture's Food Safety Inspection Service. CFS also sides with consumer organizations in supporting labels that allow shoppers to know the country of origin of their foods. CFS's relationship to the consumer group, Center for Science in the Public Interest (CSP), is complex. The two organizations are allies when it comes to tightly regulating food additives, but CFS believes that CSPI is wrong not to support labeling of genetically engineered food. When viewing CFS's activities as a whole, it partners more frequently with environmental organizations such as Earthjustice, the Environmental Working Group, Friends of the Earth, and Defenders of Wildlife than it does with consumer groups.

CFS is headquartered in Washington, DC, and has offices in California, Oregon, and Hawaii. It is currently led by its founder and executive director, Andrew Kimbrell, and has a staff of about thirty-five people. In 2011, it had revenue and expenses of about $2 million. Its website is www.centerforfoodsafety.org.

Robert N. Mayer

See also: Center for Science in the Public Interest; Food Safety Advocacy

Further Reading

Center for Food Safety Victory Report. 2013. Washington, DC: Center for Food Safety, November 25. www.centerforfoodsafety.org/reports/2735/center-for-food-safety-15-year-anniversary-victory-report.

CENTER FOR RESPONSIBLE LENDING

The Center for Responsible Lending (CRL) is a nonpartisan, nonprofit research and policy organization whose goal is to protect homeownership and family wealth. CRL's work focuses on identifying predatory lending practices—particularly those that affect low-income and minority communities—and developing practical policy solutions to address them.

CRL is affiliated with Self-Help, one of the largest community development financial institutions in the United States. Founded in 1980 by Martin Eakes, Self-Help operates credit unions in North Carolina, California, and Illinois and also does small business lending and real estate development.

In the late 1990s, Self-Help helped lead the fight against abusive subprime mortgage lending in North Carolina after seeing subprime lenders refinance its customers and other North Carolina homeowners into mortgages that incorporated wealth-draining fees and unfair or deceptive loan terms. Self-Help worked with a broad, bipartisan coalition of advocates and lawmakers to help pass the North Carolina Anti-Predatory Lending Law of 1999. This, the first such law in the country, was estimated to save homeowners more than $100 million annually.

In 2002, Self-Help established the Center for Responsible Lending in Durham, North Carolina, to expand its work to a national scope and broaden its focus to include practices outside of mortgage lending, such as payday loans. Soon after, CRL established a permanent presence in Washington, D.C., for federal activity. In 2005, CRL created an Oakland office to closely monitor predatory lending in California. All three CRL offices work together to provide a national voice against abusive financial practices.

During its first five years, CRL replicated its state advocacy efforts nationally, and began to tie that agenda to a federal strategy. CRL had immediate effect, providing technical assistance to coalitions of consumer advocates in some thirty states by providing issue expertise, policy recommendations, and strategy support.

CRL's national policy agenda broadened beyond mortgage and payday lending to include issues such as overdraft fees, credit cards, and auto lending abuses. Its efforts in all these areas involved close partnerships with AARP, the Leadership Conference on Civil and Human Rights, NAACP, the National Council of La Raza, the Department of Defense, the National Consumer Law Center, and the Consumer Federation of America, among many other groups.

During its early years, CRL's work with allies produced several key successes. These included helping halt payday lenders' use out of state banks to evade state usury limits known as the "rent-a-bank" scheme (2004), ending mandatory arbitration in mortgage contracts by Government Sponsored Enterprises (2004), and passing the Military Lending Act to protect service members and their family members against high-cost payday loans (2006). CRL also worked effectively in states with ballot initiatives. Consumer wins in Arizona, Ohio, and Montana set the stage for future payday lending victories.

CRL's influential research has raised awareness of numerous predatory lending practices and their effects on U.S. households. One of the organization's first research reports quantified the high cost of overdraft loans and bank practices that promoted this abusive product and spurred actions by regulators to rein in some of these practices. CRL studies highlighted credit card issuer tricks and traps that ultimately led to reforms in the Credit CARD Act of 2009. And more recently, CRL's research on automobile lending has brought regulator and public attention to abusive practices costing consumers more than $20 billion per year.

CRL also played a seminal role during the subprime mortgage crisis of the late 2000s. Its "Losing Ground" study, published in 2006, predicted the foreclosure crisis, and subsequent research described how foreclosures were disproportionately affecting families of color and their communities. CRL research, which has been informed by Self-Help's experience making home loans to low-income families, also shed light on the risks of exploding subprime 2/28 mortgages, loans with no documentation of income, and other "exotic" mortgage credit.

In response to the risky lending and inadequate oversight of the mortgage market that led to the 2008 financial crisis, Congress passed the Dodd–Frank Wall Street Reform and Consumer Protection Act of 2010 (Dodd–Frank); CRL played a key role in developing the mortgage provisions of the Act. Dodd–Frank reformed the mortgage market by outlining new rules for mortgage lending to prevent the market abuses that prevailed over the previous decade. CRL worked to ensure that the mortgage provisions in Dodd–Frank were designed to reorient the market back to well-underwritten, sensible traditional mortgages that build wealth for American families.

Dodd–Frank also established the Consumer Financial Protection Bureau (CFPB), an independent regulatory agency focused on ensuring that financial transactions are fair and transparent. CRL continues to work closely with CFPB and other financial regulators to address abusive financial practices that affect American families today, including debt collection abuses, payday lending, overdraft loans, and student loans.

As well as running the Self-Help Credit Union, Martin Eakes is chief executive officer of CRL. An attorney and MacArthur Fellow, Eakes is considered to be the nation's most influential consumer advocate on development finance. On a day-to-day basis, the organization is run by President Michael Calhoun, an attorney and principal author of North Carolina's 1999 anti–predatory lending law. Before joining CRL, he had worked for legal services and for the Self-Help Credit Union. Calhoun oversees a staff of forty and an annual budget of just under $7 million. In 2012, in recognition of its leadership fighting predatory lending, CRL received the MacArthur Award for Creative and Effective Institutions.

Michael Calhoun

See also: Mortgage Lending Reform; Payday Loan Advocacy

Further Reading

Delaney, Arthur. 2010. "Center for Responsible Lending in Fight with Front Group." *Huff Post Business* (March 18).

Nee, Eric. 2008. "15 Minutes with Martin Eakes." *Stanford Social Issues Review.* www.ssire-view.org.

Starkman, Dean. 2008. "Eakes! Forbes Flawed Probe of a Prescient Consumer Advocate." *Columbia Journalism Review* (March 12).

CENTER FOR SCIENCE IN THE PUBLIC INTEREST

The Center for Science in the Public Interest (CSPI) is a 501(c)(3) nonprofit health advocacy organization that focuses on nutrition and food safety. It is headquartered in Washington, D.C., and has offices in Dallas, Texas, and Ottawa, Canada.

CSPI is perhaps best known for the studies it has done on the nutritional content of movie theater popcorn, Chinese food, and other popular restaurant meals. But the organization's most significant effects have been on public policy.

For example, CSPI led the fight for passage of the 1990 Nutrition Labeling and Education Act, which required Nutrition Facts labeling on packaged foods. More recently, it helped include a requirement in the Affordable Care Act for calorie labeling at chain restaurants and lobbied for legislation that effectively eliminated most junk food from America's schools.

Funded mostly by the 900,000 subscribers to its flagship publication, Nutrition Action Healthletter, and by foundation grants, CSPI does not accept corporate or government funding.

The Organization

CSPI was founded in Washington, D.C., in 1971 by three PhD scientists who had met a year earlier while working at Ralph Nader's Center for the Study of Responsive Law. The scientists—chemist Albert J. Fritsch, microbiologist Michael F. Jacobson, and meteorologist James B. Sullivan—shared the vision of a public interest advocacy organization run by scientists. Part of that vision was to serve as a role model for other scientists. CSPI's founders believed that many scientists, if given the encouragement and opportunity, would devote their careers to public-interest activism.

The founders lived off savings or small stipends (Fritsch was a Jesuit priest living in his Capitol Hill church) and worked in borrowed office space. Their early work was eclectic. In keeping with their respective disciplines, Fritsch's projects focused on toxic chemicals, strip mining, nuclear power, and oil. Jacobson's work focused on food additives and nutrition. Sullivan focused on highways and air pollution. The three co-directors co-wrote CSPI's newsletter.

Initially, CSPI was run jointly by the three founding scientists. The departure of Fritsch and Sullivan in 1977 led to two major changes—CSPI narrowed its focus largely to food issues, and Jacobson became the organization's executive director. Since then, CSPI's staff has gradually increased from fifteen to sixty, and its annual budget from about $1 million to $20 million.

Eight veteran CSPI staffers, some of whom still work for the organization as of 2014, have played especially vital roles in the organization's growth and success. Executive director Michael Jacobson, who earned a PhD in microbiology from the Massachusetts Institute of Technology, has worked at CSPI for almost his entire career. He has authored or coauthored more than a dozen major books and reports, including *Eater's Digest, Nutrition Scoreboard, Six Arguments for a Greener Diet, What Are We Feeding Our Kids?,* and *Marketing Madness.* He has been honored by other consumer groups, government agencies, and even the supermarket industry.

Dennis Bass, an attorney, was CSPI's deputy director from 1981 to 2012, before which he worked at Environmental Action and the National League of Cities. Bass directed CSPI's administrative staff and donor programs and oversaw the development of a successful effort to increase the circulation of the *Nutrition Action Healthletter.*

Bonnie Liebman, CSPI's director of nutrition, has been with the organization since 1977. Liebman, who holds an M.S. in nutritional sciences from Cornell

University, has been the key link in formulating CSPI's policies on diet and health. She provides the scientific input on many of the organization's administrative petitions and legislative proposals, as well as writing many major articles for *Nutrition Action Healthletter*.

Bruce Silverglade began as CSPI's director of legal affairs in 1981, after having worked as an attorney at the Federal Trade Commission. He has been credited with playing a leadership role in the passage of the landmark Nutrition Labeling and Education Act. Silverglade was also the driving force behind CSPI's efforts to halt deceptive food labeling and advertising, a concern dating from his days at the FTC. Silverglade left CSPI in 2010 to join a private law firm.

George Hacker, an attorney, joined CSPI in 1982 to head its newly created Alcohol Policies Project. He organized and directed broad national coalitions in support of higher alcohol taxes, restrictions on alcohol advertising, and warning notices on product labels. Hacker authored numerous reports on alcohol issues. When CSPI disbanded its Alcohol Policies Project in 2009 for lack of funding, Hacker remained until 2013 to help lead CSPI's advocacy work to reduce consumption of soda pop and other sugar-sweetened beverages.

Margo Wootan joined CSPI as a senior scientist in 1993 after completing her doctorate in nutrition from the Harvard University School of Public Health and has served as the organization's director of nutrition policy since 2000. The author of numerous scholarly publications on food marketing, school foods, and nutrition education, Wootan created and has been leading an important national coalition, the National Alliance for Nutrition and Activity. Wootan led CSPI's efforts to stop the marketing of unhealthy foods to children, require calorie labeling at chain restaurants, and remove unhealthy drinks and foods from schools.

Caroline Smith DeWaal leads CSPI's food safety work, focusing on keeping pathogens such as *Salmonella* and *E. coli* out of the food supply. Since joining CSPI as food safety director in 1994, DeWaal has advocated stronger food-safety programs at FDA and the U.S. Department of Agriculture. Most importantly, she led CSPI's work lobbying for passage of the FDA Food Safety Modernization Act that was enacted in 2011. DeWaal serves on several USDA and FDA national advisory committees, consults with the World Health Organization on issues related to food safety and antibiotic resistance, and represents consumers' interest at the international Codex Alimentarius Commission.

Steve Gardner joined CSPI in 2004 as director of litigation after serving as an assistant attorney general in New York State and director of consumer protection in the Texas attorney general's office. Gardner has used lawsuits as a means of improving the labeling, marketing, and formulation of a number of food products. A threatened lawsuit against Kellogg led to a historic settlement agreement by which the company agreed to the first legally binding nutrition standards for foods advertised to kids. His litigation unit secured other agreements with companies as diverse as Airborne, Pfizer, and Procter & Gamble.

CSPI is overseen by its board of trustees, whose size has varied between six and fourteen people. Trustees have included scientists, attorneys, celebrities, and activists. As of 2014, former FDA commissioner David Kessler and Lynn Silver, former deputy commissioner for health promotion in New York City's health department, sit on the organization's board.

Financially, CSPI has depended upon several sources of income: foundation grants; the sale of booklets and other products; and subscription fees and donations. In the 1970s, those three sources provided roughly equal amounts of income. Work on nutrition and food safety was especially dependent upon book and poster sales, whereas the other projects enjoyed greater foundation support.

Beginning in the early 1980s, however, CSPI began earning an increasing portion of its funding from subscriptions and donations. Between 1980 and 1994, the circulation of *Nutrition Action Healthletter*, CSPI's flagship publication, increased from 30,000 to 800,000. Many of those subscribers provide donations in addition to their annual subscription fee. By 1994, subscription revenue from *Nutrition Action Healthletter* provided roughly 75 percent of CSPI's annual budget of $11 million. By 2013, CSPI's annual budget rose to $20 million from 900,000 subscribers, major donors, and foundation grants.

From its earliest days, CSPI has recognized the value of producing educational materials. In addition to *Nutrition Action Healthletter*, CSPI has produced a wide range of other publications concerning food. The book that first brought CSPI to public attention was *Nutrition Scoreboard*, which was published in 1973 and focused attention on the fat and sugar content in foods. *The Fast-Food Guide-In* book and poster versions helped focus public attention on nutritional drawbacks of the most popular foods offered by fast-food restaurants. *Kitchen Fun for Kids*, *Creative Food Experiences for Children*, and *Eat, Think, and Be Healthy* reflected the center's concern that good nutrition begin at a young age.

In 2013, CSPI launched NutritionAction.com, which offers an electronic version of *Nutrition Action Healthletter*, as well as a free "Daily Tips" e-letter and a variety of free and inexpensive reports and recipe booklets.

Its Campaigns

CSPI's major projects typically feature a mix of research, education, and advocacy. Since 1980, CSPI's scientists, writers, and organizers have been bolstered by an in-house legal staff. CSPI's scientists and policy specialists actively encourage the agricultural, food processing, and restaurant industries to improve their products and market them honestly. When necessary, the organization's legal staff seeks solutions through enforcement of existing laws, adoption of new regulations or legislation, or litigation.

One of CSPI's first major national undertakings was Food Day. CSPI sponsored that annual event from 1975 to 1977, spawning thousands of activities around the country concerning nutrition, hunger, and agribusiness. Those activities included newspaper articles and television programs, rallies in city parks, a book, and even a healthful buffet dinner at the White House in 1977.

Food Day turned out to be one of the pivotal events that helped persuade the public and policymakers that nutrition had important health effects. Until the mid-1970s, most nutrition experts had focused on the need for people to obtain adequate levels of vitamins and minerals. CSPI brought Food Day back in 2011, and by 2013 the October 24 mobilization saw about 5,000 events organized all over the country focused on promoting healthy, affordable, and sustainable diets, as well as on improving local and state food policies.

Beginning in the early 1980s, in response to the increased public demand for healthier food, many food manufacturers began promoting the supposed nutritional virtues of their products much more aggressively. CSPI began to identify numerous product labels and advertising campaigns that were clearly deceptive, if not fraudulent. After first seeking a halt to individual deceptions on a case-by-case basis, the organization began to advocate legislation to protect all consumers. That effort culminated in 1990 with the passage of the Nutrition Labeling and Education Act, which mandated clear and useful nutrition information on practically all food labels.

CSPI has long been concerned about the healthfulness of restaurant foods and with the absence of any information about their ingredients and nutritional value. By the late 1980s, CSPI, along with the attorneys general of New York State and other states, got the largest fast-food chains for the first time to disclose the ingredients from which their foods were made. That later became standard practice for restaurants, though they did not provide nutrition information on menus and menu boards.

Beginning in 1993, CSPI's nutritionists began a series of laboratory studies—the first ever—of the nutritional values of foods eaten in the most popular types of sit-down restaurants. The resulting studies of Chinese, Italian, Mexican, seafood, and other types of restaurants, as well as of movie theater popcorn, generated worldwide publicity. The enormous media coverage, in turn, prompted declines in sales at many restaurants and theaters, resulting in decisions by some major chains and independent restaurateurs both to lower the fat or sodium content of their dishes and to add a "health" section to their menus.

In this century, CSPI continued analyzing restaurant foods and publicizing its findings with Nutrition Action's "Xtreme Eating" awards. Educating Americans about the calorie content of restaurant meals helped make the case and build momentum for state and local legislation requiring calorie counts on chain restaurant menus and menu boards. After New York City and a number of other jurisdictions passed such requirements, CSPI helped include a national calorie labeling requirement in the landmark health care reform bill passed in 2010.

Even before it focused on nutrition, CSPI served as a watchdog group on food additives. In addition to publishing a book and poster on additives in the early 1970s, CSPI sought to reduce consumer exposure to potentially risky additives. As a result of CSPI's work, the Food and Drug Administration advised pregnant women to minimize or avoid the consumption of caffeine. The FDA also banned most uses of sulfite—a widely used preservative that caused serious reactions and deaths of sensitive (usually asthmatic) individuals—in fresh vegetables and also required better labeling of other foods. The U.S. Department of Agriculture set tighter limits on the use of sodium nitrite, a preservative used in bacon, hot dogs, and most other processed meats.

In the late 1990s and early 2000s, CSPI gained headlines around the world with its campaign to prohibit the use of olestra, an artificial fat substitute developed by Procter & Gamble. CSPI collected thousands of adverse reaction reports from around the country from consumers who experienced cramping and diarrhea, prompting the FDA to require a label warning consumers of the risk of "abdominal cramping and loose stools." Though the warning label was removed in 2003, olestra-containing products never sold well, and the ingredient is used in only a handful of minor varieties of potato chip.

Recognizing that pesticide use on farms endangers farmers, consumers, and the environment, CSPI has long urged reduced use of potentially dangerous agricultural chemicals. In the late 1980s, CSPI concentrated its efforts on winning passage of a federal law that defined, for the first time, the meaning of "organic" food. That facilitated the burgeoning of organic agriculture and the organic food industry.

In 1982, CSPI created a new program to focus on alcoholic beverages, which were killing an estimated 100,000 Americans a year and causing a wide range of serious health and social problems. With CSPI's encouragement, Congress increased federal taxes on distilled spirits, beer, and wine, thereby raising the cost of the product and reducing youth drinking. Congress also passed a law requiring a warning notice on all alcoholic beverages focused on drinking and driving and drinking during pregnancy.

Unlike some other consumer and environmental groups, CSPI has not opposed the use of genetic engineering to give corn, soy, cotton, or other crops useful new traits. Rather, CSPI has held that humankind should obtain the benefits from those crops while minimizing the risks. Hence, CSPI has focused on advocating a mandatory pre-market approval process for genetically engineered crops and on ensuring farmers' compliance with existing regulations. CSPI believes, as most national and international scientific organizations do, that the genetically engineered crops that are currently on the market are safe to eat and do not warrant requiring products to carry what would be tantamount to a warning label if they include an ingredient from a genetically modified crop.

CSPI has also waged a long and ultimately successful campaign to improve the nutritional quality of school meals and to eliminate the sale and advertising of soda and other junk foods on school grounds. Much of that work culminated with the passage of the 2010 Healthy, Hunger-Free Kids Act, for which CSPI gained recognition from First Lady Michelle Obama.

In the past two decades, CSPI has pushed for the elimination of partially hydrogenated oils, the artificial source of trans fat in the diet, from packaged foods and restaurant foods, estimated to be causing upward of 50,000 premature deaths per year from heart disease and other health problems. In 1993, CSPI began a decade-long campaign to require that trans fats be listed on Nutrition Facts labels, which caused sharp trans fat reductions in packaged foods. In 2004, CSPI filed a regulatory petition with the FDA urging the agency to revoke its approval of partially hydrogenated oils, and CSPI's litigation unit sued KFC and Burger King for using, but not disclosing, the discredited fat. CSPI also worked closely with officials in New York City, California, and other cities and counties to pass regulations curbing the use of artificial trans fat in restaurant and bakery foods. In 2013, the FDA published notice of its preliminary determination that partially hydrogenated oil was no longer generally recognized as safe for use in food—a regulatory move that may pave the way for the virtual elimination of artificial trans fat in food.

In 2014, a top priority is reducing the amount of sodium in packaged and restaurant foods. Excess sodium accounts for about 100,000 premature deaths annually from heart attacks and strokes. Another top priority is reducing consumption of sugar-sweetened beverages. Still another CSPI goal is eliminating artificial food dyes, which adversely affect children's behavior.

Michael F. Jacobson, Jeff Cronin

See also: Food Safety Advocacy

Further Reading

Seaberry, Jane. 1974. "Consumer Crusaders Doggedly Stay on Job." *Washington Post* (July 18): 1+.
Shinn, Annys. 2011. "Dinner with Michael Jacobson, 'Chief of the Food Police.'" *Washington Post* (February 28).
Van Vynckt, Virginia. 1989. "Consumer Advocate's Rage Turns to Resolve." *Chicago Sun-Times* (March 1).

CENTER FOR THE STUDY OF SERVICES/CONSUMERS' CHECKBOOK

The Center for the Study of Services was founded in April 1974 by Robert Krughoff (president) and Gillian Rudd (vice president). Its purpose is to provide consumers information and education to help them choose and effectively use service firms and stores.

Krughoff has always been the chief executive of the organization. With a law degree from the University of Chicago, he held several positions, including director of research and evaluation planning for the U.S. Department of Health, Education, and Welfare, before founding the center. Krughoff reports to a board of directors made up mainly of leaders from public interest organizations. The board elects its own members.

The organization's annual budget is approximately $14 million. For many years, revenues came primarily from sales of the center's publications and information services, as well as from donations received from individual consumer members/subscribers in the form of voluntary donations. In recent years, a key source of income has been conducting surveys and analyses for other organizations—for example, conducting the surveys of members of Medicare Advantage plans and Prescription Drug plans for the U.S. Centers for Medicare and Medicaid Services (CMS).

The primary functions of the center include publication of locally based magazines and operating websites (www.checkbook.org) that offer ratings of local service firms and stores, publication of local and national books and operating national websites on various consumer information subjects, provision of consumer information services on automobile purchasing and leasing, and conducting surveys and analyses for other organizations that provide information on service provider performance.

In 1976, the organization published the first issue of *Washington Consumers' Checkbook* magazine. The magazine rates auto repair shops, plumbers, hospitals, banks, and other types of service firms and stores in the Washington, D.C., metropolitan area. Ratings are based on surveys of consumers, undercover price shopping by the center's researchers to compare prices of service providers and stores, counts of complaints on file at consumer agencies, surveys of "experts" (for example, auto body shop owners' ratings of auto insurance companies), and analysis of publicly available databases (for example, hospital discharge records to calculate risk-adjusted hospital death rates), among various other things. The magazine has been published semiannually.

In 1979, the center published the first edition of *Checkbook's Guide to Health Insurance Plans for Federal Employees*. This guide, published only in book form until 2000 and since then also online at www.guidetohealthplans.org, compares health plans in terms of premiums, benefits, and actuarially estimated out-of-pocket costs. Recent versions have also compared the quality of plans on the basis of member satisfaction surveys, staffing, disenrollment rates, and various other plan quality measures. The guide has been produced annually. Recently, the online version of the guide has also included an all-plan provider directory (in some parts of the country) to make it easy for consumers to learn in which plans local physicians participate. In addition, the current version of the online guide lets consumers produce a personalized plan quality score for each plan by assigning weights to various quality measures related to customer service and claims handling, doctor quality and availability, and wellness programs. The center has provided advice and encouragement to states and the federal government on how to provide a health plan comparison tool for Health Insurance Exchanges and has provided important elements of such tools to some exchanges.

In 1982, the center published the first issue of *Bay Area Consumers' Checkbook* magazine. Additional versions of *Consumers' Checkbook* magazine were launched in 2003 for the Puget Sound (Seattle–Tacoma), Twin Cities, Chicago, Delaware Valley, and Boston areas. These magazines parallel their Washington, D.C., sister publication, with the same or similar artwork and text but their own evaluations of firms in their metropolitan areas. These magazines have also been published semiannually. At times, their collective circulation has exceeded 130,000.

Since 1995, the center has made its consumer information available online, primarily at www.checkbook.org. And its information has been available in a mobile app since 2012. Consumers can find all ratings and advice online and can search, sort, and filter to have quicker, fuller, and more current access to the ratings and other resources.

In 1984, the year AT&T was broken up, the center published the Complete Guide to Lower Phone Costs. This book evaluated consumer options for long-distance services, local phone service, and telephone equipment. The same year, the organization launched a long-distance cost comparison service. This nationwide service compared the costs of various available long-distance service providers for consumers and small businesses, based on each customer's recent months' phone bills. Comparisons were done using a computer program developed by the center that incorporated the pricing formulas of each of the more than fifty long-distance phone companies. Several years later, this service was discontinued when the differences in long-distance carriers' prices were judged by the center to be too small to justify the required fee for the analysis.

In 1985, the center published the first issue of BARGAINS in Washington, D.C. This periodical listed low-priced local stores for relatively expensive products such as appliances , home entertainment equipment, cameras, home office equipment, power tools, and sporting goods. To compile it, a list of more than 3,000 products was sent free of cost to any local retailer interested in participating. Retailers could quote prices on as few or as many items as they wished but had to sign an agreement to honor those prices until a specified date. The center's staff then sorted the prices and published in *BARGAINS* the lowest prices and the names of the stores offering them. The magazine was published semiannually in Washington and San Francisco Bay area versions until 2004. At that time, the publication was discontinued, because the center concluded that the listed prices were no longer consistently the best prices available to consumers, since many of the products (other than major appliances and heavy garden equipment) could be purchased in online marketplaces.

In 1988, the organization published the first edition of its Consumers' Guide to Hospitals. This book, based on the center's adaptation of data released by the Federal Government's Health Care Financing Administration, reported on risk-adjusted mortality rates at each of the nation's acute care hospitals. It also included information on hospitals' teaching programs, and percentages of board-certified physicians. Editions have been published periodically since then and have included risk-adjusted adverse outcome (complication) rates and results of the center's surveys of all actively practicing physicians in each of fifty-three major metropolitan areas asking these physicians for their ratings of the hospitals. This hospital guide is also available online at www.checkbook.org and at www.guidetohospitals.org.

Also in 1988, the center published *Checkbook's Guide to Washington Area Restaurants*. This guide reported ratings of restaurants based on surveys of consumers. It also included summaries of comments by professional magazine and newspaper reviewers, price information, brief descriptive text, and other details. Subsequent editions were published in the San Francisco Bay Area and the Washington, D.C., area until the guide was discontinued in 1998.

In 1991, the organization published the first issue of CarDeals newsletter. This nationwide newsletter, available both in print and online, reports on factory-to-customer rebates, factory-to-dealer incentive payments, and special financing plans offered by automobile manufacturers. It is currently published biweekly. At the same time, the center launched a syndicated newspaper feature, reporting the same information, that has been carried at times by several major metropolitan newspapers and has been used by various car-buying services. CarDeals is produced biweekly.

Also in 1991, the center began offering a service called CarBargains. This nationwide service helps consumers get the best available new car purchase price. A consumer tells the CarBargains staff the make, model, and style of car that the consumer wishes to purchase. The staff then persuades at least five dealers in a consumer's local area to bid competitively to sell this make, model, and style. The consumer is then given a report that shows each dealer's bid and the name of the responsible sales manager. CarBargains continues to serve new car purchase and lease customers.

In 1994, the center conducted a survey of 150,000 members of 250 health plans. At the time, this nationwide survey was the largest one ever conducted of health plan members to provide information for public release. A year later, the center published *Consumers' Guide to Health Plans*. This guide contained plan-by-plan ratings based on the center's 1994 member survey and included information on accreditation status, disenrollment rates, and other matters.

In 1999, the center published its first *Guide to Top Doctors*, both in print and online (at www.guidetotopdoctors.org). This guide is produced by surveying all actively practicing doctors in fifty-three major metropolitan areas, asking each to name the one or two doctors in each of thirty-five specialty fields that he or she "would consider most desirable for care of a loved one." The book and website describe the center's methods transparently and list the doctors who are mentioned most often and the number of times that each was mentioned. The center has found that doctors rated highly by peers are also associated with other measures of quality, such as lower bypass surgery death rates, than average.

From 2007 through 2009, the center sponsored a demonstration project surveying patients about their experience of care with their doctors using the Clinician/Group CAHPS survey instrument developed by the U.S. Agency for Health Care Research and Quality (AHRQ) and reported the results at the individual doctor level. This survey and reporting was done in cooperation with major health plans who identified patients in several cities with recent doctor visits. Results of the survey, which were reported free to the public, showed large numbers of statistically significant differences among doctors. The intent of this survey was to demonstrate how such information could be rigorously produced at a modest cost, with the hope that similar surveys would be conducted by the federal government or health plans or others nationwide.

The center has been in the forefront of demonstrating the feasibility of evaluating various types of local service firms and stores. In many fields, this kind of evaluation was initially met with strong industry resistance. Various firms threatened lawsuits, though none was successful. As an illustration, service providers were so unaccustomed to being evaluated that hospitals in the San Francisco area threatened to sue if the center even published their charges for emergency room visits. The center's work has provided legitimacy for such evaluations, and in many fields there is now broad acceptance of the concept of publicly disclosed firm-by-firm evaluations—now greatly expanded on the Internet.

There are several indications that the center has reached and influenced consumers. First, its magazine reports receive broad television, radio, and newspaper coverage. Second, virtually all local public libraries in the areas it serves carry subscriptions to its publications, and many offer online access. Third, in a 1981 study, a West German consumer institute interviewed a sample of *Checkbook* subscribers and learned that their purchase decisions had been based on or supported by *Checkbook* recommendations in 64 percent of the cases in which they had purchased types of services covered in recently published *Checkbook* issues. Fourth, U.S. Office of Personnel Management records show that in the first year that the center published *Checkbook's Guide to Health Insurance Plans for Federal Employees*, enrollment in the highest-rated plan increased by more than 120 percent in the Washington area.

Evaluations of service providers are now widespread. But the center's structure, policies, and methods are different from those of the ratings businesses that now heavily populate this space. The center avoids conflicts of interest and does not accept any advertising in its publications or on its website. The center has standards with regard to sample size. It does not publish its official ratings of service providers if it has fewer than ten survey ratings of the provider (and the center often has more than fifty ratings per provider). The center's rating system produces a wider range of rating scores than is produced by most online rating businesses. Moreover, the center has relatively tight controls to prevent "ballot box stuffing." It surveys primarily registered subscribers to *Checkbook* magazine or *Consumer Reports* magazine, along with a limited sample of other known residents. In this way, the center largely prevents accepting more than one rating from a service provider from the same consumer.

The center uses methods other than surveys to evaluate service providers—for example, the hospital discharge databases used to calculate risk-adjusted hospital death rates. The center also uses undercover price shopping for specified services to produce "relative price scores" for each firm it evaluates. In its early years, the organization concluded that surveying consumers about prices was not an adequate basis for price comparisons because the surveyed consumers, in most cases, had not done apples-to-apples price comparisons for carefully specified service jobs.

Given its independence and use of relatively costly methods and standards, the center faces tough competition from online ratings businesses that use less rigorous research methods and that also collect income from the service providers they evaluate. However, the center is committed to its nonprofit structure, principles, and methods.

Robert M. Krughoff

See also: Consumers Union/Consumer Reports

Further Reading

Hartjens, Peter, and Elizabeth Hartjens. 1983. *Das* Washington Consumer Checkbook: *Modell Einez Lokelen Dienstleistungsbewertungssystems.* Hohenheim, Germany: University of Hohenheim.

Krughoff, Robert. 1977. "Checkbook, A Consumer Reports for the Services." *Social Policy* 8, no. 3: 36–38.

Mohl, Bruce. 2004. "Advice for the Uncertain: Two Companies Now Offer Ratings of Area Businesses." *Boston Globe* (February 8).

Shinn, Annys. 2006. "30 Years of Obsessive Consumerism." *Washington Post* (December 18).

CENTRAL AMERICAN CONSUMER MOVEMENTS

After the civil wars and economic instability that plagued Central America from the 1970s through the 1990s, conditions finally became ripe for the development of consumer activism in Central America. Unlike the United States, where the formation of consumer groups preceded and sparked government action, consumer movements in Central America typically emerged after consumer rights were incorporated into national constitutions (e.g., Costa Rica) or established through consumer protection laws (e.g., El Salvador).

Today, consumer organizations in Central America concentrate on advancing consumer well-being, primarily by promoting health and safety as well as affordable, accessible, reliable public services. The region's consumer organizations have in common their not-for-profit character, but they have different orientations, scope, and resources. Some of them, such as the Consumer Protection Association of Honduras (ASPROCOH) or the Consumer Defense League of Nicaragua (LIDECONIC), have a general mandate—with corresponding funds—from the government. In other instances, like Costa Rica and Guatemala, the government imposes administrative duties to promote the development of consumer organizations, without the allocation of money to fulfill the requirement (unfunded mandate).

In general, consumer organizations must be officially registered with their respective governments. For example, there are twenty-eight registered consumer organizations in El Salvador and sixteen in Costa Rica, but only a handful in Honduras and Guatemala. Two of the oldest organizations in the region are Liga del Consumidor (LIDECON) in Guatemala and Ambio-Alert in Costa Rica, which were established in 1987 and 1989, respectively. Most of the organizations are relatively new, however. The youngest consumer organization became a legal entity in 2012: ADECU (Association for the Defense of Consumers and Users) in Honduras. Six of the seven countries in the region have at least one organization that has been accepted as a member of Consumers International: Four countries have a single member, and two countries have two members.

The biggest consumer associations have been able to secure funding through a combination of methods: by charging a membership fee to businesses that support their consumer protection mission and to the Chamber of Commerce, by submitting grants to international funding agencies, by providing fee-based seminars and training workshops to private organizations (e.g. developers, suppliers of goods, and banks), by reporting violations and collecting fees, and by selling advertising on their own radio programs. Many consumer associations, however, particularly in rural areas, operate without the minimum resources necessary to perform their work (computers, printers, furniture, telephone lines, etc.).

Issues

Access to safe, high-quality food for purchasing is a particular priority in Central America and was initiated, in part, by the Food and Agriculture Organization of the United Nations under the Food Security and Nutrition Program. A recent regional meeting took place in El Salvador (July 2013) to promote policies and strategies to protect the human right to food and to address food vulnerability of large segments of the population. This project, funded by the European Union, has begun to work with other regional networks and Consumers International.

Guatemala's Liga del Consumidor (LIDECON) has been very active in health and nutrition issues. LIDECON recently worked on a campaign for food fortification to decrease child malnutrition. Nicaragua's LIDECONIC, in coordination with other Nicaraguan consumer groups, has launched a campaign named TOXICOLA that exposes the toxic components of some cola drinks and other related junk food. LIDECONIC also participates in a campaign called Seeds of Identity whose objective is the protection of native seeds (and the identity of rural peasants who rely on them) in the face of agribusiness and genetically modified food. When it comes to resisting genetically modified food, Costa Rica has taken a leadership role. Seventy-seven percent of the cantons in the country are already 100 percent transgenic-free (Lopez, 2013), an achievement accomplished by the coordinated efforts of municipalities and grassroots organizations.

Consumer activists in Central America view access to clean water as a basic right. Groups in El Salvador and Nicaragua have been particularly active in this domain. For example, the Center for Consumer Defense in El Salvador organized a rally in August 2013 to demand passage of a water law that would guarantee the right of all Salvadorans to water and prevent privatization of water systems. In Nicaragua, consumer groups were part of a broad coalition whose goal was to prevent privatized water resources in rural and urban communities.

The provision of affordable and accessible public services is also of eminent priority within the region. Groups throughout the region wage campaigns against the privatization of public services and for better protection against unfair price increases. For example, Consumers of Costa Rica (CONCORI) is a nonprofit association dedicated to the promotion of mutually beneficial relations among the government, consumers, and service providers. CONCORI pressures service providers—public transportation in particular—to consider the needs of consumers. For example, it frequently reduces or blocks price increase attempts. CONCORI was also successful blocking a 75 percent postage increase (the regulator granted a 35 percent postage increase instead), establishing pricing transparency (the courts recognized a petition by CONCORI requesting the Ministry of Economy, Industry and Commerce to conduct public hearings when setting the price of products), and challenging false advertising (Delgadillo, 2012).

In addition to issues pertaining to food, water, and utilities, consumer organizations in Central America seek affordable housing and protection of real estate investments. These groups also promote corporate social responsibility and principles of social justice, including gender equity, solidarity, respect for the environment, and government transparency.

Activities

Consumer activist organizations in Central America use a variety of methods to advance consumer interests, but education is the most important. Direct consumer education is achieved through the distribution of pamphlets and fliers, as well as banners, public displays, trainings, forums, seminars, fairs, and rallies. Consumer organizations also use opportunities for increasing awareness via media releases, often by way of their own radio programs (e.g., Consumer Talk sponsored by the Panamanian Institute of Law for Consumers and Users and the National Union of Consumers and Users of the Republic of Panama).

Social networks are useful mechanisms for educating consumers about their rights, offering consumer tips, and collecting consumer complaints. For example, LIDECON in Guatemala, LIDECONIC in Nicaragua, and CDC in El Salvador have Facebook pages and Twitter accounts by which consumers can post complaints. Costa Rica's CONCORI has a webpage where it posts consumer tips, cases of false advertisements, and technical reports.

Another opportunity for increasing awareness is participation in World Consumer Rights Day (WCRD). Each year, Consumers International coordinates its member organizations in a campaign devoted to a specific consumer issue—for example, phone rights and choice in financial services. A different approach to WCRD was taken in Honduras in 2013. Osmaira Paz, president of the Asociacion de Proteccion al Consumidor, used the occasion to encourage government officials to overcome the negligence with which they carried out their work and use the day to reflect on the seriousness of their designated function of safeguarding the rights of consumers of goods and services. WCRD is but one example of how consumer activists in Central America network with other consumer organizations to leverage their influence on policymakers and increase their effect on the lives of consumers.

Most of the consumer organizations in the region are young and still developing. Their emergence has occurred between four and five decades after the rise of social movement consumer advocacy in the United States and Europe, but they continue to play an active role in advancing measures to protect all consumers in the region.

Lucy Delgadillo

See also: Consumers International; Caribbean Consumer Movements

Further Reading

Delgadillo, Lucy. 2012. "An Assessment of Consumer Protection and Consumer Empowerment in Costa Rica." *Journal of Consumer Policy* 36, no. 1: 59–86.

Lopez, Jaime. 2013. "Stay Out, Monsanto: Costa Rica is Almost 100% Transgenic-Free." *Costa Rica Star*, August 21. http://news.co.cr/stay-out-monsanto-costa-rica-is-almost-100-transgenic-free/25046/.

CENTRAL AND EASTERN EUROPEAN CONSUMER MOVEMENTS

Until the dissolution of the Soviet bloc in 1989, the economies—and therefore the situation of consumers—of the countries in central and eastern Europe were closely aligned with that of the Soviet Union and operated under a high degree of government planning. The availability and price for most goods and services were determined by government officials, leaving consumers passive and powerless. Moreover, consumers in the countries of central and eastern Europe were largely shut off from consumer goods made outside the Soviet bloc. Only in underground "black" markets did consumers exercise any real choice, but at very high prices and without any redress if something went wrong. The idea of a consumer association that worked to advance the rights of consumers to information, education, choice, and even safety had little relevance in this take-what-you-get context.

Today, much has changed. Most of the countries in central and eastern Europe have established consumer associations or specialized government consumer protection bodies. Leaving aside countries such as Russia and Ukraine that were once part of the Soviet Union, the region's largest countries in terms of population are Poland, Romania, the Czech Republic, and Hungary. Consumer activism in Poland is covered by a separate entry in this encyclopedia; this entry focuses on Romania, the Czech Republic, and Hungary. All three countries, like Poland, are relatively recent members of the European Union (EU) and have consumer associations that participate in BEUC: The European Consumer Organisation.

Of the three countries, consumer activism is best developed in the Czech Republic and Hungary. The Czech Republic has a strong economy, with a gross domestic product per capita of almost $19,000—about half that of Japan or the United Kingdom. The Czech Republic has a large and diverse set of civil society organizations, including consumer organizations. A 2011 report produced by BEUC (Fielder, 2011) described the situation of the Czech consumer movement as one of the most promising but also one of the most tragic. It is promising because the Czech Association of Consumers (TEST), which publishes a consumer magazine, dTest, is strong and is gradually developing into a full-fledged, multifunction consumer organization, not just a magazine publisher. Moreover, a sizable base of magazine subscribers has helped TEST achieve a reasonable degree of financial stability and independence. The situation is tragic, however, inasmuch as the SOS Consumers Defense Association, which was founded in 1993 and was once the most fully developed consumer association in the country, went bankrupt a few years ago amid a rift within its board of directors and among its regional members.

Fortunately, there are several important consumer associations beyond TEST and SOS. One is the Czech Consumers Association. Established in 1990, three years before the dissolution of Czechoslovakia into the Czech Republic and Slovakia, the association stresses consumer education as a preventive approach to consumer protection. Another organization is the Czech Coalition of Consumers Activities. It has about a dozen organizational members and fights for a balance of power between buyers and sellers when consummating contracts. Media coverage of consumer topics in the Czech Republic is robust, but there is no government agency explicitly tasked with consumer protection. Rather, government attention to consumer protection is divided among several ministries.

Hungary is less wealthy than the Czech Republic, but its civil society sector, at least when it comes to consumer organizations, is healthier. Hungary has about a dozen consumer associations that function at the national level. Some tackle the full gamut of consumer issues, whereas others are more specialized. The latter include organizations devoted to insurance, transportation, and environmental protection. Within its larger mission of supporting families and children, the National Association of Large Families engages in consumer education and receives a government subsidy as a consumer group for its efforts.

There are also several federations of consumer organizations. One is the National Federation of Associations for Consumer Protection in Hungary (NFACPH). NFACPH is comprised of eleven single-issue consumer organizations and has a total membership of 5,000 members. This federation works to develop a coordinated approach to consumer protection among its member organizations and offers training on consumer protection. NFACPH, which is a member of Consumers International and BEUC, participates in the development of harmonized consumer protection policies within the EU, the translation of these policies into national law, and enforcement of these laws. Another federation is the National Association for Consumer Protection (OFE). It provides consumer advocacy from its central office in Budapest and advice from forty local branches.

The main challenge facing consumer organizations in Hungary, as in most of Central and Eastern Europe, is finding a stable source of funding. Government subsidies were never generous, but today they are even less so. Several organizations have attempted to generate funds by publishing a magazine. OFE used to receive government funds to publish its magazine; in the absence of these funds, publication is solely online. The Consumer and Patient Rights Advocacy Alliance (FEBESZ) publishes a comparative product testing magazine. Competition among magazines, which is normally good for consumers, makes it difficult for any single publication to survive in the relatively small Hungarian market.

The Czech Republic and Hungary joined the European Union in 2004; Romania did so a few years later, in 2007. Moreover, Romania is less urbanized than the Czech Republic and Hungary, its economy is less industrialized, and its historic ties to Western Europe are weaker. For all these reasons, consumer activism in Romania faces a challenging environment, and only two national-level consumer organizations exist. The older of the two is the Association for Consumer Protection (APC). APC receives a government subsidy; is authorized to bring lawsuits on behalf of consumers, both individually and collectively; and works closely with European-wide organizations such as BEUC and the UK-based International Consumer Research and Testing.

The other important Romanian organization is the National Association for Consumer Protection and Promoting Programs and Strategies from Romania (ANPCPPS). Founded in 2003, ANPCPPS focuses on informing and educating consumers about their rights, giving advice, mediating complaints, conducting studies and product tests, and campaigning in the areas of food, health, financial education, and environment. It publishes *InfoCons*, the only Romanian comparative testing magazine. ANPCPPS has been a full member of Consumers International since 2012.

Viewing consumer activism in central and eastern Europe as a whole, it is difficult to know whether to be optimistic or pessimistic. One can be impressed by the achievements that have been made in a short period of time and the strong links that have been formed with other European consumer organizations. Conversely, most consumer associations in the region face governments that are stingy with their financial support for consumer associations and lack mechanisms to facilitate participation by consumer groups in consumer policy formation. If existing consumer associations can hang on until the economies in the region grow more strongly and its middle class expands, their prospects are also likely to improve.

Robert N. Mayer

See also: BEUC: The European Consumer Organisation; Consumers International

Further Reading

Fielder, Anna. 2011. "The State of the Consumer Movement in Poland." In *The State of the Consumer Nation(s): An Evaluation of the Consumer Movement in Six Countries of Central, Eastern, and South Eastern Europe*. Brussels, Belgium: BEUC.

Kozminski, Andrzej K. 1991. "Consumers in Transition from the Centrally Planned Economy to the Market Economy." *Journal of Consumer Policy* 14, no. 4: 351–369.

Stefanescu, Florica, and Sergiu Baltatescu. 2010. "The Romanian Consumer and His/her Rights: Opinions and Attitudes." *Amfiteatru Economic* 12, no. 28 (June): 297–313.

CHECKBOOK MAGAZINE

See Center for the Study of Services/Consumers' Checkbook

CHINESE CONSUMER MOVEMENT

The status of China's consumer movement is far from matching the country's impressive level of economic development. Despite China's having become the world's second largest economy, its consumer protection lags far behind that found in developed countries and, indeed, in some other developing countries.

Between 1949 and 1979, ordinary people in China relied on the government to meet basic survival needs for food, clothing, and shelter. People could scarcely dream of consuming goods and services that went beyond basic necessities, let alone make claims regarding their consumer rights. Nowadays, thanks to Deng Xiaoping's reform policies in the late 1970s and the policies that followed, the average citizen no longer struggles just to fulfill basic survival needs. Instead, they are increasingly interested in luxury products, and many people can afford spacious houses and expensive cars.

The goal of Deng's approach (which is known as "Socialism with Chinese Characteristics") was to achieve rapid yet stable economic development. There were two crucial components of Deng's reforms: achieving export-led growth and allowing some people to become rich. Deng used the term "Xiaokang society" to offer a vision of Chinese society in which most people were moderately well off and belonged to the middle class. The export-led economy has dramatically shrunk the technological gap between China and developed countries and increased the size of the Chinese middle class.

Paradoxically for a country built on a rejection of bourgeois values, the Chinese government has increasingly encouraged ordinary people to enjoy access to "modern" products and to spend time shopping. Western visitors are often astonished by the scale of the modern shopping malls that have sprung up over the last two decades. According to *The Economist*, half the world's new shopping malls are in China, which is also the world's biggest e-commerce market.

China's approach to consumer goods contrasts with the path taken by the Communist regime in the former Soviet Union, where the government suppressed popular access to Western products, which thus acquired an aura of "forbidden fruit." The present Communist government of China has taken a much cleverer stance in the hope that access to products (both international and domestically produced) will make consumers happy and, seeing the progress relative to the deprivations of past generations, less likely to press for change. For example, in March 2014, the prime minister said that China should "fully tap the enormous consumption potential of more than a billion people" ("A Billion Shoppers," 2014.) Chinese consumers are doing their part, with retail sales increasing in 2013 by 11.5 percent after similar increases in 2011 and 2012.

There are limits, of course, to this "safety valve" strategy as issues of water quality and, most conspicuously, air quality raise questions about the viability of the new affluent way of life. It is predictable that concerns regarding these basic necessities will be raised with greater urgency. Indeed, that has already happened with respect the issue of air quality. So although consumer preferences seem to be directed towards material goods such as cars, pressures are building up in the natural environment that may challenge constantly increasing consumption.

Although China's "new rich" have transformed the country into the biggest luxury goods market in the world, the vast majority of Chinese consumers are interested in avoiding the problems that plague people in other developing nations—food adulteration, unsafe products, air and water pollution—and improving their access to basic goods and services. The confidence of Chinese consumers in domestic products has been shaken by several food adulteration scandals, most notably the 2008 Chinese milk scandal, in which milk powder adulterated with melamine claimed an estimated 300,000 victims. Six infants died from kidney stones and other kidney damage, and 60,000 babies were hospitalized. (The disbursement of the victims' compensation fund remains a mystery.) The entire infant milk situation is a grand irony for the world's largest exporting country, which enjoys the honor and fame associated with being the "World's Factory."

Little by little, episodes such as the milk scandal undermine Chinese products and diminish consumer confidence. The population now has so much access to electronic media that it has become impossible for the government to suppress stories entirely in a country that is home to 1.35 billion people. So the government has, again cleverly, tolerated, even encouraged, exposure of such scandals in the knowledge that people will get to know about them anyway. The government reasons that it is better to name the guilty parties than to have a buildup of resentment against the government in general.

Perhaps because the government cannot completely control informal dissemination of news by electronic media, it has tolerated free expression of critical points of view on consumer topics . . . up to a point. At conferences and in academic institutions, there can be remarkably frank criticisms of the status quo. At Wuhan University in March 2013, for example, many Chinese speakers were fiercely critical of financial institutions, including those controlled by the state. There is also vigorous debate within China regarding the country's serious environmental problems. And government, in turn, is prepared to denounce failures of public administration. But direct criticism of government (as opposed to individual officials) is rare.

Chinese consumers—taking for granted that they cannot collectively assert their rights to safety, education, redress, and a healthy environment—have largely employed individual strategies to dealing with fears regarding safety and health. One strategy is to shun domestic products in favor of imported ones. Chinese consumers assume that consumer protections in developed countries function better than those in China, and therefore they are firmly convinced that the quality of products produced by developed countries is better than that of local products. This is apparent in the market for infant milk formula. In recent years, more than half the milk formula purchased in China has been imported, even though the price of imported formula is several times higher than locally produced versions. More recently, scared by the news from CCTV (the central national media) that massive amounts of fake imported milk products are flooding into the market, a large number of Chinese parents would rather travel to Hong Kong or even to Europe to buy their baby milk to make sure that their babies are not poisoned by products sold in China.

A second individual strategy is to lodge consumer complaints. Here the role of the Chinese Consumers' Association (CCA), a large, quasigovernmental consumer organization with offices throughout China, is crucial. During 2013, CCA provided a significant public service by handling some quarter million cases. CCA's 2013 annual summary reports that 92 percent of complaints were resolved. The result was 5 billion RMB (about $750 million) in refunds to consumers in 2012. Although the complaint-resolution activities of CCA are impressive, it is important to point out that if a business does not cooperate with the CCA, then it is extremely difficult for a case to be resolved. This causes a degree of cynicism among the public.

As a quasigovernment institution, CCA is not only restrained by its institutional competences; it is also inhibited from activities that might damage the reputation of the government. CCA is supposed to be adequately funded by the State Administration for Industry and Commerce. However, CCA and its regional brunches are frustrated constantly by funding that is insufficient to organize teams of experts capable of lobbying for consumer rights.

Overall, the CCA's complaint-handling activity does not amount to genuine consumer activism, because CCA does not synthesize the complaints into policy themes nor mount campaigns for reform. Other than sporadic, localized consumer protests, the label of "activism" is more accurately applied to the activities of environmental organizations, and it will be interesting to see to what extent consumer interests will move in that direction, for example, regarding water quality or measures to reduce pollution.

Against this backdrop of limited consumer activism in China, an important development was the opening of a new institute in 2013—the Center for International Consumer Protection Policy and Law (CICPPL) at Wuhan University. The center brings together a dozen international consumer experts for the purpose of developing both Chinese consumer legislation and international law. The center has launched work on the subjects of food safety, financial services, electronic commerce, tourism, and dispute resolution, and it is exploring the possibility of additional research on water, energy and pollution.

Domestically, there is relatively little crossover as yet between "consumer activists" and people pursuing other causes such as environmentalism. This is partly because consumer activism in the sense of independent advocacy organizations scarcely exists, as indicated earlier. Another reason is that there are potential tensions between environmental and consumer organizations in that measures to avoid pollution may raise costs, in turn increasing prices. Conversely, reducing prices or at least not getting rid of subsidies could well worsen pollution as demand for electricity (most of which is coal-based) rises. The price of energy and water is especially important to poor consumers in China, especially those who migrate to cities from rural areas. Their costs already rise dramatically when they move to urban areas. Any price increases designed to encourage conservation or reflect unsubsidized costs would be painful.

The tension between consumer and environmental priorities is a worldwide tension, of course. Paradoxically, the gravity of the environmental problems faced by China and the fact that incomes have risen so dramatically in recent years may lead to an acceptance by consumers of the need for corrective measures, even ones that increase prices. But ways may need to be found to assist the poor with the inevitable rising prices. In any event, pollution issues in China are now so pressing as to make it likely that common cause between consumer and environmental activists will be made at some level in due course.

Chinese consumer organizations are in touch with evolving international debates regarding consumer rights and consumer policy. CCA and CICPPL are members of Consumers International, and both organizations have easy access to influential consumer bodies in Hong Kong and Taiwan. However, CCA has few opportunities to turn these contacts into policy stances, because its terms of reference are limited to dispute resolution. CICPPL has regular contacts with Consumers International and is advised by a panel of international experts. In addition, a Chinese delegation to the United Nations Conference on Trade and Development is helping to revise the United Nations Guidelines on Consumer Protection. (It is worth noting, in passing, that the UN is taken very seriously by China.)

A recent development of some significance is the provision for class action lawsuits under the recently enacted Consumer Protection Act which came into force on March 15, 2014—World Consumer Rights Day, known as *san yao wu* in China. For the moment, however, only government-affiliated consumer associations, such as CCA, are allowed to launch these. To what extent this change was brought about because of "activism" or to the government understanding that it needed to take action on large-scale incidents such as food contamination is open to debate. The answer is probably that generalized discontent among the public rather than identifiable activists provided the impetus for change.

In sum, most activity on behalf of consumers in China cannot be described as "activism" in the sense in which the term is used in most countries. Rather, the government dominates consumer affairs and limits it largely to assistance in complaint resolution. The environmental challenges facing the country may change this situation. The public is aware of environmental problems, for these problems are apparent if one simply walks around in any big city. Consumer and environmental concerns are converging, and both suggest the need for citizen pressure for remedial action.

Ying Yu

See also: Consumers International; Hong Kong Consumer Movement; United Nations Guidelines for Consumer Protection

Further Reading

"A Billion Shoppers." 2014. *The Economist.* April 19. www.economist.com/news/special
    -report/21600801-chinese-consumers-are-spending-plenty-they-could-do-even
    -better-billion-shoppers.
Center for International Consumer Protection Policy and Law. http://en.international
    consumer.org/Plus/m_default/Cms/default.php.
China Consumers' Association. www.cca.org.cn/english/index.jsp.
"Doing It Their Way." 2014. *The Economist.* January 25. www.economist.com/news/
    briefing/21595019-market-growing-furiously-getting-tougher-foreign-firms-doing-it
    -their-way.
Hanser, Amy. 2004. "Made in the PRC: Consumers in China." *Context* 3, no. 1: 13–19.
"The True Meaning of San Yao Wu." 2014. *The Economist.* March 15. www.economist
    .com/news/business/21599006-chinas-new-consumer-law-has-local-and-foreign-
    firms-worried-true-meaning-san-yao-wu.

COMMUNICATIONS ADVOCACY

See Cable Television Regulation; Digital Communications Advocacy; Internet Activism; Telephone Consumer Advocacy

COMMUNITY ACTIVISM

In the past decade, community organizing has received national attention simply because earlier in his career, President Barack Obama directed the faith-based Developing Communities Project (DCP) in Chicago and served as a consultant and trainer for the Gamaliel Foundation, a community organizing institute. Although community organizing is focused on the diverse needs of particular communities, some of these needs relate to consumer protection and consumer access to essential products, such as housing and insurance.

The history of community organizing reveals several different approaches to the mobilization of grassroots organizations, and the people they represent, on a wide variety of causes. Although ACORN (Association of Communities for Reform Now) represents perhaps the best known example of community organizing, major national organizing networks and various organizing training centers express different philosophies and strategies.

One organizing approach can be linked back to the social work movement that developed in the late nineteenth century, particularly the organizing and outreach efforts of social workers associated with Jane Addams's Hull House in Chicago, the Henry Street Settlement in New York City's Lower East Side, and the settlement house movement in these and other major cities. Today, these institutions now typically function as community or neighborhood centers that offer a range of programs and services to area residents. These services often include job training and employment programs, early childhood education, afterschool youth programs, arts education and performances, English as a second language courses, literacy education, immigration counseling, and services to seniors.

In 1911, several settlement houses in New York City took the lead to form a national association called the Federation of Settlements. In 1979, the group changed its name to the United Neighborhood Centers of America and, in 2014, merged with the Alliance for Children and Families. These organizations retained a commitment to the social work model of organizing. Organizers try to strengthen communities by making linkages among community "stakeholders" through utilizing community assets and maximizing community engagement.

In part, the War on Poverty—closely associated with the presidency of Lyndon Johnson in the 1960s—built on this social work approach. The Johnson administration supported the development of community action agencies to serve as centers for multiple services in order to strengthen "community" in disorganized or underdeveloped areas. Social workers were supposed to help community residents organize to obtain needed services. These services included consumer goods and services such as affordable electric service or consumer credit.

A second approach to organizing, also focused on community institutions, has attempted to mobilize area residents to take control of these institutions, then ensure that they delivered needed services. Although some settlement houses and War on Poverty community action agencies adopted this approach, it was usually led by community development corporations (CDCs) focusing on affordable housing along with related economic development and social service functions.

Today, several thousand CDCs exist in urban and rural communities across the nation. They are responsible for the production of rental and for-sale homes and the development of property management companies. They value community organizing, especially persuading tenants to be engaged in and supportive of the maintenance of properties developed by the CDCs.

A third approach to organizing is closely associated with the Chicago-based organizer Saul Alinksy. Alinsky developed an organizing model that emphasized the mobilization of community residents for political power. In 1940, he founded the Industrial Areas Foundation to promote this model, which relied to a great extent on involving religious congregations. He also inspired a number of national networks of local community organizing, including the PICO National Network and the Direct Action Research and Training (DART), both of which were linked to faith-based groups; the Citizen Action movement, which was originally inspired by New Left groups such as Students for a Democratic Society (SDS) and by Ralph Nader, and which is now supported by a national network called US Action; and ACORN, which focused on jobs, housing, and labor protections for low-income communities.

From the early 1970s through the 1990s, ACORN effectively organized around issues such as predatory lending and voter registration in dozens of cities. However, after legal controversies about voter registration activities in some states and adverse news coverage generated by other controversies promoted by conservative groups that had targeted the organization, ACORN leaders dissolved the national organization. However, some local ACORN groups—including the Alliance of Californians for Community Empowerment and the New York Communities for Change—have continued to function on their own.

These three organizing approaches had different emphases and institutions. The neighborhood center or social work approach often focuses on community "asset building," a concept developed by John McKnight and Jody Fretzmann in their writings and their training program, the Asset Based Community Development Institute at Northwestern University.

Alinsky-oriented community organizing training sought to train organizers how to mobilize area residents against a highly visible opponent, often a large corporation, that had abused or neglected the community. This training was offered by the Industrial Areas Foundation, the National Training and Information Center/National People's Action, the Midwest Academy, and the Highlander Research and Education Center. Training on faith- and congregation-based approaches were provided by DART and the Gamaliel Foundation.

Citizen Action and ACORN tended to focus more on issues than on institutions. In most other approaches to community organizing, the priorities of local residents shaped issues and strategies. Both Citizen Action and ACORN had national agendas, such as campaign finance reform, that they tried to build support for at state and local levels.

Training programs using the community development or institution approach emphasized the linkage of community organizing to place-based strategies, including the tools and techniques of community development finance. These programs include the Community Training and Assistance Center in Boston and the Development Training Institute in Baltimore. National community development intermediary organizations, such as the Local Initiatives Support Corporation (LISC) and Enterprise Community Partners (formerly the Enterprise Foundation), also provide training and technical assistance in this area.

LISC in particular developed a "consensus organizing" approach, especially in communities without indigenous community-based organizations, that emphasized engaging in cooperative ventures with "downtown" interests. This approach depended on the building of trust between neighborhood residents and business interests, which as they worked together, realized that their agendas often did not conflict. It contrasted with the Alinsky approach that stirred conflict when communities organized politically to demand programs and other resources.

The Occupy Wall Street movement of the past several years also emphasized conflict. It was inspired in part by the anticonsumerist Canadian magazine *Adbusters*, which called for peaceful protests against corporate influence over democratic institutions. Beginning with the September 2001 "Occupy Wall Street" encampment in Lower Manhattan, Occupy groups emerged in many large cities in the United States and abroad. These groups set up encampments in public areas to protest the economic and political dominance of wealthy Americans and the institutions they controlled, which they often referred to as "the one percent."

Unlike the highly structured operations of IAF and ACORN, Occupy's organizing model was leaderless, generally anarchic, with decisions made by loosely organized "general assemblies" that determined—and frequently changed—priorities and actions. But because these decisions were not based on an articulated agenda of priorities and demands, they did not provide a lasting basis for the movement. Over time, most of the Occupy encampments dissolved, some as a result of police actions.

In several cities, though, some participants began focusing on local, often consumer-oriented issues related to financial services. Occupy our Homes Atlanta and Occupy Homes Minnesota, both part of the Occupy Our Homes national network, intervene on behalf of individual homeowners facing foreclosure and eviction. Through direct action, they try to prevent these "takings" by the banks and mortgage servicers. Another Occupy offshoot, Strike Debt, began working with Rolling Jubilee to raise money to purchase the debts of financially challenged individuals. As of early 2014, they had effectively paid off almost $15 million in debt carried by about 2,700 individuals.

Occupy-related groups also assisted residents of New York City's Far Rockaway neighborhood who had been damaged by Hurricane Sandy. In the wake of "Superstorm Sandy," when established disaster response organizations were slow to respond, these Occupy groups provided emergency disaster relief services. They did so, however, not only to assist neighborhood residents, but also to expose the inadequacy of existing systems and begin created new ones.

A related model, which enjoyed a resurgence during the recent recession beginning in 2008, was labor-related. Worker centers, supported by trade unions, which often had existed for many decades, used community organizing as a way to reach unorganized groups in urban areas, including immigrants, day laborers, taxi drivers, and domestic workers. Community organizers used local issues related to income and rights to establish relationships and trust with these populations. The community-based worker centers have developed their own national networks—notably, the National Day Labor Organizing Network, the Food Chain Workers Alliance, and the National Domestic Workers Alliance.

Even more recently, a number of community-based organizations assisted the implementation of the Affordable Care Act ("Obamacare") by helping consumers file for health insurance on state and federal insurance exchanges. More specifically, with $67 million annually in grant funds from the U.S. Department of Health and Human Services, these nonprofits are functioning as "navigators" who help lower-income consumers understand and access the ACA's health insurance options. Among the nonprofits with community outreach and organizing roots are Campesinos sin Fonteras (in Arizona), Southern United Neighbors (in Louisiana, Texas, and Arkansas), Western Maine Community Action, Urban League of Hudson County (New Jersey), and Advanced Patient Advocates (in several states). In some cases, state or county governments contracted with local organizing groups to undertake the outreach. For example, the Illinois state government awarded a grant to LISC's Chicago office, which then used door-to-door canvassing, public events, and social media to contact some 27,000 residents, enrolling nearly 3,000.

Other community-based efforts to help implement the ACA were not funded by the federal government. For example, volunteers from the Greater Bennington Interfaith Community Services worked with the Bennington (VT) Free Clinic to help the uninsured sign up for appropriate health care coverage, including Medicaid with its expanded eligibility.

Another recent development has been a new focus by some community groups not on the entire community, but on marginal populations within the community. Influenced by increasing public attention and concern about the persistence of structural inequities, the population receiving the greatest attention is African American boys and young men. In early 2014, major foundations and the White House announced a "My Brother's Keeper" initiative that seeks to break down persistent barriers to equality of opportunity. It is anticipated that much of the several hundred million dollars committed by the foundations will be granted to community-based groups to provide support to African American boys and young men through mentoring, tutoring, training, and other interventions.

Rick Cohen

See also: Energy Advocacy; Insurance Advocacy; Labor Movement; National Low Income Housing Coalition; Payday Loan Advocacy; State and Local Consumer Advocacy Groups; State Utility Advocacy; Tenant Activism

Further Reading

Boyte, Harry C. 1980. *The Backyard Revolution: Understanding the New Citizens Movement.* Philadelphia, PA: Temple University Press.

Delgado, Gary. 1986. *Organizing the Movement: The Roots and Growth of ACORN.* Philadelphia, PA: Temple University Press.

Gitlin, Todd. 2012. *Occupy Nation: The Roots, the Spirit, and the Promise of Occupy Wall Street.* New York: Harper Collins.

COMMUNITY NUTRITION INSTITUTE

The Community Nutrition Institute (CNI) began in fall 1969 with the publication of *CNI Weekly News*, later renamed *Nutrition Week*. The newsletter, which was published up to 2003, was the intellectual and financial heart of CNI, whose main mission was to inform a newly emerging profession of managers of food and nutrition about nutritional issues.

Rodney E. Leonard started and was the first editor of *Nutrition Week*. When CNI was organized as a nonprofit 501(c)(3) organization in 1970, he became its executive director and held that position until the early years of the twenty-first century. Before organizing CNI, Leonard worked in the federal government, including serving as deputy director of the U.S. Office of Consumer Affairs.

Subscriptions to *Nutrition Week* provided income that supported other programs and activities related to educational and advocacy goals. Those goals included public policies supporting community nutrition, related regulatory programs, nutrition education resources, and international agreements on product standards related to acceptable risk levels from chemicals and substance in foods and community environments.

In the mid-1990s, CNI's annual budget hovered around $400,000. About one-third of the income came from publications, and the remainder from foundation grants and contributions.

CNI was not a membership organization. As executive director, Leonard led staff development of projects that generated their own funding, such as litigation to improve meat and poultry inspection or advocacy for citizen participation in developing global standards.

CNI conceived and lobbied for the WIC program (Special Supplemental Nutrition Program for Women, Infants and Children) in 1970 to provide government-subsidized nutritional supplements to families in need. It designed the training program for the Older American Nutrition program and trained the first program managers in hundreds of communities in some twenty-five states in the 1970s. It sponsored the first graduate intern program for nutritionists to become managers of local school food programs. It developed the first nutrition labeling system implemented by the Food and Drug Administration. It initiated litigation on food safety rules and citizen participation in rulemaking that became part of case law. It helped launch World Food Day. And with CARE, it organized a community-based coalition that supported the House Select Committee on Hunger.

The organization helped train persons who later occupied key leadership positions. They include Bob Greenstein, who administered food programs under President Carter then founded and led the influential Center on Budget and Policy Priorities, and Ellen Haas, who founded and led Public Voice before becoming an undersecretary of agriculture in the Carter Administration.

In the past decade, the organization became less active then ceased to exist. For several years, longtime staffer Sheila Foley edited *CFNP Report*, which had replaced *Nutrition Week*. However, Leonard continues to comment on food safety and nutrition issues.

Stephen Brobeck

See also: Food Safety Advocacy; Public Voice for Food and Health Policy

Further Reading

Jeffs, Angela. 1991. "Agitating for Consumer Awareness: Is the Food You're Eating Fit for Consumption?" *Agricultural Times of Japan* (October): 1+.

COMPLAINT RESOLUTION

Most consumers who have complaints make no effort to resolve them, but those who do have available to them a wide range of options ranging from communicating with sellers to third-party assistance to litigation. Research shows that in any one year, about one-third of consumers think that they have a problem with a good or service purchased. But fewer than one-third of those who have these perceived problems will actually complain about them beyond griping to individuals with whom they associate. Consumers most likely to complain are those who have purchased relatively expensive products, such as automobiles or appliances, those who have high incomes and education, and those who are in their twenties or thirties.

Those with complaints are most likely to begin by communicating with the seller in person, by phone, by letter, or by email. Some sellers, especially those with great reputational risk, are more likely than other businesses to try resolving grievances. Some research finds that about half of those who complain to sellers are satisfied with the responses they receive.

A large majority of dissatisfied consumers do not pursue their grievance, but if they do, they have several options available to them. They can file their complaint with a third party, litigate, or take action themselves. Most third party groups are associated with business, government, media, or independent nonprofit organizations.

The principal business group that solicits consumer complaints is the 113 independent Better Business Bureaus (BBBs) in the United States and Canada. The BBBs are private, nonprofit organizations that are funded primarily by dues from business members. They were first organized in the early years of the twentieth century by reputable businessmen who wished to educate consumers and curb marketing abuses through voluntary efforts. Today, these BBBs and their national association, the Council of Better Business Bureaus, notifies the public of scams, reviews advertising, reviews charities, seeks to mediate a resolution to about 1 million consumer complaints a year, and provides prepurchase information about these complaints and their disposition to consumers.

BBBs seek to resolve most received complaints by contacting sellers and offering to mediate a resolution of these grievances. These complaints are most likely to be settled by businesses who wish to retain customer goodwill or receive a high rating from the BBBs. Some are mediated formally by a panel of professional arbitrators, a service for which consumers pay a fee. There are distinct mediation programs for certain types of automobile, telecommunication, and moving and storage grievances.

Over the years, BBBs have been criticized for deferring to member businesses by trusting their responses to complaints and by giving these businesses higher ratings than nonmembers. Regardless, a large number of consumers continue to contact local Better Business Bureaus for assistance resolving problems. The success of

BBBs in settling these complaints depends to an extent on the resources and skill of the local BBB and the attitude of businesses that are the subject of complaints. There is some evidence that BBBs have the most success resolving complaints against national or local businesses who are dues-paying member Accredited Businesses that have pledged to adhere to the BBB Code of Business Practices.

To receive assistance from more independent third-party groups, consumers can contact select government agencies. Many federal agencies solicit information from consumers about their grievances with sellers to more adequately regulate marketplace practices, but very few seek to resolve these individual complaints. One exception is the relatively new Consumer Financial Protection Bureau, which in 2012 and 2013 received, and sought to resolve, some 175,000 complaints against financial institutions. However, a large majority of the consumer grievances handled by government agencies are done so at the state and local levels. According to the 2013 *Consumer Action Handbook* published by the General Service Administration's Federal Citizen Information Center, in almost all states, consumers who have complaints can contact the state attorney general. In some twenty states, complainants can also contact other consumer agencies and, in almost all states, industry regulatory agencies with complaints related to those industries—for example, public service commissions with electric, gas, or phone complaints and insurance commissions with automobile, homeowner, life, or health insurance grievances. The handbook also lists more than fifty county and city consumer protection agencies, more than half of which are located in either New York or New Jersey.

Consumer agencies handling complaints first seek to persuade consumer and seller to reach a mediated settlement. If this is not possible, the agencies pursue a variety of alternatives that depend on the scope of their legal authority and their analysis of particular cases. Many agencies have the ability to issue subpoenas to uncooperative sellers and civil citations (tickets) when violations of the law are clear and no further investigation is needed. Administrative adjudicative hearings and arbitration proceedings are sometimes available to try to resolve grievances.

Another type of government option for resolving complaints is the courts. For most complainants, the most viable court option is local small claims courts, where consumers can file grievances up to $3,000 to $10,000, depending on the state where the court is located. In a small claims court, in a relatively informal hearing where legal representation is not necessary, the judge hears the complaint, talks to both the complainant and defendant, then renders a decision. Complainants often feel this decision to be fair but, in some cases, have difficulty collecting monies awarded by the judge.

Using litigation to resolve individual grievances in other courts is usually not feasible because the funds involved are not sufficient to persuade attorneys to handle the cases. The major exception is product liability lawsuits where damages are substantial and there is a possibility of an additional award for pain and suffering.

There are also various nonprofit agencies that handle individual consumer complaints. These groups include some couple dozen local Call for Action affiliates that are associated with local network television stations. Staffed largely by volunteers, these Call for Action groups receive and seek to resolve individual consumer grievances. In the past, any success reflected in part their association with television stations that might, and that sometimes did, report on the grievances.

Some of the more activist groups that have handled individual consumer complaints were influenced by the grievance procedure developed by the Consumers Education and Protection Association (CEPA). This organization was founded in Philadelphia in 1966 by Max Weiner, who had worked as a teacher and labor organizer, to organize consumers so that they could better protect themselves at a time when there were few consumer protections and agencies. The three-part grievance procedure required complainants to attend a weekly CEPA meeting during which they explained their problem, to participate in a "delegation" of CEPA members to discuss and try to resolve the complaint with the seller (if a letter sent earlier had not resolved the problem), and finally to join CEPA members in their "educational picketing" at the seller's place of business if they deemed the requested settlement to be reasonable and the seller refused to accept it. This method of resolving complaints proved to be extraordinarily effective—in part because CEPA members continued weekly pickets until sellers agreed to a resolution—and inspired other groups.

Organizations in Pittsburgh, Milwaukee, New York City, and Dallas all used this grievance procedure for a time, though the two groups that achieved greatest success employing it were Cleveland Consumer Action (CCA) and Consumer Action (Bay Area, California) in the 1970s and 1980s. At the height of its activity, CCA, which in 1970 started out as a group affiliated with CEPA brought to Cleveland by Stephen Brobeck, maintained seven local complaint groups that met weekly to hear and try to resolve grievances. Brobeck and wife Susan introduced the idea to Consumer Action head Kay Pachtner in 1975, and by the end of that decade, her group had established several of their own local complaint groups.

While CEPA was active for more than three decades, and CCA for more than two decades, the two organizations eventually folded after the departure of key leaders or after their interest flagged. This leadership required the ability to understand complaints that were often complex, to deal with market-hardened sellers, to walk picket lines each week, and to fight occasional lawsuits seeking to restrict the picketing. Although Consumer Action, now a national organization, no longer maintains complaint groups, it continues to try to resolve individual grievances submitted by phone or email.

The growing availability and use of the Internet has made available additional options to consumer complainants. Those most interested in public venting or informing other consumers of their complaints increasingly supply information to one or more of dozens of consumer complaint websites. A number of these websites target individual companies and often are called "(name of company) sucks." But a half-dozen among the many researched by the Consumer Federation of America in 2010 stand out—complaints.com, mythreecents.com, complaintsboard.com, pissedconsumer.com, consumeraffairs.com, and ripoffreport.com. Each of these websites contains accounts of complaints related to a wide variety of products. Although businesses may seek to resolve some of these grievances to reduce their reputational risk, there is no evidence that such efforts are widespread.

A few consumers have carried their complaining a step further—they have used the Internet to organize consumer opposition to a corporate practice or product. One of the most publicized efforts to use this strategy was initiated by mothers in 2010 who complained that a new Procter and Gamble diaper caused rashes. As well as voicing their dissatisfaction on a wide variety of websites, these mothers, led by Rosana Shah of Baton Rouge, Louisiana, organized a Facebook page calling on P&G to bring back the old diapers. Within months, thousands of mothers had complained on this page. This protest dissipated over a year later when the Consumer Product Safety Commission said it could find no evidence of the new diaper causing rash, and fifty-nine of the parents who had sued P&G each received a settlement of $1,000.

Stephen Brobeck

See also: Litigation; State and Local Consumer Affairs Offices; State and Local Consumer Advocacy Groups

Further Reading

"Conversation with Steve Brobeck, Consumer Advocate." 1975. *Cleveland Magazine* (July): 21+.
David, Kristin. 1990. "Beat Up on the BBB." *Changing Times* (November): 51+.
Haas, Al. 1986. "Consumed with Consumerism." *Philadelphia Inquirer* (January 2): E1.
Technical Assistance Research Programs, Inc. 1985. *Consumer Complaint Handling in America: An Update Study*. Washington, DC: U.S. Office of Consumer Affairs.
Warland, Rex H., Robert O. Herrmann, and Jane Willits. 1975. "Dissatisfied Consumers: Who Gets Upset and Who Takes Action." *Journal of Consumer Affairs* 9 (winter): 148–163.

CONFERENCE OF CONSUMER ORGANIZATIONS

The Conference of Consumer Organizations (COCO) was a national umbrella consumer that was a spinoff from the Consumer Federation of America (CFA). It included state and local groups that were often led by academics.

In the mid-1960s, a planning committee of state and local consumer leaders and educators met over a two-year period to form a national, unifying consumer body. In 1967, concluding that they could not mobilize sufficient resources to launch this organization, they joined with a national committee of Washington, D.C.–based consumer and union leaders who had already been planning Consumer Assembly, the first national consumer conference. Encouraged and sponsored by the president's special assistant for consumer affairs, Esther Peterson, this assembly was held in late 1967, and its success helped persuade planners to create CFA, which held its first annual meeting in April 1968. Father Robert McEwen was elected the organization's first president.

After several years, some state and local leaders became dissatisfied with CFA's concentration on national issues and legislation to the neglect of state and local organizational needs. They were also unhappy with the influence of national groups, especially labor unions, within the organization.

In 1973, a group of the state leaders, gathered under the leadership of Currin Shields, the head of the Arizona Consumer Council, met twice. At a national symposium organized by Shields and held in Tucson, they voted to establish a new consumer umbrella organization to be called the Conference of Consumer Organizations. The founding members were representatives from consumer groups in Arizona, Massachusetts, Nevada, Missouri, Virginia, New York, Pittsburgh, and Texas.

COCO was organized as a nonprofit educational corporation to encourage and support the formation and development of state and local consumer organizations and agencies. Its other goals were to foster dialogue with other segments of business and the public, and the promotion of educational programs at the grassroots.

The organization never had a paid, full-time staff. It published a monthly newsletter, COCO intercom, which had slightly more than 300 paid subscribers. Shields, a professor at the University of Arizona; Louis Meyer, a professor at Edinboro State College (PA); and McEwen, a professor at Boston College, were early chairmen of the group.

COCO made an effort to work with and incorporate into the organization consumer affairs representatives from government and business. It principal activity was meetings with individual companies and industry associations. These meetings helped persuade some companies, including AT&T, to create consumer advisory panels.

During the 1970s, COCO sponsored annual national meetings as well as numerous workshops and regional conferences. But during the 1980s, shrinking funds costs made it impossible to continue the conferences. Furthermore, new CFA leaders persuaded most of the individual groups to rejoin the federation. In the 1990s, the only major activity of COCO was the publication of COCO Intercom.

Stephen Brobeck

See also: Consumer Federation of America; State and Local Consumer Advocacy Groups

Further Reading

Swanston, Walterene. 1972. "Consumer Federation Waging Spirited Battle for Survival." *National Journal* (July 8): 1,126–1,136.

CONGRESSIONAL CONSUMER ADVOCACY

Periods of consumer activism in Congress have been cyclical, coming and going with shifting public mood and political fortune. Although these changes tend to make consumer protection seem like a new issue at certain times, this protection has been a governmental responsibility and a subject of congressional interest since the earliest days of the Republic. Consumer protection in Congress has always reflected congressional philosophy about the appropriate role of government in the economy.

Origins of Activism

The Constitution explicitly empowers Congress to "fix the Standard of Weights and Measures." However, the primary purpose of such measures was to assure the orderly flow of commerce. The first manifestation of an explicit consumer interest was in the Progressive Era. During that time, stretching roughly from the 1880s to 1910, Congress protected consumers against monopoly power in transportation with the Interstate Commerce Act and against monopolies, more generally, with the Sherman and Clayton antitrust laws.

Yet it is in the food and drug controversies of the early part of the century that consumer politics and policy resemble controversies from the late 1960s to the present. For several years before the passage of the Pure Food and Drug Act in 1906, Dr. Harvey Wiley, chief chemist of the U.S. Department of Agriculture, relentlessly campaigned for legislation in Congress and before the public. Wiley gained considerable fame by establishing a "poison squad," a group of volunteers who tested the effects of preservatives by ingesting them. Legislation was also pushed by labor groups, "good government" groups, and the American Medical Association.

Despite the blue-ribbon backing, pure food and drug legislation, passed twice in the House of Representatives, languished in the Senate. Ultimately, a much weakened bill passed the Senate, only then to stall in the House. The matter appeared deadlocked until the publication of Upton Sinclair's *The Jungle*, a 1906 novel that shocked the nation with its revelations of filth in the meat-packing industry. The book was quickly followed by a presidential study that confirmed Sinclair's account. The scandal, together with carefully applied pressure by President Theodore Roosevelt, pressured a still deadlocked Congress to pass, in 1906, first the Meat Inspection Act of 1906 and then the Pure Food and Drug Act. The pattern was set: Scandal and anger at large corporations, skillfully manipulated by a president and the press, forced Congress to pass consumer legislation.

A similar pattern emerged during the next episode of important congressional action on a consumer issue—the passage of the Federal Food, Drug, and Cosmetic Act in 1938. Five years of congressional attention to problems of false advertising and dangerous drugs and cosmetics still had not led to legislation when 107 persons died as a result of taking a medicine called elixir sulfanilamide, which contained a toxic solvent. Once again, a weak bill was beefed up in the wake of a scandal, and a different President Roosevelt, Franklin, signed the bill into law. Together with amendments to the Federal Trade Commission Act in the same year, Congress firmly established federal regulation of advertising and regulation of a broad category of consumer products. As with the original food and drug legislation during the Progressive period, the 1938 legislation should be seen as a product of a time of activist government—the New Deal.

The Ralph Nader Era

In the late 1960s and early 1970s, Congress was the locus of action not only in passing legislation, but also in initiating it. From 1962 to 1972, Congress perceived a need and responded to public pressure for consumer protection measures in three ways. First, the legislature passed a wide array of regulatory measures intended to improve consumer health and safety as well as to provide better information and economic protection. The major measures included the Automobile Safety Act, Kefauver–Harris Drug Amendments, Wholesome Poultry Act, Fair Packaging and Labeling Act, and Consumer Credit Protection Act.

Second, Congress created a new agency, the Consumer Product Safety Commission (CPSC), and significantly increased the power and role of existing agencies, particularly the Food and Drug Administration (FDA) and the Federal Trade Commission (FTC). The FDA was given the power to regulate not only the safety of drugs, but also their effectiveness. The FTC, under the Magnuson–Moss Act, was empowered to promulgate regulations applicable to trade practices in an entire industry, rather than just case by case. There were also attempts in Congress in the 1970s to create a "Department of Consumers," but those efforts never succeeded.

Third, Congress acted as "bully pulpit" through holding well-publicized hearings on a variety of consumer issues. Those hearings increased public support for the theory that businesses could and should be held more accountable for the safety of products and for business practices such as advertising. Probably the most profound shift was the public acceptance of the notion that injuries and deaths in automobile accidents resulted, in part, from design features of cars, as well as that manufacturers have a responsibility, which could be mandated by government, to make their products safer.

These measures were connected not only by being generally considered as consumer protection laws, but also by having a common group of supporters in Congress. This group of supporters, all Democrats, voted consistently, and as a coherent bloc, for consumerist measures. During this period, the most pro-consumer and active senators were Paul Douglas (D-IL), Lee Metcalf (D-MT), Warren Magnuson (D-WA), Gaylord Nelson (D-WI), Abraham Ribicoff (D-CT), and Thomas Dodd (D-CT). In the House of Representatives, the consumer champions were Benjamin Rosenthal (D-NY), Leonor Sullivan (D-MO), Harley Staggers (D-WV), Neal Smith (D-IA), Richard Ottinger (D-NY), and Thomas Foley (D-WA).

Groups such as Consumers Union, the Consumer Federation of America, and others were important as sources of information and legitimacy despite their limited resources and political power. These consumer advocates, including Ralph Nader, were not only lobbyists from the outside, but also key parts of coalitions supporting the consumer-oriented members of Congress. These congressmen and senators were themselves consumer activists bringing to bear their own considerable prestige and staff resources. They gained recognition and public stature by becoming "policy entrepreneurs" on behalf of a new and popular issue. Indeed, unlike in most other areas of public policy, consumer protection measures were usually initiated by Congress rather than by the president.

Business Counterattack

Passing consumer legislation that was opposed by business interests was difficult in the first place. The success of consumer advocates fighting for new protections generated not just business opposition, but also a business counterattack. This counterattack culminated in the successful effort of the business community to defeat legislation creating a new, independent agency that would serve as an advocate for consumers in federal agencies, Congress, and the courts. In this nine-year battle ending in 1978, the legislation was supported by the House, the Senate, and the president—but never, sufficiently, at the same time.

Business groups sought not only to defeat new proposals, but also to weaken consumer agencies. In the 1970s, much of their efforts were directed at the FTC. Having been granted new powers in 1974, the FTC entered into a period of activism. It began investigations and proposed consumer protection regulations affecting some of the most powerful industries in the country—insurance, the legal and medical professions, automobiles, and pharmaceuticals. After the FTC began an inquiry into television commercials aimed at children, industry opposition coalesced. A lobbying coalition of more than three dozen companies and trade associations enlisted the support of many industries affected by the commission and succeeded in persuading Congress to pass legislation that ended certain FTC investigations, including children's television advertising, and by establishing closer congressional control over all commission activities.

The business counterattack continued into the 1980s, emboldened by an antiregulation Reagan administration. For example, the CPSC was created under legislation that required it to be periodically reauthorized by Congress. By the time it was up for reauthorization in 1981, a concerted effort, supported by the Reagan administration, was made to abolish the agency. The agency survived, but its new authorizing legislation called on the CPSC to rely more on voluntary standards and less on regulation.

The congressional retreat occurred for several reasons. First, Congress gave mixed signals to the consumer protection agencies. The Appropriations Committees had requested the FTC to undertake the children's advertising initiative, but other committees sought to shut the effort down. Second, in the changing leadership of key congressional committees, key consumer "entrepreneurs" left the scene. Finally, industry pressure on Congress increased, especially when federal regulators and legislators targeted specific business practices.

By the 1980s, consumer activists in Congress—such as Senator Howard Metzenbaum (D-OH), Representative Henry Waxman (D-CA), and Representative Edward Markey (D-MA)—focused most of their efforts on defending existing consumer protections from attack. Metzenbaum was particularly effective using the restraining rules of the Senate, such as the ability to filibuster, to block anticonsumer legislation.

Congressional Restraint and Piecemeal Reforms

The election of a Democratic Senate in 1986, along with continued Democratic control of the House, had a restraining effect on the Reagan administration's antiregulation efforts. When Bill Clinton was elected president in 2000, together with a Democratic Senate and House, consumer advocates thought there were new opportunities for reform. Yet this optimism proved largely unwarranted.

A pro-business climate acted as a check on new initiatives. However, the pro-consumer sympathies of the new administration and some congressional leaders also restrained industry efforts to weaken consumer agencies and regulations.

Congress, however, did seek to protect consumers from certain adverse effects of deregulated industries, especially telecommunications and banking. Growing consumer dissatisfaction with cable television monopolies persuaded Congress to reregulate cable rate in 1992, overriding a presidential veto. Increasing irritation by consumers against recently deregulated banks for pursuing profit-maximization strategies (e.g., raising fees, increasing check holds) encouraged the legislature to pass several new consumer banking protections—limits on check holds, curbs on home equity loan practices, and required savings disclosures. All these new protections were approved by Democratic Congresses. Although the Republican Congress elected in 1994 largely deregulated cable television rates (as part of comprehensive telecommunications legislation), despite vigorous bank lobbying, the consumer banking protections have remained in place and, in recent years, even been greatly bolstered. That strengthening began in 2002, during the administration of George W. Bush, when Congress, led by Senator Paul Sarbanes (D-MD), approved major legislation (Sarbanes–Oxley) toughening securities' regulation.

Congress also sought to respond to growing consumer concerns, especially among the influential upper middle class, about certain health and safety threats. In 1989, the legislature banned smoking on all domestic airline flights. In 1990, it mandated new disclosures of the nutritional contents of food. And in 1996, it approved safe drinking water legislation. On the other hand, many in Congress argued that regulation of pharmaceuticals and medical devices stifled innovation by slowing the introduction of valuable drugs and medical devices. After hearings in both the Senate and House supported by conservative public interest groups, Congress considered, but did not pass, legislation to reduce the FDA's regulatory authority over drugs and devices. Moreover, Congress refused to approve comprehensive health care reform.

Another controversial consumer issue receiving attention after 1994 was tort reform—proposed changes in laws allowing consumers to sue to receive compensation from damages caused by defective products, medical malpractice, and fraudulent business practices. Against the opposition of most consumer advocates, in 1996 Congress passed legislation that would have curbed consumers' ability to bring product liability lawsuits. Although President Clinton vetoed this legislation, earlier he had signed into law legislation to limit the ability of consumers to sue and recover damages in cases of securities fraud.

A New Reform Era

Despite his signing of major securities reform legislation, President Bush (and his regulators) remained skeptical of most business regulations. However, changes in the world and consumer marketplace, especially related to financial services, generated new consumer concerns and popular support for new consumer protections.

These protections were advanced by a growing number of national consumer groups who worked closely together, frequently on financial services issues.

The election of a Democratic Senate and House in 2006 gave consumer activists in the legislature the opportunity to win these protections. In 2007, with bipartisan leadership from Senator Bill Nelson (D-FL) and Representative Jim Talent (R-MO), Congress approved a Military Lending Act that attempted to block the selling of payday and other high-cost loans to military personnel through a 36 percent rate cap and other restrictions. The same year, after President Bush had decried the nation's "addiction to oil," the legislature approved substantial increases in automobile fuel economy. In 2008, spurred by new concerns about unsafe imports, Congress voted for a significant increase in the budget of, and new authority for, the CPSC. Then in 2009, led by Senator Chris Dodd (D-CT) and Representative Carolyn Maloney (D-NY), the legislature approved new comprehensive credit card protections.

These reforms were only the start. In 2010, with strong support from President Obama, Congress passed three bills that would significantly restructure the American marketplace and its regulation. To greatly expand access to health care, it approved the Affordable Care Act. Among its many reforms, the legislation extended Medicaid coverage to many more Americans and provided subsidies for those who did not qualify for this coverage to purchase health insurance from new state insurance exchanges or a federal insurance exchange accessible to those in states choosing not to create their own exchanges. The same year, with leadership from Senator Dodd and Representative Barney Frank (D-MA), Congress passed comprehensive financial services regulation. As well as strengthening securities regulation and mortgage loan protections, among its many reforms, the Dodd–Frank Act established the Consumer Financial Protection Bureau (CFPB) to provide "a cop on the financial services beat." Later that year, the legislature approved the Food Safety Modernization Act that was signed into law by the president in January 2011. This measure greatly expanded FDA's authority and responsibility for ensuring that food was safe to ingest.

In part because of criticism of and some adverse reaction to health care reform, in the 2010 congressional elections, Republicans won control of the House and gained votes in the Senate. Since then, on almost all consumer issues, as well as most others, there has been a legislative stalemate. In fact, Republicans have repeatedly tried to roll back some of the reforms. For example, from 2011 to the end of 2014, the House voted to effectively repeal the ACA dozens of times. Until Senate Democrats changed the rules to limit filibusters against confirmations of presidential nominations, Republicans blocked the appointment of a permanent head of the CFPB. In his 2014 State of the Union Address, President Obama did not even pay much lip service to working with Congress, but instead announced the intention of his administration to use the powers of the executive branch to make improvements.

Consumer protection in Congress follows the general contours of federal regulation of business. In periods when Congress regulates in order to correct perceived inadequacies in the marketplace, the consumer interest is also advanced. But when Congress is more sympathetic to the view that the marketplace requires little if any government intervention, laws advancing the claims and interests of consumers are less likely to pass and are sometimes rolled back.

Mark V. Nadel, Stephen Brobeck

See also: Legislative Advocacy; U.S. Consumer Protection Agency

Further Reading

Kaiser, Robert G. 2013. *Act of Congress: How America's Essential Institution Works, and How It Doesn't Work.* New York: Alfred A. Knopf.
Nadel, Mark V. 1971. *The Politics of Consumer Protection.* Indianapolis: Bobbs-Merrill Co.
Pertschuk, Michael. 1982. *Revolt against Regulation.* Berkeley: University of California Press.
Waxman, Henry. 2009. *The Waxman Report: How Congress Really Works.* New York: Twelve, Hatchette Book Group.

CONSUMER ACTION

Consumer Action is a 501(c)(3) nonprofit consumer advocacy and education group, with offices in California and Washington, D.C., that has been seeking to advance the consumer interest for more than four decades.

In 1971, Kay Pachtner, student activist and housewife, organized a group of volunteers to deal with consumer complaints received by a telephone hotline. Calling itself Consumer Action, the group added a mobile complaint unit in an old van and added irreverent public protests to their activities. The most visible was a picket line the group set up in front of San Francisco's posh British Motors to protest a Jaguar that kept breaking down. The car dealer filed a $6 million lawsuit, but Consumer Action won the case.

In 1973, after helping the group since its inception, Neil Gendel, a young lawyer who had worked as a California assistant attorney general, joined Consumer Action as a full-time staffer. He developed the first comprehensive local survey of bank services and prices, "Break the Banks: A Shoppers Guide to Banking Services," which brought the group nationwide recognition. A year later, Consumer Action published a sharp critique of the California consumer affairs department, "Deceptive Packaging," which exposed the fact that the agency was made up of state-licensed tradespeople. Since then, Consumer Action has published surveys related to prescription drugs, bank accounts, credit cards, gasoline, and telephone services, and exposés of the food industry and need for nutritional labeling. Since the early 1970s, it has published the newsletter *Consumer Action News*.

In the mid-1970s, Consumer Action's work expanded to include reform through legislation, regulations, and lawsuits. High-profile protests, such as the 1975 "Lemonstration"—a parade of new cars with problems—brought publicity. A false advertising complaint the group filed against Bank of America resulted in a large penalty for the bank. In 1976 and 1977, Consumer Action helped the Federal Trade Commission draft new consumer protection regulations.

Pachtner and Gendel left Consumer Action in the late 1970s. Ken McEldowney, an early staff member, was appointed as executive director by the group's board of directors. McEldowney, a former consumer reporter and founder of the San Francisco group Media Alliance, brought a new perspective to the organization that emphasized helping underserved consumers, especially immigrants, minorities, and those with low incomes or disabilities.

Consumer Action began to serve these populations by preparing and distributing free, easy-to-read surveys, guides, and fact sheets in English and seven other languages. By the early 1990s, outreach staff in San Francisco and Los Angeles offices were distributing hundreds of thousands of pieces of multilingual information at no charge in California each year. The organization also created a help desk with multilingual employees—speaking Spanish and Chinese as well as English—who handle consumer complaints.

Deregulation of the telephone and banking industries in the early 1980s created consumer problems and concerns that Consumer Action began to address. In 1989, its Telephone Information Project, supported by a large penalty levied against Pacific Bell by the state public utilities commission, began providing community agencies and consumers free information about telecommunications services. In its first four years, the project distributed more than 3 million free publications. Especially notable was a 300-page *Telephone Users Guide*, prepared by longtime staffer Michael Heffer, which provided comprehensive information about the telephone marketplace and consumer services. In 1993, Consumer Action launched a Credit and Finance Project to identify and address credit and finance problems, especially those experienced by low-income, minority, immigrant, and senior consumers. Funded by court-assessed penalties against Wells Fargo Bank, the project operated a free hotline and produced fact sheets, price surveys, and a quarterly newsletter, *The Advocacy Report*.

Starting in the early 1990s, Consumer Action began to partner with selected corporations on consumer education projects. These projects allowed the organization to expand its community-based organization (CBO) network outside California. Especially far-reaching was a MoneyWi$e program, launched with Capital One in 2001, that to date has created more than thirty teaching modules and distributed millions of informational materials on housing, banking, and credit-related products.

In 1995, Consumer Action opened its National Consumer Education Resource Center, which the next year began supplying information nationally through the group's first website (www.consumer-action.org). In the same period, the organization began train-the-trainer workshops that now involve around 800 CBO staffers who learn how to use Consumer Action materials effectively. In recent years, the organization's annual National Consumer Empowerment Conference has provided additional information to these educators.

By 2010, Consumer Action's network of community-based organizations had grown to 7,500, and its distribution of free materials to consumers increased to more than 1 million annually. To support these services, the group relied not just on court awards and corporate partnerships but also on government grants and contracts.

Since then, the organization's consumer information and education activities have featured the expansion of the group's Internet presence by the creation of twelve related websites, which attract more than a half-million visitors a year. Funded by Capital One, AT&T, Microsoft, foundations, and courts, these multilingual websites have landing pages, news, and materials available in Spanish, Chinese, Vietnamese, Korean, and several other languages.

In the year ending March 31, 2009, the Help Desk responded to nearly 47,000 calls and emails requesting information and assistance, distributed more than 1 million free publications to more than 2,000 community-based organizations, and had trained nearly 800 CBO staff members in eighty-eight cities.

Advocacy has been a priority for the organization since its founding. In 2001, working with a San Francisco law firm and Trial Lawyers for Public Justice, Consumer Action was the lead plaintiff in lawsuits against Bank of America and AT&T. Victories in those cases limited bank and telephone use of mandatory arbitration clauses in consumer contracts. To boost its national effectiveness, in 2004 the organization established a Washington, D.C., office. Since then the office has been headed by Linda Sherry, a staffer since 1994, who is now the organization's director of national priorities.

Much of Consumer Action's advocacy has focused on financial services issues. In 2008 and 2009, it was a leader in helping shape and lobby successfully for the Credit CARD Act. It also worked with other consumer groups to lobby Congress, as part of Dodd–Frank legislation, for the creation of the Consumer Financial Protection Bureau and greater consumer choice about participating in high-cost bank overdraft programs. Closely related to this legislative work were Consumer Action efforts to inform consumers about mortgage modifications, foreclosure prevention scams, fake check frauds, government stimulus money scams, and other financial frauds. The group also worked with other advocates to successfully persuade the Federal Trade Commission in 2010 to reform debt settlement practices. And it worked with other groups to force the federal government to implement rules for a consumer-accessible national database of rebuilt wrecks, which started operating in January 2009.

Recently, Consumer Action has begun focusing increased attention on digital and health privacy issues. Its work includes issuing a report card for online personal health records and advocating stronger patient privacy protections at a world health care conference.

Consumer Action now has a staff of twenty-six and an annual budget exceeding $3 million. Since 1971, it has grown from a small group of San Francisco volunteers to a national organization run by professionals.

Linda Sherry

See also: State and Local Consumer Advocacy Groups

Further Reading

Navarro, Mireya. 1986. "Consumer Action: Grass Roots to Big Time." *San Francisco Examiner* (June 18): B, 1+.

Weinstein, Henry. 1975. "Inside a Consumer Group." *New York Times* (February 1975):
III, 7.

Wilson, Gregory, and Elizabeth Brydoff. 1980. "Grass Roots Solutions: San Francisco Consumer Action." In Laura Nader, ed. *No Access to Law: Alternatives to the American Judicial System* (pp. 417–459). New York: Academic Press.

CONSUMER COOPERATIVES

A consumer cooperative is a business jointly owned and democratically controlled by consumers to provide goods or services on a not-for-profit basis. Consumers organize and join cooperatives to reduce prices, increase quality, increase
availability, and even strengthen community.

For many decades, the most active consumer cooperatives have been credit
unions, rural electric cooperatives, housing cooperatives, and food cooperatives.
However, cooperatives also provide services in other areas including telecommunications, health care, and education. Moreover, other organizations such as mutual
insurance companies, mutual savings banks, and health maintenance organizations share some characteristics of consumer cooperatives.

In the mid-nineteenth century, the Rochdale Society of Equitable Pioneers
developed the cooperative model that strongly influenced U.S. consumer co-ops.
In 1844, many weavers in Rochdale, England were fired and blacklisted by mill
owners after an unsuccessful weavers' strike. The same year, to reduce the cost of
food staples, they opened a cooperative store offering these staples. By 1855, the
store sold a variety of merchandise and offered shoemaking, tailoring, drapery,
and butchering services. The cooperative also operated a wholesale division to
supply other area cooperatives and a manufacturing society that owned cotton
and wool mills.

This cooperative model embodied two principles that continue to be the distinguishing characteristics of cooperative businesses. First, profits are divided
between the members in proportion to their purchases, not the amount they have
invested. Second, each member has one vote regardless of the amount of investment in or purchases from the cooperatives, so decisions are made democratically.

In the United States, the first cooperatives were established by working people.
The first consumer cooperative was a general store opened in Philadelphia in 1864
by the Union Cooperative Association No. 1. From 1874 to 1879, the Sovereigns
of Industry, a labor organization, developed cooperative stores in the Northeast.
Other nineteenth-century consumer cooperatives included a cooperative apartment building in New York City organized in 1882 by working people; a cooperative health care group, later called the French Hospital, organized by gold miners
in San Francisco in 1849; and the 146 branch stores opened by the Mormon Zion's
Cooperative Mercantile Institute between 1868 and 1880.

However, the cooperative movement did not establish itself until the first
decades of the twentieth century. This brief history of the movement will focus
on the four most prominent types of consumer cooperatives—credit unions and
rural electric, housing, a food co-ops—and two key organizations that supported

the movement—the Cooperative League of the USA (now NCBA–CLUSA) and the National Cooperative Bank.

Credit Unions

Credit unions are owned and controlled by consumers who are both members and owners. Members pool their savings, on which they earn interest or dividends, and these savings are the primary source of funds for loans made to members. Today, there are more than 7,000 credit unions, with about $1 trillion in assets, which serve nearly 100 million members. The largest, Navy Federal Credit Union, itself has $67 billion in assets and more than five million members.

Credit unions are organized under federal or state law to allow people with a "common bond"—place of employment, community where they live, or regular association such as a church or membership organization—to join together to save and borrow. The National Credit Union Administration (NCUA), an independent federal agency with a three-person board appointed by the president, regulates all federally chartered credit unions. NCUA also administers the National Credit Union Share Insurance Fund, which insures savings in credit unions up to $250,000 per member.

U.S. credit unions trace their roots to Germany, India, and Canada. In 1908, with the help of Canadian credit union pioneer Alphonse Desjardins, the first U.S. credit union was organized in the largely French-speaking parish of St. Mary's in Manchester, New Hampshire. The St. Mary's Cooperative Credit Association was chartered in April 1909.

The person most responsible for the birth of the U.S. credit union movement, however, was Edward A. Filene, a Boston department store magnate and progressive thinker, who on a 1907 world tour, learned about and was impressed by cooperative associations in India. In 1915, Filene started the Massachusetts Credit Union Association as an example that others might replicate. He also gave $1 million of his personal wealth to help build a national credit union system in the United States.

But credit union expansion did not begin until 1921, when Filene organized the Credit Union National Extension and hired attorney Roy F. Bergengren as its head. In the next decade, Bergengren, with the help of staff and volunteers, organized hundreds of credit unions, established state credit union leagues, and lobbied to obtain state credit union legislation. He also lobbied successfully for a national credit union act, which President Roosevelt signed into law in 1934. Two Democratic Texas lawmakers, Senator Morris Sheppard and Representative Wright Patman, championed this legislation.

In 1934, the Credit Union National Extension Bureau became the Credit Union National Association (CUNA). CUNA continues to be the primary trade association of U.S. credit unions, with offices in Madison, Wisconsin, and Washington, D.C. The National Association of Federal Credit Unions (NAFCU) was founded in 1967 to represent federally chartered credit unions before Congress and federal regulatory agencies.

In 1935, Filene loaned CUNA $25,000 to form what is now known as the CUNA Mutual Group to provide affordable life insurance and other related services to credit unions and their members. Today CUNA Mutual offers a broad array of financial services products, including individual and group life and health insurance, annuities and investments, retirement and financial planning, and private mortgage insurance and auto coverage. CUNA Mutual also provides nearly all fidelity bond coverage, and most property and casualty coverage, for credit unions themselves.

In recent years, credit unions have faced many challenges including adapting to rapid technological change in financial services, adapting to new financial services regulations established by Dodd–Frank reform legislation, resisting banks who have sought to eliminate the credit union tax exemption, and dealing with the desire of the leaders of some credit unions to demutualize and eventually become banks. Empowered by the political involvement of thousands of credit union leaders from all states, the movement has not only survived but continued to grow.

This growth was helped considerably by a 1982 federal regulation that allowed credit unions to expand membership beyond narrow "common bonds." Although this regulation was overturned by the U.S. Supreme Court in 1998, it was reaffirmed by congressional legislation approved later that year. Key to the success of this defense were the efforts of longtime credit union leader Larry Blanchard—who had held positions with CUNA and NAFCU as well as NCUA—to unite disparate elements of the credit union community through an ad hoc organization known as the Credit Union Campaign for Consumer Choice.

Rural Electric Cooperatives

Today, an estimated 42 million people in forty-seven states receive electric service from rural electric cooperatives. These "customers" belong to one of 840 distribution co-ops, who themselves are served by sixty-five generation and transmission cooperatives. The customers are also co-op members, with the right to vote on board members and other decisions made at the co-op's annual meeting.

City dwellers began receiving electric service as early as 1882, when Thomas Edison built the first central station electric system in lower Manhattan. But even as late as the mid-1930s, only one in ten rural homes enjoyed electric service. The principal barrier related to the economics of service. Rural homes were so much more dispersed than urban ones that it was much more costly to serve them. As a result, investor-owned utilities (IOU) had little interest in serving these rural homes. Even today, despite the expansion of urban areas into the service territories of rural electric cooperatives, these co-ops serve an average of only about seven consumers per mile of line, compared to an average of thirty-four consumers per mile of line for IOUs.

Faced with this IOU disinterest, the farmers and ranchers who formed the core of the rural population decided to take things into their own hands. Particularly in the 1930s and 1940s, neighbors banded together to establish electric service. Long familiar with cooperative organizations that were mainstays of farming, they used this nonprofit form of organization to create rural electric cooperatives.

Local co-op leaders were greatly assisted by Executive Order 7037 of the Emergency Relief Appropriation Act of 1936, which established the Rural Electrification Administration (REA). Among other support, the REA sent out field representatives to help solve the technical problems faced by new rural electric co-ops. Co-op leaders also benefited from the enactment of the Pace Act in 1944. Introduced by Representative Stephen Pace of Georgia, this law established the REA as a permanent agency and authorized the agency to make available development loans with an interest rate of two percent and an extended loan repayment period.

The Pace Act was approved in part because of the lobbying of the National Rural Electric Cooperative Association (NRECA), which had been established in 1942 in Washington, D.C. The first head of this association was Clyde T. Ellis, an Arkansas Congressman who had earlier done battle with the state's strong IOU. He served as NRECA's chief executive officer for twenty-five years.

Since then, rural electric cooperatives have faced many challenges. They include dealing with new environmental regulations, transmission issues, and the expansion of the suburbs into rural electric service territories, which increased tensions with IOUs. These investor-owned utilities and libertarian policymakers have also, from time to time, challenged subsidized interest rates and the preference that rural electric, and public power companies, have enjoyed to electricity generated by power marketing administrations such as Bonneville and the Tennessee Valley Authority.

Led by NRECA, rural electric cooperatives dealt effectively with these challenges. They had the advantage of a U.S. Senate in which many sparsely populated states elected the same number of senators as those more heavily populated states with large urban centers. They also were assisted by strategic alliances with other co-ops, farm groups, public power, labor unions, and even consumer groups. NRECA was a founding member of, and contributed the first executive director to, the Consumer Federation of America, a national consumer advocacy group.

Housing Cooperatives

There are more than 1.2 million housing cooperative units in the United States. Members of housing co-ops vote on all important co-op decisions, elect a board of directors, and contribute to the common expenses of the co-op. These co-ops differ from condominiums in several important ways, notably that co-op members own a share of their building, not the unit in which they reside, and also must approve all new condo owners.

In the United States, cooperative housing began in New York City with "home clubs," which were designed to provide high-income consumers the advantages of homeownership without all its responsibilities. But this housing did not flourish until after World War I. In 1918, the Finnish Home Building Association established a cooperative housing development in Brooklyn. With the passage of the New York Housing Act of 1927, which provided tax exemptions and condemnation permits, thirteen housing cooperatives were built.

By 1926, even though cooperative developments existed in sixteen cities—including Chicago, Detroit, Buffalo, San Francisco, and Philadelphia—half of all housing cooperatives were located in New York City. By the end of the Great Depression, though, many had gone bankrupt.

From 1945 to 1950, cooperative housing revived, spurred by the Emergency Price Control Act of 1942 that encouraged conversions from apartments to co-ops, by Section 216 of the Internal Revenue Code, and by some state governments which provided tax benefits. However, it was provisions of the 1950 Housing Act—providing insurance and subsidized mortgages—that was the main stimulus for the development of tens of thousands of new housing co-ops. In the same period, three housing cooperative organizations were formed—the National Association of Housing Cooperatives (NAHC) to promote housing co-ops, the Cooperative Housing Foundation (CHF) to undertake related research and education, and the Federation of New York Housing Cooperatives to stimulate consumer activities and joint co-op projects.

In the 1960s, the efforts of these organizations helped establish housing co-ops in thirty cities. Since then, most co-op housing development has taken one of three forms—for-profit conversions of upper-income housing in New York City, new major cooperatives built for senior citizens, and some cooperative development initiated by for-profit developers. Since its creation in 1978, the National Cooperative Bank greatly assisted this development by providing loans. The Tax Reform Act of 1986 also helped by establishing low-income housing tax credits.

Today, the housing co-op sector is relatively stable, in part because of the services and advocacy of groups such as the NAHC and the National Cooperative Bank. In Washington, D.C., these groups focus much of their effort on ensuring that new housing laws and regulations do not discriminate against co-op housing.

Food Cooperatives

Today, more than 350 retail food cooperatives are active in the United States, with a large majority being located in New England, the upper Midwest, and the west coast. These cooperatives feature open membership, democratic control, limited return on equity, net surplus belonging to user-owners, and cooperation among cooperatives.

Beyond these principles, the organization of food co-ops may vary greatly: Some co-ops operate stores that are open to the public and offer items nearly identical to those sold in for-profit grocery stores, whereas other co-ops sell only organically produced products exclusively to members. Some food co-ops are essentially buying clubs whose members pool resources to buy in bulk, but other co-ops operate retail stores. And some retail co-ops require that all members work in the store on a regular basis, whereas others rely exclusively on a paid staff.

As early as the late nineteenth century, consumer co-ops existed in the United States that sold food as one of many products. However, it was not until the 1930s, during Roosevelt's New Deal, that large food cooperatives were first organized. Among these were the Hanover Consumer Cooperative in Hanover, New Hampshire,

and the Hyde Park Cooperative Society of Chicago. So was the Greenbelt Cooperative in Greenbelt, Maryland, which by the early 1980s operated five supermarkets,
ten furniture stores, seven automobile service centers, and a pharmacy.

The 1960s and 1970s provided a particularly supportive environment for the
creation of food co-ops. There was a growing demand for organic and locally
grown food, increasing interest in noncorporate business forms, and an upsurge
in consumerism. By 1975, an estimated 700 retail cooperatives were in existence.
However, as enthusiasm for alternatives to large supermarket chains waned, so did
food co-ops. By 1980, the number had fallen to about 340.

Since then, the food cooperative movement has been relatively stable. The number of retail co-ops has fluctuated between about 350 and 400. In addition, several
thousand buying clubs continue to operate. One hundred and thirty-six of the
larger groups belong to the National Cooperative Grocers Association. These co-op
groups include 1.3 million consumer owners who purchase $1.5 billion of product
each year. NCGA promotes the institutional development of food co-ops through
services and advocacy.

Co-op Support Organizations

In 1916, the Cooperative League of America was founded to promote and support cooperatives. Six years later, it changed its name to the Cooperative League
of the USA (CLUSA). In 1985, the organization changed its name to the National
Cooperative Business Association (NCBA), maintaining CLUSA as the name of its
international development arm. In 2013, the group merged its names and became
known as NCBA–CLUSA. Initially intended to focus just on consumer cooperatives, by the mid-1940, the organization had expanded its membership to a broad
array of producer and consumer cooperatives providing farm supply, insurance,
health care, housing, credit, and electric services.

NCBA–CLUSA represents broad co-op interests before Congress and federal
agencies. It also supports cooperatives in the United States and overseas through
training, technical assistance, publications, and other programs. Since the early
1950s, it has worked closely with the U.S. Agency for International Development
to develop cooperatives in other countries.

One of the greatest accomplishments of the organization was its leadership of
efforts to establish the National Cooperative Bank (NCB). Stan Dreyer, the president of NCBA from 1967 to 1978, played a critical role in the 1978 congressional approval of the Bank Act establishing this new financial institution. In 1981,
amendments to this law were approved to privatize the bank.

The Bank Act provided initial capitalization of $184 million to the NCB. Espe-
cially during the bank presidency of Charles Snyder during the past two decades,
that amount grew significantly—to financial assets of nearly $2 billion and total
specialized lending, investments, and technical assistance of more than $4 billion.

With these assets, NCB has expanded its services to a full line of commercial
lending, mortgage banking, development, member finance, depository, and investment banking services to customers. These customers come from a broad range of

cooperative-related industries, including housing, consumer goods, natural foods, hardware and building supply, food, health care, retirement housing, employee ownership, credit and finance, telecommunications, child care, franchising, and manufacturing. Under the Bank Act, the NCB board of directors must make its best effort to ensure that at least 35 percent of its outstanding loans are to cooperatives whose members are predominantly low-income persons or to cooperatives that provide specialized goods, services, or facilities to serve the needs of these low-income persons.

Stephen Brobeck

See also: Consumer Federation of America

Further Reading

Childs, Marquis William. 1980. *Yesterday, Today and Tomorrow: The Farmer Takes a Hand.* Washington, DC: National Rural Electric Cooperative Association.
Lee, Janet. 1993. "Food Co-ops: What Hippies Did Right." *Business Week* (November 29): 146.
Nadeau, E. G., and David J. Thompson. 1996. *Cooperation Works: How People Are Using Cooperative Action to Rebuild Communities and Revitalize the Economy.* Rochester, MN: Lone Oak Press.
Siegler, Richard, and Herbert J. Levy. 1986. "Brief History of Cooperative Housing." *Cooperative Housing Journal* 12: 12–19.
Voorhis, Jerry. 1961. *American Cooperatives.* New York: Harper and Brothers.

CONSUMER EDUCATION ADVOCACY

Advocacy for consumer education has occurred for more than a century. But until the 1960s, most interest in consumer education and related activism came from academics, and their main focus was educational institutions. Between 1899 and 1908, an interdisciplinary group of scientists met in upstate New York to discuss consumer problems. In 1909, the American Home Economics Association began as an organized continuation of these conferences. In 1912, University of Chicago economist Wesley Mitchell wrote an influential essay, first published in the *American Economic Review*, that emphasized the importance of the management of consumption by individuals and the importance of the schools in providing related skills.

From the 1920s to the 1950s, academics wrote a number of consumer education textbooks, and consumer education programs and departments were established in some schools. In 1942, the National Association of Secondary School Principals began a five-year research project to strengthen consumer education in secondary schools. And in 1953, funding from Colston Warne of Consumers Union allowed researchers and educators to organize the Council of Consumer Information, which later changed its name to the American Council on Consumer Interests. The council's goal was to advance research and dissemination related to consumer information.

Yet it was not until the emergence of the modern consumer movement in the 1960s that interest in consumer education and a subset, financial education, grew among consumer advocates, government, and business. In 1962, President John

Kennedy proclaimed four consumer rights—the right to be heard, the right to know, the right to safety, and the right to choose. To this list, in 1975 President Gerald Ford added a fifth right, consumer education.

Almost ten years before, in 1967, the legislature in Illinois had become the first state to require that high school students receive instruction in consumer education, including but not limited to installment purchasing, budgeting, and comparison of prices. Cecil A. Partee, a freshman state senator, had submitted the consumer education bill to the Illinois General Assembly. The law was supported by business groups, consumer groups, and educators.

Legislation followed at the national level in 1968, when Congress passed Public Law 90-576 with a program titled "Consumer and Homemaking Education." This law authorized funding for all fifty states in support of home economics education. In 1972, Congress authorized spending of $80 million on citizenship aspects of consumer education in amendments to the Elementary and Secondary Act. Then in 1974, similar provisions were included in Public Law 93-380, which led to the establishment of the U.S. Office of Consumer Education (OCE), for which almost $19 million was appropriated during the six years of the program's existence. While remaining focused mainly on consumer education in schools, the OCE did recognize and try to support consumer education of adults through public and nonprofit organizations.

This community-based adult consumer education was already being undertaken by local Cooperative Extension Offices that were associated with land-grant colleges and that were supported by federal funding. The 1862 Morrill Act provided for the creation of land-grant colleges in each state to provide practical education to rural families that included home management. The 1914 Smith Lever Act established Cooperative Extension Offices that were associated with and utilized the research of the colleges, most of which were part of state universities. Although the Cooperative Extension program was part of the U.S. Department of Agriculture, with the growth of urban areas and a consumer marketplace, Cooperative Extension Offices began serving urban areas and paying greater attention to consumer education, especially in the decades after World War II.

In 1981, advocates for educating consumers both inside and outside of traditional classrooms came together from such organizations as the Consumer Federation of America (CFA), the National Consumers League, and the American Association of Retired Persons (now AARP) to try to preserve support for the Office of Consumer Education within the U.S. Department of Education. This effort led to the formation of the Coalition for Consumer Education ("National" was added two years later) under the leadership of James Boyle, CFA's government affairs director. In its first few years, the coalition, incorporated as a 501(c)(3) group, was led by educator and attorney, Judith Cohart.

The Elementary and Secondary Education Act of 1980 reallocated the money for consumer education from the federal level—forcing closure of the U.S. Office of Consumer Education—to the states through block grants. Twenty percent of the money was provided to state education agencies to be used at their discretion, whereas 80 percent was given directly to local education agencies. In response, the National Coalition for Consumer Education (NCCE) prioritized developing a diverse national network to strengthen and encourage consumer education in classrooms, businesses, government, and communities.

Although the NCCE succeeded in developing this network, the effort was not well funded and met with limited success. In California, for example, the state coordinator organized a small task force to monitor the block grant process, and this group submitted the names of three well-qualified individuals for the state's Consumer Education Advisory Committee. However, this recommendation was ignored by legislators, who made political appointments.

At the national level, the NCCE advocated for the development of a center that served the broad range of national interests in consumer education, including providing leadership and coordination of consumer education concerns, such as the study of inflation, taxation, employment, and individual and family financial management.

Toward this end, it testified before House and Senate committees in both 1982 and 1983. But by the late 1980s, coalition priorities had shifted from advocacy to education activities, especially a LifeSmarts competition among high schools. In 2000, the NCCE was merged into the National Consumers League, which continued and expanded the LifeSmarts program.

In the 1990s, dramatic changes in the financial services marketplace generated increasing interest in financial education, a large subset of consumer education. Banking deregulation spurred the development and aggressive marketing of increasingly complex and often risky products, especially credit cards and, later, adjustable rate and interest-only mortgages. In the same period, employers were abandoning traditional pension plans and replacing them with contributory plans, such as 401(k)s that required more individual initiative and knowledge. In response, consumer educators shifted their main focus to helping consumers participate in a changing financial services marketplace. They were encouraged to do so by financial institutions that often saw this education as an alternative to regulation.

The coordination of an effort to advocate for personal finance education in the schools through individual courses or integration into other disciplines, such as math and social studies, was spearheaded by the American Financial Services Association under the leadership of Randy Lively. The group that eventually became known as the Jump$tart Coalition for Personal Financial Literacy was initiated in 1995 and incorporated in 1997, when it hired its first executive director, Dara Duguay, and began its development of state coalitions. The group also prepared K–12 national standards for personal finance education and established a personal finance clearinghouse. At present, Jump$tart is led by Laura Levine and has 150 partner organizations and coordinates affiliates in forty-nine states.

Duguay encouraged and helped coordinate efforts by state affiliates to persuade state legislatures to approve financial education requirements. Since then, Jump$tart efforts have been instrumental in persuading many states to require or strengthen personal finance instruction. In four states—Missouri, Tennessee, Utah, and Virginia—these laws require students to take at least a one-semester personal finance course, and in twenty other states, the laws require personal finance instruction to be incorporated into other subject matter. To ensure that teachers in these states have the tools to implement these requirements, Jump$tart and its state affiliates have developed teacher training programs.

In addition, through the leadership of the National Endowment for Financial Education (NEFE), a Financial Literacy Day was established in the year 2000. When NEFE turned the program over to Jump$tart to coordinate, it was expanded to Youth Financial Literacy Month, which later was renamed Financial Capability Month. In 2003, resolutions in the U.S. House and Senate formally recognized April as Financial Literacy Month. For more than a decade, during this month, nonprofit, government, and corporate entities have organized activities to promote the value of financial literacy.

In this period, spurred by financial abuses and consumer problems, Congress held several hearings on financial education. Largely because of the leadership of Senator Paul Sarbanes (D-MD), the Fair and Accurate Credit Transactions Act that Congress passed in 2003, contained a section on financial education. It created a Financial Literacy and Education Commission (FLEC), chaired by the treasury secretary, which brought together nineteen government agencies that provide financial education. FLEC was required to develop a national financial education strategy, a financial education website, and a related hotline.

Even before the creation of FLEC, Treasury, the Federal Reserve Board, the Federal Deposit Insurance Corporation, and the Department of Labor considered financial education to be a priority and created related programs, such as the FDIC's "Money Smart" curriculum. They were joined recently by the Consumer Financial Protection Bureau, which was created by the Wall Street Consumer Reform and Protection Act (Dodd–Frank) of 2010. This law required the new agency to create an office of financial education. This office, relatively well-funded compared to the financial education programs of other federal agencies, is emerging as the federal leader of financial education efforts. A high priority of this office has been, through evaluation of existing financial education programs and testing of new models, to learn more about the effectiveness of these programs.

During the past decade, assessment and evaluation have also been priorities for two of the leading nonprofit organizations in financial education—NEFE and the FINRA Investor Education Foundation. NEFE, headed since 2005 by Ted Beck, has been supported by an endowment, created in 1997, from the sale of financial planning assets. The FINRA Foundation—a tax-exempt foundation established in 2004 and, since 2011, directed by Gerri Walsh—is a subsidiary of the Financial Industry Regulatory Authority (FINRA), a nonprofit, congressionally authorized regulator of securities firms. The foundation has been funded by cash contributions from FINRA and by some fines imposed on securities firms.

These attempts to evaluate financial education have been welcomed by many practitioners in the field, because past research shows that it is not clear which financial education programs and strategies are ineffective, somewhat effective, or highly effective. Skepticism about the value of traditional financial education has spurred efforts to create and support alternatives that incorporate elements of this education, such as default options (especially in employee retirement programs), social marketing (e.g., America Saves), counseling (credit and mortgage counselors), and coaching.

Judith N. Cohart

See also: Center for the Study of Services/Consumers' Checkbook; Consumers Union/Consumer Reports; Journalism

Further Reading

Bannister, Rosella. 1997. "Consumer Education." In Stephen Brobeck, ed., *Encyclopedia of the Consumer Movement*. Santa Barbara, CA: ABC-CLIO.

Braunstein, Sandra, and Carolyn Welch. 2002. "Financial Literacy: An Overview of Practice, Research, and Policy." *Federal Reserve Bulletin* (November): 445–457.

CONSUMER FEDERATION OF AMERICA

The Consumer Federation of America (CFA) was established in 1968 by national, state, and local pro-consumer groups to advocate the consumer interest before the U.S. Congress and federal regulatory agencies. In the last several decades, it has broadened its mission to include advocacy on state issues, assistance to other consumer groups, and the delivery of services directly to consumers. Its role helping to unify the consumer movement is epitomized by the diversity of its membership. Today, in 2014, although a majority of its 276 member organizations are national, state, or local consumer advocacy groups, the CFA membership also includes state and local protection agencies, public power groups, credit unions, rural electric cooperatives, housing cooperatives, cooperative extension offices, credit counseling agencies, social justice groups, trade unions, and AARP.

CFA was organized by reform-minded advocates during a period of change and social protest. Many of these advocates came from organizations established earlier in the century—Consumers Union, industrial labor unions, and rural electric cooperatives, among others—who viewed the late 1960s as a time when political conditions permitted the establishment of new consumer protections and agencies.

In 1964, representatives of several of these groups headquartered in Washington, D.C., began meeting informally and planning strategy to advance consumer legislation. A year later, these activists began organizing a national consumer forum. Held in April 1966, this Consumer Assembly was cosponsored by thirty national organizations representing workers, small farmers, consumer cooperatives, and women, as well as other consumers. At the meeting, White House Consumer Adviser Esther Peterson urged the creation of a federation of national, state, and local groups to press for consumer legislation.

These organizations formed a steering committee to plan the new federation. Leaders from Consumers Union, the Association of Massachusetts Consumers, the National Consumers League, the International Ladies Garment Workers Union, the AFL–CIO's Industrial Union Department, the Steelworkers Union, the Credit Union National Association, the Cooperative League of the U.S.A., and the National Rural Electric Cooperative Association (NRECA) were among those who worked the hardest to create the new organization. At the federation's first annual meeting, held in April 1968, fifty-six charter members elected board members and appointed NRECA staffer Erma Angevine as executive director.

In developing the new organization, its founders were challenged by the fact that the organization's primary function was consumer advocacy, but at the time, few consumer advocacy groups existed, and most of these groups were run by volunteers. Moreover, the federation's income depended heavily on contributions from trade unions and consumer cooperatives (as well as from Consumers Union). To ensure that consumer groups controlled CFA, the charter defined nonconsumer organizations such as labor unions as "supporting members" and limited them to two votes at the annual meeting. Consumer groups, including co-ops, could cast as many as twenty votes if they contributed at least $200 annually.

Representatives of CFA member organizations had the authority to elect board members and to determine the consumer policies of the organization, which they accomplished at annual meetings of the organization. Recommended policies were presented at these meetings by subcommittees for individual issues areas, such as food and housing, after these recommendations had been reviewed by the chairs of all the subcommittees. Mark Silbergeld, longtime head of the Washington, D.C., office of Consumers Union, chaired this full committee for several decades. His skill played an important role in resolving differences among CFA's diverse membership.

Erma Angevine served as executive director during an upsurge of consumer activism, most visibly that of Ralph Nader and his "Nader's Raiders." Before joining CFA, Angevine had worked for major cooperative organizations, including the Consumer Cooperative Association, the Cooperative League of the U.S.A., and NRECA, where her work included directing women's activities and serving as consumer lobbyist. Her twofold mission was to take the lead on numerous consumer issues at a time when she had to build the organization from scratch. By 1969, with the help of board members, Angevine had persuaded 140 groups to affiliate with the federation. Their contributions of nearly $100,000 a year allowed her to hire two staffers.

One of Angevine's greatest challenges was seeking to resolve differences among CFA members, especially those between relatively large trade unions and cooperative groups, which contributed most of the organization's income, and much smaller state and local consumer groups, which felt they were entitled to run the organization. This disagreement culminated in the withdrawal from the federation of eight state consumer groups, which then organized the Conference of Consumer Organizations (COCO).

At the same time Angevine was seeking to build the organization, she also took the lead on numerous policy issues. As the consumer movement's chief lobbyist, Angevine involved CFA in dozens of congressional issues, developing position papers and fact sheets, mobilizing CFA members, and communicating with members of Congress and their staffers. Working closely with other consumer advocates, with cooperative and union lobbyists, and with congressional leaders such as senators Philip Hart (D-MI), Warren Magnuson (D-WA), and Paul Douglas

(D-IL) and Representative Leonor Sullivan (D-MO), she helped win passage of key consumer legislation such as that dealing with truth in lending and truth in packaging.

At the state level, CFA coordinated opposition to the Uniform Consumer Credit Code, which had been strongly influenced by creditors. Angevine monitored the actions of individual states, recruited volunteer attorneys to analyze provisions of the code, and circulated these analyses widely through the country. When she retired from CFA in 1973, she left behind a federation with a solid organizational foundation and much credibility.

Carol Tucker Foreman succeeded Angevine as executive director. The daughter and granddaughter of Arkansas politicians, Foreman had worked on Capitol Hill, in the executive branch, and in the advocacy community (Planned Parenthood) before joining CFA. This experience and her own personal skills allowed her to heighten the influence of the federation.

In this period, CFA's annual income available to support advocacy ranged from about $150,000 to $200,000, which supported five core staffers. Because of the effectiveness of Foreman and her staff, CFA was taken seriously on Capitol Hill and widely quoted in the press. High priorities were fighting inflation in the energy and food areas, and seeking to establish a federal consumer protection agency and a consumer cooperative bank. To encourage the election of a pro-consumer Congress, CFA established a Political Action Committee (PAC) that endorsed, but that did not make financial contributions to, congressional candidates. (This PAC was permissible because CFA operated mainly as a 501(c)(4) nonprofit organization. It was discontinued in the early 1990s, and CFA began functioning solely as a tax-exempt 501(c)(3) nonprofit organization several years later.)

In 1977, Foreman was appointed assistant secretary in the U.S. Department of Agriculture (USDA) and was succeeded as CFA executive director by Kathleen O'Reilly. O'Reilly had practiced law, including helping draft the first federal no-fault insurance legislation. At CFA, O'Reilly was known for her forceful consumer advocacy, testifying more than 200 times before congressional and state legislative bodies. During her tenure as executive director, O'Reilly led successful congressional efforts to reduce sugar price supports and expand protections against credit discrimination. She also worked hard on the unsuccessful effort to create a federal consumer protection agency.

In early 1980, O'Reilly left CFA to run for Congress—she later headed the Wisconsin Citizen Utility Board (CUB) for many years—and was replaced by Stephen Brobeck, who has run the federation since then. Brobeck earned a PhD in American studies in the late 1960s, then taught at Case Western Reserve University throughout the 1970s. During this decade, he also proposed the creation of, and helped lead, a grassroots consumer organization, Cleveland Consumer Action. From 1976 to 1979, he served on the CFA board.

Brobeck's greatest contributions to CFA have been as a builder. He led the expansion of CFA's membership and greatly reduced member conflict, in part by working with policy committee chairman Silbergeld to reform the policy resolutions process. He proposed and helped create new organizations such as Advocates for Highway and Auto Safety, the Coalition against Insurance Fraud, the Tele-Consumer Hotline, and America Saves. He proposed, found initial funding for, and helped lead CFA campaigns on issues including consumer debt, motor vehicle fuel efficiency, consumer literacy, and discriminatory auto insurance practices.

Under Brobeck's leadership, CFA's budget increased from $200,000 to well over $3 million, with a substantial reserve fund, which allowed the staff to grow from four persons to twenty-five. Most CFA income now comes from national foundation grants, membership contributions, and conferences and forums supplemented by *cy près* court awards.

Brobeck's recruited energetic and talented staffers, most of whom had worked earlier for another public interest group. Three policy experts and leaders have been associated with CFA for more than a quarter-century: During this period, research director Mark Cooper, a Yale PhD who has testified hundreds of times in federal and state legislative and regulatory hearings, has been a leading energy and communications expert in the consumer movement. Public affairs director Jack Gillis, who managed CFA's press relations and for a decade served concurrently as the consumer correspondent for the *Today Show*, was CFA's automobile expert as well as author of dozens of annual editions of *The Car Book*. Director of investor protection Barbara Roper has been the consumer movement's most influential and visible leader on investment issues.

Other influential policy experts and advocates were active at CFA for at least a decade. Attorney and legislative director Gene Kimmelman (from Public Citizen) has been the consumer movement's most influential communications lobbyist. Legislative director Travis Plunkett (from AARP and, before that, NYPIRG), who concentrated on financial services issues, often was cited by *The Hill* as one of the top lobbyists in Washington. Attorney and product safety director Mary Ellen Fise (from the National Consumers League) was the chief consumer advocate monitoring and communicating with the Consumer Product Safety Commission (CPSC). As product safety director, attorney Rachel Weintraub (from U.S. PIRG) succeeded Fise as the lead consumer advocate before the CPSC and recently succeeded Plunkett as CFA's legislative director. Financial services director Jean Ann Fox (from the Virginia Citizens Consumer Council), who built a nationwide network of more than 400 advocates working on high-cost lending issues, was a national and state leader on these issues. Chris Waldrop, who directs CFA's Food Policy Institute, is one of the most active and influential food safety advocates in Washington, D.C. Consumer protection director Susan Grant (from the National Consumers League) has been one of the consumer movement's leading consumer protection and privacy advocates.

Brobeck also recruited several persons who had held prominent government positions: Carol Tucker Foreman, after her service at USDA and work as an independent lobbyist, rejoined CFA to serve as senior fellow and director of the organization's new Food Policy Institute, where she continued to be one of the nation's most influential food safety advocates. J. Robert Hunter, after running the National Insurance Consumer Organization (NICO) for many years and then serving as Texas insurance commissioner, folded NICO into CFA and continued to be the nation's leading consumer insurance advocate as CFA's director of insurance. For the decade after he retired from the U.S. Senate in 1994, consumer hero Howard Metzenbaum lobbied his former Senate colleagues as honorary chairman of the federation. In 2008, Barry Zigas, who had served many years as senior vice president in charge of low-income housing at Fannie Mae, became CFA's housing and housing finance leader.

During Brobeck's tenure as executive director, two people played key roles helping him run the organization in their position as associate director—during the 1980s and 1990s Ann Lower, an energy expert who had served as Congressman Bob Eckhardt's chief of staff, and since then Nancy Register, who earlier had helped run national and local nonprofit organizations. Register also worked closely with Brobeck and Cleveland leaders to develop America Saves, a campaign launched in 2001 to help low- and moderate-income Americans save more effectively. For the past decade, she has directed this effort, which has organized nearly a hundred local savings campaigns, recruited more than 1,500 organizations to participate in annual America Saves Weeks, persuaded top Pentagon brass to support Military Saves, and convinced more than 400,000 Americans to develop a specific savings goal and plan to achieve that goal.

Lower and Register also effectively functioned as chief financial officer for CFA as well as supporting membership functions such as the state and local grants program, which was funded by Consumers Union. Also important in this area has been longtime staffer Mel Hall-Crawford, energy efficiency project director, who also led CFA's membership recruitment. They have played key roles in the evolution of CFA as an increasingly diverse organization that helps unite all types of organizations that are part of a broad consumer movement. CFA's annual Consumer Assembly, annual membership meeting, policy resolutions process, annual issue conferences, newsletter, forums, briefings, and organizational assistance including grants have helped build this unity.

During the past three decades, CFA's mission and greatest contributions have related to public policy. In the 1980s, CFA advocates devoted greatest attention to addressing, and frequently opposing, proposals related to deregulation. CFA and allied groups worked with congressional allies to thwart the Reagan administration's effort to shut down the CPSC and FTC's Bureau of Competition. Within the consumer movement, CFA was a leader in seeking stronger safety and soundness safeguards in congressional legislation that responded to the savings-and-loan crisis. Throughout the decade, CFA also led consumer movement efforts to deal with telephone deregulation and, early in the next decade, was the lead consumer advocate in persuading Congress to reregulate cable television rates. Also in the 1990s, CFA played roles in convincing Congress to require savings account and home equity loan disclosures and protections.

During the Clinton administration, Congress did little to help consumers. But during the George W. Bush administration, which followed, a new wave of congressional consumer reform began to build, cresting in 2010. CFA provided consumer leadership in passage of all the following laws: the 2002 Public Company Accounting and Reform Act of 2002 (Sarbanes–Oxley), which significantly strengthened auditing standards for publicly held companies; the 2007 Military Lending Act, which, among other reforms, capped payday and car title loans at 36 percent; the 2007 Energy Independence and Security Act, which required increases in the average fuel economy of new cars and light trucks to 35 miles per gallon by 2017; the 2008 Consumer Product Safety Improvement Act, which significantly increased the budget of the CPSC and gave it new responsibilities and authority to advance product safety; the 2009 Credit CARD Act, which prohibited numerous industry practices that had greatly expanded interest and fee income; the Food Safety and Modernization Act of 2010, which gave the Food and Drug Administration (FDA) expanded responsibility and authority to regulate food safety; and the Wall Street Reform and Consumer Protection Act of 2010 (Dodd–Frank), which included numerous new financial services protections and created the Consumer Financial Protection Bureau to serve as a "cop on the beat" of the financial services marketplace.

Leadership on these issues included preparing and releasing consumer surveys and consumer impact studies, organizing consumer coalitions, recruiting grass-roots support, and communicating with Congress through testimony, letters, emails, and conversations. Evidence of this leadership can be seen in the frequency of congressional testimony and policy-related media citations. From the 1970s to the mid-2000s, according to research for a university lecture, CFA and Consumer Union were invited to give congressional testimony far more frequently than any other consumer groups. Moreover, according to a 2006 study published in the *Quarterly Journal of Economics*, during the 1990s, among think tanks and policy groups, CFA was the consumer group most frequently cited by the media, as well as sixteenth most cited among all organizations.

During the past three decades, CFA advocates devoted even more attention to the work of federal regulatory agencies than to the work of Congress—notably, the CPSC, FDA, USDA, Federal Trade Commission, National Highway Traffic Safety Administration, Environmental Protection Agency, Federal Communications Commission, Federal Reserve Board, Federal Deposit Insurance Corporation, Office of the Comptroller of the Currency, Securities and Exchange Commission, Commodity Futures Trading Commission, and, recently, Federal Housing Administration. Through petitions, comments, research, coalitions, and individual communications with agency leaders, CFA has influenced dozens of regulations affecting consumers.

During the same period, CFA has frequently intervened at the state level, particularly when states, not the federal government, have major responsibility for overseeing and regulating consumer products and services. That is the case for insurance, nontraditional financial services such as check cashing and small loans, electricity and telephone services, and residential real estate brokerage. CFA's work in these areas has included organizing state coalitions, preparing and releasing research, filing comments, and communicating with individual regulators. CFA's achievements include helping persuade many states to preserve existing small loan protections or create new ones, improving real estate consumer disclosures and ending the subagency system, and helping convince many public service commissions to lower utility rates, or restrain increases, especially those borne by low-income consumers.

Stephen Brobeck

See also: Conference of Consumer Organizations; Consumer Cooperatives; Consumers Union/Consumer Reports; Labor Movement; Peterson, Esther; State and Local Consumer Advocacy Groups

Further Reading

Angevine, Erma. 1982. "Lobbying and Consumer Federation of America." In Erma Angevine, ed., *Consumer Activists: They Made a Difference* (pp. 331–342). Mount Vernon, NY: Consumers Union Foundation.

Brobeck, Stephen. 2009. Lecture given at the University of Utah on the consumer's right to be heard (March 24).

Cerra, Frances. 1976. "A Lobbyist for Consumers." *New York Times* (November 31): III-7.

Groseclose, Tim, and Jeffrey Milyo. 2005. "A Measure of Media Bias." *Quarterly Journal of Economics* 120, no. 4: 1191+.

Mirow, Deena. 1988. "Brobeck's Battle for Consumers Moves to Higher Level." *Plain Dealer* (September 8): C-4.

Schorr, Burt. 1975. "Winning Friends: When Carol Foreman Talks Consumerism, Congressman Listen." *Wall Street Journal* (April 9): 1+.

Swanston, Walterene. 1972. "Consumer Federation Waging Spirited Battle for Survival." *National Journal* 4 (July 8): 1,126–1,136.

CONSUMER FINANCIAL PROTECTION BUREAU

See Americans for Financial Reform; Legislative Advocacy

CONSUMER JOURNALISM

See Journalism

CONSUMER LEAGUES

The consumer league concept originated in England, spreading from there to the United States and to several European nations. In the United States, the leagues developed along with other social justice groups as part of the Progressive reform movement of the late nineteenth century.

In 1891, Josephine Shaw Lowell founded the New York City Consumers League to improve working conditions in the city's retail stores. League members believed that consumers had the ability and responsibility to eliminate child labor, reduce excessive hours of work, increase low wages, and improve working conditions.

The New York league initiated a Consumer White Label granted to manufacturers of cotton garments who met specified labor standards; it urged consumers to buy only White Label goods. After the Massachusetts Consumers League persuaded Boston's Filene's store to sell White Label cotton, conditions in factories improved.

Other consumer leagues soon were organized in Chicago and Philadelphia. These two leagues, along with the New York City and Massachusetts leagues and others committed to social justice, organized and chartered the National Consumers League (NCL) in 1899 and hired Florence Kelley as its chief executive officer. Kelley, recognizing the need for a constituency, crisscrossed the nation organizing leagues among college students and in church, women's, and community groups. In five years, she had inspired the creation of sixty-four branches in twenty states. The number of branches in the United States later peaked at ninety.

The first international conference of consumer leagues was held in Geneva, Switzerland, in 1908. The NCL sent a delegation. By 1913, consumer leagues had been organized in England, France, Holland, Germany, Belgium, Switzerland, and the United States. Only those in the United States and Switzerland survived World War I.

Kelley depended on leagues around the country for assistance in persuading congressmen to vote for consumer legislation. She, in turn, helped the leagues draft state legislation and work for better state consumer and workers laws. She drafted a model minimum wage law for the Massachusetts Consumers League. In 1912, Massachusetts enacted the first U.S. minimum wage law.

The Oregon Consumers League persuaded its state legislature to limit the workday for women to ten hours. When the law was challenged and was appealed to the U.S. Supreme Court, Kelley secured Louis D. Brandeis of Boston to defend its constitutionality. Brandeis prepared a defense based on facts drawn from ninety reports from special committees in Europe and the United States concerning squalid working conditions. This defense was the first of the "Brandeis Briefs," for which he became famous. The Supreme Court unanimously held Oregon's law constitutional.

Other leagues called on the NCL for help in resolving state issues. Brandeis continued to represent the league in many of these battles, always donating his time, until he was named to the Supreme Court.

The New Jersey Consumers League is best known for its investigation, in the early 1920s, of working conditions of girls who painted watch dials at the U.S. Radium Corporation. They visited homes of the girls, finding that eight were seriously ill and others had died. They visited the dentist who had treated the girls and learned they had symptoms of "phossy jaw," a disease caused by the use of phosphorus in manufacturing matches.

The league asked Kelley for assistance. She and Dr. Alice Hamilton obtained a report conclusively linking the adverse health effects to the handling of radioactive substances without proper protection. With this information, the NCL and the New Jersey Consumers League initiated a campaign to get radium mesothorium necrosis included in the list of compensable diseases under workman's compensation. New Jersey's governor signed the new provision into law in March 1926.

In the early 1930s, Elizabeth Magee, an Ohio Consumers League official, served as executive secretary of the state's Commission on Unemployment Insurance. She directed hearings and investigations, then wrote a report that led to passage of Ohio's 1935 law creating an unemployment insurance system.

League members included notable men and women who were dedicated to social reform, including Charles A. Beard, Sidney Hillman, Frances Perkins, Henry

Morgenthau Jr., Adolph A. Berle Jr., and Eleanor Roosevelt, as well as Florence Kelley. Many of them lived and worked in Chicago's Hull House or New York's Henry Street Settlement.

After Kelley's death in February 1932, NCL board leaders John R. Commons, a University of Wisconsin economics professor, and Nicholas Kelley, an economist who was Kelley's son, selected Lucy Randolph Mason to run the organization.

President Franklin Roosevelt's 1933 National Recovery Administration (NRA) was welcomed by consumer leagues. But when the NRA refused to accept the recommendations of its Consumer Advisory Board on industrywide codes prescribing maximum hours, minimum wages, and collective bargaining as well as abolishing child labor, the New York Consumers League organized a chain of local consumers' councils throughout the country to press the NRA. However, when the Supreme Court declared the NRA unconstitutional, many of these councils became inactive.

Despite the role played by league leaders in the New Deal, during this period many leagues were shut down. Some fell victim to lack of money or effective leadership. But the main reason many leagues did not survive is that their central mission of fighting for improved working conditions for women and children was taken over by the labor movement.

Several state leagues and the NCL survived and were revived in the 1960s and 1970s, but with more of a traditional consumer focus. Today, while NCL continues as an active national organization, the state leagues have virtually disappeared.

Erma B. Angevine

See also: National Consumers League; State and Local Consumer Advocacy Groups

Further Reading

Athey, Louis Lee. 1965. *The Consumers' Leagues and Social Reform, 1890–1923.* PhD dissertation, University of Delaware.

Harrison, Dennis Irven. 1975. *The Consumers' League of Ohio: Women and Reform, 1909–1937.* PhD dissertation, Case Western Reserve University.

Keyserling, Mary Dublin. 1982. "The First National Consumers Organization: The National Consumers League." In Erma Angevine, ed. *Consumer Activists: They Made a Difference* (pp. 343–360). Mount Vernon, NY: Consumers Union Foundation.

CONSUMER REPORTS

See Consumers Union/Consumer Reports

CONSUMER REPRESENTATION IN GOVERNMENT AGENCIES

In large part because consumers are not well organized, their representation on government executive branch decision making bodies has been spotty. Nevertheless, for many decades, there have been efforts at both federal and state government levels to increase this representation.

Federal Level

Efforts to bring about consumer or public representation on governmental decision making bodies date to the New Deal of the 1930s. The National Recovery Administration (NRA) included a Consumer Advisory Board in its organizational structure. The Agricultural Adjustment Administration (AAA) had a Consumer Council. To provide a consumer viewpoint on the revitalization of the nation's coal industry, a Bituminous Coal Consumer Counsel was established. In 1940, the National Defense Administration's (NDA) seven-member advisory commission included one commissioner appointed to represent consumer concerns. However, representatives to these agencies were not effective because they had no organized constituencies to back them up.

After World War II, the few existing consumer organizations continued to urge government to recognize the consumer interest. They achieved their first major success in 1962 when President John Kennedy sent Congress a Message on Consumer Interests, which contained a basic proclamation of consumer rights—to safety, to be informed, to choose, and to be heard.

That same year, under the Council of Economic Advisers (CEA), a Consumer Advisory Council (CAC) was appointed. Composed mainly of representatives of consumer organizations and their allies, the council's mandate was to advise the federal government on issues of broad economic policy, on government programs protecting consumer needs, and on improvement in the flow of consumer research to the public as well as to provide interested individuals and organizations a voice on these issues.

The Kennedy consumer council was the first such group appointed during relatively stable times. The council had not been in operation long, however, before it became obvious that CEA and CAC were not comfortable bedfellows. There were conflicts between consumer goals and overall economic policy. For the most part, the CEA did not take the CAC's goal and recommendations seriously. And the CAC was considered by some to be an unnecessary irritant to the business community. For their part, CAC members complained that the consumer interest was not receiving sufficient exposure, and they requested a more independent status.

Eager to divest himself of the responsibility for "servicing" the CAC, CEA Chairman Walter Heller agreed that the council could better serve its purpose if it were independent of the CEA. In February 1964, President Lyndon Johnson established by executive order the President's Committee on Consumer Interests. This new committee was to include not only members of the Consumer Advisory Council but also representatives of the major federal agencies with consumer responsibilities. Johnson also established the Office of Special Assistant to the President for Consumer Affairs and appointed a special assistant, Esther Peterson, as chair of the committee. In the administrations of presidents Ronald Reagan and George Bush, the office was increasingly marginalized, and today it no longer exists.

By the 1970s, consumer organizations began to fight for direct consumer representation in governmental decision making. Under the 1975 Magnuson–Moss Warranty–Federal Trade Commission Improvement Act, Congress substantially expanded consumer representation in this decision making and greatly increased the FTC's consumer protection responsibilities. Because many legislators felt it important to improve opportunities for the participation of diverse, legitimate groups in rulemaking, Congress appropriated $500,000 (later increased to $750,000) for a public intervenor program to reimburse the expenses not only of consumer representatives, but also of small business concerns.

The FTC program became the precedent for more than ten public participation programs in different agencies. Participants, however, could receive funding only if they could not afford to participate without reimbursement of expenses, if they had no financial interest in the outcome of issues being considered, and if they provided a viewpoint that would not otherwise be represented by agency staff or other witnesses.

Also in the 1970s, the Food and Drug Administration (FDA) provided consumer participation on the technical advisory panels that make recommendations to the agency about the approval of new drugs and devices. In this program, a consortium of consumer organizations screened the resumes of candidates for the consumer representative positions.

In the 1980s, federal public representation programs lost most of their funding, because the Reagan administration did not support them. Without government funds, consumer activist organizations usually were not able to afford participating in the programs.

Consumer groups, however, have continued, to the present day, to participate in less time-consuming advisory committees to federal agencies. Governed by the Federal Advisory Committee Act of 1972, the committees focused on health and safety issues have been most likely to have consumer participation. For example, the FDA maintains about fifty advisory committees on scientific, technical, and policy matters. Consumer representatives are expected to be affiliated with credible consumer or community-based organizations and to be able to analyze scientific data, understand research design, understand relationships between risks and benefits, and evaluate the safety and efficacy of products under review.

State Level

The history of public representation on state government decision making bodies differs from that at the federal level. Much state activity was generated by state laws requiring the appointment of citizen representatives on professional and occupational licensing boards. By the early 1990s, thousands of citizen representatives had been appointed to these boards. In California, for example, laws require all state licensing boards, except those regulating health care professionals, to contain a majority of public members.

The impetus for appointing public members came in the late 1960s in the wake of criticism that professional licensing boards were using their powers to limit competition. Restrictions on entry limited the supply of practitioners, often resulting in higher costs to consumers. Also, restrictions on advertising deprived consumers of information that could enable them to make smarter purchase decisions. Lack of enforcement and failure to discipline incompetent or unethical practitioners indicated that some boards were failing to fulfill their public protection mandate.

Some believed that these problems could be mitigated by ending exclusive self-regulation and by appointing public members to the boards to act as watchdogs and advocates of the public interest. Those supporting adding public members assumed that governors and their appointment secretaries would identify and place appropriate consumer representatives. However, little attention was paid to questions about how public members could be found, their qualifications, their roles, and their performance. Early laws defined public members solely in terms of conflict of interest, which excluded individuals with a financial stake in board decisions from public membership.

Since consumer groups often did not propose names of people to fill the new public member lists, governors turned to patronage lists. Over the years, many public members have been conscientious and played meaningful roles. Many others, however, never developed an interest in their boards, whereas others, having an interest but insufficient knowledge, were overwhelmed and often coopted by professional members with much greater expertise.

Recent evaluations of the states' experience with public representation have focused on three problem areas—weakness in identification and selection of candidates, inadequate definition of their roles and goals, and insufficient training and ongoing support. Some efforts have been made to address these areas. The Centers for Medicare and Medicaid Services Quality Improvement Organization Handbook specifies that Medicare QIOs should look for representatives to serve on their boards of directors who have an advocacy track record, especially in healthcare, who have knowledge of Medicare and advocacy organizations for Medicare beneficiaries, who are willing to develop ongoing relations with appropriate constituency groups, and who have "boardsmanship" experience on nonprofit or government bodies.

Regarding improved training and ongoing support for public members, Consumers Union has created a network of individuals who have been appointed as public members on some state boards that license physicians or who have expressed interest in receiving such an appointment. Citizen Advocacy Center (CAC), based in Washington, D.C., was created as a nonpartisan 501(3)(c) support program for public members serving on state health professional licensing boards and on the boards of directors of health certification, accreditation, and specialty organizations.

In recent years, there has been a growing movement to move beyond the appointment of a single public member to these boards. In California, for example, the overall percentage of public members of that state's health licensing boards has grown to about 44 percent. In 2005, the Schwarzenegger administration called for public member majorities on a number of health care licensing boards, including the medical board. In a number of other states, public members make up from 25 percent to 33 percent of total board membership.

David A. Swankin

See also: State Utility Advocacy

Further Reading

Citizen Advocacy Center. 1995. *Public Representation on Health Care Regulatory, Governing, and Oversight Bodies: Strategies for Success.* Washington, DC.

Friedman, Robert S. 1978. "Representation in Regulatory Decision Making: Scientific, Industrial, and Consumer Inputs to the F.D.A." *Public Administration Review* (May/June): 205–214.

Mayer, Robert N., and Debra Scammon. 1983. "Intervenor Funding at the FTC: Biopsy or Autopsy." *Policy Studies Review* 2 (February): 506–515.

CONSUMER WATCHDOG

Consumer Watchdog is a nonprofit advocacy organization that has focused most of its attention on protecting consumer rights. Since its establishment in 1985, it has been most active and influential in California but now maintains offices in Washington, D.C., and in Santa Monica, California. The organization is known for its investigative reports, creative tactics, and initiative campaigns.

Consumer Watchdog was organized by attorney Harvey Rosenfield. After Rosenfield worked for Public Citizen Congress Watch on energy issues for two years, in 1981 Ralph Nader asked him to help organize the California Public Interest Group (CALPIRG). In 1985, after working on utility and campaign issues as CALPIRG's program director, Rosenfield left the organization and established Consumer Watchdog.

Over the decades, Consumer Watchdog has worked on a broad array of consumer issues in the areas of energy, health care, telecommunications, and digital privacy, but it is best known for its advocacy on insurance issues. In 1986, the insurance industry sponsored a ballot initiative, Proposition 51, to limit damage claims on lawsuits, claiming that such restrictions would lower insurance rates in California. Although the measure was approved, Rosenfield made insurance reform his major focus. When proposed reforms were rejected by the legislature, he drafted an initiative petition to regulate California property and casualty insurance companies.

Proposition 103 remains today the most comprehensive and far-reaching set of reforms affecting property and casualty companies. Among other measures, it includes a rate rollback, greater emphasis on driving factors such as accidents and mileage in rate-setting, repeal of the industry's antitrust exemption, support for consumer interventions, and an elected state insurance commissioner. Despite vigorous opposition by insurers who massively outspent supporters of Proposition 103, aided by support from Nader, the measure won 51 percent of the vote. Refusing to admit defeat, insurers filed numerous lawsuits against the new law, but in 1994 the courts ruled that virtually all provisions of the law were constitutional, and it went fully into effect. Since then, according to an analysis by the Consumer Federation of America, it has saved California consumers more than $100 billion.

Right up until the present, Consumer Watchdog has fought to preserve the consumer rights and protections of Proposition 103. In 2010 and 2012, it led successful opposition to measures sponsored by Mercury Insurance Group that would have allowed automobile insurers to charge drivers more for having a break in their coverage, even when they did not own a car. And it has worked successfully to oppose tort reforms backed by insurers and health care providers.

Consumer Watchdog has also taken leadership on health insurance and health care issues. In 1994, the group placed a patients' bill of rights measure on the California ballot. Though the proposal was defeated, four years later the state legislature extended rights to HMO patients. In 2004, the organization chartered two private trains to take seniors to Canada to buy cheaper prescription medication. In 2009, with the City of Los Angeles, the group launched a citywide program that provided discounts on all medications. In 2014, Consumer Watchdog is sponsoring one ballot initiative to require health insurance companies to get approval for rate increases and a second ballot initiative to identify drug and alcohol abuse by physicians.

The group's work has extended to energy issues. In 1998, Consumer Watchdog sponsored Proposition 9 to block parts of utility deregulation laws passed by the state legislature two years earlier. After utilities spent tens of millions of dollars in opposition to the measure, it was defeated. But during the 2000–2001 California electricity crisis, a proposed bailout of the three major utilities, opposed by Consumer Watchdog, was defeated by the legislature.

Much of the organization's recent work has focused on consumer privacy issues. In 2002, Consumer Watchdog lobbied unsuccessfully for California legislation that would require consumer approval before financial services companies could share personal information with other companies. After the group published the partial Social Security numbers of opposing legislators, and E-Loan mounted a signature-gathering campaign, the legislature passed strong financial privacy legislation that was signed into law by the governor.

In 2008, Consumer Watchdog launched Inside Google, a project exposing hidden consumer privacy invasions by Google and other major digital providers. To date, this initiative has proposed a "do not track" right for consumers online, fought a Google attempt to corner the online market for "orphan books," instigated national and international antitrust investigations of the company, and filed complaints about Google's privacy violations that resulted in a $25 million fine levied by the Federal Trade Commission.

Consumer Watchdog is a 501(c)(3) nonprofit organization overseen by a five-member board of directors. Its 501(c)(4) affiliate, Consumer Watchdog Campaign, takes the lead on initiative petition efforts. In recent years, its annual budget of several million dollars has been supported by foundation grants, individual donations, intervenor funding, and the proceeds of legal actions.

Since the establishment of Consumer Watchdog, the organization has benefited from the leadership of Rosenfield, who now serves as its outside counsel. He has received much assistance from Jamie Court, currently the organization's president, who has written several books exposing problems and explaining reform strategies, as well as leading reform campaigns himself. The organization's current executive director is Carmen Balber, who earlier directed Consumer Watchdog's Washington, D.C., office after working for the Colorado Public Interest Research Group (CoPIRG).

Stephen Brobeck

See also: Insurance Advocacy; State and Local Consumer Advocacy Groups

Further Reading

Court, Jamie. 2010. *The Progressive's Guide to Raising Hell: How to Win Grassroots Campaigns, Pass Ballot Box Laws, and Get the Change We Voted For.* White River Junction, VT: Chelsea Green Publishing.

Kang, Cecilia. 2010. "Consumer Watchdog Targets Google." *Washington Post* (September 22).

Muir, Frederick. 1988. "Rosenfield: Hero to Some, Troublemaker to Others." *Los Angeles Times* (September 22).

CONSUMERS FOR AUTO RELIABILITY AND SAFETY

Consumers for Auto Reliability and Safety (CARS) is a nonprofit organization that seeks to improve the quality of motor vehicles and related services used by consumers. Though based in California, it has strongly influenced consumer protections in many states and has also had an effect on federal policies.

The success of CARS mainly reflects the dedication, persistence, and political skills of its leader, Rosemary Shahan. The origin of her interest in establishing new consumer protections for automobile purchases was her own personal experience with a dealer who kept her VW for repairs for more than three months in 1979. While Shahan picketed the dealer in protest, she was contacted by many other lemon owners who related their own automotive complaints. When she researched the law, she found that although manufacturers were required to buy back new cars with defects after the failure of a "reasonable" number of repair attempts, there was no benchmark for deciding what was reasonable.

Shahan then decided that resolving her own individual problem was not enough; she needed to persuade the California legislature to approve a "lemon law" that gave greater consumer protections to car buyers. She promoted this reform by handing out leaflets, giving news interviews, and communicating with legislators, who convened a hearing in San Diego where Shahan and others testified, including a Ford representative who opined that a reasonable number of repair attempts was thirty.

When the car dealer settled her complaint, Shahan used the funds to create the nonprofit Motor Voters organization. After three years of testifying, letter-writing, and other advocacy, Motor Voters and allies, including Assemblywoman Sally Tanner, persuaded the California legislature to approve legislation in 1982. This new law, and all the attention it received, including mention in a nationally syndicated humor column by Erma Bombeck, interested advocates and legislators in other states in pushing for their own lemon laws.

Connecticut lawmaker John Woodcock successfully championed one of the first of these laws, and in the next several years, many other states passed their own. Today, all fifty states have some form of lemon law to protect new car buyers. These laws have played an important role in compelling auto manufacturers to invest billions of dollars in improving the quality of their products, upgrading diagnostic equipment, training automotive technicians, building repair parts and distribution centers, and repurchasing seriously faulty automobiles.

Since its inception, the 501(c)(3) Motor Voters and its 1996 spinoff, the 501(c)(4) Consumers for Auto Reliability and Safety, which can lobby much more freely, have been leaders in improving auto safety and reliability, protecting car buyers' rights, and making new vehicles more affordable. Working on both state and national levels, CARS has played an important role in establishing new consumer protections and opposing efforts to weaken existing protections. These efforts included requiring manufacturers to install airbags and also to provide seat belt height-adjusters to protect belted children. They also included successful opposition to a federal law that would have limited the effectiveness of state lemon laws.

CARS has also engaged in successful litigation, most notably in a lawsuit against the Bush administration's Department of Justice. A court ruled that the administration was required to develop and issue rules requiring that automobile insurers report total loss vehicles to the National Motor Vehicle title Information System, thereby helping reduce frauds involving hazardous vehicles severely damaged in wrecks or floods.

For decades, Motor Voters and CARS operated on shoestring budgets and depended heavily on volunteers. While grants from the California Consumer Protection Foundation, Consumers Union, and the Consumer Federation of America helped, it was not until CARS had been approved by the courts as a recipient of *cy près* awards resulting from class action lawsuits on automobile-related issues, that the organization developed a more stable financial base.

Although Shahan remains the force behind CARS, she has been assisted by many other consumer advocates, especially Sue Woods from CALPIRG, Lucinda Sikes from Public Citizen, and Consumer Action's Cher McIntyre. Sikes and McIntyre serve on the CARS Board of Directors.

Currently, CARS is spearheading a campaign to enact federal legislation authored by U.S. Senators Schumer (D-NY), Boxer (D-CA), and McCaskill (D-MO) that would prohibit rental car companies from renting vehicles that are under a safety recall. The organization is represented in Washington, D.C., by Pamela Gilbert, a former Public Citizen advocate, former top official in the Consumer Product Safety Commission, and former Motor Voters board member. CARS is working closely with Cally Houck, the mother of two young daughters, aged 20 and 24, who were killed in a recalled Enterprise rental car.

CARS is also working to end mandatory predispute arbitration for car buyers (and other consumers and workers), severely limiting their access to judicial remedies. Its video, written and produced by Shahan and former Fox TV reporter John Mattes, features an aggrieved consumer who has been waiting for years for an arbitration hearing. It has received well over 1 million views on YouTube.

Rosemary Shahan, Stephen Brobeck

See also: Complaint Resolution; Motor Vehicle Safety Advocacy; State and Local Consumer Advocacy Groups

Further Reading

Bensinger, Ken. 2012. "Auto Safety Activist Rosemary Shahan Turns Lemons Into Legislation." *Los Angeles Times* (April 1).
"Used Car Nightmare." Video. www.carconsumer.org.

CONSUMERS INTERNATIONAL

Consumers International is the principal coordinating body of the international consumer movement. At the end of 2012, it had 240 members from 120 countries around the world. It began in 1960 as the International Organization of Consumers Unions (IOCU). At that point it was very much the product of the consumer testing bodies set up in America in the 1930s and in western Europe in the 1950s, but it soon began to defend the interests of the poor and the disadvantaged as it responded to the interests of consumer organizations across Asia, Africa, and Latin America. Its headquarters are based in London, but it maintains regional offices in Kuala Lumpur, Pretoria, Santiago, and Oman. CI's total staff is currently about thirty-five people, evenly divided between London and the regional offices, and the organization has an annual budget of approximately £4,300,000. CI is led by both a president, who heads a council and executive committee, and director general. CI's presidents are typically the heads of well-established consumer groups, whereas director generals have been recruited from both the consumer movement and the public interest sector more broadly.

Origins and Growth

IOCU arose out of the First International Conference on Consumer Testing held at The Hague in 1960, with delegates from seventeen organizations in fourteen countries. The conference was initiated and supported by three product-testing organizations—Britain's Consumers' Association (Caspar Brook), the Dutch Consumentenbond (Elizabeth Schadee), and Consumers Union (Colston Warne). It led to the establishment of a Technical Exchange Committee to supervise joint product testing, with IOCU acting as a clearinghouse for the exchange of information. With an initial annual budget of £5,000 (including £2,000 from Consumers Union), IOCU was created with an office in the Hague, a journal entitled *IOCU Bulletin*, and a council consisting of the Dutch, British, and American sponsors of the conference, plus the Belgian Association des Consommateurs and the Australian Consumers' Association.

By the time of its third meeting, in Norway in 1964, IOCU was an international movement. The Japanese Consumers' Association alone sent thirty two delegates, and the range of observers reflected an interest well beyond the comparative testing organizations that formed the IOCU's core; manufacturers' organizations sent several delegates, but so, too, did the cooperative movement, the Supreme

Cooperative Council of Poland, and the Soviet Union. In 1970, the council still consisted of the core of the five founding members, but also five co-opted members (Stiftung Warentest of West Germany and the national consumer bodies of the UK and the Scandinavian countries) and four elected members from Austria, New Zealand, Israel, and Canada. A further sixteen associate members and twenty-three corresponding members ensured that organized consumerism now reached into Asia, Africa, and Latin America, if only into the richest nations of these areas. By 1990, however, the IOCU had extended well beyond the affluent West, and an executive had been formed that included South Korea and Mauritius and had as its president Erna Witoelar of the Yayasan Lembaga Konsumen, Indonesia. Subsequent expansion into the former Soviet bloc only served to consolidate IOCU's reputation as a truly global nongovernmental organization (NGO).

Through most of its life, IOCU was sustained by the involvement and financial support of Western product-testing organizations, notably the Consumers' Association (CA) and Consumers Union (CU). Peter Goldman, CA's director from 1964 to 1987, and Rhoda Karpatkin, CU's president from 1974 to 2001, made particularly important contributions. Both served as presidents of IOCU. James Guest, also a long-serving CU president, has served as IOCU's president since 2011.

Rights and Advocacy

Much of this growth has been predicated upon an operating philosophy of consumer rights. On March 15, 1962, President John F. Kennedy made a speech to the U.S. Congress in which he acknowledged the responsibility of government to respond to the key concerns of consumer activists. He listed four consumer rights that he took to be the heart of the political philosophy of consumer activism. These were the right to safety, the right to be informed, the right to choose, and the right to be heard. These four consumer rights were adopted as the central pillars of IOCU policy, and the date later chosen for the first World Consumer Rights Day in 1983 was the anniversary of Kennedy's coming into the consumerist fold.

As organized consumerism spread into the developing world, so, too, did its conception of rights. Developing world consumer activists reoriented the organization away from the rights to choice and from product testing. Instead, they were inspired by the burgeoning environmental movement in the 1970s and the New International Economic Order proposed by the developing world states. Particularly under the leadership of the Malaysian consumer activist Anwar Fazal, who served first as IOCU's regional director for the Asia–Pacific area and then for two terms as IOCU president, from 1978 to 1984, the organization began to focus on questions of access and sustainable consumption. By the 1980s, four more rights had been added to Kennedy's original four: the right to redress, the right to consumer education, the right to a healthy environment, and the right to basic needs.

Early on, IOCU secured a foothold within the United Nations (UN). It was granted consultative status by the Economic and Social Council of the UN in 1963 and used this point of entry to place consumer rights on the international agenda. In a 1981 survey of NGOs and the number of consultative relationships they had with international governmental organizations such as the UN, IOCU was put in fourteenth place, behind such powerful bodies as the International Organization for Standardisation, the International Chamber of Commerce, the World Confederation of Labour, and the International Council of Women, but well ahead of many of the single-issue human rights, environmental, faith-based, youth, and age-concerned NGOs often associated with international civil society.

However, the other key strength of IOCU came through its campaigning networks, uniting the respectable position organized consumerism had with western governments with the radicalism emerging from consumer activists elsewhere. Three notable networks that IOCU established included the International Baby Food Action Network (IBFAN) in 1979, Health Action International (HAI) in 1981, and the Pesticide Action Network (PAN) in 1982. In addition, Consumer Interpol (1981) focused on the export of dangerous products banned or controlled in their country of origin. Led and administered by IOCU, the networks brought together a variety of NGOs and enabled many smaller groups to have a say in which issues should be brought to the attention of the UN.

Using its position on bodies such as the UN Economic and Social Council, the World Health Organization, the Food and Agriculture Office, and even the UN General Assembly, IOCU was able to push for and obtain a UN Consolidated List of Banned Products in 1982, an International Code of Marketing of Breast-Milk Substitutes, various food standards contained in the WHO's Codex Alimentarius, and, in 1985, in perhaps its greatest triumph, the UN Guidelines for Consumer Protection. The guidelines were founded on a conception of rights articulated by Kennedy and extended by IOCU. They have subsequently become the basis for national consumer protection regimes the world over. Key to the adoption of the guidelines was the lobbying of IOCU's representative to the UN, Esther Peterson, consumer adviser to two U.S. presidents.

Where the consumer movement was less successful was in attempting to create a regulatory environment for global business in a manner similar to that achieved in various national contexts. Throughout the 1980s, IOCU worked with other NGOs and the UN Commission on Transnational Corporations to set out a Code of Conduct on Transnational Corporations. Ultimately this was to no avail, and, in any case, the Uruguay Round of Trade Negotiations (1986–1994) led to the establishment of the World Trade Organization in 1995, which provided few opportunities for NGOs such as IOCU to have any real effect on the rules governing global business activity.

Retrenchment and Consolidation

For many western activists, these attempts to regulate global trade saw the consumer movement overreach itself. They felt the campaigns of the organized movement should stop at the UN Guidelines and that IOCU should merely facilitate core goals such as product testing. But for developing world activists, questions about access to consumer necessities and environmental sustainability remained key. The 1990s were therefore marked by some soul searching within IOCU.

A management review conducted in 1991 stimulated reforms and expansion at IOCU. For example, consumer groups from the developing world were accorded increased representation on IOCU committees, though in a way that placed much greater control from the headquarters. 1994 saw additional, important changes: IOCU was renamed Consumers International in 1994, and the headquarters moved to London. Global campaigns were placed under greater management control (through the Global Policy and Campaigns Unit), and much attention was given to assisting the creation and expansion of professional organizations around the world, more closely modeled on their western counterparts.

Two umbrella issues directed IOCU's work: sustainable consumption and the globalization of the world economy. The initiative on such topics was arguably being taken by a whole range of environment, human rights, and development NGOs, many of which came into their own in the 1990s and seemed to eclipse the influence and prominence formerly enjoyed by IOCU in global civil society. However, the issues enabled IOCU to steer a diplomatic path between the competing priorities of the developed and developing world consumer agendas.

During the next two decades, though, as a technology-driven globalization increasingly linked the interests of consumers in the developed and developing worlds, common agendas emerged. In 2012, Consumers International set out four programs that would guide its work until 2015: financial services; food safety, security, and nutrition; consumer justice and protection; and consumers in the digital age. In the best traditions of IOCU, these topics both focused the work of the organization around pressing concerns of both the poor and the affluent and did so in ways that allowed the organization to adapt to the competing priorities of its diverse membership. Increasingly, these priorities—such as fair mobile phone services, pro-consumer global money transfers, opposition to junk food marketing, support for healthy diets, and promotion of net neutrality—are shared by consumers worldwide and therefore thus made vibrant themes for global campaigns, including the celebration of World Consumer Rights Day.

Since the 1990s, Consumers International has emphasized international campaigns, often focused on international bodies such as the UN and its committees. But it has continued to play a critical role in analyzing consumer issues from the perspective of all consumers, poor and affluent, then helping forge a shared agenda for consumer reform (e.g., Common Agenda for Fair Mobile Phone Services). Having reached a consensus on this agenda, it then has devoted significant resources to developing tools for advocates to use locally, nationally, regionally, and internationally (e.g., Manual for Monitoring Food Marketing to Children as well as Junk Food Generation Toolkit).

The greatest success of IOCU has been in maintaining a coherent vision that unites the myriad interests that make up the world's consumer movement. If it has lost some of the energy and radicalism that marked its activities in the 1970s and the 1980s, it still remains a powerful and respected voice within the institutions of global governance. Moreover, it has proved able to adapt to a rapidly changing consumer environment—one that threatens to override the consumer voice as new markets are created and constantly adapted around the world. Key concepts such as rights, globalization, and sustainability continue to guide the organization's work, and it continues to focus on broad areas in which the interests of the poor and affluent might be united.

Matthew Hilton

See also: Caribbean Consumer Movements; Consumers Union/Consumer Reports; Middle Eastern Consumer Movements; South American Consumer Movements; United Nations Guidelines for Consumer Protection

Further Reading

Edwards, Julian. 2010. *Consumers International: Fifty Years of the Global Consumer Movement*. London, UK: Consumers International.

Hilton, Matthew. 2009. *Prosperity for All: Consumer Activism in an Era of Globalization*. Ithaca, NY: Cornell University Press.

Sim, Foo Gaik. 1991. *IOCU on Record: A Documentary History of the International Organization of Consumers Unions, 1960–1990*. Yonkers, NY: Consumers Union.

CONSUMERS UNION/CONSUMER REPORTS

Consumer Reports (CR) is the largest nonprofit consumer organization in the world. In 2011, the organization changed its name from Consumers Union (CU), which it continues to use in its advocacy work. Throughout this article, the organization will be referred to as CR.

For more than seventy-five years, the magazine *Consumer Reports* and, since 1997, the website ConsumerReports.org have served as the most popular objective sources of consumer information in the United States. But the influence of CR has extended well beyond the dissemination of consumer information. It has helped bring about major changes in public policy at the state and federal level, helped establish and support other consumer groups in the United States and around the globe, and helped change the marketplace from one whose watchword was *caveat emptor* to one where consumer rights are acknowledged and respected.

History

The stage was set for the modern consumer movement in the 1920s. Rapid business expansion and the movement toward industrial efficiency that came from standardization made it almost inevitable. Although the consumer movement owes much to the development of buyers' cooperatives, to home economics education, to economists such as Thorstein Veblen, to muckrakers such as Upton Sinclair, and to the engineer Herbert Hoover, this new social movement was virtually invented by Stuart Chase and F. J. Schlink.

When *Your Money's Worth* by Chase and Schlink appeared in 1927, it became a bestseller. The book was a guide to fraud and manipulation in foods, medicine, cosmetics, automobiles, and household equipment. It named names and provided explicit detail. It showed that consumers were victims of unchecked frauds that were rife in the marketplace.

Schlink belonged to a men's club in a Unitarian church in White Plains, New York. With his technical bent, he had prepared a series of mimeographed sheets that summarized the product experiences of members of that club and assembled them into the *Consumer Club Commodity List*. Schlink had access to much of the engineering material of the Standards Association. Wherever the ratings reflected business or governmental tests, the list indicated that. Readers of *Your Money's Worth* were invited to send in a dollar for a copy of the listing, and many did. By 1929, Schlink founded Consumers' Research, which was incorporated by New York State as a nonprofit consumer testing organization. It was the first organization of its kind in the world.

The effort suffered, however, after Schlink transplanted the new organization from New York City to the small town of Washington, New Jersey. Many employees grew dissatisfied, and when a few of them tried to organize a union, they were fired. In support, most of the employees went out on strike, and despite the intervention of the newly formed National Labor Relations Board, Schlink refused to negotiate. Eventually, striking workers and sympathetic members of the Consumers Research board of directors decided to create their own organization.

On February 6, 1936, Consumers Union of United States, Inc., was incorporated in New York. It began its operations in two rooms on East 17th Street in New York City. Engineers, journalists, academics, professionals, and others committed themselves not only to product testing, but also to joining with others to help achieve a "decent standard of living" for all consumers.

Since its founding, CR has grown to a large nonprofit organization that supports and conveys information to consumers in a variety of ways. There have been several important developments. One was the expansion and improvement of laboratory facilities, which has occurred three times: in 1954, when CR moved from New York City to Mount Vernon, New York; in 1991, when the organization renovated and relocated to a much larger building (Consumer Reports National Testing and Research Center) in Yonkers, New York, with fifty laboratories and offices for more than 500 staff; and in the late 1980s, when CR renovated a former drag strip in East Haddam, Connecticut, into a state-of-the-art automobile testing facility.

Another major development occurred in the 1980s, when CR turned to its subscribers and other supporters for some of the financial resources necessary to create its testing center. Despite prohibitions on business contributions and strict conflict-of-interest rules for individual contributions, the organization received more than 600,000 donations, which paid for half the cost of the new facilities. Since then, fundraising has become an increasingly significant source of income for the organization's operations.

A third major development, which began in the 1980s and continues to this day, was the decision to transform the organization from the publisher of *Consumer Reports* to an enterprise that uses a variety of forums and approaches to serve consumers. The most significant diversification was the creation of a Consumer Reports website, www.ConsumerReports.org, in 1997. Because CR's income was (and still is) derived mostly from consumers who pay for its information and advice, the organization made the decision to charge online users for its Ratings information. Since its inception, ConsumerReports.org has become the highest-circulation publication-based site on the Web, with some 3.25 million subscribers. Still, much nonratings advice—such as product recalls, general buying advice, and information about its testing program—is available for free to any visitor to the site.

A fourth development was the expansion of CR's advocacy role. While the organization had supported consumer causes since its founding, in 1972 CU opened a Washington, D.C., office to make federal officials more aware of the organization's research and its implications for public policy. In 1979, the board of directors voted, for the first time, to allow CR to directly lobby before legislative and regulatory bodies. In the 1970s, offices were opened in San Francisco and Austin, Texas, to work on state issues. One notable success has been the campaign to require hospitals to disclose their infection rates. When the campaign began in 2003, only two states required disclosure; ten years later, more than thirty states had passed laws requiring this disclosure.

In recent years, the organization has become more willing to use new methods to pursue its advocacy goals. It has taken out full-page ads in influential newspapers to warn consumers about problems with gift cards. It has used social networks to amass a bank of tens of thousands of first-person consumer narratives about their experience with issues CR is working on. And it has selected one food market chain as a focal point for a campaign against the sale of antibiotic-treated meat products.

Until the early 2000s, CR used only attorneys and public policy experts in its advocacy work. But realizing the effect that grass-roots activists could have, and taking advantage of the revolution in electronic communications, the organization has made contacting legislators by its online supporters a major part of its lobbying endeavors. As of 2013, CR was able to call on more than 1 million "e-activists" to send messages to legislators about issues, and more than 50,000 "super-activists" have become even more engaged, often visiting legislators or testifying to put a human face on the issues.

Governance and Leadership

CR is a membership organization. Each year, all paid subscribers are given the opportunity to vote for a slate of nominees to the board of directors. The act of voting constitutes membership. These directors govern CR. They make overall organizational policy, approve the budget, and maintain broad oversight over operations. They also appoint a president, who is charged to manage the organization.

CR has enjoyed long-term stable leadership on its board and staff. The founding president of the board, Colston E. Warne, an Amherst College economics professor, served from 1936 to 1980. He brought to the organization the conviction that the marketplace needed to be made fair to consumers and a consistent vision of how the organization could help achieve that. His successor, James A. Guest, with the new title of chair of the board, served from 1980 to 2001, when he was selected to be president of the organization. By a quirk of fate, as a boy growing up in Amherst, Massachusetts, Guest delivered newspapers to Warne.

The founding executive director (now called president), Arthur Kallet, served from 1936 to 1957. He was an engineer whose research and writing in the 1920s, with F. J. Schlink, helped lead to the founding of Consumers' Research. In 1935, he helped lead the strike that resulted in the founding of CR a year later. His leadership at CR provided the focus, shape, and identity that has marked the organization to the present. Kallett's successor as executive director was Dexter Masters, who had been editor of the magazine, and who was instrumental in having CR test milk samples for strontium-90, a radioactive byproduct from nuclear test fallout. He was succeeded, in 1963, by Wray Smith, an engineer, who left CR two years later to work for the federal government. From 1965 to 1974, CR was headed by Walker Sandbach, whose background was in the cooperative movement. His tenure as executive director was marked by healthy growth in the magazine's circulation and budget but also by some internal controversy, culminating in a brief staff strike in 1973.

From 1974 to 2001, CR was led by Rhoda H. Karpatkin, who, with her husband Marvin, had served as the organization's outside counsel since the 1950s. As noted earlier, during her tenure, the organization grew and diversified substantially, relocated to its current facilities in Yonkers, created a new automobile test facility, oversaw the creation of ConsumerReports.org, and greatly expanded CR's advocacy activities, including by opening offices in San Francisco and Austin, Texas. Karpatkin had special overlapping interests in addressing the problems of low-income consumers and those in developing countries. She was a leader and two-term president of the International Organization of Consumers Unions (now called Consumers International) and helped found and lead the Transatlantic Consumer Dialogue, a coalition of U.S. and European Union consumer organizations that develops joint consumer policy recommendations to the U.S. government and the EU.

In 2001, after chairing CR for many years, Jim Guest became the organization's president. An attorney, he served as a legislative assistant to Senator Ted Kennedy (D-MA); as Vermont's commissioner of banking and insurance, secretary of state, and secretary of development and community affairs; and as the leader of several nonprofit organizations before becoming CR's president. Guest evolved the organization into a multimedia information services provider engaging regularly with readers, who purchased more than 8 million subscriptions. He also transformed the organization's advocacy program, recruiting "e-activists" and "super-activists" from almost all states. These activists assisted advocacy staff in the organization's consumer leadership on state and federal health care issues, including passage of the Affordable Care Act, as well as supporting CR's work in many other issue areas. Like Karpatkin, Guest was a leader of, and served as president of, Consumers International.

In 2014, Guest was succeeded as the president by Marta L. Tellado, who had been serving as vice president for global communications at the Ford Foundation. Tellado began her career in the 1970s working with consumer advocates Ralph Nader and Joan Claybrook.

Resources and Functions

CR's operating revenue in 2013 was $256 million. The major share of that came from subscriptions to *Consumer Reports* magazine and the ConsumerReports.org website. The balance came from the sale of other publications and consumer information, from donations from subscribers and other supporters, and from foundation grants for special projects. CR accepts no money, products, or gifts of any sort from any commercial source, and its publications take no outside advertising.

The wording of CR's mission has changed several times over its history, but the basic theme has not, and it is best summed up by the organization's mission statement, adopted in 2005: "To work for a fair, just, and safe marketplace for all consumers, and to empower consumers to protect themselves." The primary work of the organization is information and education: comparative testing of consumer products, comparative evaluation of consumer services, research and analysis of issues affecting consumers, and advocacy on behalf of consumers in the marketplace and before legislative and regulatory bodies.

CR's testing is at the core of its work. Products that appear in the ratings are purchased at retail by anonymous shoppers around the country or online, then subjected to state-of-the-art laboratory tests and common sense use tests. Each year, thousands of products undergo stringent, sometimes months-long, comparative testing. In addition, dozens of cars and hundreds of tires are tested at the 327-acre Consumer Reports Auto Test Center in East Haddam, Connecticut.

CR researches consumer experiences to help evaluate services in the marketplace. The organization's survey research department surveys online and print subscribers for their evaluation of services such as airlines, brokerage firms, cell phone service, credit cards, diet plans, Internet service providers (ISPs), and supermarkets. The data they provide form the basis for the frequency-of-repair records, brand reliability, service ratings, and other information, which are published in *Consumer Reports*, on CR's website, and in the organization's other information products.

The results of this testing and research not only appear in the pages of *Consumer Reports* and on the ConsumerReports.org website, but also are disseminated in CR's syndicated newspaper column and online through content distribution deals with partners that include Yahoo!, Fox News, and MSN. Consumer Reports television reports are syndicated to more than ninety stations in the United States and Canada. In addition, the organization publishes another magazine, *ShopSmart*, directed toward women consumers, as well as two newsletters—*Consumer Reports on Health* and *Consumer Reports Money Adviser*.

Other vehicles that the organization uses to further its goals are new and used car pricing services and two services that are intended to more directly help consumers with their purchases—the "Build and Buy" program for motor vehicle purchases, and "Price & Shop," which connects consumers who use ConsumerReports.org product ratings with online and bricks-and-mortar retail sites offering the rated models. A Consumer Reports mobile phone app allows consumers to get product ratings information while they are shopping in stores.

In 2009, CR acquired *The Consumerist*, a popular, edgy, and irreverent consumer news and advice website. The acquisition brought with it a young, tech-savvy audience, 2 to 3 million of whom visit the site each month.

Influence

The influence of CR can be measured in several different ways. Quantitatively, one can measure how many people are reached by its information. As of 2013, average paid circulation of *Consumer Reports* magazine was almost 4 million, with the number of readers estimated at four times that. With the ConsumerReports. org website, *Consumer Reports on Health*, the *Consumer Reports Money Adviser*, and *ShopSmart* magazine, in 2013 total paid subscriptions to CR's information products totaled more than 8 million.

Millions more use free CR information, whether from its television news features or from the organization's other health, safety, and environmental websites. As an example, with the help of foundation grants, CR created CR Best Buy Drugs, an evidence-based drug comparison program that helps consumers talk to their doctors about prescription drugs to find the safest and most effective drugs that also give the best value for their health care dollar. The reports are available online and in print and are also available in Spanish.

The fact that CR has had success in acquiring and keeping subscribers, despite the proliferation of free advice on the Internet, attests to the trust the public places in the organization. For example, in a 2008 Harris poll of organizations that influence politics and business, CR placed first in the "most trusted" category, with 92 percent of respondents saying they trusted CR "a great deal" or "a fair amount." And surveys over the years typically show CR as the most-relied-on source of information, for example, for consumers looking to buy a motor vehicle.

That trust is in large part thanks to the policies that CR established in 1936, which have never varied: The organization takes no outside advertising, takes no free samples or anything else of value from any business interest, and refuses to let any company use CR material to promote its products or services. Strict conflict-of-interest rules for staff and board members ensure that nothing affects the organization's work except for the merits of the products and services evaluated.

Although the number of people reached is a significant measure of the influence of CR, there are other measures. The organization's testing and reporting has had a direct effect on sales volume for the products involved, affecting both excellent products and inferior ones. After CR rated the Suzuki Samurai sport utility vehicle "not acceptable" in 1988 because of its tendency to roll over, sales of the vehicle plummeted by two-thirds. Likewise, sales of the *Ionic Breeze* air purifier sold by Sharper Image dropped substantially after CR reported in 2003 and 2004 that the product did almost nothing to clean the air.

As well as affecting sales, CR has stimulated product improvement, both through its critiques and through regulatory action. In the 1970s, when microwave ovens were becoming popular kitchen appliances, a CR report on radiation leakage led to improved design and improved standards. After years of reports of some sport utility vehicles tipping over in its tests, the National Highway Traffic and Safety Administration in 2004 adopted a new method of measuring a vehicle's rollover propensity, and manufacturers modified their vehicles to reduce this problem.

Another effect of CR is not as measurable. CR's mission statement includes the phrase "empower consumers to protect themselves." Over more than seventy-five years, the organization has disseminated test information and other evaluations about particular products and services and how to shop for them. This information has encouraged consumers to participate in the marketplace in a more informed and assertive way. Their individual and collective attitudes and expectations about the marketplace now permeate both consumer and producer consciousness, helping raise standards for quality and performance of products and services.

Through its advocacy work, CR has had an increasingly powerful effect on consumers' welfare. In addition to its work on product and vehicle safety, CR's health experts played a key role in the passage and implementation of the Affordable Care Act in 2010, which when fully implemented will result in tens of millions of Americans being covered for the first time by comprehensive health insurance. CR was also an early and important supporter of the Dodd–Frank financial reform law, especially its creation of the Consumer Financial Protection Bureau.

Finally, almost since its inception CR has supported the growth of the overall consumer movement. The organization has promoted, helped launch, and contributed to the support of new consumer organizations, such as the Center for Auto Safety, American Council on Consumer Interests, Center for the Study of Services, Consumer Federation of America, and International Organization of Consumers Unions (now Consumers International). In addition, it has provided technical and financial support for state and local consumer organizations in the United States and in other countries.

Dan Franklin

See also: American Council on Consumer Interests; Consumer Education Advocacy; Consumer Federation of America; Consumers International; State and Local Consumer Advocacy Groups

Further Reading

ConsumerReports.org. "Our History: Timeline." www.consumerreports.org/cro/about-US/history/timeline/index.htm.
Silber, Norman I. 1983. *Test and Protest.* New York: Holmes & Meier.
Warne, Colston E. 1982. "Consumers Union's Contribution to the Consumer Movement." In Erma Angevine, ed., *Consumer Activists: They Made a Difference* (pp. 85–110). Mount Vernon, NY: Consumers Union Foundation.

COSMETIC SAFETY ADVOCACY

Since the 1930s, three periods of change have transformed cosmetic safety from an internal concern of a self-regulated industry to a high-profile issue defined by consumer advocacy and characterized by rapid market changes.

Advocates took aim at the industry in the early 1930s, when the Food and Drug Administration's (FDA) fledgling safety regulations extended only to food and drugs, not cosmetics. In a series of investigative reporting projects covering the food, drug, and cosmetic industries, advocates from the public and FDA publicized cases of injuries among cosmetic users and revealed the scope of manufacturers' reliance on potentially harmful ingredients. The work, published in three popular books and promoted in an FDA exhibit dubbed the "Chamber of Horrors," galvanized public support for reform. "Lash-Lure" eyelash dye came to epitomize this phase of consumer advocacy: Its toxic synthetic dye blinded twelve women and led to the death of another.

The work culminated in the passage of the 1938 Federal Food, Drug and Cosmetic Act (FDCA). "Organized club women" spearheaded public support during the hard-fought legislative battle. The law not only expanded FDA's authority over food and drug safety, but also extended its jurisdiction to encompass cosmetic safety for the first time. The agency could now seize cosmetic products and impose criminal sanctions if it could prove that a cosmetic on the market was adulterated (e.g., "putrid") or misbranded (e.g., falsely labeled).

This authority quickly proved inadequate. Lacking the ability to require companies to register with the agency, file ingredient information, conduct premarket testing, submit safety studies, or report adverse events, FDA was forced to regulate on a "product-by-product and after-the-fact" basis. Injury reports included allergic reactions, bacterial infections from hand creams, urinary tract infections from bubble bath, lung damage from spray propellants, and infant deaths caused by an antibacterial ingredient in baby powder.

Despite evidence of continuing safety problems, cosmetic policy reform efforts lagged for three decades. In 1960, at the request of lipstick companies, Congress rolled back the 1938 "harmless" standard for coal-tar dyes in cosmetics to allow continued use of dyes linked to organ damage, effectively extending the original law's hair-dye exemption. Representative Leonor Sullivan (D-MO) sought to strengthen FDA authority, sponsoring legislation throughout the 1960s to protect consumers from harmful products. In Consumer Reports, Consumers Union regularly published research on health risks from cosmetics, helping to keep the issue in the news.

New momentum emerged in the 1970s when Virginia Knauer, Special Assistant to the President for Consumer Affairs, engaged leading women's advocacy groups in efforts to require companies to list ingredients on product labels. The groups urged members "to seek out and to patronize companies which were willing to compete on the basis of improved safety and labeling."

By 1972, at least thirteen such advocacy groups were lending support, including the American Medical Women's Association, the National Council of Jewish Women, and the American Home Economics Association. In 1973, Senator Thomas Eagleton (D-MO) introduced the Cosmetic Safety Act in the Senate; in 1974, the administration released its own legislative proposal for stronger standards; and that same year Senator Edward Kennedy (D-MA) convened the first government hearings devoted to cosmetics regulation and safety concerns. Among those testifying were Consumers Union, advocating that companies be required to submit safety data to FDA, and consumer advocate Ralph Nader for the Washington, D.C.–based Health Research Group, who argued for premarket testing of cosmetics to bring standards in line with drugs.

The intense pressure exerted by advocacy and proposed legislation sparked change among cosmetic manufacturers and retailers. Six companies agreed to print ingredient lists on product labels, including Avon and L'Oreal, and at least three also published "not-used" lists of known allergens excluded from their products.

Threatened with the prospect of regulation, the cosmetic industry agreed to support ingredient-labeling regulations as long as other proposed changes remained voluntary. With this compromise, efforts for broad legislative reform fizzled.

FDA's labeling regulations went into effect in 1975. A significant victory for the public's right to know, the rules require companies to list ingredients and warnings on product labels. Other initiatives remained voluntary, as industry lobbyists had hoped. In 1976, the cosmetic industry's trade association launched an industry-funded science panel responsible for reviewing ingredient safety, and companies renewed their efforts to voluntarily submit ingredient lists and adverse events to FDA.

Over the next quarter-century, the cosmetic industry continued operating under this self-described "self-regulatory status." The Consumer Federation of America represented consumer interests as a nonvoting member of the industry's ingredient safety review panel.

In 2000, the Centers for Disease Control and Prevention (CDC) published a study that would inspire the third, current phase of advocacy for cosmetic safety reform. In laboratory analyses measuring levels of synthetic chemicals in urine, CDC found higher levels of compounds linked to birth defects in women of child-bearing age than in other people tested. The researchers speculated that the difference could be due to the use of these compounds in cosmetics.

This work inspired the research and advocacy organization Environmental Working Group to study and publicize the prevalence of the chemicals ("phthalates") in nail polish, fragrance and, other products. Healthcare Without Harm and Women's Voices for the Earth joined with EWG to conduct a follow-up study that found phthalates in three-quarters of products tested. Both studies earned widespread media coverage. Breast Cancer Fund, Friends of the Earth, and five other health and consumer advocacy organizations joined the effort. Together, these organizations founded the national Campaign for Safe Cosmetics, a coalition that by 2012 had grown to include more than 1,300 partner cosmetic companies and 150 endorsing organizations, with a mission of securing "corporate, regulatory and legislative reforms needed to eliminate harmful chemicals from cosmetics."

In many ways, this third phase of consumer advocacy has mirrored the second phase. Consumer groups are supplying information and engaging the public, industry is defending its ability to self-regulate, progressive retailers and companies are taking action to advance product safety, and Congress has introduced legislation to expand FDA authority.

Social media and the Internet have greatly enhanced advocates' ability to engage public support compared to past efforts. EWG's online Skin Deep Cosmetics Database, launched in 2004, allows consumers to look up safety ratings for more than 70,000 personal care products. It logged nearly 250 million searches in eight years. The campaign-sponsored "Story of Cosmetics," a video describing ingredient safety issues, attracted half a million viewers in the six months following its publication. Advocate-sponsored sign-on letters to cosmetic companies routinely secure thousands of signatures.

Over the past ten years, advocates' original research has included studies of lead in lipstick, hormonally active cosmetic chemicals in the blood and urine of teenage girls, allergens in fragrance, carcinogenic contaminants in baby products, and cancer-causing formaldehyde in hair straighteners.

Consumer groups have again taken aim at industry's self-regulatory status. A 2004 citizen petition to FDA demonstrated that the industry's safety review panel had reviewed only 11 percent of cosmetic ingredients since its founding in 1976 and that hundreds of products contain ingredients that the panel found lacked sufficient data to determine their safety in cosmetics. The industry's trade group responded with the launch of their Consumer Commitment Code. This mandatory pledge for member companies requires that they comply with the industry panel's ingredient safety findings.

Among the many retailers and manufacturers that have ramped up transparency and product safety in recent years are Johnson & Johnson, which pledged to phase out formaldehyde-releasing preservatives from baby products; L'Oreal, which is removing a hormonally active antimicrobial ingredient from its products; more than 300 companies earning "champion" status with the Campaign for Safe Cosmetics, all of which met campaign standards for ingredient safety and labeling; Whole Foods, which awards a seal to products free of certain hazardous ingredients; and Walmart, which recently announced a list of chemicals to be disclosed and phased out. Consumer advocates now consider reform efforts to be in the "retailer regulation" phase, where retailers set standards in advance of (or in place of) government reforms.

On Capitol Hill, Representative Jan Schakowsky (D-IL) has led recent efforts for reform, sponsoring cosmetic safety bills since 2010. In California, companies are required to comply with the state's Safe Cosmetics Act of 2005 (legislation sponsored by consumer groups), notifying the state of ingredients they use that may cause cancer or reproductive toxicity. In 2013, negotiations for federal reform between FDA and the cosmetics industry crumbled when leading companies left the table. Advocacy groups continue to work for change.

Cosmetics remain the least regulated of all industries under FDA purview. But periods of intense consumer advocacy have culminated in significant advances in product safety and the consumer's right to know and, to a lesser extent, expansion of federal oversight.

Jane Houlihan

See also: Prescription Drug Advocacy

Further Reading

Campaign for Safe Cosmetics (www.safecosmetics.org).

Houlihan, Jane, et al. 2014. EWG's Skin Deep Cosmetics Database. www.ewg.org/skindeep/.

Malkan, S. 2007. *Not Just a Pretty Face: The Ugly Side of the Beauty Industry*. Gabriola Island, BC: New Society Publishers.

CREDIT CARD ADVOCACY

In the 1970s and 1980s, the focus of consumer advocates on credit cards was largely on interest rates and their disclosure. These advocates opposed increases in, and the elimination of, state usury ceilings. This opposition was made difficult by the U.S. Supreme Court's 1978 decision, in *Marquette National Bank of Minneapolis v. First of Omaha Service Corp.*, to prohibit states from enforcing usury limits on credit rates if the cards were issued by companies based out of state. The advocates also supported measures such as those in the Fair Credit and Charge Disclosure Act of 1988, which required lenders to inform cardholders about annual percentage rates (APR), annual fees, and interest-free periods to make monthly payments before interest was charged. In these two decades, the consumer groups working the most actively on these issues were Consumers Union, the Consumer Federation of America (CFA), the National Consumer Law Center (NCLC), and the law reform units of the numerous legal services offices that NCLC serviced.

Beginning in the mid-1990s, however, consumer advocates began to notice and be concerned about the rapid expansion of credit card debt, fueled by aggressive card issuer marketing and credit extension, and the questionable terms and conditions of this debt which greatly increased issuer income and profits. Two prolonged battles between these advocates and card issuers ensued. The first was initiated by the issuers who sought to restrict consumer access to personal bankruptcy and who largely succeeded when Congress enacted the Bankruptcy Reform Act of 2005. The second battle was begun by consumer advocates, who fought to eliminate abusive credit card practices and largely succeeded when Congress approved the Credit Card Accountability, Responsibility and Disclosure (CARD) Act of 2009.

The Bankruptcy Reform Act of 1978 had made it easier for consumers to declare personal bankruptcy, yet throughout the early 1980s, only about 300,000 people a year filed for this bankruptcy. By 1990, however, that number had grown to more than 700,000 and, by 1996, to more than 1.1 million. The growth of these bankruptcies paralleled and was caused in part by increasing credit card debt. From August 1989 to June 1995, this debt doubled, rising from $201 billion to $402 billion (and continued growing to exceed $1 trillion in December 2008). Though all creditors were concerned about the escalation of personal bankruptcies, credit card issuers, who often had the lowest priority claim on personal assets in a bankruptcy proceeding, took the lead in organizing a national campaign to persuade Congress to restrict access to personal bankruptcy.

The political pressure of creditors was largely responsible for the creation, by President Bill Clinton in 1994, of a National Bankruptcy Review Commission to examine the federal bankruptcy code and make recommendations regarding changes. The commission's recommendations, which were released in 1997, did not include many of the sweeping bankruptcy changes that creditors had advocated, particularly the creation of a "means test" for debtor access to chapter 7 (where debts are completely discharged, as opposed to chapter 13, where the payment of all or a portion of debt is restructured). Within weeks of the issuance of the commission report, industry allies in Congress had introduced legislation that went well beyond the commission's recommendations in restricting access to bankruptcy. These restrictions included creating a complicated means test that allowed only some debtors, with monthly income below the median income of their state, to file chapter 7; allowing more unsecured credit card debt to survive bankruptcy; making private student loan debt nondischargeable; increasing the amount of debt that had to be repaid in chapter 13; and requiring debtors to receive credit counseling before filing for bankruptcy.

The early consumer opposition to this legislation was not well organized. Harvard law professor Elizabeth Warren (now a U.S. senator), who had been staff advisor to the Bankruptcy Review Commission, was particularly active in her research and public comments in criticizing the legislation. Other academics—Lawrence Ausubel at the University of Maryland, Ronald Mann at the University of Texas, and Robert Manning at the University of Rochester (*Credit Card Nation*)—also wrote and spoke about the link between credit card debt and household financial instability. In Washington, D.C., CFA executive director Stephen Brobeck debated the industry in the media, testified before Congress, and issued a series of reports criticizing credit card issuers for facilitating bankruptcy through their irresponsible marketing and issuing of credit. Legal services attorneys, such as Philadelphia's Henry Sommer, showed how the legislation would be particularly damaging to lower-income households. But it was not until the end of the 1990s that CFA, NCLC, and consumer bankruptcy attorneys took the lead in organizing a coalition to coordinate opposition efforts.

During the early 2000s, the coalition expanded to include labor, religious, civil rights, women's, and other consumer groups. Warren was the leading public critic of the legislation. Maureen Thompson, working for the bankruptcy attorneys, and CFA legislative directors Mary Rouleau and, later, Travis Plunkett were the principal coordinators of the coalition and leading lobbyists for it. Patton Boggs attorney Jonathan Yarowsky, a former congressional staff director and White House aide, was also a key lobbyist and strategist. As well as emphasizing the ruinous financial effects that the law would have on low- and middle-income consumers, the coalition pointed out that the bill took no steps to curb abusive lending by the creditors whose practices had contributed to the growth of bankruptcy filings.

The coalition's efforts were successful only in somewhat moderating the legislation and in holding off its final approval. Key here were the efforts of senior Democrats in the Senate, such as Senator Ted Kennedy (D-MA), who used procedural roadblocks to delay passage, and President Clinton, who in 2000, after legislation had passed both the Senate and House, used a "pocket veto" to stop the legislation. In 2005, nearly ten years after bankruptcy reform legislation was proposed,

Congress again approved bankruptcy legislation, which President George W. Bush signed into law.

In retrospect, consumer advocates had been "outgunned" by the industry, which spent tens of millions of dollars on their "reform" campaign. However, creditors probably would not have succeeded if most Americans had strongly opposed the reform. Public polling showed that although many Americans believed that those encountering unexpected financial difficulties were entitled to a "fresh start" in bankruptcy, they also thought some individuals were abusing the system and liked the idea of tightening laws to restrict access to "deserving" debtors.

Up until 2005, most consumer advocates had focused most of their attention to credit cards on debt and bankruptcy. But after passage of the bankruptcy law, they began concentrating on deceptive and abusive practices by card issuers, especially what Warren called their "tricks and traps." Back in 1996, the Supreme Court, in *Smiley v. Citibank*, had provided an additional motivation for issuers to employ these practices. The court expanded its 1978 Marquette decision to include fees as well as interest rates, thus further curbing the ability of states to stop anticonsumer card practices. In this period, Consumer Action, under the leadership of Ken McEldowney and Linda Sherry, was especially active monitoring these practices. In 1998, this national group issued a report on 117 cards issued by seventy-four banks that found increased use of penalty fees, late fees, over-limit fees, and shortened grace periods. From this time throughout the 2000s, they updated this report frequently and were joined by other nonprofits—Pew Charitable Trusts, Demos, US PIRG, National Council of La Raza (NCLR), and Center for Responsible Lending (CRL)—who published their own research on abusive practices. A milestone for this research was release, by the highly credible U.S. General Accounting Office in 2006, of a report documenting widespread unfair credit card practices and finding a need for more effective credit card disclosures.

At the same time that advocates, academics, and the federal government were describing questionable and unfair credit card practices—widely reported on by news media—consumers were growing more dissatisfied with their treatment by issuers. Cardholders became upset, for example, when they mailed off a payment one week after receiving their monthly bill but were then assessed a late payment fee, or when this one late payment triggered an interest rate increase from 10 percent to 25 percent. The depth and breadth of this consumer dissatisfaction was revealed when, in its 2008 request for comments on its credit card rulemaking, the Federal Reserve Board received 56,000 comment letters, a large majority of which were written by individuals describing their own problems.

Aware of a promising opportunity to achieve credit card reforms, in 2007 consumer groups organized a coalition to try to persuade Congress and regulatory agencies to take action. Coordinated by CFA's Plunkett, the coalition included not only mainstream consumer groups (CFA, US PIRG, Consumers Union, NCLC, Consumer Action, CRL, and the National Association of Consumer Advocates) but also civil rights groups (NCLR and the Leadership Conference on Civil Rights), the National Small Business Association, and labor, especially the Service Employees International Union (SEIU). The SEIU, one of the most powerful trade unions, lobbied Congress, mobilized grassroots support for legislation, and brought in members with problems to testify before Congress. U.S. PIRG's Ed Mierzwinski played a major role in coalition efforts, especially media outreach, lobbying, and communication with banking regulators.

Recruiting "victims" to testify was an important role for the coalition, helping humanize the problem. Groups including Consumer Action and Consumers Union helped identify consumers, made them available to the press, and prepared them to speak at congressional hearings. The key hearings were held by Representative Carolyn Maloney, Senate Banking Committee Chair Chris Dodd, and Senator Carl Levin, chair of the Senate Permanent Subcommittee on Investigation. Levin's two standing-room only hearings were widely reported on by news media.

The coalition coordinated a diverse array of other advocacy activities. Consumers Union delivered 120,000 "Kiss Credit Card Abuses Goodbye" postcards to members of Congress. Pew Charitable Trusts ran radio advertisements in key congressional districts and in publications covering the work of Congress. CFA convened frequent strategy and targeting meetings. And NCLC (Lauren Saunders and Chi Chi Wu) and Consumers Union (Gail Hillebrand) worked with coalition members to develop a consensus regarding specific regulatory reforms, then prepared and filed extensive comments at the Federal Reserve and other federal regulatory agencies.

All these advocacy efforts began to show results. In June 2007, the Federal Reserve issued a rule with reforms, but only to credit card disclosures. The failure of these reforms to address unfair and deceptive acts and practices spurred consumer groups and congressional leaders to seek additional consumer protections. These protections made up legislation that was introduced by Representatives Carolyn Maloney in early 2008 and passed the House in September of that year. Prodded by this legislation, in May of 2008, the Federal Reserve proposed rules related to unfair and deceptive practices and, in December of that year, finalized the rules. Both Maloney and Senator Chris Dodd moved to strengthen and codify these rules and move up their implementation date. In early 2009, Republican Senator Richard Shelby (R-AL) agreed to support Dodd's bill, and the Obama administration weighed in heavily in support of strong protections. The legislation passed the House for the second time in April 2009 by a 357–70 vote. In May of that year, it passed the Senate by the huge margin of 90–5 and was signed into law by President Obama.

The CARD Act did much to reduce and eliminate unfair credit card practices by issuers. With only minor exceptions, it prohibited card companies from hiking interest rates retroactively on balances accrued before a rate increase takes effect. It prohibited these companies from increasing a cardholder's interest rate on existing balances based on adverse information unrelated to card behavior. It disallowed over-limit fees unless the cardholder had affirmatively agreed to allow over-limit transactions. It required issuers to apply payments above the minimum amount to the card balance with the highest rate of interest. It prohibited "double-cycle" billing. And it checked irresponsible lending and aggressive marketing to young consumers without the ability to repay debt.

The pro-consumer effect of the law has been documented by two credible studies. A 2013 study led by a University of Chicago economist concluded, to the surprise of its researchers, that the law actually reduced credit card fees by $21 billion a year. Later that year, the Consumer Financial Protection Bureau (CFPB) released a report concluding that the CARD Act had eliminated the deceptive and unfair credit practices it had targeted and that the total cost of credit paid by consumers—including fees, interest, and finance charges—had declined by 2 percentage points between 2008 and 2012. The CFPB also found that although the amount of card credit decreased during the recently occurring financial crisis, creditworthy consumers still had access to $2 trillion of credit lines.

The cooperation among consumer and other nonprofit groups, which began in opposition to bankruptcy "reform" and strengthened in the fight for credit card protections, helped provide the foundation on which the even broader and more active coalition, Americans for Financial Reform (AFR), was built. AFR played a key role in generating support for congressional passage of the Dodd–Frank legislation that created the CFPB and established many other financial services reforms.

Stephen Brobeck

See also: Installment Credit Advocacy; Payday Loan Advocacy

Further Reading

Consumer Financial Protection Bureau. 2013. *CARD Act Report: A Review of the Impact of the CARD Act on the Consumer Credit Card Market* (October 1).

Manning, Robert D. 2001. *Credit Card Nation*. New York: Basic Books.

Norris, Floyd. 2013. "Card Act Cleared up Credit Cards' Hidden Costs." *New York Times* (November 7).

Warren, Elizabeth. 2014. *A Fighting Chance*. New York: Metropolitan Books.

CREDIT REPORT AND CREDIT SCORE ADVOCACY

The 1970 Fair Credit Reporting Act (FCRA) was enacted after a series of congressional hearings held by Representative Leonor Sullivan (D-MO) and Senator William Proxmire (D-WI). The hearings looked into scandals associated with the insurance investigation practices of the Retail Credit Corporation (now known as the consumer reporting agency Equifax). CRAs are colloquially known as "credit bureaus."

The FCRA, as enacted, regulated the collection and sale of both these "investigative consumer reports," largely based on subjective interviews with neighbors and employers, and the more commonly sold "consumer reports," known as credit reports, which contain factual trade lines based on bill-paying habits, as well as public record information, including tax liens and bankruptcy records. Most experts consider the FCRA, despite issues with compliance, to be the nation's most comprehensive data protection statute. Although the FCRA predated the work of a 1973 government task force on privacy, its elements largely presage that task force's Code of Fair Information Practices (FIPs). The FIPs require that data collectors collect only the data necessary for limited uses, take steps to ensure its accuracy and security, and provide opportunities for data subjects to review, correct, and control their files.

Throughout the 1970s and 1980s, the industry consolidated from local firms, with employees who made phone calls to verify information on a consumer's application, to a smaller number of firms that were among the first financial firms to use "Big Data" analytical tools, largely in automated, computerized systems. By the early 1990s, the once-local firms had aggregated nationally into an oligopoly that shrank first to five and finally to three large consumer data repositories—Equifax, Trans Union, and TRW (now Experian)—plus numerous smaller specialty credit bureaus for medical records, tenant screening, check clearing approval, and other purposes.

The mergers of firms using often incompatible computer systems with different coding led to a rise of consumer accuracy complaints. In the early 1990s, state and federal investigations led to court-ordered consent decrees between the remaining "Big Three" and the Federal Trade Commission (FTC) and numerous states. But the FTC's authority was limited—it could neither write rules concerning most parts of the FCRA, nor "supervise" the credit bureaus. Bank regulators can examine, or supervise, banks at any time for any reason. Supervisory authority functions as an early warning system. In the absence of the detailed information that could be obtained from supervision, the FTC, through 2014, has never imposed a civil penalty on any of the Big Three credit bureaus for inaccuracy or faulty dispute reinvestigation practices.

In the absence of further FTC action, despite the consent decrees, the Big Three firms did not make significant changes to improve accuracy or make the dispute process easier to navigate. Furthermore, the FCRA is a difficult law to understand. Attorneys who attempt to represent aggrieved consumers in court are usually defeated unless they become specialists who rely on the detailed FCRA manuals published by the nonprofit National Consumer Law Center (NCLC). Many of those specialist attorneys, who also handle debt collection lawsuits, along with law professors and others, in the 1990s formed the National Association of Consumer Advocates (NACA), which became an important part of consumer coalitions.

Reacting to the news stories and government investigations, in 1989 Representative Richard Lehman (D-CA) began reform hearings in his House Banking Committee consumer subcommittee. In the same year, an independent association of local credit bureaus released an accuracy study that found a 42 percent error rate in 1,500 reports examined. Advocacy reports by U.S. PIRG in 1990, 1991, and 1992, based on Freedom of Information Act Requests to the FTC, found that credit reporting was the leading complaint category three years running. U.S. PIRG's 1991 report also found that mistakes led to Kafka-esque dispute reinvestigations: consumers who complained to the FTC had already contacted the credit bureaus an average of five times or more over a period averaging twenty-three weeks with no satisfaction. In 1991, Consumers Union released "What Are They Saying About Me?"—a survey of 161 reports finding a 48 percent error rate.

Also in 1991, the Vermont Attorney General's office began highly publicized investigations of how TRW had wrongly reported that more than 3,000 residents of Norwich, Vermont had failed to pay their taxes. A similar problem occurred for Equifax the next year in Massachusetts. In both cases, agents for the firms copied lists of homeowners who had paid their taxes, not those who had not.

In 1992, the pro-consumer Banking Committee Chairman Henry B. Gonzalez (D-TX) brought FCRA reform legislation to the House floor. But, at the request of U.S. PIRG, Consumers Union, and other advocates, he pulled the bill from further consideration since it contained language, inserted at the request of banks and credit bureaus, to preempt all future state authority over FCRA matters.

Action then shifted to the states. Vermont, under the leadership of Assistant Attorney General Julie Brill (now an FTC commissioner), enacted comprehensive reform legislation that included provision of a free credit report on request. In the 1990s, six other states—Colorado, Georgia, Maine, Massachusetts, Maryland, and New Jersey—also enacted free credit report laws, whereas several other states enacted other reforms or capped the price of reports.

In 1996, Congress finally enacted reforms expanding the availability of free reports in some, but not all circumstances, providing greater privacy protections to consumers when reports were used by employers, and imposing first-time duties on creditors that "furnished" information to credit bureaus. The legislation was brokered by Senator Richard Bryan (D-NV). It passed because of his compromise provision preempting some, but not all, state actions. Unless renewed, this provision would expire in 2004.

The 1990s also saw an expansion of the use of credit scores derived from credit reports. The pioneering firm, the Fair Isaac Company, had developed the widely used FICO score. Two factors accelerated score use. First, the housing finance agencies Fannie Mae and Freddie Mac insisted on automated underwriting, using scores, for mortgages that they would securitize. Second, the rise of "instant credit" at retail locations relied heavily on scoring. But the industry resisted making scores part of reports. It pushed back against an early 1990s FTC guidance interpreting scores to be a part of the credit reports to be disclosed to consumers and gained a provision in the 1996 legislation saying that they explicitly were not.

A second 1990s trend, exacerbated by the growing issuance of instant credit, was an increase in new account fraud, commonly called identity theft. U.S. PIRG's 1996 and 1997 reports described the trend and proposed reforms to protect consumers. The crime was facilitated by easy access to Social Security numbers. These identifiers were easily obtained from college student, insurance, and military ID cards; mailing labels on tax forms sent to citizens by the IRS; and other sources. At the time, any military officer being considered for promotion to general officer rank would have his or her name and SSN appear together on a list in the printed *Congressional Record*.

The identity thief did not need to contact the credit bureau directly; the retailer, a "trusted third party," made the contact. The thief provided the retailer his own address but another consumer's name and Social Security number. In 2014, identity theft remains the leading complaint to the FTC and takes several forms: financial identity theft, medical services identity theft, tax refund identity theft, and even criminal identity theft, whereby imposters commit crimes in another's name or the imposter simply lives under another's name to avoid the stigma of his or her own previous criminal past.

The intensified use of automated systems at credit bureaus also contributed to the growing consumer problem of "mixed files," where reports issued to creditor subscribers might contain information on two or more consumers. Attorneys from NACA and NCLC alleged that this was due to bad matching algorithms, including the use of a seven-digit SSN match in "subscriber reports." Making matters worse, when a consumer requested his or her own report after credit denial, it would not contain the negative mixed file information, because disclosure to a consumer, but not a creditor, still required a nine-digit SSN match. Consequently, consumers denied credit received a cleaned-up report and could not take action to fix negative items that they could not see.

The growing use of credit scoring paralleled the real estate boom that began in the mid-1990s. Real estate agents in California, tired of telling home buyers that they did not qualify for the lowest rate "because your credit score is too low but I am forbidden by our contract with FICO from showing it to you," partnered with Consumers Union to pass the first state credit scoring disclosure law in 2000.

The national demand for solutions to identity theft and inaccurate credit reports leading to lower credit scores continued to escalate. U.S. PIRG (1998) and Consumers Union (2000) released new surveys on credit report inaccuracy. In 2002, the Consumer Federation of America (CFA) partnered with the National Credit Reporting Association, representing smaller local credit bureaus that conducted manual underwriting and verification of information on reports, to produce a study based on a review of hundreds of thousands of credit scores. Their key finding was that a significant number of consumers had a wide enough variance between scores generated from each of their three credit reports to cause them to be wrongly reported as subprime, depending on which of their reports was "pulled" by a potential creditor.

Despite all these efforts from advocates, it is likely that additional reforms would not have passed, except that creditors and credit bureaus were worried about the looming 2004 expiration of the preemption provisions in the 1996 amendments. However, advocates saw an opportunity to gain significant reforms as a condition of any extension of preemption. In 2003, Congress enacted the 2003 Fair and Accurate Credit Transactions Act (FACTA). This law established a federal portal to obtain free annual credit reports, expanded the availability of credit scores, required certain identity theft reforms, and imposed heightened accuracy requirements. Although industry convinced Congress to permanently extend some preemption provisions, consumer and community groups, in coalition with state attorneys general, persuaded legislators to protect the rights of states to enact future identity theft reforms.

None of the FACTA's identity theft reforms directly prevented identity theft, but merely helped resolve problems. In 2003, California State Senator Debra Bowen's pioneering credit report security freeze legislation was enacted. It was based on work by several consumer and privacy advocates led by U.S. PIRG, Consumers Union, and CALPIRG. If a consumer had placed a security freeze on his or her credit report, even if a thief had obtained his or her Social Security number and applied for credit in his or her name, access to the report was denied.

Advocates for U.S. PIRG and Consumers Union then prepared a "State Clean Credit and Identity Theft Model Act," incorporating the Security Freeze, a data breach notification section (again based on a new California law), and other privacy reforms. Over the next three years, in the absence of federal preemption, the two groups, aided by AARP and state attorneys general, successfully marketed the model law nationwide. Forty-six states and the District of Columbia enacted the security freeze before the Big Three bureaus capitulated and agreed to provide it throughout the country. Today, forty-nine states and the District of Columbia have breach notification laws.

Despite the enactment of the 1996 and 2003 amendments, credit reporting inaccuracies and identity theft problems continue. A 2008 NCLC report, "Automated Injustice," detailed that the reinvestigation process largely consisted of creditor and credit bureau computers confirming to each other in two-digit codes that they had the same information, but not whether it was correct.

Following the 2008 U.S. financial collapse, advocates, who had joined together as Americans for Financial Reform, worked closely with Harvard law professor Elizabeth Warren to convince Congress to establish a new Consumer Financial Protection Bureau (CFPB) in the 2010 Dodd–Frank Wall Street Reform and Consumer Protection Act. A separate provision of the act, sponsored by Senator Mark Udall (D-CO), greatly increased access to credit scores. The law granted CFPB broad authority over consumer reporting agencies. In addition to its general authority to write rules interpreting the FCRA, the CFPB was given authority to supervise, or examine, "larger" credit reporting and scoring firms. Coupled with its authority to supervise larger banks, credit card companies, and debt collectors—which together "furnish" or provide the vast bulk of information in consumer reports—the CFPB's oversight is expected to make major improvements to credit report accuracy.

In a 2012 report, the CFPB recommended that credit bureaus start sharing a consumer's full complaint with creditors during reinvestigations. Pushed to action by publication of a 2013 FTC survey showing that up to 10 million Americans could have serious errors on their credit reports, which was featured on *60 Minutes* and at a U.S. Senate Commerce committee hearing, the Consumer Data Industry Association announced that its members would begin sharing full complaint files with creditors during reinvestigations.

For years, advocates have criticized the credit bureaus' failure to fix mistakes or fight identity theft, but worse, their aggressive marketing of direct-to-the-consumer products that take advantage of fears about low credit scores. The FTC has fined Experian for deceptive marketing of its expensive (up to $20/month) credit monitoring subscription products. The bureaus also aggressively market identity theft insurance add-ons that advocates also consider a dubious bargain.

Pressure from the CFPB has also resulted in greater disclosure of credit scores. In 2013, FICO announced that it would no longer prevent creditors from showing consumers the scores that the firms had purchased from it. After Discover became the first prominent firm to adopt the voluntary reform, in 2014 the CFPB launched a public campaign to urge all banks to post credit scores on consumer account statements. Advocates hope that the initiative will reduce the amount of money, estimated to be close to $1 billion annually, that consumers spend on underperforming add-on products. In 2014, advocates continue to press Congress to make credit scores part of credit reports and to urge the CFPB to intensify its investigations and actions to improve credit report accuracy.

Edmund Mierzwinski

See also: Consumers Union/Consumer Reports; Public Interest Research Groups

Further Reading

Hendricks, Evan. 2004. *Credit Scores and Credit Reports.* Washington, DC: Privacy Times.
House Committee on Financial Services, U.S. Congress. 2007. *Credit Reports: Consumers' Ability to Dispute and Change Account Information* (June 19): v. 4.

CREDIT SCORE ADVOCACY
See Credit Report and Credit Score Advocacy

CZECH CONSUMER MOVEMENT

In 1993, Czechoslovakia split into two countries—the Czech Republic and Slovakia. Since that time, the Czech Republic has become one of the most economically vibrant countries in central and eastern Europe. The World Bank classifies the Czech Republic as a high-income country. The Republic's ranking on the UN Human Development Index is twenty-eighth, second only to Slovenia among countries in its region.

During the Communist rule that preceded the "Velvet Revolution" of 1989 (the nonviolent transition away from Communism and toward democracy), social movements were considered dangerous and discouraged by the Czechoslovakian government. That being the case, the consumer movement mainly took shape after this time, when restrictions on political activity were lifted. The economic disruptions involved in transitions to a market economy intensified the need for people to join consumer organizations. Approximately 100 consumer organizations have been created since 1990, but only a few continue to function today.

Consumer organizations were originally founded as civil associations in accordance with the Citizens Civil Law Associations Act, enacted in 1990. This legislation states that an association must have at least three members and must register with the Czech government. The act had almost no requirements for consumer organizations with respect to transparency or internal mechanisms. This will change in 2014, with new legislation regarding consumer and other civic organizations. For example, these organizations will provide basic information, such as a list of board members and official representatives, and file an annual report.

The country's first Consumer Protection Act went in to effect in 1992 and developed a framework for public administration in consumer protection. As a prerequisite for joining the European Union, the Czech Republic strengthened its consumer protection laws, and the republic was rewarded with EU membership in 2004.

Among government institutions, the chief responsibility for consumer protection lies within a small unit in the Czech Ministry of Industry and Trade. The ministry generally promotes minimizing government intervention in favor of using market forces to solve consumer problems. The ministry created the Consumer Advisory Committee, which consists of eight member consumer organizations and advises the ministry on consumer issues. Although consumer protection legislation has been developed, enforcement of these laws remains problematic. Courts are slow and expensive, serious alternative dispute resolutions do not exist, and regulatory activities remain limited.

The oldest active consumer organization is the Czech Consumer Association. Founded in 1990, this civic organization focuses on technical standardization and safety, financial services, and provides consumer advice. It also issues a seal of approval to businesses with a positive record of satisfying consumers. SOS: Consumers Defense Association of the Czech Republic, founded in 1993, was an important organization in protecting consumer interests until its recent financial demise. Initially, SOS was a local association, but it became national in scope. At its peak, SOS had branches in all fourteen regions of the Czech Republic and provided advice to more than 40,000 people per year to protect consumer interests. SOS also published a magazine (initially called *Consumer's Shield*), and the organization worked cooperatively within BEUC: The European Consumer Organisation, Consumers International, and the Trans-Atlantic Consumer Dialogue. Nevertheless, SOS's growth was not sustainable, resulting in internal fights and, ultimately, bankruptcy in 2011. People from several of the regional branches of SOS, however, started their own organizations—some with only a local focus, others with wider aspirations.

The Czech Association of Consumers TEST, or dTest, was founded in 1992, and its main focus is the publication of the consumer test magazine *dTest*. For many years, the founder and chairwoman of the organization, Ida Rozova, was the only person working at *dTest*. She did so in close collaboration with the venerable German product testing magazine *Stiftung Warentest*. In 2008, *dTest* was able to hire additional staff thanks to funding from a project financed by the European Commission and led by International Consumer Research & Testing as well as BEUC. Since that time, the organization has developed quickly, resulting in an increase in subscribers (to approximately 50,000). Today, a typical issue of *dTest* contains five tests of products and financial services. Publication of the *dTest* magazine is no longer supported from the state budget, but other activities linked to consumer rights and their promotion are.

Consumer organizations in the Czech Republic face the continuing challenge of finding a stable source of revenue to support a systematic and long-term program of activities. Many organizations began their work based on volunteerism but have transitioned to project-based financial support from the government. For the past decade, the Ministry of Industry and Trade has distributed more than 500,000 euros annually to consumer organizations to conduct projects for the benefit of consumers (Fielder, 2011). To obtain government funding, however, organizations must demonstrate that they are not completely dependent on this one financial source, which can disappear with one political decision. Each organization has its own approach to raising funds. Some typical sources are grants from municipalities, foundations, or the European Union; sale of products (magazines, brochures, etc.) and services (seminars for entrepreneurs on consumer rights, certifications, etc.); donations; and member fees.

In assessing the overall state of consumer activism in the Czech Republic, one should keep in mind that the phenomenon is relatively new, having developed in a post–Velvet Revolution society. While some issues of transparency and financial sustainability remain, consumer organizations are becoming a stable force in the country.

Karel Pavlik

See also: BEUC: The European Consumer Organisation

Further Reading

BEUC. 2011. "Strengthening the Consumer Movement in Central, Eastern and South Eastern Europe (CESEE)." Brussels, Belgium.

dTest. www.dtest.cz.

European Union. "The Czech Republic." http://ec.europa.eu/consumers/empowerment/cons_networks_en.htm.

Fielder, Anna. 2011. *The State of the Consumer Nation(s): An Evaluation of the Consumer Movement in Six Countries of Central, Eastern and South Eastern Europe.* Brussels, Belgium: BEUC (The European Consumer Organisation), September 5.

D

DANISH CONSUMER MOVEMENT

The basic structure of the Danish consumer movement was laid out in the decades before and after World War II, a time when important institutions were built in the development of the Danish welfare state and when institutions were also created or reorganized to promote the consumer cause and mitigate conflicts between business and consumers.

The Danish Home Economics Council (Statens Husholdningsråd) was established in 1935 to provide better and more reliable information to consumers and, in a broader sense, to "educate" the consumer. This institution performed many important tasks and provided useful information, but as a government institution, it could not speak on behalf of consumers in a bottom-up fashion. Amalgamating smaller consumer groups, the Danish Consumer Council (Forbrugerrådet), originally the Danish Housewives' Consumer Council, emerged in 1947 as a new umbrella organization to represent consumers from both rural and urban areas. This private initiative was both welcomed and encouraged by government.

The Danish Consumer Council is the indisputable lead organization of Danish consumers and is recognized in this capacity by both government and business. However, this does not suggest that all interests are channeled through this sole organization. Other smaller consumer organizations exist in special areas and represent specific segments of consumers, such as car owners (Federation of Danish Motorists—Forenede Danske Motorejere), shareholders (The Danish Shareholders Association—Dansk Aktionærforening), tenants (The Danish Tenant Union—Lejernes Landsorganisation i Danmark) and patients (Danish Patients—Danske Patienter). Some of these entities are even members of the Consumer Council, but unlike the Consumer Council, these organizations do not seek to represent consumers on a broad basis. Also, other nonconsumer organizations, such as unions, are members of the Consumer Council to support its general work. In sum, there is no real competition between these different organizations; consequently, the Danish consumer movement is quite centralized.

The Consumer Council receives resources and input from many organizations and sectors in Danish society. The Consumer Council relies heavily, however, on government funding. Although budget cuts are occasionally discussed, no changes in government funding have been made that have seriously affected the status of the organization. This funding makes it possible to have a highly professionalized secretariat (close to a hundred staff) that to a large extent runs the organization. Whereas it can be questioned whether there is really a vibrant associational life in the Danish consumer movement in which individual consumers are actively involved, the secretariat does a good job of remaining alert to a range of consumer issues. It provides numerous services, disseminates information to consumers, and addresses consumer problems through traditional political channels. There are instances of more confrontational consumer activism in Danish consumer politics, but these are rare.

For the average consumer, it can sometimes be difficult to understand which tasks are managed by the Consumer Council and which are covered by government bodies such as the Consumer Ombudsman (Forbrugerombudsmanden) and the general Consumer Complaints Board (Forbrugerklagenævnet). These bodies, established in the mid-1970s, were brought together under the National Consumer Agency of Denmark in 1988, but this agency merged with the competition authorities into the Danish Competition and Consumer Authority in 2010. Indeed, shifting governments have adopted different political and administrative strategies with regard to the organization of consumer policy, somewhat adding to confusion about the roles of different institutions. Under these circumstances, it has been of special importance for the Consumer Council to profile itself as an independent organization capable of voicing authentic consumer interests. Indeed, in 2013 the organization changed its Danish name to Forbrugerrådet Tænk, adding "Tænk" (Think), the name of its consumer magazine, to its name.

Over time, the Consumer Council has built its capacity and considerably broadened its engagement in consumer issues as consumption patterns have changed. From an original concern with basic commodities produced in the domestic market, today the Consumer Council focuses on an increasing number of complex consumer goods, many of which are produced abroad. The Consumer Council's guiding philosophy is that government consumer policy should advance consumer rights because transparent markets are not sufficient to protect the interests of consumers. This view permeates the council's engagement in all policy fields.

One of the main policy areas in which the Consumer Council has been engaged is food policy. Although food is a traditional and basic commodity, modern food production entails new issues with respect to food labeling and food safety. In addition, many issues addressed by the organization relate to energy, health, communication, travel, and, increasingly, the financial sector. In the past, the Consumer Council also addressed banking and insurance, but recently, it has developed stronger expertise in relation to the financial sector because its products are increasingly complex and demand significant knowledge on the part of consumers.

A key goal of the Consumer Council has always been to gain access to Danish policymaking forums, and the council, as well as some of the specialized consumer organizations, has become an insider in the formulation and implementation of Danish consumer policy. In the legislative process it is common to invite the Consumer Council into relevant committees, ask for its opinion in institutionalized hearings, and engage in a variety of informal contacts with its leaders. The influence is not as strong as the consumer movement might wish, but compared with the consumer movements of many other countries, Danish consumer participation is strong.

Participation is also formalized with regard to a number of consumer complaint boards that have emerged in many sectors since the 1970s and are recognized by the general Consumer Complaints Board. Today there are a total of nineteen permanent bodies in which representatives from the consumer movement are seated. These bodies settle conflicts between firms and consumers, and they are established to make decisions faster and more effective for the consumer. The complaint boards are good examples of recognized industry self-regulation: When a relevant industry association and the Consumer Council agree to set up a tripartite complaint board—chaired by an independent judge—and when it fulfills certain government requirements, it is recognized by the government's general Consumer Complaints Board. Interestingly, the administrative costs of consumer participation are paid for by the relevant industry.

Some patterns of participation by Denmark's consumer organizations have changed with internationalization. With the Danish admission to the European Economic Community (later the European Union or EU) in 1973, an important international pillar was added to the work of the Danish consumer movement. EU membership not only meant the expansion of new markets but also the expansion of European consumer regulation. Although Denmark is a relatively small country within the EU, its Consumer Council is a strong and active player in the European consumer movement. The Consumer Council, as well as some of the other consumer organizations, seeks to influence the consumer strategies of the Danish government, which, after approval from the EU Committee of the Danish Parliament, negotiates with the other member states of the EU to arrive at a common position. This mechanism offers interesting opportunities to influence wider European regulation, but there are also risks that achievements reached at the domestic level are thwarted by European regulation.

Danish consumer organizations work cooperatively with other consumer organizations to increase their joint effect. At one point, this cooperation was mainly confined to the organizations of other Nordic countries, but the significance of this work has dwindled in the broader process of Europeanization and globalization. Today, Danish consumer groups also participate at the EU level (BEUC: The European Consumer Organisation), at the "Atlantic" level (Trans-Atlantic Consumer Dialogue, TACD), and at the global level (Consumers International, CI). The council has become an important participant in policy formulation and strategy development with respect to European and global consumer policy.

Karsten Ronit

See also: BEUC: The European Consumer Organisation; Consumers International

Further Reading

European Union. "Denmark." http://ec.europa.eu/consumers/empowerment/cons_networks_en.htm.

Jensen, Hans Rask. 1984. *Forbrugerpolitik og organiseret forbrugerarbejde.* Copenhagen, Denmark: Akademisk Forlag.

Porter, Tony, and Karsten Ronit. 2006. "Self-Regulation as Policy Process: The Multiple and Criss-Crossing Stages of Private Rule-Making." *Policy Sciences* 39, no. 1: 41–72.

Ronit, Karsten. 2003. *Forbrugerpolitik—konflikt og samarbejde i den politiske beslutningsproces.* Copenhagen, Denmark: Forlaget Politiske Studier.

Ronit, Karsten. 2005. *Selvregulering og de private ankenævn i dansk forbrugerpolitik.* Copenhagen, Denmark: Multivers.

DEBT COLLECTION ADVOCACY

One of the incentives that drove immigration to the American colonies in the sixteenth and seventeenth centuries were harsh debt collection laws in England that provided for perpetual imprisonment of insolvent debtors, with freedom available only if someone paid the prisoner's debts. For several decades in seventeenth-century England, becoming a bankrupt was even punishable by death. Although the U.S. Constitution did not do away with debtors' prisons, it did provide for bankruptcy laws, and the first federal bankruptcy law provided for the discharge of debtors from debtor's prison.

The Industrial Revolution brought urbanization, an increase in wage-paying work, and products such as pianos for home entertainment, sewing machines that kept many immigrants from destitution, and, eventually, automobiles. Merchants sold or provided rental purchase agreements on these items and quickly repossessed the items if an installment was missed: The consumer would lose all he or she had invested in the item.

Because lending was still local, it might be hard to obtain more credit. Other merchants would post large-print "shame lists" in their store windows naming those that still owed them on credit purchases. Local merchants began to join together to set up local credit bureaus that kept records on consumers' failure to timely pay their debts. Some credit bureaus also began offering credit counseling to consumers in financial trouble and had debt collection departments that would be paid a fee by merchants to collect back payments.

Businesses in the stressful and difficult business of collecting debts sprang up in the first half of the twentieth century using home visits, typed and handwritten letters, and the telephone. The American Collectors Association was founded in 1939.

The earliest debt collection laws in the United States were laws licensing debt collectors and requiring them to have bonds. The bonds were to prevent debt collectors, hired by businesses, from running off with funds collected instead of turning them over to the businesses, minus the debt collector's commission or fees. Collection agencies had such low startup costs, requiring only small investments in equipment and facilities, that they could easily be set up by entrepreneurs, some dishonest.

In the second half of the twentieth century, the laws in many states began to be amended to protect consumers by prohibiting harassing or misleading letters and phone calls or the posting of shame lists of debtors in stores or store windows. By the early 1970s, eleven states had enacted such laws: Arizona, Arkansas, California, Connecticut, Indiana, Maine, Massachusetts, Minnesota, Nevada, Pennsylvania, and Washington.

In 1969, as part of federal government's War on Poverty, the National Consumer Law Center (NCLC) was funded to convene a meeting of fifty-five consumer credit experts from across the nation. These experts concluded that consumers were inadequately protected from predatory creditor practices and began drafting a National Consumer Act to counteract the Uniform Consumer Credit Code (1968), which national retailers were urging state legislatures to adopt.

The National Consumer Act (1970) was introduced in many states and was enacted as the Wisconsin Consumer Act, reflecting compromises by both consumer advocates and industry lobbyists. The Wisconsin Consumer Act contained a chapter protecting consumers from abusive, deceptive, and unfair debt collection laws. It was built on the existing protections in the eleven states that had earlier passed laws. These protections were sharpened and expanded by NCLC's Model Consumer Credit Act that, in the 1970s, was enacted in part by nearly a dozen states as part of the new consumer credit statutes.

In 1975, Congressman Frank Annunzio of Chicago (D-IL) introduced a consumer protection bill that bore a striking resemblance to NCLC's model provisions. In 1977, the bill passed the House by a single vote and the Senate by voice vote, with bipartisan support in both houses. The Fair Debt Collection Practices Act (FDCPA) was signed by President Carter on September 20, 1977, and became law in 1978.

The FDCPA has dozens of strong, detailed provisions, such as usually prohibiting a debt collector from informing family and friends of a consumer's financial straits and prohibiting abusive phone calls, falsely threatening suits, wage garnishment, or arrest. In broad terms, it also prohibits "abusive," "deceptive," and "unfair" debt collection conduct. It seeks to balance the legal rights and responsibilities of consumers and debt collectors so that the relationships are conducted with respect and professionalism rather than intimidation, fear, and shame. Although the FDCPA has not tamed the $51 billion debt collection industry, it has dramatically improved it.

However, it is not unusual for debt collectors to cross legal lines, and they had more opportunities to do so as consumer debt expanded rapidly in the 1990s and first decade of the new century. The Federal Trade Commission began receiving more complaints about debt collection agencies, debt collection law firms, and debt buyers than about any other business. Its 2009 report contains information about collectors' failing to properly notify consumers of lawsuits filed, collectors' filing suits based on insufficient evidence of indebtedness, courts' granting default judgments against consumers who do not appear or defend themselves, collectors' seeking to recover on debts beyond the statute of limitations, and banks' freezing funds in bank accounts that are exempt from garnishment by law.

Encouraged by this report and by the advocacy of NCLC, the National Association of Consumer Advocates, and other consumer groups, in its comprehensive 2010 financial reform legislation, Congress gave the new Consumer Financial Protection Bureau (CFPB) both enforcement and rulemaking authority over debt collections. Since then, the CFPB has reported that debt collection represents the number one source of complaints. The bureau has also announced that it is considering updating and strengthening debt collection rules.

The Fair Debt Collection Practices Act allows consumers to obtain a lawyer with only a small or no fee, which is paid by the debt collector. A directory of most of the hundreds of lawyers who specialize in enforcing that law is available at the National Association of Consumer Advocate's website, www.naca.net.

Robert Hobbs

See also: National Consumer Law Center

Further Reading

Consumer Financial Protection Bureau. 2013. *Fair Debt Collection Practices Act: CFPB Annual Report 2013* (March 20).

Hector, Colin. 2011. "Debt Collection in the Information Age: New Technologies and the Fair Debt Collection Practices Act." *California Law Review* 99: 1,601+.

Heiser, Edward J., Jr. 1974. "Wisconsin Consumer Act—A Critical Analysis." *Marquette Law Review* 57: 389+.

DECEPTIVE AND UNFAIR SALES PRACTICE PROTECTIONS

Federal and state law offer consumers important protections against deceptive, unfair, and unconscionable sales practices. The most important provisions prohibit any form of unfair or deceptive sales conduct. No matter how novel or ingenious a shady scheme, it can run afoul of statutory standards of unfairness and deception because these are broad and evolving concepts meant to adapt to any form of merchant abuse of consumers. For example, even though the concept of an Internet never existed when these laws were enacted, the standards apply effectively to Internet-related deceptive sales practices.

Examples of specific areas of consumer abuse include sales of used cars with hidden defects, unnecessary automobile repair or charges for repairs not performed, bogus trade schools, shoddy or incomplete home repair work, high-pressure door-to-door sales, late or nondelivery of mail orders, bait and switch, deceptive price advertising, overreaching credit terms, mobile home warranty problems, abusive debt collection, pyramid sales, and sale of useless insurance.

The standards were developed in response to consumer dissatisfaction with the concept of caveat emptor—let the buyer beware. Starting in the early 1900s, American courts and legislatures started moving slowly away from a pure caveat emptor approach. The Federal Trade Commission (FTC) was created in 1914 to deal not with consumer fraud, but with monopolies. The FTC Act prohibited "unfair methods of competition." In 1938, this act was expanded with the Wheeler–Lea Amendment to prohibit not only "unfair methods of competition," but also "unfair and deceptive acts and practices." In other words, a federal standard was created that merchants should not engage in unfair or deceptive practices in trade or commerce.

The deception standard was applied by the courts and the FTC to be significantly broader than common law fraud. Only a capacity to deceive needed to be shown, with no proof of the merchant's intent or knowledge of the deception, or even that consumers were actually damaged or deceived. In addition, the concept of "unfairness" was even broader than "deception." For example, selling games of chance to children could be unfair even if not deceptive.

While this standard was in place as early as 1934, it had only minimal influence on the consumer marketplace, for two reasons. First, FTC enforcement of the standard was minimal. The commission could only enjoin future conduct, not punish past conduct. Moreover, such orders only went into effect after all appeals had been exhausted. Accordingly, it might take as long as a decade for the commission to order a merchant to stop using a particular deceptive practice.

In addition, there was no private or state enforcement of the FTC Act. The only remedy for a consumer who was a victim of deception or unfairness was to complain to the FTC, which might then initiate an investigation, and eventually a proceeding, to seek an order preventing other consumers from being similarly victimized.

In the 1960s and 1970s, efforts were made to strengthen consumer protections. With the Committee on Suggested State Legislation of the Council of State Governments, the FTC proposed state legislation, patterned after the FTC Act, that would be enforced by states and by individual consumers. About the same time, the National Conference of Commissioners, the National Conference of Commissioners on Uniform State Laws (NCCUSL), and the American Bar Association (ABA) adopted the Consumer Sales Practices Act that provided private and state enforcement for deceptive and unconscionable practices. The three groups also approved a Uniform Deceptive Trade Practices Act that allowed one merchant to enjoin another merchant's deceptive conduct. Furthermore, NCCUSL and the ABA adopted a Uniform Commercial Code that allowed courts to refuse to enforce unconscionable sales agreements or unconscionable provisions in sales agreements.

In response to these model laws, and to a growing consumer movement, during the 1960s and 1970s, every state enacted a general statute prohibiting deceptive and (usually) unfair or unconscionable practices while providing state enforcement. They have been known as unfair and deceptive acts and practices, or UDAP, statutes. Injured consumers in all fifty states (and the District of Columbia) can also enforce the statutory standards.

As a result, the present standards of unfairness, deception, and unconscionability are not only federal, but also state, law. These standards are widely enforced and have real meaning in merchant–consumer transactions.

The FTC model has predominated in most states; state UDAP statutes broadly prohibit deception and unfairness. Because these statutes have broad applicability, usually provide attorney fees and adequate remedies for prevailing consumers, and are also enforced by state attorneys general, UDAP statutes are frequently used today to challenge deceptive and unfair merchant conduct. They have effectively ended the concept of caveat emptor.

In the 1970s, the FTC's own enforcement power was expanded to allow it to promulgate trade regulation rules, obtain restitution for victimized consumers, obtain civil penalties for certain illegal conduct, and preliminarily to enjoin unfair or deceptive conduct. This increased authority has allowed certain national standards and expectations to be enforced as to proper merchant conduct.

These broad standards and enforcement mechanisms, however, proved ineffective in at least one area. Sellers often attempted to separate the consumer's obligation to pay from the consumer's claims against the merchant. For example, a home improvement contractor might arrange for a home improvement loan from a finance company to a consumer, with the check signed over to the home improvement contractor. If the contractor skipped town without doing any work, the contractor got to keep the money, and the financial company could sue the consumer for repayment of the loan.

In 1975, the FTC found this situation inherently unfair and enacted the "Holder Rule." This regulation requires that any consumer loan originated by the seller or arranged by the seller contain a notice allowing the consumer to raise claims and defenses on the loan based on the consumer's complaint against the seller. In the above example, the consumer could lawfully refuse to repay the finance company because the contractor arranged the loan and the contractor had defrauded the consumer.

Over the past four decades, the National Consumer Law Center (NCLC) is the consumer advocacy group that has done the most work on UDAP-related issues. For example, NCLC has analyzed all fifty state UDAP statutes and recommended changes that were sometimes adopted. It has also engaged in successful advocacy to protect the FTC Holder Rule.

While federal law prohibits unfair and deceptive conduct in all trade or commerce, private consumers and state prosecutors cannot always remedy violations of that standard. There is no right for state agencies or individuals to use the federal law; they must instead rely on similar state laws. But in some states these laws do not prohibit unfair practices or do not apply to certain types of consumer transactions, such as utilities, insurance, credit, debt collection, real property, or regulated industries.

Jonathan Sheldon

See also: Installment Credit Advocacy; National Consumer Law Center

Further Reading

Carter, Carolyn, and Jonathan A. Sheldon. 2012. *Unfair and Deceptive Acts and Practices.* Boston, MA: National Consumer Law Center.
Naimon, Jeffrey, et al. 2010. "Under the Microscope: A Brief History of UDAP Law and Predictions for Potential Dodd–Frank Developments." *Consumer Financial Services Law Report* (October 27).
Pridgen, Lee. 2009. *Consumer Protection and the Law.* Minneapolis, MN: Thomson/West.

DIGITAL COMMUNICATIONS ADVOCACY

With the Internet at its center, the digital communications revolution, with 5 billion mobile subscribers and 2 billion Internet users worldwide, has profoundly affected and benefited consumers. Yet this revolution has also generated important consumer and public interest issues that consumer advocates have been addressing.

Universal service: Advocates have remained concerned about ensuring that all Americans have access to affordable service enabling full participation in the digital age. As online access increasingly provides an important gateway to participation in the world, lack of this access severely limits the ability of consumers to search for, purchase, and use goods and services. In the United States, there is a growing digital divide between the two-thirds who have broadband Internet service and the one-third who lack this service.

Network neutrality: Advocates believe that the first principle of communications network operation should be the obligation to operate the network in a nondiscriminatory manner. They note that this principle extends back from the common carrier regulation in the age of electronic telecommunications to the roads and canals developed in an earlier era. As the digital communications network grew, broadband network operators pushed to escape from this obligation. Advocates raised concerns about network operators that would block or slow some data transmissions for economic or technical reasons or that would selectively charge specific applications service provider fees for higher levels of service. They argued that these practices would violate the principle of network neutrality, raising consumer costs, undermining competition, and chilling innovation.

Free speech and communications as a human right: Closely related to network neutrality, but much broader, is the effect of the Internet on speech and the right to communication. Commercial threats to freedom of speech and communications are important, but they pale in comparison to threats from governments. Many public interest groups in the United States and globally believe that increasing centrality of digital communications to political, social, and economic life magnifies the importance of adherence to Article 19 of the Declaration of Human Rights.

Privacy: The easy flow of information and the ability to aggregate, analyze, and exploit it has created great concerns about privacy. Since the beginning of the Internet, public interest advocates have objected strenuously to data gathering by governments and corporations who use information to target individuals for further surveillance or marketing. In the United States, corporations that dominate the digital economy have resisted constraints on their practices and have enlisted the federal government in support of these practices.

Consumer protection: Although the Internet has dramatically increased the range of options for acquiring goods and services while slashing distribution and transaction costs, it has also posed new challenges for consumer protection. With an increasing number of instantaneous, transnational transactions taking place, difficult questions have arisen involving decisions about which laws apply and what mechanisms can be used to enforce consumer rights. For example, consumers have difficulty seeking remedies against deception by Internet-based foreign companies who sell, but have no physical base, in the United States.

Internet governance: The Internet Communications Protocol is managed by a set of voluntary self-regulatory institutions, including the Internet Engineering Task

Force (IETF), Internet Architecture Board (IAB), and Internet Society (ISOC). Day-to-day operations, such as managing the address registry, were transferred to a quasi-independent nongovernmental institution, under an agreement that preserved a special role for the U.S. government. Even before revelations about U.S. National Security Agency surveillance of Internet traffic, the role of the U.S. government and dominance of the global Internet economy by U.S. corporations was an increasing bone of contention in international policy debates. Many public interest advocates, who were highly critical of the United States' role and U.S. behavior, have also expressed grave concerns about the efforts by governments around the world to assert control over their national "Internets." These advocates fear that the Internet will become balkanized and also will be used by governments, especially those with poor records on human rights, to silence speech and local protest.

Intellectual property: Copyright holders of goods that do not require a physical embodiment—such as music, books, and video—have been pushing to eliminate the consumer ownership right by repealing the "first sale" doctrine in cyberspace. If they succeed, consumers would not be allowed to purchase a new digital product and resell it in a secondary market; they would only be allowed to license products.

Antitrust: By lowering barriers to entry and allowing users to become producers at the edge of the network, Internet and digital technologies have promoted much competition. Yet advocates have expressed strong concerns about concentration in the center of the network. In 2014, most consumers have a limited number of choices for high-speed (broadband) data service (two providers) or wireless service (four national providers). Advocates object to the ability of these providers to leverage access to consumers to set high prices and retard competition in content markets.

A relatively large number of consumer and other public interest groups have worked on these Internet issues. Different groups have taken the lead on different issues, but there has been a great deal of collaboration among those organizations interested in the same issue. Not infrequently, most of or all the groups interested in a particular issue have signed onto related congressional testimony, regulatory comments, or court filings.

The traditional consumer groups working on digital issues have been Consumers Union, Consumer Federation of America, and the National Consumer Law Center. Other groups have been identified more closely solely with Internet issues, especially privacy or network neutrality. They are the American Civil Liberties Union, the Center for Digital Democracy, the Center for Democracy and Technology, Common Cause, the Electronic Frontier Foundation, the Electronic Privacy Information Center, the Free Press, the Media Access Project, the New America Foundation, and Public Knowledge. The progressive New America Foundation, which works on a broad array of policy issues, also has prioritized Internet issues.

Mark Cooper

See also: Privacy Advocacy; Telephone Consumer Advocacy

Further Reading

Cooper, Mark. 2013. "Why Growing Up Is Hard to Do: Institutional Challenges for Internet Governance in the 'Quarter-Life Crisis' of the Digital Revolution," *Journal on Telecommunications and High Technology Law* 11, no. 1: 45–134.

Lessig, Lawrence. 2006. *Code and Other Laws of Cyberspace, Version 2.0*. New York: Basic Books.

DUTCH CONSUMER MOVEMENT

Leaving aside some early signs of consumer awareness before World War II, there have been two distinct phases in the development of the Dutch consumer movement. The first phrase began with the founding of Consumentenbond (CB) in 1953 and the gradual establishment of the government's institutional framework for consumer protection that to a large extent still prevails. The second phase began in the 1980s and lasts to the present day. It is characterized by the interaction of several trends: deregulation, technological developments, and shifts among consumers themselves. CB and other consumer organizations in the Netherlands are adapting to these trends and remain influential in the domain of consumer policy.

First Phase: The Shaping of the Institutional Framework

The consumer movement in the Netherlands today can be traced back to two predecessor developments. The first consists of consumer cooperatives, which originated in many western European countries in the late nineteenth century. The activities of these cooperatives consisted of running grocery stores, banks, and insurance companies. In the mid-1950s, the co-ops began declining; by the 1970s, they had disappeared altogether. But they left behind a tradition of organized consumer self-help.

The second forerunner of the consumer movement began with the foundation of the Netherlands Union of Housewives (NVH) in 1912. NVH's early activities aimed at eliminating threats to food hygiene. It was to a large extent because of the NVH's pressure that in 1919 a law on food safety was enacted and a food inspection department created. In the mid-1930s, at the peak of the Great Depression, two other organizations were founded that also focused on providing families with aid and information to make ends meet. Neither organization was able to adapt to the societal changes, especially the role of women, that took place in the final quarter of the last century, and they consequently disappeared.

The Dutch consumer movement as we know it today began in 1953, with the foundation of a product testing and publishing organization, Consumentenbond (CB). The first issue of its magazine noted that the consumer no long was able to make informed choices in a rapidly changing marketplace. CB set four priorities for itself: determining consumer needs, providing information about the quality and "value for money" of products, exposing dubious practices by business, and consulting and negotiating with government and business entities when consumer issues were at stake.

CB reached its first milestone, 10,000 members, by the end of 1959. CB sustained a blow when it lost a lawsuit in 1962 for having published a test that compared the nicotine and tar content of cigarettes and named the brand Lexington as having the highest content, which caused a steep fall in the brand's sales. The judge found CB liable for inadequate research: Specifically, CB used different testing methods for different cigarette brands, which resulted in measurements that differed (slightly). But the public viewed CB as the little David who took on Goliath. The public sympathy and publicity over the result of the lawsuit helped CB double its membership in the next few years. Over time, CB expanded the scope of its activities; it began providing legal assistance to its members in 1969 and pushing for measures to further competition in the market place.

In 1957, CB, together with the earlier mentioned organizations and several trade unions, founded the Consumer Contact Organ (CCO), a vehicle for applying joint pressure on the government. The CCO collapsed in 1971, however, when CB opted out, feeling constrained in its dealings with the government. The remaining organizations then founded Konsumenten Kontakt (KK), a small but effective entity that analyzed consumer problems until its dissolution in 1994. It used the results of its research to exert pressure on government, business, and local authorities to remedy these ills. CB and KK, who were allies rather than rivals, were very visible in the mass media and dominated the Dutch consumer scene in the 1970s and 1980s.

In 1970, CB, together with organizations representing specific business sectors, established a Foundation for the Resolution of Consumer Disputes (SGC) to address disputes involving purchases from suppliers affiliated with these business sectors. Dispute resolution takes place in committees that have been set up for each sector, and its decisions are legally binding for both parties. Generally speaking, these committees consist of three independent members appointed by SGC: a chairman (trained in law), a representative from the industry concerned, and a member designated by CB or other consumer organizations. Among the first participating business sectors was the travel industry, and committees have been established for sectors such as telecom, public transport, and health care. Overall, the number of participating business sectors has grown considerably: nine in 1990, twenty-four in 2000, and fifty-four at the end of 2013.

In 1975, the government issued a regulation in which it laid down the conditions for recognizing SGC's charter. These conditions, which aimed at promoting due process and impartiality in the SGC's decisions, allowed government subsidization of SGC and thereby made it less financially dependent on business funding. In this system, the Ministry of Justice subsidizes the annual costs for SGC's infrastructure, whereas businesses pay for the handling of the cases. The annual costs for the business sectors depend on the number of cases handled. Additionally, the consumer pays a low fee, varying from $35 to $175 dependent on the committee involved, which is refunded by the supplier if the committee rules in the consumer's favor. SGC's total annual costs are approximately $7–8 million. Over the years, the ministry has subsidized from 15 percent to 20 percent of SGC's annual costs of operations; businesses pay the balance. SGC has been able to considerably

reduce dispute handling time by digitizing and otherwise streamlining its processes. The average handling time for settling disputes is now about three months,
and SGC is able to oversee about 5,000 cases annually. SGC's charter complies with
the 2013 European Union (EU) directive on alternative dispute resolution. The
implementation of this directive in 2015 via Dutch legislation will certainly be a
stimulus for SGC's expansion.

Whereas CB focuses on virtually all consumer issues, the Union for the Interests of Homeowners (VEH) was established in 1974 to specialize on consumer
problems related to housing. VEH remains the only important consumer organization in the Netherlands dedicated to a single category of consumption. In 2000,
it counted more than 400,000 members; as of 2014, the number approached
700,000. VEH and CB work together in several areas of common interest. Among
other consumer groups, mention must be made of two other organizations. Rover
is a consumer organization founded in 1971 to improve public transport. Still in
operation today, it often collaborates with other consumer groups, such as CB. The
other is the Royal Dutch Touring Club. Akin to the American Automobile Association in the United States, the club serves its 4 million members by providing a
broad spectrum of paid travel-related services.

In 1979, the National Institute for Information on Household Budgeting
(NIBUD) was established. NIBUD is subsidized by the government and relevant
financial industries. At the time of publication, it plays an active role, both in
terms of offering financial advice to individuals (e.g., on how to budget) and by
providing government insight into the effects of policy proposals related to the
disposable incomes of various segments of society. In 1983, the Consumer Safety
Institute was established, fully subsidized by the Ministry of Health. The institute
is charged with monitoring and providing information on product hazards. In the
mid-1980s, the Federation of Patient and Consumer Organizations (NPCF) was
founded. NPCF consists of local, regional, and national organizations of patients
that provide support to patients and participate in the discussion and transformation of the health care system.

A Closer Look at Consumentenbond

Although CB is a single organization, its activities and influence approximate
those of a social movement. It has a democratically elected council, consisting of
seventy-five members, in which its highest authority is vested. This council autho-
rizes the budget, elects the supervisory board, and defines the priorities of the
organization by its endorsement of a strategic memorandum that is prepared every
three years. The board supervises the policymaking of the management board and
the general functioning of the bureau.

From its founding in 1953, CB's membership grew steadily (apart from a dip in
the mid-1980s lasting to the end of the 1990s) to its peak in 1997, when it had
slightly more than 650,000 members. This number equated to one out of every nine
Dutch households, a percentage unsurpassed among the world's consumer organizations. This success was presumably the result of the combined effect of CB's three

lines of action: providing excellent service towards its members (not least through its comparative testing and to a lesser extent its legal assistance), cooperating in ventures with business that serve the consumer at large, and exercising a countervailing power by applying consumer activism vis-à-vis government and businesses to remedy consumer injustices. As an example of this consumer activism, CB exposed the high costs of life insurance in the Netherlands. Although this particular action was done in a controversial manner that soured its relation with that industry for years, CB's overall approach has brought many successes and broad societal recognition. Indeed, in 2013, CB was considered one of the hundred most popular brand names in the Netherlands, ranking only a few places below KLM airlines, ING (the largest Dutch bank), and the Rijksmusuem—and ahead of McDonald's.

CB's early activities had effects well beyond Dutch borders. CB was one of the five founders of the International Organization of Consumers Unions (IOCU) in 1960. CB was especially active in the governing board of IOCU in the early years, when its headquarters were located in The Hague. In the 1990s, IOCU's headquarters moved to London; it is now named Consumers International (CI). CB also participated with consumer organizations from five other European countries in founding BEUC: The European Consumer Organisation. CB has played an active role in BEUC's operation, including by providing its president for many years and consistently serving on its board of directors.

Government Involvement

Spurred by the development of private consumer organizations, the Dutch government entered the field of consumer affairs through the subsidization of new "private" organizations. The first consumer subsidy (about $15,000) was granted by the Ministry of Economic Affairs (EZ) to CCO for comparative testing of products in 1961. Over the years, subsidies have increased, as has the involvement of EZ with respect to consumer affairs.

In 1965, the government advisory body known as the Social Economic Council—composed mainly of representatives of trade unions, employer organizations, and members appointed by government serving the general interest—established the Consumer Affairs Commission (CCA). Members of the CCA were appointed from trade unions, employers, and consumer organizations, with representatives of consumer and labor groups constituting a majority. The CCA was the first official body in which consumer organizations were represented. The CCA's task was, and with certain modifications still is, twofold: advise government on consumer policy proposals and provide a platform for consultation and negotiations between consumer organizations and industry.

Bringing together representatives of various interest groups follows the Dutch "polder model" that governs economic decision making in the Netherlands. The model dates back to the Middle Ages when people would set aside their differences and join forces when low-lying land protected by dikes threatened to flood. This tradition of finding consensus within diversity depends on negotiation and compromise. For CB, this model implies a balancing act in making deals that sometimes clearly serve the needs of the consumer and that at other times are limited by the potential of government and business.

A case in point in the negotiating model is the Advertising Code Foundation (SRC), established in 1963 with CB as a founding member. The purpose of this self-regulatory body is to ensure that companies are held accountable for their advertising practices in the Netherlands. To this end, SRC has drawn up an advertising code to be followed by companies in their advertising. Compliance with the code is monitored by the Advertising Code Committee (RCC) and the Appeals Tribunal. All major communication and advertising associations have adopted the SRC code. Apart from the general code, special code committees have been established for certain goods and services, such as alcoholic beverages, tobacco products, and sweepstakes. The number of special codes is still rising, including new codes for telemarketing (2012) and social media (2014).

Returning to the CCA, one of its first advisory actions concerned a proposal by the Ministry of Economic Affairs (EZ) to found an institute for comparative testing, SVWO, to be managed by Consumentenbond and Konsumenten Kontakt and to be subsidized by EZ. The CCA's guidelines laid down the conditions and standards for conducting and publishing test results so as to safeguard reliability and the interests of the manufacturers concerned. The subsidy made it possible to publish results of some ten to fifteen especially expensive tests annually.

CCA provides a framework for negotiations between consumer organizations and various sectors of consumer goods and services on the wording of general clauses applicable to consumer transactions. The goal is to develop general clauses whereby the interests of supplier and consumer have been taken into account in a balanced manner. The use of this framework set by CCA is one of the conditions for sectors of business to participate in the committees of the Foundation for the Resolution of Consumer Disputes previously described.

In 1974, the Minister of Economic Affairs (EZ) became the coordinating minister for consumer affairs. A year later, a directorate for consumer affairs was created around the already existing nucleus of activities at EZ. Its chief functions were helping to develop consumer policy within EZ itself and supporting other ministries in integrating consumer policy considerations in their own policies.

The increasing prominence of consumer policy within the Netherlands during the 1970s was bolstered by events within the European Community. In 1975, the Community, which had recently gone from six to eight member countries, established its first program of consumer protection. The program was based on five consumer rights that had been promulgated in 1972. These rights differed from the four rights articulated by U.S. President John F. Kennedy insofar in not explicitly recognizing the right to choose, but they acknowledged the right to the protection of economic interests.

Consumer policy developments in the Netherlands culminated in 1979, when a major government consumer policy memorandum was published and established the fundamental nature of consumer interests. According to the memorandum, the objective of government consumer policy became: "the improvement of the opportunities to satisfy needs through consumption," with an emphasis on "strengthening the position of the consumer in the marketplace" ("*Nota consument en Consumptie.*" Zitting 1978–1979, 15,716, nrs. 1–2).

Second Phase: New Challenges

Subsequent to the 1970s, Dutch consumer activism has been influenced by a number of trends. One of these has been deregulation. Emanating from the USA and UK beginning in the early 1980s, deregulation was a movement against increasing government regulation based on the belief that this regulation stifled entrepreneurial activity. The Netherlands followed suit, reviewing legislation that affected economic development and redefining government's role regarding economic actors, especially businesses. For example, SVWO was terminated in 1992 because the government no longer considered it appropriate to subsidize the regular comparative testing of products. Similarly, the need for a consumer policy directorate within the EZ was questioned. The directorate's activities were merged in 1992 with competition policy and other concerns related to the functioning of markets. The directorate's budget was reduced from $7 million to $3 million in 1997, and to even less thereafter. Subsidies for specific projects were first confined to initiatives to improve the functioning of markets and later eliminated entirely.

A further aspect of deregulation has been an effort to increase competition in the domain of services such as the public utilities, public transport and telecom. In 1998, a new competition act took effect that clamped down on agreements among firms that were anticompetitive. The national court of auditors concluded in its 2007 investigation that the new competition authority had been successful but that positive effects for the consumer were hard to quantify.

A second important trend that has influenced consumer policy has been advances in technology, especially what might be termed the "digitizing" of society. Consumers now have almost limitless access to information and channels of communication, thereby expanding their horizons. At the same time, new information and communication technologies pose threats to consumer—and citizen—privacy. Similarly, the Internet makes a global market available to consumers, but with new opportunities for consumers have emerged new forms of fraud that require consumer protection authorities to be more vigilant and active. Finally, technology has promoted greater product complexity, often accompanied by aggressive marketing practices that take advantage of a lack of consumer understanding.

Life insurance policies that include an investment component in mutual funds are a case in point. The seemingly attractive features of these policies made them hugely popular in the 1990s in the Netherlands, but a large number of these policyholders have discovered that there were many hidden costs to these policies and investment returns were far less than anticipated. Dutch enforcement authorities claimed to not have instruments at their disposal to protect the consumer against the risks involved in buying these life insurance policies, later commonly named "usurious policies." Third-party litigation awards made good for some of these losses. But the problem is far from over, as many of these life insurance policies are still running and their holders are uncertain whether their ultimate yield will be sufficient to guarantee their expected pensions or lump sum payment to settle their mortgage debts. Some 7 million of these policies have been sold, and total losses to the consumer are estimated by CB to be around $30 billion.

Third, consumers themselves have also changed. Children and young adults—who often lack experience as consumers—are more significant forces in markets, as are the growing number of older adults who sometimes face unique marketplace challenges. While consumers are better-educated overall, many still lack the math and literacy skills that are required in today's complex, information-intensive marketplace. Also, consumers appear to be less inclined to affiliate themselves with organizations, including consumer organizations.

The implications for CB of the latter two trends—technological development and changes among consumers themselves—are enormous. Before the turn of the millennium, CB was, in a sense, a monopolist within the Netherlands in terms of providing information to the consumer in an independent and transparent manner, notably through its comparative testing of products. Nowadays CB has lost this monopoly position, with many commercial websites offering comparative information free of charge, typically through the publication of customer reviews. This information is widely used, and this competition in providing consumers with product- and service-specific information is perhaps the major reason why the number of subscriptions to CB's flagship magazines has been declining since its peak of 650,000. (Its membership currently stands at about 470,000.) As is the case with product testing magazines around the world, CB also faces the challenge of gaining the interest of younger consumers in comparative testing information whose shelf life is often short in a world of rapid technological change.

The challenge CB faces is how to attract more members and gain more revenue without sacrificing the principle of providing independent and scientifically valid information. One way of coping with this conundrum is by providing intermediary services that guide the consumer through choices of products, services, or providers, as is the case for compulsory health care policies. Another way to provide intermediary services is to help the consumer to choose a company for the delivery of gas and electricity through a public auction procedure. A similar example is the public auction CB launched in early 2014 whereby firms bid to win the savings deposit business of a block customers, the first savings accounts ever marketed in this way. In all these instances, the companies winning the contract through the choice of the consumer pay CB for its intermediary services, a practice that did not exist at the turn of the millennium. Presently CB derives about 15 percent of its total revenue from these intermediary services. This type of entrepreneurial activity on the part of CB has helped compensate for the decline in government contracts to conduct specific projects, the latter having declined to the point that they now comprise less than 1 percent of CB's total income in 2012.

CB at 50 and Beyond

In 2003, on the occasion of its fiftieth birthday, CB presented a memorandum to the minister of economic affairs in which it stated that its actions to promote more competitive markets had not been accompanied by measures to guarantee the consumer an equivalent position at the market place. CB demanded, among other things, improvement of complaint handling systems, the introduction of legislation to combat unfair commercial practices, and a new system of public enforcement of consumer regulation given the deficiencies of industry self-regulation.

In 2004 the Ministry of Economic Affairs launched a "Strategic Action Program" that took into account a number of the demands CB set in its memorandum. Perhaps most notable was the decision to introduce public enforcement of private consumer protection law in addition to the existing bodies of self-regulation, acknowledging that the market and lawsuits brought by individuals were not fully capable of curbing malevolent suppliers. Because of this decision, national and cross-border enforcement of consumer protection rules was vested, starting in 2007, in one authority—the Netherlands Consumer Authority. To complement rather than supplant the private system of consumer law, public enforcement focuses on instances of collective consumer harm and inadequate self-regulatory systems.

CB has also been seeking improvements in the Dutch system of collective legal action. Until 2005, organizations representing consumers could initiate a collective action in order to seek redress for mass damage, but damages could not be awarded in this procedure. Consumer organizations could only obtain a declaratory judgment. This defect was partly remedied by the new Act on Collective Settlement of Mass Damage (WCAM) of 2005. In late 2011, the Dutch Parliament asked the government to prepare further legislation that would make it possible for representative organizations to claim for collective damages. The Ministry of Justice is considering these demands, conscious of the possible negative aspects inherent in expanding the scope for claiming damages. These efforts to expand collective legal action coincide with actions at the EU level to ensure that all member states have collective redress systems at the national level that follow the same basic principles throughout the Union, while taking into account the legal traditions of the member states.

CB continues to be viewed by the Dutch government as one of the main, legitimate representatives of consumers. CB, along with other civil society organizations, serves on the consultation panel of the Netherlands Consumer Authority. The Consumer Authority, which was created in 2007, merged in 2013 with several other government bodies to form the Authority for Consumers and Markets (ACM). ACM is unique among European countries in that it combines sector-specific regulation, consumer protection, and competition oversight in a single authority. CB will monitor and support ACM's efforts to make consumer protection and market oversight both more effective and more efficient.

Looking forward, CB and the entire Dutch consumer movement face the same challenge as the consumer movements of most other countries—adapting to a world of change in the economy and the situation of the consumer. Change is constant, giving rise to new opportunities and threats. The consumer movement, along with the Dutch government, will have to remain vigilant in preserving consumer rights.

Joop Koopman

See also: BEUC: The European Consumer Organisation; Consumers International

Further Reading

Consumentenbond. www.consumentenbond.nl.

Consumers International. 1995. *Balancing the Scales: Part 2—Consumer Protection in the Netherlands and Germany*. London, UK: Consumers International.

EURIB Top 100 of Indispensable Brands. www.rankingthebrands.com/The-Brand-Rankings.aspx?rankingID=76&nav=industry.

European Union. "The Netherlands." http://ec.europa.eu/consumers/empowerment/cons_networks_en.htm.

EAST AFRICAN CONSUMER MOVEMENTS

East Africa, as defined by the United Nations scheme, is a region comprising twenty countries. The region is also known as "the Horn of Africa" for its shape. Four countries in the region are among the ten most populous African countries: Ethiopia, Tanzania, Kenya, and Uganda. GDP per capita in east African countries is generally lower than in the rest of the continent, but there is significant variation in GDP per capita (adjusted for purchasing power parity) within east Africa—ranging from the Seychelles ($25,000) on the top to Burundi ($600) on the bottom. Similarly, growth in total national GDP during the 2007–2011 period varied greatly among east African countries, from growth exceeding 7 percent annually in Ethiopia, Uganda, and Rwanda to negligible or indeterminate growth in Zimbabwe and Somalia.

The region relies heavily on agriculture for export earnings. Major export crops include coffee, tea, tobacco, cotton, and vanilla. For several east African countries, such as Kenya, Seychelles, Tanzania, and Uganda, tourism also plays a major role in supporting their economies.

Rural areas in east Africa are highly vulnerable to water scarcity. In 2011, Ethiopia, Kenya, and Somalia suffered from an extreme drought that caused a widespread famine and ensuing high food prices for the region's consumers. Currently, more than 40 million people in east Africa face drought conditions and corresponding food insecurity (Wood Hole Oceanographic Institution, 2013). Migration to cities is no guarantee of water sufficiency. In overcrowded cities, water supplies are often insufficient and sewage treatment systems inadequate. Rapidly growing cities also face the challenge of large numbers of uneducated and unemployed young people—a source of political instability.

High birth rates and high infant mortality also pose important concerns and challenges for countries in east Africa. Notably high births rates are prevalent in Burundi, Malawi, Somalia, Uganda, and Zambia. Although infant mortality in the region has slowly decreased in the past few years, it remains high in some nations: For example, Somalia has the highest infant mortality rate, about 91 per thousand live births.

In east Africa, there are numerous consumer problems: food safety and labeling; the price and quality of water, electricity, telecommunications; and the adequacy of health services. In Rwanda, for example, the use of expired drugs in hospital stores and unsafe disposal of hazardous medical waste are particular concerns. Elsewhere, in countries such as Kenya and Sudan, less than a third of consumers have access to "improved sanitation" (e.g., a flush toilet piped to a sewer system, septic tank, or pit latrine; a ventilated improved pit latrine; or a composting toilet).

Private consumer organizations make up the majority of consumer activism groups prevalent in consumer protection. Out of the twenty countries of East Africa, eleven of them have at least one established organization under Consumers International (CI). The region has eight full members, eight affiliates, and three governmental supporters. Some countries have multiple members, whereas others have none. Kenya leads a strong consumer movement by having three full CI members, followed by Mauritius with two full members. Ethiopia, Tanzania, and the Seychelles each have a full-status CI member. Some countries are addressing their consumer problems by creating formal rights of legal redress in the country's constitution. Others are improving consumerism by improving the citizens' education and literacy levels to become more informed and sustainable consumers.

Within east Africa, a consumer movement is most developed in Kenya (see separate entry on Kenya). Kenya has several major consumer organizations, three of which are full members of Consumer International (CI)—the umbrella organization for the world's consumer movements. The advancement of Kenya's consumer organization has helped bring recognition to consumer rights in Kenya: In 2010, the Kenyan government gave legal recognition to consumer rights in its newly promulgated constitution.

Established in 1994, the Consumer Information Network (CIN) of Kenya is the country's oldest major consumer organization. Founded in Nairobi, CIN has three regional offices throughout the country. Its mission is to educate consumers about their rights and responsibilities. In addition, CIN advocates for those who do not have a voice and through constant research for improving the daily lives of consumers. The organization's areas of expertise include food safety and standards, health, sustainability, and trade. CIN joined Consumers International in 1997.

The Youth Education Network (YEN) is also a full member of the CI, having joined CI in 2005. A unique quality of this consumer organization is the focus on the next generation of consumers—the younger Kenyan citizens. Some important objectives of YEN are educating Kenyan youth to know their consumer rights and responsibilities (especially toward the natural environment) and to make informed consumer choices. YEN also encourages young people in Kenya to be actively involved in strengthening their communities. YEN has created training programs and established school clubs for consumers. In addition to using its official website, YEN also provides the public with updated, relevant news through the social media.

The African Woman and Child Feature Service (AWC) was founded in 1994 and has been an affiliate member of Consumers International since 2008. Although AWC is based in Nairobi, Kenya, it provides services throughout the east African region. AWC focuses on promoting diversity, gender equality, and literacy among women. AWC believes that advocating through the media can be an advantageous tool for educating and empowering women and children. AWC effectively uses various media to address issues affecting these two groups of consumers through a variety of media, emphasizing its website and social media. By improving the lives of its target consumers, AWC believes that it affects the country as a whole.

Tanzania Consumer Advocacy Society (TCAS) was founded in 2007 and became an affiliate member of CI in 2009. The organization aims to build a strong partnership among consumers, governmental authorities, and nongovernmental organizations (both within and without Tanzanian borders). TCAS aims to ensure that the rights of consumers are protected and that businesses are responsible and responsive to consumers' concerns and needs. TCAS also aspires to build a bridge between Tanzanian consumers and businesses. For example, it promotes financial literacy education, especially in the use of credit, by involving all parties who contribute to the economy: children, parents, educators, financial institutions, and businesses. TCAS stresses the importance of inculcating strong financial habits among Tanzania's youth—something that is important in a country where the median age is 17 years.

Though Mauritius and the Seychelles are small island countries, their consumer organizations are forces to be reckoned with when it comes to consumer activism. Both Mauritius and the Seychelles have consumer organizations that hold full membership in CI. With tourism boosting the economies of these islands, the countries also have the ability to empower and educate their citizens to become conscientious consumers and improve sustainable consumption.

French-speaking Mauritius has two organizations that are full CI members, demonstrating the influence and power of the country's consumer movement. The Consumer Association of Mauritius (ACIM) has been a full CI member since 1982. Some of ACIM's campaigns have focused on consumer education, financial services, public utilities, and sustainable consumption. Another important consumer organization is the Institute for Consumer Protection (ICP). It was originally founded in 1983 under the name Mauritian Action for the Promotion of Breastfeeding and Infant Nutrition (MAPBIN); it became ICP in 1992. ICP is known for effectively handling consumer complaints and publishing a consumer magazine called *CONSOMAG*. ICP also works to ensure that consumers are exercising their consumer rights and promoting environmental sustainability. ICP has been a full member of CI since 2009.

The Seychelles, an archipelago country of more than a hundred small islands, has its own full CI member—the National Consumers Forum (NATCOF), founded in 1994. The group's objective is to educate consumers to be responsible, resist exploitation by sellers, and advocate for themselves. In serving the general population, NATCOF conducts work with respect to consumer education, economic development, agriculture, health, and human rights. NATCOF employs social media, such as Facebook, to provide consumers with up-to-date and useful information.

Despite the vibrancy and longevity of consumer groups in some east African countries, many of the region's countries lack an organized consumer voice. Consumer activism in the region is likely to grow if economic growth and political stability continues to improve.

Kimberly Nguyen, Robert N. Mayer

See also: Consumers International; Kenyan Consumer Movement; West African Consumer Movements

Further Reading

Institute for Consumer Protection. www.icpmauritius.com.

National Consumers Forum. www.natcof.sc.

Tanzania Consumer Advocacy Society. www.tcas-tz.org/demotcas/.

Woods Hole Oceanographic Institution. 2013. "Study Provides New Insights on Drought Predictions in East Africa." January 17. www.whoi.edu/news-release/Horn_of_Africa.

ELECTRICITY SERVICE ADVOCACY

The early days of the electric industry in America were marked not by regulation, but by competition among the new electric suppliers. In the late nineteenth century, a number of American cities had many electric generating companies striving street by street to obtain customers for their new service. By the beginning of the twentieth century, however, it was generally accepted that regulation, rather than competition, was the preferred approach for the future of the burgeoning electric industry. In particular, it was recognized that it made little sense to build forests of competing electric distribution poles and lines in some districts of the city even as others went totally unserved. Electric utilities were deemed "natural monopolies"—that is, it was more economical and beneficial to society to have a single electric utility serving a particular geographic area than to let multiple utilities compete against each other to serve the same customers.

Rather than continuing to compete, electric companies across the country began to consolidate within each city and region. Some of these new utilities were municipally owned, but the majority remained in the hands of private investors. To the extent that these investor-owned utilities were not subject to competition, but were instead the recipients of government granted monopoly franchises, it was clear that the rates charged by these entities would have to be regulated. The burden of regulation fell primarily on the states, as public utility commissions were created to regulate the rates and service of electric utilities and other monopoly service providers.

By the 1920s, the consolidation of electric utilities that had begun on a local and state basis was reaching national proportions. Giant public utility holding companies were created, and those holding companies consisted of layers of corporate subsidiaries in a vast web of interlocking ownership and control. By the mid-1920s, sixteen holding companies controlled 85 percent of the nation's electricity.

The elaborate multistate holding company structure gave rise to a number of abuses that were harmful to consumers, including the "pyramiding" of corporate structures, excessive valuation of utility assets, and excessive charges on intracorporate-affiliated transactions. Many of these abuses were beyond the reach of state regulators, who could not regulate beyond their state boundaries even if they could unravel the convoluted structure of the holding companies. Another gap in state regulatory authority was exposed by the U.S. Supreme Court in 1927 when it held that state public utility commissions have no jurisdiction over interstate power transactions in *Rhode Island Pub. Utils. Comm. v. Attleboro Steam & Elec. Co.*, 273 U.S. 83.

Congress acted to correct these problems in 1935 when it passed the Federal Power Act (FPA) and the Public Utility Holding Company Act (PUHCA). The FPA established jurisdiction within the Federal Power Commission (now the Federal Energy Regulatory Commission) to regulate the interstate transmission and wholesale sale of electricity. PUHCA effectively required the breakup of the multistate holding companies into smaller companies that were either confined to one state or, in the case of "registered" holding companies, permitted to operate integrated electric utility systems in contiguous states.

The mid-1930s also saw the expansion of efforts to spread the benefits of electricity to consumers in all areas of the country. In 1935, President Roosevelt issued an executive order establishing the Rural Electrification Administration (REA). With financial assistance from the REA, hundreds of cooperatively owned rural electric companies were organized during the next decade. In addition, President Roosevelt launched very large and influential federal power agencies—the Tennessee Valley Authority and the Bonneville Power Administration.

The period from 1935 to the mid-1960s marked an era of steady growth and strong financial health for the electric utility industry, with relatively low rates and increasingly reliable service for most consumers. However, the first signs that all was not well in the industry began to appear in 1965. The great Northeast Blackout plunged much of the U.S. Northeast into darkness in November 1965. Concerns were expressed that utilities did not have adequate reserve margins to meet their capacity needs.

Many utilities began significant plant construction programs in the late 1960s and 1970s. Much of this construction represented nuclear power plants, which some early proponents had suggested would be "too cheap to meter." These construction programs occurred at a time when interest rates, and therefore the capital costs of these large construction programs, began to increase dramatically.

Meanwhile, the steady growth in electricity usage, which had given rise to the forecasts showing the need for new plants, was sharply reduced. The critical event in this period was the Arab Oil Embargo of 1973–1974, which led to a severalfold increase in oil prices that in turn led to sharp increases in electricity rates and a decline in the rate of growth in the demand for electricity.

The energy shocks of the 1970s also helped give rise to an organized utility consumer movement, highlighted by the establishment of state utility consumer advocacy offices in most states. These state offices, which now exist in more than forty states and the District of Columbia, were created to remedy the perceived unfairness of a regulatory system in which utilities were well represented by lawyers, experts, and utility personnel in matters such as rate increase requests before state public utility commissions, yet the consumers charged these rate increases were not represented. Although spiraling utility costs had a major effect on the household budgets of many consumers, individual consumers were not in a position to hire the lawyers and experts needed to defend against rate increases in complex regulatory proceedings. State consumer advocate offices were created to level the playing field and give consumers a chance to have their voices heard in an effective manner. In addition to state consumer advocate offices, a number of consumer organizations were formed at the local, state, and national levels to address utility and energy issues. Many of these organizations focused particularly on the effects of increased utility rates on low-income consumers.

Perhaps the most critical event in the history of the modern electric utility industry occurred on March 28, 1979, when a system malfunction forced the shutdown and threatened the meltdown of the Three Mile Island Unit 2 nuclear reactor near Harrisburg, Pennsylvania. Though the physical damage resulting from that accident was generally contained within the reactor walls, the financial fall-out spread to utilities and affected electricity consumers throughout the country. Nuclear plants, already facing construction delays and cost overruns, were subject to greater public and regulatory scrutiny as the inherent safety and economic via-bility of nuclear power were called into question.

No new nuclear plants began construction for some three decades after the acci-dent at TMI, and more than seventy nuclear plants that had been ordered or were under construction at the time of the TMI accident were cancelled. Those plants that had been completed faced cost overruns amounting, in many cases, to billions of dollars. Moreover, the forecast electricity demands that had been used to justify construction of many of those plants failed to materialize, leaving some utilities with extraordinarily expensive excess capacity.

This combination of events brought the electric industry under unprecedented regulatory scrutiny by state public utility commissions and consumer advocates. Whereas electric utility rate proceedings had previously been quiet affairs between utilities and public utility commission staffs, the rate cases of the late 1970s and 1980s became heated and well-publicized political, economic, and financial debates. Issues in the electric cases included whether consumers should have to pay the cost of canceled nuclear power plants, as well as the prudence and reason-ableness of the costs of completed plants, which were unneeded and uneconomi-cal by the time they came on line. One of these rate cases, *Duquesne Light Company v. Barasch*, 488 U.S. 299 (1989), went to the U.S. Supreme Court, which upheld the position of the Pennsylvania Office of Consumer Advocate that two Penn-sylvania utilities had no constitutional right to charge ratepayers for the costs of four canceled nuclear power plants. Consumer representatives in many states also spearheaded efforts to require utilities to reduce their reliance on new nuclear and coal-fired generating plants and turn instead to conservation, energy efficiency, and renewable energy resources.

Although billions of dollars of nuclear power plant expenditures ultimately were disallowed from utility rates, many more billions of dollars of costs were included in the rates. As a result, the rates charged to customers of heavily nuclear utilities increased dramatically and contributed to a major disparity in rates among utilities within states and across regions.

This great disparity in rate levels also helped give rise to another significant policy development, the introduction of competition for the sale of electricity gen-eration at both the wholesale and retail levels. Many economists and policymakers concluded that the generation of electricity was not a natural monopoly and would benefit from the introduction of competitive forces. They argued that there is no strong economic basis to restrict the generation of electricity to a single regulated entity in any given geographic area.

The move toward a competitive generation industry was given a major boost by Congress when, in 1978, it passed the Public Utility Regulatory Policies Act (PURPA). Under PURPA, electric utilities were required to purchase power from certain "qualifying" cogeneration and small power facilities at rates that were based on the utility's avoided cost—that is, the cost that a utility would incur if it built its own generating unit or purchased power elsewhere. Under PURPA, the nonutility generation industry began to flourish, and by 1990, more than half of the new electric capacity in the United States was being built by nonutility generators.

Congress gave electricity competition another boost with the passage of the Energy Policy Act of 1992 (EPAct). EPAct created a new category of independent power producers, called exempt wholesale generators, able to compete to sell power at the wholesale level. These generators were generally exempt from restrictions imposed by PUHCA, did not have to meet the special qualification requirements of PURPA, and could be owned by electric utility affiliates. Perhaps more importantly, EPAct also greatly increased the ability of third party buyers and sellers of electricity to gain access to utility-owned transmission facilities. With this increased access to transmission, the wholesale market for electricity was greatly expanded.

The congressional policy to support generation competition at the wholesale level has been implemented through a series of major generic orders by the Federal Energy Regulatory Commission (FERC). These orders further expanded the ability of generators to gain access to competitive wholesale markets and substantially restricted any ability of utilities to utilize their transmission resources to block competitive generators from selling their power to wholesale customers. These federal policies led many utilities to cede control of their transmission assets to Independent System Operators (ISOs) and Regional Transmission Organizations (RTOs), which operate the transmission systems and, in some cases, competitive wholesale generation markets on a statewide or regional basis in many parts of the country.

Although federal policy has clearly and consistently favored the creation of competitive markets and "market-based" generation rates at the wholesale level, the movement toward competition for the sale of retail generation regulated at the state level has been more uneven. Starting with California in 1996, nearly twenty states took steps to open their retail generation markets to competition. However, the national trend among states to permit competition at the retail level came to an effective halt in 2001 as a result of the California electricity crisis. That crisis arose when California's newly created electricity markets suffered electricity shortages and massive price spikes caused by market manipulation of energy marketers such as Enron. These events resulted in rolling blackouts and the bankruptcy of a major California electric utility.

After the California debacle, a few states ended their experiments with retail competition, and the majority of states continued to regulate their utility service on a traditional cost basis. However, about fifteen states, mainly from the New England,

Mid-Atlantic, and Midwest regions, though including Texas, currently allow retail customers to "shop" for the generation component of their electricity service. In those states, electric distribution service is still regulated on a monopoly basis, but the generation portion of the electric service is subject to competition. Even with respect to generation service, however, in most of these states, there is still a designated "default" supplier or "provider of last resort," for those customers who, for whatever reason, do not choose to purchase generation from an unregulated competitive supplier. For the most part, the larger industrial and commercial customers in states with retail competition have switched to competitive suppliers for the purchase of their generation supplies, while a majority of residential and small business customers still obtain generation through their state-designated default supplier. Consumer advocates in these states have generally sought to retain the benefits of reasonably priced default service for those customers who do not choose to switch to unregulated suppliers, while also assisting those customers who do choose to shop to understand their choices and to avoid falling victim to improper marketing practices.

Another recent development that has had a major effect on electric utilities and consumers is the installation of "smart" electric meters in many consumers' homes and businesses. With smart meters, utilities can charge rates that vary by the time of the day, or day of the week, rather than simply adding the kilowatt hours used over the course of the month and charging consumers the same rate for each kilowatt hour. Proponents of smart meters and "time-of-use" or "real-time" pricing contend that this approach is more economically efficient and properly charges consumers more for electric usage when the cost of providing such service is highest, such as during peak summer hours. Opponents of this type of pricing argue that it is complex and confusing to many customers and that it can be unfair to those customers who are unable to reduce or shift usage from peak periods. Consumer advocates have generally argued that these time-based rate designs should be provided to residential customers on a voluntary, opt-in basis. That is, customers who understand and believe they can benefit from these types of rates should be permitted to do so, but other customers should remain on more traditional flat rates unless they voluntarily choose the time-based rate option.

As of this writing, a number of other issues have arisen that could change how electricity is provided to American consumers. These include the growth in "distributed generation," such as solar panels on homes and businesses, where consumers can generate their own power on the customer side of the electric meter; the effect of climate change and other environmental policies that will significantly affect the use of fossil fuels, particularly coal, in the generation of electricity; and the role of energy efficiency and demand response on the services offered and the prices paid by consumers. In whatever manner these and other issues develop, however, the critical task confronting consumer representatives today and in the future remains the same—to ensure that all electricity consumers receive this vital and essential service at reasonable prices.

Sonny Popowsky

See also: Energy Advocacy; State Utility Advocacy

Further Reading

Fox-Penner, Peter. 2010. *Smart Power: Climate Change, the Smart Grid, and the Future of Electric Utilities*. Washington, DC: Island Press.

Hempling, Scott. 2013. *Regulating Public Utility Market Performance: The Law of Market Structure, Pricing and Jurisdiction*. American Bar Association Section of Environment, Energy, and Resources.

ELECTRONIC PRIVACY INFORMATION CENTER

The Electronic Privacy Information Center (EPIC) is a public interest research center in Washington, D.C. It was established in 1994 to focus public attention on emerging civil liberties issues and to protect privacy, the First Amendment, and constitutional values. A leading privacy organization in the United States, it pursues a wide range of activities, including research, litigation, congressional testimony, participation in expert panels, comments to federal agencies, and grassroots campaigns.

EPIC began in 1994 with the Internet's first online petition, the effort to stop the National Security Agency's Clipper Chip encryption scheme. A letter to President Clinton, signed by forty-two leading technology experts and legal scholars, attracted support from more than 50,000 Internet users. The petition was delivered to the White House, and the Clipper Chip proposal was eventually withdrawn.

Since then, EPIC has played a leading role on a wide range of civil liberties and privacy issues in the United States and around the world. Its initiatives include the EPIC Open Government Project, the EPIC Appellate Advocacy Project, the EPIC Domestic Surveillance Project, the EPIC Consumer Protection Project, the Public Voice Project, and the Privacy Coalition. Its websites, including www.epic.org and www.privacy.org, are among the most influential privacy websites in the world.

EPIC, a 501(c)(3) nonprofit organization, was founded and has always been led by president and executive director Marc Rotenberg. Rotenberg was a former counsel to Senator Patrick Leahy on the Senate Judiciary Committee and has been an adjunct professor at the Georgetown University Law Center faculty. EPIC staff include attorneys, law fellows, technology fellows, and administrators. They are supported by annual revenues of around $1 million, most of which represents contributions, foundation grants, and *cy près* awards. The organization does not accept funding from private companies or government agencies. It is governed by a board of directors chaired by Deborah Hurley and maintains an advisory board which includes many intellectual and policy leaders in the privacy area.

One of the priority areas in which EPIC works is consumer protection. In particular, it has focused on the responsibility of the Federal Trade Commission (FTC) to investigate and stop unfair and deceptive trade practices. In the mid-1990s, just as the commercialization of the Internet began, EPIC was the first organization to argue that the FTC's "Section 5 authority" could be used to protect the privacy of Internet users.

Since then, EPIC has pursued many successful FTC complaints concerning the misuse of user data by major Internet companies. In 2001, EPIC and a coalition of consumer groups filed a complaint concerning Microsoft Passport, a plan for single gateway access to the Internet that threatened Internet privacy and safety. Following the complaint, the FTC pursued an investigation, then announced a settlement with Microsoft that required the company to establish a comprehensive information security program for Passport and prohibited it from misrepresenting its practices of information collection and usage.

EPIC pursued similar complaints against Google and Facebook for privacy violations, again with the support of other consumer privacy organizations. In 2009, it asked the FTC to investigate Facebook's decision to change its users' privacy settings without their consent, a change that made user information more widely available to the public and to Facebook's affiliated business. The FTC investigated, agreed with the consumer privacy organizations, and established a comprehensive privacy settlement with the Internet company.

Similarly, EPIC asked the FTC to investigate Google's launch of Buzz, which forced Gmail users to sign up for Google's social network services. This complaint also resulted in settlement agreements that prohibited Google from future misrepresentations, required Google to obtain affirmative express consent before disclosing users' personal information, and required the company to establish comprehensive privacy programs subject to independent biennial assessments.

EPIC was also responsible for the largest consumer privacy settlement at the FTC before the Safari judgment in 2012. In 2005, the data broker Choicepoint agreed to pay a $15 million penalty to the FTC after a complaint from EPIC showed that the company had violated consumer protection laws.

EPIC has worked with state attorneys general to protect consumer privacy in such matters as Echometrics, a product that purported to filter Internet sites for children yet that gathered data for marketing purposes, and Google Street View, which was intercepting Wi-Fi communications as well as capturing digital imagery. The latter investigation, involving thirty-seven states, led to a $7 million settlement with Google.

EPIC has also taken leadership on issues related to student privacy, open government, and appellate advocacy. With the rapid growth of databases containing detailed student data and new systems of student identification, EPIC made student privacy a high priority. The organization submitted open government requests to uncover government treatment of sensitive data. It filed an extensive student consumer complaint with the FTC that urged the agency to protect student medical, financial, sexual, and religious information. And it joined other consumer protection groups in support of a moratorium on RFID student tracing in schools. In 2012, EPIC sued the U.S. Department of Education for weakening the Family Educational Rights and Privacy Act by broadening the permissible purposes for which third parties can access student records without first obtaining student consent. However, dismissing the case for lack of subject matter jurisdiction, the court never considered its merits.

EPIC runs one of the leading open government programs in the United States. Over the years, many of its Freedom of Information Action (FOIA) cases have been reported on the front pages of the *New York Times* and the *Washington Post*. These cases have also served as the basis for congressional hearings. For example, documents obtained by EPIC in 2012 revealed that the Department of Homeland Security was monitoring online Twitter communications.

In recent years, EPIC has successfully settled FOIA cases and obtained fees against the Central Intelligence Agency, the Federal Bureau of Investigation, the Department of Homeland Security, the Department of Education, the Office of the Director of National Intelligence, and the Transportation Security Administration. EPIC's litigation has also established favorable precedents for other open government litigators on such matters as fee recovery, expedited processing, and fee waivers. EPIC also collaborates with the Georgetown University Law Center on a FOIA clinic to train new open government attorneys.

In the past two decades, EPIC has filed more than fifty amicus briefs in federal and state courts, including twenty cases in the U.S. Supreme Court. The briefs have addressed a wide range of issues including the collection of DNA by law enforcement agencies, the reliability of controversial investigative techniques, the compelled disclosure of identity, the interpretation of various federal privacy statutes, and the rise of domestic surveillance by the National Security Agency.

EPIC has also played a significant role in seeking to reform the practice of *cy près* awards, urging courts to ensure that awards are made to organizations that are aligned with the interests of class members and that advance the purposes of the underlying legal claims. Several consumer privacy settlements have been revised in response to comments submitted by EPIC.

EPIC strongly favors Fair Information Practices, in which individuals get the rights while companies and agencies take on the responsibilities. It rejects various "notice and choice" constructions of privacy that are simply disclaimers and waivers. EPIC also supports genuine privacy-enhancing techniques that minimize the collection of personally identifiable information.

EPIC has worked closely with other organizations in the United States and abroad. EPIC established the Public Voice coalition to promote civil participation in decisions concerning the future of the Internet. It has organized conferences in a dozen countries on numerous privacy topics. For many years, it worked with the London-based Privacy International to publish *Privacy and Human Rights*, an extensive report on privacy that tracked legal developments, NGO accomplishments, and new challenges. Its Washington-based Privacy Coalition provides an opportunity for consumer privacy organizations to meet with public officials.

Since its founding, EPIC staff have testified in more than 100 congressional hearings, as well as additional hearings held by the European Parliament and federal and state agencies, and provided comments in more than 100 agency rulemakings. As well as those effects mentioned earlier, EPIC played a leading role in several successful campaigns to protect privacy after 9/11, including the end of the Total Information Awareness program and the Secure Flight screening system. Following several petitions to the Department of Homeland Security and a lawsuit, EPIC was also responsible for the removal of backscatter x-ray devices in U.S. airports.

Julia Horwitz

See also: Litigation; Privacy Advocacy

Further Reading

Burnham, David. 1983. "New Tool for Public Affairs Lobbies." *New York Times* (August 26).

Clausing, Jeri. 1999. "The Privacy Group That Took on Intel." *New York Times* (February 1).

Lohr, Steve. 2001. "Privacy Group Is Taking on Microsoft." *New York Times* (July 25).

Risen, James. 2013. "Privacy Group to Ask Supreme Court to Stop N.S.A.'s Phone Spying Program." *New York Times* (July 7).

ENERGY ADVOCACY

Today's wide array of organizations advocating on behalf of energy consumers has its roots in the early twentieth-century muckrakers who exposed the monopoly and political power of the oil and electric utility trusts, the crusading efforts of Ralph Nader in the 1960s, and the political clout of organized labor. In twenty-first century America, consumer advocates at the national and state levels publicize, agitate, organize, and lobby on behalf of Americans who purchase energy. Whether it's challenging utility rate cases, advocating alternative energy sources, or exposing corporate malfeasance, energy consumer groups owe their current existence and status primarily to organizations that came into existence in the late 1960s and early 1970s.

Among the primary intellectual forebears of consumer energy organizations were muckraking journalists, historians, economists, labor leaders, and lawyers who studied, analyzed, and challenged the growing power center in the oil, gas, coal, and electric utility industries. In 1894, Henry Demarest Lloyd, a *Chicago Tribune* reporter and precursor of twentieth century muckrakers, published *Wealth against Commonwealth*, which documented the vast power of John D. Rockefeller's Standard Oil and other monopolistic trusts. A decade later, Ida Tarbell published the now famous *The History of Standard Oil*, which remains a tour de force of investigative journalism documenting how Rockefeller's oil company eliminated competitors and controlled the oil industry. The book generated public outrage and led to a 1909 U.S. Justice Department antitrust suit against the trust. In 1911, the U.S. Supreme Court ordered the breakup of Standard Oil into thirty-four independent companies.

The predation of oil barons did not end with the breakup of Rockefeller's monopoly. The ability of wealthy oil magnates to influence government and corrupt public officials was exemplified by the Teapot Dome Scandal during the administration of President Harding. Two oilmen, Harry Sinclair and Edward Doheny, obtained oil leases by bribing Albert Fall, the secretary of the interior. An investigation led by Robert M. La Follette, a progressive Republican senator from Wisconsin and Thomas Walsh, a Democrat from Montana, exposed the crimes. That investigation led to criminal and civil lawsuits culminating in a 1927 Supreme Court decision holding that the oil leases in Teapot Dome in Wyoming and Elk Hills in California had been fraudulently obtained.

Despite congressional investigations and Supreme Court decisions aimed at promoting competition and punishing those who would corrupt public officials, the oil industry, especially the largest integrated companies that began to consolidate after the 1911 Supreme Court decision, continued to exercise great influence over the economy and policy. In 1961, Robert Engler, a political science professor, published *The Politics of Oil: A Study of Private Power and Democratic Directions*. This book documented how the oil industry influenced government at the state and national levels, undermined regulations, and influenced public policy to serve its interests. Ralph Nader called it an "early bell-ringer" in outlining the oil lobby's influence in Washington after World War II and showing how the largest companies divided up world markets.

Nader himself deserves much of the credit for parenting the consumer movement overall and the energy consumer movement in particular. Nader created or inspired numerous organizations, including Public Citizen and the public interest research groups, that worked on energy issues. Also important was the work of the law firm of Lobel, Novins & Lamont. The founders—Marty Lobel, Alan Novins, and John Lamont, who had many years of Hill and Justice Department Antitrust Division experience among them—provided intellectual and organization support for efforts aimed at reducing the outsized economic power of the major international oil companies. This firm educated many groups—advocacy organizations, labor unions, and congressional offices—on strategies to challenge the huge companies. And it was especially helpful in the founding of Energy Action.

Triggering the increased interest by consumer organizations in energy in the early 1970s was the quadrupling of world oil prices, which significantly increased the price of gasoline and home heating oil. Consumer advocates viewed the increase as the result not only of the Arab oil embargo, but also of oil company drilling and refining cutbacks and hoarding behavior. In response, President Nixon ordered his Cost of Living Council to stabilize the price of gasoline at local service stations, which encouraged Congress to approve legislation that established federal price controls on oil.

Growing pressure from major oil companies, the largest producers of natural gas, on the Federal Power Commission (FPC) to raise natural gas wellhead prices also aroused consumer opposition. Initially, this opposition was led by the American Public Gas Association, which represented the nation's municipally owned gas distribution systems. Led by executive director and general counsel Charles Wheatley, the organization communicated forcefully to the FPC and to members of Congress.

Together with organizations including the AFL–CIO, individual trade unions, the National Farmers Union, the U.S. Conference of Mayors, the National Rural Electric Cooperative Association, and the American Public Power Association, in 1973 Wheatley helped create an Energy Policy Task Force within the Consumer Federation of America. CFA was a broad coalition of consumer, cooperative, and labor groups that been organized in 1968 to lobby on behalf of consumers before Congress and the federal executive branch. The task force was chaired by former FPC chairman Lee White and directed by Ellen Berman. In response to escalating oil prices, it urged Congress to approve controls on oil and fuel prices.

In the late 1970s, the Energy Policy Task Force split from CFA and became the Consumer Energy Council of America (CECA), which until recently worked especially closely with public power companies and rural electric cooperatives to restrain fuel costs. In the early 1980s, its researcher, Mark Cooper, a Yale PhD, left CECA to join CFA as its research director, a position he continues to hold. Over the past three decades, no consumer advocate has testified before Congress, federal agencies, and state public utility commissions on energy issues more frequently than Cooper. In this time, he has undertaken research and advocacy on issues related to oil and gas pricing, motor vehicle fuel efficiency, appliance efficiency, nuclear energy, utility deregulation, and electricity rates. In the past several years, he also completed research on oil commodity speculation that was profiled by members of Congress.

The principal consumer group that organized opposition to rising oil and natural gas prices was Energy Action. In 1975, responding to escalating energy prices and exploding oil company profits, Paul Newman and several other progressive funders (Miles Rubin, Stanley Sheinbaum, Harold Willens, and Leo Wyler) formed the Energy Action Committee (later called Energy Action) to investigate rising prices, advocate before Congress, and expand the scope of energy consumer activity. Newman and his associates hired Jim Flug to lead the organization. Flug, who had worked for Ted Kennedy on the Senate Judiciary Committee, aggressively challenged the big oil companies. Employing diverse strategies including research, press events, advertising, and lobbying, Flug and Energy Action relentlessly criticized anticonsumer oil industry policies.

Beginning in 1978, a group of labor unions, statewide citizen organizations, and national consumer groups joined together to form the Citizen/Labor Energy Coalition (CLEC). Enabling CLEC's activity was the second oil price escalation generated in reaction to the Iranian Revolution. Composed of sixty national and statewide organizations, CLEC became an important political force trying to stop the decontrol of oil and gas prices being pushed by the oil industry and by President Jimmy Carter. Led by Bill Winpisinger, president of the International Association of Machinists (IAM), and directed by Heather Booth, the head of Citizen Action, CLEC together with Energy Action were the principal consumer voices in the intense public and congressional debates over energy policy.

In 1981, CLEC and Energy Action merged. Ed Rothschild, who had been CLEC's executive director, led the combined organization's research and policy efforts on energy. In the decade before that, Rothschild had worked on energy issues for the Center for Auto Safety, for the American Public Gas Association, for Senator James Abourezk, and for Energy Action before joining CLEC. From 1981 until CLEC was disbanded in the late 1980s, then until 1997 as research and policy director at Citizen Action, Rothschild was the consumer movement's most active and influential energy advocate. His priorities were stopping decontrol of oil/gas prices and consolidation within the industry and supporting greater use of renewables and energy efficiency. He also initiated a lawsuit against the federal government for failing to collect adequate royalties from their offshore oil and gas leases.

The other national consumer organization that has been a leader on energy issues is Public Citizen. Created by Ralph Nader in 1971, from 1982 through

2009 this consumer/citizen group was headed by Joan Claybrook, an influential expert on and advocate for transportation safety. But she and her organization also addressed an array of energy issues, including nuclear safety, nuclear waste, renewable energy, energy efficiency, and utility deregulation. The current director of Public Citizen's Energy Program is Tyson Slocum. Since joining the organization in 2000, Slocum has advocated on issues related to climate change, coal, oil, fracking, nuclear energy, renewables, and commodity market oversight. For the past decade, he has been the consumer advocate in Washington, D.C., who has spoken the most frequently on behalf of energy consumers.

In the 1970s and 1980s, CLEC had an extensive network of state organizations that worked on state as well as federal issues. During this period, other state consumer groups were organized to represent the interests of energy consumers. The most enduring have been consumer utility advocates that were established to intervene on behalf of consumers before public service commissions on electricity and natural gas (and telephone) issues. Most of these state groups, which in 1979 created a national association, the National Association of State Utility Consumer Advocates (NASUCA), have been directly funded by their state governments. But some have received intervenor funding allocated by public utility commissions. In California, The Utility Reform Network (TURN, which formerly stood for Toward Utility Rate Normalization), Consumer Watchdog, and the Consumer Federation of California have all used this funding to advocate on behalf of consumers. Several state Citizen Utility Boards (CUBs), instead of being funded by states, get access to utility mailings that allow them to solicit funding for their advocacy.

While most of this state advocacy is focused on regulated utilities, from time to time state groups have targeted the oil industry. For example, in 2005 under the leadership of Harvey Rosenfield and Jamie Court, Consumer Watchdog created a subgroup, Oil Watchdog, in an effort to "expose the profiteering, power, and unscrupulous practices of the oil industry." Its most important campaign was the development and promotion of a state initiative, Proposition 87, that sought to reduce oil consumption through improved energy efficiency. This 2006 ballot measure was vigorously opposed by major oil companies, which spent nearly $100 million to defeat it—and they succeeded.

Ed Rothschild

See also: Consumer Federation of America; Community Activism; Electricity Service Advocacy; Public Citizen; State and Local Consumer Advocacy Groups; State Utility Advocacy

Further Reading

Battista, Andrew. 1999. "Labor Liberalism: The Citizen Labor Energy Coalition." *Labor History* 40, no. 3: 301–321.

Engler, Robert. 1963. *The Politics of Oil, A Study of Private Power and Democratic Directions.* Chicago, IL: Phoenix Books.

Kelsey, Janet, and Don Weiner. 1983. "The Citizen/Labor Energy Coalition." *Social Policy* (spring): 15–18.

F

FAMILIES USA

For many years, Families USA Foundation has been the most prominent and influential consumer group focused exclusively on health care issues. Founded in 1982 by Phil and Kate Villers, and led since 1983 by Ron Pollack, Families USA has worked to secure meaningful national health care reform in order to achieve high-quality, affordable health coverage and care for all Americans. Among other initiatives, it was a leader in supporting health care reform during the Clinton and Obama administrations.

From the outset, Families USA has emphasized the health care concerns and needs of low- and moderate-income families as well as people in communities of color. The organization initiated and currently chairs the National Medicaid Coalition, which consists of several hundred diverse national organizations, including those representing children, seniors, women, low-income communities, health care providers, and faith-based groups.

Before becoming executive director of Families USA in 1983, Ron Pollack was the founding executive director of the Food Research and Action Center (FRAC) from 1970 to 1980, then served as dean of the Antioch University School of Law. At FRAC, he successfully argued, on the same day before the U.S. Supreme Court, two cases that protected Food Stamp benefits for low-income people and also brought a lawsuit that started the Supplemental Feeding Program for Women, Infants, and Children (WIC). At Families USA, Pollack has been recognized by *The Hill* as one of the most influential nonprofit lobbyists and was appointed by President Clinton as the sole consumer representative on the Presidential Advisory Commission on Consumer Protection and Quality in the Health Care Industry.

The senior staff of Families USA include several longtime health care reformers. Deputy executive director and government affairs director Jen Beeson, who joined the organization in 2006, previously worked on health care issues as a staffer at the House Ways and Means Committee, U.S. Department of Labor, and several nonprofit organizations. Director of organizational strategy Rachel Klein, who is leading the organization's efforts to secure optimal enrollment of people eligible for health coverage through the Affordable Care Act (ACA), worked for Families USA from 1998 to 2011, then served as founding executive director of Enroll America before rejoining Families USA in 2013. Field director Patrick Willard, who has several decades experience as an advocate and policy expert, previously worked with AARP to advocate for the ACA and its implementation. Director of enterprise and innovation Joe Ditre, who joined Families USA in 2014, had worked, since 1988, as founding executive director of Consumers for Affordable Health Care, a Maine-based advocacy organization.

The work of Families USA is supported by an annual budget of about $10 million that is funded mainly by grants from national foundations such as the Robert Wood Johnson Foundation. As an organization policy, the group does not request or receive funding from health industry organizations.

This budget supports an array of advocacy activities. They include the preparation and distribution of publications, which range from detailed health care analyses to condensed material more suitable for use in social media. Before passage of the ACA in 2010, most publications analyzed the need for health care reform and made specific recommendations for this reform. Since then, most publications have dealt in some way with the ACA—specific ideas and best practices for implementation, proposals for federal and state administrative rulemaking, need for program expansion and improvements, analyses about improving health care quality while decelerating health care costs, and defense of the ACA from ongoing attacks.

As well as preparing its own analyses, Families USA has collected stories, through its Story Bank, from individuals about their interaction with the health care system. These stores and individuals have been featured numerous times by print and broadcast media covering health care reform issues.

As part of its communications efforts, Families USA has also organized an annual Radio Row that brings together dozens of radio broadcasters to the organization's annual conference, who then interview participating consumer advocates. In addition, Families USA has organized training events for broadcasters and print journalists who serve communities of color.

Since the organization's founding, these program activities have supported Families USA's numerous advocacy campaigns. Most of these campaigns have involved mobilizing different constituencies to promote and support health care reform. During the 1990s, for example, Families USA organized ambulance and bus "drives" around the country to support rallies for this reform, especially President Clinton's proposed Health Security Act. After this legislation failed, the organization hosted multiple convocations of diverse national organizations representing insurance, hospital, pharmaceutical, physician, nurse, business, labor, and consumers interests. At these convocations, participants reached significant agreements that helped set the stage for extension of the Children's Health Insurance Program (CHIP) and, eventually, the ACA.

Since the enactment of the ACA, Families USA has helped organize campaigns to promote the state-by-state expansion of the Medicaid program. The organization has also played a leadership role in promoting campaigns designed to secure optimal enrollment of uninsured and underinsured people in ACA-related coverage.

Ron Pollack

See also: Health Insurance Advocacy; Healthcare Advocacy; Prescription Drug Advocacy

Further Reading

Aizenman, N. C. 2011. "Individual Stories are Weapon of Choice in Fight over Health-Care Law." *Washington Post* (April 9).

Fairhall, John. 1993. "Families USA Has Long Had Clinton's Ear." *Baltimore Sun* (October 16).

Lewin, Tamar. 1994. "Hybrid Organization Serves as a Conductor for the Health Care Orchestra." *New York Times* (July 28).

"Longtime Health Care Advocate Hopes for Democratic Turning Point." 2007. *Politico* (February 13). http://www.politico.com/news/stories/0207/2746.html.

FINANCIAL EDUCATION ADVOCACY

See Consumer Education Advocacy

FINNISH CONSUMER MOVEMENT

Consumer activism in Finland began with the activities of consumer cooperatives and housewives' organizations, both of which conceived of consumers as purely economic actors. Beginning in the mid-twentieth century, however, the meaning of the term "consumer" became more political. From the 1960s onward, nongovernmental consumer activism—and its support by the government—has been strong. The overall pattern of development of consumer activism has been similar to that in Finland's neighbor, Sweden, but with some unique features.

The Roots of Consumer Activism

During the 1880s, when Finland was an autonomous territory of the Russian Empire, Finnish civil society was characterized by the activities of political parties as well as various associations, including workers' associations and temperance groups. Consumer activism in Finland evolved from several of these private sector associations—most notably, women's and housewives' organizations and consumer cooperatives.

One early housewives' organization (the Martha Organization), founded in 1899 by school mistresses, aimed at improving the living conditions of common families. It focused on educating women about practices of good housekeeping, nutrition, hygiene, and financial planning. The organization was popular among women: By the late 1930s the Martha Organization had more than 60,000 members and a few hundred advisors who helped housewives in both rural and urban areas. The other women's mass organization, known as Agricultural Women, was established in 1933 and also provided household guidance services. Member enrollment in Agricultural Women grew to be even greater than the Martha Organization. Both organizations financed their activities mostly by dues and subscriptions to their publications, but also with state subsidies for their household guidance efforts.

The cooperative movement in Finland was established in the beginning of the twentieth century and quickly began to flourish. In those days, Finland was an agrarian society; two-thirds of its inhabitants made their living from agriculture and other forms of primary production, and eighty-seven percent of the population lived in rural areas. The first cooperatives were local and facilitated either agricultural production or retailing. In 1904, SOK (Suomen Osuuskauppojen Keskuskunta) was formed to help coordinate the purchases and advisory services of consumer cooperatives. These cooperatives were inspired by a cooperative ideology that strongly emphasized open membership, democracy, powerful educational objectives, and distribution of any surplus proceeds to members of the cooperative. Cooperative education warned individuals against poor-quality products and overcharging, and it taught them financial management skills Locally, cooperative ideology connected people of various social classes. Thus the Finnish cooperative movement rapidly gained members and was already a considerable movement before World War I.

The Finnish cooperative movement split in 1916. SOK represented more middle-class constituencies, whereas the newly founded Central Union of Consumer Cooperatives (Kulutusosuuskuntien Keskusliitto) represented the cooperatives that served left-wing and labor union households. Member education was particularly important in the activities of left-wing cooperatives, and it included instruction about the functioning of the economy, cooking demonstrations, and price comparisons. In 1916, the Central Union published the first magazine aimed at consumers: Consumers' Magazine (*Kuluttajain Lehti*). It first appeared in Finnish and then in Swedish. The need for household guidance aimed at housewives became all the more important thanks to the Finnish Civil War of 1917, which left many households without a male head.

Social Democrat Väinö Tanner (1881–1966) was an eminent leader of the left-wing cooperative movement and strong supporter of education activities for consumers. He served as chairman of the Central Union of Consumer Cooperatives, managing director of the cooperative retail society Elanto, and prime minister of the Social Democratic minority government in 1927. In addition to many other important roles, Tanner was appointed president of the International Cooperative Alliance (ICA) in 1927, a significant position in the international cooperative movement. He was a strong supporter of education and instruction activities

The cooperative movement represented by SOK focused primarily on providing its members with goods and services, with education and guidance being lower priorities. Some food management advisors were hired during the 1920s and 1930s, but the most significant channel of information provision was the magazine *Yhteishyvä*. Eventually, under the influence of female politician and active organizer Hedvig Gebhard (1867–1961), these cooperatives made a concerted effort to mobilize their female members. In 1941, women's committees along the lines of those in the more left-wing cooperatives were founded for the purpose of more thoroughly mobilizing cooperative members.

Consumer activism in Finland had roots beyond the cooperatives and housewives' and women's organization. One case was the Social Democratic Women's Federation. Female Social Democrats noticed that household education and guidance provided an efficient channel to attract new members. Thus the organization arranged cooking courses, lectures, and home visits. The chairperson of the organization, Miina Sillanpää (1866–1952), who served as a member of parliament for a total of thirty-eight years and became Finland's first female minister in 1927, became interested in household technology, storage methods, and the modern

American consumer society after a visit to the United States in 1931. She emphasized the need for modernization of the Finnish household.

In addition to the various organizations already described, most of which reflected the central role of women in consumption, two small farmers associations carried out household education and guidance. The first was the Small Farmers' Union (Pienviljelijäin Liitto). It was begun in 1910 as an organization of tenant farmers, who were political leftists. The second was the Central Union of the Small Farmers (Pienviljelijäin Keskusliitto), founded in 1922 by Professor Hannes Gebhard (1864–1933) as the organization of independent small farmers. During the 1930s these two organizations had 20,000–30,000 members, and they organized household education and guidance in addition to other activities. Their activity reflected the importance of Finland's agrarian population.

Organizations' Activities during and after World War II

Finland was attacked by the Soviet Union in late autumn 1939, and the Winter War that ensued lasted until March 1940. In the end, Finland managed to preserve its independence, but there were tens of thousands of casualties on both sides, and Finland lost part of its territory. During the war, the Ministry of Supply was established to organize the supply of food and raw materials, thereby essentially controlling consumer access to necessities. Difficulties for consumers in obtaining food continued during World War II as Finland first fought the Soviet Union as part of the Axis Powers (1941–1944) and then against Germany (1944–1945). Strict food rationing meant that households received very limited amounts of this precious commodity.

In times of general shortage of goods during and after the war, the role of women's and agricultural organizations stood out. Some women's organizations united to establish the Household Center (Kotitalouskeskus). The founding organizations were the Martha Organization, the Small Farmers' Union, the Central Union of the Small Farmers, and Social Democratic women. The Household Center published advisory guides and organized events. In 1944, it began testing the safety and quality of canned products, spices, and other foodstuffs.

Women's organizations had been promoting the foundation of a professorship in home economics at the university level since the 1920s. Their efforts bore fruit when a professorship in home economics was established at the University of Helsinki in 1946, the first professorship of its kind in Europe. The former executive manager of the Martha Organization, Elli Saurio (1899–1966), was appointed to the office, where she taught courses and conducted research.

Another important pioneer of household and consumer research in Finland was Laura Harmaja (1881–1954). She had been teaching home economics to students during the 1920s and was an active writer and advocate of household research. Maiju Gebhard (1896–1986) was another notable woman in the consumer movement. She was the executive manager of the household department in the research, development, and training institute of the Society for the Rationalization of Work (Työtehoseura), which was founded in 1943. The society's household department carried out research to promote efficiency in household work and promoted the use of new household technologies, such as refrigerators, freezers, vacuum cleaners, that started to flow into the Finish consumer market in the late 1940s and 1950s.

National Consumer Policy

Although Finland was still a largely agrarian society in the beginning of the 1950s and had to pay reparations to the Soviet Union, it managed to embark on a path of favorable economic development. A period of peace and gradually growing prosperity gave Finnish families the opportunity to envision a better future for consumers. Economic growth accelerated during the 1960s as Finland experienced rapid structural change. The living standard of the average citizen improved, and people moved from the countryside to cities in search of better jobs. Leisure time increased with the transition to a five-day work week. The population's overall education level improved, and enrollment at universities increased. Finland's new status as an associate member of the newly formed European Free Trade Association in 1961 significantly improved the availability of foreign products in Finland.

During the 1950s, the word "consumer" was used commonly in the left-wing cooperative movement but avoided elsewhere because of its activist political connotations. Among the middle class–oriented SOK, the words "customer" and "buyer" were preferred. Similarly, the name of a new organization established in 1957 by social democratic women—the Home Advisory Union (Kotineuvontaliitto)—did not contain the word "consumer." During the 1960s, however, the term "consumer" became more universally used.

The first governmental consumer policy in Finland was established in 1962—the Advisory Board of Consumers (Kuluttajain neuvottelukunta). In 1965, a more influential governmental organization body, the Consumer Council (Kuluttajaneuvosto), was founded along the lines of Sweden's model. Despite the displeasure of groups that traditionally advised consumers, the Consumer Council was rather active and began planning the future of consumer policy in close connection with price and competition policy. In 1965, the first "modern" nongovernmental consumer organization was founded: The Consumers (Kuluttajat–Konsumenterna). The organization did not experience a great deal of growth but was significant as a trailblazer for the consumer movement. It still operates today and is a full member of Consumers International, the world's umbrella body for consumer organizations.

During the 1960s, the state controlled and coordinated economic policy more than ever before. The Keynesian ideas of economic policy were adapted indirectly from Sweden. In 1973, consumer policy was centralized governmentally in the newly formed Commerce and Industry Board. Perhaps the most significant consumer events of 1970s were the enactment of the Finnish Consumer Protection Law in 1978 and the establishment of a Consumer Ombudsman, whose task is to monitor the observance of the legislation and to promote the realization of consumer interests. The first Consumer Ombudsman was Gerhard af Schultén.

Contemporary Consumer Activism in Finland

The latest phase in the development of consumer organizations in Finland occurred in 1990 when the Consumers' Association of Finland was reorganized into an umbrella organization with the large trade unions, significantly expanding overall membership. The association had operated as the Consumer Advice League since 1979, and before that as the Household Advice League. The secretary-general of the consumers' association was Leena Simonen; Sinikka Turunen and Juha Beurling have served as the association's secretaries-general. The Consumers' Association of Finland has continued to evolve and today is the country's most important consumer organization. As of 2011, it had sixty-four local and regional consumer associations, as well as eleven national federations, unions, and others associations representing consumer interests. Although the association collects membership fees, it also obtains a considerable share of its revenues from a state subsidy.

The association focuses on promoting consumer rights, with special emphasis on food safety, economic security, and ethical consumption. Its primary tools are producing and disseminating information, advising and educating consumers, and promoting civic activism. For example, the Consumers' Association became active in providing debt counseling beginning in the 1980s, a need that increased considerably in the beginning of the 1990s, when Finland faced an economic depression. The Finnish government responded to the debt problems of consumers as well, and in 2000 the Finnish Consumer Agency started to provide consumer counseling.

The Finnish Consumers' Association addresses additional consumer issues. These include housing costs, especially in cities; food quality and cost; availability, cost, and quality of health, banking, and transport services; and the operations of mobile phone companies. The association also has a presence at the European level. It is a member of BEUC: The European Consumer Organisation and has a representative in the Department of Health and Consumers of the European Commission.

In addition to the Consumers' Association, many civic organizations are active in consumer affairs. Two housewives organizations, the Martha Organization and Rural Women's Advisory Organization, pursue consumer interests not only in food and nutrition, but in other areas of consumer affairs as well. Together these women's organizations have more than 100,000 members. Both organizations produce advisory services, publish material, and promote sustainable lifestyles. It is especially interesting to see how Finnish consumers are responding to the challenges of environmental problems caused by the increasing consumption of the world's finite natural resources. Considering that awareness of the limits to growth is strong among Finnish youth, it is likely that environmental concerns will remain an important priority of Finnish consumer activists.

Visa Heinonen

See also: BEUC: The European Consumer Organisation; Consumers International; Norwegian Consumer Movement; Swedish Consumer Movement

Further Reading

Autio, Minna. 2006. *Kuluttajuuden rakentuminen nuorten kertomuksissa* (The Construction of Consumerism in Young People's Narratives, in Finnish with an English abstract). The Finnish Literature Society, The Finnish Youth Research Society and the Youth Research Network.

Autio, Minna, Eva Heiskanen, and Visa Heinonen. 2009. "Narratives of 'Green' Consumers—The Antihero, the Environmental Hero and the Anarchist." *Journal of Consumer Behaviour* 8: 40–53.

Heinonen, Visa. 1998. *Talonpoikainen etiikka ja kulutuksen henki. Kotitalousneuvonnasta kuluttajapolitiikkaan 1900-luvun Suomessa* (with English summary, 431–439, 'Peasant Ethic and the Spirit of Consumption: From Household Advising to Consumer Policy in the 20th Century Finland'). *Bibliotheca Historica* 33. Helsinki, Suomen Historiallinen Seura.

Ilmonen, Kaj, and Eivind Stø. 1997. "The 'Consumer' in Political Discourse: Consumer Policy in the Nordic Welfare States." In Pekka Sulkunen, John Holmwood, Hilary Radner, and Gerhard Schulze, eds., *Constructing the New Consumer Society* (pp. 197–217). London, UK: Macmillan Press.

FOOD & WATER WATCH

Food & Water Watch is a national advocacy organization working to ensure that the food, water, and fish consumed by Americans is safe, accessible, and produced sustainably. Its mission is to help create a world where everyone has access to adequate affordable, healthy, and wholesome food and clean water to meet their basic needs, a world in which governments are accountable to their citizens and manage essential resources sustainably.

Food &Water Watch was founded in 2005 by Wenonah Hauter to support and amplify online and real-world organizing through research, policy advocacy, litigation, and broad-based communications, including through several websites— foodopoly.org, factorfarmmap.org, and globalfrackdown.org. Having previously held leadership positions at the Union of Concerned Scientists, Citizen Action, and Public Citizen, Hauter is a veteran public interest advocate.

Food & Water Watch's ninety staff members are based in the Washington, D.C., national office and in sixteen state offices, from Maine to California. The group's European program, Food & Water Europe, works from an office in Brussels, Belgium. Food & Water Watch's annual budget of about $10 million is supported by individuals and foundations. The organization does not accept funding from government or corporations.

Food & Water Watch works with the more than 500,000 persons on its online activist base and with a network of volunteer activists who are linked to the field offices. The group's organizers educate and mobilize these activists and volunteers to take action on priority national, state, and local issues. These priorities include banning hydraulic fracturing (also called fracking), curtailing the use of antibiotics on factory farms, giving consumers the right to know what they are eating (through, for example, country of origin or GMO labeling), supporting food safety inspection programs, fighting potentially unsafe food imports, opposing market-based "pay-to-pollute" schemes and secret trade deals, educating consumers about the safety risks and environmental costs of bottled water, and helping communities keep water under public control.

The organization also educates policymakers and consumers about the threats posed by a highly consolidated food system that includes "factory farms," depressed rural communities, and lack of consumer choice at food stores. Hauter's book, *Foodopoly: The Battle over the Future of Food and Farming in America*, dealt extensively with this topic.

Food & Water Watch's efforts have increased public understanding of the effects of corporate control on the food system and water supplies and have won reforms for communities and consumers. The organization has helped communities ban fracking and fight water privatization. It has helped pressure the U.S. Food and Drug Administration to set limits on arsenic in apple juice and ban most types of arsenic from chicken production. It has also successfully pressured Starbucks to stop using milk produced with artificial growth hormones. And with its student activists, it has helped convince many colleges and universities to ban bottled water on campus.

Patty Lovera

See also: Food Safety Advocacy; Public Citizen

Further Reading

Hauter, Wenonah. 2012. *Foodopoly: The Battle over the Future of Food and Farming in America*. New York: New Press.
Kobell, Rona. 2012. "Waterkeeper Attorneys Join Consumer Group." *Bay Journal* (January 6).

FOOD COOPERATIVES
See Consumer Cooperatives

FOOD SAFETY ADVOCACY

Food safety concern in the United States is often historically traced to Upton Sinclair's 1906 novel *The Jungle*. This work contained such vivid descriptions of unsafe conditions in the unregulated meat packing industry that it generated popular support for new federal laws banning substances "ordinarily injurious" to people. A century later, food safety has once again come to the fore, resulting in far-reaching regulatory changes at the U.S. Department of Agriculture (USDA) and landmark legislation directing the Food and Drug Administration (FDA) to focus on preventing foodborne illness instead of just reacting to outbreaks.

The Centers for Disease Control and Prevention (CDC) estimates that each year, roughly 48 million Americans get sick, some 128,000 are hospitalized, and 3,000 die of foodborne diseases. The annual cost to society is an estimated $78 billion, including medical costs, productivity losses and long-term pain, suffering, disability, and death. Researchers have shown that food contamination can occur at any point along the farm to fork supply chain, complicating efforts to reduce contamination. In addition, emerging pathogens and new food-pathogen combinations pose additional challenges.

Pathogens

A milestone in the recent history of meat and poultry inspection was the headline-making Jack in the Box incident of January 1993. Four children died, and hundreds of others became severely ill, after eating hamburgers tainted with E. coli O157:H7 in fast food restaurants. Five U.S. slaughter plants and one in Canada were identified as likely sources of tainted beef sold to the Jack in the Box chain by the Von Corporation.

Newly inaugurated President Clinton called for congressional hearings on this incident. Under pressure from consumer advocacy groups such as the Consumer Federation of America, Center for Science in the Public Interest, and STOP Foodborne Illness, USDA's Food Safety and Inspection Service (FSIS) declared E. coli O157:H7 an adulterant, thereby forcing meat packers to test for the pathogen. FSIS also began a new sampling program for raw ground beef in grocery stores.

Nearly two decades later, in the wake of a widespread outbreak of E. coli infection in Europe associated with bean sprouts contaminated with the uncommon O104:H4 pathogen, advocates and regulators focused attention on the "Big Six" non-O157 strains—E. coli O26, O45, O103, O111, O121 and O145. In 2012, FSIS declared the "Big Six" to be adulterants and began testing beef trim for them.

USDA also required meat and poultry plants to adopt Hazard Analysis Critical Control Point (HACCP) systems. However, in September 2013, the Safe Food Coalition—whose members include the Consumer Federation of America, Consumers Union, Center for Science in the Public Interest, STOP Foodborne Illness, the National Consumers League, Food & Water Watch, the Center for Foodborne Illness Research and Prevention, and the United Food and Commercial Workers Union—urged USDA to abandon its pilot HACCP-based Inspection Model Project (HIMP), which would streamline and speed up processing of poultry. The coalition cited a Government Accountability Office (GAO) investigation that found inadequate evaluation by USDA of the pilot HIMP projects.

Consumer advocates also asked USDA to stop treating certain foreign meat and poultry inspection programs as "equivalent" and reevaluate the inspection programs in countries such as Australia and Canada. Australia had shifted inspection responsibilities from government officials to company employees, raising questions about adequate oversight. Canada, in 2012, recalled millions of pounds of beef contaminated with E. coli O157:H7, of which 2.5 million pounds entered the United States.

Antibiotic Resistance

Concerns about improper use of antibiotics in food animals came to a head in fall 2013, when an outbreak of salmonellosis was linked to antibiotic-resistant *Salmonella heidelberg* in chicken products produced by Foster Farms in central California. At least 300 people were sickened by the pathogen and reported their illness. The pathogen was unusually virulent—more than two-fifths of those who reported their illness were hospitalized. It was also resistant to several commonly prescribed antibiotics, according to the CDC.

Consumer advocates have long been concerned that overuse of antibiotics in animal agriculture contributes to the emergence of antibiotic resistance in pathogens. A 2013 report by the Pew Commission on Industrial Farm Animal Production concluded that the current system of farm animal production is not sustainable and poses unacceptable risks to public health and the environment as well as unnecessary harm to the animals themselves.

The Foster Farms incident came amid promises by the Obama administration to ensure that antibiotics for livestock would be used only to address disease problems and not to enhance growth or otherwise improve production. FDA announced plans to ask drug companies to stop marketing antibiotics for growth promotion.

The Foster Farms incident also renewed interest in a petition, filed in 2011 by the Center for Science in the Public Interest (CSPI), asking USDA to declare antibiotic-resistant *Salmonella* an adulterant, which would allow the department to recall meat products based on testing rather than lengthy epidemiological investigations. In May 2013, more than one dozen consumer and health advocacy organizations urged Agriculture Secretary Tom Vilsack to act on CSPI's two-year-old petition.

On Capitol Hill, legislation was introduced in both the House and Senate that would ban the use of antibiotics for all production purposes while still allowing ill animals to be treated with the drugs. Representative Louise Slaughter (D-NY), a microbiologist by training who has been a long-time critic of current animal drug policy, introduced the House bill in March 2013.

FDA Food Safety Modernization Act

Signed into law in January 2011, the FDA Food Safety Modernization Act (FSMA) is considered by consumer advocates to be the most significant food safety legislation since the 1930s. This law set in motion sweeping reforms to FDA's oversight of domestic and imported food products.

Supported by both consumer advocates and food industry trade associations, FSMA represented a bipartisan legislative response to widely publicized foodborne illness outbreaks in the United States and abroad. Some of these outbreaks, such as peanut butter contaminated by pathogens, were homegrown. But fears grew that imported foods would also cause illness. In China, infant formula adulterated by unscrupulous manufacturers sickened and even killed babies, raising a cloud of suspicion about all products imported from that country.

The concerns about Chinese imports extended to imports from other countries, which are substantial. FDA estimates that 15 percent of the U.S. food supply is imported, including 50 percent of fresh fruits, 20 percent of fresh vegetables, and 80 percent of seafood. Yet FDA has resources to inspect only about 2 percent of imported food.

The FSMA law directs the FDA, working with a wide range of public and private partners, to build a new system of food safety oversight focused on preventing foodborne illness rather than merely investigating illness outbreaks. Processors of all types of food are now required to evaluate the hazards in their operations and have a plan in place to take corrective actions. FDA now has new enforcement tools, including mandatory recall, allowing it to remove contaminated food from the market. The agency has been required to design a product tracing system for foods it designates as posing a "high risk."

FSMA also required FDA to set science-based standards for the production and harvest of fruits and vegetables and implement risk-based inspection of food processing facilities. All high-risk domestic facilities must be inspected by 2016 and no less frequently than every three years thereafter.

As for food products coming into the United States, FDA can now require that importers verify the safety of food from their suppliers and reject foods from facilities or countries that refuse its inspection. The agency promised to work more closely with foreign governments and increase inspection of foreign food facilities.

Rollout of regulations to implement FSMA has been a slow process, with some deadlines set by Congress missed by a year or more. In 2012, frustrated by the Obama Administration's delay in proposing required regulations, the Center for Food Safety filed suit in the U.S. District Court for Northern California to demand action. This court ruled that FDA was required to meet a final rules deadline of June 2015. In February 2014, FDA reached a court-approved settlement with the Center for Food Safety and the Center for Environmental Health on deadlines for publishing final rules for FSMA. The agreement shifted the final rule deadlines beyond the June 2015 deadline set by the U.S. District Court in 2013. The new deadlines are August 30, 2015, for preventive controls for human food and for animal food; October 31, 2015, for produce safety, foreign supplier verification, and third-party accreditation; March 31, 2016, for sanitary transportation; and May 31, 2016, for intentional adulteration.

Full implementation of FSMA was also threatened by budget cuts to FDA and by a proposed farm bill amendment that would delay new regulations pending "scientific and economic analysis" of their effect. The Center for Food Safety pointed out that FDA already conducts such analysis as part of its rulemaking process.

GMO and Right to Know

Do genetically engineered (GE) foods, commonly known as genetically modified organisms (GMOs), jeopardize food safety? The biotech industry, major food companies, and leading scientific organizations in the United States and elsewhere insist that GE foods are safe to eat, noting that none of these foods has been linked to a single case of illness since they were first introduced in 1996. However, many consumer advocates remain uneasy about the widespread adoption of such "materially different" foods, in part because FDA lacks legal authority to formally approve foods or ingredients made from GE crops.

Advocates have asked Congress to amend the Federal Food, Drug, and Cosmetic Act to require a mandatory pre-market approval process open to public participation and review. They acknowledge that formal approval of GE crops might lengthen the approval process but argue that this approval would ensure both greater safety and public confidence in this safety. They also argue that labeling would allow any future health risks, such as allergens, to be more easily traced back to the source. In 2011, the Codex Alimentarius, a United Nations-sponsored food standard setting organization, gave the green light to member nations to institute GE labeling if they choose to do so.

Citing a 2007 campaign promise made by then candidate Barack Obama, advocates began demanding biotech food labeling at both the state and federal levels. In 2011, the Center for Food Safety launched a petition drive asking FDA to require GE labeling. The *Just Label It* campaign garnered 1.2 million signatures by 2012, but FDA did not respond. At the state level, advocates in California collected signatures for a 2012 ballot initiative that would require GE labeling. Proposition 37 triggered a multi-million-dollar advertising battle pitting GE labeling advocates against the biotech industry and its food industry allies. Outspent by nearly $40 million, Prop 37 advocates were defeated by 2 percentage points in the November election.

Regrouping in 2013, advocates succeeded in persuading legislatures in more than twenty states to consider labeling legislation. Connecticut and Maine both enacted GE labeling bills, but implementation of their bills was conditioned on other states enacting similar legislation. In Washington State, voters rejected a ballot Initiative 522, similar to California's Proposition 37, by 55 percent to 45 percent.

Over the past two decades, the following advocates and their organizations have been particularly active and influential: Barbara Kowalcyk at the Center for Foodborne Illness Research and Prevention; Andrew Kimbrell at the Center for Food Safety; Michael Jacobson, Caroline Smith DeWaal, and Gregory Jaffe at the Center for Science in the Public Interest; Carol Tucker Foreman and Chris Waldrop at the Consumer Federation of America; Jean Halloran and Michael Hansen at Consumers Union; Tony Corbo at Food & Water Watch; Sandra Eskin now at Pew Charitable Trusts; Nancy Donley at STOP Foodborne Illness; Bill Marler, a Seattle-based foodborne illness attorney; Tom Neltner, Erik Olsson, and Maricel Maffini at Natural Resources Defense Council; and Margaret Mellon and Doug Gurian-Sherman at the Union of Concerned Scientists.

Stephen Clapp

See also: Center for Food Safety; Center for Science in the Public Interest; Food & Water Watch; Product Safety "Victim" Activism

Further Reading

Bottemiller, Helena. 2012. "The Food Safety Modernization Act—One Year Later." *Food Safety News* (January 20)
Nestle, Marion. 2007. *The Politics of Food Safety*. Oakland: University of California Press.
Pew Commission on Industrial Farm Animal Production. 2013. *Putting Meat on the Table: Industrial Farm Animal Production in America* (October).
Scharf, Robert. 2012. "Economic Burdens from Health Losses due to Food Borne Illness in the United States." *Journal of Food Protection* 75: 123–131.
Tavernese, Sabrina. 2013. "F.D.A. Says Importers Must Audit Food Safety." *New York Times* (July 26).

FRENCH CONSUMER MOVEMENT

Before World War II, the relationship between buyers and sellers was dominated in France, as it was elsewhere, by the idea that contracts were negotiated on equal terms by knowledgeable and willing parties. There was therefore little need for government consumer policy. As the movement toward a mass consumption society accelerated after World War II, including a system of distribution that included numerous intermediaries between producers and consumers, the notion that consumers were able to protect themselves without any government support became incompatible with the reality of marketplace transactions. Moreover, the rules of civil and criminal procedure left consumers on their own to enforce their rights, typically with the burden of proof when bringing legal actions.

It is in this context, and aided by the political unrest of May 1968, that the modern French consumer movement developed in the 1960s. By the end of that decade, the government-funded National Consumption Institute (Institut National de la Consommation, or INC) was created, and the first fundamental consumer protection laws were passed and began to operate.

Although family associations and consumer cooperatives had existed in France for a long time, there was not a politically oriented consumer movement until the end of the 1960s. At that time, consumer organizations were established and multiplied, buoyed by the example of the U.S. consumer movement. The articulation of consumer rights by President John F. Kennedy and the considerable efforts of Ralph Nader played an important role in giving birth and inspiration to the French consumer movement. The movement was also stimulated by several tragedies, such as the death of thirty-six infants in 1972 due to adulterated talcum powder.

The 1960s and 1970s were the golden age of consumerism in France. The movement had a strong grassroots character and an aggressive political posture. Consumer organizations were able to mobilize their members to participate in price surveys, political rallies, and product boycotts. Gunnar Trumbull, in a study comparing the consumer movements of France and Germany, summarized the strategy of the French movement with the word "confrontation." According to Trumbull, "the French groups took on the status of a watchdog to industry, looking out for transgressions, mobilizing against high prices and dangerous products, and filing frequent lawsuits" (p. 46).

France's consumer movement quickly earned itself a place within government consumer policymaking. In 1960, the government created the National Consumption Council (Conseil National de la Consommation, or CNC) as a discussion forum for consumer groups and government officials. The CNC was composed of fourteen consumer representatives and fourteen ministerial members, and it met regularly and frequently.

The major consumer organizations in France also coordinated their efforts to increase their influence in public policymaking. In 1972, eleven organizations established the Coordination Committee for Consumer Organizations (Comité de Coordination des Organisations de Consommateurs, or CCOC). The CCOC successfully lobbied for consumer protection legislation, for example, to allow a cooling-off period for door-to-door sales and to permit advertisements to name specific competitors.

Leaving aside, for the moment, governmental or quasigovernmental consumer organizations, the French consumer movement has had three main strands over the last fifty years: strictly consumer associations, some of which cover a wide range of consumer issues while others focus on specific products or services such as housing or transportation or public utilities; family-oriented organizations; and labor union-based organizations. Among these numerous organizations, the two most prominent are the Federal Union of Consumers (l'Union Fédérale des Consommateurs, or UFC) and Consumption, Housing, and Environment (Consommation, Logement et Cade de Vie, or CLCV). Both UFC and CLCV were founded in the early 1950s, have roughly half a million members each, run networks of local offices, and are largely independent of government funding or influence. By virtue of their history and stature, UFC and CLCV are France's only full members of Consumers International (the umbrella organization for the world consumer movement) and are France's only members of BEUC: The European Consumer Organisation.

A key indicator of the legitimacy of specific consumer organizations in France is whether they are authorized by the French government to bring lawsuits on behalf of collective consumer interests—legal actions that individual consumers rarely have the incentive or capacity to bring. Beginning in 1973, consumer organizations could apply for authorization if they met certain conditions: a primary objective of assisting and defending consumers, independence from business organizations, at least 10,000 members, and more than a year of continuous operation. Approximately twenty organizations have satisfied these criteria and consequently are permitted to act as private prosecutors for consumers for the purpose of halting harmful business practices. (Only labor unions have a similar right, something they achieved at the beginning of the twentieth century.) While consumer organizations, in theory, can make claims for collective damages, in practice the rules and procedures for doing so are impractical. For example, each claimant must be named individually in the lawsuit. Beginning in 2013, however, France allowed class action lawsuits whereby private attorneys can file lawsuits in the name of a group of consumers, not all of whose members can be identified.

France has two organizations that publish product-testing magazines. One is *Que Choisir?* (Which to Choose?), published by the UFC beginning in 1960. The other magazine, *60 Millions de Consommateurs* (60 Million Consumers), has been produced by the INC since 1966. Both magazines still exist, but whereas UFC's magazine relies primarily on subscriptions for its financial survival and provides a key revenue stream for a fully private organization, the INC enjoys a significant government subsidy and can be considered a quasigovernmental entity.

Having two product-testing magazines might seem like a blessing for French consumers, but it can be a curse as well. By concentrating revenues from magazine sales in the hands of a single consumer organization, countries such as the United States, the United Kingdom, and the Netherlands have been able to build consumer organizations that are both well funded and largely independent of government influence. But In France, the government, via the INC, has undercut the potential strength of private consumer organizations, especially the UFC.

Given the competition between UFC and INC, it should not be surprising that INC's existence is controversial within the French consumer movement. Some consumer organizations regard INC as an indispensable technical institute that supports the educational and lobbying work of French consumer organizations and helps carry out research with its counterparts in other European countries. Other consumer groups, especially UFC, view the INC as too dependent on the government and would prefer to see its role redefined to more directly serve consumer organizations.

The contrast between the funding sources of the UFC and INC should not obscure the fact that government financial support for private consumer organizations is extensive in France. Family associations and union-affiliated consumer groups have received government subsidies. Indeed, Trumbull observes that "the prospect of receiving these funds helped to induce family and labor groups to move into the field of consumer advocacy" (2006, p. 59). Government support of consumer organizations is the rule in most European countries, stemming from traditions of intervention by public authorities to protect the economic interests of consumers and other politically weak citizen groups. Reflecting the same philosophy, licenses of public broadcasting networks in France require them to broadcast programs dealing with consumer topics. The production of these programs is the responsibility of the INC or regional technical centers for consumers, not of private consumer groups such as UFC or CLCV.

As the European Union (EU) has become more active in the field of consumer policy, the consumer movements in many European countries have directed their attention to regional rather than national policymaking. The dominant form of consumer policymaking has become a two-step process: The EU issues a consumer policy directive, then the member states of the EU transpose the directive into national laws within a specified period of time. Thus the power of consumer groups to influence consumer policy depends, to a large extent, on their ability to collaborate regionally with other consumer organizations. Yet, for a variety of reasons, the French consumer movement has not been powerful in this new political environment. Part of the reason may be the predominance of the English language in the scientific and technical universe—combined with the fierce French pride in their language and consequent insistence on using it. More important, however, is the absence of a single consumer organization that speaks for French consumers at the international level. Whereas the INC can address some technical issues of relevance to consumers, its status as a government-funded body undermines its legitimacy as a voice of consumers. At the same time, the large number and diverse interests of France's private consumer groups makes coordination difficult and prevents any single organization from serving as the commonly recognized representative of the French consumer at the European level.

The limited role played to date by French consumer organizations in the consumer policymaking of the EU could change in the future. As an original member of the European Economic Community (the forerunner of the EU), France enjoys prestige. More concretely, its number of representatives within the European Parliament is second only to that of Germany. In addition, France is well suited to serve as a bridge-builder within the EU by virtue of its geographic position between the northern and southern European countries, its simultaneous embrace of modernity and traditionalism, and its experience with economic liberalism and state intervention.

In the future, the movement will probably be more streamlined and more aggressive. Recent economic difficulties have influenced individual consumers to become more responsible, more aware, and more demanding. Constant budgetary restrictions imperil not only the private consumer associations but also the INC. Fortunately, French consumer organizations enjoy an important asset—the trust of the French populace. According to a 2012 national survey reported in July 2013 edition of *The Consumer Conditions Scorecard*, France ranked second only to the Netherlands among twenty-seven EU countries in terms of citizen trust in their national consumer organizations—certainly a strong base on which to build.

Robert N. Mayer

See also: BEUC: The European Consumer Organisation; Consumers International

Further Reading

Chambraud, Agnes, Patricia Foucher, and Anne Morin. 1994. "The Importance of Community Law for French Consumer Protection Legislation." *Journal of Consumer Policy* 17: 23–38.

European Commission. 2013. *The Consumer Conditions Scoreboard*, 9th ed. Luxembourg: Office for Official Publications of the European Union.

Trumbull, Gunnar. 2006. *Consumer Capitalism*. Ithaca, NY: Cornell University Press.

FRONT GROUPS

When a group such as a corporation, trade association, labor union, or environmental organization engages itself in a public policy debate, it is beneficial if the group can plausibly claim that its position benefits "the general public," or at least the vast majority of it. Similarly, in matters of consumer policy, competing interest groups typically assert that they represent the preferences of "consumers." Consumer groups such as the National Consumers League, Consumers Union/ Consumer Reports, and the Consumer Federation of America, by virtue of their extensive track records of advocating policy positions that promote consumer well-being, view themselves as having earned the right to speak with legitimacy for consumers. The opponents of these traditional consumer groups (typically individual businesses or trade associations) are not so quick, however, to cede this political high ground.

One method by which business groups seek to delegitimize the policy positions of traditional consumer organizations is to impugn them as irrational zealots or fearmongers motivated by the desire to increase donations to their organizations. A variant of this approach to undercutting traditional consumer activists is to describe them as "elitists" who seek to impose their conception of what is good for consumers on consumers, who—it is implied—have a much different notion.

There is a second major method by which business groups seek to strip the positions taken by traditional consumer groups of their mantle of being in the consumer interest. This method involves establishing "front groups"—new and generally short-lived groups that present themselves as legitimate consumer groups but that are established, funded, and controlled by business organizations to take positions opposing those advocated by traditional consumer groups. By giving a patina of legitimacy to arguments against consumer protection, front groups can pose a serious tactical challenge for traditional consumer groups.

The use of front groups is certainly not confined to consumer politics. Indeed, they are commonly found in debates regarding environmental and labor policy. For example, broad-based–sounding groups such as the Consumer Energy Alliance and Energy Citizens Alliance are widely regarded as fronts for the fossil fuel industry in its efforts to thwart cleaner energy sources and contest climate change. Similarly, groups such as Save Our Secret Ballot and the Center for Union Facts provide business groups a way of opposing the policy initiatives of organized labor. (Labor unions are themselves frequently accused of hiding behind front groups.) This entry, however, focuses on the role of front groups in consumer politics.

Some caveats: Whereas front groups are sometimes blatantly used to hoodwink the public or give cover to policymakers who have little real regard for consumer welfare, many consumer policy debates involve genuine differences of opinion regarding what is in the best interests of consumers. This is especially true when a policy debate pits two consumer values against each other, such as safety versus price or privacy versus convenience. As a result, one person's front group may be another person's authentic champion. In addition, the receipt of some corporate funding should not automatically taint an organization as a front group, for several respected and longstanding consumer organizations receive a portion of their funding from business sources.

It is therefore unfair to label any group whose position differs from those of traditional consumer groups as a front group. The term is most usefully applied when an element of deception is involved regarding a group's origins, goals, leaders, and supporters. A group that is called "Consumers for . . ." but that is run out of a public relations firm, funded entirely by a corporation or trade association, and that goes out of existence as soon as a consumer policy decision has been made probably deserves the epithet "front group." Still, there is no consensual and objective set of criteria for identifying a front group, and no front group would admit to being one. So claims—in the media, research reports, and in this entry—that a group is a front are necessarily judgment calls.

What do front groups accomplish for their creators and funders? First, front groups create the impression of grassroots public support for the positions of their corporate benefactors. In carrying out this legitimating function, front groups can organize petition drives, enter into lobbying alliances, or testify at hearings. Second, and closely related, front groups provide a vehicle for larger scale activities that might seem overly self-interested if associated with the front group's sponsor. For example, a front group can pay for millions of dollars of issue advertising without divulging the source of its funds. Third, front groups add to the work load of traditional consumer organizations, forcing them to devote resources to countering the impression made by front groups.

There are two primary prerequisites for functioning effectively as an industry front group in the domain of consumer policy. The first is having adequate financial and human resources. Obtaining resources is typically not a problem, because the cost of establishing a front group is generally only a small portion of a corporation or trade association's lobbying budget on a particular issue. The other prerequisite is more challenging—creating a plausible (if typically ingenuous) argument that an industry's position in a consumer policy debate is more "pro-consumer" than the position taken by traditional consumer activists.

Most often, the argument that the front group is the true consumer champion is framed negatively. They contend that a particular consumer protection policy will harm consumers by raising prices, restricting choices, or stifling innovation; thus opposing the policy is claimed to be the pro-consumer position. In other cases, the argument is more positive. It accepts that consumers indeed have a problem, but it asserts that consumers are best served by conducting further study, giving competition or technology more time to correct the problem, educating consumers rather than regulating business, or leaving solutions to state or local officials.

Corporate-funded front groups have been involved in a wide variety of consumer policy debates, but they appear to be used most often in four issue domains: "vice" products (e.g., tobacco, alcohol, fast food); food in general, especially genetically modified food; pharmaceuticals; and telecommunications. Proposed restrictions on consumer vices are especially likely to produce front groups, because the interests of producers align with those of their customers (some of whom are literally addicted) who want no further restrictions on access or increase in prices. For example, the National Smokers Alliance, which operated in the United States during the 1990s, was funded by the tobacco industry (Philip Morris, in particular) and launched by the large public relations firm Burson–Marsteller. The alliance claimed three million members, but they were not expected to do anything other than let the tobacco industry lobby in their name (Kuntz, 1997).

The Center for Consumer Freedom was funded by the tobacco industry as well, but it lobbies on behalf of the alcohol, fast food, meat, and other industries that purvey potentially unhealthy forms of consumption. In recent years, the center has played a leading role in resisting restrictions and taxes on soft drinks. The center was established in 1996 with initial funding from Philip Morris, but today its contributors include major companies such as Coca-Cola, Wendy's, and Tyson Foods (Warner, 2005). The center's website states that it opposes "a growing cabal of activists [that] has meddled in Americans' lives [including] self-anointed 'food police,' health campaigners, trial lawyers, personal-finance do-gooders, animal-right misanthropes, and meddling bureaucrats." The site claims that the center "isn't afraid to take on groups that have built 'good' images through slick public relations campaigns," but ironically, the center is directed by Rick Berman, who is the president of the Washington, D.C.–based public relations firm Berman and Company. The center gets some credit, however, for being transparent about its leadership.

The use of front groups in policy debates regarding food is common enough that the Center for Food Safety published *A Guide to Food Industry Front Groups* (Simon, 2013). The guide cites the Sensible Food Policy Coalition for its work in deflecting restrictions on marketing to children and New Yorkers for Beverage Choices for its opposition to size limits on soda cups. The guide profiles ten other "front groups," plus six manufacturer-funded institutes.

A specific food issue that has attracted front groups has been whether to mandate labeling for genetically modified foods. In 2012 and 2013, statewide votes took place on this question in California and Washington, respectively. The voting results were close in both states, especially in California, but in both instances, the opponents of labeling—notably biotechnology companies that sell genetically modified seed, large-scale farmers, food manufacturers, and retailers—won. Labeling proponents blamed their losses, in part, on the activities of front groups such as the Coalition against the Costly Food Labeling Proposition in California. In Washington, a group called No on 522 served as a mechanism by which companies such as Coca-Cola, Pepsico, and Nestle could spend more than $1 million each to defeat the initiative without their names' appearing in campaign advertisements or materials (Shannon, 2013).

The pharmaceutical industry has also made ample use of front groups. During the 1990s, it set up groups to oppose President Clinton's prescription drug benefit bill, to support President Bush's version of the bill, and to prevent state governments from excluding certain expensive brand-name drugs from lists of approved drugs for Medicare and Medicaid enrollees. Today, these front groups lobby for the repeal of the Affordable Care Act ("Obamacare"). For instance, the 60 Plus Association and the Seniors Coalition were designed to appear similar to, but to counteract, the public policy efforts of AARP, the nonpartisan but liberal-leaning advocacy group. These front groups—which are active on issues beyond those involving pharmaceuticals and receive funding from other industry sources—claim that their policy positions promote stronger competition and give consumers greater control, but supporting industry positions seems to be their main function.

A final issue domain in which front group accusations have been common is telecommunications. Here, front groups seem to have been used as part of intra-industry struggles in an environment of rapid technological and regulatory change. For example, in the late 1990s, the long-distance carrier AT&T established front groups with names such as Consumers' Voice to ensure access ("interconnection") to local lines at low rates and to keep regional Bell operating companies (RBOCs) from entering long-distance markets. RBOCs such as Ameritech and SBC, for their part, used front groups such as Keep America Connected to try to block competitors from accessing their networks while remaining able to move into new markets themselves. Ten years later, when telecom companies like Verizon and SBC sought to deregulate the cable television industry, they funded Consumers for

Cable Choice and Consumers for Competitive Choice to give the appearance that grassroots consumer groups sided with them.

More recently, front groups have weighed in on the telecommunications debate over net neutrality—the idea that Internet service providers should provide access on equal terms to all content and applications, regardless of their nature or source. Traditional consumer groups and companies such as Google, Amazon, and Microsoft strongly support net neutrality, fearing discrimination and censorship in a system in which speed of transmission could depend on how much users can pay. Broadband service providers, cable television firms, and phone companies generally oppose net neutrality and have a strong economic incentive to lobby against it. These groups have provided the primary funding for consumer-sounding groups such as Hands off the Internet, Broadband for America, American Consumer Institute, and Americans for Prosperity. Their core argument is that government regulation (as represented by a policy of net neutrality) will impede the development of the Internet and constrict consumer choice. Yet most analysts believe that consumers and startup companies benefit under a system of net neutrality.

Some corporate front groups have achieved a level of longevity that perhaps deserves its own category and terminology. By virtue of their engagement across a large number of issues and across a period of ten years or more, groups such as Americans for Prosperity, Citizens for a Sound Economy, Consumer Alert, and the American Council on Science and Health do not pretend to be spontaneous expressions of consumer opposition to the policies supported by traditional consumer organizations. Nevertheless, these organizations do not publicize that they have no real membership rolls, receive virtually all their funding from corporate or pro-business foundations, and take advantage of inclusive-sounding words—such as "Americans," "Citizens," and "Consumer"—in their titles to advance a business agenda.

In summary, it appears that use of industry-funded front groups in consumer politics is an important feature of U.S. consumer politics, but there is little evidence about whether, to what extent, or how they influence policy outcomes. Their effectiveness is likely greatest under two conditions: (1) ambiguity in what constitutes the pro-consumer policy and (2) opacity in who funds and controls a front group. When front groups can make a plausible case that they, not traditional consumer advocates, have the best interests of consumers in mind, these groups are likely to be convincing to voters (if not the press and policymakers). Similarly, when front groups can hide their connections to industry groups who stand to gain or lose in a consumer policy debate, these groups are likely to influence policy outcomes, especially ballot initiatives and referenda. Consumer activists can address these challenges by compellingly articulating their view of what is in the best interests of consumers and by pressing for more transparent and speedy mechanisms of campaign finance disclosure.

Robert N. Mayer

See also: Initiatives and Referenda

Further Reading

Center for Consumer Freedom. 2014. "About." www.consumerfreedom.com/about/.

Kuntz, Tom. 1997. "Word for Word: The National Smokers Alliance: Got a Light? How about the Flame of Freedom," *The New York Times*, September 21. www.nytimes .com/1997/09/21/weekinreview/word-for-word-national-smokers-alliance-got-light-about-flame-freedom.html.

Mayer, Robert N. 2007. "Winning the War of Words: The 'Front Group' Label in Contemporary Consumer Politics." *The Journal of American Culture* 30, no. 1: 96–109.

Shannon, Brad. 2013. "Report: Pepsi, Coke, Nestle Contribute More Than $1 Million Each to Fight I-522." *The Olympian*, October 18. www.theolympian.com/2013/10/18/2782420/ report-top-donors-to-grocer-pac.html.

Simon, Michele. 2013. *A Guide to Food Industry Front Groups.*" Washington, DC: Center for Food Safety (May).

Warner, Melanie. 2005. "Striking Back at the Food Police," *New York Times*, June 12. www .nytimes.com/2005/06/12/business/yourmoney/12food.html?pagewanted=all&_r=0.

FUNERAL CONSUMER ADVOCACY

Although it is one of the most emotionally fraught and potentially costly purchases for any household, the American funeral is often overlooked as a target for consumer protection activities. Funeral services are purchased infrequently, often by those who are reluctant to be "smart shoppers" for services that have emotional and even spiritual significance. However, there is a long history of consumer advocacy relating to funerals and the funeral and cemetery industries.

Post–Civil War America saw the rise of the commercial funeral business, an industrial outgrowth of the local undertaker/furniture maker in small towns. Before the late nineteenth century, most families were intimately involved with the care of the dead, including the preparation of the body and the viewing—most often in the home. With urbanization and professional medicine came the removal of death and "death care" from the homes into emerging "funeral homes."

By the early twentieth century, commentators and critics began writing about the increasing cost of funerals. The Metropolitan Life Insurance Company published a landmark study of 15,000 bills for funeral services, submitted on behalf of policyholders, which found that many bills, often for the poor, contained "excessive expenditures." Social workers, clergy, and labor activists criticized the funeral home business for taking advantage of consumers' feelings of guilt to encourage lavish spending. By 1950, the U.S. Department of Labor identified twenty-eight member-owned funeral service cooperatives in the United States, most of which were outgrowths of farm cooperatives.

In 1939, the modern funeral consumer movement began when Seattle minister Fred Shorter organized the Peoples Memorial Association (PMA), now the largest member-owned funeral cooperative in the country. PMA contracted with a local funeral home to offer simple cremations at a reduced price to members. Although the founding vision of PMA was to create a member-owned co-op with its own physical plant, it was not until 2007 that PMA launched such a co-op, adding its own funeral service to the network of private funeral homes in PMAs list of contract providers.

In the 1950s, mainstream media began paying closer attention to burial costs. "The High Cost of Dying," an article published in *Collier's* magazine in 1951, took the trade to task for misleading and fraudulent sales practices. Other exposés followed, the most widely discussed of which was journalist Jessica Mitford's *The American Way of Death*, published in 1963. The first book-length examination of the funeral industry written for the general public, this publication explained how funeral homes capitalized on family grief to oversell expensive services. The book sold 1 million copies and was the basis for an hour-long CBS documentary titled *The Great American Funeral*.

Throughout the 1950s and 1960s, dozens of nonprofit consumer groups, called Memorial Societies, were created to work for simple, low-cost burials and cremations. With the help of the Cooperative League of the USA (now the National Cooperative Business Association), in 1963 these local societies formed a national organization, the Continental Association of Funeral and Memorial Societies (CAFMS). In 1996, this organization became the Funeral and Memorial Societies of America. In 1999, the organization changed its name to the Funeral Consumers Alliance. Since 2003, the organization has been headed by Joshua Slocum, whose background as a newspaper reporter included investigating funeral practices.

The 1960s surge in public interest in funeral costs carried through the 1970s as consumer activists, AARP, and others worked with the Federal Trade Commission (FTC) to research consumer abuses. In 1978, the FTC published a 526-page report documenting widespread deception in the funeral trade, along with a proposed trade rule to protect consumers. The report found that funeral homes routinely refused to disclose prices by phone or in writing, that undertakers frequently made up nonexistent legal requirements for services, such as embalming, to increase costs, and that consumers were at a great disadvantage in their bargaining with funeral directors.

The industry's largest trade association, the National Funeral Directors Association, fought implementation of the trade rule, claiming consumer abuse was the result of a few rogue practitioners. Evidence of widespread mistreatment, however, convinced the FTC to put the Funeral Rule into effect in 1984. The rule requires funeral homes (but not cemeteries) to disclose prices in writing and by phone, to refrain from misrepresenting the law, and to allow consumers to choose funeral goods and services, typically bundled, a la carte. The rule was amended in 1994 to ban "casket handling fees," financial penalties levied on customers who purchased a casket from a third-party source. The FTC found it was common for funeral homes to charge several hundred dollars for "handling outside merchandise," a practice that thwarted the Funeral Rule's intent to protect consumer choice.

Since 1984, consumer groups have pushed for expansion of the rule to cover cemeteries, crematories and other death-related vendors. In 1999, consumer advocates, FTC staff, and funeral industry groups testified before the Senate Special Committee on Aging about the insufficient protection by and inadequate enforcement of the Rule. In 2002 and 2004, Senator Chris Dodd (D-CT) worked closely with the Funeral Consumers Alliance to introduce federal legislation that would elevate the Funeral Rule from a regulation into a statute. The bills would also have expanded the rule to cover cemeteries and other death-related businesses. Both bills were tabled, as was a similar bill introduced by Congressman Bobby Rush (D-IL) in 2009.

Joshua Slocum

See also: AARP; Consumer Cooperatives

Further Reading

Bowman, Leroy. 1959. *The American Funeral: A Study in Guilt, Extravagance, and Sublimity.* Washington, DC: Public Affairs Press.

Federal Trade Commission. 1978. *Funeral Industry Practices: Final Report to the Federal Trade Commission and Recommended Trade Regulation Rule.* Washington, DC.

Roberts, Daryl L. 1997. *Profits of Death: An Insider Exposes the Death Care Industry.* Chandler, AZ: Five Star Publications.

Slocum, Joshua, and Lisa Carlson. 2011. *Final Rights: Reclaiming the American Way of Death.* Hinesburg, VT: Upper Access Publishing.

G

GERMAN CONSUMER MOVEMENT

Consumer policy in Germany originated and is embedded in the post–World War II "social market economy"—a new kind of free-market capitalism combined with a strong commitment to social insurance and, since the 1980s, paired with environmental responsibility. The German consumer movement is a reflection of the country's political traditions, cultural values, economic development, social conditions, and historical trajectory. For example, the majority of consumer organizations are government-run or depend partly or fully on government financing, with only a small number of privately run, member-financed consumer organizations (such as the Consumer Initiative, Food Watch, and some online communities) having developed in recent years. Consequently, a historical perspective helps to explain the current state of Germany's consumer policy.

Private consumer cooperatives were well established by the mid-nineteenth century and provided an opportunity for consumer empowerment. These cooperatives can be regarded as a precursor to modern consumer activism in Germany. As of the 1920s, consumer cooperatives were still important, especially with respect to construction of urban housing. During the Nazi era (1933–1945), opportunities for German citizens to participate in a democratic political system were limited, including participation in consumer cooperatives.

After World War II, Germany was divided into two nations. The Allies developed a market economy in West Germany (which later evolved into the German model of a social market economy), whereas East Germany adopted a policy of strict economic command and control under the Soviet Union. Consumer organizations grew steadily in importance in West Germany, but the idea of consumer organizations had little relevance in East Germany's planned economy, with its strictly regulated products and prices. After the fall of the Iron Curtain and national unification in 1990, West German governance structures, including consumer policy, were fully adopted in the new East German states, and organizations there had to start nearly from scratch.

In West Germany during the 1950s, a variety of civic organizations focused on consumer policy issues. The first umbrella organization for consumer groups, the Federation of Consumer Organizations (AgV), was founded in 1953. It included such diverse partners as the German Tenant Association, the German Association of Housewives, and the Organization of Consumer Co-operatives. To facilitate product comparison by consumers, AgV promoted packaging standardization, consumer education, and consumer advice. The first consumer advisory center opened in Hamburg in 1957 and provided consumers with personalized information. Gradually, all German states—including those in the former East Germany—established similar state-run centers.

In the 1960s, the "economic miracle" decade, consumer policy was linked primarily to economic and competition policies. West Germany's first Minister of Finance and "father" of the social market economy, Ludwig Erhard, was the first major politician to highlight the necessity of the "empowered sovereign consumer" for economic prosperity. He called for a strict competition policy, an approach that neoliberals like Erhard regarded as the best form of consumer policy. Moreover, West Germany had limited experience with consumer institutions per se (whether public or private), which made it difficult for the country to establish effective consumer protection and comparative product testing. Despite these challenges, one of West Germany's consumer successes during this time was the establishment in 1964 of Stiftung Warentest, a national institute for product testing. Consumer advocates, some nominated by trade unions, held important positions in this new institute, as did representatives from business, consumer cooperatives, and the credit sector. As a departure from West German consumer policy, which typically blocked the development of consumer protection institutions, the state founded and funded Stiftung Warentest.

Today, Stiftung Warentest continues to offer comparative and neutral information on products and services with the aim of empowering consumers in ever more complex markets. Fifty years after its founding, the Stiftung has become a broadly recognized and trusted institution among both consumers and producers. Regular polls show that the Stiftung Warentest is consistently one of the most trusted institutions in West Germany. Although Stiftung Warentest was never meant to be a government agency for product testing, the allocation of public funds ensured that its relations with the state remained close.

By the 1970s, consumer policy reached its height in West Germany. Public and scientific debate on the role and financing of consumer policy and its institutions became more prominent. In 1971, the government published its first report on consumer policy—the only one of its kind for almost thirty years. (Additional reports appeared in 2004, 2008, and 2012.) Driven mainly by the closing of ranks between consumer organizations and the powerful German unions, this reports reflects a common understanding of consumer policy's multiple goals: to create economic benefits for consumers, to safeguard consumers' life and health, to secure open access to goods and markets, and to offset social differences for vulnerable consumers.

As was common throughout Europe, consumerism in Germany in the 1980s and 1990s was shaped by the concepts of liberalization and privatization. Accordingly, the conviction that good competition policy is the best consumer policy regained significance in the political sphere, along with the idea that consumers are sovereign when markets are competitive. Consequently, consumer organizations lost some of their political significance, and the consumer movement became less united.

In 2000, the AgV was merged with other specialized, mostly state-funded consumer organizations and foundations to regain political visibility for consumer interests. This joining of forces create a new, larger, much more powerful umbrella organization for the forty-one German consumer associations and consumer advice centers known as the Federation of German Consumer Organizations (Verbraucherzentrale Bundesverband, or "vzbv"). Although vzbv receives its funding from the German Ministry of Consumer Protection, it is not run by the government and is an independent nongovernmental organization (NGO) that spearheads and coordinates the organized German consumer movement. All major consumer organizations are members of vzbv, except for a very small number that have chosen not to join. The federation operates on four levels: It lobbies for effective consumer policy on the national and European level, engages in mediation and lawsuits, advocates the availability of consumer advice and information, and promotes consumer education. Its immense network allows vzbv to work closely with consumers, which in turn enables the organization to identify consumer and market problems, develop suitable solutions, act as a market watchdog, and serve as policy consultants. In 2012, vzbv established the Foundation for Consumer Protection to empower the public through improved consumer information, education, and advice. The foundation is the stimulus and funding agency for diverse consumer-related projects carried out by a variety of organizations.

Unlike other European countries, and against regular calls to follow suit, Germany has not established explicit consumer legislation. Rather, consumer law is based on the German civil code, as well as other diverse areas of law that focus primarily on market participation. These areas include the regulation of consumer debt, tourism, and pharmaceuticals.

An important concern of the German consumer movement has been food safety. The 1950s were particularly critical for the development of consumer policy with respect to food. A substantial knowledge base resulted from the development of food research institutes, and food policy decisions became more evidence-based. The establishment of the Food and Agriculture Information Service in 1977 led to an increased focus on consumer advice and information in the food sector. Germany's first Federal Ministry of Consumer Protection, Food, and Agriculture was established in 2001, primarily in response to Europe's shock over the food scare commonly referred to as "mad cow disease" (bovine spongiform encephalopathy, or BSE). A gradual development of a more coherent overall government policy on food safety was supported institutionally by two new federal institutions that report to the ministry: the Federal Institute for Risk Assessment and the Federal Office of Consumer Protection and Food Safety. The effect of food scares, particularly BSE, on the profile of consumer protection in Germany was mirrored at the European level with the formation of the European Commission's Health and Consumer Protection Directorate General (DG SANCO) in 1999. This directorate has become the key institution for consumers in Europe and issues almost all the laws that are consumer-relevant.

The latest political developments in the governmental institutions of consumer protection are a sharp departure from the past. Whereas consumer protection has traditionally been linked to food and agriculture, the current "Grand Coalition" has moved the bulk of consumer policy to the Ministry of Justice and created a new

Federal Ministry of Justice and Consumer Protection. This has several potential consequences that cannot be fully evaluated at this time. On the one hand, consumer policy is now closely linked to its major instrument: consumer law. This might strengthen its position as a policy field in general and also in the parliament (German Bundestag), where consumer issues were often subordinated to the powerful interests of the food and agricultural industries. Moreover, the team-up with the Ministry of Justice seems to fit better with the cross-cutting nature of consumer policies, which cover different domains besides food. However, the influence and power of a policy field also depends on fiscal budgets allocated to political initiatives, and the Ministry of Justice has not traditionally managed big budgets.

In response to increased cross-border shopping by Germans and consumers in neighboring countries, two European Consumer Centres (ECC) have been established—one at the French–German border in Kehl and another at the Polish–German border in Frankfurt/Oder. The ECC-Net, created in 2005, includes both public and private actors and consists of a set of centers that work together to provide consumers with information on international commerce and aid the resolution of cross-border complaints and disputes. On the international level, there is much exchange and mutual learning. For instance, vzbv is one of the largest and most powerful members of the European umbrella organization of consumer organizations—BEUC: The European Consumer Organisation. Stiftung Warentest is a member of Consumers International (CI) and is active in international outreach and training projects, especially those that promote consumer testing organizations worldwide.

In a summary, the consumer movement in West Germany developed more sporadically than many other nations, but the consumer organizations that eventually emerged are well integrated with government consumer policy institutions. Consumer policymaking itself in Germany is fragmented, a situation that may stem partially from the country's historical development and its federal system. The fact that Germany has not accepted a federal consumer policy strategy may be an indication of a lack of serious, coherent, and systematic political consumer representation. However, the latest policy programs of political parties currently administering national affairs indicate that this lack of interest may soon change. Policymakers across the political spectrum are realizing the increasing need and opportunity to focus on consumer issues. In facing current issues, such as the transition to a stable, "green" economy based on renewable energy, policymakers may find it useful to take a consumer perspective by actively engaging with consumer organizations and consumers themselves.

Lucia Reisch

See also: BEUC: The European Consumer Organisation; Consumers International

Further Reading

Gasteiger, Nepomuck. 2010. *Der Konsument. Verbraucherbilder in Werbung, Konsumkritik und Verbraucherschutz 1945–1989.* Frankfurt, Germany: Campus Verlag.
Kleinschmidt, Christian. 2010. "Comparative Consumer Product Testing in Germany. *Business History Review* 84, no. 1: 105–124.

Reisch, Lucia. 2004. "Principles and Visions of a New Consumer Policy." *Journal of Consumer Policy*, 27, no. 1: 1–42.

Thøgersen, John. 2005. "How May Consumer Policy Empower Consumers for Sustainable Lifestyles?" *Journal of Consumer Policy* 28, no. 2: 143–177.

Wahlen, Stefan, and Kaisa Huttunen. 2012. "Consumer Policy and Consumer Empowerment: Comparing the Historic Development in Finland and Germany." *International Journal of Consumer Studies* 36, no. 1: 2–9.

H

HEALTH INSURANCE ADVOCACY

Although reformers have sought "universal health insurance" for more than a century, only in the past three decades has this issue fully engaged consumer groups and their allies at federal and state levels. In the early 1980s, broadening health insurance coverage became a high priority for a number of these organizations as well as for newly established groups with a specific focus on health insurance. Almost all organizations working on health insurance reform favored the creation of single-payer health insurance programs and for more than a decade devoted most of their energies to winning acceptance of these programs at the federal and state level. But after achieving only modest gains, reformers increasingly were willing to accept reforms that retained key features of the existing insurance system. By the late 2000s, virtually all liberal and left groups seeking health insurance reform united behind support for President Obama's Affordable Care, which was approved by a Democratic Congress in 2010.

The principal goal of these national and state advocacy groups has been to expand access to health care services through increasing their availability and lowering their cost to individuals and families. They have faced the challenge of changing a complex system based on government-funded insurance to the elderly (Medicare) and poor (Medicaid) and employer-provided insurance to most of the non-elderly. In a true single-payer system, such as those in Canada and most European countries, government covers basic health care costs for the entire population. Proposed transitions to this system in the United States typically face intense opposition from health insurers, who would be put out of business, and many health care providers and consumers, who are apprehensive about changes to the health care system.

Vigorous advocacy by consumer, health care, and allied organizations for single-payer programs and less radical reforms began in the 1980s. In the late 1980s, health reform coalitions were organized in several dozen states, often in association with national groups such as Citizen Action and Families USA, which themselves were established in the previous decade. One of the most active, for example, was Health Access in California, which brought together a broad array of health care, civil rights, senior, labor, religious, and traditional consumer groups, including Consumers Union and the California Public Interest Research Group (CALPIRG). The central focus of these coalitions was expanding access to affordable health care coverage in their states. But they also supported the efforts of Citizen Action, Families USA, and Jobs with Justice, a labor/community coalition, to work for national single-payer legislation that was introduced in 1991 by Representative Marty Russo (D-IL) and more than fifty other House members.

The political difficulty of enacting single-payer reform at either the federal or state level led advocates to debate the merits of supporting less far-reaching reforms that would retain essential features of the current system. In 1993 and 1994, some of these advocates—such as Families USA and labor groups—fully committed their organizations to passage of President Clinton's Health Security Act, which featured "health alliances" that would preserve both employer-provided coverage and participation of the commercial insurance industry. Other advocates did not make this full commitment. Citizen Action, which eventually did endorse the legislation, organized the Campaign for Health Security, a broad-based effort of consumer, religious, senior disability, labor, farm, and provider organizations to educate the public and mobilize support for comprehensive health insurance reform based on single-payer.

After Congress refused to approve the Health Security Act, many advocates continued to work at the state level not only for expanded affordable coverage for different groups, such as children, but also for single-payer insurance. Unable to persuade state legislatures to adopt radical reforms, in several states, they organized initiative campaigns. The single most influential state initiative was Proposition 186 in California, which was led by the Health Access coalition. The overwhelming defeat of this single-payer measure in 1994, 73 percent to 27 percent, provided support for the view that it was to difficult to win strong popular support for radical health insurance reform.

Although coalitions in several other states continued to work for single-payer programs, over time, many de-emphasized this goal as a program priority. (To date, only Vermont has adopted a system with single-payer features.) Families USA, convinced that national reform could not be achieved without broad-based support from health insurers and providers as well as citizen and labor groups, organized a series of convocations with these stakeholder groups that reached significant agreements that helped make possible passage of President Obama's Affordable Care Act in 2010.

When President Obama proposed health care reform that included greatly expanded Medicaid coverage and the creation of state and federal insurance exchanges to provide consumers with competitive options, almost all groups supporting health insurance reform enthusiastically joined the campaign for legislation. Citizen Action groups (now part of USAction), other leftist groups, and big service workers and public employee unions (SEIU and AFSCME) worked together in the Health Care for America Now (HCAN) coalition, primarily to mobilize support for the legislation at the grassroots. More traditionally liberal groups—such as Families USA, Consumers Union, and AARP—not only sought to generate grassroots support, but also worked closely in Washington, D.C., with the Obama administration, labor groups, and health care providers to advance the legislation. Both Consumers Union and Families USA collected stories from "victims" of health care coverage and undertook extensive media outreach.

After the legislation's enactment in 2010, many of these organizations continued to work on behalf of the new law, trying to fend off attacks from Republicans, provide information to consumers, and facilitate enrollment of the uninsured. Consumers Union, for example, developed HealthCareHelper to provide personalized information to consumers. And Families USA helped organize state campaigns to promote state Medicaid expansion and to enroll the uninsured.

Stephen Brobeck

See also: Consumers Union/Consumer Reports; Families USA; Healthcare Advocacy

Further Reading

Hoffman, Beatrix. 2008. "Health Care Reform and Social Movements in the U.S." *American Journal of Public Health* 98 (September): S69–S79.

Kirsch, Richard. 2011. *Fighting for Our Health: The Epic Battle to Make Health Care a Right in the United States.* Albany, NY: Rockefeller Institute Press.

Starr, Paul. 2011. *Remedy and Reaction: The Peculiar American Struggle over Health Care Reform.* New Haven, CT: Yale University Press.

HEALTHCARE ADVOCACY

Consumer advocacy on healthcare has expanded significantly in recent years and has also become far more effective. Most of that advocacy now surrounds the Affordable Care Act (ACA), the Obama administration's health reform initiative. Debate on the law began in 2009 and has not abated, even after passage of the act in March 2010. Most recently, consumer groups have sought to support and guide the law's implementation and beat back attempts to repeal or significantly alter it. Less well known is that consumer advocacy on healthcare issues was becoming increasingly potent before 2009. That helped build support for healthcare reform and ultimately shaped the specifics of the final ACA bill.

Broadly speaking, consumer advocacy in healthcare—pre- and post-ACA—has focused on expanding insurance coverage, restraining cost growth, and improving care quality and safety. Hundreds of consumer organizations—some national, many state-based and local—have led or joined efforts to address the wide array of problems that arise from the unique complexity of the patchwork U.S. healthcare and medical system—a system that accounts for close to one-sixth (and fast approaching one-fifth) of our economy.

Consumer Issues

Both separate from and connected to implementation of the ACA, the following issues are at the forefront of consumer advocacy focused on healthcare services and care delivery.

Payment reform: Providers (doctors, hospitals and others) receive most of their income from private insurers (both employer-based and individually purchased coverage) and government (Medicare and Medicaid). A growing number of doctors, around 25 percent, opt for salaried positions but most still get paid through a fee-for-service system in which they are compensated for every service they provide, procedure they perform, or test they give. Put another way, providers get paid for the *quantity of care* they deliver, not its *quality*.

With studies—from highly credible sources such as the RAND Corporation—estimating that 25 percent to 30 percent of all care is unnecessary and that another 25 percent is ineffective, consumer groups are pressing for changes in how providers get paid. They advocate a system in which payment is increasingly linked to performance, quality of care, and results. This will be a major transition and take years, with an eventual end to open-ended fee-for-service payment. Under the ACA, Medicare payments to providers begin to be linked to performance on quality-of-care measures. Consumer groups who are leaders in this area include AARP, the National Partnership for Women and Families (NPWF), and Catalyst for Payment Reform.

Price variability and transparency: Research shows that fee-for-service prices for health care services are highly variable and often excessive. Even in a single city, according to monitoring by the Center for Medicare and Medicaid Services, the price for some procedures can vary by fivefold or more. For example, the average hospital fees for the treatment of heart failure ranged from $21,000 to $46,000 in Denver, Colorado, and from $9,000 to $51,000 in Jackson, Mississippi. An investigation by the *New York Times*, published June 3, 2013, found that the highest price charged for a colonoscopy in seventeen cities ranged from $2,116 in Nashville, Tennessee to $8,557 in New York City. Consumer advocacy—led by AARP, Consumers Union, and NPWF, among other groups—is focused on requiring doctors and hospitals to make public the fees they charge so consumers can comparison shop, even when treatment is mostly paid for by insurance.

Out-of-pocket costs and medical debt: Soaring medical prices have driven employers and insurers to shift costs to consumers—through higher premiums, deductibles, co-pays, and co-insurance (the percentage of the bill you pay). A fifth of middle-income families spend 10 percent or more of their incomes on healthcare. Millions of low-income seniors who live mostly on Social Security payments spend an even higher proportion. Medical expenses are the leading cause of medical debt and personal bankruptcy in the United States. Consumer advocates want to limit the shift in cost to consumers and families, limiting their exposure to no more than 10 percent of income.

Public reporting of data on providers: Insurers, employers, and government are now requiring hospitals and doctors to measure the quality of their care, in part due to new payment initiatives in the ACA. These requirements yield data that can, when appropriately packaged and explained, steer consumers to providers who deliver high quality care at an affordable cost. Consumer groups are pushing insurers and government to collect high-quality data that is meaningful and actionable for consumers.

Consolidation in the healthcare industry: Healthcare is structured in a way that perennially pits payers against providers. Payers want more accountability and value for their dollar, and as much competition as possible to yield both. Providers want to be paid as much as possible. Employers, insurers, government, and consumers thus have an interest in making sure, for example, that hospitals compete on price and service and do not gain too much market power. These stakeholders also have an interest in assuring robust competition among health insurance companies.

On local, state, and federal levels, consumer groups are mobilized to prevent excessive concentration of market power amongst both insurers and providers. It's a never-ending struggle for balance. The ACA has been criticized for creating some momentum to consolidation in both the insurance and hospital industries. Consumer groups have pledged to monitor this issue to ensure that growing concentration does not allow unwarranted price increases.

Structure of care delivery: Healthcare in the United States is highly fragmented. People needing treatment for serious conditions often get shuttled among providers and institutions, with the doctors they see often not coordinating on a coherent course of care. As a result, quality suffers. Consumer groups—led by the NPWF's Campaign for Better Care—support efforts being made by employers, insurers, and Medicare to incentivize providers to better coordinate care, through payment and system reforms.

Patient safety and medical errors: A widely publicized 1999 report from the National Academy of Science's Institute of Medicine (*To Err is Human: Building a Safer Health System*) galvanized a movement to improve patient safety. The report estimated that as many as 98,000 people in the United States die each year from preventable medical errors. Since then, consumer and patient groups, and families who had experienced harm, have played a major role in shaping policy and marketplace reforms to address this issue through testimony, lobbying, grassroots activism, and media outreach. That advocacy has spurred significant regulatory change at the federal and state level. Among consumer leaders in this area are Consumer Union's Safe Patient Project, the Leapfrog Group, and Mothers against Medical Error.

Overtreatment, undertreatment, and evidence-based medicine: Decades of research shows that medical care frequently yields poor results. There are two related problems. Many people, especially people of color and those with low incomes, fail to obtain needed care. On the other hand, millions of Americans receive care that is ineffective, unnecessary, or inappropriate.

This misallocation of resources has many causes but reflects poor knowledge and poor application of the medical knowledge that does exist. Despite enormous progress made in medicine over the past twenty years, the evidence gap in medicine is very real. Some studies indicate that anywhere from 25 percent to 50 percent of care delivered lacks evidence for effectiveness.

Consumer advocates have joined forces with many others in a long-term struggle to improve the evidence base of medicine and care itself and to educate both providers and consumers on the need to weigh treatment choices carefully. The Lown Institute in Boston and its consumer advocate Shannon Brownlee—author of *Overtreated: Why Too Much Medicine is Making Us Sicker and Poorer*—has taken a lead role on this issue. National consumer groups such as AARP and Consumers Union strongly supported the establishment in the ACA of the Patient-Centered Outcomes Research Institute. PCORI's job is to fund research that directly compares treatment options and effectively disseminates the findings to providers and consumers.

Patient engagement and "participatory medicine": Initiatives to educate consumers on the importance of becoming engaged patients dates back to the 1970s, with activists such as author Thomas Ferguson, a medical doctor. The movement's core messages remain largely the same as they were then, but in the digital era they now emphasize the advantages of becoming an "e-patient." That can involve using online and mobile health tools to monitor your health; joining an online patient support network; using your doctor's web portal to get test results, make appointment, and email questions; rating your doctor or hospital online; and compiling your medical records in an electronic personal health record (PHR).

Consumer groups helped push legislation in 2009 that pays doctors to adopt and use electronic health records (EHRs). As part of that legislation, doctors must make treatment summaries and medical records available to patients in electronic format beginning in 2014. Consumer-led groups such as the Center for Advancing Health, the Center for Technology and Democracy, and the Society of Participatory Medicine are leaders in this area.

Access to care: Expanding insurance coverage remains the principal aim of advocacy surrounding access to care. But this effort also now encompasses increasing the number of primary care doctors and support for community clinics that serve low-income, mostly uninsured, people. Consumer groups and advocates for the poor successfully lobbied to increase funding in the ACA for the network of 1,200 community health centers operating throughout the nation. The law commits $11 billion to expanding the clinics from 2012 to 2017.

Medicare: Led by AARP, most consumer groups with a healthcare portfolio monitor Medicare policy and regulations. Some, such as the National Committee to Preserve Social Security and Medicare, primarily lobby Congress to head off disruptions to the program or reductions in benefits. Others, such as the Medicare Rights Center and the Center for Medicare Advocacy, provide direct services to Medicare Beneficiaries and fight legal battles around beneficiaries' access to care.

End-of-life care: Studies show that care at the end of life remains suboptimal. Too many people die in hospital intensive care units instead of where most would rather die—at home. Too few people get good hospice care. Too few have advance directives specifying which care they want, or do not want, at life's end. Consumer advocacy in this area centers on enhancing access to hospice and palliative care services at home and reducing the overuse of intensive, often futile treatment when that treatment clearly risks reducing and not enhancing quality of life.

Strategy and Challenges

When advantageous, consumer groups now routinely partner with employer, union, provider, and even insurance trade and lobby groups to push for reforms in care and services. In the run-up to passage of the ACA, many such liaisons were formed, formal and informal. Most notably, NPWF (which receives some funding from healthcare businesses) has a formal relationship with the Pacific Business Group on Health, a coalition of sixty large California-based employers. Jointly, the two groups operate the Consumer–Purchaser Alliance (CPA). With funding from the Robert Wood Johnson Foundation, the alliance lobbies the government on health care regulations and advocates for quality improvement and payment reforms. Other alliance members include AFL–CIO, AARP, the National Business Group on Health, and the Midwest Business Group on Health. AARP, NPWF, and other CPA participants are also active participants in a multi-stakeholder organization called the National Quality Forum (NQF). NQF is charged by the ACA with evaluating the performance and quality measures providers must now use.

Consumer organizations have also worked with provider groups, including the American Medical Association and American College of Physicians, on quality improvement and performance measurement issues. One organization providing a forum for this collaboration is called the AQA Alliance.

Though haltingly at times, and not without missteps and controversy, these collaborations of consumer and industry groups have proved effective over time. In particular, they have, on occasion, clarified strategic directions that the Medicare program has followed. And in the years before the ACA was crafted, these collaborations set the system on a path towards reforms in care delivery that are now embodied and propelled forward by the ACA.

In the past decade, the work of these national organizations and coalitions has been strengthened by groups representing patients with particular diseases. More than 1,000 now exist. Some lobby and seek to influence legislation, regulations, and Medicare policy. Others are more oriented towards providing support services for patients.

National consumer groups on the liberal and progressive end of the political spectrum worry that many patient advocacy groups receive funding from and appear to be aligned with industry, particularly pharmaceutical and medical device companies. They often point to the National Health Council as illustrative of this "conflict of interest" problem. The NHC is a Washington, D.C.–based coalition of about 100 patient advocacy organizations, disease-oriented groups (including the American Cancer Society and American Heart Association), and healthcare companies (including *all* the major pharmaceutical companies). The NHC and patient advocacy groups that receive funding from industry defend their role and argue that they positively affect health reform—in particular, the research priorities of industry and government.

Like almost every other aspect of modern life, healthcare advocacy is being transformed by social media. This development is so new that it is hard to know where exactly it will lead. It is likely, however, that one prominent outcome will be a substantial enhancement in people's awareness of the health system's shortcomings and the need for continued reform in how services are provided and paid for. Notably, millions of people with medical conditions and diseases are now actively engaged in patient support websites and online social networks. Some of these networks (for example, patientlikeme.com) have developed sophisticated new tools that allow patients to participate in research. Almost every day, a person or family posts a petition on change.org seeking support and help for a loved one in dire medical circumstances. And almost all patient and consumer groups have active Facebook and Twitter presences.

Consumer groups active in healthcare advocacy are now firmly entrenched in the implementation of the ACA. But they remain at a significant disadvantage in terms of funding and resources compared to hospital, physician, drug, and other industry groups. According to the Center for Responsive Politics, the healthcare industry spent just under $500 million on lobbying in 2013, more than any other industry. By comparison, AARP, the largest consumer lobby in healthcare, spent $9.6 million in the same year.

At the ground level, this disparity plays out in many ways. One persistent challenge is fielding advocates who have the technical expertise to match that of industry lobbyists. On some issues, one consumer advocate who may not have an advanced degree must contend with industry lawyers, PhD economists, and IT experts. However, at least now, unlike decades ago, there is usually at least one consumer advocate involved.

Steven Findlay

See also: Consumers Union/Consumer Reports; Families USA; Health Insurance Advocacy; Prescription Drug Advocacy; Public Citizen

Further Reading

Brownlee, Shannon. 2008. *Overtreated: Why Too Much Medicine is Making Us Sicker and Poorer.* New York: Bloomsbury USA.

Consumers Union and Robert Wood Johnson Foundation. 2013. *Addressing Rising Healthcare Costs: A Resource Guide for Consumer Advocates* (November). www .consumersunion .org/healthcost/HealthCareCosts-BriefingBooklet-DigitalVersion .pdf.

Ferguson, Thomas, ed. 1980. *Medical Self-Care: Access to Health Tools.* Mono, Ontario: Summit Books.

Kohn, Linda T., et al. 1999. *To Err is Human: Building a Safer Health System.* Washington, DC: National Academy Press.

RAND Corporation. "Health Care Reform Publications." www.rand.org/health/browse-health/healthcare-reform.html.

HOMEOWNERS INSURANCE ADVOCACY

See Insurance Advocacy

HONG KONG CONSUMER MOVEMENT

The Hong Kong Consumer Council is the only statutory consumer protection body in Hong Kong, one of two special administrative regions of the People's Republic of China. The council was established by the Hong Kong government in 1974 when the region was a British territory. The council has twenty-two members, including a chairman and vice-chairman. These members are drawn from a variety of professions and are appointed by the chief executive of Hong Kong. As of 2012, the council had more than 140 staff operating in its headquarters, divisional offices, and consumer advice centers in various districts.

The council's financial resources are mainly drawn from government grants, with about 5 percent of its budget coming from the sale of publications. In spite of the heavy reliance on government funds, the council enjoys considerable independence in formulating its policies on consumer protection as well as discharging its statutory duties.

Although the change of sovereignty back to China in 1997 signified a new era for Hong Kong, there were no significant changes to the council in terms of its powers or its consumer protection policies. Indeed, as the council has developed strong collaborative ties with consumer bodies in mainland China to enhance consumer interests, the council has become better known and more influential in the region and the world.

Vision and Activities of the Council

The council is committed to enhancing consumer welfare through empowering consumers to protect themselves and engaging in the public policy process. Over its four decades of activity, the council has moved far beyond its traditional function of complaint handling. Today, its activities also include: generating and disseminating the results of scientific product testing; educating consumers, especially vulnerable groups such as children, the elderly, and recent immigrants; helping consumers with legal recourse with problems that cannot be resolved via complaint handling; advocating for greater competition and better business conduct; seeking government action to promote consumer interests; cooperating with consumer organizations in mainland China; and participating in the international consumer movement. These activities are described more fully below.

Empowering consumers with information and education is a core activity of the council. The council places high priority on testing consumer products to provide unbiased comparative test results. The publication of these results helps consumers make rational choices, alerts them to product hazards, and induces improvement in product quality and safety. The council's monthly announcement of test results via *Choice*, with its emphasis on brand-specific information, attracts immense media and public interest. The magazine was initially available only in paper form, but today it can also be accessed via electronic media. In the course of a year, the council publishes more than forty test reports (and an additional 100 research reports). The council also collaborates with International Consumer Research and Testing to conduct international comparative tests on a wide range of consumer products.

The council complements information with consumer education, both of which are crucial to consumer empowerment. Through systematic activities that target three vulnerable groups—namely, young people, senior citizens, and new immigrants—participants in consumer education programs acquire the skills and know-how necessary to become rational consumers who are aware of their rights and responsibilities. Adopting the principle of "training the trainers," the council provides support to other stakeholders and educational institutions to enable them to run their own consumer education programs. Every year, more than 200 educational talks, visits, workshops, and seminars are organized for stakeholder and educational institutions, as well as other interested parties such as teachers, parents, women, and disadvantaged groups. In its product testing and other information dissemination activities, the council is mindful that promoting and supporting sustainable consumption—not just seeking the best product at the lowest price—is important as well.

Helping to resolve consumer–business disputes remains a central component of the council's activities. The council has a consumer hotline and seven consumer advice centers; these constitute an extensive network in offering convenient service to consumers. A team of complaint officers is responsible for handling consumer complaints. To address consumers' concerns speedily and effectively, the council makes inquiries, lodges complaints, and tries to resolve disputes. Over the past ten years, the council has received more than 100,000 consumer inquiries and currently receives more than 20,000 consumer complaints annually. Complaints against telecommunication services have constantly remained on top of the complaint list, followed by telecommunication equipment, and electrical appliances.

Although the council can help resolve consumer complaints, they may also refer complaint cases to the Consumer Legal Action Fund (the Fund) of which the council is the Trustee. The fund aims to give consumers access to legal solutions by providing consumers with financial support and legal assistance to pursue their claims. In considering the merits of a case, the Fund's Management Committee not only considers the benefits for the individual complainant but also potential community benefits, particularly for groups with similar grievances in cases involving significant public interest and injustice. Over the years, the fund has considered more than 1,200 applications, and assistance has been given to more than half of them.

In addition to providing information, education, complaint handling services, and legal support for consumers, the council encourages businesses and professional associations to establish self-regulatory codes of practice and advises government officials. In a market-based economy such as Hong Kong, the council has a key role in ensuring that best practices and competition in the marketplace lead to economic efficiency and consumer satisfaction. The council studies various aspects of marketplace behavior to identify concerns of consumers as well as encourage responsible trade practices and fair competition. Many study reports of competition have been published by the council, covering anticompetitive actions of banks, supermarkets, telecommunication, broadcasting, energy suppliers, and property sellers.

In 2005, the council launched a *Good Corporate Citizen's Guide* to promote corporate responsibility. This guide lays the groundwork for corporations to respect individuals, communities, and the natural environment. Businesses accepting the guide commit to adhere to high ethical standards when devising or implementing business strategies and abide by laws and regulations. The guide has been adopted by more than twenty trade associations across diverse industries.

Recognizing disputes related to unfairness in consumer contracts, especially consumer service contracts, the council published in 2012 a study entitled *Unfair Terms in Standard Form Consumer Contracts*. The report called on businesses to adopt fair terms in standard form consumer contracts. It was well received by business groups, who have, in turn, made improvements in response.

The council has worked well with the government over the years and has advocated for the enactment of many consumer protection laws. The council keeps abreast of developments in the law that affect consumers, and it attempts to submit its views on consumer issues as early in the policy process as possible. Locally, the council's regular liaisons with more than ten government bureaus and thirty government departments are well established, facilitating its work in addressing specific consumer issues that fall within their purview.

Serving on public and government boards is an important means by which the council presents the views of consumers. By serving on relevant boards/committees, council representatives express consumer concerns and seek to enhance consumer protection relating to a host of consumer issues, including consumer health and safety, residential properties, financial and telecommunications services, regulating travel and real estate agency business as well as environmental protection initiatives. The council's views are formulated with first-hand knowledge of consumer needs acquired through surveys, complaints, and direct contact with consumers and traders. As of 2012, representatives of the council served on more than sixty public advisory committees and boards of regulatory or statutory bodies.

The council has long maintained close relationships with consumer organizations and related bodies from the mainland (more than 3,200 consumer associations in the whole country) through exchange of information, referral of complaints, meeting with their delegations, and providing training to their staff. Starting in

2004, memorandums of cooperation were signed with consumer associations in major cities/provinces in the mainland. The council's network in the mainland has facilitated the dissemination of consumer information to the mainland through the Internet. The council's Shopsmart website provides consumer information to mainland visitors and is hyperlinked to twenty-eight mainland organizations.

As a final dimension of the council's activities, it is an active participant in the international arena of consumer protection. For example, the council's leaders have held important leadership positions (including the presidency) in Consumers International (CI)—the umbrella organization of the world consumer moment with more than 240 members from 120 countries. As another illustration, the council signed a memorandum of understanding with the United Nations Conference on Trade and Development .(UNCTAD) in which the council agreed to help build the organizational capacity of consumer organizations in six developing countries (Bhutan, Botswana, South Africa, Lao, Ecuador, and Oman). These cooperative efforts foster the council's role in promoting consumer rights in the international arena, and the council's chief executives have been frequent speakers at international and mainland conferences on consumer protection. Across its various areas of work, the council upholds the core values of being driven by the welfare of consumers, maintaining openness in its activities, being independent of undue influence, protecting the privacy of personal data, and being accountable, fair, and proactive.

Accomplishments and Assessment

The council has advocated for the enhancement of consumer protection through legislation and has been at the forefront of the public debate during the consultation period of various pieces of legislation. More than twenty consumer protection laws were enacted or revised since the inception of the council.

In the summer of 2012, three historic pieces of important consumer legislation were passed—long-awaited laws regarding competition, the sale of residential properties, and unfair trade practices. The council worked in a sustained fashion to rally support for these laws; in the case of the Competition Ordinance, the council first advocated such a bill in 1993. The law regarding residential sales was a priority for the council, because buying a home is often the most expensive and significant purchase in a consumer's life.

Across its nearly four decades of operation, the council has earned a reputation for being driven by the core values of promoting consumer welfare, maintaining openness in its activities, being independent of undue influence, protecting the privacy of personal data, and being accountable, fair, and proactive. The council's high status among international consumer organizations was recognized by its selection to host in Hong Kong the CI World Congress in 2011. (The council also hosted this conference in 1991.) The 2011 Congress achieved a record high in the number of delegates attending in the history of the CI World Congress. The success of the Congress gained the council much goodwill and a wide recognition of its international standing in consumer protection.

Robert N. Mayer

See also: Chinese Consumer Movement; Consumers International

Further Reading

Consumer Council. www.consumer.org.hk/website/ws_en/.
Shui, Pamela Chan Wong. 1997. "Hong Kong Consumer Movement." In Stephen Brobeck, ed., *Encyclopedia of the Consumer Movement* (pp. 304–306). Santa Barbara, CA: ABC-CLIO.

HOUSEHOLD PRODUCT SAFETY ADVOCACY

Activism for improved food and drug safety began at the end of the nineteenth century and eventually led, in 1906, to congressional passage of two laws to improve this safety. However, Congress did not seriously address household product safety hazards until the 1950s and early 1960s, and then only by dealing piecemeal with specific hazards that were extensively reported on by the press. In 1953, as a response to fires involving children wearing flammable clothing, the Flammable Fabrics Act was enacted to authorize federal regulators to create flammability standards. In 1956, as a response to children being trapped inside household refrigerators, the Refrigerator Safety Act was enacted to require that refrigerators manufactured after October 1958 be easily opened from inside.

In 1960, the Federal Hazardous Substances Act was enacted to require warning labels on hazardous household chemical products. In 1966, Congress approved amendments to this law giving federal regulators the authority to ban household substances and toys containing these substances. In 1969, the Child Protection and Toy Safety Act extended statutory authority to children's products presenting electrical, mechanical, and thermal dangers to users. In 1970, the Poison Prevention Packaging Act was enacted to require products, which contained hazardous substances that could be ingested by young children, to be placed in packaging with child-resistant closures.

In 1967, Congress established the National Commission on Product Safety to address broader issues of product safety. This commission was championed by Senator Warren Magnuson (D-WA), chairman of the Senate Commerce Committee, who had been convinced by Michael Pertschuk and other committee staffers that the federal government needed an agency to deal with household safety hazards. Pertschuk, chief counsel to the committee (and future chairman of the Federal Trade Commission), served on the commission, which researched product safety hazards and held regional hearings. Its report, released in 1970, was instrumental in persuading Congress, in 1972, to approve the Consumer Product Safety Act. In the House, the leadership of Congressman John Moss (D-CA) was particularly effective in mobilizing support for the legislation. The final bill, signed into law by President Richard Nixon, created a new, independent federal regulatory agency with the authority to set mandatory safety standards for consumer products and to recall dangerous products from consumers, store shelves, and the entire distribution chain. This agency, called the Consumer Product Safety Commission (CPSC), took over responsibility for enforcing the product safety statutes approved earlier by Congress.

Although consumer advocates including Ralph Nader and the Consumer Federation of America's Erma Angevine had supported this legislation, its most effective advocates had been Senator Magnuson, Congressman Moss, and Pertschuk. Throughout the remainder of the 1970s, consumer groups focused more of their attention on the creation of a federal consumer protection agency than on the organization of a strong and effective CPSC. Leadership here was taken by Commissioner R. David Pittle, a former engineering professor, and his two legal counsel—Robert Adler, who as a legal services attorney had worked with Pittle in Pittsburgh organizing a local consumer group, and Janne Gallagher, a Baltimore Legal Services attorney.

Congress had given the CPSC broad responsibility for numerous products in and around the home but a relatively modest budget of under $40 million. The impossibility of agency staff's quickly developing standards for numerous products ultimately forced the commission to allow affected businesses to participate in, and sometimes lead, the standard-setting activities. The effectiveness of these standards depended, to a large extent, on the leverage CPSC leaders were willing to exert over those writing the standards. A tough stance by the commission, for example, pressured leaders of the chain saw industry to agree to a strong voluntary standard for that product. In 1975, in part because of the effective advocacy of Andrew McGuire, whose pajamas had caught fire when he was seven years old, the commission set flammability safety standards for children's pajamas.

The main focus of product safety advocates in the early 1980s shifted to the preservation of the CPSC itself. The Reagan administration proposed eliminating the agency and, when that failed, tried to emasculate it. The administration supported legislation, approved by Congress, that prohibited the agency from promulgating mandatory safety standards if compliance with a voluntary standard would largely reduce the risk of injury and there would be "substantial compliance." They cut the commission's budget and staff by about 30 percent. Most damaging of all, they appointed antiregulation commissioners, notably Chairman Terence Scanlon, who supported all these weakening measures, as well as many others.

During the 1980s, three national consumer groups—Consumers Union, Consumer Federation of America (CFA), and U.S. PIRG—led opposition to the Reagan Administration's weakening of the CPSC. At Consumers Union, R. David Pittle, who became technical director after leaving the CPSC in 1982 (and continued serving in that capacity until his retirement in 2005), oversaw that organization's efforts. At CFA, product safety director and general counsel Mary Ellen Fise, who specialized in household safety issues, was a product safety leader before Congress and the CPSC from 1984 up to 2002. She worked closely with Pamela Gilbert, U.S. PIRG's product safety advocate from 1984 to 1989 and Congress Watch's director from 1989 to 1994. Among other accomplishments, Gilbert led successful efforts to persuade Congress to pass a law requiring labeling of hazardous art and craft materials, which went into effect in 1990. Since 1986, U.S. PIRG has released annual reports on toy safety that have led to a number of product recalls.

Despite having to play continuous defense, these advocates did help persuade Congress to enact a law directing the CPSC to institute a ban on the sale of lawn darts after several well-publicized child deaths from this toy. They also supported Commissioner Stuart Statler's efforts to regulate all-terrain vehicles (ATVs), which resulted in a compromise negotiated settlement between the commission and ATV manufacturers.

Overall, the 1980s was a dismal decade for product safety advocacy, but things improved in the 1990s when President Bill Clinton appointed Ann Brown chair of the commission. Brown, who was well-connected in Democratic Party circles, had served as a vice president of CFA and had undertaken annual toy safety surveys. Brown appointed Pamela Gilbert as executive director of the agency, and together they worked with some success to raise the public profile of the agency, increase staff morale, increase regulatory activity, even persuading the Clinton Administration and Congress to modestly increase the commission's budget.

The agency under Brown's leadership was also more responsive to consumer groups. For example, the commission approved a strong voluntary standard making baby walkers safer in response to a petition submitted by CFA, Consumers Union, the American Academy of Pediatrics, and the National Safe Kids Campaign, whose lead advocate was Alan Korn. Beginning in this decade, Carol Pollack-Nelson, who earlier had served as senior human factors psychologist with the CPSC, began product safety initiatives that eventually included petitions to the agency to eliminate hazardous cords in window covering, to make bunk beds safer, to require barriers on the glass door of gas fireplaces, and to require stronger standards for hunting tree stands and safety harnesses.

By the late 1990s, new product safety advocates had joined national consumer groups. In 1997, attorney Sally Greenberg was hired by Consumers Union as senior product safety counsel and spent a decade in this position working on safety issues related to household products, motor vehicles, food, and drugs before being appointed president of the National Consumers League. In 1999, attorney Rachel Weintraub began working as an advocate on issues, including product safety, at U.S. PIRG. Then in 2002, she moved to CFA, where she has specialized in household product safety issues and, since Fise's departure in 2004, has served as the organization's product safety director (and later, legislative director).

The most important product safety development since the creation of the CPSC was the enactment of the Consumer Product Safety Improvement Act (CPSIA) in 2008.

This comprehensive law, intended mainly to improve the safety of children's products, severely limited levels of lead and phthalates allowed in children's products, required third-party testing of products subject to CPSC safety rules, increased penalties for violating these rules, mandated creation of a database of product safety complaints accessible to the public, and significantly increased the budget and staffing of the agency.

This legislation largely reflected growing concern about the safety of products manufactured in China, especially children's products containing lead. In the House, the chief sponsor of legislation was Bobby Rush (D-IL), and its most effective advocates were Henry Waxman (D-CA), Jan Schakowsky (D-IL), and Ed Markey (D-MA). In the Senate, Daniel Inouye (D-HI), Mark Pryor (D-AR), Dianne

Feinstein (D-CA), Barbara Boxer (D-CA), and Bill Nelson (D-FL) made essential contributions.

These congressional leaders were encouraged and supported by a coalition of consumer, environmental, and safety groups coordinated by CFA's Weintraub. She worked closely with the director of Consumers Union's Washington office, Ellen Bloom, who earlier in her career had worked for Senator Howard Metzenbaum (D-OH). Don Mays—who earlier had served as Consumers Union's director of testing, then returned to the organization in 2005 as a senior director working on safety issues—contributed much technical expertise. Nancy Cowles of Kids in Danger and Cindy Pellegrini of the American Academy of Pediatrics were particularly effective members of the coalition.

The CPSIA required or encouraged the CPSC to issue a number of safety rules, and to date, they have issued several—on baby bath seats in 2010, on cribs in 2011, on independent product testing in 2011, and on handheld infant carriers in 2013. In 2011, the agency began posting information about unsafe products on its new website, SaferProducts.gov. CPSC Chairman Inez Tenenbaum and Commissioner Robert Adler, both appointed to their positions in 2009, were instrumental in the development of these standards and website. Among public interest organizations, CFA (Weintraub), Consumers Union (Ami Gahdia), and KID (Cowles) were especially active communicating with the agency about these rules.

Stephen Brobeck

See also: All-Terrain Vehicle Advocacy; Cosmetic Safety Advocacy; Product Safety "Victim" Activism; Tobacco Activism

Further Reading

Adler, Robert S. 1989. "From 'Model Agency' to Basket Case—Can the Consumer Product Safety Commission Be Redeemed?" *Administrative Law Review* 41: 61+.

Felcher, E. Marla. 2002. *The U.S. Consumer Product Safety Commission: The Paper Tiger of American Product Safety*. Washington, DC: Understanding Government Report.

Lemov, Michael R. 1983. *Regulatory Manual Series: Consumer Product Safety Commission*. Colorado Springs, CO: Shepard's/McGraw Hill.

HOUSING COOPERATIVES

See Consumer Cooperatives

INDIAN CONSUMER MOVEMENT

As in other countries, India's consumer movement originated from the necessity of protecting and promoting the interest of consumers against fraudulent, unethical, and unfair trade practices. The movement initially reflected a common perception that retailers and manufacturers were out to maximize profits by any means, fair or foul, with scant regard for the well-being of consumers. When the basic tenet governing the legal position of consumers was "buyer beware," careful shopping was the only form of consumer self-defense. Over time, however, an emerging consumer movement found ways of bringing pressure on business firms (as well as government) to correct conduct that was unfair or otherwise contrary to the interests of consumers.

Genesis

The consumer movement as an organized effort may be said to have begun in India when Gandhian Shri R. R. Dalvai, inspired by the precepts of Mahatma Gandhi, formed the Madras Provisional Consumers Association (MPCA) in 1947. One can even identify pro-consumer activity as far back in time as 1915, when the Passengers and Traffic Relief Association (PATRA) was set up in Mumbai. The first consumer organization in India to have a substantial impact however, was the Consumers Guidance Society of India (CGSI). CGSI formed in 1966 in response to an infamous episode in which forty people were struck with dropsy (severe swelling) and glaucoma after consuming groundnut oil adulterated with toxic argimon oil. When it was clear that the culprits would never be brought to justice, nine housewives were outraged and energized to organize a movement to fight for consumer rights. They formed the CGSI to resist consumer exploitation of all types. The CGSI, in the initial years, established branches in various places to undertake a program of consumer education, including publicity and exhibitions. CGSI also started publishing an English-language magazine, *Keemat*, to disseminate consumer information.

The consumer movement gained momentum in the 1970s. The Bangalore-based Karnataka Consumer Service Society (KCSS) formed in 1970 and had strong influence. Apart from creating awareness among the public about consumer issues, it also organized seminars in schools on consumer education. Today, however, KCSS is nearly defunct.

In 1973, in the southeastern port city of Vishakhapatnam, the Vishakha Consumer Council was established and highlighted the problems faced by low-income consumers when trying to use ration cards to purchase milk and liquefied petro-leum gas. Several other organizations were set up in large cities (Pune, Mumbai, Jamshedpur) during the 1970s. These organizations took up the cause of consum-ers who were being overcharged by traders for basic products needed for everyday life. In response, these organizations purchased items in bulk at wholesale rates and resold the goods at much lower prices.

In 1978, the Consumer Education and Research Center (CERC) was set up in Ahmedabad. Since then, the center has protected consumer rights and brought about positive changes by various means. CERC established its own laboratory for testing consumer products, such as pharmaceuticals, food items and domes-tic appliances, and disseminates its testing results. CERC also effectively uses the Indian legal system to protect consumers.

Growth

The 1980s saw continued, if sporadic, growth in consumer organizations. Jagrat Grahak was formed in 1980 in the city of Baroda, to deliver consumer education through seminars and publications; it also runs forty-five complaint centers. Con-sumer Unity and Trust Society (CUTS) started modestly in 1983 in the city of Jaipur as a small voluntary group of citizens. Today, CUTS is an impressive international organization that raises consumer awareness at the grassroots levels and operates advocacy centers. These centers operate not only in major Indian cities such as New Delhi and Calcutta but also in five overseas locations (Lusaka, Zambia; Nairobi, Kenya; Accra, Ghana; Hanoi, Vietnam; and Geneva, Switzerland). CUTS works with several national, regional, and international organizations, including Consum-ers International. Additional consumer organizations, such as Voluntary Organiza-tion in the Interest of Consumer Education (VOICE), formed in the early 1980s.

In 1986, the landmark Consumer Protection Act (CoPRA) was enacted to protect consumers from exploitation. Though not quite a panacea for all consumer prob-lems, the act provides consumers with practical means of redress when problems occur. With the enactment of this law, consumers are in a position to declare "sellers beware." In addition to substantially improving the rights of individual consumers, the law triggered the rapid growth of India's consumer movement. By the end of the twentieth century, there were hundreds of consumer associations in India.

CoPRA also stimulated coalition building among consumer organizations. Sev-eral federations of consumer associations were formed to derive the benefits of a collective and unified approach. Today, more than a dozen state-level bodies have been formed to network consumer groups and pursue issues of common inter-est. In addition, a number of federations/councils were established with members from all over the country. The latest of these national coalitions is the Consumer Coordination Council (CCC). CCC was founded in 1992 by a group of consumer activists from various consumer organizations, who met at the behest of Friedrich–Naumann–Stiftung, a German foundation. Today, CCC is a national coalition of more than eighty leading consumer organizations in the country. Some broad coali-tions are difficult to maintain because of internal misunderstandings and internecine conflict. In the case of CCC, dominance by a few individuals who lack the necessary managerial skills and fundraising capability has undermined its credibility.

The consumer movement in India has enlarged in scope and coverage during the last two decades. However, out of the 1,000-odd consumer associations, only a few can be regarded as well organized and effective in their work of educating consumers, advocating their causes, fighting court cases for them, handling consumer complaints, initiating public interest litigation, and representing consumers as members of official committees and consultative bodies.

Present Challenges

In 1991, India initiated reforms to move the economy away from socialism and toward free markets. In the ensuing decades, these liberalization policies radically changed the Indian marketplace by opening up India to foreign trade and investment. For consumers, the reforms meant greater participation in a globalized market, with its attendant benefits and challenges.

Today, though India's consumer organizations and government authorities in India struggle to keep up with the rapid pace of technological developments brought by globalization, they also face major challenges with respect to "traditional" consumer areas, such as ensuring food safety, honest trade practices, affordable financial services, and effective redress. The movement, once largely confined to middle class citizens in urban center, is now having a presence in semi-urban and rural areas, but the movement needs to be strengthened further in such locales.

Consumer organizations in all countries face the ongoing task of obtaining adequate financial resources. In India, the creation of Consumer Welfare Fund (CWF) by the government has helped some organizations by providing grants in aid, but membership subscriptions and contributions remain the main source of finance for the majority of these voluntary organizations. Most consumer organizations, with a few exceptions such as CUTS, struggle to hire full-time professionals who can provide expertise and continuity to their organizations.

India can be justly proud of the international visibility of its consumer organizations. In addition to the important international work carried out by CUTS, especially in Africa, India is well represented among the members of Consumers International—the umbrella organization for the world's consumer groups. Indeed, India has more full members and affiliates of Consumers International than any other country, and by a wide margin.

Almost three decades after the enactment of CoPRA in India, the goal of fully realizing consumer rights in India is still a distant dream. Progress has been made, but gaps in protection remain, and mechanisms of policy implementation and enforcement remain weak. To ensure further progress, many organizations formed in 1970s and 1980s will have to successfully pass on leadership to a new generation of consumer activists.

George Cheriyan

See also: Consumers International

Further Reading

Cheriyan, George. 2012. *State of the India Consumer 2012*. Jaipur, India: Consumer Unity and Trust Society. www.cuts-international.org/CART/consumersup/pdf/Report_State_of_the_Indian_Consumer-2012.pdf.

Jain, T. R., Mukesh Trehan, and Ranju Trehan. 2009–2010. *Indian Business and Economy*. New Delhi, India: V.K.: 280.

Narayanaswamy, Sromovasa. 1999. *Milestones of the Consumer Movement*, October 31. www.hindu.com/folio/fo9910/99100380.htm.

INDONESIAN CONSUMER MOVEMENT

Indonesia is the fourth most populous country in the world, the largest economy in southeast Asia, and, according to the World Trade Organization, the twenty-sixth largest exporting country in the world. Nevertheless, as of 2012, the International Monetary Fund still listed Indonesia as a developing economy. Furthermore, because Indonesia consists of nearly 17,500 islands, specific challenges can be difficult to address on a national level. Indonesia continues to face unemployment and poverty, limited infrastructure, corruption, and labor unrest.

Political instability in the 1960s led to the deterioration of the economy and a resulting change in government leadership and structure. The "New Order" administration, ushered in by the change, brought regulation to financial policy but also generated economic nationalism in the region. Conditions improved, but distrust of international trade contributed to a tenuous economic system.

The consumer movement in Indonesia originated with the establishment of the Indonesian Consumers Organization (Yayasan Lembaga Konsumen Indonesia, or YLKI) in 1973. This organization, the first of its kind in the country, focused on protecting consumers. Because many people in the region lacked affordable food, clean water, and health care, YLKI focused on access to basic services as well as ensuring that consumers received good value in their purchases. In addition, YLKI sought to shift consumer purchases from imported to locally produced goods—but only if local producers improved the quality of their products. Early on, YLKI focused on monitoring products and services and handling consumer complaints. The organization disseminates information through their monthly consumer magazine, *Warta Konsumen*. Over time, the organization's services have grown to include legal services, research, and education.

Indonesia was hard hit by the Asian financial crisis of 1997, and the government experienced yet another major change in political leadership and structure. Not only thanks to significant administration changes, but also thanks to advocacy efforts and pressure on the government over many years, the Consumer Protection Law was enacted on April 20, 1999. The legislation created organizations within the government to support consumer rights. The National Consumer Protection Agency (Badan Perlindungan Konsumen Nasional, or BPKN) was established to make recommendations to the government on how to promote consumer protection policy, conduct research, disseminate information, and receive complaints. The president of Indonesia appoints from fifteen to twenty-five members of BPKN, who in turn appoint their own chairman and vice-chairman to run the agency. Another government organization is the Consumer Dispute Settlement Body (Badan Pen-yelesaian Sengketa Konsumen, or BPSK), a quasijudicial body that was organized to settle consumer disputes, conduct investigations, and hand down verdicts on consumer protection violations. Its decisions can be appealed to district courts and the Supreme Court. Initially set up with ten BPSK offices, the goal is to eventually have one in every district in Indonesia.

The 1999 legislation prohibits false advertising of products, sets labeling standards, and makes businesses responsible to compensate for damages or losses to the consumer. Furthermore, the law recognizes the role of nongovernmental organizations (NGOs) that promote consumer protection. The law requires consumer organizations to register and file reports of their activities with the government. There are currently more than 250 consumer protection NGOs listed with the Ministry of Trade. Consumer protection NGOs in Indonesia operate to enhance consumer awareness of rights and obligations, receive consumer complaints and assist in resolution, and prepare class action suits.

Sources of financial support for consumer organizations in Indonesia are varied and include philanthropic organization grants, local government funding, and consumer donations. Financial support from the government conveys legitimacy to an organization, but with a possible loss of autonomy.

YLKI continues to be Indonesia's most important consumer organization. Over time, it has become more aggressive in defending consumers. YLKI has successfully postponed or eliminated price increases for various services such as toll roads and telephones. The organization has lobbied for a safer water supply and cheaper generic drugs. Furthermore, YLKI has engaged the legal system in class action suits against housing developers, oil companies, and electric companies. Most recently, YLKI has been involved with public service campaigns to increase consumer awareness of harmful lifestyle choices such as smoking and consumption of unhealthful foods.

It is common in Indonesia for consumer activists to work with individuals or organizations in other social sectors—such as environmentalists and farmers—to pursue common goals. For example, YLKI has campaigned and brought legal action against genetically modified food in cooperation with other civil society organizations. Similarly, consumer activists work alongside environmental activists to reduce imports of electronic and other forms of toxic waste.

In spite of strong economic nationalism in the Indonesia, its consumer organizations have been involved with the international community since the beginning of the consumer movement in the nation. YLKI joined Consumers International in 1974 and is a full member, and two other organizations, the Institute for Consumer Development and Protection and the Yogyakarta Consumer Foundation, are affiliate members that joined in 1990 and 2012, respectively. YLKI's Erna Witoelar held the highly prestigious post of president of Consumers International from 1991 until 1997. This kind of involvement in CI gives Indonesia an opportunity to develop relationships with consumer organizations internationally. Consumer activists in Indonesia face continuing challenges. A large portion of consumers in Indonesia continue to be unaware of their rights. Sellers and manufacturers are able to exploit this lack of consumer awareness to take advantage of consumers in the region. Although the Consumer Protection Law of 1999 has set an important standard for businesses to meet, consumer activists in Indonesia will continue to press for improvements in the government infrastructure for consumer protection.

Leslie Durham, Robert N. Mayer

See also: Consumers International

Further Reading

Boston University Center for Finance, Law & Policy. *Indonesia.* www.bu.edu/bucflp/countries/indonesia/.

Indonesian Consumers Organization. n.d. *Empowering Consumers, Enhancing the Nation.* Jakarta, Indonesia.

Indonesian Consumer Organization. www.ylki.or.id.

"Consumer Protection Law Is Just the Start." 2000. *The Jakarta Post.* April 16. www.thejakartapost.com/news/2000/04/16/consumer-protection-law-just-start.html.

Makarim and Taira S. 2012. *Indonesia: The Law on Consumer Protection.* January 23. www.mondaq.com/x/160974/Consumer+Law/The+Law+on+Consumer+Protection.

INITIATIVES AND REFERENDA

One of the political tools that consumer advocates have at their disposal is the ballot initiative. Efforts to persuade legislators to vote in favor of consumer protection measures may be thwarted by the lobbying skills and resources of business interests, but ballot initiatives put power directly in the hands of voters. If people are convinced that an initiative is in their interests as consumers, they can enact it. Only about half of U.S. states allow the ballot initiative (or its cousin, the referendum), but in those that do, consumer advocates have made effective use of this mechanism of social change. (Cities can also be the locus of ballot initiates, as when voters in Berkeley, California, in 2002 enjoyed the aroma but did not quaff an initiative to require all coffee sold in the city to be certified as organic, shade-grown, or Fair Trade.)

Although the subjects of many ballot initiatives (e.g., immigration reform, marriage equality, or congressional term limits) are far afield from consumer issues, many pertain directly to the physical and financial well-being of consumers. For example, ballot initiatives pertaining to automobile and health insurance, payday loans, tobacco products, genetically modified food, and marijuana have the ability to set policies with enormous implications for consumers.

The terms initiative and referendum are often used interchangeably, but there is a difference between them. Initiatives permit citizens to propose (or "initiate") a legislative measure by filing a petition bearing a minimum number of valid signatures. Referenda, in contrast, do not require the petition process; they occur when a government body, typically a legislature, "refers" a proposed or existing law to the citizenry for their approval or rejection. Constitutional amendments and bond issues best exemplify referenda items. From the point of view of making consumer policy, initiatives are more important. The term initiatives will be used in this article to encompass both forms of citizen lawmaking.

The initiative process developed largely during the Progressive era, a period that saw a number of efforts to make government more open, accountable, and honest. Whereas Progressivism was a national phenomenon, the initiative mechanism was established primarily in midwestern and western states. In these two sections of the country, Populism combined with Progressivism to accentuate the need for direct democratic involvement in government decision making. In the Northeast, by contrast, the large number of immigrants may have discouraged the middle and upper classes from supporting the initiative process. In the South, the large number of blacks who gained the right to vote after the Civil War made initiatives less attractive to the dominant, white population. Today, the majority of states that allow their citizens to propose laws are located west of the Mississippi, with Michigan and Massachusetts being two notable exceptions.

This article narrowly construes consumer ballot initiatives as those dealing with traditional consumer issues such as safety, product price and quality, and information, but it is possible to construe consumer initiatives as including the provision of public services, clean government concerns, and environmental quality.

A second caveat concerns the difficulty of distinguishing initiatives that seem genuinely aimed at helping consumers from initiatives that are sponsored by business interests even when they claim to be looking out for consumers. In some cases, one will observe "dueling" initiatives on the state ballot, as when California voters faced four propositions in 1988 regarding automobile insurance and two initiatives in 2005 dealing with the price of pharmaceutical products. In the latter instance, Proposition 78 was sponsored by the drug companies, whereas Proposition 79 was backed by consumer, health, and senior groups. (Both propositions failed to pass.)

Knowing the names of the groups that support or oppose an initiative does not necessarily help in determining whether the proposed law will be good for consumers. When mainstream consumer organizations such as Consumers Union or AARP officially support an initiative, it is a fair assumption that the initiative is intended to benefit consumers. But one would have needed to be more careful, for example, with respect to a 2012 Missouri initiative to limit the interest rates on payday loans. Two groups—both sounding as if they were looking out for the consumers—took opposing positions on the initiative. Missourians for Responsible Lending supported the measure, while the industry-backed Missourians for Equal Credit Opportunity opposed it.

A final qualification in the study of consumer ballot initiatives is that there may be important differences among consumers in terms of the benefits and costs of a proposed policy. For example, a ballot initiative to establish lifeline utility rates to make electricity, natural gas, or water more affordable to low-income people is a subsidy for one group of consumers that is paid for by another, wealthier group of consumers or by the utility's investors. Thus consumers may have divergent views concerning whether a ballot initiative is "good for consumers," which may explain the defeat of many initiatives that purport to help consumers.

With these caveats and qualifications in mind, below are examples of a range of consumer-oriented ballot initiatives. Most of these initiatives deal with consumer health and safety, consumer information and choice, or consumer prices. The majority of initiatives have addressed these issues with respect to food, tobacco, marijuana, insurance, and financial services.

A landmark initiative involving food safety was overwhelmingly passed (67 percent versus 37 percent) in California—Proposition 65 ("The Safe Drinking Water and Toxic Enforcement Act"), in 1986. Among other features, the proposition required that all products containing certain chemicals (e.g., food with certain additives or pesticide residues) bear a label stating, "WARNING: This product contains chemicals known to the State of California to cause cancer and birth defect or other reproductive harm." In a similar vein, a number of states have tried to require a label for food made with genetically modified ingredients. Oregon voters snubbed the first such initiative in 2002 by a sizable margin, but more recent initiatives in California (2012) and Washington (2013) lost by very narrow margins after heavy campaign spending, especially by the antilabeling, industry-financed side.

Tobacco is probably the subject of more initiatives than any other consumer product. Some initiatives pertain to where someone may smoke, as in Florida's successful Amendment 6, which in 2002 prohibited smoking in the workplace. Other initiatives involve the taxation of tobacco products and include the amount of the tax or how it is spent, or both. Most proposals to increase cigarette and tobacco taxes pass, because smoking is generally considered a vice that should be discouraged, and smokers constitute the minority of voters. (Even some smokers support these initiatives, believing that higher prices will help them quit.) In 2002, Arizona voters doubled the tax on a package of cigarettes, but Missouri voters that same year balked at the idea of quadrupling it. A successful California initiative in 1998 was notable. Proposition 10 earmarked much of a $0.50 per package tax increase for programs to promote early childhood development. It helped the campaign for the initiative that popular actor and director Rob Reiner was its figurehead.

Although tobacco-related initiatives have ebbed in recent years, the number of marijuana-related initiatives has surged. Some initiatives have sought to deter marijuana use through harsh sentencing requirements, but most ballot campaigns have attempted to make marijuana more readily available and less legally fraught. These latter initiatives provide proof of the adage "If at first you don't succeed, try, try again." The first marijuana-related initiative took place in Oregon, where a ballot measure to decriminalize the possession or growing of marijuana for personal use was defeated 74 percent to 26 percent in 1986. In 1996, however, California voters approved the use of marijuana for medical purposes. In 1998, voters in Washington, Oregon, Nevada, and Alaska followed the lead of California, but a similar measure in Arizona failed to pass. Today, almost half the states allow use of marijuana for medical purposes, so the battleground has become legalization of marijuana for any use, medical or not. Whereas California voters narrowly defeated a legalization initiative in 2010, the dam broke in 2012 when both the Colorado and Washington electorates approved legalization (with regulation) of "weed."

Several hotly contested initiative battles have dealt with automobile or health insurance issues. A 1988 California initiative to reduce automobile insurance premiums received strong support from consumer champion Ralph Nader and was narrowly approved by the voters, but efforts to introduce no-fault automobile insurance in California via the ballot box have fallen short of passage. (Under a no-fault policy, policyholders are indemnified for losses by their insurance company regardless of whether they caused or contributed to an accident.) In Michigan, the home of the U.S. auto industry, voters rejected so-called reform proposals that would have limited their benefits and rights under the state's no-fault auto insurance system. In 2010, a Michigan initiative to cut insurance premiums by 20 percent (and 40 percent for drivers with good records) failed to qualify for the ballot despite the support of mainstream consumer organizations such as the Consumer Federation of America.

Initiatives dealing with health insurance reforms have been put to the voters in several states. Most of these have attempted to expand coverage or lower its cost, but some have pushed back against efforts to limit consumer choice of health insurance alternatives. Roughly a hundred years ago, in 1918, a referendum in California tried to create a publicly funded health insurance system. Though unsuccessful, this campaign preceded by many decades the creation at the federal level of the Medicare and Medicaid programs. Again in California, Proposition 166 in 1992 had the ambitious goal of requiring all employers to provide health insurance coverage to employees working as few as 17.5 hours per week, but voters rejected the idea by more than two to one.

In 1997, an initiative proposed allowing people in Washington to choose their doctor or keep their current doctor if they changed jobs or insurance plans, but heavy opposition from major employers and voter confusion about the initiative's purpose contributed to a heavy defeat. Voters in nearby Oregon roundly rejected an initiative in 2002 that would have established a state-paid universal health care system, and voters in Massachusetts defeated a more timid initiative in 2000 that would set up a council to study the idea. Signing into law of the federal Patient Protection and Affordable Care Act in early 2010 sparked pushback in the state of Arizona where, in November, voters passed largely symbolic Proposition 106 to prevent any new rules from forcing state residents to participate in any government-organized health insurance program.

Restrictions on payday lending are a final example of a consumer issue addressed by direct democracy. Payday loans come in many forms, but they most commonly involve borrowing a few hundred dollars for a short amount of time, with the loans secured by a post-dated check. Consumer advocates hate these loans because of their extremely high interest rates, often in the range of 400 percent or 500 percent based on an annual rate. Voters in Ohio and Arizona passed judgment on these loans in 2008. Ohio's electorate chose to limit these loans to 28 percent annual percentage rate (APR). This cut deeply into the profitability of payday loans and effectively shut them down in the state. The main opponent of Ohio's initiative was an industry-backed group called Ohioans for Financial Freedom, whereas the high frequency with which borrowers roll over their payday loans every two weeks suggests that these loans are anything but liberating. Meanwhile in Arizona, voters rejected an initiative sponsored by the payday loan industry that would have raised the cap on payday loans from 36 percent to 391 percent. In 2010, Montana voters capped payday interest rates at 36 percent, and a similar referendum narrowly missed being placed on the ballot in Colorado.

Although backers of pro-consumer initiatives have enjoyed some notable successes over the years, a number of questions can be raised about the advisability of using the ballot box to make consumer policy. First, the vast majority of consumer-oriented initiatives and referenda fail to pass. Whether this is attributable to spending by their industry opponents or the basic resistance of voters to change, the low rate of success raises a simple and fundamental question about the utility of citizen lawmaking.

Second, most public policy issues are complex and have impassioned partisans on both sides. The legislative process, whatever its shortcomings, provides an opportunity for compromise among competing interest. Initiatives, in contrast, present take-it-or-leave-it solutions. Initiatives are probably most useful when they force reluctant legislators to take action rather than substitute for it. In California in 2003, for example, the threat of a ballot initiative is credited with stimulating state legislators to resurrect and pass a landmark law on financial privacy. The threat of an initiative campaign may be as effective as actually mounting one.

Third, most initiative campaigns are conducted via the mass media. Consumer organizations are typically no match for the well-financed public relations efforts of industry groups, who often present voters with simplistic, and even misleading, information. Voters are rarely in a position to make well-informed and farsighted decisions. Finally, considering low voter participation in the United States and the higher propensity of older, whiter, and more affluent people to vote, the initiative process is ill suited to advance the interests of society's less advantaged citizens.

In response to these criticisms of initiatives, it would be fair to ask: Is the initiative process any less capable of making informed decisions, any less insensitive to disadvantaged citizens, and any less vulnerable to corporate campaign spending than other methods of making consumer policy? Clearly, consumers are better off with the initiative mechanism than without it, but a transparent and less partisan legislative process at the federal and state levels would be better still.

Robert N. Mayer

See also: Insurance Advocacy; Front Groups

Further Reading

Ballot Initiative Strategy Center. http://ballot.org.
Ballotpedia: An Interactive Almanac of U.S. Politics. http://ballotpedia.org/Main_Page.
Ellis, Richard J. 2002. *Democratic Delusions: The Initiative Process in America.* Lawrence: University of Kansas Press.
Initiative and Referendum Institute. www.iandrinstitute.org.
Matsusaka, John G. 2004. *For the Many or the Few.* Chicago, IL: University of Chicago Press.
Schmidt, David D. 1989. *Citizen Lawmakers: The Ballot Initiative Revolution.* Philadelphia, PA: Temple University Press.

INSTALLMENT CREDIT ADVOCACY

For many decades, installment loans have permitted consumers to afford and purchase motor vehicles and other durable goods, but these loans also have sometimes been unfair to borrowers. This article discusses two important installment loan policy issues that have engaged the attention of advocates and regulators, during the past forty years, as the dominant political and economic philosophy moved toward one of deregulation. The first issue involves two trade regulation rules adopted by the Federal Trade Commission (FTC) that made installment credit safer for consumers as the nation entered the deregulatory era. The second issue reveals how individual attorneys used the courts to expose a market practice seriously in need of reform by the end of the twentieth century.

The FTC has authority to promulgate rules restricting unfair or deceptive trade practices. Beginning in the mid-1970s, it used this authority to implement two important rules that helped redress serious imbalances in the respective rights and remedies available to consumers and their creditors.

The first FTC rule limited the effect of the "holder in due course" doctrine. That is a legal principle that separates the consumer's obligation to pay for goods or services from the seller's obligation to provide the promised value and to do so in compliance with the law. For example, if a home improvement contractor enters into a retail installment sales contract with a homeowner, it may then "assign" (or sell) that contract to a lender. If the contractor fails to do the work, or otherwise fails in its part of the bargain, the holder doctrine would usually enable the lender to insulate itself from the consumer's claims arising out of that seller's misconduct and continue to demand payment for the goods or services from the consumer. The result was to make it difficult for consumers to hold sellers accountable for misconduct. In turn, the lenders who took over those contracts had little incentive to monitor their seller–partners.

In 1975, the FTC enacted the "Preservation of Claims and Defenses Rule," which made it feasible for consumers to pursue claims arising out of the sale. It did so by the simple means of promulgating a rule requiring retail sales contracts to include a clause saying that consumers can bring claims against the holder of the contract that they could have brought against the seller. This rule has been important in giving consumers the ability to enforce their own legal and contractual rights, and therefore to help police the retail installment sales market.

Although the holder-in-due course doctrine limited consumer's remedies when the seller's part of the bargain failed, standard boilerplate installment loan contract terms gave creditors extraordinary remedies against consumers who fell behind on payments. For example, wage assignments allowed creditors to take a consumer's wages without a court order and also to threaten the seizure of other household goods—to in effect "clean out the house"—even though the goods may have had little value as collateral to the lender.

After a ten-year process, the FTC issued a "Credit Practices Rule," effective in 1985, that limited or prohibited some of these unfair boilerplate clauses. The effect was to make consumers a little safer from those disproportionate remedies as the consumer credit market was being deregulated over the next three decades.

While the legal and economic environment was changing, so, too, was the installment loan market. In the last quarter of the twentieth century, that market segment fragmented. Old-line finance companies moved into larger-balance, home-secured lending; high-cost, small dollar payday and auto title lending displaced the old finance company small-dollar loan market; and credit cards replaced retail installment sales agreements for most retail purchases except vehicles. However, installment credit remained the primary means for Americans to buy vehicles.

At the turn of the twenty-first century, a second installment loan issue played out at the intersection of consumer protection and civil rights—discrimination in pricing auto finance credit. The opportunity for discrimination is embedded in a typical situation, called "indirect auto lending," in which the dealer functions as an active intermediary between the buyer and the ultimate lender. Most consumers finance their car purchases, and the majority do so through the dealers from whom they buy the vehicle. However, commonly the dealer does not make decisions about the credit worthiness of the buyer, nor does it ultimately keep the loan as an account of its own. Instead, the dealer submits the application and proposed deal to one or more lenders. The lender makes the credit decision and, for approved loans, informs the dealer what terms are acceptable. Among those terms is the interest rate, called the "buy rate," that represents the lender's evaluation of the credit risk on the deal, given the borrower's credit profile and the collateral. That rate, however, may well not be the one that the dealer then presents to the buyer.

The terms of the agreements between dealers and lenders often permit the dealer to charge a higher rate—sometimes called the "dealer markup"—to the consumer. The dealer then keeps all or part of the difference between the higher rate the consumer actually pays and the lender's lower risk-based "buy-rate." The lender might share the resulting excess revenue from that rate hike with the dealer. None of this is transparent to the buyer. The industry's justification for the markup is that it represents a fee for the dealer's services in arranging the financing. Yet as the average profit on individual auto sales narrowed, dealers became more dependent on finance-related revenue and more willing to boost this revenue in unfair and discriminatory ways

One of the first people to uncover and challenge the discrimination resulting from this practice was a private lawyer from Nashville, Clint Watkins. Watkins received two independent car-related referrals from the local legal services program. Curious how these African American clients, whose cases involved different dealers and different lenders, had been charged car loan rates of about 20 percent, he began to investigate.

In the absence of direct explanations from sellers and lenders, investigatory hurdles related to credit pricing are extremely high. Evaluating automobile finance lending for price discrimination is much more difficult than it is with mortgage lending. The Home Mortgage Disclosure Act (HMDA) has reporting requirements that give regulators and the public some baseline empirical data to facilitate monitoring for discrimination in the mortgage market, but there is no equivalent for installment lending. Therefore, finding sufficient information to be able to control for variables, including legitimate credit risk as well as race or national origin, presents major challenges.

Watkins nonetheless pursued the issue, finding a way to combine sources of information that allowed his paralegal to review files of dealer-arranged loans, to see if their findings warranted further investigation. Their initial, preliminary investigation indeed found higher dealer mark-ups for minorities. That set the stage for a series of lawsuits against several of the major automobile finance companies over the six-year period from 1998 to 2004. These cases eventually provided firm empirical evidence of discriminatory credit pricing in the auto finance market and brought the problem to national attention.

Along with Watkins, the team consisted of Gil Gilmore and Michael Terry, class action specialists at the National Consumer Law Center. Professors Mark Cohen from Vanderbilt University and Ian Ayres from Yale provided the rigorous analysis of data that is fundamental in credit discrimination cases. The team eventually obtained sufficient information to evaluate over 35 million consumer files from borrowers over all the country, representing loans from seven lenders affiliated with auto manufacturers and five major financial institutions. The analysis found that African Americans received dealer markups more often than similarly situated white borrowers and that they paid higher markups than the white borrowers who did get the markups—on average by hundreds of dollars and in some cases by thousands of dollars.

The lawsuits were settled, so there were no definitive judicial findings issued on the cases. Even though the defendants disputed both the evidence and their legal liability, as part of the settlements, automobile lenders imposed temporary caps on the amount of markup that dealers were permitted to impose. The last of these temporary caps under the settlements expired in 2010, though those temporary limits may have become the generally accepted standard.

Regulatory agencies, state officials, and the Department of Justice continued to monitor the markup practice. In 2013, the Department of Justice and the Consumer Financial Protection Bureau's first joint fair lending enforcement action involved alleged discrimination resulting from unjustified dealer markups. The work of several attorneys, starting from a legal services referral, not only saved many borrowers much money, but also brought much-needed sunshine into this shadowy side of pricing automobile finance credit.

Kathleen Keest

See also: National Consumer Law Center

Further Reading

Cohen, Mark A. 2006. *Imperfect Competition in Auto Lending: Subjective Markup, Racial Disparity, and Class Action Litigation.* Vanderbilt Law & Economic Research Paper No. 0701. http://papers.ssrn.com/sol3/papers.cfm?abstract_id=951827##.

Federal Trade Commission. 1980. *Credit Practices: Staff Report and Recommendation on Proposed Trade Regulation Rule.*

Federal Trade Commission. 1978. *Report of the Presiding Officer on Proposed Trade Regulation Rule: Credit Practices.*

Rossman, Stuart T. 2002. "Financing Fair Driving: Race Discrimination in Retail Car Loans." *Clearinghouse Review,* 36: 227+.

INSURANCE ADVOCACY

Because insurance in the United States is mainly regulated by individual states, much consumer advocacy has been directed at the states, often through the National Association of Insurance Commissioners (NAIC), the association of state insurance regulators. However, this advocacy has also targeted Congress, federal agencies, and individual insurers. This article will review consumer activism related to three main types of insurance purchased by consumers—automobile, homeowners, and life—and how these insurance products are regulated. Health insurance advocacy is treated by another article in this encyclopedia.

Insurance Regulation

Insurance has been regulated by the states since New Hampshire first created a board of insurance commissioners in 1851. One of the earliest advocates for strong insurance regulation was Elizur Wright, who was a member of the Massachusetts Board of Insurance Commissioners. Wright not only sought to check anticonsumer practices of insurers, but also proposed federal regulation of the industry. In 1869, in *Paul v. Virginia*, the U.S. Supreme Court ruled that insurance was not interstate commerce and thus not subject to federal regulation.

However, many years later in 1944, in *United States v. Southeastern Underwriters Association* the U.S. Supreme Court reversed its earlier decision, declaring insurance interstate commerce. In response, the industry persuaded the states, which feared losing the power to collect insurance premium taxes, to join it in lobbying Congress to cede regulatory power to the states and to provide the industry with an antitrust exemption that would continue to allow state regulation. Together, they persuaded Congress to pass the McCarran–Ferguson Act, which conferred a permanent moratorium on enforcement of the federal antitrust laws on insurers.

For decades, consumer groups have objected to this antitrust exemption as anticompetitive and anticonsumer. In the 1980s, the National Insurance Consumer Organization (NICO) took the lead in fighting for elimination of this exemption. In the 1990s, Consumers Union (CU) and the Consumer Federation of America (CFA), which had absorbed NICO, sought to persuade Congress to do away with the exemption. The lead advocates were Linda Lipsen, CU's legislative director, and J. Robert Hunter, CFA's director of insurance. (Hunter had earlier served as federal insurance administrator, then as founder and director of NICO, then as Texas insurance commissioner.) They found a sympathetic ear in Representative Jack Brooks (D-TX), who persuaded members of the House Financial Services Committee he chaired to approve legislation eliminating the exemption. However, neither the House nor the Senate voted on this legislation.

Insurance reform is particularly challenging for consumer advocates, because individual states are largely responsible for consumer protection, yet in most states, insurers can overwhelm advocates with superior resources to lobby state legislatures and insurance departments. In fact, most states have no consumer group that has great expertise in automobile, homeowner, or life insurance issues. Except in a few large states, notably California, national groups often must take the initiative and then look for support among state consumer, community, and other nonprofit groups.

That inequality was particularly evident at national meetings of the National Association of Insurance Commissioners. In the 1980s, NICO's Hunter was often the only consumer advocate having insurance expertise at these meetings. However, pressed by Hunter and other advocates, in 1990 the NAIC created a program to fund the expenses of participating consumer advocates. Today, at meetings attended by hundreds of industry representatives, from fifteen to twenty funded advocates provide insurance commissioners with consumer points of views. For the past fifteen years, dealing with property/casualty issues and several life issues, the Center for Economic Justice's (CEJ) Birny Birnbaum has been a consumer leader at these meetings. Birnbaum was chief economist for the Texas Insurance Commission in the early 1990s, when it was led by Hunter. Since 2000, he has led the CEJ.

Despite this program, in the states insurers still usually have much greater influence with regulators than consumer advocates have. As well as superior resources, the industry benefits from the "revolving door" between commissions and insurers. Insurance commissioners frequently work for the industry before becoming a regulator and then, when their term as commissioner ends, return to the industry. This practice was extensively documented in a study with unusual origins. In the wake of the tumult caused by voter approval of California's Proposition 103 (see below), the Professional Association of Insurance Agents (PIA) hired consumer icon Esther Peterson to recruit several leading consumer advocates—NICO's Hunter, Public Citizen's Joan Claybrook, and CFA's Stephen Brobeck—to work with PIA in researching regulatory issues of mutual interest. From 1988 to 1990, the working group, called the Consumer Insurance Interest Group, produced extensively researched reports not only on the revolving door issue, but also on the inadequate resources available to state insurance departments. These reports helped convince several states to increase these resources.

In the 1960s, 1970s, and early 1980s, insurance commissioners—including James Hunt in Vermont (later affiliated with NICO then CFA), James Stone in Massachusetts, Howard Clark in South Carolina (later affiliated with NICO), and Herb Denenberg in Pennsylvania—had sought to protect consumers. But criticism of the industry in the late 1980s and early 1990s persuaded some governors to appoint consumer advocates as insurance commissioners—NICO's Hunter in Texas, NICO's Jay Angoff in Missouri, and Oregon PIRG's Joel Ario in Oregon (and later Pennsylvania). Moreover, voters elected pro-consumer commissioners in other states—John Garamendi in California, Kathleen Sebelius in Kansas, and John Morrison in Montana. Despite political and budgetary constraints, all were able to advance consumer interests, in part because of their access to information about the industry.

One regulatory issue debated for many years by consumer advocates has been the desirability of the federal government's taking on major responsibility and authority for regulating insurers. Some national advocates believe that they would have more opportunities to reform anticonsumer insurer practices if the primary regulator of the industry were a federal agency. Their model is the relatively new Consumer Financial Protection Bureau. Other national advocates and most state advocates, however, fear that federal preemption of state regulation would lead to the establishment of weak, pro-industry regulation—like much of banking and securities regulation until recently—that would undercut effective consumer protection in those few states, particularly California, currently having such protections.

The Dodd–Frank Wall Street Reform and Consumer Protection Act of 2010 did create a Federal Insurance Office (FIO) within the Treasury Department to monitor the insurance sector, including monitoring whether "traditionally underserved communities and consumers have access to affordable non-health insurance products." And CEJ, CFA, and other advocates have asked this office to investigate issues related to CFA's automobile insurance research. However, to date the FIO has not seriously pursued this issue but has instead released a lengthy report favoring further insurance deregulation that was sharply criticized by advocates.

Automobile Insurance

More than nine-tenths of American households own cars, and their drivers are required by all states except New Hampshire to carry automobile insurance liability coverage to protect other drivers in at-fault accidents. In 2012, consumers spent $168 billion on this liability coverage as well as on collision and comprehensive coverage. For more than three decades, national consumer advocates have monitored and criticized automobile insurer policies and practices. In the 1980s, the lead advocacy group was NICO. Since then, CFA and CEJ have provided this leadership.

Before this time, however, a consumer automobile insurance issue generated controversy and change. In a 1965 book, professors Robert Keeton and Jeffrey O'Connell proposed replacing the traditional liability system with a no-fault approach in which there would be no or limited liability for negligent driving. Instead, drivers would purchase sufficient insurance to cover their losses in any accident they experienced, regardless of fault. The two experts argued that such a no-fault system, by eliminating all the costs of determining fault and holding negligent drivers responsible, would reduce system-wide expenses and allow rate reductions.

In the 1970s, Consumers Union was the lead consumer group supporting no-fault legislation. This proposal was opposed not only by trial lawyers concerned about loss of income but also by those who felt that a fault-based system encouraged safe driving because it forced negligent drivers to take responsibility for resulting accident losses. Public Citizen was most vocal among public interest groups in criticizing no-fault.

In the early 1970s, sixteen states passed no-fault automobile insurance laws. However, since 1976, several of these states have repealed or substantially modified these laws, and no other state has adopted a true no-fault plan. This declining popularity reflected several factors, including the belief of drivers that they should not be required to cover the costs of accidents for which they were not at fault, and escalating losses resulting from the rise in fraud rings that took advantage of no-fault systems. Over the past two decades, though, consumer advocates have not participated very actively in these state debates.

In the early 1990s, however, there was a unique no-fault proposal, "pay at the pump," that stimulated much discussion and controversy, especially in California. Developed by journalist Andy Tobias, this proposal involved paying for a low level of liability coverage through a fee added to every gallon of gasoline purchased, thus reducing the role and costs of insurance agents as well as achieving any no-fault savings. Tobias spent his own money to try putting a pay at the pump proposal on the 1993 California ballot, but the combined weight of opposition from insurance agents, trial lawyers, and oil companies forced him to give up this initiative.

As enthusiasm over no-fault waned, consumer advocates became more interested in strengthening state regulation. In California, in 1985 influential State Assembly Speaker Willie Brown commissioned a study by NICO's Hunter about improving automobile insurance regulation, then presented it to the state legislature the next year. When it turned out that Brown simply wanted to use the study to raise funds from the insurance industry, the lack of legislative action prompted Steven Miller, the head of the Insurance Consumer Action Network (ICAN), to use Hunter's study to develop a comprehensive reform proposal to be submitted to California voters as Proposition 100. Working with Ralph Nader, Consumer Watchdog's Harvey Rosenfield developed an even tougher reform proposal, Proposition 103, which aggressively regulated rates, mandated good driver protections, repealed the state antitrust exemption, and rolled back automobile insurance prices by 20 percent. Outspent massively by an apoplectic insurance industry, the consumer advocates nevertheless prevailed, winning 51 percent of the vote in the state's 1988 election. When the courts finally ruled in 1994 that virtually all provisions in the proposal were constitutional, including the rate rollbacks, its reforms were fully implemented. Recent research by CFA has shown that, because of rate regulation, California has experienced the lowest rate increases among states over the past two decades.

Proposition 103 encouraged reform efforts in other states. Several have provided ways for consumers to be represented in rate hearings and other matters before insurance departments. The Office of Public Insurance Counsel in Texas and the Intervener Compensation Program of California have been the most effective of these programs. All these reform efforts also encouraged some regulators and insurer groups to reach out to consumer groups. The NAIC's consumer participation program and PIA's Consumer Insurance Interest Group resulted from this outreach. So did two new organizations proposed by CFA's Brobeck to try to restrain insurer losses, thus allowing lower premiums. Advocates for Highway and Auto Safety, founded in 1989, and the Coalition Against Insurance Fraud, established in 1993, represent joint efforts by consumer advocates and insurance companies that continue today.

The consumer movement's most recent automobile insurance reform campaign was initiated by the Consumer Federation of America in 2011. Led by Hunter,

Brobeck, and financial services director Tom Feltner, with the assistance of former Consumer Watchdog leader Doug Heller, the initiative seeks to provide low- and moderate-income drivers with affordable, nondiscriminatory liability coverage. It has released a half-dozen reports showing that because automobile insurers use discriminatory factors such as occupation and education in their pricing, most insurers charge lower-income drivers far higher premiums than higher-income drivers. The campaign has persuaded the NAIC to create a working committee on low-income automobile issues, convinced a member of Congress to develop related legislation, and pressed the relatively new Federal Insurance Office to collect information about industry practices. However, apart from documenting high and discriminatory prices, the initiative has focused most of its efforts on building support among national and state groups, particularly those of the latter that are located in the jurisdictions of targeted state insurance departments.

Homeowners Insurance

The homeowners insurance marketplace is not as large as the automobile insurance marketplace—only about $65 billion in annual premiums paid by roughly one-half of all households. Yet, it has been the scene of major protests, primarily by housing, community and civil rights groups, related to redlining and natural disasters. Insurance redlining—insurers' refusing to write policies in geographical areas because of their racial or ethnic character—has been criticized by local housing, community, and civil rights groups since the 1960s, but largely took a back seat to mortgage redlining protests until the 1980s. During this decade, activists tried to extend the progress they had made in forcing disclosures and reducing discriminatory practices in the mortgage loan marketplace to the related homeowners insurance marketplace. Groups such as National People's Action and ACORN led local protests and also encouraged litigation by organizations such as the ACLU and the NAACP, which argued that federal prohibitions against mortgage redlining also applied to insurance redlining. In the early 1990s, the Sixth and Seventh Circuit Courts of Appeals ruled that the prohibitions did apply. Since 1995, fair housing organizations across the country have filed lawsuits and administrative complaints resulting in favorable settlements with large insurers that have included State Farm, Allstate, Nationwide, American Family, and Liberty Mutual.

Homeowners insurance policies have also been a focus of consumer and community groups dealing with the effects of large natural disasters such as hurricanes, floods, tornados, and earthquakes. In the wake of these disasters, insurers invariably have tried to restrict coverage and raise rates substantially. With much assistance from CFA's legislative director Travis Plunkett, CFA's Hunter, who had managed the federal flood program as federal insurance administrator, served as the chief consumer expert in monitoring and criticizing these industry practices. He also advised members of Congress, governors such as Florida's Charlie Crist in the wake of Katrina, and a growing network of community groups that sought to address the adverse impacts of the restrictive coverage and escalating rates. In the early 2010s, for example, Alabama's Michelle Kurtz has organized a multistate, grassroots insurance reform coalition to address coastal insurance issues related to hurricanes. The most active group in the country addressing the adequacy of insurance claims payments related to natural disasters has been United Policy-holders (UP). Founded by Amy Bach and Ina Delong in 1991, and led by Bach since then, UP has worked closely with attorneys seeking fair claims settlements, including by filing more than 300 amicus briefs in court cases.

For decades, consumer advocates have criticized force placed automobile and homeowner insurance policies, imposed by lenders to protect their security inter-est, for the extremely low loss ratios and high prices of these policies. Only recently, however, have several large states taken action to curb these high prices for home-owner policies. A 2010 article in American Banker provoked both litigation and the attention of some policymakers. With encouragement by CFA's Hunter and CEJ's Birnbaum, New York, Florida, and California insurance departments have acted to lower premiums for force placed homeowner policies.

Life Insurance

Historically, life insurance has played a role in helping protect household incomes and facilitate saving. Term insurance has helped ensure that on the death of a wage earner, his or her dependents have resources to cover living expenses for a time. And cash value policies, especially whole life, have offered both death benefits and a tax-deferred way to save regularly for retirement.

However, for decades these cash value policies have been the source of contro-versy. Required disclosures, especially the so-called illustration of future yields, are difficult to understand and are subject to manipulation by agents and other salespersons. Agents have financial incentives to sell cash-value policies, rather than the term policies appropriate for many households, and to churn customers from one policy to another.

From the 1970s until recently, Joseph Belth and James Hunt have been lead critics of many of these practices. Belth, a longtime professor at the University of Indiana, produced numerous books, articles, blogs, and the monthly period-ical *The Insurance Forum*, which was published from 1974 to 2013. Hunt, a life insurance actuary, served as Vermont insurance commissioner in the late 1970s, then later served as a life insurance expert first for NICO and then for CFA, where he continued his consumer service evaluating cash-value life insurance policies. Both Belth and Hunt were frequently consulted by journalists such as Jane Bryant Quinn, policymakers, and other consumer advocates for information and advice. Their criticism and that of others helped persuade the Federal Trade Commission to prepare a study in the late 1970s showing that cash-value life insurance investments provided much lower yields than did many comparable investments. This report was so threatening to the industry that it persuaded Congress to limit FTC research on insurance issues to that specifically requested by Congress.

All this criticism of cash-value policies, along with changes in the financial services marketplace, led to dramatic declines in consumer purchases of these policies. Today, only about one-fifth of households hold such policies, and the lion's share of these assets are held by wealthy families for their tax benefits. As a result, consumer advocates no longer see reform of cash-value policies as a priority. They are content to continue advising consumers, mainly through the press, not to purchase these policies unless they intend to hold them for at least ten to fifteen years, after which time the policies usually provide reasonable yields.

Consumer advocates funded to participate in meetings of the NAIC for the past several decades—particularly CEJ's Birnbaum, University of Georgia professor Brenda Cude, and Center for Insurance Research leader Brendan Bridgeland—have advised insurance commissioners on a variety of life insurance-related safety and soundness, investment, and structural issues. The issues they have addressed include credit insurance pricing, small-face life insurance abuses, viatical/life settlements and STOLI (Stranger-Originated Life Insurance) transactions, retained asset accounts, misuse of Death Master File records on annuity policies, insurer use of the Interstate Insurance Product Regulation Compact to override individual state protections, and the adequacy of state solvency regulation.

For several decades, consumer advocates have also focused much attention on life insurance sold with consumer credit products, chiefly automobile and other installment loans. These advocates, particularly Hunt in the 1980s and 1990s and Birnbaum in this century, have documented the exceptionally poor value offered by most credit insurance products, which typically return well under 50 percent of premium dollars to policyholders in claims benefits. Advocates cite "reverse competition" as the explanation for low payout ratios. Insurers compete with each other for bank sellers by offering high fees that sometimes represent more than half of premium dollars. Banks then sell the credit life policies of only one insurer at relatively high prices. The lack of consumer choice and high prices is one reason why all states regulate credit insurance rates.

The reports by Hunt and Birnbaum on credit insurance products, which were extensively reported on by the press, and their testimony in many states did help persuade many state regulators to lower allowable rates in the 1990s. Their advocacy also convinced the NAIC to toughen the standards in its consumer credit insurance model law and regulation and to develop a model law for credit personal property insurance. Hunt's efforts to stop financed single premium credit insurance (FSPCI) were joined by CEJ in the 1990s and by fair lending groups several years later. This advocacy persuaded federal regulators to approve reforms that eliminated most FSPCI use.

This and much other criticism of credit insurance products persuaded many consumers not to purchase them. Also influential was the decision of many banks to sell not credit insurance, but rather equivalent debt-consolidation products that were not subject to regulation by state insurance departments. However, these latter products have been severely criticized by CEJ and other consumer advocates. Faced with pressure from both advocates and regulators, recently major banks such as Capitol One and Bank of America have stopped selling these policies.

Stephen Brobeck, J. Robert Hunter, Brenda Cude

See also: Advocates for Highway and Auto Safety; Consumer Federation of America; Consumer Watchdog; National Insurance Consumer Organization; Tort-Related Consumer Advocacy

Further Reading

Banks, McDowell. 1994. *The Crisis in Insurance Regulation.* Westport, CT: Quorum.

Covaleski, John M. 1995. "Insurers Fret as Consumer Groups Merge." *Best's Review/Property-Casualty* 92 (June): 40+.

Kimball, Spencer L., and Herbert S. Dennenberg. 1969. *Insurance, Government, and Social Policy: Studies in Insurance Regulation.* Homewood, IL: R. D. Irwin.

Klein, Robert W. 2009. *The Future of Insurance Regulation in the United States.* Washington, DC: Brookings Institution Press.

Squires, Gregory D., ed. 1997. *Insurance Redlining: Disinvestment, Reinvestment and the Evolving Role of Financial Institutions.* Washington, DC: Urban Institute Press.

INTERNATIONAL ORGANIZATION OF CONSUMERS UNIONS

See Consumers International

INTERNET ACTIVISM

A great deal of the activity of consumer advocates is devoted to helping individuals make better purchasing decisions and obtaining speedier redress for individual consumer problems. In addition, companies such as TripAdvisor, Yelp, Angie's List, eBay, Craigslist, Airbnb, JustShareIt, and Prosper have unlocked the power of consumer-to-consumer sharing of information and selling of goods and services. The essence of consumer activism, however, is attempting to change business practices to benefit consumers collectively. Thus, although consumer organizations have effectively used the Internet to educate consumers and help them achieve redress, this entry focuses on the use of the Internet to bring about change in business policy—either directly by putting pressure on firms or indirectly by enlisting the power of government to force change. Specifically, the Internet has enhanced the effectiveness of two methods of changing business behavior: exercising collective buying power and pressuring governments.

Collective buying power can be applied to punish firms, as in the case of boycotts, or reward them, as when buyers direct their patronage to firms that stand out in providing value for consumers. The exercise of collective buying power is not a new method of consumer activism. In the United States in the late nineteenth century, the National Consumers League employed a seal of approval to direct its members to purchase products made and sold under "clean and healthful" conditions. The benefit for consumers was a clear conscience. Also in the nineteenth century, consumers in England, Scotland, and France formed cooperatives to obtain goods and services at prices below those available to them as individuals in the marketplace. In the 1960s and 1970s, U.S. consumers engaged in local boycotts to protest the high price of everyday grocery items such as meat, milk, sugar, and coffee. During the mid-1980s, U.S. consumer advocate Ralph Nader organized an energy cooperative, Buyers Up, to drive down the cost of obtaining home heating oil. Buyers Up operated in Takoma Park, Maryland, Philadelphia, New York, and other East Coast cities. Members paid a small membership fee but then saved hundreds of dollars a year in fuel costs. In all these instances, protesters not only sought benefits for themselves (whether economic or psychological), but also hoped to stimulate improvements in the marketplace for all consumers.

Although the use of collective buying power has long been an important form of consumer activism, the Internet has greatly expanded its potential. High transaction costs once made pooling purchase power difficult or prohibitive, but Internet technology has diminished these costs and ignited an explosion of collective buying activity. Websites such as Groupon and Living Social offer prenegotiated discounts to groups of consumers, but the initiative remains with the sellers. In contrast, consider the origins of the Chinese group-buying phenomenon known as Tuangou. Hundreds of consumers met online and agreed to mob an electronics store in Guangzhou at an appointed time. Their spokesmen then negotiated a group discount on the spot. Eventually, this practice has become institutionalized to the point that websites prenegotiate discounts that will be honored as long as a specified minimum number of consumers commit to a purchase. In essence, the deal is "triggered" at that point, and the offer will typically last only a few hours or days. The basic model has spread to other countries, but, in theory, the buyer and seller need not be in the same location as long as an item can be ordered via the Internet and then delivered. The website BigTrigger is an example. It specializes in photography goods and services. It arranges deals between vendor and buyers, both of whom can be located anywhere in the United States.

Collective buying can take the form of a reverse auction in which businesses bid for the business of a group of consumers. This model has been successful in England. Local government units are helping to organize groups of residents for the purpose of negotiating a better price for their electricity or natural gas. Once a sufficient number of residents are signed up and committed to switch their business to the lowest bidding company, an intermediary such as the company iChoosr receives bids from multiple energy companies and then notifies the winner. Switching auctions that took place in England during June 2014 saved energy consumers approximately $1.5 million (Smithers, 2014).

Whereas many of the websites just cited are primarily designed to offer the economic benefits of collective purchasing, they are also political inasmuch as they challenge previous ways of doing business and put pressure on firms to serve consumers better. Some websites harness collective buying power in a more explicitly political fashion. In the wake of the massive oil spill in the Gulf of Mexico in 2010 attributable to British Petroleum (BP), the social media website Facebook was used to organize a boycott of BP products; the organizers claimed a million boycott adherents. The website Carrotmob.com employs group purchasing to convince businesses to improve their energy efficiency, reduce water use, plant trees, provide scholarships for a summer camp, and purchase sustainably harvested or locally sourced food. Boycotts and collective switching campaigns organized online in response to consumer anger are essentially forms of picketing, except the line that consumers are discouraged from crossing is virtual rather than tangible.

In some cases, a petition directed at a business can serve as an implicit boycott threat or as an adjunct to a collective switching campaign. The website Change.org specializes in petition advocacy. In 2011, the website was the locus of a successful petition drive against imposition of a new $5 per month charge by Bank of America on debit card accounts. The petition drive was supplemented by Bank Transfer Day, an Internet campaign that encouraged consumers to switch their accounts from commercial banks such as Bank of America to credit unions. Shortly after the petition drive and switching campaign, Bank of America dropped its proposed new fee. In the United Kingdom, the website 38 Degrees performs a function similar to Change.org. The site invites users to generate petitions on consumer, environmental, or other matters of national or local important.

In addition to enhancing collective buying power as a tool of consumer advocacy, the Internet facilitates activist efforts to pressure governments into forcing business to make changes. In 1962, U.S. president John F. Kennedy described the right of consumers "to be heard," by which he meant that the views of consumers should receive full and sympathetic consideration in the formulation of government policy. Consumer advocates have tried to exercise this right, either organizing direct input from consumers or, when necessary, speaking in the name of consumers.

The Internet has added amplitude to the voice of consumers. For example, it has made it much easier for consumer activists to amass signatures on petitions that can be presented to government agencies. In a 2014 example, Consumers Union and several other U.S.-based advocacy organizations gathered 400,000 signatures on a petition opposing Comcast's proposed takeover of Time Warner Cable; the petition was presented to the Federal Communications Commission and the Department of Justice. In 2013, Americans for Financial Reform joined with other activist groups to generate pressure via a petition drive on Republican lawmakers who were delaying confirmation of Rich Cordray as the first director of the Consumer Financial Protection Agency. When the U.S. Copyright Office ruled in 2012 that consumers needed the permission of their cell phone carriers to switch providers even after completion of their contract terms, more than 100,000 people protested by signing an online petition directed at the White House. Two years later, Congress passed and the president signed the Unlocking Consumer Choice and Wireless Competition Act and overturned the earlier action.

In addition to petition initiatives, the Internet has made it easier for consumer organizations to organize letter-writing campaigns, typically directed at legislators. For example, Consumers Union, the policy arm of Consumer Reports, has more than 800,000 "e-activists" whom it periodically asks to transmit letters to government decision makers on top-priority matters of policy. The organization Public Citizen employs the same method. It has urged its members to write their congressmen to oppose the controversial trade agreement known as the Trans-Pacific Partnership and overturn Supreme Court decisions that have lifted restrictions on donations by corporations and wealthy individuals to election campaigns.

In addition to petitions and letter-writing campaigns, the Internet has encouraged consumers to submit comments on pending regulatory actions at agencies. In 2014, the Federal Communication Commission (FCC) received 800,000 public comments on its proposed rules regarding net neutrality—the position strongly favored by consumer groups that all Internet service providers should transmit all Internet content at equal cost and equal speed. The Internet not only facilitates the submission of comments, but also makes it possible for the government to release them for public scrutiny as well. The campaign for net neutrality also used the Internet in 2014 to generate more than 4,000 phone calls to the FCC within one week.

The recently established Consumer Financial Protection Bureau has made a special commitment to receptivity with respect to consumer comments. The bureau solicits comments from consumers both before it fashions a new regulation and after it has proposed one. For example, the bureau has sought consumer input in advance of rulemaking on topics such as student loans, mortgage closings, and problems of elderly consumers.

Looking to the future, the Internet holds vast potential as an organizing tool for consumer activists. It can disseminate information *to* consumers at lighting speed but serve as well as a powerful means of obtaining information *from* consumers. The Internet allows consumers to assemble quickly in a given physical location, yet it can make organizing consumers across geographical boundaries easier as well. As a general matter, the Internet promotes transparency and participation, both of which are core values of consumer advocates. It is likely, then, that the Internet will only grow in importance as a tool of consumer advocacy.

Robert N. Mayer

See also: Boycotts; Consumers Union/Consumer Reports

Further Reading

Bachman, Katy. 2014. "Internet Activists Campaign over Net Neutrality Escalates," *AdWeek*, May 12. www.adweek.com/news/advertising-branding/internet-activist-campaign-over-net-neutrality-escalates-157594.

Bates, Richard. 2012. *Get It, Together*. London, UK: Consumer Focus, April. www.consumerfocus.org.uk/publications/get-it-together-the-case-for-collective-switching-in-the-age-of-connected-consumers.

Smithers, Rebecca. 2014. "Collective Energy Switching Auction Saves Consumers £232 Per Household," *The Guardian*, August 6. www.theguardian.com/money/2014/aug/06/energy-switching-saves-gas-electricity-bills.

The Economist. 2006. "Shop Affronts." June 29, www.economist.com/node/7121669.

INTERNET GOVERNANCE
See Digital Communications Advocacy

INVESTOR PROTECTION ADVOCACY

The term investor protection refers to efforts to guard the rights and promote the interests of those individuals who provide financing for private corporations and public entities through the purchase of securities. At the most basic level, investor protection regulations seek to ensure that investors receive accurate information on which to base their investment decisions, that outside investors are protected from misappropriation of their funds by powerful insiders, that shareholders have a say in the operations of the companies they own, that transactions are conducted in fair and orderly markets, that investment professionals, such as broker–dealers and investment advisers, treat their customers equitably, that fraud in all its varieties is prevented and punished, and that those who are wronged have a right to redress. Investor protection regulations are typically not designed to protect investors from the risk of loss that is inherent to investing in securities. Although there have been securities markets operating in the United States since its founding, systematic investor protection regulation is a relatively recent phenomenon, and organized advocacy to promote investor protection is more recent still.

The modern investor protection regulatory regime originated during the buildup to and aftermath of the 1929 stock market crash that ushered in the Great Depression. Concerned that citizens in his state were being targeted with sales of fraudulent investment schemes, Kansas Banking Commissioner Joseph Dolley helped shepherd the first modern statute governing securities sales through the Kansas state legislature in 1911. The law, which required companies to register with the state banking commission before offering stocks and bonds for sale in the state, was aimed at preventing fraud and barring unfair business practices. By 1913, another twenty-three states had followed Kansas's lead in adopting securities laws, and when the U.S. Supreme Court held the laws constitutional in 1917, the movement gained additional steam. By 1933, every state but Nebraska had adopted state securities legislation, many based directly on the Kansas model. Although an important step forward, the state laws suffered from two major flaws: Most were riddled with loopholes, and even the best of them could too easily be evaded by individuals operating across state lines.

The federal government was much slower to respond to evidence of widespread fraud and abuse in the markets. A variety of factors ultimately came together to prompt the federal government to act, chief among them: the lingering stock market devastation of the early 1930s, the election of Franklin Roosevelt as president in 1932 on a platform of reform, and the appointment of Ferdinand Pecora to head up the previously languishing Senate Banking Committee investigation of securities industry practices. With a flair for the dramatic, Pecora provided the headlines that galvanized public support for direct federal regulation of the securities markets. Meanwhile, Roosevelt provided the necessary willingness to assert federal regulatory authority to rein in the abuses that had been brought to light, challenging those who viewed federal action as unconstitutional.

Advised by some of the best legal minds of the day, the Roosevelt Administration conceived of a regulatory regime that continues to provide the bedrock on which modern investor protections are based:

The Securities Act of 1933 required companies to register their securities before selling to the public, providing detailed financial and other information in the process. It also prohibited deceit, misrepresentations, and other fraud in the sale of securities.

The Securities Exchange Act of 1934 created the Securities and Exchange Commission (SEC) and gave it broad authority to enforce the 1933 act and to oversee the securities industry, including brokerage firms, transfer agents, clearing agencies, and industry self-regulatory organizations (including the exchanges).

The Investment Company Act of 1940 regulated the organization of mutual funds and other companies that "engage primarily in investing, reinvesting, and trading in securities, and whose own securities are offered to the investing public." It set rules to minimize conflicts of interest and to promote full disclosure to investors in these securities. The Investment Advisers Act of 1940 regulated those industry professionals who are in the business of giving advice about securities for compensation.

The newly created SEC got off to a strong start under its first chairman, Joseph P. Kennedy. Although a controversial nominee, Kennedy confounded his critics by securing generous funding for the agency, staffing it with some of the nation's top corporate law experts, and pursuing a "balanced" policy that combined action against fraud with promotion of beneficial business interests. These early achievements were quickly eroded, however, first as focus shifted to fighting World War II, then from an apparent lack of interest in the Truman Administration, and finally from a belief in the Eisenhower Administration that business was overregulated. The agency, which had reached a peak of 1,723 employees in 1941, saw its staff reduced to 666 employees by June of 1955, even as both the stock markets and securities fraud were enjoying a postwar boom. Although Congress subsequently increased SEC funding, and efforts were made in the Kennedy Administration to revive the agency, funding increases continued to be outpaced by the growth in the markets the SEC was charged to oversee—a problem that persists to this day.

The creation of the nation's original investor protections was a largely top-down affair, led first by state banking officials and then by the Roosevelt administration's "brain trust." A bottom-up investor advocacy movement did not really begin to emerge until the late 1980s and early 1990s. Not surprisingly, the increased attention to investor protection issues by consumer organizations at this time coincided with a dramatic upsurge in market participation by middle income American households. Consumer Federation of America (CFA) and AARP were the first of the national consumer groups to devote significant resources to investor protection issues, with other groups playing more of a supporting role. Concerned about the growing dependence of middle income, often financially unsophisticated Americans on securities investments to fund their retirement, these groups focused primarily on issues related to the standards applying to the professionals investors turned to for advice (broker–dealers, investment advisers, and newly emerging financial planners), abusive products and practices targeting these less sophisticated investors, the clarity of disclosures—particularly for the mutual funds that were a favorite among middle-income investors—and the fairness of systems to provide investor redress.

Although consumer groups began to plan an increasingly important role on investor protection issues in the late 1980s and early 1990s, primary leadership at this time came from two other quarters. Representatives John Dingell (D-MI) and Edward J. Markey (D-MA) who chaired, respectively, the Energy and Commerce Committee and its Securities Subcommittee, took a strong interest in investor protection issues. From the mid-1980s until the Republicans took control of the U.S. House of Representatives in 1994, they used their leadership positions to draw attention to securities market abuses and propose legislative solutions, often winning bipartisan support. Among the issues they addressed, with differing levels of success, were penny stock reform, limited partnership rollups, government securities regulation, financial planner regulation, investment adviser oversight, and arbitration reform.

State securities regulators, acting through the North American Securities Administrators Association (NASAA), were strong allies to Chairman Dingell and Markey in their efforts to strengthen investor protections. Drawing on the experience and expertise of its member regulators, NASAA helped document and publicize abusive practices encountered by state securities regulators, particularly abuses targeting less sophisticated middle-income investors, and offered expert testimony in support of legislation to address those abuses.

Consumer groups supported these investor protection efforts but did not, for the most part, take the lead during this period in developing a pro-investor agenda. One exception was financial planner regulation, where CFA in particular played a more prominent role both in defining the problem and identifying appropriate solutions.

Meanwhile, the 1992 election of Bill Clinton as president and his appointment of Arthur Levitt to chair the SEC created a new opportunity to promote investor protections through regulatory means. But the administration's record did not always please investor advocates. On the one hand, Levitt created an office of investor assistance at the SEC, promoted plain English disclosure, sought to reduce conflicts in broker–dealer compensation practices, increased accountability for failure to supervise, and sought to enhance auditor independence, but on the other, he also gave early support to the move to restrict shareholder class action lawsuits, succumbed to congressional pressure to weaken his auditor independence rules, and made it easier for brokers to evade regulation as investment advisers while marketing themselves to the public as objective advisers. A side effect of the attack on shareholder class action lawsuits was that it galvanized more active consumer group involvement in investor protection issues. Several consumer groups that had previously played a more peripheral role on investor protection issues, including Consumers Union, U.S. PIRG, and Public Citizen, became actively engaged in efforts to defeat legislation restricting shareholder rights.

Ultimately, a series of market failures from the bursting of the tech stock bubble in 1999 through the financial crisis of 2008 led to significantly ramped-up consumer group involvement in investor protection issues. During this period of market scandals and disruptions, groups that had previously played a largely supporting role for an investor protection agenda developed by others became more active in defining and pursuing a pro-investor agenda. In response to the accounting scandals at Enron and other major public companies, for example, CFA published research which helped to define the policy options Congress should pursue to strengthen auditor independence and oversight, worked closely with staff in drafting legislation, and testified in support of legislation. CFA worked closely with other national consumer groups (Consumers Union, Public Citizen, U.S. PIRG,

Consumer Action) to lobby for passage of the Sarbanes–Oxley Act and to ensure its effective implementation. CFA also continued to take the lead throughout this period in advocating heightened standards for broker–dealers providing advice and recommendations, working closely with AARP, Fund Democracy, and others to raise awareness of the issue and prompt a policy response.

In addition, important new players joined the scene during this period. Founded in 2000, Fund Democracy brought new energy and expertise first to issues related to mutual fund regulation and then to a broader set of investor protection concerns. When market timing scandals at several prominent mutual fund companies provided an opportunity for reform, for example, Fund Democracy took the lead in working with other consumer groups to develop a mutual fund reform agenda and communicate that agenda to both Congress and the SEC.

Two other influential groups emerged in the wake of the 2008 financial crisis—Americans for Financial Reform (AFR) and Better Markets. In addition to providing significant in-house expertise on a variety of financial regulatory issues, AFR played a crucial role in coordinating the activities of a broad coalition of groups and experts in support of financial reform legislation and regulations. With extensive expertise on derivatives and other market structure issues, Better Markets has sought to advance financial reform by exposing failings in the financial and regulatory system and by working through the regulatory process to correct those failings. Groups such as CFA, U.S. PIRG, Public Citizen, AARP, and Consumers Union worked both through AFR and independently to ensure that financial reforms adopted in response to the near collapse of the global financial system were commensurate with the extent and seriousness of the market abuses and regulatory failures. Among other contributions, AFR helped to cement an already existing relationship between consumer groups and labor in support of financial market reforms.

For more than two decades, other consumer advocates, policymakers, and the press have looked in particular to three individuals for expertise and leadership. Barbara Roper, CFA's director of investor protection, began work in the area in the 1987, when she released a study of financial planners. Since then, her work has included consumer leadership on major legislation—Sarbanes–Oxley, Dodd–Frank, and the JOBS Act—as well as on numerous regulatory issues. Before organizing Fund Democracy in 2000, Mercer Bullard, who is also a law professor at the University of Mississippi, worked for the SEC as an attorney in the Division of Investment Management. As the SEC's chief accountant during the Clinton administration, Lynn Turner headed the agency's effort to strengthen auditor independence rules. Since leaving the SEC, Turner has been a leading voice on corporate governance, financial reporting, and other investor issues. Helping draft Sarbanes–Oxley, he also worked on Dodd–Frank and against the JOBS Act. In the past decade, the three have been joined by Damon Silvers, policy director of the AFL–CIO. Silvers has been the labor movement's chief voice on investor protection issues. Active during drafting and implementation of Sarbanes–Oxley and Dodd–Frank, he was a member of the Congressional Oversight Panel for the Troubled Asset Relief Program (TARP). All four advocates have worked closely together.

Today, investor advocates face significant challenges. Well-funded industry lobbyists still greatly outnumber investor advocates and are relentless in their efforts to weaken and roll back pro-investor regulations. The SEC, the primary agency responsible for implementing investor protection regulations, is seriously underfunded in relation to the growth of industry and the agency's responsibilities. Both Congress and even consumer-friendly administrations tend to be very responsive to industry concerns. And industry has recently perfected the strategy of challenging regulatory agencies that seek to adopt rules on the grounds that the agency has not sufficiently considered their costs and benefits. This tactic has proven particularly effective against the SEC. Despite these challenges, the investor protection movement has evolved, over the last few decades, into a broad, collaborative movement that brings considerable expertise and energy to its efforts to guard the rights and promote the interests of those individuals who provide financing for private corporations and public entities through the purchase of securities.

Barbara Roper

See also: AARP; Consumer Federation of America

Further Reading

Armour, John, and Joseph A. McCahery. 2006. *After Enron: Improving Corporate Law and Modernising Securities Regulation in Europe and the U.S.* Oxford, UK: Hart Publishing.
SEC Historical Society. www.sechistorical.org.
Seligman, Joel. 2003. *The Transformation of Wall Street: A History of the Securities and Exchange Commission and Modern Corporate Finance.* New York: Aspen Publishers.

ITALIAN CONSUMER MOVEMENT

The Italian consumer movement can largely be equated to the country's consumers organizations. The first such organization, National Consumer Union (Unione Nazionale Consumatori), was established in 1955. It remained the sole consumer organization in Italy until the 1970s, when four additional organizations were founded: Consumers League (Lega Consumatori) in 1971, Altroconsumo in 1973, Confconsumatori in 1976, and Cittadinanzattiva in 1978). The number of consumer organizations grew during the 1980s and 1990s. The creation of Casa del Consumatore in 2000 brought the total number of official Italian consumers organizations to eighteen, where it stands today.

Most consumer organizations claim to be independently funded, but the situation is more complicated. Some consumer organizations, such as Federconsumatori, are financed by Italian trade unions, such as the Italian General Confederation of Labor. Other consumer groups, such as Lega Consumatori, have connections with Catholic associations, which in turn are connected with the Radical Party (Partito Radicale). Cooperation among consumers organizations is limited—an exception being Consumers' League (Intesa Consumatori), a formal coalition of four major consumer organizations.

If an Italian consumer organization is recognized by the government as "nationally representative," it is eligible to be part of the National Council of Consumers and Users (Consiglio Nazionale dei Consumatori ed Utenti, or CNCU), a government body hosted by the Department of Treasury (Ministero dell'Economia e Finanza). (The prerequisites for being nationally representative include a minimum of 30,000 members, having local branches in at least five of the twenty Italian regions, and being active for at least three years.) Membership in CNCU allows consumers' representatives to make proposals for new laws to advance consumer interests, provide comments and suggestions on other proposals sponsored by members of the Italian parliament, and promote research and studies on consumer issues.

Consumer organizations that are members of the CNCU are also eligible for government funding. All of them receive public funds, except the Association for the Rights of Consumer and Users (ADUC), which ideologically rejects any kind of public funds and never asked to be part of the CNCU. Data for 2003–2012 show that consumer organizations enrolled in CNCU received, on average, $260,000 per year. (Financial support to consumer groups during the first half of this period was much higher than in recent years.) Until 2007, most of this money came from fines collected by the national government for violations of consumer rights or anticompetitive behavior.

The Italian crisis that began in 2009 and resulting constraints on the government's budget reduced dramatically the financial support allocated to consumer organizations. The fact that the balance sheets of most of these organizations relied on public funds represented a big challenge for the Italian consumer movement overall. At the same time, public concern grew regarding both the total amount of public funds devoted by the government to the consumer interest organizations and the criteria used to distribute these funds. Newspapers and other media stressed how a lack of scrutiny of the self-reported data used as input in the funding distribution process and a lack of transparency on the financial reporting of these organizations suggested the need for radical reform of the system by which the government subsidizes consumer organizations.

Although public funds are the main source of income for most of the consumer interest organizations, there are other potential sources of funds. Some organizations charge for providing educational and professional services (e.g. seminars, conference, counseling) to both private and public entities. Membership fees are also used, but they are not a main source of income because of their low level (typically $1 to $50 per year).

Many consumer organizations focus on a broad range of consumer issues, but some are more specialized. For example, some groups focus on consumer problems in only one of the following areas: banking and other financial services; food and beverages; medical services from doctors and hospitals; and consumers of public utilities, such as energy, water, and transportation.

In terms of their activities in support of consumer protection, almost all the organizations provide some kind of advisory or support service to consumers with specific problems, including consumers who are considering legal action against a firm or a government body. Beyond this similarity, however, there are important differences in approaches to consumer protection. Some consumer organizations stress the role of education about consumer rights and the consequences of specific choices. Also in the domain of education, some organizations provide comparative test results for products and services so that consumers are more knowledgeable about the market opportunities. Other organizations believe that lobbying is the most effective tool to protect consumers. Some organizations work with the government to promote effective consumer legislation, whereas other consumer groups try to apply direct pressure on companies to reduce prices or improve quality.

Consumer organizations also employ litigation in pursuit of consumer rights, although some organizations view legal action as a primary strategy while others consider it a last resort. Recently, the Italian Consumer Code, in addition to coordinating all existing consumer protection provisions, introduced class action as a form of legal action. This is widely considered the most relevant achievement of the Italian consumer movement in the last twenty years.

The introduction of class action filled a huge gap in legal consumer protection in Italy, but other achievements of the consumer movement should be mentioned as well. Improvements in product certification (e.g., for wine and extra-virgin olive oil), clear explanations about the meaning of "Made in Italy" product labels and controls on counterfeit products, and other issues related to product labeling can be considered significant achievements of the Italian consumer movement because of their effect on the everyday experience of Italian consumers.

Italian consumer organizations contribute to consumer protection in Europe and the world. Although some Italian organizations have no foreign interactions, two take part in the European Consumer Organization (BEUC), and five are members of Consumers International. Participation in these international organizations provides an opportunity for Italian consumer activists to learn from others as well as providing lessons from their own experience.

Gianni Nicolini

See also: BEUC: The European Consumer Organisation; Consumers International

Further Reading

Altroconsumo. www.altroconsumo.it.
European Union, *Italy*. http://ec.europa.eu/consumers/empowerment/cons_networks_en.htm.

JAPANESE CONSUMER MOVEMENT

According to the Japanese Consumer Affairs Agency, as of 2011 there were 2,430 consumer groups in Japan. There were 166 national groups, 418 at the level of prefectures (Japan's largest subnational jurisdictions) and 1,846 local-level groups. Many of these groups were formed either in the 1960s and 1970s or during the 2000s. In the former period, the eruption of serious consumer problems and the growth in general of citizen movements stimulated the formation of consumer groups. In the 2000s, along with new consumer problems shaped by deregulation and the information technology, reforms to the taxation, incorporation, and litigation systems were advantageous for the formation of additional consumer groups.

Judging from the sheer number of groups, Japan may seem to be a country where consumer groups flourish. But the quantitative increases do not necessarily mean qualitative enhancements. Among the range of organizations defined as consumer groups in the survey mentioned above, women's and family groups, life improvement groups, and even small residents circles are included. The profusion of diverse and sometimes weak consumer-related organizations makes it difficult to understand the universe of Japanese consumer groups clearly.

Major Consumer Organizations

Among Japan's consumer groups, Consumers Japan (CJ) deserves special consideration. (CJ's Japanese name is *Shodanren*, which translates to the National Liaison Committee of Consumer Organizations.) CJ was founded in 1956 and has worked as the primary umbrella organization for Japan's major consumer groups. As an indicator of CJ's importance, it is currently the only Japanese full member of the Consumers International, a position that allows it to represent Japanese consumer groups on a global level.

CJ's member organizations are diverse. These organizations include those whose members are primarily housewives, renters, workers, members of consumer cooperatives, and consumer affairs specialists working mostly for local governments and in business settings. This national organization also counts among its members twenty-three organizations that are themselves umbrella organizations for consumer groups in individual prefectures. CJ's policies are decided by board members representing this wide variety of member organizations. CJ's secretary-general becomes a member of the board of directors, leads an executive staff of about ten people, and functions as the representative of the Japanese consumer movement.

One of the most influential members of CJ, and also one of the oldest consumer groups in Japan, is the Japan Housewives Association (*Shufuren*). Shufuren was established in 1948 during the postwar reconstruction period and remains active and relevant today. Shufuren has tackled a variety of consumer problems relating to the price and safety of products and services. The high price of rice and utilities, high consumption taxes, and genetically modified foods are examples of problems that Shufuren has addressed. In recent years, Shufuren has intensified its interests related to environmental protection. Shufuren has only about 200 individual members, but it has ninety-six organization members. It owns and manages a building called Housewives Hall (Plaza F). This building contains a hall that can be rented for ceremonies, thereby serving as a source of revenue. Equally important, Shufuren's own offices, as well as those of Consumers Japan (CJ), are located in Plaza F, making this building the base of Japan's consumer movement.

Two additional consumer organizations—Japan Consumers' Association (JCA) and Consumers Union of Japan (CUJ)—were founded along the lines of the U.S. consumer information publishing organization Consumers Union. This organizational model is based on obtaining financial resources by publishing consumer information magazines but with revenue left over to spend on consumer interest advocacy.

Beginning with its establishment in 1961, the Japan Consumers' Association issued the magazine *Monthly Consumer* to provide consumers with information about products and services. In its heyday, JCA's magazine had approximately 50,000 subscribers. Unlike Consumers Union in the United States, JCA received funds from industry groups and, later, subsidies from the Ministry International Trade and Industry. Hence JCA's autonomy from business and government was questioned. Declining sales of the magazine led to its discontinuation in 2011. Today, JCA's main activity is training and certifying consumer advisors known as consumer life consultants.

The Consumers Union of Japan was founded in 1969. It remains an organization funded purely by its members, who receive a bulletin titled *Consumer Reports*. CUJ aspires to be totally free from business and government influence, and among members of Consumers Japan, it is the most radical. It takes uncompromising positions on issues such as the safety of pesticides, imported beef, and genetically modified food. CUJ also opposes nuclear power—a reflection of its priorities with respect to peace and the natural environment. At one point, CUJ had about 10,000 members, but that number has declined to about 1,500 today. Along with Consumers Japan, CUJ is active on the world level, and it is an affiliate member of Consumers International.

The Japanese government operates a network of locally based centers to which consumers can turn for information and advice. Working at one of these centers requires certification as a consumer counselor, consumer life consultant, or consumer life advisor. The Japan Association of Consumer Affairs Specialists (JACAS) was founded in 1987 to represent the consumer experts who work at the consumer centers operated by prefectural and local governments. JACAS has a membership of about 2,000. Consumer counselors are qualified by the National Consumer

Affairs Center of Japan (NCAC), a quasigovernment organization that is the center of a countrywide consumer complaints information network (and that once was a product testing agency). JACAS has a close relationship with NCAC, and its office is located in the NCAC building.

The Nippon Association of Consumer Specialists (NACS) is also a professional organization for consumer specialists working for businesses rather than consumer advice centers. NACS currently has approximately 3,500 members. These members are consumer life advisors qualified by NACS itself or consumer life consultants certified by JAC.

Rounding out the description of Japan's most important consumer organizations is the Japanese Consumer Cooperative Union (JCCU). Founded in 1951, JCCU is a coalition of 343 consumer cooperatives across the country. Although some co-ops are small, others are large, expertly managed, capital-intensive operations. The total number of individual co-op members in Japan is about 27 million, amounting to about 3.3 trillion yen (approximately $33 billion) in annual business sales. Importantly, JCCU has acted as a patron of Japan's consumer movement by taking advantage of its ample financial and human resources. Until recently, for example, JCCU loaned and salaried its own employees to serve as the staff for Consumers Japan.

Each year, Japan's consumer organizations attend the National Consumer Conference. The themes of the conference are diverse. In the fifty-first conference, held in 2013, the themes were consumer policy, peace, food, social security, environment, and nuclear power plants. The previous year, in response to the Great East Japan Earthquake and the Fukushima nuclear accident, victims relief, the siting of nuclear power plants, and the overall selection of energy sources were dominant major themes.

Recent Achievements

Since the 1990s, Japanese consumer groups have achieved, in cooperation with lawyer organizations and lawyers-turned-politicians both in the ruling and opposition parties, several landmark consumer laws. The Product Liability Act of 1994, Consumer Contract Act of 2000, Food Safety Basic Law of 2003, Consumer Safety Act of 2009, and Consumer Education Act of 2012 are representative accomplishments. But the introduction of a consumer group litigation system in 2007 and the establishment of Consumer Agency in 2009 were victories of historic proportion for Japanese consumer groups.

Under a consumer group litigation system established in 2007, consumer groups that meet certain stringent requirements can file lawsuits on behalf of consumers to require companies to refrain from specific actions ("injunctive relief"). Currently, only eight consumer groups are authorized as the qualified consumer groups. A new law passed in late 2013 goes a step further. It creates a collective consumer damage recovery litigation system under which qualified consumer groups can make claims to recover collective monetary damages, thereby bringing Japan close to having a class action legal mechanism for the first time. The privilege of qualified consumer groups to bring these collective lawsuits does not extend to other public interest groups, such as those focusing on environmental and human rights issues.

In 2009, a new government entity—the Consumer Affairs Agency—was established at the ministerial level to coordinate consumer policymaking that had been distributed among several ministries and agencies. The new agency took over, in whole or in part, implementation and enforcement of numerous consumer protection laws that had previously been the under the jurisdiction of the Fair Trade Commission, the Ministry of Agriculture, the Ministry of Health, Labor and Welfare, the Ministry of International Trade and Industry, and the Quality-of-Life Policy Bureau of the Economic Planning Agency.

The Consumer Affairs Agency is under the jurisdiction of the Minister of State for Consumer Affairs and Food Safety. These ministers are generally recruited from the majority party in the National Diet (Japan's bicameral legislature). The consumer agency itself is administratively controlled by its director-general. Although the equivalent posts in other ministries and agencies are occupied by top career civil servants, the director-general post in the Consumer Affairs Agency is open to appointees from outside the state bureaucracy. Notably, the agency's third and current director-general is Hisa Anan, the former executive director of the important consumer organization, CJ.

To summarize the characteristics of Japanese consumer groups from an internationally comparative perspective, Japan tried but failed to succeed at replicating the model of the United States and elsewhere by which consumer organizations achieve financial independence via the sale of consumer magazines containing comparative product testing information. Second, Japanese consumer groups do not have mass-based memberships. Their members have been composed of a relatively small number of socially conscious people, especially housewives. The aging of these activists and a decrease in membership are serious problems that threaten the survival of Japan's consumer organizations. Third, the concerns of Japanese consumer groups are no longer confined to obtaining safe and high-quality products at reasonable prices. The interests of these groups increasingly extend to the natural environment, peace, and human rights. Japan's prolonged economic downturn could increase consumer interest in price and quality issues, but it is unclear whether a consumer movement in Japan with a narrow focus on traditional consumer issues will re-emerge.

Takuya Inoue

See also: Consumers International

Further Reading

Anderson, Mori, and Tomotsune. 2014. *A New Class Action System in Japan.* Tokyo, Japan. January. https://www.amt-law.com/en/pdf/bulletins4_pdf/140114.pdf.

Maclachlan, Patricia L. 2002. *Consumer Politics in Postwar Japan.* New York: Columbia University Press.

Maclachlan, Patricia L. 2004. "From Subjects to Citizens: Japan's Evolving Consumer Identity." *Japan Studies* 24, no. 1: 115–134.

JOURNALISM

For well over a century, journalists have played three important consumer roles. They have evaluated individual products. They have provided advice about how to purchase, use, and resolve problems with products. And they have investigated and sought to expose unfair business practices.

The roots of consumer journalism can be found in the early nineteenth century, when the industrial revolution led to the mass-production of consumer products and created sufficient wealth for many people to be able to afford these products. Into this cultural vacuum stepped journalists of "manners," who wrote mainly for magazines and provided advice about how the rising middle class should live and consume products. One of the most influential and successful of America's earliest magazines of manners was the *Saturday Evening Post*. In 1830, a strong competitor to the *Post* appeared—*Godey's Lady's Book*, the first magazine directed solely to women. Just before the Civil War, a more critical type of magazine appeared. Two of the most successful were *Harper's New Monthly Magazine* (1850) and *Frank Leslie's Illustrated Magazine* (1856). Leslie's, for example, campaigned against the sale of "swill milk"—milk produced by cows fed on the grain waste discharged by New York–area whiskey distillers.

The Emergence of Muckraking Journalism

In 1893, America slid into its first modern depression. For the next four years government fumbled with ways to cope with industrial and financial excesses, including those harming consumers. A new generation of consumer journalists, who were deeply suspicious of what passed for progress and who hoped to bring about social and political reform, emerged.

Joseph Pulitzer was a newspaper publisher who invented a new type of tabloid journalism to reflect this public anger, "yellow journalism." Pulitzer bought the enfeebled *New York World* in 1883 and turned it into a "truly democratic" newspaper in the Jacksonian "common-man" tradition. The "yellow journalism" practiced by Pulitzer was very successful, and the *New York World* soon had one of the largest daily circulations of any newspaper in the world. Its reporters and editorial writers documented with angry clarity all kinds of evils. Soon the Pulitzer journalists were joined by colleagues writing for other newspapers, magazines, and books.

One of the most controversial and successful imitators of the *New York World* was the *Denver Evening Post*. Crusaders Henry H. Tammen and Frederick G. Bonfils bought the paper in 1895. In daily editorials, titled "So the People May Know," Tammen attacked the local water company, the coal companies, purveyors of alleged fresh food, and many other special interests. In a campaign unique to the *Post*, Tammen and Bonfils accused Denver's major department stores of being little more than "junk shops . . . filled with a confusion of the commonest and coarsest rubbish." When the stores withdrew their advertising from the newspaper, the *Post's* writers broadened their attacks to the stores' shoddy merchandise and exorbitant pricing.

These angry investigative reporters and editors around the country came to be known as the "muckrakers," a sobriquet given them by President Theodore

Roosevelt in a 1906 speech. By then, the muckrakers worked for many publications. The most impressive work was being published in *McClure's*, whose managing editor, Lincoln Steffens, serialized his "Shame of the Cities," later publishing his articles in book form. *McClure's* also published Ida Tarbell's exposé of John D. Rockefeller Sr. and the Standard Oil company, Burton J. Hendrick's enraged "Story of Life Insurance," and Raymond Baker's series on America's rapacious railroads. Elsewhere, Charles E. Russell took on the beef trust in *Everybody's* magazine, and *Collier's* serialized "The Great American Fraud," Samuel Hopkins Adams's exposé of the patent medicine industry. Edward W. Bok, editor of *Ladies' Home Journal*, worked the same mine, running exposés of the patent medicine industry at every opportunity, and refusing to carry their advertising. In 1906, Upton Sinclair, aided by a $500 advance from the socialist magazine *Appeal to Reason*, published *The Jungle*, a shocking fictional look inside the meat-packing industry (e.g., dead rats in the sausage, missing workers turning up in the lard).

The Jungle is often cited as the most influential of the muckraking genre. The general public read the book, and so did members of Congress. Within a year after its publication, Congress passed two landmark consumer laws—the Meat Inspection Act and the Pure Food and Drug Act. The former made the government responsible for ensuring the quality of any meat shipped in interstate commerce. The latter did the same for grains, most processed foods, and all patent medicine in interstate commerce.

Muckraking consumer journalists continued their print crusades, but the rising public outcry for action and the responses of Congress and the president took the steam out of the muckraking movement. One of the last magazines to pursue cleanup campaigns in this period was *Hampton's Broadway*, founded in 1898.

The Development of Product Testing

Less sensational but no less important for the development of consumer journalism was the approach taken in 1900 by the editors of *Good Housekeeping*. Alarmed by the extent of the "muck" being raked up, the editors set up an "experiment station" to test the items they planned to write about in subsequent issues. In this way, they could assure their readers that the consumer articles published in the magazine could be believed and trusted. Two years later, the editors decided to accept advertisements only for products that they had themselves tested in their "experiment station." In 1909, *Good Housekeeping* upgraded its "experiment station" to an "institute," installed a modern laboratory, and settled upon an oval seal with the legend "Tested and Approved by the Good Housekeeping institute conducted by Good Housekeeping magazine." The oval seal was shown prominently in the advertising of those products that successfully came through the institute's testing program.

In 1912, the editors of *Good Housekeeping* hired Harvey W. Wiley to join the institute to direct a new *Good Housekeeping* bureau of foods, sanitation, and health. Wiley had been a chemist at the U.S. Department of Agriculture in Washington D.C., where he and a small staff had contributed much data to support the landmark Pure Food and Drug and Meat Inspections Acts of 1906. Wiley and his staff had earned themselves the name of "The Poison Squad" because they tested an array of suspicious foods and patent medicines by ingesting them themselves. Wiley wrote a monthly "Question Box" for *Good Housekeeping*, one of consumer journalism's most popular and longest-running columns. He continued writing it until shortly before his death in 1930.

In the mid-1930s, Rexford G. Tugwell, an assistant secretary of agriculture in President Franklin D. Roosevelt's New Deal administration, drafted a Food, Drug and Cosmetic Act. When enacted in 1938, the law established a new federal agency, the Food and Drug Administration, with the power to conduct a wide range of consumer protection activities, including product testing. A companion law, the Wheeler–Lea Act, gave the Federal Trade Commission (FTC) new authority to regulate food and drug advertising. With the authority of these laws, Tugwell and other New Dealers objected to the *Good Housekeeping* seal on grounds that it was "misleading and deceptive." In 1941, the FTC ordered the magazine to "cease and desist" from saying that the sealed products were really "tested and approved." Reluctantly the magazine agreed. However, its table of contents contained a blanket endorsement that all products advertised in the magazine "are good ones."

In the 1920s, the government established the National Bureau of Standards to test products that were purchased by government agencies. One of the bureau's engineers, F. J. Schlink, thought that the kind of objective, disinterested testing done by and for the government ought to be extended to the private consumer as well. In 1927, he joined forces with economist–writer Stuart Chase, who two years earlier had published *The Tragedy of Waste*, an exposé of the consequences of America's rapid industrialization. Together Schlink and Chase published *Your Money's Worth: A Study in the Waste of the Consumer's Dollar*, a critique of the consumer's impotence in a marketplace shaped and degraded by shoddy goods and false advertising.

Schlink became one of the country's best-known writers as a result of the success of *Your Money's Worth*. Impressed by the public's response, he left government in 1929 and established Consumers' Research as a product testing organization. He wrote up his test results and published them in his new journal, *Consumer Bulletin*, which contained no advertising.

One of the testing engineers hired by Schlink was Arthur Kallet. Using data generated at Consumers' Research, in 1932 Kallet and Schlink published *100,000,000 Guinea Pigs*, an account of government fumbling and inaction with regard to foods and drugs of doubtful integrity and safety. The Kallet–Schlink book was a sensation and became required reading within the Tugwell circle of New Deal reformers.

In 1936, as a result of political labor conflicts, Kallet left Schlink and Consumers' Research to start Consumers Union and its own magazine, *Consumer Reports*. After nearly eighty years of publication, this publication remains the preeminent example of pure consumer journalism—factual, objective, advisory, and focused on what consumers need to know.

During the Great Depression and World War II, virtually every newspaper and magazine carried articles to help consumers cope with adversity, scarcity, and poverty. For the first time, the federal government began disseminating consumer information. The Department of Agriculture mailed thousands of recipes, gardening tips, home repair tips, and other helpful items to local, regional, and national publications. During the 1930s and 1940s, the department's Extension Service and public information staffs helped develop a new generation of writers, editors, and illustrators to produce reliable, believable consumer journalism. Many of these professionals remained with the government, but others returned to hometown newspapers, state universities, state government offices, or the national media to continue providing consumer information to the public.

After World War II, the U.S. economy began a long and sustained economic boom. Consumer writers of this era were enthusiastic about the expanding array of new goods and services, and reported on each important product development. During this period, consumer journalism and consumer advertising developed a partnership. Newspaper and women's and service magazines circulating in expanding suburbs offered advertisers special pages, sections, or editions focusing on consumer needs, thus creating a selling-oriented, consumer-friendly "editorial environment" within which local or national advertisers could present their own messages. To help write and edit these new articles and sections, publishers employed consumer public relations writers. This new, rising subset of consumer journalism included persons trained in journalism who worked directly for manufacturers and service and professional groups to write articles in which their products were presented in a positive light.

The New Consumer Journalism

During the 1960s and 1970s, the public insisted on new consumer protections. Journalists played an important role in the development of consumer awareness and expectations. During this time, consumer reporting as a distinct specialty within the journalism profession was accepted. One reason for this acceptance was the work of Morton Mintz, an investigative national affairs reporter for the *Washington Post*. Covering thalidomide and other drug-related stories in the 1960s, Mintz wrote in the best muckraking tradition of Tarbell, Steffens, and Sinclair. While continuing to cover the drug industry, Mintz soon branched out to report on other consumer issues. He also inspired other journalists, who increasingly worked closely with reformers in Congress, federal agencies, and new nonprofit consumer advocacy groups. One of these journalists was Stanley E. Cohen, who in his forty-two years editing *Advertising Age* sharply criticized industry advertising and labeling practices.

A major influence on consumer journalism in this period was Ralph Nader, whose investigative work on the Chevrolet Corvair drew the attention of its manufacturers, General Motors. The company tried—and failed—to stop Nader from proceeding. In 1965, Nader had published *Unsafe at Any Speed*, which concluded that America's annual toll of 51,000 highway deaths could be significantly reduced by industry improvements to motor vehicles. Several years later, he recruited hundreds of students—called "Nader's Raiders"—who researched and published reports on the failure of many government agencies and programs.

In response to increased media interest in consumer topics, university departments of journalism began adding a "consumer reporting" elective. Graduates with that training were hired not only by Washington-based publications and wire services, but also by the national and regional media. Consumer journalists—such as Molly Sinclair and Caroline Mayer of the *Washington Post* and Marian Burros of the *New York Times*—were hired by newspapers. And consumer reporters—such as Betty Furness for WNBC in New York, Roberta Baskin for WTTW in Chicago, Tom Vacar for KTVU in Los Angeles, Silvia Gambardella for WCCO in Minneapolis, Lea Thompson and Elizabeth Crenshaw for WRC in Washington, D.C., and Herbert Denenberg for WCAU in Philadelphia—were given daily time slots for special television reports. The National Press Club in Washington, D.C., recognized the value of this journalism by establishing an annual awards program for excellence in consumer reporting.

The 1980s were often called the "Me Decade" because so much attention was given to earning more money to purchase a wide array of products, including expensive clothes, a second home, and costly vacations. The assignment to cover these trends and trendy people fell to consumer writers who already knew something about quality, prices, sources, taste, and manners. This assignment also included coverage of health and medical news, physical fitness, diet and weight control, interpersonal relations, marriage and divorce, childrearing, and other aspects of personal, family, and social life. The articles often appeared in newspaper sections titled "Life," "Style," "LifeStyle," "Today's Living," "Contemporary Life," and "Home," or in such new or redesigned magazines as *Self*, *Working Women*, *Kiplinger's Personal Finance Magazine*, *Money*, and *Modern Maturity*.

By the 1990s, the new consumer journalism was still being practiced, but not as extensively as fifteen or twenty years earlier. Nevertheless, consumer activists who documented a widespread abuse could usually find journalists to cover it, even if these reporters were not defined narrowly as consumer journalists. One type of consumer journalism that did flourish, however, was coverage of consumer issues by television news magazine shows. *60 Minutes* was the first program of this type. By the mid-1990s, programs of this kind aired on most evenings. Hard-hitting consumer stories were often developed by broadcast journalists, such as Lea Thompson, Erin Moriarity, and Roberta Baskin, who had earlier done consumer reporting for local television stations. Others followed, including Betsy Ashton, Paula Lyons, Jean Chatzky, Jack Gillis, Arnold Diaz, and Herb Weisbaum.

In the same period, consumer groups continued to publish popular guides to consumer products. Public Citizen Health Research Group's *Worst Pills Best Pills*, developed by Dr. Sidney Wolfe, and the Center for Auto Safety's *The Car Book*, prepared by Gillis, were just two examples of consumer guides that usefully supplemented the voluminous product-related information published by *Consumer Reports*. Also noteworthy is Consumers' Checkbook, an evaluator of local consumer services, which was established in Washington, D.C., in the 1970s and which since then has expanded to six other urban areas—San Francisco, Seattle, Minneapolis, Philadelphia, Boston, and Chicago.

Recent Challenges

Increasingly, however, investigative journalism was weakened by several developments. The first was the decline of print journalism as Americans increasingly turned first to broadcast journalism, then to the Internet, for information about consumer products and sales practices. This erosion of readership was aggravated by increasing criticism from corporate advertisers about critical coverage of consumer services. Metropolitan daily papers in particular often faced daunting challenges from local businesses—especially home sellers, car dealers, food stores, and financial institutions—on whose advertising their profitability greatly depended.

Some newspapers pushed back. For example, the *Louisville Courier-Journal* and the *Toledo Blade* announced moratoriums on ads from insurers selling health and accident policies after readers complained about unfair sales practices and misleading disclosures. The ban, which lasted a month, cost the *Courier-Journal* $250,000 in ad revenues. Many other newspapers refused to buckle under to advertiser pressure. Yet over time, the resistance of many weakened. Some newspapers that had published running lists of food inspection violations ceased their publication. And, after the *San Jose Mercury News* published a personal finance piece with hard-hitting information about how to purchase a car only for car dealers to pull $1 million of advertising, the newspaper repudiated the article and gave the dealers free space to respond.

Litigation by business also chilled critical coverage of consumer products, especially by network television stations. One of the most highly publicized lawsuits was by General Motors against NBC's *Dateline*, which had carried a piece on the danger of exploding gas tanks in some GM vehicles. Because NBC had not disclosed that it had triggered the filmed explosion, it settled the lawsuit, which sent a chill throughout the consumer journalism community.

A major exception to this trend was increasing print and broadcast coverage of unfair financial services practices. This coverage was made possible in part by the release of dozens of reports by consumer advocacy organizations such as the Center for Responsible Lending, USPIRG, National Consumer Law Center, and Consumer Federation of America. These reports exposed unfair practices in products as diverse as mortgage loans, car loans, student loans, credit cards, debit cards, payday and car title loans, and investment products. Journalists writing about business and finance frequently reported on the findings of these reports, often in columns syndicated in many newspapers. The journalists, who also used many other sources, included Jane Bryant Quinn (*Newsweek*), Michael Sorkin (*St. Louis Post-Dispatch*), Jeff Gelles (*Philadelphia Inquirer*), Michelle Singletary (*Washington Post*), Ken Harney (*Washington Post*), Humberto Cruz (*Fort Lauderdale Sun Sentinel*), Chris Jensen (*Cleveland Plain Dealer*), Kathy Kristof (*Los Angeles Times*), and Liz Pulliam-Weston (*Reuters*).

The coverage of these critical reports by reporters, columnists, and editorial writers played an important role in informing the public and policymakers of growing abuses in a financial services marketplace in which consumer and investor products were complex and opaque, as well as in establishing new consumer protections. Early in the second decade of the new century, Congress approved the

Credit Card Protection Act, which proscribed many specific industry practices, and more comprehensive reform, closely identified with co-sponsors Senator Chris Dodd and Congressman Barney Frank, which among other consumer protections created an independent Consumer Financial Protection Bureau.

Also a victim of declining newspaper readership and advertiser pressure were consumer action and help lines. Newspaper columns that responded to consumer requests for information and assistance have largely disappeared. Also less active are Call for Action affiliates run by local network television stations. These programs seek to resolve individual consumer complaints by talking to and mediating with sellers. First created in 1963, in their early years some of these programs were not averse to using the threat of news coverage as leverage to resolve problems. Today, the some couple dozen surviving programs, which rely heavily on the assistance of volunteers, have greatest success in resolving problems involving reasonable consumers and merchants.

Since the rise of the Internet, individual consumers have become more active evaluating products and exposing sharp business practices. There are now dozens of popular websites that include either product reviews, such as ConsumerSearch.com, or consumer complaints, such as mythreecents.com and pissedconsumer.com. Less expensive to maintain than traditional news sources, these new sources may well continue to grow in number and influence. In this information environment, research and reports by publications that professionally test and report on a wide range of products with no dependence on advertisers, such as *Consumer Reports*, will be of even greater importance for consumers.

The Internet has also made possible the emergence of new nonprofit organizations that specialize in investigative journalism that often treats consumer issues. The most active and influential of these groups is ProPublica, which was founded by Paul Steiger, a former managing editor of the *Wall Street Journal*, and that is funded mainly by foundations. "Seeking to uncover unsavory practices in order to stimulate reform," ProPublica recently has published well-researched reports on high-cost loans, college debt, the housing crisis, health care–related safety issues, Obamacare, and other consumer topics. Other Internet-based organizations, such as the Center for Public Integrity and the *Huffington Post*, have also helped compensate for severe cutbacks in investigative reporting by national print and broadcast media. However, to date, little has compensated for the loss of this reporting at local and state levels.

Theodore O. Cron, Stephen Brobeck

See also: Consumers Union/Consumer Reports

Further Reading

Endres, Kathleen L., and Theresa L. Lueck, eds. 1995. *Women's Periodicals in the United States: Consumer Magazines.* Westport, CT: Greenwood Press.

Lieberman, Trudy. 2013. "The Rise and Fall of Consumer Journalism." *American History of Business Journalism* (March).

Lieberman, Trudy. 1994. "What Ever Happened to Consumer Reporting?" *Columbia Journalism Review* 33, no. 3: 34–40.

K

KENYAN CONSUMER MOVEMENT

The history of Kenya's consumer movement is closely linked to initiatives by Consumers International (CI), the umbrella organization for the world's consumer organizations. During the 1980s, CI worked to establish international standards for consumer protection applicable to both more and less developed nations. CI's efforts culminated in 1985 with the adoption of the United Nations Guidelines for Consumer Protection, giving a boost to consumer activism in Kenya. In 1994, CI (then operating as the International Organization of Consumers Union) opened a regional office in Zimbabwe to foster the development of consumer organizations throughout Africa. The first Kenyan organization joined CI in 1997. Since that time, consumer organizations in Kenya have continued to grow, especially the Kenya Consumer Organization (KCO); Consumer Information Network (CIN), whose leader Samuel Ochieng was CI president; and Consumer Unity and Trust Society (CUTS Nairobi), an offshoot of the Indian-based Consumer Unity and Trust Society (CUTS International). The efforts of these organizations have contributed to the enactment (or updating) of various consumer protection statutes and the establishment of various government institutions to address consumer concerns.

Consumer organizations in Kenya work cooperatively with the Kenyan government to protect consumer interests in the country. Among the government institutions working closely with consumer organizations are the Kenya Bureau of Standards, the weights and measures department of the Ministry of Trade, the Competition Authority of Kenya (formerly Monopolies and Prices Commission), the Communications Authority of Kenya (formerly Communications Commission of Kenya), the Anti-Counterfeit Authority, and the Central Bank of Kenya (CBK). Nevertheless, there is a gap between the official role and actual effects of these government institutions in protecting consumers. This gap is, in part, a result of inadequate human and financial resources being devoted to consumer protection work, but a lack of clear roles among the government institutions and a paucity of political will to address consumer challenges in the country are also barriers.

Before 2010, consumer protection in Kenya consisted of several laws dealing with various consumer protection issues. For example, the Standards Act of 1974 established a code of practice to ensure that the production process for food products met international best practices for safety and information disclosure. The Medical Practitioners and Dentists Act of 1977 limited participation in medical practice to practitioners with proven qualifications. The Trade Descriptions Act in 1979 provided deterrence for false or misleading statements by businesses regarding various aspects of goods, including their identity, composition, quantity, size, and method of production. As a final example, the Food Drug and Chemical Substances Act 1992 was designed to curb the sale of unwholesome, poisonous, or adulterated food.

In 2010, the piecemeal approach to consumer protection was superseded by a new national constitution that fully recognized consumers' rights as part of its Bill of Rights. Article 46 of the Constitution grants consumer the rights to: goods and services of reasonable quality; information necessary to gain full benefit from products and services; protection of consumer health, safety and economic interests; and compensation for loss or injury arising from defects in goods or services. Specifically, Article 22 of the Constitution entitles every person the right to institute court proceedings claiming that a right has been denied, violated, infringed, or threatened. In addition, Article 42 of the Constitution entitles every person the right to a clean and healthy environment, and a court for enforcing this right is provided for under Article 70.

Two years later, continued efforts by several leading consumer organizations in Kenya stimulated enactment of a Comprehensive Consumer Protection Act 2012. The principal objectives of the act are to promote and advance the socioeconomic welfare of consumers in Kenya and establish a consistent enforcement regime for consumer protection legislation. Among numerous features, the act prohibits unfair trade practices in consumer transactions; provides for improved standards of consumer information; promotes responsible consumer behavior; and advances a consistent legislative and enforcement framework relating to consumer transactions and agreements. Regulations to guide the implementation of this act are in development process, but a Consumer Advisory Committee (housed under the Ministry of Trade, Tourism and East African Affairs) has already been appointed to help fully realize the goals of the Act.

Like in other developing countries in the world, Kenya's consumers continue to face many challenges in the marketplace. Consumer education programs are inadequate, leaving the majority of Kenyan consumers in a vulnerable position that makes them easy prey for unscrupulous businesses. According to complaints received by CUTS Nairobi, consumers are afflicted by substandard goods and services in various sectors of the economy, including energy, water, financial services, medicines, and telecommunications. The situation is made worse by ineffective market surveillance and weak enforcement of regulations by the responsible government institutions. Moreover, Kenya has not underscored the crucial importance of consumer rights protection in its bilateral and multilateral trade negotiations. The country needs to make a stronger political commitment to sound consumer protection policies (including effective enforcement), consumer education, and additional measures that will help realize a strong consumer movement in Kenya. Most fundamentally, the consumer movement in Kenya needs the support of the ordinary Kenyan consumers to be more visible and formidable. In the interest of this fledgling democracy, consumer activists and scholars in the country should think deeply about how that can be achieved.

Daniel Okendo Asher

See also: Consumers International

Further Reading

Asher, Daniel Okendo. 2012. *The State of the Kenyan Consumer Report 2012*. Nairobi, Kenya: CUTS.
CUTS Nairobi. www.cuts-international.org/ARC/Nairobi/.

KOREAN CONSUMER MOVEMENT
See South Korean Consumer Movement

L

LABOR MOVEMENT

For more than a century, some trade unions and consumer groups have worked on the same issues and provided mutual support. From the 1890s through the 1920s, the top priority of middle-class consumer groups was to win improvements in the wages and conditions of workers, especially women and children. During the 1960s and 1970s, labor provided critical financial and legislative support to the consumer movement. Since then, despite weaker institutional ties, consumer groups and trade unions have worked closely together on such issues as bankruptcy reform and improved regulation of the financial services marketplace.

During the Progressive period, the only consumer groups in existence were Consumer Leagues and their national organization, the National Consumers League (NCL). The principal goal of these organizations was the improvement of the wages and working conditions of workers, especially those of women and children. Both the leagues and unions also joined together in support of pure food and drug legislation. Food safety reforms had appeal to labor not just because they promised to improve consumer health and safety, but also because they created opportunities to improve dismal working conditions in the food industry, especially the meat-packing plants exposed in Upton Sinclair's novel, *The Jungle*, published in 1906.

The consumer leagues, giving special attention to such job security protections as unemployment compensation, continued supporting worker protections into the 1930s and beyond. Increasingly, these leagues were backed by labor groups. In 1942, for example, the Consumers League of Ohio was supported by seven union locals. At the end of the war, thirteen other union groups were making contributions. By 1957, when the league worked with labor in support of minimum wage legislation, eighty-four unions participated in the consumer group. Three years later, when the league joined unions in opposition to "right-to-work" laws, forty-seven other union groups joined.

Also during the 1930s, because of a labor dispute, dissident staffers left Consumers Research to establish a new product testing organization, Consumers Union. Leaders of Consumers Union were strongly pro-labor and created an organization whose labor union remains influential to this day.

In the 1950s, consumer groups continued their support of trade union issues. In the early years of that decade, to prevent the relocation of poultry processing plants from the unionized North to the non-unionized South, the Amalgamated Meatcutters Union launched a campaign for poultry inspection. Supported by NCL and progressive women's groups, the union persuaded Congress to pass the nation's first poultry inspection law in 1957. During the next decade, the union lobbied Congress to strengthen this law, which it did in 1968. A year later, again with support from consumer advocates, the Amalgamated began a campaign to pass a fish inspection law. It finally succeeded in the 1990s when the Food and Drug Administration increased oversight of fish handling.

An important link between consumer groups and trade unions was Esther Peterson. Having worked for two unions and the AFL–CIO in the 1930s, 1940s, and 1950s, and having served as assistant secretary of labor in the early 1960s, Peterson had great credibility and influence with labor. But she also was strongly committed to advancing the welfare of consumers. When she proposed the creation of a consumer federation that would include trade unions as well as consumer groups, Jacob Clayman of the AFL–CIO's Industrial Union Department, John J. Sheehan of the Steelworkers Union, and other labor leaders supported the effort, contributing both money and organizational skills. The Consumer Federation of America (CFA), organized in 1967 and 1968, included as members several dozen labor groups, several of which were represented on the federation's board of directors.

During the late 1960s and 1970s, these labor groups contributed about 40 percent of CFA's budget and supported many of its legislative campaigns. The political skill and clout of labor lobbyists such as Evelyn Dubrow of the International Ladies Garment Workers Union (now UNITE) and Arnold Mayer of the Meatcutters Union (later United Food and Commercial Workers Union) were in no small measure responsible for the passage of consumer laws ranging from truth in lending to truth in packaging. Sheehan and Kenneth S. Kovack of the Steelworkers Union also provided important support for these efforts. For more than twenty years, Kovack served as secretary-treasurer of CFA.

During this period, labor gave much more to CFA than it requested of CFA. In part, this generosity reflected the fact that the industrial unions, the strongest union supporters of the federation, were relatively affluent and exercised considerable political influence with federal policymakers. In part, it resulted from the commitment of trade unions to serve the needs of their members not only as workers but also as consumers. In fact, unions such as the United Auto Workers (UAW) created extensive consumer programs to assist their members. The Community Services Department of the AFL–CIO encouraged member unions to provide consumer education and other consumer services. For many years, consumer journalist Sidney Margolius published a consumer column for many labor publications.

Outside Washington in several states, trade unions supported consumer-labor coalitions that mirrored CFA. These groups included the Ohio Consumers Association, the Consumer Federation of California, and the Michigan Consumer Federation. As with CFA, labor supplied funding for these largely volunteer-based groups and also contributed political savvy and support on consumer policy issues.

Since then, strong institutional ties between trade unions and the National Consumers League have continued. Today, four of NCL's board members have a labor affiliation, and two of five of NCL's most important programs—Stop Child Labor and Wage Theft—focus more on labor than on consumer issues.

By comparison, trade unions are far less active in CFA. Only the UFCW continues to actively participate in CFA, and this is partly because of complementary interests in protecting and strengthening federal meat and poultry inspection programs. Moreover, labor groups now contribute less than 1 percent of CFA's total revenues.

The withdrawal of trade unions from CFA mainly reflected their need to focus more attention on narrow labor issues in a period when trade unions were threatened by tough new challenges threatening their very existence. In the area of communications, conflicts between even consumer and labor groups emerged. In a ten-year fight over rewriting the nation's telecommunications laws, communications workers allied themselves with regional phone companies while most consumer groups were often aligned with their long-distance competitors. Conflicts also surfaced on some trade issues. In general, consumer groups tended to favor free trade, whereas labor groups tended to support "fair trade" laws that sought to "level the playing field" for products manufactured inside and outside the United States.

However, in the past two decades, consumer and labor groups have continued to work closely on several issues, notably those involving financial services. When creditors sought to pass federal legislation that weakened bankruptcy protections for insolvent households, the AFL–CIO and several affiliated unions joined consumer groups in opposition. Their letters and visits to members of Congress were especially helpful in strengthening this opposition, which succeeded in moderating and delaying passage of the legislation.

Of even greater consequence was trade union support for financial services reforms that grew more important and politically feasible as a result of the worldwide financial crisis beginning in 2007. Trade union groups supported new consumer protections for credit card holders, approved by Congress in 2009, and comprehensive financial services reforms, approved by Congress in 2010. Labor and consumer groups worked especially closely together in support of the latter, the Dodd–Frank Wall Street Reform and Consumer Protection Act, within the Americans for Financial Reform (AFR) coalition. The AFL–CIO's Damon Silvers was particularly active and influential in AFR. While labor's chief interest was reform of corporate governance, derivatives, and shareholder rights, it also strongly supported consumer reforms such as the creation of the Consumer Financial Protection Bureau.

Despite some differences, most consumer groups and labor groups continue to view each other as allies. They are linked by their shared commitment to promoting social welfare, by their belief that government has a critical role to play in advancing this welfare, and by their historic partnership.

Stephen Brobeck

See also: Americans for Financial Reform; Consumer Federation of America; Investor Protection Advocacy; National Consumers League; Peterson, Esther

Further Reading

Barkin, Solomon. 1973 "Trade Unions and Consumerism." *Journal of Economic Issues* 7 (June): 317–321.

Kirsch, Larry, and Robert N. Mayer. 2013. *Financial Justice: The People's Campaign to Stop Lender Abuse.* Santa Barbara, CA: Praeger.

Warne, Clinton L. 1973. "The Consumer Movement and the Labor Movement." *Journal of Economic Issues* 7 (June): 307–316.

LATIN AMERICAN CONSUMER MOVEMENTS

See Central American Consumer Movements; South American Consumer Movements

LEGAL ADVOCACY

See Litigation

LEGISLATIVE ADVOCACY

In the past several decades, the U.S. Congress has approved many pro-consumer reforms. Just between 2007 and 2010, for example, it enacted major financial services, health care, food safety, product safety, and energy legislation. These reforms may seem surprising considering that business and other special interest groups usually have considerable resources at their disposal to mobilize opposition. In a typical campaign, they spend millions, even tens of millions, of dollars to influence congressional voting. They employ these resources in diverse ways that include lobbying members of Congress in Washington, DC, and in home districts, influencing other groups to support this lobbying, buying advertising, contributing to campaigns, and offering the prospect of employment after Congress.

How then have consumer advocates been so successful persuading Congress to pass consumer legislation? The critical difference is that they are advocating for all Americans—at least as consumers—rather than for a narrow interest group. And if they are successful in building support among many consumers (who also vote), members of Congress must take this concern seriously. This article will discuss how consumer advocates seek to build this support. It will also note those conditions which affect their success. And it will illustrate points mainly using advocacy before Congress for the establishment of the Consumer Financial Protection Bureau (CFPB), one of the most significant consumer reforms in the history of the nation.

Consumer advocates use strategies employed by other lobbyists. They prepare research and analysis, communicate their findings personally and through media, build coalitions, develop grasstops support, and work with congressional allies. The research and analysis, if the press takes it seriously, can be especially effective. One could argue that nearly two decades of reports of anticonsumer financial services practices by consumer groups was a necessary condition for congressional creation of the CFPB.

Since the early 1990s, groups including U.S. PIRG, the Center for Responsible Lending, National Consumer Law Center, Consumer Action, and the Consumer Federation of America (CFA) had prepared and released critical studies of mortgage, credit card, auto, payday, and other high-cost lending that was extensively reported on by news media. This research revealed egregious lender practices that, national surveys confirmed, a large majority of Americans wanted regulators to stop. These practices were so offensive that the typical lender response—additional regulation will restrict the availability of credit—was taken less seriously by legislators. In fact, increasingly Americans thought that lenders had gone overboard not just using "tricks and traps," but also aggressively marketing expensive credit to those who could not afford it.

However, to succeed consumer advocates must not only dramatize problems but also develop workable solutions that the public will support. Elizabeth Warren, now a U.S. senator but then a Harvard law professor, proposed the creation of a new federal agency that could address a broad range of credit related problems. This proposal quickly won strong support from consumer advocacy groups working on financial services issues. These groups joined together and helped create a much broader coalition that mounted the most ambitious and successful consumer advocacy campaign ever waged in the United States.

Coalitions are important for many reasons. They mobilize and use resources more efficiently than individual groups working on their own. More importantly, they provide an opportunity to create and implement a unified strategy. Coalitions involving consumer groups vary in their breadth. Some, such as the one which earlier fought successfully for credit card reforms, are informal and include mainly consumer groups. At the other extreme, other coalitions, such as some food safety coalitions, include industry groups whose interests are congruent with those of consumers. In a few instances, such as Advocates for Motor Vehicle and Highway Safety created by consumer advocates and auto insurers, ad hoc coalitions have been transformed into a new, permanent organization.

The coalition that fought to create the CFPB was not this broad, but it included organizations—most importantly, labor, women's, community, and civil rights groups—whose top priority had not been consumer issues. This coalition, called Americans for Financial Reform (AFR), effectively coordinated the work of numerous organizations. Despite varying priorities among its more than 250 affiliated groups, AFR was able to mobilize the resources of these members, plus foundation support, to speak with one voice to Congress and the media on the importance of Wall Street reform and the creation of a new financial services agency to protect consumers.

AFR also had the resources to mobilize some support for the proposed CFPB in congressional districts. Although the coalition lacked the presence and voice of a financial services industry that was well established in every state and district, AFR was able to recruit some local support. This support is important because, other factors being equal, legislators pay more attention to local consumer advocates—their constituents—than to advocates based in Washington, D.C.

For consumer advocates, lobbying essentially means communicating with legislators and their staff. Because of limited resources, advocates work especially closely with congressional leaders—often committee chairs—who share their consumer concerns and agree to "champion" legislation. Advocates and staffers communicate frequently about concepts and language for this legislation, then about winning the support of other legislators. The CFPB would probably not have been established without the leadership of Senator Chris Dodd (D-CT), chairman of the

Senate Banking Committee, and Barney Frank (D-MA), chairman of the House Financial Services Committee. Advocates from AFR, U.S. PIRG, and CFA were especially active communicating with the staffs of these two congressional leaders.

Helpful to advocates in their campaign were the findings of national opinion surveys. These surveys showed that upwards of four-fifths of Americans wanted Congress to take action to stop abusive financial services practices, and about three-fifths supported the creation of a new federal agency to take responsibility for curbing these practices. Legislators gain information about public opinion in their state or district in many ways—from individual communications of consumers, from reports in the press that legislators assume have influenced the thinking of their constituents, and also from public opinion surveys. If legislators, even those in very pro-business and antigovernment districts, are convinced that their constituents strongly support a consumer reform, they ignore this support at their political peril.

The CFPB was incorporated into the Wall Street Reform and Consumer Protection Act—commonly known as Dodd–Frank—that Congress enacted in 2010. Its creation represented the most important consumer financial services reform since the creation of a federal deposit insurance system during the Great Depression of the 1930s. But effective consumer advocacy, while a necessary condition, was not a sufficient condition for its passage. Several other stars had to align. Most important were fresh memories among all Americans of a financial crisis, caused largely by irresponsible industry practices, that brought on the nation's worst economic crisis since the Great Depression. A large majority of the public largely blamed Wall Street and big banks for the crisis. So, when an extensive financial services industry argued against fundamental reforms, their voices were ignored by the public and many legislators; other legislators who disliked government regulation muted their opposition.

However, it should also be emphasized that the CFPB would not have been established as a strong independent agency had Democrats not controlled Congress and the White House. Back in the 1960s and 1970s, Republicans including Senator Jacob Javits (R-NY) and Senator Frank Percy (R-IL) had led efforts to establish new consumer reforms. But in the twenty-first century, almost all congressional leadership for such reforms has come from Democrats. Influenced strongly by the Tea Party and antiregulation business groups, a large majority of Republican legislators are wary of, and usually opposed to, new consumer protections. On Dodd–Frank, on a couple critical votes, the White House and congressional Democratic leaders did need the support of several moderate Republicans—all from New England states—yet this support nearly did not materialize.

In general, when consumer advocates work closely together, target egregious practices, persuade the press to report on these practices, and arouse broad public concern, they have the best opportunity to persuade legislators to approve new protections. When there is little public attention to issues, especially when these issues are complex, industry lobbyists can effectively employ their superior resources to manage congressional outcomes.

Stephen Brobeck

See also: Congressional Consumer Advocacy

Further Reading

Brobeck, Stephen. 2003. "Consumer Advocates Inside the Beltway." *Inside the Minds: Political Powerhouses.* www.Aspatore.com.

Brobeck, Stephen, and Robert N. Mayer. 1997. "Coalitions." Brobeck, ed., *Encyclopedia of the Consumer Movement.* Santa Barbara, CA: ABC-CLIO.

Kirsch, Larry, and Robert N. Mayer. 2013. *Financial Justice: The People's Campaign to Stop Lender Abuse.* Santa Barbara, CA: ABC-CLIO.

Pertschuk, Michael. 1987. *Giant Killers.* New York: W. W. Norton & Company.

Warren, Elizabeth. 2014. *A Fighting Chance.* New York: Metropolitan Books.

LIFE INSURANCE ADVOCACY

See Insurance Advocacy

LITIGATION

What is consumer litigation? Everyone is a consumer, and so every lawsuit in which any individual is a party could be called a consumer case. But this article will use a more narrow definition. Consumer cases will be limited to those in which the dispute is about a product or service that an individual has acquired and the dispute is over the meaning of a contract and the various conditions surrounding it. This definition excludes disputes over real property, including property that an individual may rent and inhabit, but it includes leases for cars, phones, furniture, or other property besides land or buildings. It also excludes cases involving physical injuries from a defective product. The legal basis for the consumer's argument may arise under the law of contracts, but it also may arise under a variety of other federal or state legal authorities.

A second limiting feature of this article is that it will not discuss cases in which there is a significant dispute about the facts giving rise to the consumer's claim. There are two reasons for this exclusion. First, it is very hard to tell a meaningful story about the myriad of cases, in which the facts are contested, that also have broader implications for consumer litigation. Second, this litigation is most significant when it makes new law that benefits not only the parties who prevailed in a case, but also those who are similarly situated and come after them. That happens most often when there are no significant factual disputes. For these reasons, the cases this article discusses are what are often referred to as "law reform" cases. Many of them are undertaken with a series of related problems in mind, as illustrated by those involving the legal and other professions discussed below.

Broadly speaking, there are three ways that consumer litigation cases arise. The first is defensive: A consumer is sued and raises a legal defense. Second, the consumer sues the seller, claiming harm of some kind to him or her personally. Third, a case such as one in the second category is filed, but the complaint specifically asks for relief, often money damages, on behalf of an entire group (class) of similarly situated individuals. In many situations, the same legal issue could arise whether the consumer brings suit (i.e., is the plaintiff) or is sued, but they are treated separately, because it is much easier to be strategic on the offense than on the defense. Similarly, some cases in the second category seeking monetary relief might be susceptible to class treatment, but for reasons discussed below, they are brought as individual actions. This article will feature primarily cases in that category, most of them handled by the Public Citizen Litigation Group, which for the past several decades has been the nation's most active law reform litigating organization.

Finally, a word about the defendants/opposing parties in these cases. In most of these cases, the opposing party is a private entity, but in some cases a government or quasigovernment agency has issued a rule, or a legislature has enacted a statute, often at the behest of an industry, that has serious adverse effects on consumers. The minimum fee schedule system established by the Virginia State Bar, and the Virginia law forbidding the truthful advertising of the price of prescription drugs, both discussed below, are two examples of anticonsumer laws that were overturned in the courts. There are many other things that governments do, or often refuse to do, that can harm consumers—for example, failing to ensure that automobiles are safe in a crash, that food labels are not misleading, or that approved pharmaceuticals are safe for their intended uses. Those and scores of other problems could become the basis of lawsuits brought by consumers, but they raise a very different set of issues and are not part of this article.

Defensive Litigation

Good examples of this kind of case are fairly recent arrivals on the litigation scene, having literally been created by the Internet. The Litigation Group's initial Internet litigation foray arose when a California homeowner was sued by the Terminix Company for trademark infringement because she had said some disparaging things about Terminix on her website. She was unhappy because Terminix had inspected her home for termites, gave it a clean bill of health, and then refused to fix a serious problem that arose. In 1993, she sued the company under her contract (*Virga v. Terminix*) but lost when her expert witness did not show up for the trial. Terminix then sued her for libel for the statements about its performance on her website, but she prevailed. The company then brought the trademark suit in its home state of Tennessee, and that is when she called for help.

The Litigation Group saw this suit as a first strike at consumers who dared to complain and to use one of their few weapons—the Internet—to strike back at companies that do not perform up to standards. It agreed to defend her fully on the merits and also object to where the suit was brought, which it did. But the Litigation Group did something else: After filing papers, it sent a copy to the Wall Street Journal, which published a lengthy story on the case. Shortly thereafter, Terminix dropped the case. This was the beginning of a whole new area of Litigation Group work, representing consumers who are fighting back on the Internet—sometimes openly and other times anonymously—to protect against retaliation. Some of the cases were withdrawn when the company realized that the consumer had experienced counsel, but others went to judgment, in which the consumer interest was validated, in a variety of cases, with legal theories based on claims of libel, theft of trade secrets, and trademark misuse.

Two other examples of efforts to have major effects on consumers arose in cases in which the plaintiff was an individual, but the most significant defenses were so broad that they actually or virtually eliminated the plaintiffs' claims. In those cases, Litigation Group lawyers became counsel in an effort to stave off defeat for the current plaintiff as well as future plaintiffs.

The first involves the doctrine of preemption under which a claim based on a state law is precluded (preempted) because there is a federal law dealing with the subject of the lawsuit that not only sets a floor governing the conduct that companies covered by the law must follow, but also bars states from setting a higher or different standard. Preemption is found not only in areas affecting consumers (as the term is used in this article), such as banking, airline frequent flyer programs, and advertising rules for cigarettes, but also in laws affecting rights and benefits for employees and the safety of drugs and medical devices, as well as some features of products such as cars, motor boats, and locomotives. These cases typically arise when a consumer (or other affected person) brings a lawsuit for money damages based on the defendant's negligence or other wrongful conduct and the defendant seeks dismissal on the ground that it complied with the federal law and that the state law, which demands that the company do more or something different, is allegedly preempted. Although the Litigation Group would rarely have filed the case, it often intervened to oppose preemption, which a former colleague referred to as a "get out of jail free card."

The other example is technically a subset of preemption, but has developed into a specialized area of its own. The cases involve contracts containing an arbitration clause, which the defendant wrote into the contract and now seeks to enforce, to bar the consumer party from using the courts to resolve a dispute. The U.S. Supreme Court has had many recent cases involving general claims of preemption and specific claims relating to arbitration, based on the Federal Arbitration Act. Overall, for a court that has often favored corporations over individuals, it has come down somewhere in the middle on preemption generally, but has ruled (almost always 5–4) in favor of requiring arbitration. Perhaps the most anticonsumer decision of this kind (*AT&T Mobility LLC v. Concepcion*) involved a case brought on behalf of a class of 30 million AT&T cell phone owners who bought service contracts and received a "free" phone. However, they were not told that they each owed about $32 in sales tax for their free phone. In 2011, the court held that the arbitration clause and a companion ban on class actions required each consumer to sue on his or her own, in arbitration, which meant that almost no one would do so.

Offensive Litigation

In 1972, Allegheny Airlines, now U.S. Airways, made a terrible mistake: Ralph Nader had a confirmed seat on a flight from Washington to Hartford, where he was to give a talk before a large audience. He was running late, but he was still on time when he arrived at the gate. He was told that the plane was full and that he would not be allowed to board. The airline also refused to ask other passengers whether they would be willing to give him their seat. Because he missed the event, Nader brought suit for breach of contract and other violations for being denied the right to board a flight for which he had a confirmed seat (*Nader v. Allegheny Airlines*).

The case has a long history, and eventually Nader was denied his claim for money damages. He may have lost the battle, but he won the war, because he unearthed practices, followed by the entire industry, whereby carriers routinely deceived passengers into believing that they would have a seat when there was a substantial likelihood that they would not. The airlines insisted that they never "overbooked" a flight, but that was because they had defined "overbooking" as intentionally selling more seats for a flight than they expected to have passengers. What they did do was "oversell"—for example, by selling 105 seats for a 100-seat flight, expecting five passengers not to show. But if only three did not show, two people would not have seats, and the carrier would say that it had not "overbooked" the flight.

When this practice became public, it did not take a court order to bring about change. The Civil Aeronautics Board (now extinct) issued a rule that set requirements for dealing with oversold flights, mandating minimum payments for being denied boarding, and setting up gateside auctions in which passengers with flexible schedules could participate. Without Nader's lawsuit, consumers might still be hearing that airlines never overbook and that "we are very sorry that there is no seat for you on this flight and we will get you on the next flight we can, but with no compensation of any kind."

A second example of offensive litigation involves the practice by which many attorneys set their fees. For many years, bar associations in more than thirty states had been publishing what they called minimum fee schedules, which lawyers followed. In Virginia, the bar had issued opinions saying that it was unethical for lawyers to charge less in a bid to attract clients. As a result, when a potential client would visit a lawyer and the issue of fees came up, the lawyer would turn to his or her bookshelf, reach for the fee schedule, and express regrets that "this is the least that the bar allows me to charge." Lawyers, like everyone else not in a regulated industry, can charge whatever price they please, but when competitors agree to charge the same price, that looks like a violation of the federal antitrust laws—unless somehow lawyers are different. The Litigation Group took on the Virginia system (*Goldfarb v. Virginia State Bar*) and, in 1975, obtained an 8–0 Supreme Court ruling that lawyers were just as subject to the antitrust laws as everyone else, unable to use fee schedules to fix prices.

A third example of offensive consumer litigation, which had an enormous ripple effect in a wide range of commercial activities, was the Litigation Group's 1976 challenge to the Virginia law, similar to that in thirty-four other states, which barred pharmacists from advertising the price of prescription drugs (*Virginia Pharmacy Board v. Virginia Citizens Consumer Council*). It was perfectly legal for pharmacies to compete over price, but consumers had no way of easily learning which pharmacy charged the lowest price. Consumers were forced to communicate personally with pharmacies in person or by phone and, if the latter, had no assurance of being quoted a price. Relying on the rights of consumers to receive truthful information, and applying the First Amendment's protection of free speech to apply to commercial, as well as political and ideological speech, the Supreme Court ruled 8–1 that the law was unconstitutional.

A year later, the court applied the same principle (but only by a 5–4 vote) to total bans on lawyer advertising, another rule of "Lawyers' Ethics" that made it more difficult for consumers to find lawyers who could handle their particular matter at a reasonable price. The advertising cases and the minimum fee schedule case were part of a long-term strategy to increase the availability and affordability of legal services. This advocacy later included cases challenging the extent of the monopoly that lawyers have (and that keep out potentially qualified and lower-cost alternatives) and impose residence and local office requirements for admission to the bar, which keep out lawyer competitors, thus harming consumers.

Staying on offense is a good strategy because it maximizes the likelihood that cases will be decided on favorable facts and that the timing best suits the cause. But cases are often beyond the control of those who bring them, which means that consumer law reform litigators must always be on the lookout for important cases even when the consumer is the defendant.

Class Actions

Most of the cases discussed above sought legal rulings that would have effects far beyond the parties to the lawsuit. In a class action, the plaintiff seeks actual relief—generally money damages—for the wrong that the defendant has committed, which can raise the stakes considerably. Consumer class actions are very common under the securities and antitrust laws as well as under a variety of consumer protection statutes and general contract law. Because of the potential for very large damage awards or settlements, these cases attract commercial law firms which specialize in these areas. In addition, because these cases are very large, and the factual and legal issues often quite complicated, they require a major investment to fund the lawsuit, which most public interest groups do not have. Because these cases are commercially viable, the rules of the Internal Revenue Service, applicable to public interest law firms, discourage and perhaps even preclude those firms from taking on fee-generating cases like these, especially where attorneys in private practice are available to handle them. For these reasons, the Litigation Group and similar non-profit organizations rarely bring such cases (although the minimum fee schedule case was a class action with only 2,400 class members).

There is one aspect of consumer class actions in which the Litigation Group has played a major role. Many class actions settle, and under the applicable rules, a judge must approve the settlement. That is required for several reasons. Both judgments and settlements apply to all class members (unless they choose to exclude themselves and sue, or not, on their own), and the judge is there to protect the class from possible overreaching by the individuals who brought the case (by taking special benefits for themselves) or by the lawyers receiving an unreasonable fee, which comes out of the recovery of the class members. To assist the judge in assessing the fairness of a settlement, including attorneys' fees, the rules permit class members to object to some parts of the settlement. But because most class members will not have lawyers or have the means to hire one given their small stake in the case—think of the case with the $32 tax for the free cell phone—the

Litigation Group has stepped in to assist class members in assuring that they are receiving fair deal as, in effect, consumers of the settlement who are paying for it by surrendering their claims.

Most consumer cases involve no great principles of law, and many turn on their unique facts, but that is true of most lawsuits. This article is about the small group of consumer cases that seek to do more than help an individual consumer prevail. The goal of these cases is to move the law in a direction that provides more protection for consumers in the long haul, often as part of a long-term strategy like that for the cases involving the legal profession.

Alan B. Morrison

See also: Public Citizen; Tort-Related Consumer Advocacy

Further Reading

Craig, Barbara Harrison. 2004. *Courting Change: The Story of the Public Citizen Litigation Group.* Washington, DC: Public Citizen Press.

Mauro, Tony. 2004. "Moving On: A Nader Protégé with Friends in High Places." *Legal Times* 27–21 (May 24).

LOBBYING
See Legislative Advocacy

MALAYSIAN CONSUMER MOVEMENT

Malaysia has been one of the leading advocates of a more development-oriented approach to consumer protection that focuses more on the needs of the poor than on the demands of the affluent. This is largely a result of the national and international influence of the Consumers' Association of Penang (CAP).

CAP was formed in 1969 in the immediate aftermath of the riots that followed the national elections of that year. Organized consumerism offered a way forward on a range of social and economic issues that were otherwise tainted by the politics of race and an increasingly authoritarian regime. Ever since its formation, the organization has been strongly associated with the voice of its president, S. M. Mohamed Idris, who was still in office as of 2015. Through the pages of *Utusan Konsumer,* he has advocated an approach to consumer protection focused on securing access to safe and reliable basic goods and services for all consumers, rich and poor alike.

In the 1970s, CAP targeted a number of Malaysian consumer issues that also addressed global problems. For instance, it highlighted the adulteration of common household goods and the inappropriate advertising of products such as breast-milk substitutes by multinational corporations. Additionally, CAP increasingly turned to environmental issues, leading to the formation of *Sahabat Alam Malaysia* (SAM; Friends of the Earth Malaysia), a sister organization of CAP. CAP also focused on questions of development, most famously by providing an alternative model of economic growth for the villagers of Kuala Juru, which inspired a range of copycat initiatives. CAP's interventions frequently brought it to the attention of the authorities, and in 1987 its legal officer, Meena Raman, was detained without trial as part of Operation Lalang, which rounded up more than a hundred members of Malaysian civil society.

Throughout its existence, CAP has maintained an international point of view. CAP inspired the formation of the Third World Network in 1984, which continues to act as a hub for South–South NGO cooperation. From its earliest years, CAP also played an active role in the International Organisation of Consumers Unions (IOCU). Notably, CAP's secretary and driving force, Anwar Fazal, became president of IOCU in 1978, serving two terms and arguably steering the global consumer movement through eight of its most active and vocal years.

Despite CAP's global importance, it is but one of a number of consumer organizations operating within a federal constitutional system. The Selangor Consumers' Association has operated from within the capital, Kuala Lumpur, since 1965. Drawing on more elite social connections, it advocated a more consensual and collaborative role with the state. In 1971, the Selangor Consumers' Association led to the formation of the Federation of Malaysian Consumer Associations (FOMCA), an umbrella organization that has enabled the spread of organized consumerism throughout the country. It has done so by accepting state funding for most of its activities, a decision which has brought more access to the decision making process but also a potential threat to its independence of operation. CAP certainly thought so, and it refused to join FOMCA. Although relations between CAP and FOMCA have improved in recent years, the tensions between these two organizations have characterized the strengths and weaknesses of Malaysian consumer protection ever since. Although CAP can speak as the voice of the people, it can also be ignored by those it seeks to persuade. FOMCA, by contrast, has been a partner in government at times but is aware that funding will be cut if it strays too far from what is politically acceptable.

In 1985, ERA Consumer, an organization originally based in Perak State, joined FOMCA. Josie Fernandez, a former volunteer at CAP, sought to bring CAP's focus on the poor and disadvantaged to other states within Malaysia. ERA has brought attention to the plight of the Orang Asli, an indigenous population, and has also highlighted problems affecting women consumers. It quickly took on a more national profile and later transferred its activities to Kuala Lumpur, whence it has worked closely with FOMCA ever since (often sharing key personnel).

Relations between consumer groups and the state have become closer over time. Since 1974, FOMCA's contacts with government have been through the Division of Consumer Affairs within the Ministry of Trade. (Today, consumer policy in Malaysia resides in the Ministry of Domestic Trade, Co-operatives, and Consumerism.) In 1999, the Consumer Protection Act (written with the assistance of Sothi Rachagan, a member of the Selangor Consumers' Association and later a regional director of IOCU) formalized some of these connections, including the launch of a National Consumer Policy in 2002. A year later, Fernandez assisted in this by drawing up the Consumer Master Plan for the period 2003–2013, which, as is so often the case with Malaysian regulations, has been more enthusiastic in its intentions than its implementation.

At the same time as the government was accepting responsibility for consumer policy, its openness to a human rights agenda created new opportunities for Malaysian consumer activities. This openness has enabled the radicalism of CAP to be combined with the more mainstream consumer rights agenda of FOMCA, and it has enabled both organizations to work with human rights and other civil society groups. The language of human rights rejuvenated consumer protection in the 1990s, and it enabled FOMCA to launch some high-profile campaigns, such as the fight in 2000 against the Indah Water Consortium, an ill-fated sewage privatization project.

Nevertheless, the consumer protection mechanisms in Malaysia are by no means as extensive as in Europe and North America, and FOMCA remains a fragile organization in comparison to its Western counterparts. Moreover, the distinctive nature of Malaysian consumer activism, especially that associated with CAP, appears increasingly antiquated. Although CAP continues to offer basic consumer services for its clients, its moralistic critiques of many new trends in consumer culture and lifestyle fit uneasily within an increasingly affluent country. Here, a new generation of shoppers appears more willing to embrace, rather than question, the proliferation of goods throughout society. It is difficult to see how consumers brought up in a world far removed from poverty and disadvantage will take to a nationalistic message with the experiences of village life (the *kampong*) very much at its center. Still, the country remains an important hub for the international consumer movement, and Consumers International's regional office in Kuala Lumpur remains a crucial mechanism for the circulation of staff and ideas that have their origin in Malaysian consumerism.

Matthew Hilton

See also: Consumers International

Further Reading

Hilton, Matthew. 2009. *Choice and Justice: Forty Years of the Malaysian Consumer Movement.* Penang, Malaysia: Universiti Sains Malaysia Press.

Hilton, Matthew. 2007. "The Consumer Movement and Civil Society in Malaysia," *International Review of Social History* 52, no. 3: 373–406.

MIDDLE EASTERN CONSUMER MOVEMENTS

The term "Middle East" has no single definition, but it is generally considered to include portions of Southwestern Asia and Northern Africa. It is generally understood to include, at minimum, Egypt, Sudan, Israel, Jordan, Lebanon, Syria, Turkey, Iraq, Iran, Saudi Arabia, and the other countries of the Arabian Peninsula.

With exception of Israel, the consumer movement in the Middle East region is relatively new compared to movements in Europe, the United States, and many Asian countries. The movement's emergence in the Middle East has corresponded with the growth of free markets, more affluent lifestyles, and new consumer habits. From an emphasis on accumulating goods, consumer concerns have migrated toward improving quality of life and minimizing environmental harm. Despite this shift, many consumers are still unaware of the concepts of "consumer protection" and "consumer rights." This "consumer illiteracy" creates fertile conditions for consumer fraud. There is thus a great need for consumer activists in the region, as well as substantial obstacles for them to overcome. The singularity of the region's culture, traditions, and religious values suggests that it will be difficult to replicate the successful experiences of Western consumer organizations in the countries of the Middle East.

The overriding issue faced by consumer movements in the Middle East is the paternalistic role that governments tend to play. In most of the countries, governmental agencies or departments in charge of consumer protection try to monopolize all consumer protection and awareness activities, leaving civil society associations financially unsupported and marginalized. Although some governments in the Middle East are beginning to back the consumer movement in keeping an eye on fraudulent merchants and illegal or unfair dealings (notably Yemen and Saudi

Arabia), other governments view civil society associations as rivals rather than partners in consumer protection. Thus, consumer education faces a double task—informing consumers of their right and convincing governments of the importance of a civil society movement dedicated to consumer protection.

As a result of a strained relationship with governments, consumer associations typically do not actively participate in the policymaking processes related to consumer laws and rights. To some extent, consumer associations lack the specialized experts that would allow them to contribute to policymaking, but a more important reason is that governments do not want to actively involve consumer organizations. Governments only want consumer association to "rubber-stamp" their decisions. There are exceptional cases in which consumer associations have been engaged in such processes, but there is still much room for improvement.

Even when governments acknowledge the importance of consumer associations, government prefer that these organizations define consumer issues narrowly in terms of seller fraud and problems with the performance of goods and services. This marginalizes the role of consumer associations with respect to issues such as the natural environment, health, money laundering, and intellectual property rights. Similarly, governments in the Middle East are wary of leaders in the field of consumer protection who approach consumer issues from the perspective of human rights. Governments in the Middle East often resist the idea of human rights (for example, freedom of speech and religion and the rights of women), viewing the consumer movement's demands for human rights as an interference in state policy and a Trojan horse of alien ideologies.

In addition to a problematic relationship with government, consumer organizations face the challenge of funding their operations. Here they face a major dilemma. Without government financing, these organizations can rarely achieve their goals. They are run by volunteers, some of whom see their work primarily as a means of obtaining an influential position in the government or of finding a lucrative business opportunity rather than serving the interests of consumers. Other organizations are "one man shows," wherein a sole fighter tries to play the impossible role of consumer defender for an entire nation. Knowing that consumers believe that their government supports businesses over consumers, the consumer associations play the role of victim to elicit support, trust, and financial contributions. In the long run, some of these organizations may attain financial self-sufficiency via member donations, grants from international organizations, contracts to conduct educational and research projects. At present, however, consumer associations tend to disappear or remain in name only without government financial support.

But government financial support can be problematic for consumer associations as well. When consumer associations are partially or totally backed by the government, questions arise regarding transparency and legitimacy. The consumers that these organizations seek to represent and benefit may be dubious about the independence of these associations and may, as a result, ignore their role. In this situation, consumers lack trust in the role of either government or consumer associations in consumer protection.

To address public skepticism about the government's commitment to consumer protection and stave off the need for consumer associations, some governments in the Middle East have rushed to establish consumer protection agencies (typically as departments within ministries). This has helped gain consumers' trust in some countries, as in the Sultanate of Oman with the establishment by royal decree in 2011 of the Public Authority for Consumer Protection. By pursuing a broad agenda of consumer education, protection, and complaint handling, the Public Authority has won the trust of consumers, and the authority has marginalized the role of the longstanding Oman Association for Consumer Protection, which was perceived by some consumers as ineffective.

Even when new consumer protection agencies have not been created, many countries in the Middle East have enacted new consumer protection laws or used existing laws in ways that are favorable to the consumer. Countries that have passed specific consumer protection laws include Tunisia, Oman, Lebanon, Egypt, United Arab Emirates, Qatar, Yemen, Syria, and Iraq. However, the general concern of consumers and consumer organizations is how forcefully these laws will be implemented and applied. For example, laws on consumer redress are complex; getting a complaint resolved via a lawsuit may take years.

Some consumer associations prefer to pursue the consumer cause without the existence of a specific law. These organizations claim that laws drafted by the government without input from consumer groups often diminish their role and restrain them from defending consumers. For example, in Morocco, the consumer protection legislation prohibits consumer organizations from representing the consumer before the consumer protection agency, thus taking away the little bit of power they have and paralyzing their work. In this situation, consumer groups prefer the absence of a law that could take more than it provides.

Despite the numerous barriers to consumer organizations in the Middle East, several associations have achieved a considerable measure of influence and permanence. An important indicator of a consumer association's stature is joining Consumers International (CI), the umbrella organization for the world consumer movement. Consumer organizations in Oman, Jordan, and Sudan are full members of CI, and groups in Yemen and Turkey are affiliate members.

Consumer movement organizations in the Middle East have also recognized the importance of unifying their efforts. Given similarities in traditions, language, and habits, a consumer campaign in one country can be expanded within the region to achieve massive and significant results for additional consumers. Federations among consumer groups have begun to take shape in the region.

One example of joint activity is the Arab Federation for Consumers. Established in 1998, it is a coalition of consumer protection associations in more than a dozen Arab countries. The organizations seek to advance consumer interests through cooperative action and in coordination with the institutions of joint Arab action, particularly the Economic Unity Council. Another federation is the Maghreb Union for Consumer Protection. The union was founded in 2013 to coordinate activities of consumer associations in the Maghreb countries (Morocco, Algeria, Tunisia, Libya, and Mauritania). The organization's aims include creating awareness among consumers in the Maghreb region, as well as fighting commercial fraud, counterfeiting, and the manipulation of Maghreb consumers. As a final illustration of joint action, the first Arab Forum for Consumer Protection convened in Alexandria in February 2014.

Further solidarity among consumer organizations will likely be advanced by the establishment by CI of a new office for the region in Muscat, capital of the Sultanate of Oman, to serve the region's associations and to help them work jointly to overcome difficulties in the campaign for consumer rights. The main objectives of the office are to gain a better understanding of the region's consumer organizations and to help them develop relationships both among themselves and with consumer organizations around the world. In this way, the region's consumer associations will be able draw lessons from a global perspective.

By way of an overall assessment, one can observe that some consumer organizations have succeeded in improving consumer rights and increasing consumer awareness, but for the most part, consumer organizations have not been able to make their presence felt among consumers in the Middle East. The region, commonly known for political turmoil, has been working to solve other, "more important" problems, and consumer issues are seen as secondary. This may be a narrow view, as was demonstrated lately during the Arab Spring, where one of the main causes of discontent was the rise of commodity prices. Therefore, it is imperative to create a roadmap for a strong consumer movement—including changes in both government and consumer behavior—to clear the way for the development of the "more important" plans of the region.

Aziza Mourassilo

See also: Consumers International

Further Reading

Mahajan, Vijay. 2013. "Understanding the Arab Consumer." *Harvard Business Review* 91, no. 5: 128–133.

Sengupta, Rijit, and Udai S. Mehta. 2012. *Understanding the State of Domestic Competition and Consumer Policies in Select MENA Countries.* Jaipur, India: CUTS Centre for Competition, Investment & Economic Regulation. www.cuts-ccier.org/pdf/Competition_and_Consumer_Policies_in_MENA_Countries.pdf.

MORTGAGE LENDING REFORM

Over the past eighty years, mortgages and mortgage regulation have undergone several transformations. During the Great Depression of the 1930s, widespread home loan foreclosures inspired federal and state reforms that created simple, affordable, standardized mortgage loans that, from the 1940s to the 1990s, helped millions of Americans join the middle class. But by the end of the latter decade, complex and often highly risky loans emerged and were aggressively marketed, helping trigger the financial crisis and Great Recession of the late 2000s. In the aftermath of this crisis, legislators and regulators approved new regulations to make mortgages safer and more understandable. Consumer and housing advocates played a key role in the establishment of these new protections.

The modern mortgage developed as an outgrowth of the Great Depression of the 1930s. Before that time, home buyers typically paid 50 percent down and financed the rest with a five-year loan that required a large balloon payment or refinancing at the end of the term. Loans were made and held by local banks, many of whom failed in the early 1930s as homeowners struggled to pay their loans and depositors made runs on banks to withdraw deposits. Out of this disarray, the federal government and state governments stepped in to buy and restructure the loans in order to help homeowners afford them and remain in their homes. In 1934, the federal government established the Federal Housing Administration (FHA) to provide home loans with low down payments and lengthy terms, greatly increasing their affordability. The states did their part by approving mortgage loan reforms such as limits on fees, interest rates, and prepayment penalties.

The federal government also created government agencies to help ensure that mortgage lenders had money to lend. Previously, lenders such as savings and loans were limited in the amount of their mortgage loans they could make by the amount of deposits they held. In 1938, the National Federal Mortgage Association ("Fannie Mae") was established. Much later—in 1970—a companion organization, the Federal Home Loan Mortgage Corporation ("Freddie Mac"), was created. These two organizations developed a system to buy home loans from lenders, package them into securities, and sell the securities to investors. As a result, mortgage credit became more available to home buyers and at a lower cost.

Under this structure, and with the growth of the post–World War II economy, homeownership levels increased, exceeding two-thirds of all housing units by the late 1990s. However, many creditworthy families of color were denied this opportunity. For many years, FHA specifically excluded most nonwhite families from obtaining FHA home loans. Private lenders did the same, redlining communities and refusing to lend there.

Civil rights and community groups fought this discrimination, helping persuade Congress to pass the 1968 Fair Housing Act and the 1974 Equal Credit Opportunity, which outlawed discrimination in housing and lending, respectively. However, discriminatory practices, many much subtler, remained persistent and widespread.

In this period, housing and consumer advocates also convinced Congress to approve additional lending protections in new laws it enacted. Building on the many years of work by Senator Paul Douglas, the Truth in Lending Act was enacted in 1968, requiring for the first time standard disclosures of interest rates, fees, and other key loan terms for all loans, including mortgages. A key disclosure was the annual percentage rate, or APR, a measure of the overall costs of a loan over time including both interest and other charges. However, the law did not limit the rates and fees that could be charged. The 1974 Real Estate Settlement Procedures Act (RESPA) specifically addressed fees and charges related to mortgage loans. It required the completion of a new form—the so-called HUD 1—in which all fees paid in connection with the loan transaction were disclosed. The act also prohibited the payment of referral fees in connection with the loan.

Until the 1980s, most states had usury laws that limited the amount of interest and fees that could be charged on home loans and other credit. However, the high inflation of the late 1970s pushed up interest rates so that in states with low interest rate limits, loans became difficult to obtain. Instead of simply allowing states to raise the rate limits, Congress approved a new law—the Depository Institutions Deregulation and Monetary Control Act of 1980—that eliminated usury limits on mortgage loans while giving states a limited period to pass new limits or preserve their right to do so in the future. When few states met this deadline, most state mortgage interest rate limits ended. National bank regulators then provided lending institutions with a way to avoid even the remaining rate limits. These regulators ruled that states could not regulate the interest rates of banks domiciled in another state. Predictably, big banks selected home states with few or no limits, such as Delaware or South Dakota.

This lending deregulation was part of a larger banking deregulation that led, in the late 1980s, to the savings and loan crisis and, in the next decade, to irresponsible and imprudent mortgage lending practices that destroyed home equity and that led to millions of home foreclosures. Key perpetrators of these practices were subprime lenders who pushed homeowners to refinance mortgages at high fees and interest rates. The scope of this lending broadened considerably as large national companies entered the market and Wall Street began buying these loans and packaging them into securities.

In 1994, encouraged by housing and consumer advocates led by the National Consumer Law Center (NCLC), Congress passed the Home Ownership Equity Protection Act (HOPEA) to provide some consumer protections for very expensive subprime loans. This act depended on the Federal Reserve exercising new authority to monitor and prohibit unfair and abusive lending practices. However, the Federal Reserve chose not to exercise this authority until 2009, after the financial crisis was already in full force.

Experiencing the fallout from this predatory lending—with whole communities' being devastated by home foreclosures—states began enacting laws to curb the unfair practices. These laws addressed the issues of high fees, prepayment penalties, loan flipping, and other abuses. In 1999, North Carolina was the first state to enact one of these laws. Groups including the Center for Responsible Lending (CRL), NCLC, ACORN, and AARP worked with local coalitions, and similar laws were passed in many other states. Banks fought back by arguing to federal regulators that federal law made them exempt from state regulation. Regulators, notably the Office of the Comptroller of the Currency, often agreed, and courts largely demurred to the regulators.

By the 2000s, subprime lending had grown to make up nearly one-fourth of all mortgage loans, and unsafe, anticonsumer lending practices had spread through much of the mortgage market. Mortgage brokers and lenders were paid large fees for steering borrowers into these loans, and the Wall Street firms securitizing the loans also earned hefty fees. So not surprisingly, the volume of these products exploded, becoming, at the peak of the housing boom, the dominant mortgages. No-documentation or stated-income loans, where the loan file contains only an income figure with no documentation, began comprising nearly half of subprime loans and a third of other loans. Negative amortization loans, where borrowers pay less than the accruing interest each month, now were aggressively marketed to consumers who could barely afford the initial reduced payments, much less later larger ones.

As early as 2000, community and consumer advocates were issuing warnings about the dangers of these loans, which were driving a mounting number of home-owners into foreclosure. However, their voices were drowned out by the financial industry's defense of the products and by the complacency of federal regulators, who failed to see the coming financial crisis. In fact, these regulators continued efforts to block states from establishing new protections.

The flood of foreclosures from the many unsustainable mortgages was delayed as borrowers who could not afford their loan payments refinanced their loans, paying the arrearage by adding it to the loan principal. However, once housing prices leveled off and then fell, millions of these loans failed, accelerating and sustaining the plunge in housing prices. As a result, tens of millions of other homeowners also suffered losses, as did many investors, helping trigger the most serious recession since the 1930s. Families of color, who had been targeted by many subprime lenders, were hit especially hard, many losing all or most of their home equity. These losses greatly increased the wealth disparities between them and white households.

In 2010, in response to the housing crisis and subsequent financial collapse, Congress enacted the Wall Street Reform and Consumer Protection Act, com-monly known as Dodd–Frank for its leading Senate and House sponsors. This law, which represented the most comprehensive financial services reform since the 1930s, addressed a broad range of issues related to mortgage market reform. The act required that lenders make a determination of the borrower's ability to repay the loan and that they document the borrower's income and debts as part of this process. It updated and added key protections for high-cost and subprime loans, including prohibiting prepayment penalties and closing loopholes in the coverage of existing laws. It also restricted the steering of borrowers to riskier loans and reduced the ability of federal banking regulators to use preemption to undercut state mortgage protections. The act improved servicing standards so that borrow-ers received fair accounting of their payments and so that those who faced hard-ship and fell behind would have a better chance of having their loans modified to reduce these payments. And it established a market wide regulator, the Consumer Financial Protection Bureau (CFPB), with a broad mandate to supervise mortgage companies that had operated under weak and fragmented regulators.

Consumer and housing groups fought hard for these reforms. They joined civil rights, labor, and community groups to form a new coalition, Americans for Financial Reform (AFR), which worked for all the reforms in the Dodd–Frank legislation. CRL, NCLC, the Consumer Federation of America, Leadership Confer-ence on Civil and Human Rights, NAACP, National Council of La Raza, US Public Interest Research Group, and AARP were especially active seeking new mortgage lending protections. They found congressional champions in Representatives

Mel Watt (D-NC) and Brad Miller (D-NC) and Senators Jeff Merkley (D-OR) and Carl Levin (D-MI), among others.

The enactment and implementation of the Dodd–Frank Act mortgage provisions, combined with the creation of the CFPB, reformed the mortgage market in a fundamental way. New basic standards have ended many past practices that harmed consumers and the economy. Equally important, any new abusive practices face scrutiny and oversight by the CFPB. Advised by consumer and housing groups, the CFPB has already issued regulations that implement the requirement that lenders make only loans that borrowers can afford to repay; have adopted detailed protections for loan servicing; and have instituted a new, clearer consumer disclosure form that mortgage lenders are required to provide. The resulting mortgage market, in 2014, is much safer for consumers than it has been in several decades.

Michael Calhoun

See also: Americans for Financial Reform; Congressional Consumer Advocacy; Center for Responsible Lending; Legislative Advocacy; National Consumer Law Center; National Low Income Housing Coalition; Tenant Activism

Further Reading

Immergluck, Dan. 2009. *Foreclosed: High-Risk Lending, Deregulation, and the Undermining of America's Mortgage Market.* Ithaca, NY: Cornell University Press.
Kirsch, Larry, and Robert N. Mayer. 2013. *Financial Justice: The People's Campaign to Stop Lender Abuse.* Santa Barbara, CA: Praeger.
Schwartz, Alex F. 2010. *Housing Policy in the U.S.* New York: Routledge.
Sherman, Matthew. 2009. *A Short History of Financial Deregulation in the U.S.* Washington, DC: Center for Economic and Policy Research.

MOTOR VEHICLE FUEL ECONOMY ADVOCACY

The original Corporate Average Fuel Economy (CAFE) standards were passed in 1975, by solid margins in both the U.S. House and Senate, as a response to the 1973 oil embargo. They were considered to be economic and national security necessities with environmental and consumer benefits as important secondary benefits. The standards set sales-weighted, fleetwide fuel economy averages that each manufacturer had to meet. They were intended to double fuel efficiency by requiring that each manufacturer's passenger car fleet average 27.5 miles per gallon (mpg) by 1985. The most active advocates for the law were the Center for Auto Safety, Friends of the Earth, Environmental Action, and the Sierra Club.

After passage of the law, fuel economy gradually increased throughout the early 1980s. In 1985, under pressure from Ford and General Motors, the Reagan Administration lowered the standard to 26 mpg. This standard, however, was raised to 26.5 mpg in 1989 and to 27.5 mpg in 1990. However, in this period, the light truck standard was lowered from 20.5 to 20.0 mpg.

During this time, the Center for Auto Safety, Environmental Action, and the Sierra Club were at the forefront of trying to prevent weakening of the standards.

In 1986, the Center for Auto Safety, Environmental Policy Institute, Public Citizen, and Union of Concerned Scientists sued the National Highway Traffic Safety Administration (NHTSA) to force it to issue the standards on time and within the letter of the law, which called for the maximum feasible fuel economy to be set. However, the lawsuit did not succeed.

While much of the debate about CAFE focused on implications for national security and the environment, the effect of reduced gasoline consumption on consumer pocketbooks was also an issue. Advocates, such as Clarence Ditlow of the Center for Auto Safety and Dan Becker of the Sierra Club, argued that higher fuel economy requirements would also save consumers money.

In 1990, an attempt by Senators Richard Bryan (D-NV) and Slade Gordon (R-WA) to raise fuel economy by 40 percent was killed on the Senate floor by filibuster. In 1995, when the Clinton administration attempted to raise the light truck fuel economy requirements, the Republican-controlled Congress passed a rider to an appropriations bill that stripped such authority from the administration. This rider remained in effect until 2000 in spite of numerous, but unsuccessful, efforts by congressional advocates of higher standards.

During the early 2000s, vehicle fuel economy changed little. In fact, because of the consumer shift from cars to SUVs, which had to meet lower standards, some advocates said that fleetwide average fuel economy actually declined.

In the face of federal inaction, California, the only state permitted to set its own standards, used its authority under the California Air Resources Board (CARB) to do so. In 2002, the state legislature passed the Pavley Global Warming Bill (AB1493), which required reductions in greenhouse gas emissions from light duty vehicles. Although the bill focused on clean air, vehicles using less fuel also reduced consumer costs. Because federal law allows states to adopt California's standards when they are stricter than federal guidelines, a number of states adopted these requirements.

These more stringent state requirements were significant, because carmakers had little choice but to meet them, especially in the huge California market. Predictably, because they much preferred uniform national standards to a patchwork quilt of separate state rules, they grew less critical of higher federal standards.

In 2005, the Consumer Federation of America and Consumers Union joined forces with the Center for Auto Safety, Clean Air Watch, the National League of Cities, the United States Conference of Mayors, the Environmental Council of States, and the National Environmental Trust to help defeat the proposed Gasoline for America's Security Act of 2005. This legislation proposed to weaken a number of important environmental and energy regulations, in the name of energy security, while ignoring the lack of fuel economy improvements.

Also in 2005, in order to bring greater consumer focus on the fuel economy issue, the Consumer Federation of America began to release a series of surveys and reports. These surveys showed that Americans were greatly concerned about future gasoline prices and U.S. dependency on Mideastern oil and supported higher fuel economy standards even when they increased vehicle costs. Research undertaken by CFA's research director, Mark Cooper, also demonstrated that despite vehicle price increases, because of decreased fuel consumption, higher standards would lower consumer costs.

In 2007, a Democrat-controlled Congress approved legislation—the Energy Security and Independence Act—that required an increase in CAFE standards for cars and light trucks to 35 mpg by 2020. The bill also called for the "maximum feasible levels" to be enacted for 2030 without actually setting a requirement.

President George W. Bush, who earlier had lamented the "nation's addiction to oil," signed the bill into law, but his administration's NHTSA, responsible for setting mileage requirements, and the U.S. Environmental Protection Agency (EPA), responsible for setting emissions requirements, never issued final rules. In addition, in 2007, the EPA notified Governor Schwarzenegger of California that it was denying the state's request for a waiver from the Clean Air Act, which would have enabled it to raise mileage standards via more stringent emissions standards.

President Barack Obama and his administration were far more supportive of higher fuel economy standards. President Obama directed the EPA to reconsider California's waiver request and to accelerate the increase in standards to 35.5 mpg by 2016 under a plan worked out by EPA and NHTSA. The plan was finalized in 2010 and was called "Phase 1 of the National Program" covering vehicle model years 2012–2016. It represented an historic agreement between federal regulators (EPA and NHTSA), state regulators (CARB), and automobile companies that resulted in significant increases to both fuel efficiency standards and global warming pollution standards.

An important factor allowing this higher standard was a 2007 U.S. Supreme Court decision in a case between EPA and the commonwealth of Massachusetts. The court found that greenhouse gases were, in fact, a pollutant that could be regulated under the federal Clean Air Act. This decision empowered the EPA to act more aggressively than it had in the past.

Once the standard was set for 2012–2016, environmental and consumer groups began pushing for even higher standards after this period. The Consumer Federation of America released new reports showing the affordability of these higher standards and new national consumer surveys demonstrating consumer desire for stronger standards. In 2010, with Consumer Action and twenty state and local consumer organizations, CFA sent a letter to the President asking for a goal of 60 mpg by 2025.

In 2011, the Obama administration took advantage of the confluence of a number of unique situations as it developed "Phase 2 of the National Program." These included the bailout of the car companies by the U.S. government, the ability of California to set its own standards, union concerns that U.S. automakers would lose market share if they did not build more fuel efficient vehicles, the globalization of the auto industry, and the growing consumer demand for more fuel efficient vehicles. These factors helped bring disparate parties together to reach consensus on "Phase 2" standards, which would cover the 2017–2025 model years.

On the advocacy side, a key element in the finalization of "Phase 2" standards were efforts by several environmental groups—Union of Concerned Scientists, Natural Resources Defense Council, and Sierra Club. At the center of the effort, among others, was Dan Becker, who launched the Safe Climate Campaign in 2008 after directing the Sierra Club's Global Warming Program and serving as the first "green" co-chair of the Blue Green Alliance, which solidified union involvement in the environmental effort. Consumer Federation of America (CFA) and Consumers Union released new surveys showing that consumers supported higher fuel standards, and CFA disseminated a new analysis showing consumer pocketbook savings with these higher standards.

As the new requirements were debated, a reoccurring criticism, especially by car dealers, was that consumers would be forced to buy cars that they really did not want. In making this argument, the critics appealed to fears of overzealous government regulation and the imposed reduction of market choices. Regulators addressed this concern by basing standards on the size of the vehicle, thereby improving the fuel efficiency of each vehicle category but not forcing fuel efficiency conscious consumers to buy vehicles that did not meet their needs. Although some in the environmental movement feared this would open the door to larger, less fuel-efficient vehicles, CFA saw it as a compromise that respected consumer choice and that, in the long run, would result in significant increases in fuel efficiency across all vehicle types.

In August 2012, the Obama administration approved new CAFE standards requiring 54.5 mpg by 2025. Remarkably, thirteen of the fourteen major automakers selling in the United States agreed to the mandate. The only industry opposition came from car dealers who said they would not be able to sell the new fuel-efficient vehicles because of their higher prices.

Because Congress has limited NHTSA to setting standards for only a five-year period, there will be a midterm evaluation of the new standards by EPA and NHTSA in 2018. Advocacy groups are gathering data and working on arguments in support of the original plan of reaching 54.5 mpg by 2025. Increasing consumer demand for more fuel efficient vehicles could well play a major role in the outcome of the mid-term evaluation.

Jack Gillis

See also: Center for Auto Safety; Consumer Federation of America; Energy Advocacy

Further Reading

National Research Council, The National Academies. 2002. *Effectiveness and Impact of Corporate Average Fuel Economy (CAFE) Standards.* Washington, DC: National Academy Press.

Vlasic, Bill. 2012. "U.S. Sets Higher Fuel Efficiency Standards." *New York Times* (August 28).

Yacobucci, Brent et al. 2012. *Automobile and Truck Fuel Economy (CAFE) and Greenhouse Gas Standards.* Washington, DC: Congressional Research Service.

MOTOR VEHICLE SAFETY ADVOCACY

The emergence of the modern consumer movement in the 1960s is closely identified with advocacy related to motor vehicle safety. In 1965, Ralph Nader's book

318 MOTOR VEHICLE SAFETY ADVOCACY

Unsafe at Any Speed was published. It criticized automobile companies for knowingly designing unsafe vehicles and targeted General Motors' rear-engine Corvair as being particularly dangerous. The response of GM, which hired private detectives to investigate Nader, led to a March 1966 U.S. Senate hearing at which Nader's senator, Abraham Ribicoff (D-CT), demanded that GM's president apologize to Nader. Because of extensive press coverage of the event and issue, Nader became an instant consumer hero. He then helped initiate and institutionalize consumer advocacy on this issue that continues to the present day. This advocacy has made essential contributions to safety improvements that, in the past half-century, have saved hundreds of thousands of lives.

Nader is still known for his early leadership on motor vehicle safety issues, but since the 1970s, much of the national leadership on these issues has been taken by two organizations he established—Public Citizen and Center for Auto Safety—and two leaders he recruited—Joan Claybrook and Clarence Ditlow. Claybook, an attorney, ran Public Citizen's lobbying arm, Congress Watch, before being appointed by President Jimmy Carter to head the National Highway Traffic Safety Administration (NHTSA) in 1977. She then returned to Public Citizen in 1982 as president, a position she held until her retirement in 2009. Ditlow, who has worked closely with Claybrook since the early 1970s, was a leader of the Nader-inspired public interest research group before being appointed head of the Center for Auto Safety in 1975. Since then, Ditlow, with training in chemical engineering and two law degrees, has headed the center. Since the mid-1970s, both Claybrook and Ditlow have been the consumer advocates who have provided the most commentary to the press, and advice to Congress and regulators, about motor vehicle safety issues.

During this time, other individuals and organizations have also played important advocacy roles on these issues. William Haddon Jr., a physician, served as the first administrator of the newly created National Traffic Safety Agency and the National Highway Safety Agency, from 1966 to 1969, when he became president of the Insurance Institute for Highway Safety (IIHS), which he headed until his death in 1985. At the two new agencies, Dr. Haddon was responsible for setting the first federal safety standards for motor vehicles, and throughout his career, he effectively advocated for increased research on many highway safety issues, including crash-testing of vehicles, and for mandatory installment of airbags. He also developed a matrix—listing pre-crash and post-crash events on one side of the grid and vehicle, driver, and environment across the top—that is still used by safety professionals to organize their analysis of vehicle crashes. Haddon was succeeded as IIHS president by Brian O'Neill, who oversaw the development of crash testing at the organization's Vehicle Research Center, which opened in 1992. Since 2006, Adrian Lund has headed the organization. Since its founding in 1959, IIHS has been funded mainly by automobile insurers.

Since it was organized in 1936, Consumers Union/Consumer Reports (CU) has evaluated the safety of motor vehicles, with increasing effectiveness after it built a vehicle test track in the late 1980s. Particularly during the leadership of Executive Director Rhoda Karpatkin (1974–2001) and Technical Director David Pittle

(1982–2005), CU used its product safety expertise to publicize safety hazards, advise regulators, and communicate with Congress.

Since its founding in 1989, Advocates for Highway and Auto Safety has been a leading force in improving motor vehicle safety laws and regulations as well as state highway safety laws. From its inception until 2011, President Judith Stone led the organization, which represents a coalition of auto insurers and safety advocates. Consumer advocates who have served as board members—including Claybrook, Ditlow, and Jack Gillis—provided key support. Gillis, public affairs director of the Consumer Federation of America since the early 1980s, has also published thirty-three editions of *The Car Book* with the Center for Auto Safety. Recently, Claybrook has served as co-chair of Advocates, where she has worked closely with its current president and longtime collaborator, Jacqueline Gillan.

Nader's advocacy, GM's reaction, and the resulting public and congressional attention sparked enactment, in September 1966, of the National Traffic and Motor Vehicle Safety Act. This law created the first federal auto safety regulatory agency to set motor vehicle safety standards for new cars sold in the United States, to conduct research to support such standards, and to oversee vehicle safety defects about which manufacturers were required to notify vehicle owners. Officially named the National Highway Traffic Safety Administration in 1970, the agency was authorized to make grants to states to help fund state highway safety programs. The new law also required the agency to issue safety performance standards for vehicle crash worthiness, including vehicle design.

In the late 1960s, under Haddon's leadership, the agency issued dozens of federal motor vehicle safety standards, ranging from dual braking systems to collapsible steering columns to side impact protection. During the early 1970s, the agency designed a program to develop new small car experimental safety vehicles. This program was responsible for models with improved safety levels that, as of 2014, NHTSA still has not required new vehicles to meet.

In 1970, NHTSA issued a vehicle safety standard for air bags to protect vehicle occupants in frontal crashes. These nylon bag-shaped devices, which inflated automatically, were intended to complement safety belts, not supplant them. Although GM accepted the standard, announcing that all GM cars would be equipped with air bags by 1975, Ford Motor Company resisted. Its leaders persuaded President Richard Nixon to revoke the air bag standard and instead require that all cars, beginning with 1974 models, be equipped with safety belts and shoulder straps that must be hooked for the car to start. Because of public resistance to this constraint on drivers, Congress revoked the requirement and vetoed any future rule requiring vehicles to be equipped with air bags.

In the late 1970s, during the presidency of Jimmy Carter, when Joan Claybrook was administrator of NHTSA, the agency became much more active. It issued a number of new safety standards related to antilock brakes for large trucks, bumper strength, the comfort and convenience of safety belts, child restraint crashworthiness, and, for pickup trucks, standards that already applied to cars, including dual braking and collapsible steering assemblies. NHTSA also issued a revised safety performance standard for installation of automatic crash protection that required occupant protection with air bags or automatic safety belts. The standard was to take effect over a three-year period. Although both automobile companies and public interest groups sued NHTSA—the companies to postpone the rule and the citizen groups to have it take effect more quickly—the agency won in the U.S. Court of Appeals. Attempts in Congress to overrule the air bag standard did not succeed.

In this period, NHTSA also increased its investigations and actions against individual auto companies. The agency successfully sued Firestone over a safety defect in production of all its tires from 1974 to 1977, forcing the company to recall more than 8 million of these tires in use. It also began an investigation of Ford Motor Company vehicles that jumped from park to reverse. Although Ford persuaded the Secretary of Transportation to prohibit NHTSA from requiring a recall—shortly before the 1980 presidential election—the agency put related documents into the public docket, which made it easier for individual consumers to sue for relief. In the late 1970s, the agency also acted to resolve a huge backlog of safety defect investigations. Its efforts to develop enforcement actions or close out the cases persuaded some auto companies to initiate recalls to avoid penalties. In 1977 alone, the companies recalled 12 million cars.

In 1978, NHTSA began crash testing new cars to evaluate their safety characteristics. (In 2000, at the direction of Congress, the agency added a test for rollover risk. Then in 2005, Congress required the agency to place crash test results on new car price stickers.) To help ensure that this information reached consumers, NHTSA created *The Car Book*, which it announced on the Phil Donahue television show in 1980. This announcement and other media coverage generated requests for 450,000 copies of the book. When the administration of President Ronald Reagan decided not to publish *The Car Book*, the NHTSA staffer who managed the project, Jack Gillis, resigned from the agency and began publishing it himself with the Center for Auto Safety.

With one major exception, the administrations of President Reagan and President George Bush did little to improve motor vehicle safety. In the eight Reagan years, only one safety standard—for a high-mounted brake lamp—was issued. And in the four Bush years, the only standards issued were to require pickup trucks and SUVs to meet the same standards as cars. In fact, during the Reagan administration, a new regulatory council headed by Vice President Bush issued a report—Actions to Help Detroit—that led NHTSA to revoke the safety standard covering air bags and other standards, including improved fields of view. The revocation of the air bag standard was challenged by a lawsuit against the Department of Transportation filed by the State Farm Insurance Company with the support of other auto insurers and consumer and safety organizations. The court of appeals ruled in favor of State Farm in a decision upheld by the U.S. Supreme Court, which instructed the Department of Transportation to reconsider the rule in light of the court's decision.

Despite opposition from automobile companies, in 1984 the new secretary of transportation, Elizabeth Dole, reissued the rule with a caveat that made the rule palatable to the White House. Automatic restraints would be installed over a three-year period beginning with 1988 models, but if by April 1989 states approved effective mandatory seat belt use covering two-thirds of the U.S. population, the rule would be suspended. This possibility motivated auto companies to work hard to persuade states to pass seat belt laws, and they might have succeeded in meeting the two-thirds requirement if not for a countermove by insurers and safety advocates. At the suggestion of Michael Sohn, a State Farm attorney at the Arnold and Porter Law firm, consumer and safety groups persuaded Willie Brown, speaker of the California House, to pass a seat belt use law that would be automatically revoked if California's population were counted to revoke the automatic restraint rule. When the automobile companies could not persuade enough remaining states to pass laws, the air bag rule was retained. Yet the safety belt laws now existed in many states, providing protections complementing those of air bags. In 1991, consumer and safety groups persuaded Congress to require air bags in cars and light trucks, on both the driver and passenger sides, to be phased in for these vehicles by 1997 models.

Several years later, a major air bag controversy arose. When manufacturers began installing passenger side air bags in 1994, reports surfaced of serious safety risks to small children and infants. That problem—which NHTSA had informed manufacturers how to avoid back in 1980—was addressed by Congress when in 1988 it enacted a law requiring new air bag tests for different-sized occupants. Also, there was a joint effort by auto companies, insurers, and safety advocates to urge families to place children under age 9 in the back seat.

In 2000, a serious tire-related safety hazard was uncovered. Anna Werner, at the CBS-affiliate in Houston, reported that Ford Explorers with Firestone tires had experienced more than twenty serious rollover crashes resulting from exploding tires. When NHTSA opened an investigation, Ford resisted providing information. But when later in the year, Werner reported that Firestone had recalled the same tires in Saudi Arabia because of explosion complaints, Ford forced the tire company to recall millions of tires. Joan Claybrook, who had earlier been interviewed by Werner, joined with Arkansas trial lawyer Tab Turner in calling for additional Firestone tires to be recalled and for improvements to the rollover-prone Explorer. They also asked Congress to hold hearings and pass legislation that would require a rollover prevention standard and criminal penalties for companies that knowingly and willingly sold unsafe defective products. Congress then enacted legislation that contained no new criminal penalties but that did require increased civil penalties, new car rollover tests, new dashboard information about tire inflation, and Early Warning Reports by make and model provided by automobile and parts manufacturers to NHTSA when the companies received claims about related injuries or fatalities. When the Bush administration refused to make these reports public, Public Citizen used litigation to force NHTSA to release some of the data.

Rollover crash deaths, however, continued to mount in number and, by 2005, exceeded 10,000 annually. In response, Public Citizen and Advocates for Highway and Auto Safety urged Congress to enact legislation that would require NHTSA to issue new standards for rollover prevention and crash worthiness. Senator John McCain (R-AZ) first introduced the bill. After he left the Senate Commerce

Committee, Senator Trent Lott (R-MS) took leadership of this legislation and guided it to passage. However, a NHTSA led by appointees of President George W. Bush issued only minimal standards to comply with most requirements of the new law, although it did establish a safety standard requiring a dynamic side impact test that forced manufacturers to install side impact air bags. The agency also issued an electronic stability control rule designed to prevent rollovers after being urged to do so by suppliers of the new system.

During the administration of President Barack Obama, new auto safety problems surfaced. After reports of sudden acceleration in many Toyota models, consumer advocates called for Congress and NHTSA to address the threat. Yet, despite hearings and an investigation, neither body acted. Although Toyota did retrofit a brake override system in many of its vehicles, it blamed a rogue floor mat for much of the problem. A class action lawsuit against Toyota, still in process as of late 2014, forced Toyota to reveal problems with the electronic systems—problems it had previously denied.

Receiving even more public attention has been the very recent disclosure of defective ignition switches in Saturn Ions and Cobalts made by GM. Jostled by a driver's knee or heavy set of keys, these switches could turn off power steering, power braking, and air bag inflation systems. The controversy was fueled by evidence, uncovered by the Center for Auto Safety and major media outlets, that GM had covered up the problem. Congressional hearings confirmed the cover-up and faulted NHTSA for failing to investigate related complaints. As of August 2014, legislation supported by consumer advocates to require NHTSA to take steps that would help prevent future mistakes, and also to be more transparent, was being considered by Congress.

During both Republican and Democratic administrations, consumer and safety advocates have faulted NHTSA for not aggressively enforcing existing safety laws and for failing to issue timely new safety standards. Nevertheless, pushed by these advocates over the past half-century, federal legislators and regulators have approved numerous measures that have contributed substantially to dramatic improvements in driving safety. From 1966 to 2012, the number of annual motor vehicle fatalities declined from more than 50,000 to fewer than 34,000. Equally significant, the fatality rate per mile driven has declined by nearly 80 percent.

Joan Claybrook

See also: Advocates for Highway and Auto Safety; Center for Auto Safety; Consumers for Auto Reliability and Safety; Product Safety "Victim" Activism

Further Reading

Claybrook, Joan and David Bollier. 1985. "The Hidden Benefits of Regulation: Disclosing the Auto Safety Payoff." *Yale Journal of Regulation* 3-1 (fall): 87–132.

Coniff, Ruth. 1999. "Joan Claybrook, Consumer Advocate." *The Progressive* (March).

Jensen, Christopher. 1988. "This Man Gives the Auto Industry Nightmares." *Plain Dealer* (July): D-1.

Nader, Ralph. 1965. *Unsafe at Any Speed: The Designed-in Dangers of the American Automobile*. New York: Grossman Publishers.

NADER, RALPH (1934–)

It is hard to imagine the rise of the modern consumer movement without the leadership, resourcefulness, and sheer persistence of Ralph Nader, a self-described "public citizen" who has been at the forefront of scores of progressive campaigns over the past fifty years.

Born in Winsted, Connecticut, and educated at Princeton University and Harvard Law School, Nader first gained national attention in 1965 as the 31-year-old author of *Unsafe at Any Speed*. The book indicted unsafe automobile design in general, and General Motors' Corvair in particular. When it became publicly known that General Motors had hired private detectives in an attempt to dig up information that might discredit Nader, a Senate subcommittee looking into auto safety summoned the president of General Motors to explain his company's harassment and personally apologize to Nader.

This incident catapulted auto safety into the public spotlight, leading to a series of landmark laws that have prevented hundreds of thousands of motor vehicle–related deaths and injuries. The episode also certified Nader in the public mind as the fierce, incorruptible advocate for the "little guy," a reputation that he has parlayed into one of the most influential careers in American politics. Without ever holding public office, Nader has used his considerable talents as an organizer, activist, legal analyst, and pamphleteer to rally public opinion to help push through dozens of reforms in business, government, and various professions.

The range of issues that Nader has addressed is broad, including consumer protection, congressional reform, openness in government, nuclear power safety, defense of the civil justice system, renewable energy, food and drug safety, air and water pollution, fair taxation, product liability protection, union democracy, and government procurement, as well as consumer reforms in insurance, banking, pension law, and telecommunications. Nader has even sponsored consumer initiatives to reform university governance, educational testing, daily newspapers, women's health care, legal services, and professional sports.

More than anyone, Nader transformed "consumerism" into a movement that could effectively counter the power wielded by business in the marketplace and by government policymakers. Before 1965, most consumer reforms were prompted by tragedy and sporadic congressional leadership. They were rarely instigated by consumers themselves. Nader's leadership gave the consumer movement a proactive, visionary dimension. Through a process that he once described as "documenting your intuition," Nader spent the latter half of the 1960s investigating a host of abuses against individuals by American business and government. His

Nader Reports spurred passage of new laws addressing unsanitary conditions in meatpacking and poultry production, the danger of natural gas pipelines, radiation emissions from television sets and x-rays, and hazardous working conditions in coal mines and other industrial workplaces.

To expand his efforts, Nader recruited a task force of law students to investigate the Federal Trade Commission (FTC), the agency charged by Congress with protecting consumers from shoddy products, fraudulent business practices, and deceptive advertising. The team's report, released in 1968 (and published commercially two years later), found the FTC "fat with cronyism, torpid through an inbreeding unusual even for Washington, manipulated by the agents of commercial predators [and] impervious to governmental and citizen monitoring." It sparked a congressional investigation and a major overhaul of the FTC. It also produced admiring publicity for the citizen-investigators, burnishing Nader's public image even further.

After this success, Nader hired several dozen undergraduate and law students in the summer of 1969 to investigate a still-wider array of government and corporate abuses—incompetence and corruption at the now defunct Interstate Commerce Commission, the health hazards of air pollution and pesticides, and the Food and Drug Administration's lax oversight of the food industry, among other abuses. In 1970, according to Nader's Center for Study of Responsive Law, more than 30,000 students—and one-third of the Harvard Law School—applied for 200 summer jobs that Nader created from the proceeds of his publishing and paid appearances. Journalist William Greider, then a *Washington Post* reporter, dubbed the crusading students "Nader's Raiders," and the moniker stuck.

In subsequent summers, new "raids" were launched against the nation's worsening water pollution; the secrecy, conflicts of interest, and concentration of power at First National City Bank (now Citibank); the indignities and frauds practiced by nursing homes; the dangerous use of pesticides on agricultural crops; and the despoliation of land in California by developers and speculators. By 1972, seventeen Nader books had been published.

Unlike muckrakers of the early 1900s who unmasked scandal then moved on, Nader wanted to experiment with new strategies of citizen action and to establish organizations that could empower ordinary consumers. His ambition was to reinvigorate the possibilities of citizenship in a modern society dominated by institutional giants—multinational corporations, government bureaucracies, labor unions, bar associations, and universities.

Nader's chief vehicle for advancing his reform agenda was the citizen advocacy group—modestly funded organizations of a few researchers and attorneys who investigate a given field, publish reports, organize citizens and other allies, lobby Congress, petition regulatory agencies, and litigate in court. For his Washington, D.C., headquarters, the Center for Study of Responsive Law, Nader has provided the moral leadership, political and legal advice, and seed financial support for a sprawling network of more than four dozen groups that he has founded. Although most of them are now formally independent of Nader, they frequently collaborate as the occasion arises. Perhaps the most significant of Nader's institutional creations is Public Citizen, a membership organization founded in 1972 that now consists of five quasiautonomous groups: Congress Watch, the Health Research Group, the Litigation Group, the Energy Program, and Global Trade Watch.

A few recurrent themes tend to animate most of Nader's campaigns. The first is challenging the "seller-sovereign" economy with a "consumer-side" vision. Nader has believed that a "seller-sovereign" marketplace, unchecked by meaningful mechanisms of accountability, naturally tends to generate anticonsumer abuses ranging from price-fixed products and services to deceptive packaging to unsafe products to overselling credit and insurance. These insights prompted Nader, in 1970, to launch a nine-member task force of law students to document the concentration of corporate power in America and its anticompetitive effects. This research has been followed by campaigns against the legal profession's price fixing and ban on advertising, the anticompetitive effects of industry standard-setting groups, the territorial monopolies of beer brewers, and the special antitrust exemption that allows two newspapers in a single city to share facilities, among other anticompetitive practices.

To help stimulate competition in the marketplace, Nader also sought to generate greater quantities of reliable consumer information about products and services. The consumer movement has won mandatory disclosures related to diverse issues including car safety, appliance energy efficiency, loan costs, prescription drug risks, and constituents of food products.

When economic regulation of markets has artificially limited competition, Nader has vigorously supported deregulation. His advocacy played a role in the deregulation of the trucking and airline industries in the late 1970s, for example. However, Nader has always opposed lax antitrust enforcement and deregulation of health, safety, and environmental protections.

Because government subsidies can inflate prices and retard innovation in the marketplace, Nader has been a staunch critic of various government subsidy programs—for nuclear power, supersonic jets, agribusiness interests, synthetic fuels development, and dozens of obscure tax subsidies. To gain greater influence over corporate decision making, in the 1970s Nader sought to secure formal consumer representation in corporate governance. "Project GM" agitated for three seats for public representatives on the company's board of directors. Although the effort failed, it did illustrate the value of mounting dissident shareholder campaigns, a tactic later adopted by dozens of other citizen advocates. The 1976 book by Nader, Green, and Seligman, *The Taming of the Giant Corporation*, was Nader's most ambitious effort to achieve greater public accountability in corporate governance through federal chartering of large corporations.

In the 1970s, Nader was one of the leading champions of consumer cooperatives as a way to assert greater consumer autonomy in the marketplace. When the co-op movement did not achieve the heights that Nader envisioned for it, he modified his tactics by promoting "group buying" experiments that aggregated consumer purchasing power without the organizational overhead of a co-op. One such Nader-launched innovation, Buyers Up, a purchasing organization for home heating oil, served consumers in several East Coast cities.

In the 1990s, Nader applied the lessons of group buying to the nation's largest consumer, the federal government, to the benefit of consumers. Nader persuaded the U.S. General Services Administration (GSA) to ask automobile manufacturers to respond to a bid request for 5,000 automobiles equipped with airbags, which would be an addition to the federal government's fleet of cars. The GSA decision was instrumental in finally convincing automakers to offer airbags in automobiles.

A second theme in Nader's campaigns has been developing new mechanisms to foster government accountability. Nader's original campaigns against corporate abuses in the marketplace usually called on government to pass legislation or issue regulations. But Nader's groups found that corporate abuses were often ignored or even defended by legislators and regulators representing big business interests. Accordingly, Nader launched a series of initiatives to ensure that the procedures of the democratic process—in Congress, the executive branch, and the judiciary— were open to public scrutiny and not corrupted by influence-peddling and conflicts of interest.

The first major crusade to reform government was the Congress Project, a 1971 attempt by hundreds of college students to profile every member of Congress and six key congressional committees. The project exposed the little-known world of "protocol, alcohol, and Geritol" to an American public that barely knew how Congress operated. A subsequent book based on the research—*Who Runs Congress?*— eventually went through four different editions and a print run of more than 1 million copies, making it the best-selling book ever written about Congress.

The Congress Project, soon institutionalized as Congress Watch, advocated "sunshine laws" that opened up congressional committees to the public and new procedural reforms that weakened the power of entrenched committee chairpersons. Over the past two decades, Nader and Congress Watch have been leading advocates for campaign finance reform, ethics reforms, and bans on lobbyist-paid gifts and travel. Nader has also waged highly vocal campaigns against congressional pay raises.

Within the executive branch, Nader repeatedly sought to ensure the integrity of decision making by prohibiting secret deliberations, the withholding of public documents, and the stacking of advisory panels with industry representatives. Nader forces played a critical role in winning passage of the landmark 1974 amendments to the Freedom of Information Act, which has been an important tool for rooting out waste, abuse, and other wrongdoing in government and industry.

A widespread practice that Nader and his associates have fought is the private taking of what Nader calls "taxpayer assets"—federally owned forests, minerals, grazing lands, waterways, coastal lands, airwaves used for television and radio, and government-generated research and information. Over the years, Nader and his associates have documented these "private takings" in the development of California lands, the exploitation of Alaska's natural wealth, the commercialization of basic drug research, the "privatization" of government databases, and the commercialization of the public's airwaves.

A third focus of Nader's campaigns has been to mobilize the energies of key constituencies to serve a public interest agenda. One example is Nader's influence on American journalism, whose watchdog capacities Nader has repeatedly sought to invigorate. His groups' research and reports have acted as agenda setters for reporters, suggesting fruitful lines of inquiry and promising sources. His influence has also been felt through the Nader-founded Capitol Hill News Service, which in the early 1970s pioneered investigative reporting about Congress. By founding the Freedom of Information Clearinghouse, Nader also tried to educate journalists about how they can obtain government documents under the Freedom of Information Act, providing litigation support when necessary.

In the legal profession, Nader has mobilized plaintiff's attorneys to form Trial Lawyers for Public Justice in order to advocate legal reforms. Nader has also been a leading champion of public interest law, securing various new funding mechanisms to support such advocacy and exhorting a generation of law students to pursue such jobs. To help spur the idealism of young people, over the years he helped found a network of student-run public interest research groups (PIRGs) on college campuses. Some PIRGs, such as New York PIRG, have been major forces in their states for consumer and environmental reforms.

Nader's crusades range from the local to the global. In Elmhurst, Illinois, and in his hometown of Winsted, Connecticut, a foundation he helped launch retained a "Community Lawyer" in 1990 to help citizens exercise their rights and participate in local government. In 1988, he spearheaded a campaign for California auto insurance reform that resulted in the passage of Proposition 103, which introduced greater regulation of consumer products, prohibited anticompetitive industry practices, and, according to an analysis by the Consumer Federation of America, has saved California consumers $100 billion through 2013. Nader has also promoted citizen activism abroad especially in less-developed countries. His monthly magazine *The Multinational Monitor*, founded in 1980, has been a unique source of investigative reporting about international corporate behavior. In 1990, Nader encouraged activists to oppose GATT (General Agreement on Tariffs and Trade) negotiations, which he felt would degrade consumer and environmental protections, undermine democratic processes, and give multinational companies undue influence in Third World markets.

During the past two decades, Nader has perhaps been most widely known for running for president of the United States four times. Yet he continues to work out of his office at the Center for Study of Responsive Law, with the help of a small, dedicated staff, writing articles and books and initiating citizen campaigns that continue to include a consumer focus. Recent articles he penned criticized the "wild and cruel gap between debtors and creditors" and explained the many ways the Canadian health care system was superior to "Obamacare." Nader also initiated, through his Princeton class of 1955 and Harvard Law School class of 1958, alumni-supported public interest groups as models for older alumni at universities and law schools.

The legacy that Nader has achieved over several decades of advocacy has been considerable. It can be seen in entirely new bodies of legislation and case law, dozens of new governmental programs designed to protect the public, industries that are more competitive and innovative, and far more plentiful consumer-oriented information. He has also helped bring into being a national network of activists and supporters, whose careers, strategies, and ideals he has strongly influenced. To a great extent, many of these contributions have been so integrated into American society and culture that they are now taken for granted.

David Bollier, Stephen Brobeck

See also: Air Travel Advocacy; Center for Auto Safety; Motor Vehicle Safety Advocacy; National Insurance Consumer Organization; Public Citizen; Public Interest Research Groups; Telecommunications Research and Action Center

Further Reading

Bollier, David. 1991. *Citizen Action and Other Big Ideas*. Washington, DC: Center for Study of Responsive Law.
Cox, Edward, et al. 1970. *The Nader Report on the Federal Trade Commission*. New York: Grove Press.
Gorey, Hays. 1975. *Nader and the Power of Everyman*. New York: Grosset & Dunlap.
Green, Mark J., et al. 1972. *Who Runs Congress?* New York: Bantam Books.
McCarry, Charles. 1972. *Citizen Nader*. New York: Saturday Review Press.
Martin, Justin. 2002. *Nader: Crusader, Spoiler, Icon*. New York: Basic Books.
Nader, Ralph, et al. 1977. *Taming the Giant Corporation*. New York: WW Norton & Company.
Nader, Ralph. 1965. *Unsafe at Any Speed: The Designed-in Dangers of the American Automobile*. New York: Grossman.

NATIONAL ASSOCIATION OF CONSUMER ADVOCATES

The National Association of Consumer Advocates (NACA) is a national 501(c)(6) nonprofit association of attorneys and consumer advocates committed to representing the interests of consumers, especially those of modest means. The organization's mission is to promote justice for all consumers by maintaining a forum for communication, networking, and information sharing among consumer advocates, particularly regarding legal issues, and by serving as a voice for its members and consumers, especially to public policymakers.

NACA's story begins with the War on Poverty and the creation of the federally funded Legal Services Corporation (LSC). In its early years, LSC helped fund legal aid attorneys, most of whom were strongly committed to making the country a more fair and just place for all residents. These attorneys, acting as both traditional lawyers as well as community organizers, fought for reforms in areas such as health care and public benefits, migrant and worker rights, fair and safe housing, tenants rights as well as consumer protection.

As part of this reform era, with legal aid lawyers playing a leading role, Congress and state legislatures approved statutory federal and consumer protection laws. From state Unfair Deceptive Acts and Practices (UDAP) statutes to the Consumer Credit Protection Act of 1968, laws were created not only to protect consumers, but also to give them the power to protect themselves through their own private enforcement.

With legal support from the National Consumer Law Center (NCLC), which was created in 1973, legal aid attorneys used these new laws to try to both provide redress and end abuses against individual consumers and groups of consumers. These lawsuits not only helped stop bad business practices, but also provided a new source of organizational funding through the awarding of attorneys' fees under the fee shifting provisions included in the new statutes. This success, which required a substantial level of expertise, spurred the development of a new, specialized practice of consumer protection law.

With this successful effort to protect consumers came a substantial corporate backlash. During the Reagan administration of the 1980s, LSC funding was reduced substantially, leading to closed legal aid offices, attorney layoffs, and a significant reduction in services, particularly consumer protection litigation. Then, in the 1990s as part of Republican efforts to reduce the size and influence of the federal government, Congress approved further reductions in support for, and further restrictions on, legal services. Federal funding for legal aid support centers, including NCLC, was completely eliminated. New restrictions included limitations on the ability of traditional legal aid programs to collect attorneys' fees and to bring class action lawsuits.

These cuts and restrictions led to a slow but steady exodus of consumer protection lawyers from legal aid programs. With their knowledge and experience, and the litigation support of NCLC, some of the more entrepreneurial attorneys set out to become the first private attorneys in the United States to specialize in consumer protection law. In late 1994, with NCLC's federal funding eliminated and its existence threatened, a group of twelve of the most successful consumer lawyers created an organization, NACA, to provide support for the now federally defunded NCLC and for any and all attorneys interested in practicing consumer protection law.

Today, about 1,800 attorneys and other consumer advocates belong to NACA, which is governed by a twelve-person board. Since 2001, the organization has been led by executive director and general counsel Ira Rheingold. Before joining NACA, Rheingold served for many years as a legal aid attorney, first at the Legal Aid Bureau of Maryland, where he specialized in homeless, public benefits, and public housing issues, then at the Legal Assistance Foundation of Chicago, where he created the Foreclosure Prevention and Senior Housing Law Projects.

The organization has an annual operating budget of approximately $1.2 million, almost all of which comes from members through dues, donations, conference registrations, and *cy près* awards. To work toward economic and legal justice systems that treat all consumers with dignity, respect, and fairness, NACA not only assists members in their work as traditional consumer attorneys, but also organizes these members and their clients into a community that speaks to policymakers about consumer problems and the need for marketplace and legal reform.

NACA provides substantive, practical, and entrepreneurial resources to its members. These resources include specialty forums where advocates share the latest courtroom and business strategies, case law, and regulatory updates; almost weekly webinars on various aspects of consumer protection law; and annual in-person conferences. Its "Standards and Guidelines for Litigating and Settling Consumer

Class Actions" provides guidance to all attorneys about the ethical prosecution, defense, and settlement of class action cases. Furthermore, NACA offers mentorship opportunities for new attorneys and has begun a systematic outreach to law schools to inform students about the psychic and financial rewards of a career dedicated to fighting for consumer justice.

NACA uses the knowledge gained by members in their representation of consumer clients to challenge unfair and deceptive corporate practices in areas including debt collection, credit reporting, mortgage origination and servicing, auto sales and repossessions, and usurious small dollar lending. The organization shares this knowledge and insight—especially consumer "horror stories"—with local and national media, regulators, and legislators, which has allowed the group to be a leader in the fight against predatory financial services practices.

Over the past two decades, NACA has worked on dozens of policy issues involving unfair and deceptive practices, often in collaboration with other consumer organizations. Examples of its work include: helping to draft legislation that provided consumers protection against the purchase of rebuilt wrecked or severely damaged cars and then working successfully to defeat legislation that would have allowed such cars to continue to be sold, helping draft mortgage origination and servicing guidelines that later became part of the Dodd–Frank Act (which included a ban on forced arbitration in mortgage contracts), and playing a lead role in founding and coordinating the "Fair Arbitration Now" coalition, an effort that joined consumer, civil, and employment rights organizations in a campaign to end the use of forced arbitration clauses in contracts imposed by corporations on consumers and employees.

Ira Rheingold

See also: Litigation; National Consumer Law Center

Further Reading

National Association of Consumer Advocates. www.naca.net.

NATIONAL CONSUMER LAW CENTER

The National Consumer Law Center (NCLC) is the most active nonprofit organization seeking to advance the interests of low-income consumers on pocketbook issues. It is best known for its advocacy, research, litigation, and treatises on consumer law. The organization also serves as the hub of a community of lawyers practicing consumer law, providing this community with information and networking opportunities, particularly at its annual National Consumer Rights Litigation Conference. It is located in Boston, with an office in Washington, D.C., and associated experts elsewhere in the country.

NCLC's advocacy has focused on subjects ranging from insurance and warranties to housing and access to markets. The primary emphasis over the years, however, has been consumer credit, debt and finance problems, deceptive practices, and the affordability of necessities such as home heat, telephone, and utility services.

NCLC was founded in 1969 at the Boston College School of Law. Professor William Willier, a commercial law professor and consumer advocate, was the motivating force in getting the center started, with the active support of the law school's dean and future congressman, Father Robert Drinan. The group's first executive director was Richard Hesse, formerly a legal services attorney in New Jersey and later a professor of law. During his tenure, NCLC established itself as a national representative of the interests of low-income consumers.

In 1975, Mark Budnitz succeeded Hesse. Budnitz left the clinical law program at Boston University School of Law to join the center, where he had previously served as litigation director. During his tenure, the organization expanded its advocacy into areas of energy law and policy. In 1979, Robert Sable succeeded him. Sable was former civil director of the Cleveland Legal Aid Society, then served as deputy director of NCLC. During his tenure, the center expanded its publications and diversified its funding base.

The current executive director, Willard Ogburn, replaced Sable in 1987. Ogburn had previously worked for the Congressional Legislative Reference Service, in the Office of Management and Budget in the Executive Office of the President, as Massachusetts deputy commissioner of banking, and as a legal services attorney in Cleveland. Under his leadership, the center has grown considerably, created a consumer law movement, and increased its influence on public consumer protection policies.

The NCLC board has included many distinguished members, including a U.S. senator, a future federal judge, a state solicitor general, and the president of the American Bar Association. However, throughout its history, the strength of NCLC has mainly been its staff of experienced legal experts. Some of the longer-serving specialists include Robert Hobbs, consumer credit and debt; Jonathan Sheldon, deceptive practices, credit regulation, and publications; Margot F. Saunders, consumer credit and utility regulation; Charles Hill, utility regulation and services; Ernest Sarason, consumer credit; Kathleen Keest, usury and credit regulation; Carolyn Carter, financial services and credit regulation; Mark Leymaster, usury and credit practices; John Rao, bankruptcy and mortgages; Chi Chi Wu, credit reporting and tax services; Elizabeth Renuart, consumer credit regulation; Stuart Rossman, litigation; Deanne Loonin, student loans, vocational education; Charlie Harak, energy policy and utility regulation; Margaret Rigg, warranties and taxation issues facing low-income Americans; John Howat, energy policy and policy analysis; Olivia Wein, energy, telecom, and utilities; and Alys Cohen, federal consumer finance policies.

Initial funding for NCLC was provided by the Federal Office of Economic Opportunity (OEO) as part of the nation's War on Poverty. OEO was then funding new legal services neighborhood organizations to help ensure that low-income Americans had access to lawyers and the ability to protect and assert their rights in court and in public affairs. To support and complement the work of local legal services offices, OEO funded a small number of national backup centers, beginning with the Center on Social Welfare Policy and Law at Columbia University School of Law and followed shortly by other centers including the National Housing Law

Project at Boalt Hall, Berkeley, the Center for Law and Education at Harvard Law School, and the National Consumer Law Center at Boston College School of Law. Since then, NCLC has worked closely with legal service programs that now serve all parts of the country.

In 1973, NCLC separated from Boston College for financial reasons, incorporated as a 501(c)(3) nonprofit organization, and moved into space in downtown Boston. Today, NCLC owns its own historic building in Boston's financial district.

Through 1995, the largest single source of financial support was OEO funding and funding from one of its successors, the Federal Legal Services Corporation. Since then, only a very small portion of NCLC's annual budget—which in recent years has been more than $8 million—has come from public funds, including short-term contracts with federal and state agencies such as the U.S. Department of Justice and state attorneys general. Nongovernment funding sources include foundations, donors, court awarded attorneys' fees, other court-awarded funds, publications, conferences, training events, and the provision of services such as expert witness testimony and program design.

Many consumer protections in state and federal law reflect NCLC expertise or advocacy. Shortly after its founding, the organization successfully challenged an industry-financed effort to reshape state credit laws. The National Conference on Uniform State Laws, using industry funds, drafted and proposed a Uniform Consumer Credit Code (UCCC) for adoption by each state that contained many provisions detrimental to consumers. In response, NCLC drafted a National Consumer Act and, later, a Model Consumer Credit Act, and also joined with local advocates to oppose adoption of the code unless it was amended. As a result, the code was withdrawn and revised to include many improvements recommended by the center. In years following, the National Consumer Act and the Model Consumer Credit Act served as models for state law provisions. Today, NCLC's Model Family Financial Protection Act serves as a basis for reforming and modernizing state consumer protections.

Most major federal consumer financial protection laws adopted since the center's founding also have been influenced by the expertise of its staff and their policy proposals. In the late 1970s, the Truth in Lending Act, the Fair Credit Reporting Act, the Fair Debt Collection Practices Act, and the Bankruptcy Reform Act included concepts and language submitted by NCLC. NCLC's Model Consumer Credit Act, introduced as a federal bill by Senator William Proxmire (D-WI), helped shaped many of these laws. More recently, the Home Ownership and Equity Protection Act of 1994, the Credit CARD Act of 2009, and the Wall Street Reform and Consumer Protection Act of 2010 contained recommendations from NCLC, such as the latter legislation's limits on the ability of financial institutions to use pre-emption to undermine or ignore state consumer protection laws.

In addition to helping shape laws, NCLC undertakes litigation, including participation in groundbreaking cases before federal and state courts, including the U.S. Supreme Court. The cases have established constitutional due process rights of consumers, especially debtors; expanded standards of deception and unfairness; secured appropriate interpretations of consumer protection laws; and caused hundreds of millions of dollars of illegal overcharges by oil companies to be set aside for the benefit of low-income households. For example, in the center's first decade or so, the organization participated in a series of cases before the U.S. Supreme Court—*Swarb v. Lennox, Fuentes v. Shevin, Memphis Light, Gas & Water Division v. Craft*—that secured fundamental due process rights for consumers, such as being served with a complaint and being represented in court. More recently, as co-counsel in national class action cases under the Equal Credit Opportunity Act, NCLC succeeded in curbing large auto loan markups to African American and Hispanic customers. And in another case, NCLC and a team of lawyers successfully challenged reporting by the three major credit bureaus of debts discharged in bankruptcy as debts still owed.

The center has also participated extensively in federal and state agency rulemaking. For example, it was the most effective public interest group in influencing the many regulations issued by the Federal Reserve Board related to the Truth in Lending Act. It helped shape the Federal Trade Commission's Credit Practices Rule, as a compensated FTC Public Advocate, by presenting 180 witnesses and cross-examining 200 other witnesses in a series of hearings held in several cities. Moreover, it was instrumental in creating, fostering, and helping implement "percentage of income payment plans" issued by state public service commissions.

Much of NCLC's advocacy is based on investigative reports or public policy analyses addressing particular industry practices, emerging consumer problems, or the unfair treatment of distressed households. This research is often reported on by the national press and used by policymakers. Some of the most influential publications include a series of reports analyzing the harmful effects of energy and utility costs on low-income households, which focused greater industry and public policy attention on the issue; a study of the financing of home improvement scams and second mortgage abuses, which influenced the Home Ownership and Equity Protection Act of 1994; an investigative report of financial scams aimed at military personnel and veterans, which helped persuade Congress to pass the Military Lending Act that capped interest rates on high-cost loans at 36 percent; and a report identifying the junk fees and restrictions that states allowed on unemployment compensation delivered on bank debit cards, which generated state reforms.

Perhaps the most lasting impact of NCLC activism has been the creation of a community of lawyers in all parts of the country who practice consumer law. Before the founding of modern legal services for the poor, perhaps only a dozen lawyers practiced consumer law for a living. In the 1970s, NCLC trained and assisted a growing number of consumer lawyers in public service. In 1992, the organization started supporting and seeking to increase the number of private consumer lawyers. A year later, it incorporated the National Association of Consumer Advocates (NACA), a membership organization of practicing consumer lawyers. Today, several thousand attorneys make a living representing aggrieved consumers. NCLC supports these attorneys by organizing a annual Consumer Rights Litigation Conference, annually presenting a Vern Countryman Consumer Law Award, organizing dozens of training events each year, serving as co-counsel in important cases, and encouraging communication among these legal practitioners.

An important NCLC service to consumer attorneys is a series of comprehensive consumer law practice manuals that it prepares and publishes. The organization's twenty-volume Consumer Credit and Sales Practice Series is a widely used collection of practice materials on topics ranging from unfair deceptive acts and practices and credit reporting to student loan law, fair debt collection, and foreclosures. These manuals cover not just federal law, but also the laws of all fifty states and the District of Columbia, including all relevant laws, regulations, agency interpretations, and case law. They are often cited by courts, including the U.S. Supreme Court.

Willard Ogburn

See also: Litigation; National Association of Consumer Advocates

Further Reading

National Consumer Law Center. Consumer Credit and Sales Practice Series (20 titles).
Rothschild, Donald P., and David W. Carroll. 1977. *Consumer Protection: Text and Materials.*
   Cincinnati, OH: Anderson Publishing Co.

NATIONAL CONSUMERS LEAGUE

The National Consumers League (NCL) is America's first national consumer and worker advocacy organization. It was founded in 1899 by leaders of consumer leagues in New York City, Philadelphia, Boston, and Chicago who believed that consumers had the ability and obligation to raise the living standards of the disadvantaged, especially women and child workers. Today, as a 501(c)(3) organization headquartered in Washington, D.C., NCL continues to focus on worker issues and also on consumer issues such as telemarketing and Internet fraud and medication safety.

Leaders of the four consumer leagues selected Florence Kelley, Illinois's chief factory inspector, as NCL's first chief executive. Kelley, who had lived at Hull House in Chicago, moved to Henry Street Settlement in New York City and opened NCL's first office there in May 1899. Under Kelley's leadership, NCL researched industrial conditions and supported legislation to prohibit child labor, set minimum wages, limit working hours and night work, abolish sweatshops, and improve other working conditions.

NCL also campaigned to prevent the sale of unpasteurized milk and to pass state and federal pure food and drug laws. In 1905, it investigated conditions under which food products were prepared and the working conditions of employees who produced them. In 1906, it established a permanent food committee and played a role in securing President Theodore Roosevelt's support for the Federal Food and Drugs Act, which he signed into law in June of that year.

The League's plan of action was to "investigate, educate, agitate, and legislate." It worked to secure child labor laws that would effectively safeguard working children in every state. The league led the effort to create a federal Children's Bureau, which President William Howard Taft signed into law in April 1912.

NCL members in several states secured maximum labor hour laws, and Kelley was instrumental in the 1912 passage in Massachusetts of the first state minimum-wage law. In 1907, Kelley and Brandeis's sister-in-law, Josephine Gold-mark, asked Louis D. Brandeis of Boston to defend, *pro bono*, the constitutionality of Oregon's ten-hour workday for women before the U.S. Supreme Court. This was also the first "Brandeis Brief," comprising largely social evidence with far less reliance on legal argument. The league raised funds to print the brief and pay court expenses. In *Muller v. Oregon*, the Supreme Court in 1908 unanimously agreed that the law was constitutional. Before President Woodrow Wilson appointed him to the Supreme Court in 1916, Brandeis also orally defended nine women's labor laws or filed briefs prepared under his direction by Goldmark, the League's publications secretary from 1903 to 1917. In each instance, state and federal courts sustained the laws as constitutional.

After Brandeis joined the Supreme Court, Felix Frankfurter, who was then a Harvard Law School professor, continued NCL's legal efforts, also *pro bono*, working with Kelley, Goldmark, and later Mary Dewson, the league's research secretary. When Frankfurter also joined the Supreme Court, Dean Acheson, who after law school went to Washington to clerk for Brandeis and ultimately became secretary of state under President Harry Truman, donated his time.

In 1924, at Kelley's invitation, Dr. Alice Hamilton, authority on industrial diseases and a professor of industrial toxicology at Harvard's School of Public Health, agreed to consult with NCL's committee, which was conducting an investigation into the dangers posed by workplace fumes and dust to the health of women and child workers. Hamilton also helped draft model legislation aimed at protecting these workers. When the New Jersey Consumers League reported an alarming death rate among women engaged in painting luminous watch dials, with Dr. Hamilton's help, NCL and the New Jersey Consumers League helped the women's families sue U.S. Radium Corporation. Dr. Hamilton and Kelley then took their data to the federal government, urging the surgeon general and the U.S. Public Health Service to study industrial poisons and develop standards. In 1928, the Surgeon General called a conference of experts on radium, which prepared a report on the subject that helped persuade the U.S. Public Health Service to call for effective, continuous inspection of dial painting factories and for standards for use of radioactive mixtures and for working conditions of those using such mixtures.

In 1920, NCL was a leader in establishing the Women's Bureau in the Labor Department. During that decade, the league helped educate and mobilize the public in support of national health insurance legislation, pioneered promotion of workers' compensation laws, supported compulsory state-administered employment insurance, advocated for federal infant and maternity programs, investigated migrant agricultural workers' living conditions, and helped organize the Southern Council for Legislation for Women and Children in Industry.

After the 1929 stock market crash, many of the state leagues reported that minimum wage, sweatshop, and child labor laws were being ignored. NCL convened a conference in New York City, inviting labor department officials from eastern states. The group agreed that labor standards committees should be organized in as many states as possible and that model state minimum wage legislation should be drafted. A committee of Felix Frankfurter, Benjamin V. Cohen, Josephine Goldmark, and Mary Dewson drafted legislation basing wage rates on "reasonable value of services rendered" rather than "cost of living." New York was the first state to enact the law (in 1933).

Kelley, who had guided NCL's activities for thirty-two years, died in February 1932. Directors named her son Nicholas, an economist, as board chairman. With the help of the League's president, University of Wisconsin economics professor John R. Commons, Kelley selected Lucy Randolph Mason to run the organization. Mason had been serving NCL as its southern representative while on the staff of both the League of Women Voters and the Young Women's Christian Association in Richmond, Virginia. Mason was an activist particularly concerned about low wages, poor working conditions, and racial discrimination in the South.

NCL board minutes of the time claimed about 2,500 members and twelve active branches. In 1933, Congress enacted the National Industrial Recovery Act, which set a minimum wage, and President Franklin Roosevelt urged governors of industrial states to enact minimum wage laws similar to those that NCL had drafted. Four years later, the U.S. Supreme Court upheld Washington State's law.

Eleanor Roosevelt, along with other Junior League members, had become a member of NCL when she was a young girl. Roosevelt was assigned to work at the Rivington Street settlement house, where she taught girls calisthenics and dancing. She also investigated sweatshops. Roosevelt later served as NCL vice president, an office she held while first lady until her death in 1962.

Frances Perkins was vice president of the league until she assumed her official duties as secretary of labor and the first woman cabinet officer appointed by FDR. As head of the New York Consumers League, Perkins had witnessed the tragic 1911 Triangle Shirtwaist Factory Fire, she and worked in New York State to put in place fire safety regulations thereafter. Josephine Roche, another vice president, became assistant secretary of the treasury. Dewson, the league's research secretary, subsequently headed the Democratic Party's women's division and, in 1935, became a member of the Social Security Board. John G. Winant, NCL president, was named chairman of the Social Security Board in 1935.

After his election in 1948, President Harry Truman sought to amend the Fair Labor Standards Act to increase the minimum wage, to expand Social Security eligibility, and to increase benefits for retired workers. NCL worked for these liberalizing amendments, and their enactment helped the league celebrate its fiftieth birthday.

In 1958, NCL relocated its headquarters to Washington, D.C. Under a succession of executive directors, it focused attention on migratory labor, licensing of private employment agencies, problems with consumer regulatory agencies, and protection of workers using radioactive materials.

In 1976, NCL's board selected Sandra L. Willett to head the organization. She steered the league toward new consumer issues. The organization developed an Assertive Consumer Project, training citizen leaders who, in turn, educated consumers about credit, warranty rights, and assertive behavior. To build consumer participation into government processes, the league contracted with the Consumer Product Safety Commission to involve industry, consumers, and technicians in standards setting. After Barbara Warden succeeded Willett in 1982, NCL focused greater attention on the rapidly changing health care system.

From 1985 to 2007, NCL was led by Linda Golodner, who earlier had worked as a congressional staffer before running her own public affairs firm. During her tenure, NCL participated in dozens of coalitions and advisory committees, providing a consumer perspective on issues ranging from clean air and water to health care reform. It hosted conferences, forums, workshops, and legislative briefings on consumer issues, including privacy, health care reform, medication safety, financial services, safe drinking water, and consumer fraud. NCL's brochures, handbooks, and manuals, along with the *NCL Bulletin*, were widely distributed to consumer advocates and educators nationwide.

To address the burgeoning problem of telemarketing fraud, in 1982 NCL established the National Fraud Information Center (NFIC). Its director, Susan Grant, formerly with the office of the district attorney in Northwestern Massachusetts, represented NCL internationally through her participation in the Transatlantic Consumer Dialogue (TACD) and the OECD Committee on Consumer Policy. By 1996, NFIC had expanded its focus, launching www.fraud.org to address rapidly expanding and increasingly sophisticated Internet fraud. By phone and online, NFIC provided assistance to thousands of consumers, organizations, and law enforcement agencies fighting fraud.

From its earliest years, protecting children from exploitative working conditions has been a top NCL priority. In 1989 the league cofounded, and since then has cochaired and administered, the national Child Labor Coalition, a group of organizations dedicated to stopping child labor violations and injuries worldwide by raising public awareness through media outreach, an annual report, and the *Child Labor Monitor* newsletter. In 1987, the Secretary of Labor appointed Golodner to the DOL Child Labor Advisory Committee, which she chaired. The coalition developed a model state law that several states incorporated into their legal codes. During the 1990s, NCL annually surveyed state departments of labor about the status of children in the workplace, including information regarding safety issues and compliance efforts, and published the survey results. In 1998, NCL launched the Children in the Fields campaign, with the American Farmworker Opportunity Programs, to highlight the plight of children working in U.S. agriculture. In 1999, through its Child Labor Coalition, NCL was a lead organizer of the Global March against Child Labor, which successfully pressured the International Labour Organization to adopt ILO Convention 182 on the worst forms of child labor. NCL was instrumental in persuading Congress to ratify the convention.

In 1996, President Clinton appointed Golodner to the Apparel Industry Partnership (AIP), which addressed unfair labor conditions in the apparel and footwear industries, and the group's members elected her chair. The following year, the AIP presented a code of conduct and procedures for implementation to the White House and established the Fair Labor Association (FLA). Since 1999, with active NCL involvement, FLA has helped improve the lives of many workers around the world by offering tools and resources to companies, delivering training to factory workers and management, conducting due diligence through independent assessments, and advocating for greater business accountability and transparency.

In response to media disclosures of child labor in the cocoa fields, NCL worked with international labor federations and unions as well as those in the cocoa industry to address these child labor concerns. In 2001, Senator Tom Harkin (D-IA) and Representative Eliot Engel (D-NY) developed a protocol to establish the International Cocoa Initiative (ICI). NCL was a signatory and Golodner served on the ICI's founding Board of Directors.

In 2007, Golodner was succeeded by Sally Greenberg, a consumer attorney and lobbyist for Consumers Union. Under Greenberg leadership, NCL has strengthened its connections to the consumer advocacy community and organized labor while also making new connections between the two groups. In 2008, NCL launched a consumer–labor coalition to bring labor and consumer activists together on issues of joint concern. The same year, NCL joined other national consumer groups in crafting a Consumer Manifesto with seven enumerated consumer protection priorities, including re-establishing the White House Office of Consumer Affairs and sending it to President Barack Obama and all members of Congress.

Today under Greenberg, NCL continues its consumer leadership on labor issues by cochairing and staffing the CLC with the American Federation of Teachers. Coordinated by NCL's Reid Maki, formerly with the Association of Farmworker Opportunity Programs, the CLC includes separate domestic and international subcommittees that advocate to protect working children in the United States and abroad. In recent years, NCL has also joined forces with advocates for low-income workers in support of increased state and federal minimum wages, including tipped wages for restaurant workers, paid sick leave, and family leave.

NCL's Fraud.org helps consumers avoid being victimized by telemarketing and Internet scams. Headed by John Breyault, formerly director of the Telecommunications Research & Action Center, Fraud.org works closely with national, state, and local law enforcement agencies, including the U.S. Department of Justice and the Federal Communications Commission. Since the early 1990s, the league has also convened the Alliance against Fraud, bringing together representatives from government, business, consumer groups, and the media to marshal forces against all types of fraud.

NCL's health agenda features a national campaign, launched in 2011, entitled Script Your Future, directed by attorney and longtime health advocate Rebecca Burkholder, that is raising awareness among patients, family caregivers, and healthcare professionals about the importance of taking medications as prescribed. Script Your Future is a coalition that now includes more than 135 businesses, professional and trade associations, and patient advocacy groups, along with federal agencies including the FDA and AHRQ. In addition to the national campaign effort, NCL has established and supports local *Script Your Future* coalitions in six cities across the country.

NCL's LifeSmarts teen financial literacy and consumer education program, which the league acquired from the National Coalition on Consumer Education in 2000, teaches marketplace and citizenship skills to teenagers through a national online and in-person competition, culminating in a national championship held annually in a different city. Conducted in partnership with state-level volunteer consumer advocates and educators at regional Federal Reserve Banks, state attorneys general offices, and nonprofit groups, LifeSmarts annually reaches hundreds of thousands of high school students. Under the leadership of Program Director Lisa Hertzberg, formerly on the staff of the Minnesota Attorney General, the program has experienced steady growth.

NCL's communications department, headed for the past decade by Carol McKay, manages the League's primary websites—Nclnet.org, Fraud.org, LifeSmarts.org, ScriptYourFuture.org, and StopChildLabor.org. SavvyConsumer blog and league-hosted webinars complement NCL's Web presence.

NCL is a 501(c)(3) nonprofit organization governed by an elected board of directors. Directors include citizens and representatives of public interest organizations, labor unions, academic institutions, and trade associations. Resources include revenue from individual and organizational contributions, conferences, grants from foundations and federal agencies, publications sales, *cy près* awards, and events that has recently ranged from $2.4 to $3.6 million annually.

Erma B. Angevine, Larry Bostian, Linda F. Golodner

See also: Consumer Education Advocacy; Consumer Leagues; Labor Movement

Further Reading

Keyserling, Mary Dublin. 1982. "The First National Consumer Organization: The National Consumers League." In Erma Angevine, ed., *Consumer Activists: They Made a Difference* (pp. 343–360). Mount Vernon, NY: Consumers Union Foundation.

Sklar, Kathryn Kish, and Beverly Wilson Palmer, eds. 2009. *The Selected Letters of Florence Kelley.* Urbana-Champaign: University of Illinois Press.

Storrs, Landon R. Y. 2000. *Civilizing Capitalism: The National Consumers' League, Women's Activism, and Labor Standards in the New Deal Era.* Chapel Hill: University of North Carolina Press.

NATIONAL COOPERATIVE BANK

See Consumer Cooperatives

NATIONAL INSURANCE CONSUMER ORGANIZATION

The National Insurance Consumer Organization (NICO was established in 1980 by J. Robert Hunter and Ralph Nader. For fifteen years, it was the leading consumer group in the nation on issues pertaining to insurance. It advocated reforms before federal and state governments and sought to educate consumers about these reforms and about sensible purchase practices. In 1995, the organization was folded into the Consumer Federation of America (CFA) as its "Insurance Group."

Hunter and Nader established NICO because consumers purchase hundreds of billions of dollars of insurance products each year, but there was no organization in the country speaking out on behalf of these insurance consumers. In 1945, by passing the McCarran–Ferguson Act, Congress largely exempted the insurance industry from the application of the nation's antitrust laws, allowing insurers to collude with each other on pricing and other decisions exempted from federal review. Also in that year, it delegated authority to regulate insurance to the states but set no standards for the state's regulatory efforts, nor did it put in place routine oversight of these efforts by the federal government.

For several decades, the large majority of insurance commissions failed to protect insurance consumers adequately. One reason for this neglect was the close ties of most insurance commissioners to the industry: studies by the U.S. General Accounting Office and others revealed that about half of state commissioners came from the industry and that about half returned to the industry.

Hunter had been the Federal Insurance Administrator under Presidents Gerald Ford and Jimmy Carter. He wrote a paper outlining the need for an organization to redress the imbalance in power between the insurance industry and the consumer. Nader read the paper and suggested that Hunter undertake such an effort. He agreed to do so and established NICO with the assistance of funding contributed by Nader.

NICO's first board was made up of Hunter; Howard Clark, a former South Carolina insurance commissioner; and James Hunt, a former Vermont commissioner of banking and insurance. Hunter was a casualty actuary, Hunt a life actuary, and Clark an insurance lawyer.

The first study published by NICO was a 1980 report on the then prevalent practice of rates being set by insurance companies without giving consideration to their investment income. Using auto insurance as an example, NICO showed that rates could be reduced by about $5 billion if this factor was reflected. The NICO report led to a multiyear study of the issue by the National Association of Insurance Commissioners (NAIC) and, in 1984, eventual adoption by the NAIC of the methods proposed by NICO. Texas was the first state to adopt these methods, which resulted in a decline in rates.

NICO also campaigned for the creation of independent public advocates dealing with insurance in each state. It pointed out that commissioners have a conflict when insurers make proposals to them. If the commissioners act like judges, only the insurers' sides are heard. But if the commissioners act like consumer advocates, then the fairness of their decisions are in question. As a result of NICO's efforts, states including Texas and Oregon established consumer advocates.

NICO also led a campaign to repeal the federal antitrust exemption conferred by the McCarran–Ferguson Act. Under this exemption, states can choose to "deregulate" while collusive activities continue. Without the exemption, states choosing to deregulate would be able to do so and be certain to have the competing insurers operating at arm's length; states who chose to regulate would have to meet a tougher "state action" level of regulation. Although the House Judiciary Committee voted out related legislation, it was not approved by either house of Congress.

In addition to these and other advocacy efforts, NICO undertook efforts to educate consumers. It published information for buyers of different insurance products and obtained wide dissemination of this information both through direct order and, even more significantly, through the media. In the process, NICO—especially

Hunt on life insurance issues and Hunter on all other insurance issues—became the leading consumer spokespersons to the media on consumer insurance matters. NICO also published a bimonthly newsletter for its several thousand members. When the organization merged with CFA, memberships ceased.

NICO also undertook to help establish other consumer groups and assist existing national and state groups to advocate on behalf of consumers. The involvement of NICO with several groups in California led to the state legislature's assigning a study on consumer problems. Although the legislature failed to act on the study's recommendations, their refusal triggered the organization of separate ballot initiatives by two groups. In 1988, California voters passed one of the initiatives, Proposition 103. NICO's general counsel, Jay Angoff, who later served as insurance commissioner of Missouri, was a key campaigner for the reform.

The passage of Proposition 103, and related insurance reforms introduced in the following year in more than forty states, put the insurance industry on notice that they were now receiving much closer public scrutiny. After passage, some insurer groups even reached out to NICO and to other consumer groups to try addressing mutual concerns. The National Association of Professional Insurance Agents, for example, persuaded Esther Peterson, NICO, CFA, and Public Citizen to work with them to study the quality and resources of state regulation to try to upgrade the quality of such regulation. Research by this Consumer Insurance Interest Group (CIIG) convinced many that state insurance departments needed additional resources and greater autonomy.

In this period, both Hunter and Hunt began to work closely with Stephen Brobeck, CFA's executive director. They prepared studies on auto insurance and credit life insurance. The latter research, which documented what was called the "worst consumer insurance rip-off" in the country, led to reform of credit insurance pricing in about twenty states. Shortly thereafter, the organization began offering Hunt's service to evaluate the cash value insurance policies held by individuals.

In 1993, Hunter left NICO to become Texas insurance commissioner. When he returned in 1995, the NICO Board and that of CFA decided to merge NICO into the federation as its "Insurance Group," with Hunter as CFA's director of insurance and Hunt as the organization's life insurance actuary.

J. Robert Hunter

See also: Consumer Federation of America; Insurance Advocacy; Nader, Ralph

Further Reading

Geisel, Jerry. 1986. "Industry 'Gadfly' Draws Praise, Scorn." *Business Insurance* February 17: 1+.

Pendleton, Scott. 1994. "Regulating Insurance in Texas." *Christian Science Monitor* (September 22).

NATIONAL LOW INCOME HOUSING COALITION

The National Low Income Housing Coalition (NLIHC) is a 501(c)(3) nonprofit group that seeks to advance the housing interests of low-income households, especially renters. Since the mid-1970s, the organization has undertaken research, public education, communications with policymakers, and work with members to try to ensure that low-income people have affordable and decent homes.

Cushing Dolbeare was largely responsible for the founding of the NLIHC. Dolbeare was a well-informed, passionate, and persistent advocate on low-income housing issues. In 1974, in response to the Nixon administration's moratorium on federal housing programs, she organized the Ad Hoc Low Income Housing Coalition, an advocacy group. A year later, she helped establish the Low Income Housing Information Service (LIHIS) to provide information, public education, and assistance to state and local advocacy groups. In 1978, the NLIHC was incorporated as the National Low Income Housing Coalition. In 1996, the two organizations merged.

Dolbeare wrote dozens of articles, books, and reports about the nature, causes, and solutions to the housing problems of low-income people. She designed the methodology for Out of Reach, NLIHC's annual report on the gap between housing costs and wages of these individuals. She also developed widely cited reports on the disparity between the cost of tax-based subsidies benefiting homeowners and direct spending on housing assistance for low-income households. From 1977 to 1984, and again from 1993 to 1994, Dolbeare served as the NLIHC's executive director. However, from 1974 until her death in 2005, she remained active in the organization.

NLIHC has recently been led by president and CEO Sheila Crowley, who joined the organization in 1998. Crowley earned a PhD in social work; worked for two decades in Richmond (VA), including eight years as executive director of a multi-purpose homeless service and advocacy organization; and served as a Democratic staffer on the Housing Subcommittee of the U.S. Senate Banking Committee before joining the NLIHC in 1994. She heads a staff of sixteen that operates on an annual budget of about $2.5 million. Most funds come from foundation grants and support from several hundred national, state, local, and individual members located in forty-seven states and the District of Columbia.

In the past several decades, the NLIHC has focused most of its attention on issues related to low-income rentals in public and private housing. Much of its work seeks to ensure that the federal funding continues adequate funding to ensure an adequate stock of this housing, adequate operations and maintenance of government-owned housing, and adequate direct subsides, including vouchers, to low-income renters. Today, NLIHC also deals with the effects of regulations on housing discrimination and the effects of landlord foreclosures that harm low-income tenants.

Stephen Brobeck

See also: Mortgage Lending Reform; Tenant Activism

Further Reading

Edson, Charles L. "Affordable Housing—An Intimate History." In American Bar Association, *History and Regulatory Foundation of Affordable Housing.* http://apps.americanbar.org/abastore/products/books/abstracts/5530024%20chapter%201_abs.pdf.

Schudel, Matt. 2005. "Cushing N. Dolbeare Dies at 78; Lifelong Fair Housing Crusader."
   Washington Post (March 19): B07.

NETHERLANDS CONSUMER MOVEMENT

See Dutch Consumer Movement

NETWORK NEUTRALITY

See Digital Communications Advocacy

NORWEGIAN CONSUMER MOVEMENT

In Norway, government action on behalf of consumers has militated against the formation of private consumer organizations. The first governmental consumer institution in Norway was established in 1936. Over time, governmental institutions of consumer protection have gained considerable public legitimacy, thereby explaining the lack of general-purpose, private consumer organizations in Norway.

Norwegian consumer institutions developed in four phases. The first phase, the foundation, took place from 1936 to 1940. At that time, consumer issues were narrowly defined and linked to the economic management of the home. Thus, the first institution, established in 1936, was the Norwegian Advisory Service for Home Economics. It had twenty regional offices around the country. During World War II, the service played an important role in educating consumers in dealing with shortages of food and clothing.

The development phase, from 1950 to 1960, was a period when government consumer institutions were established—in particular, the Norwegian Consumer Council in 1953. The council was a response to the call for consumer information from women's organizations, which were, in turn, linked to labor and farmer movements or to consumer cooperatives. Although the new consumer institutions of this era were established by the government, with total financial support from Parliament, they were granted a high degree of political independence. Nevertheless, the tension between governmental financial support and political independence has remained one of the main characteristics of Norwegian consumer policy for more than fifty years.

The Norwegian Consumer Council began distributing the consumer magazine *Forbrukerrapporten* (Consumer Report) during the postwar period and continued publication through 2010. The Declaration Committee for Consumer Goods was also established during this second phase of consumer policy formation as a way to obtain voluntary agreement with producers regarding labeling of consumer goods.

The third phase, from 1968 to 1978, can be conceptualized as the reorganization of consumer policy. Consumer information was augmented with new consumer laws that focused on consumer protection. The right to redress was ensured by a general act covering the sales of goods, a new door-to-door sales act, and a consumer credit act. Consumers were also protected against misleading advertising by the Marketing Control Act of 1972.

Political authorities in Norway were not content with merely adopting new laws. New institutions were established and old ones reorganized to meet the provisions of the new legislation. The Marketing Control Act established the Consumer Ombudsman (CO) to encourage compliance with laws as well as the Market Council to serve as an appellate body for decisions by the CO. Both the Consumer Council and National Institute for Consumer Research (SIFO) were reorganized to meet evolving demands. The Consumer Council strengthened its links to civil society by establishing a National Biannual Congress, and a government-financed consumer complaint board was introduced to ensure consumers of their right to redress. The research of SIFO shifted from the household focus of home economics to societal challenges facing consumers. The shift is evident in SIFO's extensive research on environmentally sustainable consumption and other forms of consumption motivated by ethical or political considerations.

The fourth phase, from the early 1980s to present, is characterized by deregulation, new governance, and an adaption to the consumer policy of the European Union. Norway witnessed a deregulation in the markets for energy, housing, television, and telecommunication; and there was partial deregulation of business hours for shops. Within the banking and finance industries, Norway has seen not only deregulation, but some new areas of regulation. For example, the new Debt Settlement Act passed the parliament in the 1990s. Norway has also made changes in its product safety regulation and laws regarding product liability as a result of the European Economic Area (EEA) agreement between Norway and the European Union (EU), which allowed Norway to participate in the internal market of the EU without joining it.

Consumer Organizations

As a result of the historic development of Norway's consumer institutions described above, today there are three important government organizations: SIFO, the Consumer Council, and the Consumer Ombudsman. Established in 1939, SIFO is the oldest of the Norwegian consumer organizations. The institute has changed several times in role and organizational structure during the many decades of its existence. One fundamental change took place in 1972 when two government bodies merged—one based on a home economics model of providing information to homemakers and another with a tradition of conducting research, including product testing. In the 1980s, two structural changes took place at SIFO: It built up its competence in social science research as its product testing activities were moved to other institutions or closed down. In essence, as the concerns of Norwegian consumers shifted from "the kitchen" to the marketplace and society, this was reflected in the research activity of the institute.

Today, SIFO is an independent research institute with fifty employees. The institute receives 60 percent of its funds from the government and the other 40 percent from commissioned research projects. Although the Norwegian Research Council is the most important financial contributor to these projects, SIFO has also participated in more than twenty projects funded by the European Union (EU) during the last decade.

Although SIFO is the oldest of Norway's three main consumer institutions, the Consumer Council is the largest and most important. It has 130 employees and ten regional offices. It was founded by the government in 1953 at the urging of Norwegian women's organizations. As a result, these organizations gained representation on the board of the Council. In 1972, links between the Consumer Council and the civil society were strengthened through the establishment of a biannual consumer congress. In 2002, this congress was replaced by a Consumer Political Forum with twenty-five representatives from public authorities, research institutions, and a large variety of nongovernmental organizations This new forum functioned as an advisory body to the Consumer Council. The forum was disbanded in 2009, and since that time, the Consumer Council has had no formal links to the civil society. As a consequence of this development, the Consumer Council has also left Consumers International—the umbrella organization for the world's consumer associations.

The council does receive significant input, however, from individual consumers—more than 100,000 annually (Forbrukerrådet, 2011). Traditionally, consumers used telephone or personal contacts to gain consumer information or help in complaint handling cases. In 2012, the Consumer Council handled more than 5,000 consumer complaints (Forbrukerrådet, 2011). Over the years, however, these personal methods of contact have been replaced by technology-guided systems and various consumer portals dedicated to specific subjects such as for financial services. Another sign of the changing times with respect to consumer information delivery came in 2010, when the council ceased publication of its magazine, *Forbrukerrapporten* (Consumer Reports).

The Consumer Council receives all its funding from the Norwegian government, and this type of public funding of watchdog organizations is typical of Nordic political culture. The council's board members are appointed by the Ministry of Children, Equality, and Social Inclusion. In spite of these close formal links to political authorities, the council acts very much as an independent consumer organization. At one point in its history, the council had close links to women's organizations, trade unions, consumer cooperatives and other nationwide organizations, and national and local governments. The Norwegian Consumer Council has gradually weakened links to civil society groups, however, and functions today mainly as an independent governmental institution.

The Marketing Control Act, which passed the Norwegian Parliament in 1972, established two new consumer institutions: the Consumer Ombudsman (CO) and the Market Council. The main task of the CO is to implement the Marketing Control Act by protecting the consumer against misleading advertising and standard contracts. The Market Council functions as an appeal body for the ombudsman decisions. The Consumer Ombudsman is the official English name of the institution. However, in 1980 it changed the Norwegian name to the more gender-neutral Consumer Ombud.

The Consumer Ombud is appointed by the government, has approximately thirty employees, and runs on government funding. Within this framework, the CO is an independent administrative body that seeks to keep a running account of business practices and ensure conformity with the provisions of the Marketing Control

Act. The CO annually receives thousands of complaints from members of the public and, based on its judgment of their significance, undertakes corrective action.

Examined as a whole, Norwegian consumer institutions are dualistic in the sense that they exhibit a high degree of independence yet are financed primarily by the government. (This model is found in all five Nordic countries, with some minor differences.) Although these institutions advocate for consumers and sometimes taken into account the views of civil society organizations, they set their own agendas and, in the case of SIFO, enjoy traditional academic freedoms.

Role in the Global Consumer Movement

Beginning in the late 1970s and lasting for more than two decades, cooperation among the five Nordic countries (Denmark, Finland, Iceland, Norway, and Sweden) was the main driver of Norwegian consumer policy. This included action with respect to consumer information and education, consumer rights, household financial management, and consumer research. It also served as an opportunity for interaction among all Nordic consumer organizations. One specific outgrowth of this cooperation was the development of the Nordic Swan, a successful multinational ecolabel.

Gradually, as a result of European integration, the Norwegian consumer movement has oriented itself to the consumer policies of the entire European Union. This is the case even though Norwegian voters twice have rejected joining the European Union (1972 and 1994). Moreover, Norway (along with Iceland and Liechtenstein) joins with the member countries of the European Union in the European Economic Area. Thus the agenda for the Norwegian consumer movement is closely aligned with that of the other countries in Europe.

Although Norway is not a member of the European Union, the Norwegian Consumer Council has been active within BEUC: The European Consumer Organisation. The council also participates in the activities of the European standardization institutions, such as the European Association for the Co-ordination of Consumer Representation in Standardisation (ANEC). The European connection has to a large degree replaced the Nordic cooperation within the framework of the Nordic Council of Ministers. Another consequence of this strengthening European connection has been the withdrawal of the Norwegian Consumer Council from membership in Consumers International (CI). As indicated above, the council no longer has strong links to civil society organizations, and there is no true "consumer movement" in Norway. Thus, council membership in an activist organization such as CI is not very germane to its activities. Also, if Norwegian consumer institutions are going to act on an international level, the consumer topics addressed by BEUC are far more relevant to the policy concerns of Norway than the global issues tackled by Consumers International.

Recent Consumer Issues

Norwegian consumer institutions are well established and enjoy a good deal of support from consumers. However, it is possible to identify three challenges for the consumer movement in Norway: globalization of supply chains, deregulation in a market economy, and climate change.

The internationalization of economic activity creates new possibilities and opportunities for Norwegian consumers. The result of this process has been lower prices for many consumer goods and a greater choice of products. For example, thanks to falling textile prices, sales of clothes in Norway have increased substantially in the last two decades. At the same time, the negative environmental and social aspects of textile production have been put on the political agenda in Norway, as in most European countries. To date, Norwegian consumer organizations have found it difficult to develop consumer information (for example, through labeling systems) that is capable of influencing practices in the global supply chains for products.

Deregulation and the growth of a market-based economy influence consumers in many of the same ways as internationalization does. More and lower-priced products find their way to the market, thereby enhancing the consumer's right to choose. On the other hand, deregulation (for example, in the financial sector) may threaten the consumer's right to safe, reliable products.

Norway is not a formal member of the EU, but the Norwegian Consumer Council and the Consumer Ombud have nevertheless been attentive to consumer rights at the European level. These Norwegian consumer organizations take part in the discussion of proposed EU consumer directives. Norwegian groups are particularly wary of directives that, in the name of harmonization, involve weakening consumer protection in some European countries. A case in point was the 2008 proposal by the EU to implement a consumer rights directive focused primarily on electronic commerce. The directive would have prohibited individual countries such as Norway from having policies that were stronger than the provisions of the directive. Norwegian consumer organizations helped modify the directive, and when it was passed in 2011, most of the disputed issues were resolved in favor of strong consumer protection.

Finally, the linkage of consumption to the natural environment and climate change has become increasingly important to both environmental and consumer organizations in Norway. To date, however, Norway's consumer institutions have been hesitant to take seriously environmental challenges and climate change. Neither the Consumer Council nor the Consumer Ombudsman has given priority to consumer responsibility and green consumption. The main concern of the Council and CO remains "value for money spent." The potential of moving consumption in the direction of sustainability has, however, been one of the main research areas at SIFO. The institute has been involved in more than twenty projects financed by the Norwegian Research Council and programs of the European Union—a hopeful sign for the future.

Eivind Stø

See also: BEUC: The European Consumer Organisation; Consumers International; Danish Consumer Movement; Finnish Consumer Movement; Swedish Consumer Movement

Further Reading

Forbrukerrådet (Consumer Council). 2011. *Annual Report 2011*. Oslo, Norway. www
.forbrukerradet.no/forside/_attachment/1129608?_ts=137e11d5aa4.

Ilmonen, Kai, and Stø, Eivind. 1997. "The Consumer in Political Discourse: Consumer
Policy in Nordic Welfare States." In Sulkunen, Holmwood, Radner, and Schulze, eds.
Constructing the New Consumer Society (pp. 197–217). London: Macmillan Press.

P

PAYDAY LOAN ADVOCACY

Payday loans are short-term loans with repayment tied to a borrower's scheduled payday. Key features are high rates—typically 400 percent annual percentage rate (APR) or more—a single balloon payment due on the borrower's next payday, and payment taken directly from the borrower's bank account, either using a personal check held by the lender or using authorization to electronically debit the borrower's bank account.

Payday loans are marketed as a way to meet short-term credit needs but are often used continuously, with the typical borrower taking out ten loans per year. Research shows that using payday loans financially harms most borrowers.

In the early decades of the twentieth century, most states set usury limits on small-dollar loans, based largely on model legislation from the Russell Sage Foundation, whose priority was to protect the poor and the vulnerable. However, as many states raised or eliminated these limits during the inflationary 1980s, deregulated rates either permitted payday lending, or new laws were enacted to explicitly authorize these loans. Consumer advocacy against payday loans has concentrated on these state laws and related regulations, though it has sometimes also focused on city councils, federal regulatory agencies, and Congress. Over the past two decades, consumer advocates and public officials have fought over legislative carveouts for payday loans, permissible loan terms, the proliferation of unlicensed online payday lending, and the use of shams and ruses to evade state rate caps or regulation, such as lenders claiming to broker or arrange loans for banks, a practice dubbed "rent-a-bank" payday lending by advocates.

Widespread opposition to payday lending from national and state groups has featured research, networking, litigation, and campaigns, with the following contributions by organizations: industry reports by Jean Ann Fox of the Consumer Federation of America (CFA); research on the law and consumer protections from the National Consumer Law Center (NCLC), led by Elizabeth Renuart and Lauren Saunders; polling and focus groups on consumer attitudes, as well as marketplace research, by Pew Charitable Trusts; national coverage and state advocacy by Consumers Union; surveys of payday loan stores by USPIRG, state PIRGs, and other state consumer groups; the convening of advocates in states and filing amicus briefs in support of state regulators and private litigation by AARP; research on payday loan effects and staffing of state campaigns by the Center for Responsible Lending (CRL); advocacy against bank payday lending by National People's Action and affiliates; and national leadership and state support by civil rights groups such as the NAACP. Faith groups and religious leaders have also played an important role in state advocacy, as have organized labor and state credit union leagues. Academics and journalists have undertaken their own research on payday loan markets and consumer effects.

An important initiative to encourage and support these state efforts was CFA's creation of a national network of state and local advocates who shared information and tactics using an e-mail list, monthly telephone conferences, and an annual conference attended by dozens of leaders. The email list grew from the initial six participants in 1999 to nearly 400 participants, from some 200 organizations, by 2014. This network enabled small groups and lone advocates to draw from shared expertise and successful campaigns to influence legislation, ballot initiatives, and enforcement actions. State organizations also supported federal advocacy with Congress and regulatory agencies.

State and Local Advocacy

From the late 1990s through 2005, payday lenders had the upper hand in persuading state legislatures either to carve out exemptions for payday lending from state usury laws or to preserve the deregulated rates that allowed them to continue their lending practices. In 2005, Michigan was the last state to authorize payday lending. Since then, consumer advocacy campaigns to repeal payday loan authorization or impose limits on these loans have put the industry on the defensive in many states.

Despite a low loan rate cap, Georgia was rife with payday loan operators. Local advocates—including AARP, Georgia Watch, and the Georgia chapter of the NAACP, with support from CRL—sought to shut down these operators. The Attorney General sued the lenders, and in 2004, the state legislature enacted a law that made payday lending a racketeering violation and specifically prohibited banks from arranging loans on behalf of storefront lenders.

North Carolina authorized payday lending in 1997 but permitted this law to expire in 2001 after the banking commissioner had documented its adverse effect on consumers. However, using creative tactics, payday lenders continued to operate. It was not until 2006 that the Banking Commissioner and Attorney General, through enforcement actions, shut down these lenders. A broad coalition—including the Community Reinvestment Association of North Carolina (CRA-NC), Self-Help Credit Union, NAACP, and AARP—supported these state efforts and, in recent years, successfully worked to prevent the reauthorization of payday lending by the legislature.

Despite its constitutional usury cap, Arkansas enacted a check cashing law designed to permit payday lending by check cashers. A diverse coalition led by Hank Klein, the head of the largest credit union in the state, waged a multiyear campaign to prohibit this lending. Their tactics included research reports on all payday lenders, a website, press releases, and repeated interventions at the Arkansas Supreme Court by attorney Todd Turner, who challenged the constitutionality of the check cashing law. When the court eventually held the law unconstitutional, the legislature repealed it, and Attorney General Dustin McDaniel shut down storefront and online payday lenders.

Even though West Virginia had a 36 percent small loan rate cap and had never authorized payday lending, "rent-a-bank" lenders had been able to avoid these restrictions and make loans. After the state's attorney general brought a series of enforcement actions against these rent-a-bank lenders and online lenders, they stopped operating in the state.

When consumer advocates have failed to persuade state legislatures to curb payday lending, the advocates have sometimes resorted to state ballot initiatives. In 2010, Montana voters approved a 36 percent rate cap on all forms of small loans, including payday and car title loans. The coalition was led by AARP, the Service Employees International Union, the Montana Catholic Council, Montana Community Foundation, and Rural Dynamics. After losing a lawsuit over the ballot language, the industry stopped fighting the initiative. In 2012, Missourians for Responsible Lending, a coalition of faith and community groups, collected 180,000 signatures of registered voters to put rate-cap reforms on the ballot. However, industry's stalling tactics succeeded in keeping the initiative off the ballot.

Payday lenders have also sought to use state ballot initiatives to eliminate consumer protections. In 2008, the Ohio Coalition for Responsible Lending, with research from Policy Matters Ohio, helped persuade the state legislature to pass a strong bill curbing payday lending through a 28 percent rate cap and other loan limits. When the industry launched a ballot initiative to overturn the rate cap, the coalition vigorously opposed it. Despite industry spending of about $15 million on the campaign, Ohio voters rejected the ballot measure by two to one. However, payday lenders have been able to exploit weaknesses in other Ohio lending laws to continue making triple-digit–rate loans, and these practices have been upheld by a decision of the Ohio Supreme Court.

In Arizona, unable to persuade the state legislature to grant permanent authorization for payday lending, in 2008 the industry launched a ballot initiative to carve out a legal exemption to the state's small loan rate cap of 36 percent. Opposition to this measure was led by the No on 200 coalition, itself led by the Center for Economic Integrity, chaired by state Senator Debbie McCune-Davis, and assisted by CRL. The campaign included press outreach, testimony at ballot forums held by the secretary of state, billboards showing a shark-toothed villain, and rallies at the state capital with Attorney General Terry Goddard. AARP led statewide communications, and CFA's Fox debated the industry lobbyist on Public Television. Churches held a day of solidarity against usury, the Military Officers Association of America spoke out for service members and veterans, and the Arizona Credit Union League distributed flyers through member credit unions. Despite industry spending of $13 million, Arizona voters defeated the lender's measure, which allowed authorization for payday lending to expire in mid-2010.

In many states where repeal or low rate caps were not politically feasible, consumer coalitions sought to make payday loans less harmful. After campaigning by the Monsignor John Eagan Campaign for Payday Loan Reform, led by Citizen Action Illinois and the Woodstock Institute, Illinois enacted loan limits and closed loopholes that limited payday installment loans. In Washington State, advocacy by groups including Poverty Action and Columbia Legal Services won a limit of eight loans per year at licensed payday lenders. That resulted in a two-thirds decline in the number of loans. Colorado was one of the first states to authorize payday lending, but after the state attorney general's office researched this lending and Coloradans for Payday Lending Reform worked for reform, the legislature revised the existing law to require at least a six-month loan term. Although interest and fees remained high, a 2010 decision by the Attorney General's office to make up-front fees refundable has discouraged loan flipping—expensive and unnecessary refinancing encouraged by lenders.

The fight over payday lending has been waged at the local government level as well. Frustrated by state legislatures' refusal to curb expensive lending, many cities and counties have taken action to curb these loans. As of late 2013, more than 150 city, town, and country governments had enacted zoning ordinances, substantive protections, or moratoriums on new lenders. Consumer leaders include the Coalition of Religious Communities in Utah, Texas Appleseed and religious groups in Texas, the California Reinvestment Coalition, and Alabama Appleseed and Alabama Arise, a religious coalition.

Federal Advocacy

When lenders have failed to win permissive state authorizing legislation, they have turned to other devices to make high-rate loans, such as claiming that the loans were coupon sales with a rebate, Internet access with a rebate, or pawns. The most widely used tactic has been "rent-a-bank" payday lending at storefronts. State and national advocacy groups have fought this side battle with a variety of tools. CFA and USPIRG researched and published reports that identified lenders and partner banks and called on federal regulators to stop this practice. In 2000, the Office of the Comptroller of the Currency (OCC) and the Office of Thrift Supervision (OTS) issued advisory letters to banks, making it clear that partnering with payday lenders would draw scrutiny. In fact, the OCC letter stated that bank charters were not property to be rented out to help storefront lenders evade consumer protections. The OCC examined and took enforcement action to terminate payday lending by four national banks named in CFA reports.

However, about a dozen small state-chartered banks, regulated by the Federal Deposit Insurance Corporation (FDIC), made it possible for payday lenders to operate in states where payday products were not legal. Community reinvestment groups and consumer advocates filed Community Reinvestment Act (CRA) letters for every bank that was partnering with a payday lender in an effort to jeopardize the bank's CRA rating. In 2003, protests against the FDIC included CRA-NC (now Reinvestment Partners) staging a "basketball game" outside the FDIC building in Washington, D.C., which pitted the "peeps" (consumers) against the "sharks" (payday lenders) with the FDIC Chairman portrayed as a referee who strongly favored the sharks. In 2006, when the FDIC had new leadership, it issued tough guidelines and, through enforcement actions, terminated state bank partnerships with payday lenders.

Following defeats and stalemate in many states, in 2009 payday lending groups began trying to persuade Congress to authorize their payday loan lending practices and preempt state laws. The House Financial Institutions Subcommittee on Credit held a hearing at which CFA testified. With much opposition from state groups, especially Woodstock Institute and Citizen Action Illinois, bill sponsors were persuaded to withdraw their support for proposed legislation.

The 2010 Dodd Frank Wall Street Reform and Consumer Protection Act gave the new Consumer Financial Protection Bureau (CFPB) authority to supervise and examine all payday lenders but prohibited this agency from setting a federal usury cap. Consumer advocates such as USPIRG, CFA, NCLC, and the Americans for Financial Reform coalition had frequently cited payday loan abuses as an important reason to create a new consumer agency.

Congress did take action to protect one important group of Americans from payday and other high-cost loans. Military financial counselors had long complained about the harm caused by payday lenders clustered around the gates of military bases. The well-publicized maps created by Cal State Northridge geography professor Steve Graves in a law journal article, authored with law professor Christopher Peterson, graphically illustrated that predatory lenders were targeting the troops. With backing from military, veteran, and consumer groups, Senator Elizabeth Dole (R-NC) won a 2005 request for the Department of Defense (DoD) to study the effects of predatory lending on the military. The resulting study—in which CFA, NCLC, CRL, the National Association of Consumer Advocates, and military charities were consulted—made the case for new credit protections that were then requested by DoD. An amendment to the defense authorization legislation, now called the Military Lending Act (MLA), banned payday and car title loans, set a federal 36 percent rate cap, and established other credit protections as defined by DoD rules. In 2010, CFA issued a report on the impact of the MLA and the need for stronger enforcement tools and broader coverage. In late 2012, Congress added enforcement tools for the new CFPB and the FTC, and required the Department of Defense to study emerging problems and propose new rules. In September 2014, the DoD, with encouragement from a broad-based coalition organized by the CFA, proposed new rules that incorporated many reforms recommended by advocates.

One unique feature of a payday loan is direct payment from the borrower's next pay or benefits deposited to his or her bank account. Since borrowers give permission for the lender to withdraw deposited pay or benefits before other obligations are paid, advocates have argued that the payments are a new form of wage assignment, a credit practice deemed unfair by the FTC many years ago. This fight has been led at the federal level by the NCLC, CFA, and CRL. As a result, loan features are now prohibited on prepaid cards that receive deposited federal benefits. Advocates supported federal legislation to prohibit loans secured by electronic access to borrower bank accounts and also supported strict supervision of third-party payment processors by bank regulators.

At the state level, New Yorkers for Responsible Lending urged the New York Department of Financial Regulation and the New York Attorney General to halt illegal online lenders by stopping their access to the electronic payments system. As a result, in 2012 New York sent sixty-five cease and desist letters to illegal online lenders, alerted all banks in the state about the risks of processing payments for illegal loans, and urged the industry self-regulatory group to make sure that banks were complying with their rules. Consequently, some banks withdrew from the payday loan processing business. In related work, federal bank regulators issued stronger guidance on third-party payment processors.

Jean Ann Fox

See also: State and Local Consumer Advocacy Groups

Further Reading

Fox, Jean Ann. 2012. *The Military Lending Act Five Years Later*. Report by the Consumer Federation of America (Washington, DC).

Kiel, Paul. 2013. "How High Cost Lenders Fight to Stay Legal." *ProPublica* (August 2).

Montezemolo, Susanna. 2013. *Payday Lending Abuses and Predatory Practices*. Report by the Center for Responsible Lending (Durham, NC).

Payday Lending in America: Who Borrows, Where They Borrow, and Why. 2012. Report by the Pew Charitable Trusts (Washington, DC).

PAYMENT PROTECTION ADVOCACY

Some consumers have experienced serious problems using payment devices, including checks, credit cards, debit cards, and prepaid cards. Consumer organizations have played a leading role in improving the law governing payment devices and the systems that process payments. National organizations that have been particularly active protecting consumers in their payment transactions include Americans for Financial Reform, Consumer Action, the Center for Responsible Lending, Consumer Federation of America, Consumers Union, the National Association of Consumer Advocates, the National Consumer Law Center, National Council of La Raza, Public Citizen, and U.S. Public Interest Group. Their advocacy has included conducting research, issuing reports, and communicating with legislative and regulatory policymakers. The groups share the same policy goals and typically work with each other in ad hoc coalitions.

Checks

Despite the growing popularity of new forms of payments, American consumers continue to write billions of checks every year. The Uniform Commercial Code (UCC) is the source of most of the law governing checks. The UCC, however, does not protect consumers. A revision of the UCC was considered for many years, culminating in the adoption of the present version in 1990. During the revision process, lawyers from the National Consumer Law Center (NCLC) and Consumers Union attempted to promote and safeguard the interests of consumers as revisions were being made. The revised UCC, however, failed to protect consumers, because the revision process was dominated by banking interests who were intent on drafting law that would permit banks to implement technological advances without legal restriction. Nevertheless, consumer advocates were able to block proposed elements of the UCC that would have made it even more unfavorable to consumers.

Remotely created checks are checks originated by companies such as telemarketers and payday lenders. The checks are sent by companies to financial institutions in order to withdraw funds from consumer accounts at those institutions. The checks do not contain the consumer's signature, but the companies contend the consumer authorized the withdrawals. Typically, businesses first withdraw the consumer's funds electronically. When the consumer disputes the validity of the withdrawals and stops the electronic withdrawal as permitted by federal law, the business switches to remotely created checks for which little legal protection exists. Consumer advocates have testified before Congress and federal regulatory agencies, urging that these checks be prohibited.

Credit Cards and Prepaid Cards

The Truth-in-Lending Act includes important protections for consumers when there are billing errors and unauthorized use of credit cards, but consumers need more protection than the law provides. In 1970, NCLC published the National Consumer Act (NCA) to counter the creditor-friendly Uniform Consumer Credit Code (UCCC) promoted by the Uniform Law Commission. The NCA included provisions on credit card protections. While drafting the NCA, NCLC received expert advice from several national organizations. NCLC followed with the Model Consumer Credit Act that also included protection for consumers using credit cards. Portions of these model acts were enacted by some states and served as an alternative that helped stop the effort in many states to pass the UCCC. Over the years, card issuers developed many product features that were deceptive and costly, such as allowing cardholders to exceed credit limits for a hefty fee in addition to charged interest. In response, consumer organizations supported a bill in Congress designed to restrict several of these "tricks and traps." Their efforts culminated in passage of the Credit Card Accountability, Responsibility and Disclosures Act of 2009 (whose provisions are summarized in the entry on credit card advocacy).

After years of advocacy by consumer organizations, Congress and the Federal Reserve imposed some restrictions on fees and expiration dates for gift cards. However, many low income consumers who do not have bank accounts use general purpose reloadable prepaid cards. These are not regulated. Consumer organizations have urged the Consumer Financial Protection Bureau (CFPB) to prohibit overdraft fees on prepaid cards. In addition, the consumer groups contend that credit features should not be allowed on prepaid cards, because there is no underwriting and the cards can be used to evade usury laws—laws which make payday loans illegal—and legal protections that benefit members of the military.

Electronic Fund Transfers

Electronic fund transfers (EFT) include direct deposit of pay and government benefits, debit cards, preauthorized transfers, online bill payment, and fund transfers using automated teller machines. Congress established the National Commission on Electronic Fund Transfers to consider whether federal legislation was needed to protect consumers using EFT. The Commission invited NCLC to testify before the commission, and its testimony stressed the need for federal legislation to protect consumers. Congress passed the Electronic Fund Transfers Act (EFTA) in 1978, a statute that contains important consumer safeguards, such as limits on unauthorized transfers. The Federal Reserve Board issued EFT regulations supplementing the act until that authority passed to the Consumer Financial Protection Bureau (CFPB). The national consumer organizations have actively participated in the agencies' rulemaking process.

The National Automated Clearinghouse Association (NACHA), a private organization, issues rules that banks and other payment processors voluntarily agree to comply with when they send electronic payments through the Automated Clearinghouse network. Consumer groups have submitted comments to NACHA on proposed rules urging protection beyond those required by government regulations.

Electronic Benefit Transfers (EBT) is an electronic payment system used by states to deliver needs-based government benefits such as the Supplemental Nutrition Assistance Program and Temporary Assistance to Needy Families. Federal legislation provides for these government benefits to be delivered electronically to recipients. During the years when critical decisions were being made about the design of EBT systems, recipients of these benefits were represented by consumer advocates who testified before Congress on the need for recipients to have the same protections as those guaranteed under the EFTA.

The Treasury Department actively encourages electronic delivery of funds from benefits programs administered by the federal government, such as Social Security, Supplemental Security Income, and Veterans Assistance. Recipients of those benefits can receive their funds through direct deposit if they have bank accounts or through a "Direct Express" card account, a prepaid card offered by a bank approved by the Treasury Department. However, check cashers, currency dealers, money transmitters, convenience stores, liquor stores, and prepaid card distributors not approved by Treasury have entered into arrangements with banks in which the bank "fronts" for the unapproved company and that company becomes the only company from which recipients can receive their benefits. These companies charge high fees in order for recipients to access their accounts. In addition, this arrangement forces recipients to come to the company, where they are vulnerable to predatory practices. Consumer organizations have therefore advocated that the EFTA apply to EBT recipients so that they will enjoy the same protections as other consumers.

Overdrafts

A major source of income for financial institutions has been revenue from overdraft fees imposed when consumers write checks, pay with debit cards, or make ATM withdrawals and the institution claims that the consumers' accounts do not contain sufficient funds to cover the withdrawal. Consumer advocates contend that institutions manipulate the processing of these fund transfers in order to maximize overdraft fees. Some consumers have complained that overdraft fees were levied by their bank even though their account had sufficient funds. For many years, courts rejected consumers' legal challenges to these fees. Consumer organizations persisted, advocating for protection in Congress and before federal agencies. Finally, in 2009, the Federal Reserve Board issued a regulation restricting overdraft services for consumers using debit cards and making ATM withdrawals. Most importantly, the new rule required explicit customer consent to these services. In addition, the FDIC issued a guidance that recommended reforms affecting overdraft fees for checks as well. NCLC, along with private consumer lawyers, challenged bank overdraft fees in federal court. A national rule may be forthcoming in the future. Under the Dodd–Frank Consumer Financial Protection Act of 2010, the CFPB has the authority to issue regulations governing overdraft services.

Remittances

Every year millions of people living in the United States, many of them low-income consumers, send billions of dollars to relatives and others in foreign countries. Until 2014, there was no federal regulation of these payments. Pursuant to the Dodd–Frank Act, the CFPB issued proposed regulations to require much greater transparency and disclosure of the costs of remittances. However, the proposed regulation also imposed liability for loss on consumers if the consumer sending the remittance made an error in the account number of the recipient, despite the CFPB's acknowledgement that few such errors occur. Fourteen national and state consumer organizations and eight law professors submitted a comment opposing the imposition of any liability on consumers. Consumer advocates contended that if the loss was put on the financial institution sending the payment containing the error, the loss to financial institutions would be minimal, because there are few errors and the loss would be spread out among many institutions. In contrast, putting the loss on individual low-income consumers would cause great hardship to each consumer who made an error. The advocates pointed out that imposing liability on the institutions would incentivize them to develop technology that would further minimize the risk of errors.

Future Challenges

Advances in technology will facilitate the trend toward consumers paying less often with cash and checks, and more frequently by using pre authorized electronic transfers, online bill-paying, debit cards, and prepaid cards. As mobile banking and mobile payments increase and ATMs perform more functions, bank branch offices will close. The development of new types of virtual or cryptocurrencies and the establishment of novel types of nonbanks will likely outmode the law and severely challenge the regulators who enforce it. Lack of security and privacy protection will pose a threat to consumers from both the companies with which consumers do business and cyberthieves. All these developments will have a particularly harsh effect on low-income consumers, who can least afford the losses they incur when payment problems arise. Consumer organizations will play a major role in ensuring that consumers are protected from these future threats.

Mark E. Budnitz

See also: Credit Card Advocacy

Further Reading

Budnitz, Mark E. 2005. "Consumer Payment Products and Systems: The Need for Uniformity and the Risk of Political Defeat." *Annual Review of Banking and Finance Law* 24: 247.

Budnitz, Mark E. 2010. "The Development of Consumer Protection Law, the Institutionalization of Consumerism, and Future Prospects and Perils." *George State University Law Review* 26: 1,147.

PETERSON, ESTHER (1906–1997)

During the past half-century, Esther Peterson probably did more than other single person, other than Ralph Nader, to advance the consumer movement and consumer protections. Born into a conservative Mormon family, Peterson earned a bachelor's degree from Brigham Young University in 1927 and a master's degree from Columbia Teacher's College in New York City. In 1930, while teaching, she worked with the National Consumers League, which for years had advocated for the interests of women and child workers.

After marrying Oliver Peterson, when he joined the Office of Price Administration in 1944, she moved with him to Washington, where she worked with the International Ladies Garment Workers Union, then with the Amalgamated Clothing Workers Union. Later in the 1940s, she and her husband, who was now working for the foreign service, lived in Sweden and Belgium for several years.

After World War II, she rejoined the labor movement as a lobbyist, helping persuade Congress to expand the coverage of the Fair Labor Standards Act to guarantee a minimum wage and maximum working hours for workers. Her work with Senator John F. Kennedy (D-MA) led, in 1961, to her appointment as director of the Women's Bureau of the Department of Labor and later as an assistant secretary of labor, a position she held through 1968.

In 1963, after proposing the creation of a subcabinet-level consumer adviser to the president, Kennedy asked Peterson whether she would take the job. Although Kennedy died before Peterson could accept, President Johnson renewed the offer, this time as special assistant to the president for consumer affairs. Peterson accepted, and served in that position through 1967. During this period, she also chaired the president's Committee on Consumer Interests.

As special assistant, Peterson saw her role as coordinating government–consumer activities, locating the gaps, and stimulating local and private consumer groups. Her specific goals were to establish premarket testing for cosmetics; expand authority to require hazard warnings on rugs, cosmetics, and pressurized containers; require the Agriculture Department to certify the safety of pesticides before they were marketed; extend the federal government's authority to inspect meat and poultry that did not cross state lines; allow the Federal Trade Commission to issue temporary cease-and-desist orders while hearings were held on possibly hazardous products or misleading advertising; and enact truth in packaging and truth in lending bills.

Many of these goals were achieved. During Peterson's tenure as special assistant, legislation was enacted on truth in lending, truth in advertising, open dating, unit pricing, meat and poultry inspection, occupational safety, and truth in packaging. She also proposed the creation of a federation of consumer organizations and convened meetings that led to the founding of the Consumer Federation of America in 1968.

In 1970, Peterson worked as consumer adviser to Giant Food and persuaded them to adopt unit pricing and open dating policies. Giant's adoption of these policies was instrumental in the acceptance of improved consumer disclosures by other large food chains.

In 1977, President Carter reappointed Peterson as special assistant to the president for consumer affairs, a position she held through 1980. One of her chief goals was the establishment of a federal office of consumer protection. Widespread business opposition to this proposal, and the refusal of some consumer advocates to support compromise legislation, led to its congressional defeat.

In the 1980s, Peterson supported numerous progressive causes. This work included helping organize the United Seniors Health Cooperative and the Consumer Insurance Interest Group, a coalition of insurance agents and consumer advocates that sought to persuade state governments to strengthen their regulation of the insurance industry.

During this period, however, Peterson's greatest consumer contribution came in 1986, when she led the campaign to persuade the UN to adopt its Consumer Protection Guidelines. Working with the International Organization of Consumers Unions (now Consumers International), she was instrumental in convincing the UN General Assembly to approve minimum health and safety standards. Most important, these standards set goals for developing nations to attain.

Stephen Brobeck

See also: Consumer Federation of America; Consumers International; Labor Movement

Further Reading

Halamandaris, Val J. 1990. "Champion of the Underprivileged: A Tribute to Esther Peterson." *Caring People* (July): 2–13.

Peterson, Esther, and Winifred Conkling. 1995. *Restless: The Memoirs of Labor and Consumer Activist Esther Peterson*. Washington, DC: Caring Publishing.

PEW CHARITABLE TRUSTS

The Pew Charitable Trusts is a large, independent, and activist foundation that, in the past decade, has undertaken consumer research and advocacy in areas such as food safety and financial services. Based in Philadelphia, it maintains an office in Washington, D.C., and has an annual operating budget of around $300 million.

Pew was built by the family of Joseph Newton Pew (1886–1963), founder of the Sun Oil Company, between 1948 and 1979. In 1986, the trusts began work on federal public policy issues, and in 1994, it extended that interest to state policy issues. In 2004, it created the Pew Research Center, a separate operating subsidiary that, among other work, undertakes the nation's most extensive and credible public opinion polling.

In 2004, when the Pew Charitable Trusts became a public charity, it gained greater flexibility to take on a more activist role. Like the Ford Foundation, for example, Pew works in a dozen broad areas, including arts and culture, economic policy, environment, health, and family financial security. But unlike Ford, Pew uses its extensive resources not just to make grants, but also to undertake research and policy initiatives.

This research and advocacy has included work that touches on consumer interests related to the Internet, motor vehicle fuel economy, children's nutrition, prescription drugs, and the use of antibiotics in animal feed. However, Pew has worked most closely with other consumer groups in the areas of food safety and financial services. In fact, most of its leaders in these two areas had experience working for national consumer groups. Food safety expert Sandy Eskin and financial services experts Susan Weinstock and Travis Plunkett had all worked for the Consumer Federation of America. Eskin had also directed Georgetown University's Produce Safety Project, Weinstock had also helped lead AARP's utility advocacy, and Plunkett had also worked for New York PIRG and AARP. Financial services expert Nick Bourke had done consulting for industry.

Pew's work on food safety, launched in 2008, has focused on strengthening the Food and Drug Administration's authority to ensure the safety of the foods it regulates. Pew organized a broad coalition to advocate for the FDA Food Safety Modernization Act (FSMA), legislation enacted in 2011 requiring the agency to develop prevention-based rules for all the foods it regulates and to establish a new oversight system for imported food. Since then, Pew has worked to see that the law is fully implemented through the rulemaking process and that the FDA has sufficient resources to monitor the oversight envisioned in the law. It has also issued reports analyzing the U.S. Department of Agriculture's meat and poultry regulation and proposing improvements to this system.

Pew began work on consumer financial services in 2007 with a focus on improving the safety and transparency of the credit card marketplace. The foundation's reports helped convince policymakers to include certain uniform standards and proscribe harmful practices in the 2009 Credit CARD Act. More recent reports have analyzed small-dollar loans (primarily payday loans), overdraft lending, and checking accounts and have recommended reforms to better inform and protect consumers. Its small-dollar loan work has involved business leaders in the testing of model policies and practices, and has built support for federal and state reforms. Its model disclosure box for checking accounts has been adopted by many of the nation's large banks and credit unions. And it is in the process of developing a similar uniform disclosure box for prepaid cards. In 2013, Pew began research on a range of issues including retirement and short-term saving policy, family balance sheets, and the market effects of payday lending reforms.

Stephen Brobeck

See also: Credit Card Advocacy; Food Safety Advocacy; Payday Loan Advocacy

Further Reading

Strom, Stephanie. 2003. "Pew Charitable Trusts Will Become Public Charity." *New York Times* (November 7).

Wooster, Martin M. 2007. "The Pew Charitable Trusts." *The Great Philanthropists and the Problem of Donor Intent* (pp. 44–52). Washington, DC: Capital Research Center.

PHILIPPINE CONSUMER MOVEMENT

The Philippines is a country where monopolies abound in almost all sectors of the economy. The owners of such monopolies wield vast influence over government agencies and officials who are supposed to protect the ordinary citizen. In this environment, Filipino consumers have become vigilant in protecting their rights from abusive and oppressive business practices.

In the 1970s and 1980s, Filipino activists spearheaded the formation of the Consumer Movement of the Philippines (Kilusang Mamimili ng Pilipinas, or KMPI), the Organization of Workers Consumers (Samahan ng mga Manggagawang Konsumer, or SAMAKO), and the Citizens Alliance for Consumer Protection (CACP), which incorporated consumer issues into the fight against dictatorship during the years of martial law under President Ferdinand Marcos. These organizations were considered more assertive than their predecessors from the 1960s and 1970s, such as the Consumers Federated Group of the Philippines and the Consumer Union of the Philippines. The CACP, for example, went against large corporations on the issue of expensive medicines and exposed how companies were pushing for infant formula in hospitals. Unfortunately, these consumer organizations were not able to sustain themselves and have been dormant (Vermeer, 1981).

Nonetheless, Filipino consumers have continued to come together on certain issues to air their grievances, hold abusive firms accountable, and push for changes in government policy. One of the major consumer issues is the cost of fuel, water, and electricity. The campaign network Coalition against Oil Price Increases (CAOPI), a prominent network in the 1980s that was revived in 2012, gathered together oil consumers from all sectors of society to press for government action against high oil price increases. In the 2000s, Water for the People Network (WPN) and People Opposed to Warrantless Electricity Rates (POWER) were formed to oppose the government privatization policy and its effect on consumer access to power and water services.

Campaigns by networks such WPN and POWER were—and continue to be—crucial in exposing the oppressive practices of utility firms such as high prices and fees for electricity and water. In 2002, strong public protests forced the power distribution giant Meralco to stop the collection of the controversial "purchased power adjustment," a cost automatically passed on to consumers no matter whether the power bought by distributors was generated or used. In 2013, the government's water regulatory office decided to junk the water firms' petition for rate hikes after the WPN and other consumer groups discovered onerous charges in water bills, such as pass-on costs of corporate income taxes and donations.

The price of utilities is just one example of an issue that stirs the commitment of Filipinos. During the early 1990s, consumer groups also expressed their outrage over a lottery by Pepsi in which consumers increased their purchases of the soft drink in an effort to win 1 million pesos (about $40,000) if their bottle cap was marked with winning numbers. However, Pepsi announced the wrong winning number, and instead of a single 1-million-peso winner, up to 800,000 bottle caps marked with the winning "49" were printed. Tens of thousands of winners soon began demanding their money, but Pepsi refused to pay. In their rage, some consumers stoned Pepsi delivery trucks and several Pepsi plants. Today, social media also play an important role in airing consumer complaints regarding poor services of mobile phone, Internet, airline, and credit card companies.

At present, the Philippine consumer movement is built around tactical objectives such as opposing price increases, resisting abusive practices, reforming monopolies, and scrutinizing industry privatization and deregulation. Several campaigns have yielded positive results for consumers; however, a broad, sustained movement for Filipino consumer protection is still lacking. Unlike developed countries where consumer movements tend to focus on the right to choice and safety, the most pressing consumer issue in the Philippines is the high cost of basic products and services. The movement has yet to develop proactive mechanisms to address grievances and promote redress on a variety of consumer welfare issues.

Notably, most of Filipino consumer activists are part of people's organizations pushing for the interests and welfare of marginalized groups in society. For instance, the women's umbrella organization Gabriela, which has been active in promoting the rights and welfare of women since the 1980s, includes consumer issues in its campaigns. Examples of these issues are the high prices of rice, food, fuel, and utilities. The group formed the consumer alliance Consumer Alert (Alerto Mamimili) at the height of increasing prices of basic commodities in the early 2000s. Similarly, the broad-based New Patriotic Alliance (Bagong Alyansang Makabayan, or "Bayan") and its organizations have spearheaded the formation of CAOPI, POWER, and other campaign-oriented consumer alliances like Consumers Action for Empowerment (focusing on access to medicines) and TextPower (campaigning for fair practices in telecom services). Likewise, the Philippine Peasant Movement (Kilusang Magbubukid ng Pilipinas) formed the alliance Rice Monitor (Bantay Bigas) to campaign against the so-called rice cartel that currently dictates the prices and supply of rice in the country. The alliance is also active in campaigning against the effects of a rice liberalization policy that has removed subsidies for both consumers and farmers. Recently, the organization also exposed the issue of rice smuggling and its effect on rice prices and income of Filipino farmers.

Meanwhile, the cause-oriented research group IBON, established in the late 1970s during the martial law period to be an alternative source of socioeconomic information, has contributed in the formation of these campaign-based consumer alliances by providing advocacy support through research on various consumer issues such as water, power, and food. The research group also provides secretariat work in several consumer coalitions as well as doing lobby work in Congress and government agencies. IBON, a member of Consumers International, also reaches out to broader networks of consumers with its publications, campaign materials, forums, and consumer assemblies.

Funding of campaign coalitions and people's organizations in the Philippines relies mostly on donations from members and allies. These groups also conduct their own income-generating activities to support their campaigns. Fundraising activities include selling campaign materials that promote their advocacy (statement shirts, buttons, bags, calendars, etc.), publishing and selling books on consumer issues, and holding fundraising events such as concerts, dinners, sports events, and protest fashion shows.

There are many other issue-based organizations in the Philippines. These include the National Association of Electricity Consumers for Reforms, Inc. (NASECORE), Water for All Refund Movement, Ecowaste Coalition (plus many other environmentalist-based consumer groups), National Center for Commuter Safety and Protection (NCCSP), Coalition for Consumer Protection and Welfare, Inc. (formerly 349 Coalition), Consumer Rights for Safe Food, Parents Enabling Parents Coalition, and Consumer Oil Price Watch—led by businessman Raul Concepcion—among others. Ordinary consumers who are not part of any consumer group or alliance have resorted to bringing their numerous grievances to the traditional media, Internet-based social media, or by contacting concerned government agencies like the Department of Trade and Industry and National Telecommunications Commission.

All in all, despite the numerous organizations and coalitions in the Philippines, the advocacy for consumer rights has been more short-term and tactical than long-term and strategic. Filipinos have yet to see the development of a broad, national consumer rights movement that can synthesize, initiate, and support sustained campaigns including legal actions and engagement in policy advocacy. Some opinionmakers believe that new technology, such as social media, can be leveraged to create such a movement.

At present, Bayan, IBON, and allied organizations are working to build an umbrella consumer organization that will address the need for an organized consumer movement in the Philippines. Members of the network would include individuals, consumer groups, homeowners associations, cooperatives, members of the media, academic bodies, and other concerned organizations. The proposed umbrella organization will be launched in 2014, and it will apply as a unifying starting point the eight basic consumer rights found in the UN Guidelines on Consumer Protection. The organizers are also looking to align the network to the international consumer movement.

Rhea Padilla

See also: United Nations Guidelines for Consumer Protection

Further Reading

Ibarra, Venus. 1998. *Consumerism and Pharmaceutical Companies in Belgium and in the Philippines: A Comparative Study on the Awareness of the Basic Rights of Consumers.* Discussion Paper No. 19, Centre for ASEAN Studies. http://webh01.ua.ac.be/cas/PDF/CAS19.pdf.

Tan, Michael. 2007. "Wanted: Consumerism. *Philippine Daily Inquirer.* January 9. http://opinion.inquirer.net/inquireropinion/columns/view/20070109-42494/Wanted:_consumerism.

Tan, Michael. 2009. "A New Consumerism." *Philippine Daily Inquirer.* February 27. http://showbizandstyle.inquirer.net/lifestyle/lifestyle/view/20090227-191268/A_new_consumerism.

Vermeer, Ruth Simmons. 1981. "The Consumer Movement: A Historical Overview." *Life Today* (November): 20–21.

POLISH CONSUMER MOVEMENT

Among central and eastern European countries, Poland's consumer movement emerged the earliest and has become one of the region's most durable and diverse. Even prior to the breakup of the Soviet bloc, Poland had an important consumer organization—Consumer Federation (Federacja Konsumentow, or FK). Since then, consumer activism in Poland has gained strength as part of the nation's development of a robust civil society and market economy. The consumer movement in Poland is complemented by governmental consumer protection bodies. The Office for Competition and Consumer Protection (Urzad Ochrony Konkurencji i Konsumentow—UOKiK) is in charge of consumer policy and promotes the collective interests of Polish consumers.

Consumer activism in Poland originated with the establishment of FK in 1981. FK is the largest and the best-known consumer organization in Poland, with about forty local units around the country. In 2011, FK had approximately a thousand individual members. There was a staff of five, with volunteers doing a great deal of additional work. The organization's main activities include consumer representation, information provision, and education. One of FK's primary activities is running a national hotline known as "Consumer Infoline." With the assistance of government funding, FK's local units offer consumers assistance, including legal advice.

The Association of Polish Consumers (Stowarzyszenie Konsumentow Polskich—SKP) is also an important consumer organization. Founded in 1995 as a research and advocacy organization, SKP employs experts on consumer protection (twenty-three as of 2011). Its main activities include offering free legal advice; disseminating consumer information and running education campaigns for local consumer ombudsmen, seniors, and young consumers; providing consumer representation; and working cooperatively with partners such as local consumer ombudsmen, other civil society organizations, and state agencies. Beginning' in 2010, SKP has brought together consumer protection institutions and organizations in the Polish Consumer Knowledge Fair to celebrate the World Consumer Rights Day (March 15), the world's biggest consumer educational event.

Both FK and SKP are recognized as experts in the field of consumer protection. They are consulted by the national government, as well as local entities, on how best to protect consumer interests, and they are well covered in the media. Both organizations are active in promoting alternative dispute resolution systems (ADRs) and responsible business practices. Both FK and SKP are members of Consumers International, the international association of consumer organizations, and BEUC: The European Consumer Organisation.

PRO-TEST is a private foundation that publishes an online magazine containing comparative test results for products and services. Because the two major Polish consumer associations do not conduct comparative testing, the magazine fills an important gap. So far, paid circulation of PRO-TEST's magazine is small, but increasing affluence in Poland suggests that the publication's prospects for growth are good. PRO-TEST is a member of International Consumer Research and Testing (ICRT).

Consumer activism is not well developed at the local level in Poland. Although more than 800 institutions list consumer protection among their activities and meet the basic legal requirements for being organizations, many do not actually take an active role in consumer activism. One reason is that beginning in 1999, local, government-funded consumer ombudsmen have provided free advice and legal information (including assistance in bringing consumer disputes to court) to consumers. There are more than 366 local consumer ombudsmen based in all Polish districts. Local governments thereby satisfy most consumer demand for consumer education and information at the local level.

A second reason is that unlike many other European countries, there is little government funding in Poland for consumer organizations, especially local ones, and only officially designated consumer organizations are eligible to receive government support. There is no national or local budget line for funding consumer organizations in Poland, but consumer organizations can apply for funding from state, regional, or local budgets by participating in the calls for proposals on projects that promote and protect consumer rights. The majority of these calls for proposals concern providing consumer advice. Ironically, the resulting consumer expectation that advice and information should be available free of charge hinders the development of membership-based consumer organizations that charge for their services. With public funding as their main source of income, consumer organizations face an unstable funding environment. The system of public funding is focused on the short term, with projects usually lasting no longer than one year. This limits the opportunity for strategic planning. Another issue is that the main criterion for granting funds is the cost of the proposed project. This leads to a strong price competition among organizations.

The main consumer problem remains weak enforcement of consumer rights, particularly related to retail sales. Seeking redress via civil litigation is not cost-effective for most consumer disputes. ADR systems represent an alternative and are relatively well developed in Poland, but they are available only in select markets. Consumer organizations have no legal power (and not enough resources) to participate in collective legal actions.

A span of more than thirty years of consumer activism in Poland has resulted in significant developments. The current system of consumer protection was established thanks to consumer organizations that introduced consumer policy to consumers, business, and politicians. For example, in the 1990s, FK lobbied successfully for the engagement of local government in consumer policy; during the next ten years, SKP successfully trained local consumer ombudsmen in consumer policy and legislation. Accession to the European Union in 2004, with its corresponding requirements in terms of consumer policy, was the next step in development of consumer protection in Poland. However, the consumer movement is still underfunded and not granted a partnership position by public institutions.

Grazyna Rokicka

See also: BEUC: The European Consumer Organisation; Consumers International

Further Reading

Fielder, Anna. 2011. *The State of the Consumer Movement in Poland.* In *The State of the Consumer Nation(s): An Evaluation of the Consumer Movement in Six Countries of Central, Eastern, and South Eastern Europe.* Brussels, Belgium: BEUC: The European Consumer Organisation.

Mazurek, Malgorzata, and Matthew Hilton. 2007. "Consumerism, Solidarity and Communism: Consumer Protection and the Consumer Movement in Poland." *Journal of Contemporary History* 42, no. 2: 315–343.

PRESCRIPTION DRUG ADVOCACY

The safety, efficacy, and accessibility of medicinal drugs have long been issues of keen interest to consumer activists in the United States. At the turn of the twentieth century, groups of female consumers—including the National Consumers League (NCL) and the General Federation of Women's Clubs—mobilized to support a push for federal-level regulation of both food and medicines. The effort was spearheaded by Harvey Wiley, chief of the Department of Agriculture's Bureau of Chemistry. Publicity surrounding Wiley's research into the effects of chemical food additives on the bodies of healthy volunteers, combined with muckraking articles in publications such as *Ladies Home Journal* and *Colliers* about food adulteration and the large volume of ineffectual or unsafe drug products on the market, galvanized these consumers. This legislative initiative engaged middle-class consumers, appealing to their desire to be protected from hidden sanitary and chemical threats. However, some reformers—including settlement house worker and founder of NCL Florence Kelley—supported the legislation as one of a range of reforms aimed at making twentieth-century consumer society more humane, including labor laws for women and children, workers' compensation mechanisms, tenement regulation, and provision of basic nutrition and medical services for poor people.

The Pure Food and Drug Act of 1906 that resulted from Progressive-era consumer activism laid crucial groundwork for what became the federal Food and Drug Administration (FDA) and instituted regulation of so-called "ethical" drugs (listed in the *U.S. Pharmacopoeia* and prescribed by physicians). But this law was limited in its effect on the trade in patent medicines—the heavily marketed, proprietary products composed largely of water and addictive substances that made up the vast majority of medicinal drugs consumed by Americans in the first few decades of the twentieth century. When new consumer movement leaders came to prominence in the 1920s and 1930s by excoriating the excesses of advertising, the poor quality of consumer products, and the marginalization of consumers' interests in government in a series of popular publications, patent medicines figured prominently in their screeds. These muckraking activists founded the first consumer-oriented product testing organization, Consumers' Research (CR), in 1929, and their widely read 1932 book, *100,000,000 Guinea Pigs* by Arthur Kallet and F. J. Schlink, helped stimulate a legislative movement toward a new food and drug law that culminated with passage of the Food, Drug, and Cosmetic (FDC) and Wheeler–Lea Acts of 1938.

The interwar period and the Great Depression exposed political and ideological divisions between consumer advocates, and this polarization became evident in the renewed debate around the federal regulation of drugs. By the time the laws were passed, liberal and radical strains of the consumer movement had emerged, taking different positions on the legislation. CR turned toward a conservative brand of libertarianism and withdrew from debate over the drug law, whereas liberal consumerists took a middle-of-the-road approach, seeking discrete protections for FDA authority. The more radical contingent, which wanted government to be forceful in keeping dangerous and ineffectual products off the market, formed the unionized, consumer product-testing organization Consumers Union (CU) by breaking off from CR in 1936.

CU identified with radical groups engaged in forms of direct action for social, political, and material ends—organizing unemployment councils, unions, collectives, rent strikes, and boycotts—and favored cross-class unification of consumers. Leftist physician Harold Aaron directed CU's work on patent medicines and the food and drug law. Aaron was affiliated with the increasingly self-conscious and professionalized practice of "social medicine," by which some in the medical field sought to address social and political factors affecting public health. Their primary objective in the interwar period was securing national health insurance, for which CU also advocated strongly.

In the conservative political environment of the postwar period, CU and other institutions associated with social medicine either moderated their approach or disappeared. At the same time, there were substantive transformations in the realm of pharmaceuticals and national health policy. Amendments to the FDC Act codified in detail the distinction between prescription and over-the-counter drugs but preserved drug companies' ultimate prerogative to determine which of their own products qualified, just as powerful new "wonder drugs"—antibiotics, hormones, and psychotropic medications—significantly altered clinical medicine and epidemiology. American health care policy and biomedical research cleaved to an acute illness model, focusing on clinical care and use of new pharmaceuticals rather than on preventive interventions in disease-causation. Scientists and physicians such as Harold Aaron at CU, Wilhelm Hueper at the National Cancer

Institute, and Barbara Moulton at the FDA quietly laid foundations of a critique of this increasingly pharmaceutically centered national health policy. Moulton, a reviewer of new drugs for the FDA, later testified in hearings, held by Senator Estes Kefauver, that led to significant reforms to the Food Drug and Cosmetic Act in 1962. She also became a source for journalist Morton Mintz, who broke the story of thalidomide, a tranquilizer inducing birth defects, that facilitated passage of the 1962 amendments. Mintz wrote the most extensive and widely read work of pharmaceutical muckraking of the 1960s, *The Therapeutic Nightmare*.

Over the next decade, as prescription drugs became more central to medical care, and as pharmaceutical companies became more powerful, lawmakers beginning with Kefauver raised questions about drug prices and advocated affordable prices for patients. At the same time, a new generation of reformers scrutinized the safety and efficacy of drugs. Liberal critiques from Mintz and a few congressmen in the early to mid-1960s opened debate. Advocates who began to focus on drugs in the 1970s intended to address issues of the affordability, safety, and efficacy of specific drugs, but also to reform the political, economic, and social construction of the diseases these drugs aimed to treat. These consumer advocates developed critiques of pharmaceuticals and related policies that drew on more radical thought from within the civil rights and antiwar movements of the late 1960s. They called into question the substance of scientifically based knowledge about health and illness, as well as the institutions that conferred physician authority. Leading this new wave of advocacy around prescription drugs were Sidney Wolfe, a physician who had been active in a medical group involved in the civil rights movement, and activists within the women's health movement, who responded to new concerns about the safety of hormones used by millions of women to regulate fertility and affect pregnancy.

Between 1971 and 1972, Wolfe partnered with Ralph Nader to found the Health Research Group (HRG) as an autonomous division of the larger consumer advocacy organization, Public Citizen. HRG focused on a range of issues in the areas of healthcare delivery and occupational safety and health, but prescription drugs were an emphasis from the start and were the subject of the many of HRG's most successful initiatives. After journalist Barbara Seaman highlighted the potential adverse effects of oral contraceptives in a popular book, *The Doctor's Case against the Pill*—resulting in high-profile Senate hearings in 1970 and, soon after, an insert that disclosed the risks of the drugs in every package prescribed—women's groups and HRG continued to monitor the risks and benefits of "the Pill" and advocate for federal and corporate transparency in matters related to these drugs. When it became apparent that the widespread use of the synthetic hormone diethylstilbestrol (DES) as a post-coital contraceptive was failing to prevent pregnancies and was associated with cancer in the daughters of women who used it, a student named Belita Cowan spearheaded an effort to educate others and restrict the drug's use. Along with women's groups, Nader helped Cowan bring the issue national attention in 1972. HRG staff researched the drug and became a regular presence in debates over the safety and efficacy of synthetic and conjugated estrogens for controlling fertility and treating symptoms of menopause and post-menopausal changes. HRG often worked collaboratively with the National Women's Health Network (NWHN), which Seaman and Cowan helped found in 1975 as a national political action organization and women's health clearinghouse. During this decade, NWHN was the only consumer group, besides HRG, that participated extensively in FDA proceedings concerning drugs.

Women's health advocates and HRG honed an aggressive, multipronged approach to altering FDA policy and actions in relation to specific products, using press releases, letters, citizen's petitions, lawsuits, and communications with congressional subcommittee leaders. HRG developed and elaborated this approach throughout the 1970s and 1980s, as the group applied similar strategies to other drug classes than fertility-related hormones, including antibiotics, drugs for diabetes and high cholesterol, and drugs for anxiety and pain. In many instances, HRG urged the FDA to use stronger drug warning labels, restrict prescription of certain drugs, and sometimes remove drugs from the market altogether. HRG filed the first-ever citizen petition seeking stronger restrictions on a drug, precipitating an FDA advisory committee meeting that resulted in a stronger warning label on the antibiotic erythromycin estolate.

In 1974, the group entered a fierce debate that had been raging over the safety of the sulfonylurea class of oral hypoglycemic drugs, persuading Senator Gaylord Nelson (D-WI) to hold hearings on these medicines, testifying before FDA advisory committees, and ultimately—because FDA did not place additional warnings on the drugs until 1984—publishing its own book appealing directly to consumers not to use these drugs. In 1977, after an FDA advisory committee unanimously recommended withdrawing approval for another antidiabetes drug, the biguanide phenformin, HRG successfully petitioned FDA to exercise for the first time its power to immediately remove a drug from the market as an "imminent hazard." In the late 1970s, HRG also brought scrutiny both to the early cholesterol-lowering drug clofibrate, which ultimately resulted in a black box warning and a vast contraction in the drug's use, and to the painkiller Darvon, approval for which FDA withdrew thirty-two years later at the group's renewed urging. In the early and mid-1980s, much of HRG's advocacy focused on multiple nonsteroidal anti-inflammatory drugs, several of which were eventually removed from the market. Alongside unions, senior citizens' groups, and professional pharmacists, HRG also advocated successfully for consumer access to more affordable generic forms of prescription drugs—first in state-level struggles against antisubstitutions laws, and later in national-level efforts to facilitate FDA approval of generics.

The Health Research Group was not successful in every initiative regarding a specific drug. And although HRG had some high-profile victories and carved out a spot for itself in high-level debates over drug regulation, the relatively radical reforms for which Wolfe and his team advocated in the 1970s never materialized. These reforms included requiring therapeutic superiority of a new drug over existing drugs for FDA approval, coordinating the testing of experimental drugs, mandating patient-education procedures for prescribing, and promulgating of a National Formulary of medically essential drugs for which (and only for which) the government would reimburse through its healthcare financing programs.

Other advocates, such as Philip Lee—two-time assistant secretary for health, under presidents Lyndon Johnson and Bill Clinton—pursued a similar range of reforms in the 1970s and subsequent decades but used a less public, less litigious, and more politically collaborative approach. As many of these reforms began to seem elusive in the mid-1970s, HRG began employing new and more aggressive strategies. The antibiotic clindamycin and DES became the basis for the HRG's first "clearinghouses"—bodies of information about drugs that the group sold to plaintiffs' attorneys for use in tort suits on behalf of clients harmed by those drugs. In this period, lawyers began to win impressive awards and settlements for clients, claiming injury from prescription drugs, and brought the first mass toxic substances litigation against pharmaceutical companies. In collaboration with the Litigation Group, another charter division of Public Citizen, HRG also brought its own lawsuits against the federal government to gain access to drug information in FDA's possession or to compel the agency to take action.

Two of the more successful legal battles brought Wolfe and HRG to a new level of engagement in FDA politics and public visibility in the early 1980s. They involved the group's efforts to compel FDA, first, to act on the findings of the retrospective efficacy review of prescription drugs approved before the 1962 amendments to the FDC Act and, second, to complete the safety-and-efficacy review of pre-1962 over-the-counter (OTC) drugs. HRG had a significant effect on these extensive regulatory undertakings, and at the same time, Wolfe became a regular presence on popular media outlets, taking his concerns about drugs straight to consumers. Amid its efforts to expedite FDA action in removing ineffective pre-1962 prescription drugs, HRG published its first book, *Pills That Don't Work*, which made one of the best-seller lists. Sales of this publication were boosted enormously by Wolfe's appearance on the daytime talk show *Donahue*. Over the next three decades, HRG published multiple books that advised consumers directly about which specific drugs were and were not safe and effective. Many of these publications became mass-market best-sellers, helping fund all the activities of Public Citizen.

The 1980s solidified HRG's place in the national debates over drug regulation, but the group spent much of the decade fighting against the Reagan administration's efforts to roll back regulations to increase the U.S. pharmaceutical industry's competitiveness in an increasingly global marketplace. At the same time, political, economic, social, and epidemiologic changes also drove an expansion and diversification of consumer activism around prescription drugs. In the mid- to late 1970s, a growing number of health professionals and activists had begun to decry double standards for consumer protection against pharmaceutical-related risks in the industrialized and developing worlds. Newly forming consumer groups in poorer nations began to call attention to the marketing of drugs they saw as unsafe, ineffective, or inordinately expensive. In 1977, when the World Health Organization (WHO) published a list of 182 "essential" drugs deemed adequate to meet 90 percent of developing countries' need for pharmaceuticals, these groups advocated vigorously that governments adopt regulatory policies structured around this essential medicines list.

The expansion of the consumer movement in the developing world occurred with crucial assistance from the International Organization of Consumers Union (IOCU, later Consumers International), which represented consumer organizations from the United States, Western Europe, and Australia and which received a portion of its original funding in 1960s from CU as it gingerly re-entered politics. In 1981, multiple groups, which had been involved in successful efforts to secure the WHO's adoption of the International Code of Marketing of Breast-Milk Substitutes and an effort to see the antifungal/antiprotozoal drug Clioquinol banned in Japan, came together to form a new organization, Health Action International, that continued to advocate vigorously for drug safety and access. A new Nader-affiliated publication, *The Multinational Monitor*, had begun reporting on the conduct of multinational corporations overseas in the late 1970s; in 1982, it formed a new organization, Essential Information, to support the international expansion of consumer activism by facilitating information exchange among groups.

In the United States, one result of this ferment around international pharmaceutical issues was a revisiting, in the early 1980s, of a problem associated with poorly controlled antibiotic use over which some physicians, and even the CU publication *Consumer Reports*, had expressed concern as early as the 1950s—drug-resistant bacteria. In the late 1970s, Stuart Levy, an American doctor and microbiologist who had studied the transference of antibiotic resistance between animals and humans, became aware of the extent to which human populations in the developing world continued to act as reservoirs for infection and, increasingly, yielded drug-resistant strains of bacteria. Levy and colleagues concerned about antibiotic resistance began urging governments to adopt standards for antibiotic prescription, distribution, advertising, and dispensing that were uniform internationally.

To carry out and support research and advocacy around the issue, Levy founded the Alliance for the Prudent Use of Antibiotics. This renewed attention to the problems associated with antibiotic consumption, both internationally and domestically, and triggered congressional hearings in 1984, but it did not result in the adoption of any new U.S. policy that would exert more centralized control over the prescription of antibiotics. Neither did the even more intense scrutiny of antibiotic use generated during the 1990s, when the emergence in industrialized nations of new infectious pathogens such as the AIDS virus and the resurgence of old bacterial scourges such as tuberculosis—sometimes in new, drug-resistant strains— re-invigorated the surveillance and infection-control operations of state health departments and the Centers for Disease Control and Prevention.

The era of AIDS did, however, see a change in the face of consumer activism around prescription drugs the world over. In the late 1980s, new grassroots formations of AIDS activists in the United States—most prominently, the AIDS Coalition to Unleash Power (ACT-UP)—began advocacy around prescription drug issues. With the objective of obtaining treatment, these groups began emulating some of the aggressive advocacy techniques of civil rights, consumer, and women's health advocates, quickly affecting debates over pharmaceutical policy in which HRG had long been involved. AIDS activists became participants in FDA policymaking related to AIDS drugs and helped expand the numbers of HIV-positive people eligible for federal programs that subsidized treatment. At the same time, the drug industry and its political allies used the renewed scrutiny that AIDS activists brought to the drug-approval process to pursue long-desired deregulatory agendas at the FDA.

These efforts eventually resulted in reforms—not only to the assessment of drugs for life-threatening illnesses, but also to evaluation of all drugs—on an order that the pharmaceutical industry's political allies had sought in the early 1980s but had never attained. HRG remained a powerful institutional player, but the landmark legislation that was a byproduct of this reinvigorated reform drive, the Prescription Drug User Fee Act (PDUFA) of 1992, shifted a large portion of the financial burden of new-drug review from government to the industry itself. This change weakened the congressional influence over FDA conduct, which had been a major tool of HRG's advocacy, and gave manufacturers greater influence within the agency. In the late-1990s, PDUFA began to take effect in ways shaped by the surging "new Right." By the early 2000s, the state of U.S. drug regulation was coming under scrutiny in popular and medical press outlets, and the 2004 removal of Vioxx from the market intensified this attention. Vioxx was the first in a new class of nonsteroidal anti-inflammatories about which HRG had raised safety concerns. Whistleblowers within the FDA testified in congressional hearings, and prominent physicians, including former editors of the *New England Journal of Medicine* Jerome Kassirer and Marcia Angell, became outspoken critics of the pharmaceutical industry's role in medicine.

Beginning in the early 1990s, transformations in the AIDS epidemic also shaped domestic activism in other ways and mobilized new forms of activism at the global level. The experiences of women and minorities within the American AIDS activism movement and the rapid spread of the disease in poor and minority communities— even as AIDS drugs began to revolutionize treatment—re-introduced questions about deeply rooted social determinants of health and illness and splintered the movement in the United States. The epidemic also continued to spread at explosive rates in the developing world while ratification of trade-liberalizing treaties facilitated profound change in the pharmaceutical industry worldwide.

In the late 1990s, global trade activists began to highlight the human consequences of free trade agreements and structural adjustment policy, and an overlapping group of reformers, including many veterans from the AIDS and consumer activist movements, took up the issue of drug prices in the developing world. Drug prices were never the primary focus of HRG's activism, though the group did periodically champion national single-payer health insurance and policies to facilitate development of lower-cost generic versions of drugs. In light of the advancement of the epidemic globally and the economic obstacles that stood between millions of patients and life-saving treatment, activists chose to focus intensively on distinguishing prescription drugs from other commodities subject to international trade agreements. With important leadership from Bronx-based AIDS physician Alan Berkman, multiple international and U.S.-based organizations, including the Consumer Project on Technology, Essential Information, Doctors without Borders, ACT-UP, and Health Action International, combined to form the Health

Global Access Project Coalition, which used high-profile advocacy in venues that included the Office of the U.S. Trade Representative and the World Trade Organization to support grassroots level initiatives seeking compulsory licensing and parallel importation of crucial drugs.

In 2000 and 2001, global treatment activists achieved a series of substantive gains. Prices of antiretroviral drugs dropped significantly amid increased competition in 2000, and the United Nations announced its intention to found the Global Fund to Fight AIDS, Tuberculosis, and Malaria—developments that treatment activists seized upon to advance their agenda of expanding access to medications. In South Africa, Brazil, and Kenya, treatment activists confronted the brand name pharmaceutical industry, successfully pressing for new laws and court rulings that facilitated production or importing of affordable generic drugs. In more recent years, however, the shifting international political environment, and the same deep, structural factors that also facilitate the spread of the epidemic in poor countries, have slowed treatment activists' progress.

The landscape of consumer advocacy around prescription drugs has changed a great deal, not only since Florence Kelley joined Harvey Wiley in seeking to curb snake oil sales, but also since the 1970s, when women's health activists and other consumer representatives began asserting that access to safe and effective medicines was citizens' right. HRG's publications evaluating specific drugs now figure among many such assessments available online. These evaluations have been generated by a variety of sources—those that are for-profit or not-for-profit and those that have obscure funding sources or that are staunchly independent. The latter include the UK-based Cochrane Collaboration, which began conducting meta-analyses of research on pharmaceuticals and other clinical interventions in the early 1990s in pursuit of a more "evidence-based" approach to medicine, undistorted by bias from researchers' and corporations' interest in obtaining particular outcomes.

The AIDS activism movement inspired other patients and health service consumers to organize, self-educate, fundraise, and engage in advocacy with a new level of vigor. It also inspired industry representatives to seek alliances with, fund, and even create such groups when possible. The number of such groups in the United States, many having significant pharmaceutical industry funding, has grown exponentially in the twenty-first century. The AIDS epidemic also, however, spurred a global movement to protect patients' access to essential medicines as a basic human right. The efforts of HRG and others to empower consumers and strengthen the U.S. government's role in protecting consumers' interests in prescription drugs continue, as does advocacy to increase access to medicines worldwide. Historically, these different strands of consumer activism have operated largely in parallel, but as advocates of safe, effective, and affordable healthcare and medicinal drugs find their efforts stymied by corporate interests, they may find opportunities to develop new, coordinated strategies both domestically and abroad.

Ava Alkon

See also: Families USA; Health Insurance Advocacy; Healthcare Advocacy; Public Citizen

Further Reading

Alkon, Ava. 2012. "Late 20th-Century Consumer Advocacy, Pharmaceuticals, and Public Health: Public Citizen's Health Research Group in Historical Perspective" (PhD diss., Columbia University).

Greene, Jeremy A. 2007. *Prescribing by Numbers: Drugs and the Definition of Disease*. Baltimore, MD: Johns Hopkins University Press.

Tone, Andrea, and Elizabeth Siegel Watkins, eds. 2007. *Medicating Modern America: Prescription Drugs in History*. New York: New York University Press.

Wolfe, Sidney, et al. 2005. *Worst Pills, Best Pills: A Consumer's Guide to Avoiding Drug-Induced Death or Illness*. New York: Pocket Books.

PRIVACY ADVOCACY

Consumer privacy advocates seek to increase control by individuals over their personal information gathered by those selling goods and services and, to a lesser extent, by governments. These activists have focused particular attention on information related to financial, health care, and communications services. Their concerns range from psychological loss of privacy to marketing manipulation to discrimination (e.g., by insurers or employers) to data breaches, including identity theft. Related to the loss of control over personal information is loss of privacy through physical intrusion such as telemarketing calls.

The concern of consumer advocates about these privacy issues reached critical mass in the 1990s, when several national privacy groups were founded. What chiefly provoked this concern was a digital revolution in which computers, the Internet, smartphones, and video equipment allowed quantum increases in the storing, sharing, analysis, use, and abuse of personal information. To this concern, one industry leader of the revolution—Scott McNealy, CEO of Sun MicroSystems—opined in 1999: "Privacy is dead. Get over it." In response, consumer and privacy advocates built organizations and coalitions to immediately keep personal privacy on life support, with the long-term goal of establishing fundamental individual privacy rights that would fully revive the patient.

With few exceptions, the early advocates for personal privacy were not consumer organizations; most were academics or journalists. In the 1960s and 1970s, computer scientist Willis Ware, MIT president and presidential science advisor Jerome Wiesner, Harvard law professor Arthur Miller (*Assault on Privacy*), and Columbia law professor Alan Westin (*Privacy and Freedom*) were instrumental in bringing privacy concerns to the attention of the larger society. So were Ralph Nader, who pushed Congress to update privacy laws, and Vance Packard, who in 1964 published *The Naked Society*. Journalists such as David Burnham (*New York Times* and author of *The Rise of the Computer State*), Evan Hendricks (*Privacy Times*), and Robert Ellis Smith (*Privacy Journal*) began writing about privacy in the 1970s and continued this coverage of privacy issues into the current century.

In the earlier period, the most influential organization advocating for increased privacy was the American Civil Liberties Union (ACLU), and it continues this advocacy today. Many leading privacy advocates—including Jerry Berman, Marc

Rotenberg, JanLori Goldman, Jay Stanley, and Chris Calabrese—got their start or spent time at the ACLU—working on privacy issues. With individual advocates, the ACLU supported the first important consumer privacy legislation—the Fair Credit Reporting Act of 1970, which required credit investigations and reporting agencies to give consumers access to records—that was championed by Senator William Proxmire (D-WI) with House leadership from Representative Leonor Sullivan (D-MO).

The post-Watergate era provided an opportunity for significant legislative progress, including the Privacy Act of 1974, which established comprehensive privacy safeguards for records held by federal agencies. Yet because this law did not extend these safeguards to data held by private companies, privacy advocates began working on developing "sectoral legislation" that aimed to establish privacy laws for specific industries and practices. An early victory came in the form of privacy subscriber provisions in the Cable Act of 1984. Two years later, Congress enacted the Electronic Communications Privacy Act and, in 1988, passed the Video Privacy Protection Act, one of the first laws to establish privacy safeguards for new digital services. Senator Patrick Leahy (D-VT) successfully championed both bills.

In the 1980s, organizations dedicated solely to working on privacy issues began emerging. Computer Professionals for Social Responsibility (CPSR) was incorporated in 1983, initially focusing on the use of computers in warfare. In succession, Marc Rotenberg, who today heads the Electronic Privacy Information Center (EPIC), organized the ACLU's Privacy and Technology Project, worked for Senator Leahy on privacy issues, headed the DC office of CPSR, and founded the Public Interest Computer Association.

In the 1990s, Congress approved a broad range of new privacy protections related to autodialers, phone records, medical records, children's data, and financial information. The Telephone Consumer Protection Act of 1991 restricted telemarketing calls, including those of autodialers. The Telecommunications Act of 1996 required phone companies to gain consumer approval before using information about calling patterns to market new services. The Health Insurance Portability and Accountability Act (HIPAA) of 1996 required standards for protecting the privacy of health information about individuals. The Children's Online Privacy Protection Act of 1998 limited the ability of commercial websites and online services to collect information about children 12 years old and younger. The Financial Modernization Act of 1999 ("Gramm–Leach–Bliley") required financial institutions to notify customers of information practices.

National consumer organizations—including U.S. PIRG, Consumers Union (CU), and Consumer Federation of America (CFA)—supported most of this legislation. But so, too, did a growing number of new public interest groups focused exclusively on privacy issues. In 1990, former industry leader Mitch Kapor, Jerry Berman, and others created the Electronic Frontier Foundation (EFF) as an advocate for digital rights. In 1991, Kathryn Montgomery and Jeff Chester organized the Center for Media Education (CME) to address online privacy issues related to children. In 1992, Beth Givens and others founded the Privacy Rights Clearinghouse (PRC) to educate and advocate for consumers on issues related to consumer credit, direct marketing, and data breaches. In 1994, Jerry Berman left EFF to organize the Center for Democracy and Technology (CDT) to "promote democratic values and constitutional liberties in a digital age." Also in 1994, Marc Rotenberg founded EPIC. In 2001, Jeff Chester left CME to organize the Center for Digital Democracy (CDD) to oppose the monopolistic practices of consumer information companies. In 2003, Pam Dixon founded the World Privacy Forum to research and to educate consumers about privacy issues, especially in the digital area.

Most of these new organizations worked on a broad array of privacy and related digital information issues, which included government access to phone calls and emails. But they also joined with established consumer groups to try protecting consumer information collected, used, and sometimes abused by corporations. In the financial services area, it was common for mainstream groups—notably, U.S. PIRG, CU, CFA—to join with financial services advocates—such as Americans for Financial Reform, Center for Responsible Lending, National Consumer Law Center, National Association of Consumer Advocates—and with privacy organizations—including CDD and Privacy Times. Yet, on most other consumer privacy issues, the members of ad hoc coalitions included roughly equal number of consumer groups—e.g., CU, U.S. PIRG (Edmund Mierzwinski), Consumer Action (Linda Sherry and Ruth Susswein), CFA (Susan Grant), Consumer Watchdog (John Simpson)—and privacy groups—CDD, EFF, PRC, Privacy Times, EPIC, CDT (Ari Schwartz then Justin Brookman), Privacy Rights Clearinghouse—as well as the ACLU. In the health privacy area, two groups played a leading role—the Health Privacy Project, which was organized by JanLori Goldman to ensure effective implementation of the 1996 health privacy law, and Patient Privacy Rights, which was founded in 2004 by Dr. Deborah Peel, who organized the Coalition for Patient Privacy.

These advocates communicate regularly with each other. EPIC convenes monthly privacy meetings and submits *amicus curia* legal briefs to appellate courts on related technology and civil liberties concerns. U.S. privacy and consumer groups often coordinate group letters and regulatory comments to policymakers, often to the Federal Trade Commission.

Many of these organizations also cooperate with public interest groups in other countries. Since 1995, both U.S. and European consumer groups have worked together in the Transatlantic Consumer Dialogue to address issues of common concern, which include data privacy, unsolicited electronic mail, child privacy, the use of RFIDs (radio-frequency identification tags), mobile privacy, privacy and security in relation to smart meters, cloud computing, consumer privacy protections in cross-border data flows, and the growing influence of large U.S. Internet companies. Privacy International, founded in 1991 by Simon Davies and based in London, has helped shape strategies used by U.S. advocacy groups. International privacy frameworks, such as the OECD Privacy Guidelines and the EU Data Protection Directive, have also influenced the work of U.S. privacy organizations.

In 2007, recognizing the implications for privacy of the increasing use of online behavioral tracking and targeting, U.S. consumer and privacy groups called for effective "do not track" tools for consumers. They also participated in an effort by the World Wide Web Consortium to set technical standards for honoring "do not track" requests. Though industry opposition thwarted this initiative, some browsers now make available no-tracking options to users, and advertisers maintain a program providing limited consumer controls on the use of data gleaned through online tracking. Advocacy by consumer and privacy groups was also instrumental in the decision by the White House to issue a "Privacy Bill of Rights" in 2012, which articulates principles for improving consumer privacy online. These principles, however, have not been enacted into law by Congress.

"Big data," the "Internet of Things," and mobile payments present new challenges and concerns about privacy and potential discrimination. The revelations about the National Security Agency's collection of individuals' personal data are heightening concerns about government surveillance and the relationship between the federal government and the commercial entities from which much of that data is derived. Other privacy issues on which consumer and privacy groups now focus attention relate to personal data about students, health-related data not covered by HIPAA, new technologies such as facial recognition and drones, data brokers, data security, and the impact of trade agreements on privacy laws and regulations.

Stephen Brobeck, Susan Grant

See also: Center for Digital Democracy; Credit Report and Credit Score Advocacy; Digital Communications Advocacy; Electronic Privacy Information Center; Privacy Rights Clearinghouse

Further Reading

Bennett, Colin J. 2008. *The Privacy Advocates: Resisting the Spread of Surveillance.* Cambridge, MA: MIT Press.
Burnham, David. 1983. *The Rise of the Computer State.* New York: Random House.
Gurak, Laura J. 1997. *Persuasion and Privacy in Cyberspace: The Online Protests over Lotus MarketPlace and the Clipper Chip.* New Haven, CT: Yale University Press.
H-S Li, Joyce. 2003. *The Center for Democracy and Technology and Internet Privacy in the U.S.* Lanham, MD: Scarecrow Press.
Miller, Arthur. 1971. *Assault on Privacy: Computers, Databanks, and Dossiers.* Ann Arbor, MI: University of Michigan Press.
Rotenberg, Marc, et al., eds. 2015. *Privacy in the Modern Age: The Search for Solutions.* New York: The New Press.
Rule, James B., and Graham Greenleaf. 2008. *Global Privacy Protection: The First Generation.* Cheltenham, UK: Edgar Elgar.
Westin, Alan F. 1970. *Privacy and Freedom.* Oxford, UK: Bodley Head.

PRIVACY RIGHTS CLEARINGHOUSE

The Privacy Rights Clearinghouse (PRC) is a 501(c)(3) nonprofit consumer education and advocacy organization based in San Diego, California. Since its founding in 1992, it has been a state and national leader in advancing consumer rights and interests regarding informational privacy.

The PRC's mission is to engage, educate, and empower consumers. Its goals are to raise consumer awareness of how technology and other societal trends affect personal privacy and to give individuals tools to safeguard their privacy. In addition to educating consumers, the PRC represents them in public policy proceedings. The organization advocates for consumer control over their personal information and for commercial transparency regarding the collection and use of this information.

The PRC was founded and continues to be directed by Beth Givens. The organization was established with funding from the Telecommunications Education Trust (TET), a program of the California Public Utilities Commission. Since TET funding ceased in the early 1990s, the PRC has been funded mainly by foundation grants and class action *cy près* awards. Its annual budget has ranged from $100,000 to more than $400,000. This budget has supported a staff of one to five, and currently, four persons.

From 1992 through 1996, the PRC was a program of the Center for Public Interest Law in the University of San Diego's School of Law. In late 1996, the PRC moved to the San Diego-based Utility Consumers' Action Network (UCAN), where it operated under the fiscal sponsorship of that organization's nonprofit umbrella. In 2014, the PRC separated from UCAN to become an independent organization.

The PRC has maintained robust consumer information and education services. Before the Internet was widely used, the organization maintained a toll-free telephone hotline. The group's earliest consumer guides were mailed in paper form to consumers and to other organizations who in turn distributed them. In 1994, the PRC launched an online "Gopher" site and, in 1996, a full-fledged website. The telephone hotline and the paper guides were eventually replaced by online communications and a website.

Today, the PRC operates an online complaint center that responds to privacy-related questions and complaints from consumers nationwide. The organization also distributes more than seventy fact sheets that it has developed on topics including online privacy, smartphones, credit reporting, debt collection, data breaches, medical records privacy, workplace issues, identity theft, and telemarketing. These fact sheets, many of which have been translated into Spanish, are posted on the PRC's website, www.privacyrights.org, which has become the organization's primary vehicle in communicating with the public. The website also includes PRC's consumer "alerts" and policy statements. Among the most popular sections of the site is PRC's chronology of data breaches. Chronicling thousands of security lapses involving sensitive personal information since 2005, the breach list is updated virtually daily and has been referenced in numerous news stories.

The PRC has been a national leader in informing the public about privacy-related problems and helping consumers solve these problems. In 1994, it was the first consumer group to spotlight identity theft and provide assistance to victims. It was also the first consumer organization to develop consumer guides on the Financial Services Modernization Act (2000), also known as Gramm–Leach–Bliley, as well as among the first to publish a consumer guide on the medical privacy rule under HIPAA (2003).

The PRC is among the few consumer organizations that provide information and assistance to individuals regarding employment background checks. It has also taken leadership on the issue of online data brokers. With expanding consumer use of mobile devices, it has given attention recently to smartphone privacy and security. In 2013, the organization released a study on mobile health and fitness apps. Findings highlighted the invisible capture and transmission of sensitive personal information for third-party advertising and data analytics.

The PRC also has represented consumers in a wide range of public policy proceedings. Staff members have testified or submitted written comments on privacy-related concerns to the California legislature, U.S. Congress, Federal Trade Commission, and other state and federal agencies. These testimonies and comments often incorporate the experiences of individuals who have contacted the organization. In this way, the PRC serves as a "societal feedback loop."

Consumers' concerns have changed over the years. In the early 1990s, the PRC's top complaints were about credit reports, junk mail, telemarketing, Social Security numbers, and medical records. From the mid-1990s into this century, the issue most frequently raised by complainants was identity theft, which became a significant national issue. More recently, the top complaints have been about online data brokers and employment background checks, as well as other issues related to emerging technologies and the Internet.

Although PRC staff members have worked closely with national privacy groups, they have focused particular attention on privacy protections in their home state of California. The PRC has organized an annual state legislation strategy meeting with California-based consumer group representatives and academics. This collaboration has resulted in support for and passage of many strong privacy-related laws. These laws have given California consumers an opt-in right to limit sharing of personal financial information with third parties and an opt-out right for affiliate sharing, limited the use of credit checks by employers in hiring decisions, expanded the data breach notice law beyond financial incidents to include medical information and, more recently, usernames and passwords, strengthened the rights of victims of identity theft, limited the display of Social Security numbers, and promoted public transportation privacy. These laws, overall, provide California consumers with stronger privacy protections than those available to consumers in other states and have served as a model for privacy protections established by other states.

Beth Givens

See also: Privacy Advocacy; State and Local Consumer Advocacy Groups

Further Reading

Frank, Mari and Beth Givens. 2013. "Identity Theft   It Could Happen to Anyone: The Problem, Safeguards, and Solutions." In Dale L. June, ed. *Protection, Security, and Safeguards: Practical Approaches and Perspectives.* Boca Raton, FL: CRC Press.

Miller, Cheryl. 2014. "Opening the Privacy Files." *The Recorder,* January 3. www.therecorder.com/id=1202636103165?slreturn=20140104184001.

PRODUCT SAFETY ADVOCACY

See Household Product Safety Advocacy

PRODUCT SAFETY "VICTIM" ACTIVISM

Some of the most effective activists for product-related safety reforms have been those who suffered a personal loss related to a consumer product. Most of these so-called victims, who went on to found organizations dedicated to mitigating product-related hazards, were motivated by the death of their child or other family member.

This article briefly describes seven organizations that have had some staying power and national influence related to the safety of motor vehicles, household products, or food. That influence has derived mainly from the stories, energy, and persistence of the victims, not from substantial revenues. Only Mothers against Drunk Driving (MADD) has had a multi-million-dollar annual budget. The other six groups have usually had annual budgets well under $500,000.

Motor Vehicle Safety Groups

MADD was founded in 1980 by a Sacramento mother, Candy Lightner, whose 13-year-old daughter was killed, in a hit-and-run accident, by a convicted drunk driver who was not severely penalized. By 1985, bolstered by a television movie about Lightner, MADD had more than 600,000 members, 360 chapters in all fifty states, and an annual budget approaching $10 million. A year earlier, the organization had been instrumental in persuading Congress to approve the National Minimum Drinking Age Act, which imposed a federal penalty on states that permitted those younger than age 21 from purchasing and possessing alcoholic beverages. Within a year after the U.S. Supreme Court upheld the law in 1987, every state was in compliance with this law.

Under Lightner's leadership, MADD fought not only for increased penalties for convicted drunk drivers and expanded enforcement efforts, but also for higher alcohol taxes. After the defeat of its tax campaign in California, the organization decided to become more mainstream, including decreasing the number of activists, and increasing the number of industry representatives, on its board of directors. It also moved its headquarters to Texas and accepted a grant from the Anheuser-Busch Company, the nation's largest brewer. During this period, Lightner left the organization.

Since then, MADD has focused mainly on stopping drunk driving, preventing underage drinking, and supporting the victims of this drinking and driving. In the 1990s, the organization lobbied Congress and the states for a lower legal limit for blood alcohol content (BAC) in drivers. In 2000, Congress approved a lower level, and by 2005, all states had as well.

MADD continues to involve victims of drunk driving, especially on victim effect panels in which convicted drunk drivers listen to victims of drunk driving. Its current national president is Jan Withers, whose daughter was killed by a drunk driver. Several other victims serve on the organization's board of directors.

MADD's 2012 revenues of $38 million included individual contributions, corporate grants and contributions, government grants, and victim impact panels to which drunk drivers made contributions. No alcoholic beverage companies are listed as sponsors.

Since 1995, KidsAndCars.org has sought to prevent child injuries and deaths related to motor vehicles. It was founded, and continues to be led, by Janette Fennell, who was kidnapped and left for dead, with her husband, in the trunk of their car. Fennell led a successful campaign to convince automobile manufacturers and the federal government that trunk entrapment was a serious problem. After 2001, all vehicles sold or leased in the United States were required to have an internal trunk release mechanism. Since then, Fennell has worked on other vehicle-related hazards to children, including power window strangulations, vehicles being locked into gear, and lack of driver visibility when backing up. She deserves some credit for reforms in 2005 and 2008 transportation laws that require power windows to reverse direction when obstructed and an expanded field of view for drivers when backing up. In 2013, KidsAndCars joined with three national consumer groups to sue the U.S. Department of Transportation for failing to promptly issue a rear visibility rule. In April 2014, the day before the court hearing, the National Highway Traffic Safety Administration issued the rule, which effectively requires rear view cameras in all new cars.

Since 2005, Concerned Families for ATV Safety have worked to reduce injuries and deaths among children driving all-terrain vehicles (ATVs). The group was founded by three mothers—Carolyn Anderson, Sue Rabe, and Carol Keezer—who lost children who were driving ATVs. It supports other families who have lost children, informs parents and policymakers about the dangers of children riding on ATVs, and works with national consumer groups, especially the Consumer Federation of America, supporting related reforms.

Household Product Safety Groups

Kids in Danger (KID) is a nonprofit group dedicated to improving the safety of child products ranging from cribs and bunk beds to high chairs and car seats to toys and play yards. The organization was founded in 1998 by two Chicago parents, professors at the University of Chicago, whose infant son Danny Keysar was killed by a previously recalled crib. KID focuses attention on several audiences—on parents to whom it supplies information such as product recalls, on designers and engineers who help create and develop child products, and on policymakers such as the Consumer Product Safety Commission. KID has also participated in the development of voluntary standards for children's products within ASTM and other standard-setting organizations.

KID executive director Nancy Cowles has worked closely with national consumer groups on improved regulation and legislation, including the Consumer Product Safety Improvement Act. This legislation included a provision, named after Danny Keysar, that requires both the promulgation of mandatory standards for infant and toddler products and third-party testing to ensure that products comply with the standards. KID has also promoted state reforms, such as a law that prohibits the sale or lease of any child product that has been recalled, first passed by Illinois in 1999.

Parents for Window Blind Safety is a nonprofit organization that was established in 2002 to support parents whose children have been seriously injured or killed by dangerous cords, to educate consumers about the dangers of these cords, to encourage industry to make safer products, to test these products, and to encourage policymakers to establish safer standards. Its founders, Matt and Linda Kaiser, lost a child who was strangled by a window blind cord. They have worked closely with the Consumer Federation of America to encourage Congress and the Consumer Product Safety Commission to approve safer standards.

Food Safety Groups

STOP Foodborne Illness is a national nonprofit organization that seeks to prevent illness and death from foodborne illness. The organization was founded in 1993 by Roni Austin, whose daughter died in an *E. coli* outbreak associated with Jack in the Box hamburgers, and by Nancy Donley, whose son died after eating *E. coli*–contaminated ground beef. For two decades, Donley led the organization and served as its principal public spokesperson.

STOP supports other victims of foodborne diseases through peer-to-peer mentoring and a free help line, but its principal impact has been through its consumer advocacy. The organization has participated actively in national food safety coalitions working to achieve reforms, including requirements for testing and zero tolerance for pathogens in school lunch meat and a decision by the U.S. Department of Agriculture to declare six strains of *E. coli* as adulterants in ground beef. Its unique contribution to these coalitions has been providing the voices of victims who have lost loved ones to foodborne diseases. However, STOP has also helped persuade states, such as California, to pass their own food safety laws.

The Center for Foodborne Illness Research & Prevention (CFI) is a national nonprofit organization that works for a science-based food safety system which prevents foodborne illness. CFI was organized in 2001 by a mother, Barbara Kowalcyk, and a grandmother, Patricia Buck, of a boy who died from an *E. coli*–related complication. Today, Kowalcyk serves as the organization's CEO and director of research while Buck holds the position of director of outreach and education. The group works closely with other consumer advocates for improved food safety and can claim some credit for progress in this area, particularly in advocating for enhanced data sharing and collecting.

CFI's influence is based not only on sympathy for victims of foodborne illnesses, but also on the credentials of Kowalcyk, a PhD, and the organization's board members. The latter include other victims, research experts, and consumer leaders such as Teresa Schwartz, a George Washington University law professor who earlier served as deputy director of the Federal Trade Commission's Bureau of Consumer Protection and, for two decades, as a board member of Consumers Union. CFI has been asked to undertake research by organizations including the Food and Drug Administration and Pew Charitable Trusts. It, and the stories of Kowalcyk and Buck, were featured in the 2010 Oscar-nominated documentary *Food, Inc.*

Stephen Brobeck

See also: All-Terrain Vehicle Advocacy; Food Safety Advocacy; Household Product Safety Advocacy; Motor Vehicle Safety Advocacy

Further Reading

Fell, James C., and Robert B. Voas. 2006. "Mothers against Drunk Driving (MADD): The First 25 Years." *Traffic Injury Prevention* 7: 195+.
Mohl, Bruce, and Patricia Wen. 1998. "Are Consumers Getting Enough Protection? *Boston Globe* (June 30): 3.
Yeoman, Barry. 2000. "Dangerous Food." *Redbook* (August 1).

PUBLIC CITIZEN

Public Citizen is a nonprofit advocacy organization that for several decades has been among the nation's most active and influential public interest groups. Founded in 1971 by Ralph Nader, Public Citizen seeks to counter corporate lobbying by representing the public before federal and state legislative, executive branch, and judicial bodies. The group has been a leader in addressing issues such as congressional lobbying and ethics reform, drug and medical device safety, Wall Street reform, corporate accountability, public access to the courts, campaign finance reform, expansive trade agreements, freedom of information, and renewable energy. It employs researchers, lobbyists, and lawyers, enabling the organization to lobby for legislation, to petition regulatory agencies to ensure that laws are implemented in the public interest, and to seek judicial relief when they are not.

Public Citizen has a $15 million annual budget and approximately 100 employees. The organization receives funding from foundation grants, memberships, and individual donations. To preserve its independence and integrity, it does not accept funding from the government or from corporations. The organization has offices in Washington, D.C., and in Austin, Texas.

Public Citizen was conceived by Ralph Nader while he attended Harvard Law School in the late 1950s. As a law student, he became disillusioned by learning that lawyers were trained to serve mainly corporations, not the public. In the 1960s, he rose to public prominence with the publication of *Unsafe at Any Speed* and the subsequent revelation that General Motors had hired private detectives to investigate him. Having captured the attention of reform-minded students, he recruited hundreds of them to work on research exposing harmful corporate practices and the acquiescence of government agencies to these practices. The dozens of books and studies produced by "Nader's Raiders" were widely reported on by the press and encouraged reporters to undertake their own investigative reports.

Aware of the need to institutionalize this advocacy, Nader decided to form an organization, Public Citizen. In March 1971, he purchased advertisements in thirteen publications and mailed letters asking for financial support. By the end of May 1972, more than 60,000 people had donated a total of more than $1.1 million for the new group.

Nader served as the first president of Public Citizen. The next permanent president was Joan Claybrook, who had worked with Nader on the Congress Project. In 1977, Claybrook was appointed Administrator of the National Highway Traffic Safety Administration (NHTSA), but when she left this agency in 1982, she returned to Public Citizen as its president, holding this position until her retirement in 2009. She was succeeded by Robert Weissman, the organization's current president. Weissman was previously editor of *Multinational Monitor*, a Washington, D.C.–based journal that Nader had created to track the activities of multinational corporations, particularly in the developing world.

Public Citizen's work is carried out through program groups and projects, including: Congress Watch, the Health Research Group, the Litigation Group, the Energy Program, and Global Trade Watch.

Congress Watch

Public Citizen's Congress Watch division grew out of Nader's "Congress Project," which produced reports on the secretive operations of congressional committees and cobbled together in-depth profiles of every member of Congress running for re-election in 1972. About a thousand people, many of them students, worked on the project. The research included hundreds of personal interviews, a 633-question survey, and investigations in each congressional district. Some of those who worked on the Congress Project later became noted journalists: James Fallows, Evan Thomas, E. J. Dionne, David Ignatius, Frank Rich, Margaret Carlson, and Walter Shapiro. A resulting book—*Who Runs Congress?*—sold so many copies that it topped one of the *New York Times* best-seller lists for a month. Through the work of the Congress Project, Public Citizen became one of the first public interest groups to bring citizen pressure on Congress to curb corporate abuses, government waste, secrecy, and conflicts of interest.

The success of this project prompted Nader to create the Congress Watch program at Public Citizen. Joan Claybrook, who helped lead the Congress Project, became the first Congress Watch director.

Since its inception, top priorities of Congress Watch have included improving congressional ethics and enacting campaign finance reform. Staffers have worked to slow down the revolving door between government and business, curb lobbyist-funded gifts and travel, boost disclosure of campaign contributions and funding of political advertising, increase public access to information and meetings, and ensure more protections for whistleblowers. In addition, the group has uncovered "corporate welfare"—government subsidies to industry—and has fought for much legislation establishing new consumer protections. After the 2008 financial crash, for example, it pushed for strong legislation to prevent the kinds of Wall Street abuses that led to the meltdown. Congress Watch has also worked to safeguard the regulatory system and civil justice system from industry attacks.

Congress Watch was a leader in advocating a number of reforms approved by Congress: creation of the Consumer Product Safety Commission (1973); the Sunshine Act, requiring senior government officials to keep records (1976); congressional reform, banning many gifts and requiring lobbyists to register (1995); the McCain–Feingold campaign finance law, banning "soft money" and regulating issue ads by interest groups (2002); lobbying and ethics legislation (2007); reforms to the Consumer Product Safety Commission (2008); the creation of the Consumer

Financial Protection Bureau after the 2008 financial crash (2010); and the STOCK Act, which prevents insider trading by members of Congress and their staff (2012).

Health Research Group

Another program group that has existed since the organization's founding is the Health Research Group. Its longtime leader, Dr. Sidney Wolfe, started the group with Nader in fall 1971. Wolfe, who was a researcher at the National Institutes of Health when he met Nader, created a distinctive niche at Public Citizen by combining thorough medical research with aggressive consumer advocacy and public education.

The Health Research Group's first offensive came in a letter to the Food and Drug Administration (FDA) urging the agency to remove Red Dye No. 2—a food, drug, and cosmetic additive—from the market. The letter was the first of hundreds of letters and petitions that Wolfe and his staff sent to FDA during the next four decades. After five years, FDA agreed to remove Red Dye No. 2 from the marketplace. By 2014, the group had successfully petitioned for the removal of more than two dozen drugs from the market, including the painkiller Bextra, the diet drug Meridia, and the dietary supplement Ephedra.

When addressing an issue, the Health Research Group collects scientific evidence of harm, petitions the appropriate federal agency, publicizes the evidence and the petition, and sometimes works with Public Citizen attorneys and lobbyists to lobby Congress or sue an agency. With Public Citizen lawyers, the Health Research Group has forced the Occupational Safety and Health Administration to limit workplace exposure to a group of common carcinogens (1974), to the industrial chemical benzene (1978), to the pesticide DBCP threatening farm workers (1978), to cotton dust (1983), to asbestos (1985), and to grain dust in the air of grain elevators or mills, which can explode when ignited by sparks or hot metal (1987). The Health Research Group has also petitioned for dangerous medical devices to be removed from the market (such as silicone gel breast implants), pushed for structural reform of the health care system (calling for a single-payer, Medicare-for-all system), and publicized unethical clinical trials.

The Health Research Group educates patients through books, guides, and online posts. These publications include the "Questionable Doctors" series, which listed physicians who had violated criminal or ethical rules through offenses such as misprescribing drugs, having improper sexual relations with patients, and being guilty of negligence or incompetence. They also include annual rankings of the performance of state medical boards and the book, *Worst Pills, Best Pills*, which has profiled hundreds of commonly prescribed medicines and warned patients of particularly hazardous medications and potentially dangerous interactions. This book, published periodically, has sold hundreds of thousands of copies and contains information that is now online at worstpills.org. Health Research Group also publishes a monthly newsletter.

Litigation Group

Founded in 1972 by Nader and Alan Morrison, the Public Citizen Litigation Group has been one of the most active and influential public interest law practices in the nation. Its influence extends to many areas of law: freedom of information, open government, union democracy, lawyers' ethics, food safety, occupational safety and health, the constitutional separation of powers, and the right to free speech and anonymity on the Internet. Its lawyers have argued more than sixty cases before the U.S. Supreme Court.

Morrison was a 33-year-old attorney with the U.S. Attorney in the Southern District of New York City when he joined Nader in forming the Litigation Group. Some of the most important cases it has won involve the Constitution's separation of powers doctrine, which limits any one branch of government from acquiring too much power. In 1972, for example, when President Richard Nixon refused to spend money that Congress had appropriated for specific highway programs, the Litigation Group represented the chair of every standing Senate committee. The case, *State Highway Commission of Missouri v. Volpe* and argued by Morrison, led to a court decision against a presidential impoundment of funds.

In 1990, the Litigation Group founded the Alan Morrison Supreme Court Assistance Project with the goal of helping rectify an imbalance in practice before the court. Although business clients can often afford to hire experienced Supreme Court practitioners and the government is represented by the Office of the Solicitor General, public interest groups have been forced to use small firm practitioners with little or no Supreme Court experience. The Litigation Group project offers assistance to lawyers who lost in lower court but wish to appeal to the Supreme Court, and to lawyers who are trying to keep cases from reaching the Supreme Court. This assistance takes the form of writing briefs and preparing for oral arguments. During any one Supreme Court term (usually from October to the summer of the following year), Public Citizen lawyers typically are involved in fifteen to twenty cases. These cases often involve access to courts issues, class-action procedures, claims of government misconduct, or situations in which workers, tort plaintiffs, or civil rights claimants have won awards of significant damages or have established important rules of law.

Morrison left Public Citizen in 1992 to teach. Since then, attorneys David Vladeck, Brian Wolfman, and Allison Zieve have, in succession, directed the group. Vladeck later served as director of the Federal Trade Commission's Bureau of Consumer protection.

Energy Program

Originally called the Critical Mass Energy Project, the Energy Program group was a key organizer of the antinuclear movements of the 1970s and early 1980s. In 1974, Nader and Claybrook convened the first national antinuclear conference, which they called "Critical Mass '74." The new program group was founded to carry out the work of that conference. Staffers used the Freedom of Information Act to document malfunctions at the nation's nuclear reactors. They also documented and publicized accidents, near-accidents, and emergency shutdowns; testified before Congress; and filed petitions with the Nuclear Regulatory Commission.

As the nation's energy landscape evolved, so did the focus of this program group. In the 1980s, Critical Mass intensified its advocacy of safe, renewable energy alternatives. In the 1990s, it began addressing issues pertaining to food and water. In 2005, then-director Wenonah Hauter formed a new organization, Food & Water Watch. The Energy Group also was a leading critic of Enron's market manipulation and BP's corporate culture, which resulted in the Gulf oil disaster in 2010. Today, led by Tyson Slocum, the Energy Program opposes tax breaks for the fossil fuel industry, promotes renewable energy to combat climate change, and advocates fairness in electric utility rate setting.

Global Trade Watch

Global Trade Watch was created in 1995 to promote government and corporate accountability in the expanding trade relations of a globalizing world. The group's founder, Lori Wallach, a Harvard-trained lawyer, was working as a lobbyist for Public Citizen's Congress Division when she noticed that industry representatives were boasting that stronger pesticide and food labeling laws would not be allowed under the General Agreement on Tariffs and Trade (GATT). This discovery that trade agreements were being used by large corporations to undermine domestic health, safety, and environmental laws persuaded then Public Citizen President Joan Claybook to encourage Wallach to raise funds to create a new Public Citizen group to address related issues.

Under Wallach's leadership, Global Trade Watch has played a unique role in addressing the public interest implications of global trade relationships, especially those involving the United States. It has educated the press, policymakers, and the public about how trade agreements, such as the North American Free Trade Agreement (NAFTA) and those created by the World Trade Organization (WTO), have constrained federal, state, and local governments from regulating issues related to food and product safety, financial services, local development, access to essential services, and the environment.

Still led by Wallach, today the group designs and undertakes national and international campaigns related to WTO, NAFTA, the Central America Free Trade Agreement (CAFTA), and various bilateral U.S. Free Trade Agreements (FTAs). It conducts research, monitors trade pact outcomes, publishes books and reports, maintains an online trade data center, educates the public, and coordinates with domestic and international allies and partners.

Other Public Citizen Initiatives

Texas office: In 1984, Public Citizen opened an office in Austin to help ensure affordable local phone services after the deregulation of the Southwestern Bell telephone system. Even though the phone company withdrew its proposed rate hikes, Public Citizen decided to maintain the office. Headed since 1985 by Tom "Smitty" Smith, the Texas team initially focused on campaign finance reform and lobbying disclosure. It led successful legislative efforts to establish a Texas ethics commission and to limit campaign finance spending on Texas judicial campaigns.

During the past two decades, this office has focused much attention on reducing the state's electricity reliance on coal and increasing use of renewable energy sources. Its efforts have been instrumental in blocking seventeen of twenty-two proposed coal-powered plants and six of eight proposed nuclear plants in the state. The group also helped persuade the state to implement a requirement to generate 10,000 megawatts of electricity from renewable sources by 2025, a goal surpassed in 2010 in large part because of increased use of wind power.

Auto safety: With leadership from Claybrook, who had headed NHTSA, Public Citizen prioritized stronger auto and truck safety rules. Public Citizen was a leader in winning battles for mandatory air bags and tire pressure monitors, stability and roof-strength standards in SUVS, and rear-view backup in all vehicles.

Commercial Alert: Established as a Public Citizen project in 2011, Commercial Alert seeks to prevent the commercial culture from exploiting children and subverting higher values related to family, community, the environment, and democracy. It has worked to reduce hospital marketing of infant formula and advertising in schools.

Democracy Is for People: The main goal of this campaign, launched in 2010, is to gain support for a constitutional amendment to enable states to restrain campaign spending. Initiated after the Supreme Court's 2010 ruling in *Citizens United v. Federal Election Commission*, which freed corporations to spend unlimited sums in elections, Democracy Is for People works with national and state activists to build support for the amendment. By June 2014, sixteen states, approximately 550 towns and cities, more than 150 members of Congress, and President Barack Obama had indicated support for an amendment.

Global Access to Medicines: This Public Citizen program was established in 2009, when Weissman became president. It works with partners worldwide to improve health outcomes and save lives by promoting the use of measures to lower pharmaceutical costs, including increased generic competition. Challenging the drug industry's patent-based monopolies, the program supports civil society groups and public agencies with analysis and technical assistance.

Angela Bradbery

See also: Air Travel Advocacy; Food & Water Watch; Litigation; Nader, Ralph; Prescription Drug Advocacy

Further Reading

Bollier, David. 1989. *Citizen Action and Other Big Ideas: A History of Ralph Nader and the Modern Consumer Movement.* Washington, DC: Center for Study of Responsive Law.

Coniff, Ruth. 1999. "Joan Claybrook." *The Progressive* (March 1).

Craig, Barbara. 2004. *Courting Change: The Story of the Public Citizen Litigation Group.* Washington, DC: Public Citizen Group.

Sperling, Dan. 1986 "Sidney Wolfe." *USA Today* 19 (March): D4.

Witt, Elder. 1986. "Attorney Morrison: Constitutional Gadfly." *Congressional Quarterly* 19 (April): 875.

PUBLIC INTEREST RESEARCH GROUPS

The state public interest research groups (PIRGs) are nonprofit, nonpartisan, public-interest advocacy groups that address a broad range of problems related to consumer protection, product safety, health care services, financial services, college affordability, campaign finance, government budget transparency, voter registration, tax reform, and public health. Although initially inspired and assisted by Ralph Nader, the PIRGs have always been independent and self-sustaining.

Organizational Development

The PIRGs grew out of the student activism of the 1960s and early 1970s, including that involving Nader's Raiders, which investigated government and corporate abuses. After meetings with student activists, Nader and his associates proposed a model for institutionalizing self-sustaining student activism that was described in a book *Action for a Change*, which he wrote with Donald K. Ross. (Ross later became the first executive director of New York PIRG and also wrote the *Public Citizens' Action Manual*, which described sample citizen projects that influenced state PIRG activities.)

The model included a mechanism for giving individual students the ability to direct a portion of their student activity fees to their campus PIRG. This form of labor checkoff, and the PIRG chapters it funded, would be established after a majority petition drive of the student body and negotiations with campus administrators. Early efforts were widely supported by faculty and some administrators, who saw the PIRGs as providing opportunities for leadership and academic credit fieldwork opportunities. Although most PIRGs have been supported by the voluntary fees, renewable every two to three years based on ongoing student referenda, some groups have been funded through a student government contract.

As the PIRGs grew in number and in influence, both on campus and in statehouses, their funding mechanism was increasingly challenged by opponents. In 1983, the Mid-Atlantic Legal Foundation, one of several corporate-funded "public interest" law firms established in the 1980s, brought a suit against Rutgers University on behalf of student Joe Galda. Although the court in *Galda v. Blaustein* rejected the lawsuit, the decision resulted in the modification of the Rutgers fees to make them waivable instead of refundable. The checkoff and other PIRG fee mechanisms have, in general, withstood other legal, campus, and legislative challenges, including congressional legislation proposed by Representative Gerald Solomon (R-NY)—which would have denied federal funds to any campus where student fees were used by groups "seeking to influence public policy"—that was defeated, 263–161.

In 1977, the PIRGs created their first national association. This National PIRG Clearinghouse was located first in Ames, Iowa, at Iowa PIRG's offices, then was moved to Washington, D.C., where it conducted association and grant-seeking functions. Lacking sufficient resources, it was dissolved in 1979. However, in 1982, the PIRGs established the Fund for Public Interest Research (now the Fund for the Public Interest), which has conducted door-to-door canvassing campaigns for PIRGS and other allied groups. These canvasses not only raise funds but also are used to educate and build support from citizens for PIRG campaigns. In 1983, several state PIRGs formed U.S. PIRG, a federation of state PIRGs and the national advocacy office. In 1992, the PIRGs organized an environmental organizing training school, Green Corps.

In the mid-2000s, the groups began dividing into separate state environmental groups, with a national arm known as Environment America, and state PIRGs, still associated with U.S. PIRG and working mainly on consumer protection and government reform issues. All these groups are part of the Public Interest Network, or TPIN, but each group pursues its own agenda and raises its own funds. About 200 staff work for the PIRG groups in some thirty states, supported by annual budgets totaling about $15 million.

Instrumental in establishing these joint projects was Douglas Phelps, who was executive director of Massachusetts PIRG during its rapid growth in 1978 and 1979, when it emerged as one of the nation's most influential state-based citizen groups. For example, to gain approval of a refundable beverage container deposit law ("bottle bill"), MASSPIRG undertook several legislative attempts, a successful veto override, and defeat of an industry-sponsored repeal initiative. Phelps now serves as president of U.S. PIRG and several other affiliated network organizations.

PIRG student leaders who now serve as senior staff of the PIRGs or affiliated organizations include former CALPIRG board chair Andre Delattre, now U.S. PIRG director; former Oregon PIRG student board chair and executive director Maureen Kirk, now a senior TPIN official; and former ConnPIRG board chair and executive director Edmund Mierzwinski, now U.S. PIRG consumer program director. Since 1989, Mierzwinski has been U.S. PIRG's chief consumer spokesperson in Washington and the PIRG representative who has worked most closely with other national consumer organizations, including Consumer Reports (formerly Consumers Union) on whose board he now serves.

Many others who started as PIRG campus or canvassing staff have been with the organization or network for twenty-five years or longer. The following leaders and their current positions include Janet Domenitz, MASSPIRG director; Blair Horner, NYPIRG legislative director; Gene Russianoff, NYPIRG senior counsel; Wendy Wendlandt, TPIN political director; Ed Johnson, canvass director for the Fund; Rich Hannigan, TPIN publications director; and Margie Alt and Anna Aurilio, Environment America executive director and legislative director, respectively. PIRG alumni include many public officials, including President Barack Obama, who was a NYPIRG campus project director in 1985.

National Advocacy

The national office U.S. PIRG, established in 1983, has been the federal lobbying office for the state PIRGs. The organization has been funded by dues contributions from member state PIRGs and individual memberships from its own canvass operations. It is affiliated with the U.S. PIRG Education Fund, its tax-deductible research and education arm, funded mainly by foundation grants. Gene Karpinski, who had been field director of Nader's Public Citizen Congress Watch and Norman Lear's People for the American Way, served as the organization's first director and held this position until 2006.

Lobbying by U.S. PIRG has focused on taking successful state PIRG ideas to the national level. For example, after passage of legislation, supported by MASSPIRG and NYPIRG, of state legislation restricting bank check holds, U.S. PIRG advocated successfully for a federal check hold law, enacted in 1987. The organization also played an important role in the passage of other financial services legislation, including the 1991 Truth in Savings Act, the 1988 Home Equity Loan Disclosure Act, and the 1988 Fair Credit and Charge Card Act. More recently, the PIRGs were instrumental in the formation and leadership of Americans for Financial Reform, the coalition that worked with Harvard law professor Elizabeth Warren, now U.S. Senator (D-MA), to establish the Consumer Financial Protection Bureau as part of the Wall Street Reform and Consumer Protection Act of 2010.

U.S. PIRG's product safety work has emphasized children's health. Since 1986, annual PIRG "Trouble in Toyland" reports have resulted in Consumer Product Safety Commission (CPSC) recalls and other actions against more than 150 toys. When an effort by U.S. PIRG, Consumers Union, and Consumer Federation of America (CFA) to enact a federal toy safety label requirement failed, the PIRGs sought state protections. In 1992, ConnPIRG persuaded its state legislature to pass the nation's first toy safety labeling law, which was upheld in federal courts after the industry filed suit to overturn it. Federal legislation passed two years later. In 2008, after a year that saw dozens of recalls of millions of imported toys, U.S. PIRG, CFA, and Consumers Union took the lead in helping persuade Congress to reauthorize and strengthen the CPSC by passing the Consumer Product Safety Improvement Act.

Although the state environmental groups created in the mid-2000s undertake most of TPIN's environmental advocacy, the PIRGs continue to work on some environmental issues from a consumer perspective. For example, they oppose nuclear power generation because of its cost and attendant nuclear waste problem. This environmental advocacy builds on successful state campaigns, such as toxics use-reduction laws and bottle bills in Massachusetts, Oregon, and several other states. Moreover, U.S. PIRG and state PIRGs have worked on food safety issues, including the labeling of genetically modified foods and elimination of antibiotics from animal feed, as well as issues related to toxic chemical products in the home.

U.S. PIRG and state PIRGs have also supported tough campaign finance reforms and have published numerous reports on political action committees (PACs) since the U.S. Supreme Court ruled unconstitutional most corporate limits on donations and other contributions to influence political campaigns. The groups have worked to end corporate tax shelters, improve state budget transparency, and expose wasteful government spending, partnering with the conservative National Taxpayers Union on a series of reports on this spending. The groups have also urged a fairer tax system, with recent emphasis on closing offshore tax loopholes and on eliminating the "carried interest" loophole that allows hedge fund managers to use an effective tax rate of 15 percent.

At state and local levels, PIRGs have opposed proposals advanced by investment banks and other special interests to urge governments to privatize parking lots, university housing, bridges, and toll roads. Since 2008, annual PIRG reports have ranked state and local government budget and spending transparency, which has encouraged some governments to improve their rankings.

State Advocacy

The greatest strength of PIRGs has been the grassroots reach of the state PIRG campuses and canvasses. This advocacy has included generating letters to public officials, holding district meetings, organizing state and national lobby days, and organizing state coalitions on issues. Tactics have included legislative and ballot initiative campaigns, litigation, economic development projects, and publication of reports and consumer guides.

PIRGs have prepared hundreds of investigative reports and consumer guides on numerous topics, including hearing-aid sale abuses, small claims courts, landlord–tenant relations, the Clean Water Act, rising bank fees, credit bureau errors, nursing home conditions, playground safety, airline complaints, overpackaged products, toxic consumer products, nuclear waste transportation safety, campus consumer problems, meat grading and inspection, energy alternatives, and unfair property tax assessments. PIRGs often collaborate with other organizations on these reports, for example, a 1993 national bank fee report undertaken with CFA was released at press conferences by PIRGs and CFA local groups in twenty-three states.

Since the 1970s, state PIRGs have initiated many reforms. In the 2010s, PIRGs in Alaska, Massachusetts, Michigan, New York, and Vermont helped enact low-cost generic drug pricing laws. Connecticut and Oregon PIRGs conducted studies of poor nursing home conditions that precipitated reforms. A 1977 CALPIRG report highlighted on *60 Minutes* exposed price fixing and fraudulent beef grading in San Diego stores and led to an end to the practice. A 1974 NYPIRG campaign led to passage of the state's Freedom of Information Act. Multiyear NCPIRG research and advocacy on brown lung disease exposed dangerous working conditions in textile mils and failed state enforcement, and a NCPIRG textile workers petition to the Federal Occupational Safety and Health Administration (OSHA) led to cotton dust standards that have significantly reduced the incidence of brown lung. NYPIRG's Straphangers Campaign, begun in 1979, continues today to advocate for an adequately funded, cleaner, and safer New York City subway and bus system.

In the 1980s, PIRG legislative successes ranged from roles in passage of the nation's first new-car lemon law (ConnPIRG, 1982) to passage of the first state Superfund law for hazardous waste cleanup (NYPIRG, 1981). Oregon PIRG's 1987 credit card solicitations disclosure law contributed to the 1988 passage of a federal law. A 1984 Colorado PIRG campaign led to establishment of a state Consumer Counsel agency to protect utility customers. A 1984 Oregon PIRG (OSPIRG) citizen ballot referendum established a government-chartered nonprofit Citizens Utility Board (CUB) with the same goal. OSPIRG was outspent 40–1 but still prevailed. CUB and the Colorado agency have stopped billion of dollars of rate hikes in each state.

A 1990 Michigan PIRG campaign resulted in the nation's toughest "polluter pays" law for Clean Water violations; by 1995, it had recovered $100 million in penalties. NJPIRG's 1991 Pollution Prevention Act helped reduce hazardous waste generation by 50 percent over the next ten years. A 1997 Ohio PIRG exposé led to new USDA rules preventing washing and reselling of expired eggs, after Ohio PIRG attorneys had defeated a multi-million-dollar lawsuit by an egg company for alleged disparagement of its perishable product. CALPIRG reports in 1996 and 1997 on financial identity theft led to passage of the first state law criminalizing the practice.

In 2003, Congress enacted major credit reporting amendments but failed to adequately address the problem of identity theft. U.S. PIRG and Consumers Union drafted a model state law addressing the issue. With the aid of local AARP chapters, state PIRGs launched reform campaigns. From 2004 to 2008, forty-six states enacted the model law's data breach notification provisions, and forty-nine gave consumers the right to place a security freeze on their credit reports.

Other PIRG victories since 2000 include Oregon PIRG's 2003 campaign to establish a state-run prescription drug buying pool, MASSPIRG's 2004 campaign for state rules reducing mercury pollution at power plants, NJPIRG's 2008 effort to convince the governor to reject a proposal to privatize the New Jersey Turnpike, and a 2009 NYPIRG-led campaign that succeeded in updating the state bottle law to include plastic water bottles and to generate $120 million annually in state revenues. In this decade, both NYPIRG and MASSPIRG joined with their state firefighters' associations to persuade state legislators to approve fire-safe cigarette bills to reduce the risk of upholstery fires.

Other Strategies

Ballot initiatives: When legislative efforts have failed, PIRGS have qualified many questions for state ballots. A number of these initiatives have focused on eliminating special interest money from the political system. Others have dealt with solid waste and recycling. A San Francisco ballot initiative to ban ATM surcharges fees was approved by resident citizens, though the law was later invalidated in the federal courts.

Litigation: Historically, PIRG litigation has focused on violations of the federal Clean Water Act and Clean Air Act. Since their Clean Water Litigation program in the early 1980s, the PIRGS, with the National Environmental Law Center (NELC), has won more than eighty clean water lawsuits and recovered more than $40 million in fines and penalties. New Jersey PIRG established a foundation, endowed by penalties, that has provided funds to groups undertaking antipollution work in New Jersey watersheds. In 1995, PIRG and NELC attorneys settled a case against Shell Oil, which had been illegally dumping toxic materials into San Francisco Bay.

NYPIRG lawsuits have also been instrumental in ensuring that college students retain the right to vote at their school addresses. Minnesota PIRG litigation has ranged from a successful case against Ford for misleading television advertising of the durability of pickup trucks driven off-road to an unsuccessful 1984 U.S. Supreme Court case challenging the constitutionality of Representative Gerald Solomon's (R-NY) amendment that required draft-eligible students to be registered for the draft before receiving financial aid.

Economic development: The PIRGs have established several economic development projects. For more than thirty years, NYPIRG has run a heating oil–buying cooperative for its several thousand members. In 1991, several state PIRGs founded a socially responsible, sustainable investment fund family, Green Century Funds, which also lobbies corporations and files shareholder resolutions to advance environmental stewardship and corporate accountability.

Field organizing campaigns: PIRGs have the ability to run field campaigns that mobilize staff and volunteers to urge thousands of citizens to take action—to attend a rally, to sign a petition, to send a letter to Congress or the statehouse, or to answer a survey. For more than thirty years, beginning in 1972, students, staff, and citizen volunteers of NJPIRG's "Waterwatch" streamwalked and monitored water quality at hundreds of rivers and streams, providing numerous reports of violations and NJPIRG with data to support passage of remedial legislation. Similarly, for many years, Florida PIRG's "Save Our Shores" campaign has collected petition signatures on beaches, published reports, and undertaken other opposition to oil drilling off its coasts.

In 1979, NYPIRG, with Musicians United for Safe Energy, organized a "No Nukes Rally" in Battery Park, New York City, attended by more than 200,000 persons. In 1980, the PIRG Campaign for Safe Energy picketed presidential candidate events around the country to protest nuclear power, which resulted in the insertion of a safe energy plank in the Democratic platform. In 1990, PIRGs coordinated a national Clean Air Campaign in the course of which more than 300 environmental groups generated more than 500,000 Clean Air postcards sent to Congress, ensuring passage of tough amendments to the law. The April 1995 National Earth Day Rally, chaired by Karpinski and staffed primarily by the PIRGs, brought more than 200,000 people to the Capitol Mall to "send a message" to Congress. The rally was part of a larger campaign that included a "Free the Planet" student conference attended by nearly 2,000 students in Philadelphia in February 1995, where PIRG and other organizations announced an environmental bill of rights petition drive. After attaining more than 1 million signatures on the petition, PIRG students organized on campus in support of the bill's twenty-five recommended reforms.

Since 1984, the National Student Campaign for Voter Registration has registered hundreds of thousands of students and others to vote. The kickoff conference brought nearly 2,000 students to a national conference in Boston. Beginning in 1985, student PIRG Hunger and Home campaigns have staged hundreds of rallies and raised millions of dollars for local food banks and shelters.

Edmund Mierzwinski

See also: Nader, Ralph; State and Local Consumer Advocacy Groups

Further Reading

Center for Public Interest Research. 2002. *The State PIRGs: 30 Years of Action in the Public Interest.* Washington, DC.

Griffin, Kelley. 1987. *Ralph Nader Presents More Action for a Change.* New York: Dembner Books.

Nader, Ralph, and Donald K. Ross. 1972. *Action for a Change.* New York: Grossman.

Ross, Donald K. 1973. *A Public Citizens' Action Manual.* New York: Grossman.

PUBLIC POWER

Public power is the oldest form of electric utility ownership in the United States. Butler, Missouri, turned on arc lamps atop its courthouse on December 6, 1881, and continues to operate its own municipal electric system today. More than 814 publicly owned electric systems have been in existence 100 years or more. These and newer public power systems were created and are sustained by the activism of consumers and citizens seeking affordable, reliable electric service.

Today, according to the American Public Power Association, about 2,000 publicly owned electric utilities serve nearly 15 percent of all U.S. electric consumers. Twelve of the country's thirty largest cities are served in whole or in part by public power. Moreover, municipal utilities, utility districts, state authorities, joint action agencies, and other public entities supply about 10 percent of the nation's generating capacity.

Public power systems differ from investor-owned utilities (IOUs) in several respects. First, public power systems are nonprofit institutions that belong to the citizens they serve while the IOUs are organized for profit and owned by stockholders. Second, public power systems are service-oriented, with no built-in economic bias toward a particular technique or technology. Because IOUs are normally guaranteed a rate of return on plant investment, they are encouraged to build capital-intensive projects. Third, citizens of communities served by public power direct the activities of these systems through the selection of city councils and governing boards and through participation in the formulation of policies and programs. Fourth, because municipal utilities are both distributors and users of electricity, their interest is in delivering service in cost-effective ways.

In the 1870s, investors developed equipment to produce and harness electricity for lighting buildings and streets. In the late nineteenth and early twentieth centuries, public power systems and IOUs competed over local franchises. By 1900, there were some 800 municipal electric systems and about 2,200 private electric utilities. The largest concentration of public power systems was in Great Lakes states and the central part of the nation. Most served small communities that could not obtain electric service from privately owned companies. However, by 1895, municipal systems served Anaheim, California; Jacksonville, Florida; Tacoma, Washington; and Austin, Texas.

The number of public power systems peaked at 3,066 in 1923, then declined because of an accelerating trend toward consolidation among private electric utilities who sought to elimination competition. By the late 1920s, sixteen corporate empires controlled more than 85 percent of the nation's power supply (as well as railroad, coal companies, water companies, and other operations). These private companies waged a campaign to discredit "government in the power business" as a threat to democracy. Between 1924 and 1934, the private companies bought out more than 1,500 municipal systems.

Advocates for consumers fought back. In 1928, Congress ordered the Federal Trade Commission (FTC) to investigate political and financial practices in the private utility industry. After four years, the FTC issued a study that charged private companies with abusing the public trust and misleading attacks on public power. Led by reformers, an aroused public supported tighter regulation of private utilities and the encouragement of "consumer-owned systems" run by municipalities or cooperatives.

In the 1930s, Congress created three major federal power-related agencies affecting public power. The Tennessee Valley Authority was established in 1933 to develop resources in the Tennessee River Valley. These resources included power production through dams and power plants to which municipal systems were given first purchase rights at cost-based rates. The Rural Electrification Administration was created in 1935 to promote the establishment of electric cooperatives serving rural consumers who had no access to electric service. In coming decades, these rural cooperatives served as important allies of public power systems when both were attacked by private utilities.

The Bonneville Power Administration was established in 1937 to market hydropower throughout the Pacific Northwest. Municipal systems were given first purchase rights to this power at cost-based rates. Subsequently, other federal power agencies were created. In 1995, five of these agencies marketed power from 132 hydropower projects in the West, Southwest, and South.

During this period, public power also began to expand the scope of its operations at the state and local levels, and several state power authorities were established in the 1930s. In the 1930s and 1940s, public or people's utility districts (PUDs) were created as areawide government entities to provide electric and water services. Today, most of the 100-plus PUDs are in Washington, Oregon, Nebraska, and California. In the 1940s, Nebraska became an all-public power state by public mandate.

Between 1950 and 1970, local public power systems focused on improving power supplies. An important strategy was to create joint-action agencies—groups of municipal systems that built facilities large enough to serve a number of cities and towns. By the late 1980s, more than fifty of these joint-action agencies were in existence.

In the early 1990s, anticipating widespread deregulation of electricity markets, the federal government created Regional Transmission Organizations (RTOs) to facilitate the exchange and pricing of power. However, over the past two decades, many public power systems have argued that the wholesale rates set by these RTOs, which the power systems pay, are "neither just nor reasonable." Large power generators are being overcompensated by purchasers, including public power systems, to the detriment of utility ratepayers.

Public power leadership on this issue, and many others, has come from the American Public Power Association (APPA), the national service organization for publicly owned electric utilities. Formed in 1940, the APPA has always included a large majority of public power systems. APPA supports members with advocacy and information and supplies representation before Congress, the courts, and federal agencies. Since the late 1960s, it has worked closely with two consumer advocacy organizations—Consumer Federation of America and Consumer Energy Council of America—which it helped establish.

During its life, APPA has sought to protect and preserve the public power option. It has been in the forefront of efforts to apply the antitrust laws to the electric industry, ensure that benefits of high-voltage transmission are available to all utilities on fair and equitable terms, and preserve cost-based rates as a measure of consumer protection. APPA has also supported those communities that wished to substitute public power for private power. In the past decade, seventeen of these communities established public power utilities. Although thirteen communities sold public power systems, most were purchased by neighboring rural electric cooperatives, which are also community-controlled.

Stephen Brobeck

See also: Electricity Service Advocacy; Energy Advocacy; State Utility Advocacy

Further Reading

American Public Power Association. 1987. *Public Power in America: A History*. Washington, DC: American Public Power Association.

Radin, Alex. 2003. *Public Power, Private Life*. Washington, DC: American Public Power Association.

Rudolph, Richard, and Scott Ridley. 1986. *Power Struggle: The Hundred Year War over Electricity*. New York: Harper & Row Publishers.

PUBLIC VOICE FOR FOOD AND HEALTH POLICY

Public Voice for Food and Health Policy was a national nonprofit organization that used research, education, and advocacy to promote a safer, healthier, and more affordable food supply for all Americans. It was founded by Ellen Haas in 1982 and led by her until 1993, when she became undersecretary for food, nutrition, and consumer services at the U.S. Department of Agriculture (USDA). Earlier, Haas had been a leader in the grassroots protests against rising beef prices, which led to the creation of the Maryland Citizens Consumer Council. After that, she worked for the Community Nutrition Institute.

In 1993, Haas was succeeded by Mark S. Epstein, an attorney who had earlier been executive director of the Oregon Natural Resources Council. In 1996, Epstein was succeeded by Arthur Jaeger, who had been serving as the organization's public affairs director. In 1999, the organization was folded into the Consumer Federation of America (CFA).

At the organization's peak, Public Voice had a budget of more than $1 million, derived largely from government, foundation, and corporate grants. This budget supported a full-time staff of seventeen. The organization's annual National Food Policy Conference, which was continued by CFA, has represented the leading annual consumer forum for food policy stakeholders.

Public Voice played a leading role in campaigns for improved nutrition labeling, healthier school food programs, stronger pesticide and food safety laws, "greener" and more consumer-friendly farm legislation, and tougher meat, poultry, and seafood inspection standards. It successfully petitioned USDA for an improved beef grading system, helped secure passage of legislation requiring more informative food labels, organized a national campaign to enact a mandatory federal seafood safety inspection program, and pressured USDA to improve nutritional standards for the school lunch program. It was also the lead consumer organization in campaigns to reform anticonsumer federal sugar, peanut, and dairy programs.

Stephen Brobeck

See also: Consumer Federation of America; Food Safety Advocacy

Further Reading

Sinclair, Ward. 1986. "Ellen Haas: Bringing a New Approach to the Consumer Movement." *The Washington Post* (August 18): A, 15.

R

REAL ESTATE BROKERAGE ADVOCACY

During the past half-century, consumer advocates have focused on real estate brokers and brokerage sporadically. This lack of attention reflects several factors, including the infrequency with which individual consumers use brokerage services, the absence of many complaints about price and service, the great political influence of the National Association of Realtors (NAR) at federal and state levels, and the limited number of ways national consumer groups can seek federal remedies for an industry regulated at the state level.

The first strong criticism against real estate agents and brokers in the post–World War II period was by journalists who exposed "blockbusting" tactics that took advantage of the segregation of African Americans in urban areas, where housing costs were abnormally high. Especially influential was a 1962 article in the *Saturday Evening Post*, which documented the practice of real estate agents' moving black families into all-white neighborhoods, then encouraging panicked and commission-generating sales by whites.

In the 1960s, civil rights and community groups took the lead locally in fighting this practice through legislation and litigation. A series of court decisions and the Fair Housing Act of 1968, which established federal causes of actions against blockbusting, curbed this real estate practice.

The first comprehensive critique of the structure and practices of real estate agents and brokers was an extensively researched report issued in 1983 by the Los Angeles Regional Office of the Federal Trade Commission, which documented anticompetitive practices in the industry. In earlier decades, the industry had created a system based on cooperation between listing and buyer brokers (called "cooperative brokers") in which the former collected brokerage fees, then shared them with the latter. This system was enforced by the industry (i.e., the NAR and its state affiliates) through its development and control of local Multiple Listing Services (MLS) on which agents and brokers depended for listings and information about listings.

The FTC report described this system in detail and criticized the industry in particular for high and uniform prices ("commissions") and for its discrimination against agents and brokers that offered lower prices or exclusive buyer brokerage. The most egregious feature of the industry system was that of subagency, in which agents working with buyers were considered subagents to sellers and thus unable to negotiate terms favorable to their buyer clients.

This report aroused much concern in the industry but did not immediately generate much activism for reform. That advocacy occurred nearly a decade later, when a growing number of lawsuits, along with press coverage generated by a series of reports by the Consumer Federation of America (CFA), persuaded the industry that it could not continue the subagency system. Beginning in 1991, CFA's executive director, Stephen Brobeck, aided by researcher Patrick Woodall, released reports describing an anticompetitive system, with high uniform prices and systematic discrimination against buyers, that was controlled by an industry cartel that dominated most state regulatory bodies.

The CFA reports received much national news coverage but little local news coverage until syndicated housing columnist Ken Harney exposed subagency in columns that appeared in numerous local newspapers. Recognizing that after buyers understood that their cooperating brokers could not be their fiduciary representative, the public would reject the traditional subagency system, the industry responded by advocating improved disclosures and even joined with CFA to release principles on which these disclosures should be based. But improved disclosures approved by many states did not prove sufficient to stem rising dissatisfaction with subagency, and there ensued a debate within the industry that led it to abandon traditional subagency and consider alternatives including "disclosed dual agency" and "transactional brokerage." The industry never reached agreement on one "solution" to the problem, as reflected by the variation today in state real estate agency laws.

During the 1990s and early 2000s, CFA worked closely with other opponents of the existing system, including the American Homeowners Grassroots Alliance (headed by Bruce Hahn), the Real Estate Café (formed by Bill Wendel), and the National Association of Exclusive Buyer Brokers (NAEBA). CFA's principal goal during this period was to introduce real competition into pricing. This effort was greatly aided by a run-up in housing prices that led higher-income sellers and buyers, for example, to question the value of a $30,000 commission, at 6 percent, on the sale of a $500,000 home.

While real estate agents and brokers grew more willing to lower the 6 to 7 percent level that was the unpublicized industry standard in most areas, they were reluctant to go much below 5 percent. They were supported by a MLS system that listed the commission level for cooperating brokers. If a listing broker listed a 2 percent level or lower, he or she risked cooperating brokers' not showing their listed properties.

As well as issuing reports, the consumer coalition opposed state laws discriminating against alternative brokers, especially antirebate and minimum service statutes, and urged the FTC and Department of Justice to take action. By the late 1990s, the "information revolution" was in full swing, and websites listing houses for sale began to proliferate, threatening the dominance of the MLS. The NAR responded by creating its own website available to the public, but continued to maintain separate local websites, with more detailed information on properties and commission splits, accessible only to NAR members.

In the 2000s, the Department of Justice began vigorously challenging, through a series of reports and lawsuits, anticompetitive practices that discriminated against "innovative brokers." By 2008, it had succeeded in eliminating antirebate and minimum service laws and in greatly reducing MLS discrimination against these alternative brokers. DOJ was encouraged to take these actions not only by consumer advocates but also by companies, such as Lending Tree, that wanted more freedom to price and offer different levels of service.

Today, the principal monitors of real estate brokerage practices are the FTC, DOJ, and journalists, such as Harney, who write about housing issues. Consumer advocates are focusing little attention on these practices, with one exception—the broker role in title insurance. For the past decade, real estate brokers have been criticized for collaborating with title insurance companies, often in formal partnerships, to steer customers to high-priced services. Douglas R. Miller, who runs an independent title insurance company as well as a nonprofit advocacy organization, Consumer Advocates in American Real Estate, has led this advocacy. He has been supported by national groups, with CFA and its director of insurance, J. Robert Hunter, being particularly active. Recently, the Consumer Financial Protection Bureau has begun investigating alleged kickbacks between title insurers and real estate brokers.

Stephen Brobeck

See also: Consumer Federation of America

Further Reading

Carter, Matt. 2002. "From Subagency to Non-Agency: A History." *Inman News* (February 17).
Christie, Les. 2006. "Consumer Group Goes after Real Estate Industry." *CNN Money* (June 19).
Federal Trade Commission and U.S. Department of Justice. 2007. *Competition in the Real Estate Industry* (April).

REGULATORS, CONSUMER ADVOCATES AS

A number of consumer leaders have been appointed to federal or state regulatory positions. President Carter, for example, selected Public Citizen's Congress Watch director Joan Claybrook to head the National Highway Traffic Safety Administration (NHTSA), Consumer Federation of America executive director Carol Tucker Foreman to run the U.S. Department of Agriculture's (USDA) food safety programs, and activist congressional staffer Michael Pertschuk to chair the Federal Trade Commission (FTC). He also reappointed Pittsburgh activist and professor R. David Pittle to a second term as a Consumer Product Safety Commission (CPSC) commissioner. President Clinton appointed longtime consumer advocate Ann Brown to head the CPSC and Public Voice president Ellen Haas to administer the USDA's food nutrition and welfare programs. President Obama appointed longtime consumer advocate Robert Adler, who spent most of his career in government and academia, as a CPSC commissioner.

At the state level, governors have selected several consumer advocates as insurance commissioners—longtime industry critic Herb Denenberg in Pennsylvania, former Congress Watch lobbyist Jay Angoff in Missouri, Public Interest Research

Group (PIRG) leader Joel Ario in Oregon, and National Insurance Consumer Organization founder and president J. Robert Hunter in Texas. Several consumer advocates, including Sharon Nelson, who worked as a staff member and later a board member for Consumers Union, have served as public utility commissioners. Other activists—most notably Esther Peterson as White House consumer adviser to two presidents—were appointed to influential government positions that did not carry with them regulatory powers.

These and other appointments of consumer advocates to regulatory positions confronted most appointees with several dilemmas. The activists were forced to redefine their consumer roles and, in so doing, were often compelled to deal with issues such as their relationship to advocacy groups, elected officials who appointed them, and career civil servants working for them. These issues also included their priorities as regulators, particularly the time they spent on administrative matters versus policy issues, and their policy priorities.

A unique dilemma faced by activists is adapting to a regulator role different from that of advocate. The principal function of an advocate is to promote aggressively the interest of consumers to the exclusion of other interests such as those of sellers. A regulator is also supposed to promote the consumer interest but must do so within constraints imposed by government mandates and statutes. One constraint is the expectation, or even requirement, that the regulator consider the impact of any decisions on society, including business. That is the central purpose of cost–benefit analysis, which regulators have increasingly been required to employ over the past three decades before adopting regulations.

Typically, regulators also are burdened with far greater administrative responsibilities than advocates. When Foreman led CFA, she managed a staff of five persons; at USDA she supervised the work of thousands. As Pertschuk lamented in his book, *Revolt against Regulation*, "You can get worn down by the day-to-day problems of hiring, firing, and fights over turf. You have to worry about having enough parking spaces in the garage, about lawyers getting filing cabinets."

The accountability of regulators also differs from that of advocates. For all practical purposes, some activists are accountable to no one but themselves. Others are accountable only to their peers or to leaders of their organization including members of a board, who in consumer groups typically give staff great discretion. On the other hand, regulators are accountable to many—a governor or president, other executive branch officials (e.g., NHTSA is accountable to the secretary of transportation), and a legislative body that oversees their work and approves their funding. Because they are public officials, the work of regulators is scrutinized far more closely by the press than are the activities of activists.

Another major challenge faced by most advocates-turned-regulators is dealing with critics. Some of the toughest criticisms received by President Carter's consumer appointees were leveled by other advocates. As reported by news media, Nader criticized Claybrook for "a trail of averted or broken promises" and for failing to resign over delays in required installation of airbags, as widely reported by the news media. Activists faulted Pertschuk for not moving quickly enough to consider a ban on television ads for candy and sugar-coated cereals.

The opposition to regulators from business and conservatives was much fiercer and more sustained. Not just farm groups, but also one conservative columnist attacked Foreman, calling her the "dragon lady of USDA." Automobile manufacturers found fault with most of Claybrook's decisions. Many industries organized a coalition to fend off initiatives from the Pertschuk-led FTC, and succeeded in persuading Congress to reduce the authority of the commission. Opposition from meat industry lobbyists and the school foodservice to Haas's efforts to improve the nutritional value of school lunches eventually forced her resignation.

Businessmen and conservatives most often claimed that regulators imposed onerous, anticompetitive burdens on sellers. Given the opportunity, they also complained about the alleged favoritism of regulators. Because Foreman was married to a high-ranking labor official, and because her department awarded a small contract to the Consumer Federation of America (which she had headed), Foreman was a prime target of these attacks.

Regulators have responded to business and conservative criticisms in different ways. In general, over the past several decades they have tried to accommodate their opponents' interests to a greater extent. In the late 1970s, for example, Pertschuk refused to try to mollify many congressional and business critics. On the other hand, in the early 1990s, Hunter made a point of meeting with and accommodating any legitimate concerns of legislators and industry leaders. And in the 2000s, Brown sought not only to meet with congressional leaders and business groups, but also to develop partnerships with these groups.

In general, consumer advocates working as regulators significantly advance the consumer interest. They have opportunities to succeed because of their authority within their own agency, influence over the disposition of agency resources, regulatory authority, access to the president and Congress, and credibility with the press and general public.

Several regulators considerably strengthened their agencies through reorganization and morale-building. Because the Texas insurance department had been wracked by poor management and scandal, Hunter was compelled to devote most of his time as commissioner to rebuilding the agency. Even from skeptical legislators and industry leaders he received praise for these efforts. When Brown became chair of the CPSC, which had suffered severe budget cuts and much criticism for more than a decade, many agency staff were dispirited and demoralized. Brown acted quickly to infuse the agency with a sense of purpose and importance.

As regulators, consumer advocates have had opportunities to issue regulations establishing new consumer protections and enforce old regulations more effectively. Pertschuk's FTC, for example, was able to promulgate and implement trade regulation rules governing funeral practices. It also had the opportunity to develop innovative penalties for deceptive advertising, such as mandatory counterads correcting deceptive ads. At the CPSC, Pittle was instrumental in the development of safety standards for lawnmowers, chainsaws, toys, toxic chemicals, and other potentially hazardous products. At NHTSA, Claybrook was largely responsible for the issuance of standards for airbags and passive restraints. Though revoked by President Reagan, the airbag/passenger restraint standard was reissued to comply with a 1983 U.S. Supreme Court decision.

Consumer advocates working as regulators also have the chance to identify new issues and put them on the public agenda. Through the completion of detailed, critical studies of complex products, Pertschuk's FTC laid the foundation for reform of several financial services products. FTC reports on life insurance and residential real estate brokerage services, for instance, remain today the most informative documents on these subjects. By initiating crash testing of cars at thirty-five miles per hour, and releasing results of this testing (and other information) in *The Car Book*, Claybrook pressured auto manufacturers to improve the crashworthiness of their vehicles.

As regulators, advocates sometimes have opportunities to lobby issues even more effectively than in their past role of consumer advocate. As a USDA assistant secretary, for example, Foreman helped persuade Congress to eliminate the requirement that recipients pay something for food stamps. As insurance commissioner, through research and lobbying of insurers, Hunter and his department persuaded insurers voluntarily to hire more minority agents and write more policies to underserved areas.

Particularly in the late 1970s, regulators were able to build support for their initiatives by making funds available to advocacy groups to participate in regulatory proceedings. Pertschuk's FTC, for example, made available more than $1 million for this purpose. Even when these regulators were not able to make or help shape pro-consumer policies, they sometimes succeeded in using the position as a bully pulpit to put issues on the national agenda. For example, efforts begun by Foreman at USDA to increase the usefulness of food labeling helped lead, more than a decade later, to the passage of congressional legislation and the issuing by FDA of effective nutritional labeling regulations. Claybrook's advocacy for and education on airbags contributed significantly to decisions made by government and industry more than a decade later that ensured the installation of these safety devices.

Consumer advocates working as regulators must make difficult judgments about how aggressively to pursue stronger consumer protections. However, their decisions have contributed significantly to progress toward a more consumer-friendly marketplace.

Stephen Brobeck

Further Reading

Mayer, Caroline E. 1978. "A Rude Awakening for Activists in Government." *U.S. News and World Report* 84 (March 6): 52+.

Pertschuk, Michael. 1982. *Revolt against Regulation: The Rise and Pause of the Consumer Movement*. Berkeley: University of California Press.

Rosenbaum, David E. 1976. "Public Affairs Groups, Now on Outside, Expect Access to Power Under Carter." *New York Times* (December 1): II, 6.

REGULATORY ADVOCACY

Federal regulatory agencies write and enforce rules that affect all aspects of the consumer marketplace. These agencies have diverse consumer-related responsibilities ranging from inspecting food to establishing automobile safety standards to regulating monopoly utilities to overseeing investment banks. The role of consumer advocates is to help ensure that the rules finalized and enforced by regulatory agencies actually serve the consumer interest.

Advocacy before federal regulatory agencies is an especially important aspect of the work of consumer activists. Regulatory agencies, which are part of the executive branch of government, also exercise legislative functions through the promulgation of regulations that have the force of law, as well as judicial functions through enforcement of their rules. Some agencies, such as the departments of transportation, health and human services, and agriculture, are cabinet-level agencies. Others, such as the Consumer Product Safety Commission (CPSC) and the Securities and Exchange Commission (SEC), are independent.

Advocates have two approaches available for influencing these agencies: They can seek to influence an agency directly to persuade it to use its existing authority to address a particular issue. Alternatively, they can work through Congress to pass legislation that either gives the agency new authority or directs it to use its existing authority to address an issue. One of their most effective strategies to direct an agency to prioritize a specific issue is to support legislation that requires an agency to promulgate certain rules within a defined time period. For example, the Consumer Product Safety Improvement Act, passed in 2008, required the CPSC to promulgate mandatory regulations for toy standards, testing standards, and standards for specific infant and toddler products. These laws also often require agencies to conduct studies on specific issues, which can later serve as a basis for regulatory action.

Both legislation and rules are most likely to be adopted when there is a crisis receiving significant press coverage. Numerous recalls of toys and other consumer products led to the passage of the Consumer Product Safety Improvement Act. Frequent foodborne illness outbreaks created public concern supporting approval of the Food Safety Modernization Act. A financial crisis that threatened a worldwide economic depression led to passage of the Dodd–Frank Wall Street Reform Act in 2010. In these and other cases, a lack of mandatory standards was identified as a source of problems. During congressional testimony in 2011, CPSC Commissioner Robert Adler stated that in the past three decades, his agency had promulgated only nine mandatory standards.

Passing this kind of legislation requires members of Congress who are committed to reform and organized consumer advocates who thoroughly understand the issue, who have formulated specific provisions of legislation, who have research to support these provisions, and who can engage other groups and experts in the legislative process. The same sort of preparation by advocates is important in helping ensure that regulatory agencies issue effective rules. The advocates must have great legal and technical expertise and be deeply engaged in the regulatory process.

This engagement starts with providing examples and publishing research that demonstrates the need for the rule being considered. It is also important for advocates to make specific recommendations about the most effective regulatory approach for addressing the problem. Advocates need to organize other advocates, other experts, nontraditional allies, and individuals, especially "victims," to communicate not only to the agency but also to the public through the media during the notice and comment periods. If there are public hearings, it is essential for advocates to testify and use the hearings to try to gain additional public attention. Making a strong case for regulation is especially important today because rules are assessed by the regulatory agency and by the Office of Management and Budget in terms of their costs and benefits.

In addition, it is important for advocates to have strong personal relationships with leaders and staff of regulatory agencies to ensure that they understand consumer views and are knowledgeable and respectful of the consumer advocacy. When a rule is being considered, it may also be useful to persuade congressional leaders to hold oversight hearings focusing on the rulemaking progress of an agency.

Another important way for consumer advocates to influence the agenda of a regulatory agency is to file a petition urging the agency to promulgate a rule to address a particular problem. The Administrative Procedures Act provides citizens with the ability to petition an agency to take a specific action. Each agency has its own rules for citizen petitions. Over the past three decades, for example, Consumer Federation of America and other consumer groups have filed petitions at the CPSC on products, including baby bath seats, product registration, all-terrain vehicles, window coverings, and adult bed rails. Even when these efforts do not result in mandatory rules, they do force the agency to work on the issue and establish a record that could eventually lead to regulation.

If an agency abandons rulemaking or issues inadequate rules, litigation can be an effective strategy for advocates to employ. In 2002, through a lawsuit Public Citizen Litigation Group forced the National Highway Traffic Safety Administration to revise a rule about underinflated tire warnings so that it effectively implemented a law. Submitting amicus curiae ("friend of the court") briefs can also be an effective strategy in opposing industry lawsuits that seek to prevent or weaken agency action.

In all regulatory advocacy efforts, it is important to have access to information from the agency, from industry, and from other experts. It may be important to file official requests for this information through the Freedom of Information Act to obtain information and may be necessary to involve congressional allies in such efforts.

As noted above, one of the most effective strategies for persuading regulatory agencies to protect consumers is to engage Congress. However, congressional involvement has the potential to harm as well as benefit consumers. Congressional leaders not infrequently criticize the pro-consumer efforts of regulators. More recently, some legislators have been trying to pass legislation that would limit the ability of all agencies to issue new consumer protections. These bills would restrict the agencies by requiring proposed rules to be subject to extensive cost–benefit analysis, additional reporting and analytical requirements, and approval of both houses of Congress. Consumer advocates have been devoting increased time to try thwarting these congressional initiatives.

Rachel Weintraub

See also: Consumer Representation in Government Agencies; Legislative Advocacy

Further Reading

Avner, Marcia. 2002. *The Lobbying and Advocacy Handbook for Nonprofit Organizations.* Nashville, TN: Fieldstone Alliance.

A Citizen's Guide to Influencing Agency Action. www.administrativelawreview.org/publicresources/CitizenGuide.pdf.

Pertschuk, Michael. 1987. *Giant Killers.* New York: W. W. Norton & Company.

RESEARCH

One of the most influential activities of consumer advocates has been research. One could even argue that studies and reports by consumer groups have had as much effect on public policy and corporate practices as any other activist activity, if not more. In fact, several extensively researched books—notably Upton Sinclair's *The Jungle* (1906), Arthur Kallet and F. J. Schlink's *100,000,000 Guinea Pigs* (1932), and Ralph Nader's *Unsafe at Any Speed* (1965)—symbolize periods of consumer reform. More recently, hundreds of books, studies, and reports by dozens of consumer groups have collectively exercised great influence on national public opinion, legislation, regulation, and corporate practices.

Consumer advocates undertake research about consumer attitudes and behavior, corporate practices, and government policies, in part, to achieve better understanding. But their main goals are action and change, usually by government or corporations. Advocates typically treat research as "ammunition" to be used in "battles" for reform. Corporations too use research in these battles, but they also have the resources to employ other "weapons," including issue advertising, organization of front groups, extensive grassroots campaigns, and the development of relationships, lubricated by campaign contributions, with many members of Congress or state legislators. Consumer activists, because they usually lack such extensive resources and because they have a public interest orientation that favors fact-driven public policy, rely much more heavily on research.

Subjects: Advocates research three broad subjects—consumers, corporations, and government. Although these activists sometimes try to understand what consumers know or do not know—often to better target education or advocacy—they most frequently seek to learn about problems consumers face and consumer attitudes related to solutions of these problems. Problems run the gamut through all consumer goods and services from sales practices, to pricing, to product quality and safety. A principal source of information about these problems is consumer complaints to government agencies. Federal agencies including the Federal Trade

Commission (FTC), Food and Drug Administration (FDA), National Highway Traffic Safety Administration (NHTSA), Consumer Product Safety Commission, and Consumer Financial Protection Bureau (CFPB) pay particular attention to the complaints they receive from consumers. When these data are accessible to the public, consumer advocates often "repackage" and release them. For decades, an important source of information for auto safety advocates, which they then summarized and disseminated, has been the accident reports of NHTSA. A recent example of repackaging government data is U.S. PIRG's 2014 release of a summary and commentary on data about credit card complaints that had been collected by the CFPB.

Activists also seek to learn more about how consumers regard current corporate practices or proposed reforms. While consumer groups often survey their own members or constituents, they also employ survey firms to question a representative sample of consumers nationwide. The resulting data are more broadly representative of the attitudes of all consumers and have greater credibility with the press and policymakers. For many years, for example, the Consumer Federation of America (CFA) has employed a national survey firm to learn how consumers would regard reforms ranging from the creation of a consumer financial protection agency to increases in motor vehicle fuel economy standards. Survey findings have then been incorporated into CFA's advocacy materials.

An even greater focus of consumer advocates in their research has been the marketplace—individual products, corporate practices, and marketplace structure. The health and safety of individual products has been a particular priority of their investigations. Since its founding in the 1930s, Consumers Union/Consumer Reports has "tested" the safety of hundreds of different types of individual products. Just in the past several decades, the Center for Science in the Public Interest has commissioned laboratories to assess the nutritional value of dozens of foods and meals served by restaurants and other vendors, such as movie theaters. Consumer activist research related to safety also includes the annual holiday season evaluations, by Public Interest Research Groups, of the safety of new toys.

Research on financial products and related corporate practices has also received much attention from consumer advocates, especially since the deregulation of the banking industry in the 1980s. For the past couple decades, Consumer Action and U.S. PIRG have been the most active in surveying the prices and practices of financial institutions related to products such as checking and credit cards. In the past several years, perhaps the most influential research by advocates in this area has been undertaken by the Pew Charitable Trusts. Its reports on credit cards, checking accounts, payday loans, and other financial products have been taken seriously by the media and policymakers. Also going well beyond marketplace surveys have been the dozens of reports by CFA, the National Consumer Law Center (NCLC), and Center for Responsible Lending on all aspects of payday loans and other types of high-cost lending, which have often included detailed analysis of existing and proposed public policies.

Not just individual products and corporate practices but also the structure of the marketplace has been a focus of some advocacy groups, particularly those with staff who have expertise in economics. For the past two decades, American Antitrust Institute head Albert Foer, who earlier worked in the FTC's Bureau of Competition, has analyzed the consumer effects of corporate mergers and competition. Since the 1980s, CFA Research Director Mark Cooper, a Yale-trained PhD, has been jousting with antiregulation experts in the areas of energy and communications, often producing reports approaching 100 pages that contain exhaustive literature reviews.

The performance of government, especially federal agencies, has been the main focus of the research of several consumer groups, especially those related to Ralph Nader. Nader's *Unsafe at Any Speed* was as much a condemnation of the failure of the federal government to regulate auto safety as it was criticism of the practices of automobile manufacturers. His "Nader's Raiders," most of whom were undergraduates or graduate or professional school students, then researched a whole series of books—including *The Chemical Feast*, *Vanishing Air*, and *Interstate Commerce Omission*, all published in 1970—that lambasted the failure of government agencies to protect consumers. Public Citizen, Nader's flagship organization, continued this tradition of analyzing and criticizing federal agencies, especially NHTSA and the FDA.

Consumer advocates have completed much research and analysis on specific public policies. For proposed legislation, much of this research focuses on related consumer needs and how new laws or regulations will help meet them. Activists have also analyzed existing laws and regulations in terms of their harm or insufficient benefits to consumers. All major consumer groups have undertaken, often together, criticism of proposed or existing deregulation measures. In the past several years, major consumer groups have joined with other public interest organizations to oppose legislation that would severely limit federal regulatory agencies, for example, by requiring congressional approval of each new regulation they issue. Also recently, NCLC and CFA issued a report on the Military Lending Act of 2007, which concluded that the law had increased consumer protections but should be amended to close its loopholes.

Research by others: Although most research used by advocates is generated by them, they also often find the research of others to be helpful. This research ranges from that of investigative reporters to that of academics. The advantage of the investigative journalism over scholarly work is that it is more likely to be relevant, timely, and interesting to a broad audience. Like that of Progressive-era "Muckrakers," recent investigative reporting has focused on issues of public concern and has often been completed and published within a period of months. Moreover, this reporting usually has included dramatic examples of problems and abuses.

On the other hand, thoroughly researched work by scholars on controversial policy issues is also sought by policymakers considering consumer reforms. For example, the early anecdote-laden reports that first appeared in the 1990s on high-cost lending abuses were later supplemented by careful research on consumer effects published more than a decade later. Together, both types of research helped convince state and federal policymakers to try eliminating these abuses. Government reports also often assist advocates in making their case for reform. After many studies and reports by consumer groups on credit card abuses, a 2006 U.S. General Accounting Office report confirmed the existence of many of these abuses and helped convince Congress to pass related legislation.

Effects and criticism: It is difficult to identify major new consumer protections that were not influenced by consumer activist research. In some cases, just the release of the research and its dissemination to the press and regulators have been largely responsible for reforms. For example, within two years after release of two critical reports on credit life insurance by the National Insurance Consumer Organization and CFA in the late 1980s, more than a dozen states had placed new limits on prices charged by credit insurers. Moreover, largely because extensive news coverage of the reports, sales of credit insurance products declined by more than one-third. The ability of consumer research to influence the marketplace is seen most frequently in the product modifications, often to motor vehicles, generated by Consumers Union/Consumer Report's release of its product test results.

Research published by consumer advocates tends to be very empirical, emphasizing facts about the marketplace and the experience of consumers with this marketplace. But in part because an important goal of these advocates is that their research be noticed and lead to policy change, some have questioned its objectivity and reliability as a guide to reform. There is no question that much advocacy-related research contains bias, not just in topics selected, but also sometimes in sources consulted, data used, and the analysis and presentation of these data. However, particularly when it attracts much attention, this research is rigorously scrutinized by the subjects of any criticism and by those objecting to its policy recommendations. For important policy issues, the press and policymakers note these responses and undertake their own evaluation of the original research. Aware of the possibility of this intense scrutiny, most experienced consumer advocates take great pains to ensure that their studies and reports can withstand tough third party assessments.

Stephen Brobeck, Robert N. Mayer

See also: American Council on Consumer Interests; Journalism

Further Reading

Nader, Ralph. 1965. *Unsafe at Any Speed: The Designed-In Dangers of the American Automobile.* New York: Grossman Publishers.

Kallett, Arthur, and F. J. Schlink. 1932. *100,000,000 Guinea Pigs: Dangers in Everyday Food, Drugs, and Cosmetics.* New York: Vanguard Press.

Sinclair, Upton. 1906. *The Jungle.* New York: Doubleday.

RURAL ELECTRIC COOPERATIVES

See Consumer Cooperatives

RUSSIAN CONSUMER MOVEMENT

For most of its history, the Soviet Union operated a planned economy in which the availability, quality, and price of consumer goods was determined by the government rather than market forces. Accordingly, consumers had a largely passive and powerless role. Moreover, the government prioritized the production of public goods (e.g., buses) over private ones (e.g., cars). Soviet consumers were largely shut off from consumer goods made outside the Soviet bloc (the countries whose economic and political policies were closely aligned with those of the Soviet Union) and from contact with Western consumer organizations.

During the mid-1980s, the dual policies of *perestroika* and *glasnost*, spearheaded by General Secretary of the Communist Party Mikhail Gorbachev, brought the beginnings of change in the situation of consumers in the Soviet Union. *Perestroika* aimed at restructuring the economic system in a more consumer-oriented direction via increased efficiency and the introduction of limited, free market reforms. *Glasnost* called for less corruption and more openness on the part of government. The associated easing of government censorship allowed the media to be more honest about economic problems and include greater information about developments outside the Soviet bloc.

While the various economic and political reforms were ultimately insufficient to solve longstanding problems in the Soviet Union, the reforms did provide a climate in which the first consumer organizations in the Soviet Union emerged. In 1989, several consumer associations formed the Federation of Consumer Societies of the USSR to lobby for improved legal rights for consumers. After the dissolution of Soviet Union at the end of 1991, the organization became the Inter-Republican Confederation of Consumers Societies (KonfOP) and was welcomed as a member of Consumers International, the umbrella organization of the world consumer movement. Owing partly to the efforts of KonfOP, the first law on the protection of consumer rights in Russia was passed in 1992, and it has been amended by the Russian parliament on multiple occasions.

KonfOP remains one of the two most important consumer organizations in the Russian Federation today. It has approximately forty member organizations and works to bring consumer rights to the level enjoyed by people living in the European Union. Since the early 1990s, it has published a comparative testing magazine, *SPROS* (Demand), to help consumers make informed choices about products and services, conducting roughly seventy independent tests per year. KonfOP addresses a wide variety of consumer problems, ranging from food adulteration and deceptive advertising to bank overcharges and poor treatment of airline passengers.

In recent years, KonfOP has been particularly active in the area of tobacco control. It has opposed exaggeration by cigarette companies of the benefits of "light" cigarettes and supported government measures to restrict cigarette advertising and the locations at which cigarettes can be purchased. The organization's long-time director, Dmitry Yanin, was awarded the prestigious Judy Wilkenfeld Award by the U.S.-based Campaign for Tobacco-Free Kids for his efforts. Of course, calling for restrictions on tobacco and alcohol are politically safe issues in Russia, as prime ministers Vladimir Putin and Dmitry Medvedev have also spoken out strongly against these vices and helped passed strong legislation to reduce their consumption.

The other leading consumer association in Russia is the Consumers Union of Russia. Established in 1990 and accepted as an affiliate member of Consumers International in 2008, the Consumers Union of Russia is a federation of more than a hundred regional and local consumer associations. The organization's main activities are representing consumer interests in governmental bodies, seeking improvements in consumer rights legislation, educating consumers and providing them with legal assistance, and conducting independent product testing. As an example of a specific issue of interest to the Consumers Union of Russia, its chairman, Peter Shelisch, spoke out in 2013 in favor of restricting advertising to young people of fast food.

Despite the improvements in consumer protection achieved at the urging of groups such as KonfOP and the Consumers Union of Russia, significant barriers to consumer mobilization exist in Russia. Democratic rights, including freedom of the press and freedom of assembly, are essential to a strong consumer movement but are incompletely realized in today's Russia. A politically active middle class has also been a typical prerequisite for consumer activism. While incomes and wealth have increased in Russia over the last decade, income inequality, which shot up after the dissolution of the Soviet Union, has remained high, stunting the growth of a large middle class. Finally, the persistence from Soviet times of a "dependency culture" by which people believe that the government, not citizen action, is the only source of social change, constitutes a final barrier to consumer activism. Nevertheless, one factor helps support a Russian consumer movement: Educational attainment in Russia is extremely high by international standards, and education tends to promote rising economic aspirations and civic participation.

Robert N. Mayer

See also: Consumers International

Further Reading

Auzan, Alexander A., 1995. "Changes in the Behaviour of Russian Consumers under Recent Reforms." *Journal of Consumer Policy* 18: 73–84.

Schrad, Mark Lawrence. 2014. *Vodka Politics: Alcohol, Autocracy, and the Secret History of the Russian State.* New York: Oxford University Press.

Treadwell, Amy B., and William Alex Pridemore, 2004. "Purchasing Power: Consumer Empowerment and Adaptation to the Free Market in Russia." *Journal of Consumer Policy* 27: 451–474.

SAVINGS ADVOCACY
See Truth in Savings Advocacy

SERBIAN CONSUMER MOVEMENT
The consumer movement in Serbia has a long history, beginning when Serbia was still one of six republics within the country of Yugoslavia. Despite the organization of the Yugoslav economy under socialist principles, including government control of the economy and a low priority placed on consumer luxuries, the first consumer council in Serbia was established on June 8, 1955, in the city of Leskovac. Within a few years, there were nearly 600 consumer councils nationally. These early consumer councils were not the result of self-organization by consumers, however, their representatives being nominated by government officials. The councils were essentially an interventionist control tool in the planned economic system.

From 1959 until 1965, both at the federal level of Yugoslavia and within the Republic of Serbia, a network of "family and household" boards functioned at the municipal level. The network composed of these organizations was particularly active in comparative product testing. In 1963, a new Yugoslav constitution gave official recognition to municipal-level consumer councils; a few years later, the Socialist Union of the Working People of Yugoslavia argued for an expanded role for citizens at the local level, including arbitration bodies to resolve consumer complaints. By 1974, there were 3,000 active consumer councils throughout Yugoslavia. In addition, the first consumer codes were established in the early 1970s as tripartite agreements between consumer councils, municipalities, and government-owned enterprises. The first code was signed in Osijek, Croatia in November, 1970, and the first in Serbia was signed in April 1971, again in the city of Leskovac.

The Constitution of 1974—Yugoslavia's fourth and final constitution—was notable for consumers. It was the first constitution in the world to explicitly promote interests of consumers and their associations. By 1975, the number of consumer councils had grown to approximately 12,000, including some that operated beyond specific municipalities at the republic level. Nevertheless, the consumer movement of Yugoslavia (and therefore Serbia) operated primarily within local governments, which provided funding and direction to the work of consumer representatives. Consumer arbitration councils, comprised of representatives of both consumers and chambers of commerce, were an important development. In addition, some municipal councils established so-called consumer clubs that organized various information and education campaigns as well as provided free legal aid to consumers. All this took place within a country run by a single political party, but one in which citizens enjoyed a substantial level of freedom, in which their voices were heard, and in which their representatives were elected in an open and transparent process.

The fall of Yugoslavia in 1991, followed by an economic downturn, hyperinflation, and UN sanctions targeting the Serbian economy, all contributed to a diminution in consumer activism and organization. New laws on local self-governance did not foresee an active role of citizens as consumers, and consumer councils were not obligatory. Many councils dissolved; only a very few turned into nongovernmental consumer associations. Although the mid-1970s may be described as a golden period for Yugoslavia's consumer movement, the mid-1990s were a black time. Nevertheless, some consumer organizations survived and, after democratic changes in 2002, continued their operation in the nongovernmental sector. In May 2004, the first joint session of members of the Union of Consumer Organizations of Serbia and Association of Consumers of Serbia was held, encompassing around thirty consumer organizations, and by May 2005, a National Organization of Consumers of Serbia (NOPS) had been established. All this occurred before Serbia formally gained its independence in June 2006.

A new law on consumer protection was adopted in 2010, replacing the relatively vague Consumer Protection Law of 2005. This new legislation implemented a substantial part of the European Union's "acquis communautaire," the set of laws and commitments that would be required for Serbia to become a member of the Union. A key feature of the 2010 law was establishing procedures whereby consumer associations can represent and protect collective consumer interests. This augments the Associations Acts of 2009, which sets the criteria for nonprofit, nongovernmental organizations. Nevertheless, consumer organizations in Serbia generally struggle with a lack funding. Although the Serbian government will occasionally fund specific projects conducted by consumer organizations, these organizations do not have a stable source of funding from the government or elsewhere.

There are currently more than seventy consumer organizations in Serbia—a large number for a country of only about 7 million people. Not all these organizations are officially registered and thereby empowered to represent the collective interests of consumers, however. Although the requirement for consumer organizations to register was likely intended to raise their level of professionalism and prevent oversaturation, in practice, registration has not achieved these aims. There are around thirty registered organizations. All are broad in their areas of focus and desired competence, with the exception of one that specializes in protecting banking clients. As a result, the most important consumer organizations are federations of consumer organizations. These are the National Consumer Organization of Serbia (twenty-two member organizations), the Association of Consumers of Serbia APOS (five member organizations), and the Consumers' Centre of Serbia (thirteen member organizations). (The first two of these federations are affiliate members of Consumers International, an indication of their independence and commitment to building their organizational capacity.) Some of these umbrella associations operate consumer advice enters, are represented in the government-run National

Council of Consumer Protection, and are seen as project partners by the Department of Trade, Services, Prices, and Consumer Protection within the Ministry of Trade, Tourism, and Telecommunications.

Besides inadequate funding, Serbia's consumer organizations suffer from a lack of expertise. The major federations are usually run by a small number of people who, in some cases, lack professional education or see consumer activism as their second job. A small number of professionals work voluntarily on a pro bono basis, but a strong consumer movement will require full-time, paid, professional leaders.

Tatjana Jovanic

See also: Consumers International

Further Reading

Markovic, Milic. 2005. *Pola veka zastite potrosaca* (Half century of consumer protection). Leskovac, Serbia: Organizacija Potrošača.

Fejős, Andrea. 2013. "The Impact of EU on Consumer Protection Enforcement in Serbia." *Journal of Consumer Policy* 36, no. 3: 247–268.

Papović, Goran; Fejős, Andrea. 2008. "The Role of Stabilization and Association Agreement in Consumer Protection" (Uloga Sporazuma o stabilizaciji i pridruživanju u zaštiti potrošača). *Challenges of European Integration* 1: 45–60.

Vilus, Jelena. 1977. "Self-Management and Protection of Consumers in Yugoslavia." *Journal of Consumer Policy* 1, no. 2: 165–171.

SLOVENIAN CONSUMER MOVEMENT

Slovenia is among the countries with the highest standard of living among formerly communist countries. After declaring independence from Yugoslavia in 1991, it joined the European Union (EU) in 2004 and adopted the euro as its national currency in 2007. For almost twenty years, Slovenia was a success story in terms of its transition to democracy and a market economy, but the worldwide economic crisis in 2009 unveiled numerous problems, shortcomings of its development model, and questionable ethics within its political and economic systems. The country's GDP plummeted, and the unemployment rate doubled (though it remained less than the EU average). As of 2014, the country was facing a multifaceted crisis for the fifth year in a row, a situation that could not help but affect Slovenia's consumer movement.

Slovenia's primary consumer organization—the Slovene Consumers' Association (Zvezapotrošnikov Slovenije, or ZPS)—was founded in June 1990 by Breda Kutin, an economist and former head of research at the home economics institute, Domus. ZPS was modeled after Western consumer organizations, which have paying members, a product-testing magazine, and involvement in issue campaigning and consumer policymaking. From its modest beginning, ZPS developed into professionally run organization on par with many of the older and well established consumer organizations in Europe. ZPS is known by 91 percent of Slovenia's population and is widely recognized as a dynamic, ambitious, and effective association of consumers ("Perception . . . ," 2009). It is a long-standing and active member within international-level umbrella organizations, such as Consumers

International, BEUC: The European Consumer Organisation, and International Consumer Research & Testing. ZPS's president, Breda Kutin, served as a council member of Consumers International for fourteen years (1994–2007) and as a BEUC vice president for three terms, as well as as a steering committee member of the Transatlantic Consumer Dialogue.

Despite its accomplishments, ZPS faces many challenges in achieving economic self-sufficiency. Slovenia is a small country in terms of both geographic size (7,800 square miles) and population (2 million). Equally important, Slovenia has a strong socialist heritage, where consumers reach out for assistance from nongovernmental organizations that they expect to be funded by the national government. Indeed, the Consumer Protection Act, adopted in 1998 and amended several times, provides a legal basis for acknowledging consumer organizations as the legitimate voice of consumers and therefore for government funding of consumers associations such as ZPS.

The Consumer Protection Program, adopted by Parliament for the first time in 2001 as the first of a series of five-year policy plans, provided significant financial support to non-government consumer organizations and ZPS in particular. The funds were used for consumer counseling, publishing consumer magazines, and other programs for the benefit of consumers. But reliance on government funding has both benefits and drawbacks.

One of the most successful activities during the early years of ZPS's existence was helping overindebted consumers complain in 1991–1992 about massive increases in the amount of their mortgage payments. ZPS effectively lobbied the Ministry for Environment and Housing and the Parliament, resulting in a housing fund being set up through which 3,500 consumers were able to transfer their high-interest rate contracts from commercial banks into low-interest loans from the housing fund. Their mortgage interest rate was reduced dramatically—from an annual rate of 14 percent rate to 2 percent. As a result, consumers saved approximately 18 million euros.

One of the most important activities of ZPS is to shape case law in the field of consumer protection, in which no significant court rulings previously existed and in which government measures are not effective, nor even in place. An important ZPS campaign involved a 2006 court action against the largest bank in Slovenia at the time (NLB Bank) after the bank decreased the interest rates paid on savings accounts even though these rates were part of a contract. Before going to court, ZPS tried to reach an acceptable settlement with the bank. However, the bank's offer to approximately 40,000 clients was not acceptable. It would have meant that on average only 60 percent of the unpaid interest to which consumers were entitled would be paid them by the bank. As Slovenia's legal system does not permit class action lawsuits, ZPS had to file 160 individual lawsuits with claims ranging from 400 to 20,000 euros per contract. Eventually the Slovenian Supreme Court ruled in favor of ZPS members on most counts. In all, NLB Bank paid out approximately 12 million euros to their savers in 2009 (Kutin et al., 2010).

There have been many other successful campaigns. One was against an additional monthly fee introduced by mobile phone for services that consumers rarely use. Another was against banks that introduced identical ATM fees for cash with-drawals on the same day, in breach of competition law. A further instance occurred when Slovenia entered the Eurozone in 2007, at which time ZPS was alert to the possibility that sellers might use the currency transition to raise prices. Accord-ingly, ZPS implemented a campaign to monitor prices. The campaign kept prices unchanged and thereby increased the visibility and credibility of ZPS. In 2013 and 2014, ZPS brought legal action against usurious loans offered by nonbank financial institutions and over subscriptions for unwanted services that are "crammed" into mobile phone bills without the consent of consumers. In the latter case, the trial court decided that providers should be more transparent in advertising the price of commercial messages and that consumers should always be given the option to stop being a subscriber to the service.

During its twenty-four-year existence, ZPS has been committed to providing consumers with impartial information. Starting in 1991, ZPS began the continu-ous publication of a comparative testing magazine, *VIP*. Today, ZPS runs the main website in Slovenia devoted to consumer protection. In 2013, the site had more than 810,000 unique visitors and was listed as one of the top hundred most-visited online portals in the country. ZPS is also highly active in social media, with more than 26,500 Facebook fans and more than 2400 followers on Twitter.

ZPS's research arm, the International Consumer Research Institute (MIPOR), was founded in 1993 by the Slovene Consumers' Association and the British Consumers' Association (known since 2004 as Which?). MIPOR conducts comparative testing of products and services and serves as the publisher of the consumer magazine *VIP*. MIPOR also carries out projects relevant to consumer protection policy in areas such as financial services, healthcare and patient rights, telecommunications, housing, and product safety. Of particular importance was the publication in 2000, with funding from the European Union, of *Guidelines for Consumer Policy in Central and Eastern Europe*. The results of MIPOR's research are published as scientific reports and serve as the basis for articles in *VIP*. The quality of the research conducted by MIPOR lends legitimacy and credibility to the Slovene Consumers' Association (ZPS) in its effort to inform consumers, lobby legislators, and carry out additional activities in the field of consumer protection.

MIPOR has also been very active in promoting alternative dispute resolution (ADR) mechanisms in Slovenia. In spite of organizing several roundtables and research studies, Slovenian consumers still lack proper ADR in key consumer fields such as banking, insurance, telecommunications, energy, and the like.

From 2006 to 2014, MIPOR coordinated information campaigns that the Euro-pean Union was implementing in central and eastern Europe. With its role in six information campaigns launched in twelve new member states of the EU, MIPOR has gained considerable experience in the field of organizing and running informa-tion campaigns on consumer rights. In addition, the EU financed a project carried out by MIPOR that provide consumers with new Web applications (e.g., product pickers, mutual fund comparisons, video clips) that advance consumer protection by giving Slovenian consumers easier access to important information.

In 2010, ZPS celebrated its twentieth anniversary. To mark this milestone, it organized an international forum, "Consumers in the Financial Crisis and the Way Out," with the assistance of BEUC and the Transatlantic Consumer Dialogue. ZPS brought together key stakeholders in the field of financial services. The meeting resulted in the Ljubljana Declaration, in which consumer organizations called for reforms in the field of the supervision of financial markets.

In contrast to the high point represented by ZPS's twentieth anniversary, recent years have brought a decrease in what had originally been strong financial support from the government for independent consumer activism. The Consumer Protection Office, a body of the Ministry of Economy that was established in 1996, was widely viewed as ineffective. After years of constant criticism against the office, it was disbanded in 2011, with its roles and responsibilities transferred to the Ministry of Economy.

Unfortunately, the end of the Consumer Protection Office was not a good development for consumer protection in Slovenia. Officials in the Ministry of Economy did not fully appreciate the need for effective consumer policy and a strong consumer movement. When the ministry was criticized for confining its financial support to only ZPS, it reacted by withdrawing all financial support to both major consumer organizations, ZPS and MIPOR, in 2013 and 2014—without an attempt to explain their reasons or the legal basis for their action.

In 2013, government officials also decided to stop the implementation of the National Consumer Protection Program adopted by the Parliament in June 2012. The ministry reversed its decision to have ZPS provide free legal advice to Slovenian consumers. The ministry also took over operation of the European Consumer Center, whose aim is to provide free consumer counseling with respect to cross-border buying. The center had been operated by ZPS since 2006 and was recognized as one of the best-run centers in the EU. Finally, the government ended funding for *VIP*—Slovenia's only comparative testing magazine. All this was done even though the National Consumer Protection Program for 2012–2017 provided grounds for these activities to be in the hands of independent consumer organizations.

The sudden cut of state funding presented a challenge for ZPS and necessitated the reorganization of its resources. Whereas the scope of ZPS activities had previously been broad, the organization entered a period of scaling down its activities. It can be argued that expanding competition and enhancing consumer protection are pillars for the recovery of the Slovenian economy from the worldwide recession. Yet, as part of an austerity campaign, Slovenia turned into the opposite direction. Slovenia needs to rethink the importance of protecting its consumers.

Regardless of the current situation, ZPS has attempted to remain active in representing consumers, both at the national and international levels. It enables consumers to access useful information and advice, mainly through its online portal and consumer magazine, *VIP*. The magazine has improved greatly since its early days when it primarily printed test results produced by other organizations; today, *VIP* contains some of its own test results. The magazine also publishes a quarterly financial services supplement focused on market research and testing of banking services. Following the example of the German product-testing organization, *Stiftung Warentest*, ZPS introduced a quality certification label called *VIP Test* to permit the careful useful by business of test results to promote their products. Despite all this activity, the magazine has only about 7,000 subscribers. This subscriber basis is too small to support the magazine's expansion, let alone address ZPS's most pressing challenge—finding a stable and independent source of funding.

To help find a sustainable operating model without state financing, ZPS has turned to BEUC for assistance. The early results are promising. With the help of BEUC's capacity building program for consumer organizations in central, eastern, and south-eastern Europe (CESEE program) and support from some BEUC members, ZPS has a pilot project in place that is aimed at developing new business models for consumer organizations by fostering for-pay consumer services and significantly increasing the number of magazine subscribers. If successful, the new business model will help ZPS not only survive, but also achieve long-term growth.

Breda Kutin

See also: BEUC: The European Consumer Organisation; Consumers International

Further Reading

BEUC: The European Consumer Organisation. 2012. *Analysis of the Consumer Movement in Central, Eastern, and South-Eastern Europe.* Brussels (October). www.ec.europa.eu/consumers/reports/cesee2_2012_report_en.pdf.

Guidelines for Consumer Policy in Central and Eastern Europe. 2000. London, UK: Consumers International.

Kutin, Breda, Matja Videčnik, Meta Stegenšek, and Živa Drol Novak. 2010. *20 Years on the Side of Consumers.* Ljubljana, Slovenia: Slovene Consumers' Association (May).

Perception and Attitude towards ZPS and VIP Magazine. 2009. Valicon Marketing Consulting and Marketing (February).

SMOKING
See Tobacco Activism

SOUTH AMERICAN CONSUMER MOVEMENTS

Today, consumer protection in South America (and Latin America in general) has gained an important place in national and regional public policy development. This high level of consumer protection would have been difficult to predict in the 1970s and 1980s. (The latter decade was described as the "Lost Decade" because most countries in South America were ruled by dictatorships and experienced social and economic crisis.) During this period, a few consumer organizations were established—among them, the Colombian Confederation of Consumers in 1970, Consumer Action (ADELCO) in Argentina in 1980, and the Brazilian Institute for Consumer Defense (IDEC) in 1985. There were also a few attempts to address consumer rights through legislation. Consumer laws were enacted in Venezuela in 1975 and Colombia in 1981, but the laws were weak. The region was not yet ready to fully embrace consumer protection.

In 1985, the unanimous approval by the United Nations General Assembly of the Guidelines for Consumer Protection was a landmark not only for the

South American consumer movement, but for consumer movements through-out the world. The guidelines set a list of consumer rights and brought to the region greater interest in consumer issues. Consumer groups started to appear in every country, and governments began to pay attention to these new rights. (By 2013, it became apparent that the Guidelines for Consumer Protection needed to be updated in light of consumer issues, such as electronic commerce and data protection, that had emerged since 1985. South American countries have been important participants in this revision process, with Brazil co-chairing one of the working groups.)

The last part of the 1980s and the first half of the 1990s were a time in which consumer protection advanced, as many countries in the region regained democracy. The resulting emphasis on individual political rights helped make consumer rights a prominent issue as well. In addition, the unpopular push by several South American governments to privatize public services such as electricity delivery focused attention on problems of access to basic goods and services. In response, consumer rights provisions began appearing in newly updated and reformed constitutions as well as specific laws.

To date, consumer rights are mentioned in eight constitutions in South America: Argentina, Brazil, Paraguay, Peru, Bolivia, Colombia, Ecuador and Venezuela. Laws containing consumer protections were either new laws or updated versions of older laws. The countries that drafted new laws were Brazil in 1990 with its Consumer Defense Code, Peru in 1991, Argentina in 1993, Chile in 1997, Paraguay in 1998, Uruguay in 1999, and Ecuador in 2000. In 1992, Venezuela replaced its existing consumer protection legislation of 1975 (replaced in 2010 by new legislation). Many of these laws have in turn been further modified or updated recently: in Argentina (2008), Ecuador (2011), Peru (2011) and Chile (2011). Bolivia is the only country in the region that does not have a comprehensive consumer protection law.

To fully understand consumer activism in South America, one must take account of the role of Consumers International's Office for Latin America and the Caribbean (ROLAC). The office was established in 1986 in Montevideo, Uruguay, and in 1991, it moved to Santiago, Chile. ROLAC played a significant role in the development of consumer protection in the region by raising awareness of the need to address consumer rights. When it began its work, only a few countries in the region had consumer legislation, so one of its first tasks was to develop a Model Law for Consumer Protection to serve as a prototype for national laws. During the last two decades, virtually every South American country has used this model as a source in drafting its consumer protection legislation.

In the 1990s, facing the controversial trend toward privatizing government-owned companies, ROLAC focused on consumer protection with respect to public utilities such as water and electricity. A program called Consumers and Public Utilities (CONSUPAL) helped consumer groups defend consumer rights in the context of the new private companies. This work resulted in consumer bills of rights, or charters, for the different services and set a standard for consumer protection that was applied in other regions around the world. In the twenty-first century, ROLAC's work has focused on financial services and the growing influence of new technologies on consumer behavior. Nevertheless, more "traditional" issues such as food, advertising, consumer education, sustainable consumption, and global trade are counted as important topics for the work of ROLAC. In the case of consumer education, for example, ROLAC fostered the creation of a consumer education network for the region and initially acted as a secretariat, afterwards leaving the coordination of the network to its members.

Regional Participation

The 1990s experienced the development of regional consumer protection agreements involving governments and/or consumer organizations. The Southern Cone Common Market (MERCOSUR)—initially composed of Argentina, Brazil, Paraguay and Uruguay, with Venezuela joining in 2012—has a working group on consumer protection known as Technical Commission No. 7 (CT7) that addresses consumer issues such as tourism, redress, and contracts. A Charter of Consumer Rights by MERCOSUR's presidents was issued in 1998 as an attempt to harmonize legislation among the trading bloc's members. The effort to have a more comprehensive declaration was ultimately set aside, however, because for Brazil, adoption would mean lowering its national level of protection. The CT7 continues to meet at least twice a year to discuss matters of common interest.

In 2002, the Andean Community of Nations (CAN)—comprised of Bolivia, Colombia, Ecuador and Peru, with Chile as an observer—created the Andean Roundtable on the Promotion and Protection of Consumer Rights. The roundtable brings together government agencies and consumer associations to discuss issues such as tourism, redress, and competition.

An umbrella organization was launched in 2003 as an initiative of the Consumers International Regional Office for Latin America and the Caribbean to unite government agencies within Latin America. Initially called the Latin American Consumer Protection Government Agencies Forum, the name changed to Ibero–American Forum of Consumer Protection Government Agencies (FIAGC) with the addition of Spain to the forum in 2006. (Portugal is an official observer.) The presidency of FIAGC rotates annually among member nations, and its annual meeting is held in the country where the current presidency resides. FIAGC works to harmonize consumer protections on topics such as cross-border transactions, contracts, tourism, financial services, standards, and participation by civil society organizations. All South American countries are members of FIAGC.

As a final example of cooperation within the South American region on consumer matters, the Latin American Parliament (PARLATINO) established a commission on consumer protection. The commission has worked with Consumers International in creating a Model Law for Consumer Protection, launched in 1998. The commission still gathers regularly, at least twice yearly.

The consumer rights movement in South America also cooperates with movements in Central America and North America. The Organization of American States (OAS) has paid more attention to consumer protection in recent years and has developed the Consumer Safety and Health Network to help countries with online information about defective products and recalls. OAS is also developing a Rapid Alert System on product safety that will allow countries to act quickly in cases where consumer safety may be at imminent risk.

Consumer Protection Today

Today, consumer associations can be found in all South American countries, and many older associations have compiled a history of successes that can be measured in decades. It is not a stretch to say that many of these associations were the motor that drove the governments of South America to act on behalf of consumers, and consumer organizations continue to amplify the voice of millions of people who were previously unheard. These associations advanced through great effort, mainly through the work of volunteers, and grew through innovation and creativity.

Most consumer organizations in the region lack a reliable source of funding, so a common dialogue among South American consumer organizations relates to how to fund their activities and ensure long-term survival. The model of producing magazines and recruiting members that has worked for some organizations in more developed countries has failed in most South American associations, with some exceptions. But just the effort to run a revenue-generating magazine, even when unsuccessful, strengthened the reputations of these organizations. Some associations, however, have received funding from their governments, such as in Argentina (subsidies), Chile and Brazil (project funding), and Peru (remission of a percentage of fines collected by a government agency).

In the past, government consumer agencies in South America were weak or nonexistent, but now each country has a consumer protection agency, and they often have adequate powers and resources. The structure of these agencies varies from country to country: in Brazil, a secretary of state for consumer protection in the Ministry of Justice; in Bolivia, a vice ministry of defense of consumer rights in the Ministry of Economy; in Argentina, an undersecretary of consumer protection under the Ministry of Economy; in Paraguay and Uruguay, directorates in the Ministry of Economy; in Chile, the National Consumer Service (SERNAC); and in Ecuador, a directorate under the Ministry of Industry and Productivity. In Peru, Colombia, and Venezuela, autonomous agencies deal with consumer protection. These bodies are, respectively, the National Institute for Defense of Competition and the Intellectual Property Rights, the Superintendence of Industry and Commerce, and the Institute for the Defense of People in their Access to Goods and Services. All these agencies have a reasonable degree of independence, and in some countries, such as Peru and Colombia, they also deal with other aspects of economic regulation related to consumer protection.

Many countries in South America have developed detailed policies and strategic plans relating to consumer rights for both public and private sectors. There are some aspects that need to be strengthened—most notably, enforcement, which is still weaker than it should be. But it is clear that consumers are now more empowered and aware of their rights. Every year, consumer complaints grow in number, suggesting developing consumer involvement. One of the challenges for the consumer movement is to look at the nature and causes of these complaints, not just their quantity. Another challenge is to find creative ways to ensure the financial sustainability of consumer associations while maintaining autonomy from political parties and corporations.

Although the region is now more economically stable, the distribution of wealth and income is still highly uneven, so the need to focus on simple aspects of consumer protection, such as by ensuring that all consumers can fulfill their basic needs, is still the major focus for consumer activists. Prices of basic items such as food, shelter, and public services require constant attention, because price inflation has been an issue in some countries. Furthermore, financial services have to be closely monitored and regulated to avoid consumer problems in the use of credit. At the same time, consumers in South America are increasingly taking advantage of the opportunities of modern life, including both shopping and paying bills online. As the South American consumer movement continues to fight for the rights of consumers of all income levels, it is inspired by the view that consumer rights are not just economic rights, but mainly human rights.

Antonino Serra Cambaceres

See also: Brazilian Consumer Movement; Caribbean Consumer Movements; Central American Consumer Movements; Consumers International

Further Reading

Consumers International. 2010. *50 Years of the Global Consumer Movement.* London, UK: Consumers International. www.consumersinternational.org/media/33263/ci50 ebook-english.pdf.

Rhodes, Sybil. 2012. *Social Movements and Free-Market Capitalism in Latin America.* Albany, NY: SUNY Press.

SOUTH KOREAN CONSUMER MOVEMENT

In a 1997 article discussing the South Korean consumer movement, the authors, Kee-Choon Rhee and Jinkook Lee, mentioned four current challenges: the increase in international trade, overconsumption, the possibility of a Korean reunification, and overcoming centralization. Today, Korea is almost fully globalized, and South Koreans are experiencing the same global consumer problems as consumers in other developed nations. The challenge of overconsumption was abruptly "solved" by the financial crisis of 1997–1998, when South Korea's currency, the won, was drastically devalued. This resulted in considerable difficulties for individual households and a fairly drastic reduction in consumer spending. The possibility of Korean reunification is still an ongoing matter, but it is less urgent than it was in the late 1990s. Centralization issues were addressed, at least in part, as a system of local self-government was adopted in 1990 and the number and influence of regional consumer associations increased.

The most dramatic change in consumer policy since 1997 was passage of the amendments to the Consumer Protection Act in 2007. The law, enacted in 1979, represented the first involvement of the South Korean government in protecting the rights of consumers. The amendments to the law in 2007 not only changed the content of the law, but also resulted in a new name, "The Framework Act on Consumers." The revised law was based on a new paradigm that recognized consumers as independent, rational economic players rather than as objects of manipulation who needed extensive consumer protection. The amendments emphasized both rights and duties of consumers. The right to a safe environment was added to the seven rights listed in the previous version of the law. These original rights were: the right to health and safety in consumer products, the right to be informed, the right to choose, the right to be heard, the right of redress, the right to be educated, and the right to representation in the marketplace. The three duties of consumers outlined in the new law are to choose goods wisely and to exercise their fundamental rights, to obtain the knowledge and information required to promote their own interests, and to live resource-saving and environmentally friendly lives. Changes to the law meant that consumers must play a positive role in the improvement of their lives and in the development of the national economy.

In addition to changes involving individual consumers, there are a few clauses in the law that relate to consumer organizations. For example, the law lays out the activities of consumer organizations, implements a system of registration for consumer organizations, and provides government subsidies to support activities of consumer organizations. The purpose of these clauses was to strengthen consumer organizations and thereby promote their independence.

In addition to government subsidies, consumer organizations in South Korea obtain funding from membership fees as well as grants for research and education from various organizations and businesses. Each organization has its own funding formula, but most suffer from a general lack of funding. The funding problem is most apparent in the small number of people employed by these groups.

Until the 1990s, the South Korean consumer movement mainly focused on safety issues, particularly those related to food, drugs, and consumer appliances. As the economy and well-being of consumers grew, the focus of consumers and consumer organizations shifted to issues related to quality of life and environmental protection. Additionally, South Korean consumers have recently shown interest in information privacy, financial services, and sustainable consumption.

Consumer organizations have also changed their methods of promoting consumer welfare. Whereas in the past they relied on aggressive methods such as boycotts or demands for increased regulation, today the consumer organizations are more likely to rely on less confrontational methods, such as consumer education, information dissemination, and court-based redress.

A special feature of the Korean consumer movement is the existence of the Korean National Council of Consumer Organizations, which is a federation of consumer protection organizations. The National Council was established in 1976, when four consumer groups came together. Today, the council has ten member organizations. The purpose of the council is to stimulate consumer activity, support member organizations, and to achieve the goals of the member groups more effectively. The ten member groups act independently but jointly promote interests of the consumer nationally. The Bureau of Consumer Protection in the Korean Fair Trade Commission, the main consumer protection agency of the South Korean government, engages in joint activities with the council, reinforcing the important role of each body in protecting the consumer interest.

South Korean consumer activists are also becoming more involved in international consumer activities. Five Korean consumer groups are registered members of Consumers International (CI), including the Korean National Council of Consumer Organizations. Korean consumer groups actively participate in CI-hosted events such as seminars, workshops, and conferences. Furthermore, to find solutions to consumer issues emerging globally, South Korean consumer groups cooperate with CI and other international consumer organizations.

As the South Korean consumer movement has spread, academics have become involved, thereby increasing the movement's influence. Academics bring needed expertise, experience, and human resources to the consumer movement. For example, Dr. Kee-Choon Rhee, who was instrumental in introducing consumer sciences as a field of study in South Korean and who was responsible for launching the Department of Consumer Sciences at Seoul National University, contributed significantly to the growth of consumer advocacy groups in South Korea. Furthermore, South Korea has recently seen the growth of more academic consumer organizations, such as the Korean Society of Consumer Policy and Education.

In the last few years, the consumer movement has changed tremendously in several important ways. First, there has been a transition in leadership. Traditionally, the Korean consumer movement was directed by leaders of women's associations. As these founders of the consumer movement have begun to step aside, new leadership is emerging, though it is still predominantly female.

Second, whereas earlier consumer groups in South Korea tended to embrace a large number of consumer issues, a number of new groups within the South Korean consumer movement are more focused on specific products or services, such as on telecommunications, insurance, genetically modified foods, and medical services. These new single-issue groups tend to be more professional in their methods and bring a high level of expertise to issues, both of which have increased their visibility and influence. None of these single issue groups have joined the National Council of Consumer Organizations to date. The future of the consumer movement will depend on synergies that develop between single-issue groups and the more established groups.

A final challenge facing the consumer movement in Korea is lack of public support. The public has yet to embrace the goals and ideals of consumerism, undermining the movement's influence. A potential goal of consumerists could be to raise the visibility of the organizations with the general public. This could help solve issues related to human resources and money, and it could turn consumers activists into the primary voice of the consumer rather than government bodies and elected officials. At least in part, this could offset the overwhelming power of business in the Korean economy.

Jung Sung Yeo

See also: Consumers International

Further Reading

Rhee, Kee-Choon, and Jinkook Lee. 1997. "South Korean Consumer Movement." In Stephen Brobeck, ed. *Encyclopedia of the Consumer Movement* (pp. 522–525). Santa Barbara, CA: ABC-CLIO.

Rhee, Kee-Choon, and Jinkook Lee. 1996. "Review of Consumer Activism in Korea, 1910–1995: A Political–Economic Approach." *Journal of Consumer Policy* 19, no. 3: 365–392.

SPANISH CONSUMER MOVEMENT

The origins of the Spanish consumer movement trace back to 1962, when, under the auspices of the National Movement (an amalgamation of political forces that supported Franco's authoritarian regime), housewives' associations were created on a provincial level. The Spanish consumer movement as it is known today, however, began after Franco's death in 1975, when King Juan Carlos presided over democratic reforms. In December 1975, the first consumer organization independent from the preexisting regime was constituted: the Organización de Consumidores y Usuarios (OCU). Its founder, Antonio García-Pablos, abandoned Franco's Internal Commercial and Consumption Council both because of its ineffectiveness in protecting the consumer interest and because he wanted to establish an independent, privately financed consumer association inspired by the Anglo-Saxon model.

Since 1975, the Spanish consumer movement has grown in strength and diversity. This growth has been encouraged by recognition of the right of free association and new demands from the citizenry, improvements in living conditions and consumption patterns, the establishment of three levels of territorial governance (municipalities, provinces, and autonomous regions), and Spain's accession into the European Union in 1986. The semigovernmental housewives' associations, in existence since 1968, modified their articles of association in 1977 to transform themselves into a more consumer-oriented federation, known today as the Confederación Española de Organizaciones de Amas de Casa, Consumidores y Usuarios (CEACCU). Later, the Unión Cívica de Consumidores y Amas de Hogar—today Federación Unión Nacional de Consumidores y Amas de Hogar de España (UNAE)—was established by Margarita Font Melis and Margarita Fernández de Lis as a unit of the federation.

The evolution of older organizations was apparently endorsed by the favorable attitude (at least formally) of the new Spanish legal system toward consumer organizations. Specifically, Section 2 of Article 51 of the 1978 Spanish Constitution essentially established that public authorities, both national (the state) and regional (the autonomous regions), must encourage consumer organizations and accept their input in matters affecting consumers. In 1979 the Asociación General de Consumidores (ASGECO), originating from an older national federation of cooperatives, was created to serve as a collective voice for consumer cooperatives. Today, the ASGECO embraces other classes of consumer organizations as well.

In the early 1980s, Spain witnessed an explosion of consumer organizations, fostered by the Autonomous Regions as well as by the political parties and trade unions. Demands for consumer protection, it was discovered, attracted voters, especially after the 1981 tragedy involving adulterated cooking oil, in which the government's regulatory apparatus was shown to be a failure. Two years later, from eleven independent associations based in the Autonomous Regions, the Confederación de Consumidores y Usuarios (CECU) was created. In addition, the Unión de Consumidores de España (UCE) was formed in 1984 under the auspices of the Spanish Workers Socialist party and the socialist trade union, the General Union of Workers. In 1986, the Federación de Usuarios Consumidores Independientes (FUCI) was created, emerging from fifteen independent associations in diverse Autonomous Regions.

Despite all this activity, the establishment of national regulations specific to consumer organizations did not occur until 1984. As part of the former General Consumer Protection Act 1984, Chapter VI was dedicated to the right of consumers to be consulted and participate, through their organizations, in the development of consumer policy. In 1990, this chapter was further developed by Royal Decree 825, in which the state's legal statute regarding consumer associations was established, a census of consumer organizations taken, an advisory council created, and the conditions enumerated under which consumer associations can access certain benefits granted by Spanish law (e.g., subsidies and membership in consultative bodies). Today, this subject matter is covered by Title II (Articles 22–39) of the General Consumer Protection Act 2007 and various royal decrees.

Organizational Features and Activities

The consumer organizations in Spain are diverse. Some focus on a broad range of consumer issues, whereas others are devoted to issues specific to a sector of the economy. For example, the Asociación de Usuarios de Bancos, Cajas y Seguros (ADICAE) was established in 1988 by Manuel Pardos to address banking issues. Organizations also vary in their mix of private and public funding sources. Some groups are private associations under the Right of Free Association Act 2002. Consumer cooperatives, too, rely primarily on private funding and are subject to laws governing private organizations. In contrast, many consumer organizations are governmental in nature. Regardless of their private or public status, these organizations must operate in a democratic fashion.

The framework of Spanish consumer organizations is particularly complicated because consumer protection is shared by the state and the autonomous regions—a division of responsibility on which Spain's Constitution Court has insisted in its decisions. This arrangement is the reason for the creation of the Sectorial Consumption Conference in 2006 to facilitate information exchange, collaboration, and coordination between the national and regional levels.

The consumer associations are empowered to bring legal actions in the courts in matters such as misleading advertising and unfair methods of competition, as well as damages caused by defective products. Furthermore, they are empowered to seek injunctions to protect the collective interests of consumers. Depending on the nature of the claim and the type of organization, they can take advantage of various benefits (e.g., exemption from court fees).

Spain's consumer associations participate, to varying extents, in the global consumer movement and especially in the European Union, either maintaining collaborative relations with consumer associations in other EU member states or participating in several bodies that represent consumer interests (such as BEUC: The European Consumer Organisation, the European Consumers Consultative Group, and the European Economic and Social Committee). Spanish consumer organizations also participate in international bodies such as Consumers International (CI). Nine Spanish organizations are affiliated with CI, the most of any European country.

Problems and Challenges

After an emergent phase, Spanish consumer organizations have been advancing on the road to consolidation. The absence of a unified, tightly coordinated movement is not explained entirely by the relatively late development of the Spanish consumer movement. The sheer number of organizations is a barrier; as of the end of 2006, there were around 400. Although the total number of members was estimated to be about 3 million in 2003, many small organizations had only a few active members. This low participation rate is due, to a great extent, to the weak structure of Spanish civil society, especially the lack of a tradition of private, voluntary associations. Furthermore, the existence of some consumer associations is a direct response to the availability of government subsidies. In fact, it is possible that some associations—the so-called phantom associations—have been created for the main purpose of obtaining subsidies—which in 2012 totaled about $4 million.

Linked to the problem of exaggerated affiliation figures are two others: a lack of transparency and concerns about political servility. In relation to the lack of transparency, the fact that there is no duty of registration of consumer associations under Spanish regional law (in contrast to Spanish state law, which establishes a duty to register in the census handled by the National Consumption Institute (INC) for the statewide consumer associations) has given rise to "opaque" regional or local consumer organizations that raise doubts about their composition, political orientation, and actual goals. In addition, the relationships among the main consumer organizations are not always peaceful, peppered with exchanges of reciprocal defamatory remarks. This has a negative influence in consumers' confidence in these organizations.

Even the prominent Consejo de Consumidores y Usuarios (Council of Consumers and Users) is not exempt from criticism. Established under public law, the council is the major government-sanctioned body for the representation and consultation of Spanish consumers. It is composed of the major regional consumer associations together with several national ones. Despite efforts to improve both the representative nature and structure of the council, its main shortcoming—its ineffectiveness as a representative body of the Spanish consumers—has not been addressed.

Although Spain is a member of the European Union in which consumer protection has a high level of importance, the overall priority accorded to consumer protection policy at the national level in Spain is still low compared to many other policies. This explains the consistently late incorporation of European Union directives on consumer protection into Spanish law as well as the slow revision of the General Consumer Protection Act of 2007 and other provisions on consumer protection. The shortcomings of Spain's consumer protection legislation are especially evident in areas in which there is little input from the European Union or in which problems afflict vulnerable groups, such as the elderly and children.

As a rule, the lack of protection for Spanish consumers is not due to deficiencies in the consumer protection laws, but to their lack of effective enforcement. This is easily seen in the case of telecommunication services—the most contentious sector of activity as measured by consumer complaints (1.6 million in 2010). Regulations governing telecom services are adequate, but telecom operators frequently ignore these rules and behave abusively. In other consumer domains, such as food production and sale, government control and inspection is inadequate (usually because of a lack of resources). Lax enforcement of consumer protection laws is exacerbated by a lack of information and education of Spanish consumers (despite the efforts of consumer associations) and the scarcity of consumer association personnel trained in consumer protection matters.

When Spanish consumers experience serious problems, they often have difficulty gaining access to justice. In 1993, steps were taken to facilitate the resolution of consumer conflicts by means of a specific consumer arbitration system—free of fees for both consumers and businesses and whose decisions are fairness-based. This system was further institutionalized by the General Consumer Protection Act of 2007 and Royal Decree 231 of 2008. Consumer associations take part by having representatives on some of the arbitration panels. Nevertheless, the effectiveness of the system is still limited, because businesses can choose not to submit to arbitration and can limit the scope of the decision power of the arbitration court. Furthermore, two significant sources of consumer complaints—banking services and insurance—have a separate and administrative law–based complaint system that is more committed to the transparent functioning of financial markets than to satisfying the private economic interests of consumers. Consumers still have to make a claim before the ordinary courts if they want to obtain redemption, restitution, or compensation. Although consumer associations have been active in the domain of financial services and judges have been sensitive to consumer needs, the extension of the consumer arbitration system to financial services would likely bring faster and fairer resolution of such disputes, and thereby contribute to social equity.

Pedro-José Bueso Guillén, Manuel-Ángel López Sánchez

See also: BEUC: The European Consumer Organisation; Consumers International

Further Reading

Alcalá Fernández, L. J. 2003 "El movimiento consumierista en España. Asociaciones y arbitraje de consumo," *Distribución y Consumo* 69 (May–June): 86–92.

Bercovitz Rodríguez-Cano, Rodrigo, ed. 2009. *Comentarios del Texto Refundido de la Ley General para la Defensa de los Consumidores y Usuarios y otras leyes complementarias.* Madrid, Spain: Aranzadi–Thomson Reuters.

Marín López, Manuel Jesus. 2009. "Título II. Derecho de representación, consulta y partici-
    pación y régimen jurídico de las asociaciones de consumidores y usuarios." In Rodrigo
    Bercovitz Rodríguez-Cano, ed., *Comentarios del Texto Refundido de la Ley General para
    la Defensa de los Consumidores y Usuarios y otras leyes complementarias* (pp. 317–568).
    Madrid, Spain: Aranzadi–Thomson Reuters.
Reyes López, Maria Jose. 2012. *Manual de Derecho Privado de Consumo*, 2nd ed. Madrid,
    Spain: La Ley.
Ruiz González, Jose Gabriel. 2010. *Las asociaciones de consumidores*. Valencia, Spain: Tirant
    lo Blanch.

STATE AND LOCAL CONSUMER ADVOCACY GROUPS

State and local consumer advocacy groups have played important roles not only in working for consumer protections in cities, counties, and states, but also in supporting the work of national groups before Congress and federal regulatory agencies. Before the 1960s, few of these organizations existed. However, in that decade and succeeding ones, hundreds of grassroots groups were organized to promote individual and collective consumer interests. Many of these consumer groups are still active today. They have increasingly allied themselves with other organizations that have a broader social justice focus but work on individual consumer issues, often related to financial services.

During this country's first two centuries, individuals and small groups occasionally protested seller practices, but these spontaneous protests were neither organized nor continuous. Not until the nineteenth century, when the expansion of cities and the development of national markets helped create the conditions for consumerism, did consumer advocates and consumer groups emerge.

Between 1891 and 1903, state-based consumer leagues were organized in twenty states. Their highest priority was to improve the working conditions of women and children. The leagues urged consumers to purchase products made only by producers who provided adequate working conditions. They lobbied for legislation that would curtail child labor, limit the workweek, and improve workplace conditions. These groups also supported the establishment of pure food laws to address problems identified by scientist Harvey Wiley and muckrakers such as Upton Sinclair. Their efforts culminated not only in the establishment of some state and local protections, but also in the passage by Congress of the Pure Food Act in 1906.

During the first half of the twentieth century, much grassroots consumer activism was undertaken by women's groups. Especially in the 1930s and 1940s, members of organizations such as the General Federation of Women's Clubs, National League of Women Voters, National Women's Trade Union League, American Association of University Women, American Home Economics Association, National Congress of Parents and Teachers, and League of Women Shoppers initiated most grassroots advocacy against business abuses and in support of consumer reforms. Their actions ranged from voicing complaints against individual sellers to lobbying for reforms such as accurate textile labeling.

Only in the late 1960s and 1970s, however, did state and local consumer advocacy become a powerful force in our society. In this period, hundreds of state and local consumer groups were established to assist individuals and influence public policy. A 1969 survey by Consumers Union identified thirty-eight state or local self-identified consumer groups. A 1983 survey by the Consumer Federation of America (CFA), however, listed nearly 400 organizations working on consumer issues. By 1992, another CFA survey reported that the number of groups exceeded 400.

These organizations were part of a larger social movement. Grassroots consumer leaders drew inspiration from various sources, including the civil rights movement, the antiwar movement, the labor movement, and Ralph Nader. However, their principal impetus to action was concern about specific local and state consumer problems they often experienced, along with a determination to solve them.

Most state and local groups performed at least one of three general functions—public policy advocacy, complaint resolution, and consumer education and information dissemination. Many of these groups concentrated their work in a single product area. In the 1983 survey by CFA, 391 state and local advocacy groups reported the following priority areas: utilities (175), health (106), housing (95), food (63), energy (38), banking (27), taxation (24), and transportation (15).

In this period, many state and local consumer advocacy groups could be sorted into four categories—public interest research groups (PIRGs), other multi-issue state advocacy organizations, utility advocacy groups, and local consumer action groups.

PIRGs: In the 1970s and 1980s, PIRGs were organized on college and university campuses in more than twenty states. At the outset they were inspired by Ralph Nader and organized under the direction of Donald Ross but were established as independent groups controlled by local boards of directors chiefly consisting of students. In the early years, virtually all funding came from student activity fees. The PIRGs emphasized statewide advocacy on consumer, environmental, good government, and student issues The groups also developed student services such as providing information about local products. They continue active today and are described in greater detail in a separate entry.

State advocacy groups: The oldest type of grassroots group is state advocacy organizations made up almost exclusively of volunteers. By the 1960s, consumer leagues—especially those in Oregon, Louisiana, Ohio, Nevada, Wisconsin, Iowa, and New Jersey—had evolved into this kind of organization. In that decade and the next, they were joined by similar groups that often had the words "consumer council" in their name: Pennsylvania Citizens Consumer Council, Maryland Citizens Consumer Council, Virginia Citizens Consumer Council, North Carolina Citizens Consumer Council, Association of Massachusetts Consumers, and Idaho Consumer Association.

These organizations were usually run and supported by middle-class professionals. Many leaders were academics, including Father Robert McEwen (Massachusetts), Lee Richardson (Louisiana then Maryland), Currin Shields (Arizona), Helen Nelson and Jim Brown (Wisconsin), Louis Meyer (Pennsylvania), and Clinton Warne (Ohio). Others, such as Dermot Shea (Massachusetts) and Phyllis Rowe (Arizona), were active for many years in state politics.

The principal focus of these groups was persuading states to establish effective consumer protections. Their tactics emphasized communications with elected officials through letters, testimony, and personal conversations. They usually published newsletters to keep their own members informed and encourage them to communicate with policymakers. Annual budgets of these groups were supported mainly by annual dues and rarely exceeded a few thousand dollars.

These volunteer groups provided skilled professionals with opportunities to influence public policy but weakened, and often disappeared, as their leaders aged and died. Today, few of these groups are still active.

Utility advocates: It was no accident that the issue area of greatest interest in the 1980s was utilities. Factors including the Arab oil embargo; the construction of large, expensive power plants; the deregulation of oil and gas prices; and the deregulation of telephone service combined to arouse consumer concern about the cost of electric, gas, and telephone services. In 1978, the Citizen/Labor Energy Coalition began organizing regional coalitions to fight rising electric rates and the construction of nuclear power plants. In 1979 in Wisconsin, the first Citizen Utility Board (CUB) was organized. CUBs were promoted by Ralph Nader as citizen-supported advocacy groups that would represent consumers before state public utility commissions. Other CUBs were organized in Illinois, New York, Oregon, and the San Diego Area (Utility Consumers Action Network or UCAN).

One key to the success of CUBs was gaining access to monthly utility bills for inserts informing consumers of their programs and soliciting memberships and contributions. However, after the U.S. Supreme Court ruled in 1986 that utilities could not be compelled to distribute this information, CUBs became much more difficult to organize and sustain. Today, CUBs still exist in Wisconsin, Oregon, Illinois, and southern California, but they rely on other funding sources, including state intervenor funding.

In the late 1970s and 1980s, most states began to fund consumer counsel offices that represented residential customers in rate cases. The trade association for these utility advocates, the National Association of State Utility Consumer Advocates (NASUCA), was established in 1979. The work of all these utility advocates, most of whom are active today, is discussed in a separate entry.

Local consumer action groups: In the late 1960s and 1970s, consumer advocacy groups were organized in a number of cities. They included the Consumers Education and Protection Association (Philadelphia), San Francisco Consumer Action, Chicago Consumer Coalition, Cleveland Consumer Action, Concerned Consumers League of Milwaukee, Seattle Consumer Action Network, Ft. Wayne Consumer Center, Pittsburgh Alliance for Consumer Protection, Niagara Frontier Consumer Association, and Harlem Consumer Education Council.

Most of these groups were organized by young college-educated activists who saw the consumer movement as part of a larger progressive movement to create a more just, democratic society. Max Weiner, the founder of Consumers Education and Protection Association, participated in leftist groups in the 1940s and 1950s.

Ken McEldowney of San Francisco Consumer Action and Stephen Brobeck of Cleveland Consumer Action had been active in Students for a Democratic Society (SDS) in the 1960s. Florence Rice of the Harlem Consumer Education Council was inspired by the civil rights movement, and Dan McCurry of the Chicago Consumer Coalition participated in southern voter registration drives.

Several of these groups were influenced by the complaint-organizing model first developed by Max Weiner in Philadelphia, as discussed in the entry on complaint resolution. However, most local action groups undertook a broad range of advocacy and education activities. They lobbied city councils and state legislatures and mounted initiative campaigns, also seeking to assist individual consumers through information, education, and complaint resolution. For example, after Cleveland Consumer Action collected sufficient signatures on an initiative petition to create a city consumer office, the Cleveland City Council passed legislation establishing such an agency.

Most of these local organizations employed at least one full-time staffer whose salary was supported by membership dues, government grants, and/or foundation grants. Yet the influence of these organizations was often greater than their budgets suggest, because the groups relied heavily on volunteers.

Like many of the state advocacy groups, however, these local action groups depended heavily on the commitment of a few individuals. And when these people moved on to other challenges, interest in their organizations flagged. Today, only San Francisco Consumer Action (now Consumer Action), which expanded throughout California to then become a national consumer group with an office in Washington, D.C., is very active.

If many non-PIRG state and local groups active in the 1970s have little or no presence today, what state and local groups are currently working on consumer issues? Although there has been no recent inventory of all state and local advocacy groups working on consumer issues, the state and local consumer membership of CFA provides a representative sampling of the most active groups that are most likely to identify themselves as consumer organizations. At present, there are 100 such groups. Twenty-four are PIRGs, most of which have been active for least three decades. Another twelve are state advocacy groups. These organizations count several that have been in existence for more than four decades, such as VCCC, but they also include newer groups with small professional staffs that work on a array of consumer issues—notably, Consumer Federation of California, Georgia Watch, and the Maryland Consumer Rights Coalition.

Another fourteen groups focus on a single issue area. In light of the growing financial abuses in the 1990s and 2000s culminating in a major financial crisis, and the creation of the Consumer Financial Protection Bureau, it is not surprising that most of these single-issue organizations work on financial services issues. Some groups—such as the Woodstock Institute (based in Chicago) and the New Economy Project (formerly the Neighborhood Economic Development Advocacy Project based in New York City)—work mainly on mortgage and high-cost credit issues. Other groups—including the Center for Economic Integrity (Arizona), United Policyholders (California), and the Citizens for Home Insurance Reform

(Massachusetts)—work mainly on insurance issues. In other issue areas, Consumers for Auto Reliability and Safety (CARS), based in California, is particularly active and influential.

Among CFA's state and local member groups, there are also sixteen social justice organizations. These groups include Alabama Arise, Alabama Appleseed Center for Law and Justice, Florida Consumer Action Network, Kentucky Equal Justice Center, New Jersey Citizen Action, Economic Fairness Oregon, Tennessee Citizen Action, Texas Appleseed, Virginia Poverty Law Center, and the Washington Community Action Network. Although these organizations do not identify themselves as consumer groups, they do work on consumer issues. Most of these issues are financial, many involving high-cost credit issues related to payday lending. But all work on other social justice issues such as social welfare benefits, tax equity, and workers rights.

One reason these organizations affiliated with CFA was because they had joined with consumer groups in coalitions to work for financial service reforms. Nationally, eight-one groups, mainly state and local organizations, belong to CFA's high-cost lending network, which for more than a decade has served as a resource for groups working on both state and federal issues. In many individual states, there are credit reform coalitions. New Yorkers for Responsible Lending, for example, is made up of 161 separate consumer, community, legal, civil rights, and religious groups. From 2011 to 2013, the coalition addressed check cashing, credit report, payday lending, mortgage servicing, mortgage foreclosure issues, and debt collection issues.

These coalitions, and earlier ones working on utility issues, represent the most effective way state and local advocacy groups have fought for new protections against abusive corporate practices. As the entries on credit and energy advocacy suggest, these alliances have had success passing laws that established these protections and opposing attempts to weaken them.

Stephen Brobeck

See also: Community Activism; Complaint Resolution; Conference of Consumer Organizations; Consumer Action; Consumer Federation of America; Consumer Leagues; Consumer Watchdog; Consumers for Auto Reliability and Safety; Energy Advocacy; Public Interest Research Groups; State Utility Advocacy; Tenant Activism; TURN; Virginia Citizens Consumer Council; Woodstock Institute

Further Reading

Herrmann, Robert O. Edward J. Walsh, and Rex H. Warland. 1988. "The Organizations of the Consumer Movement: A Comparative Perspective." In E. Scott Maynes, ed., *The Frontier of Research in the Consumer Interest.* Columbia, MO: American Council on Consumer Interests.

Mirow, Deena. 1976. "Frenzy Gone: Activist Groups Here Take a Calmer Tack in Consumer Crusade." *Plain Dealer* (September): 24+.

"U.S. Consumer Groups Livelier Than Ever." 1976. *U.S. News and World Report* 81 (December 6): 90–91.

STATE AND LOCAL CONSUMER AFFAIRS OFFICES

State and local consumer affairs offices were created to help ensure that consumers are adequately informed and protected. Although there are differences among these offices, most handle individual consumer complaints and implement consumer–merchant education programs. Many also administer state Mini-FTC Acts, license selected businesses, administer cable television franchises, and advocate the consumer interest locally, statewide, or in Washington, D.C.

These offices exist at the state level in the office of the attorney general or in state government departments, at the county level, and at the city level. In all states, the state attorney general plays a role in protecting consumers. A separate entry (attorneys general) describes this role, which has been of great significance nationally. In fact, for twenty-one states, the federal government website, USA.gov, lists only the attorney general (and sometimes local district attorney offices) as offering consumer services. For twenty-two states, this website lists other state offices, often within a department of commerce, as providing consumer services.

In twelve states, the website lists at least one county or city office as offering consumer services. Most of these states are located in the Northeast or Upper Midwest, though six Florida counties maintain consumer offices. A number of county offices—such as Montgomery and Howard counties in Maryland, Fairfax county in Virginia, and Broward and Palm Beach counties in Florida—are supported by relatively affluent populations. And a number of county and city offices serve large cities, including New York, Chicago, Los Angeles, Miami, Cleveland, Orlando, Tampa, and Boston. Nearly every New Jersey county maintains a consumer office.

Agencies vary greatly in size and authority. They range from single-person offices, whose responsibility is primarily mediation of complaints, to large departments with hundreds of employees responsible for enforcing many consumer protection laws and regulations.

State and local government consumer offices first appeared in the late 1800s and early 1900s, when some state legislatures passed laws guaranteeing the accuracy of weights and measures in the sale of goods. However, state, city, and county consumer protection offices with wide-ranging authority to prevent deceptive trade practices were not created until the late 1950s, with most being established during the 1970s. This growth resulted in large part from a Federal Trade Commission (FTC) initiative that encouraged states and localities to enact laws, often called Mini-FTC Acts, to protect the public from deceptive and unfair trade practices.

Many of these offices survive today. Yet many others have been shut down, and others have experienced budgetary cutbacks. This weakening of some agencies reflects factors including strongly held antigovernment views held by some citizens, diminishing resources for government, and the lack of an organized consumer constituency. There is no longer even an association for these agencies apart from the National Association of Attorneys Generals (NAAG). In 1976, the National Association of Consumer Agency Administrators was created to link and support local and state agencies, but in the 2000s this association grew less active and then disappeared. For more than two decades, the Consumer Federation of

America (CFA) has coordinated an annual complaint survey and report in which dozens of consumer offices have participated. And for the past several years, CFA has organized sessions for state and local protection agencies at its annual Consumer Assembly.

The principal roles played by state and local consumer offices have been complaint handling, consumer and merchant education, law enforcement, licensing, and advocacy. The most visible role for these offices has involved complaint resolution. Consumer agency staffers who handle complaints first attempt to persuade the parties to reach a mediated settlement. Should this prove impossible, agencies pursue a variety of alternatives. Many agencies can issue subpoenas to uncooperative merchants and civil citations (tickets) when violations of law are clear and no further investigation is needed. Administrative adjudicative hearings and arbitration proceedings are sometimes available to bring cases to closure. Some offices not only refer complainants to small claims court, but also helps clients file and present their cases.

Agencies with substantial enforcement powers are better able to mediate complaints successfully. Volunteer mediators and arbitrators are often used to resolve consumer–merchant disputes and augment professional staff resources. When patterns of deceptive trade practices are found, agencies move beyond individual complaint handling and use other means to prevent these marketplace problems (and resulting complaints).

Consumer education is the most frequently used preventive activity. Telephone advice lines, brochures, pamphlets, speeches, press releases, television and radio shows, and websites provide information and advice to the public on a wide range of topics ranging from leasing a car to choosing a contractor to filing a small claims complaint. This information is usually free, but some agencies with shrunken budgets now charge for printed materials and telephone advice. Other agencies suffering budget cuts have been forced to discontinue services offered through toll-free numbers.

Some agencies inform consumers by disclosing merchant complaint records, which not only helps buyers make wise decisions, but also encourages merchants to resolve grievances. And many agencies help merchants understand their legal responsibilities by issuing advisories about new legislation or organizing classes to explain existing laws.

Most strong agencies administer a Mini-FTC Act and use law enforcement tools provided by such consumer protection legislation. Often these offices are executive-branch agencies that report to a governor, mayor, or county executive; others are located in the offices of state attorneys general or are attached to the office of the local district attorney. Mini-FTC acts contain broad language prohibiting business practices that are misleading or deceptive, such as failure to honor warranties or disclose important information. Agencies can use subpoena power to investigate allegations of law violations, then employ civil penalties, restitution, and court orders to remedy violations.

Some state and local protection offices license businesses such as auto repair shops, home improvement contractors, and landlords. Licensure sometimes requires proof of technical competency and financial ability and often establishes certain rules under which the licensed business must operate. It also brings in revenue to pay for regulation and, through license revocation or suspension for continued violation of consumer laws, represents an effective enforcement tool.

A few consumer offices contain weights and measures programs to ensure accuracy and fairness by testing devices, checking scanners for verification of pricing accuracy, and inspecting certain products. A few offices are charged to represent the consumer's interest before utility commissions. And these agencies may have responsibilities for franchising and overseeing cable television providers.

Many consumer protection offices function as advocates who seek to identify potentially deceptive or other unfair practices, then address these abuses by helping develop, then support corrective legislation or regulation. For example, Walter Dartland, Consumer Advocate for Metro Dade–Miami, led opposition to a Southern Bell Company proposal to the Florida Public Service Commission (PSC) to approve local measured service (LMS). This opposition included a statewide campaign collecting 350,000 signatures opposing LMS. The PSC rejected the Southern Bell proposal.

Other offices are not quite as active but still engage in advocacy by providing pro-consumer comments or testimony on proposed legislation or regulation. Often these proposals resulted from complaints or investigations received by consumer offices. Thus, the offices played an important role in the passage of "lemon laws" requiring manufacturers to fix defective cars or buy back the vehicles. The consumer offices then often enforce these laws.

State and local consumer offices typically cooperate with other law enforcement authorities, including the local police, Federal Bureau of Investigation, and postal authorities. The consumer agencies are often the first to hear from victims of a scam, whereas the law enforcement authorities can offer resources and the threat of large fines and jail time for law-breakers.

Barbara Gregg, Stephen Brobeck

See also: Complaint Resolution; State Attorneys General

Further Reading

GSA Federal Citizen Information Center. 2014 Consumer Action Handbook (USA. govconsumer).
Richardson, S. Lee. 1995. "State and Local Consumer Protection." In Kenneth J. Meier and E. Thomas Garman, eds. *Regulation and Consumer Protection* (pp. 393–406). Houston: DAME Publications, Inc.

STATE ATTORNEYS GENERAL

Central to the work of the attorneys general of the fifty U.S. states (the "AGs") is the weighty responsibility to maintain competitiveness, fairness, and safety in the marketplace. As the chief law enforcement officers of their states, they collectively stand at the forefront of the American consumer movement by performing a range of consumer protection functions including: mediating individual consumer complaints, designing innovative educational campaigns and other measures that prevent harm to consumers, and helping shape consumer protection policies about state and national matters. They usually have the formal authority to decide when and how to commence legal actions to enforce a state law or to act on behalf of a state and in the name of the public interest. In many states, AGs are the most visible consumer advocates, public or private.

The power of AGs to punish consumer fraud and to address consumer problems is of long standing, and it has expanded substantially over recent decades. Once, AGs confined themselves largely to bringing conventional court actions. Over the recent past, however, AGs have developed more creative enforcement approaches that include seeking formal multidistrict judgments, broad consent decrees, permanent cease-and-desist orders, and corrective advertising. Increasingly, they have joined together with other AGs to embrace class actions and multi-jurisdictional proceedings. They also have adopted approaches that depend less on the judicial system than on moving public opinion through press releases, educational efforts, and national "shaming" of bad actors using the media.

As the global economy has become ever more interwoven, and as electronic transactions have become ubiquitous, the role of AGs in pursuing those who do business inside a state but whose physical presence is outside a state has become correspondingly significant. It is not exceptional to find AGs acting in collaboration with federal consumer protection agencies to bring their collective resources to bear against large domestic and international corporations based elsewhere. AGs also are engaging in international action in coordination with their counterparts elsewhere in the world.

Development of the Office

The office of the attorney general is a venerable institution. Well before the adoption of the U.S. Constitution, common-law powers of the AG were expansive. The office of the attorney general represented the interests of the eighteenth-century English Crown in conflicts with corporations, trusts, and associations. The Crown, not surprisingly, conferred on its protectors sweeping powers of oversight.

In the United States, the legal foundation for the consumer protection function of the attorneys general flows generally from judicial constructions that state and federal courts have given to state "police powers." The powers to intervene to protect the health and citizens of a state are most notably reserved to the states by implication from the principle of federalism in the Tenth Amendment to the Constitution.

The institutional office of the AG is thus rooted in hundreds of years of Anglo-American common and constitutional law. The expansion of the AG's consumer protection authority has occurred organically; it has expanded with the growth of the size and statutory authority of administrative agencies that depend on the AG to bring the power of the government to bear on those who violate newly established rules designed to address new ways of cheating or endangering consumers. As a result, consumer protection responsibilities of the AGs now pervade the functions of state agencies that regulate the insurance, banking, and public utility industries; that oversee food safety and public health; and that license professions and occupations.

Consumer protection efforts by the AG have also emerged in response to particular public outcries that no other office could remedy and that could be addressed by reference to broad general powers. AGs typically act as lawyers with political ambitions, and they recognize that standing up for justice in the marketplace may represent a social imperative and a political opportunity.

Beyond law enforcement, the AG's formal role generally includes providing legal advice and counsel to the governor and state agencies about who to prosecute and what priorities to establish. Most AGs do not control criminal law enforcement and prosecution within their jurisdictions, however; in most states, the authority to initiate criminal cases is vested primarily, if not exclusively, in local prosecutors.

The modern role of AGs in consumer protection dates from the tenure of New York attorney general Louis Lefkowitz, who began a concerted campaign against consumer frauds in the late 1950s. He relied primarily on his inherent common law powers and his authority, under the corporation laws, to seek to enjoin the activities or annul the charter of a corporation, association, or partnership that conducted its business in a persistently fraudulent manner. From this beginning, Lefkowitz fashioned a full-fledged consumer protection program, winning passage of legislation expanding his enforcement powers and creating a program for redress of individual consumer problems.

Other attorneys general began parallel consumer protection programs based on their asserted powers under state law. In Minnesota, for example, Attorney General Walter Mondale became celebrated for aggressive use of ill-defined common law powers to investigate abuses by a national charity for victims of polio and for using the limited powers available under corporation laws to pursue dishonest home improvement contractors and door-to-door sales schemes. By 1960, the Council of State Governments had recommended that principal authority for enforcing state consumer protection laws usually reside with the AGs, and most attorneys general had established consumer protection programs, or even bureaus, that varied substantially in size and quality.

By the end of the 1970s, almost every state had adopted a basic consumer protection act, sometimes referred to as a "Little FTC Act" or UDAP (unfair and deceptive acts and practices) statute. These civil statutes tend to follow one of three general models. The first parallels provisions of the Federal Trade Commission Act in prohibiting "unfair methods of competition and unfair or deceptive acts or practices" in trade or commerce. The second prohibits "false, misleading or deceptive acts or practices in the conduct of any trade or commerce." The third prohibits an itemized list of specified deceptive trade practices, followed by a catch-all prohibition against "any other act or practice which is unfair or deceptive to the consumer."

Under all these statutes, the effect on the authority of an AG is similar: The AG is given broad power to act against almost any deceptive practice harmful to consumers. In addition, as states have gained experience with a wide range of consumer problems, attorneys general have helped to develop and enact many supplemental statutes needed to address abuses encountered in particular industries. Common problem areas include investment schemes, debt collection, alternate lending, tele-marketing, Internet service providers, auto repair, home improvement, pyramid selling schemes, landlord–tenant relations, land sales, collection practices, chari-table solicitations, door-to-door sales, hearing-aid sales, prearranged funeral sales, false and misleading advertising, and health clubs.

In the 1980s and 1990s, state AGs emerged as national consumer protection leaders. In large measure this phenomenon was a spontaneous and unexpected reaction to regressive developments at the national level where, through much of the decade, federal consumer protections were scaled back or abandoned. With federal agencies often unable or unwilling to act—whether through lack of staff, budget, or will, state attorneys general repeatedly found themselves drawn into issues that had long been the exclusive domain of the federal government. The result was the convergence of multistate consumer protection activities—a devel-opment that quickly catapulted attorneys general into the thick of national con-sumer law enforcement and policymaking.

Multistate Collaboration

In earlier years, states occasionally cooperated in pursuit of a common objective; a prominent example was the collaboration in the late 1970s of more than forty states in litigation against a major automaker for substituting engines from one of its divisions into more expensive cars sold by another division. In the 1980s however, joint investigations, negotiations, and occasionally joint litigation efforts became a standard operating procedure. Several dozen states, for example, collab-orated in settling a case of alleged fraud at the nation's largest automobile transmis-sion repair chain, as well as on another regarding alleged odometer tampering in connection with the sale of new vehicles by a major manufacturer.

In 1997 the AGs prevailed in the first of several successful efforts to reduce youth smoking, and in 1998 the AGs of forty-six states entered into a master agreement with major tobacco companies requiring them—in exchange for a release from tort liability—to, among other things, fund tobacco cessation efforts and compensate both victims of tobacco related diseases and the states for health costs related to tobacco-related illnesses. By pooling staff and resources, the AGs found themselves able to address abuses by even the largest corporations and to take on other issues previously beyond their apparent capacity to address.

Multistate collaboration quickly moved from joint investigation of a single case to the creation of working groups to investigate industrywide problems. Ad hoc multistate working groups formed to study fraud, deception, and other abuses involving airline fares, car rental practices, ambulance safety, all-terrain vehicle safety, health claims in food advertising, product energy-saving claims, new-car "lemon laws," environmental advertising claims, pay-per-call practices, telemar-keting, credit reporting, sweepstakes, mortgage escrows, auto leasing, unlicensed medical providers, and pharmaceutical marketing.

As states gained experience with this process, they began to use multistate working groups not only to investigate specific companies, but also to develop voluntary guidelines, proposals for federal reforms, and model state legislation to address industrywide problems. This process continued onward, with multistate groups increasingly combining individual enforcement actions with systematic proposals for policy reforms that were often developed in public dialogue with the affected businesses and other interested parties.

By the first decade of the twenty-first century, joint initiatives involving state AGs and federal agencies had become routine and sometimes massively significant. A 2003 settlement with the Household Finance Corporation returned $484 million to consumers; a settlement with Ameriquest in 2006 returned $325 million. These cases were both multistate and multiagency: They linked not only state consumer protection divisions, but civil rights divisions from AGs offices, as well as state banking regulators and county attorneys. Working together, state officials settled the claims and implemented distribution of funds.

In the years after the international economic collapse that began in 2008, AGs brought scores of collective actions against bad actors in the financial sector. Perhaps the largest of these settlements, in 2012, involved the U.S. attorney general, the secretary of HUD, and a coalition of forty-nine state attorneys general who accused five of the nation's largest mortgage servicers of fraud and other abuses; the coalition succeeded in reaching a $25 billion joint federal–state settlement with Bank of America Corporation, JPMorgan Chase & Co., Wells Fargo & Company, Citigroup, Inc., and Ally Financial, Inc. (formerly GMAC). The group obtained an agreement disgorging unlawful gains and creating standards for mortgage servicing in the future.

AGs have used their authority to protect consumer interests that have involved other than purely economic harm. They have pursued data privacy invasion. They have pursued marketers and manufacturers for fraudulent health claims about foods and beverages, as well as for selling dangerous beverages. And they have intervened to prevent collusive class action settlements in which manufacturers conspired with plaintiffs' lawyers to close down litigation and to try to invalidate oppressive contract provisions. They have punished major pharmaceutical companies for illegally promoting off-label uses of drugs they produced (e.g., marketing a drug approved for the treatment of the shingles virus as a palliative chronic lower back pain).

Broad Consumer Protection Approaches

At the heart of the attorney general's role is the duty to enforce the state's consumer protection laws. In most jurisdictions, the attorney general is also invested with broad investigative powers, enabling him or her to demand the production of documents and to take depositions or pose interrogatories before filing a civil action. The attorney general is also typically invested with at least one grant of sweeping consumer protection authority, as well as a series of more narrowly drawn protections. When an attorney general is successful in proving the violation of the consumer protection laws, the remedies available in most states are equally broad and typically include restitution to consumer victims, such injunctive relief as may be necessary to remedy the harm done and ensure that the misconduct does not recur; monetary civil penalties to the state; and reimbursement to the state for the costs of investigation and litigation. Because the law enforcement responsibilities of the AGs cover the spectrum of consumer transactions, the cases brought under these statutes are diverse. Frequent areas of litigation, in addition to those previously mentioned, include fraudulent telemarketing schemes, often involving phony sweepstakes or prize offers; deceptive practices in connection with the advertising, sale, or repair of cars and trucks; home repair frauds; abuses in connection with credit practices and collections; and get-rich-quick business opportunity schemes.

Most AGs have no legal authority to bring litigation on behalf of individual consumers. They represent the state, and their litigation is brought in the interest of the state or the public in general, although it often results in restitution to individual victims.

As attorneys general become more prominent as consumer advocates, public requests for assistance increase, and in response, most states gradually develop programs for informal assistance to individual consumers who encounter problems in the marketplace. In many states, this assistance includes information, referral services, and consumer tips on many consumer issues, often offered through toll-free telephone hotlines that, in some states, handle as many as several hundred thousand calls annually. Some also offer assistance through storefront offices. Where permitted by state privacy laws, these services may include records of complaints about particular businesses.

In many states, the office of the attorney general accepts individual complaints for voluntary mediation; although this process depends on the goodwill and cooperation of the parties, states have found that most complaints can be resolved to the satisfaction of everyone involved. Some states incorporate the use of volunteers as mediators, and a few use arbitration mechanisms.

The function of consumer education has generally evolved as an adjunct to the AG's law enforcement and complaint-handling functions. Almost all information programs include a website and print information on the most common consumer problems, ranging from simple pamphlets in some states to comprehensive books in others. In some states the consumer education programs take the form of public/ private partnerships in which corporations, trade associations, consumer organizations, and others combine efforts to help raise the consumer literacy of students and other consumers.

Considering the role of the AGs as law enforcers, their experience in handling individual consumer problems, and their position as independently elected officials, it is not surprising that AGs have emerged as prominent advocates for policies and laws to protect consumers' interests better. This has taken a variety of forms. In many states, the AG has long been a primary source of consumer legislation. AGs helped develop not only the basic consumer protection statutes of most states, but also many of the industry-specific statutes written in response to particular prob-lems, including the "lemon laws" that have been enacted in every state.

The influence of the state AGs extends to federal legislation and rules through the National Association of Attorneys General and multistate working groups. Federal legislation addressing telemarketing fraud, for example, stems from the problems state AGs experienced in protecting against long-distance fraudulent schemes. Similarly, rules on child-safe packaging and nutritional labeling origi-nated with state-level proposals.

Finally, several of the most successful policy initiatives of the AGs focus on framing the public debate on emerging issues. These initiatives, which are often coordinated with enforcement actions, typically include public hearings, written reports, and recommendations for voluntary industry self-regulation. Programs about predatory lending, smoking, smoking cessation and electronic cigarettes, and motor vehicle repair are good examples.

Critics—particularly business associations and corporate lobbyists—have assaulted the modern expanded consumer protection role of the AGs, arguing that their powers permit too much discretion to be exercised by essentially political actors. In 1999, four Republican AGs created the Republican Attorneys General Association to stop what they called "government lawsuit abuse" and redirect state legal efforts away from national tort and consumer cases and back to "traditional" crime fighting.

With few exceptions, however, neither AGs nor federal or state legislators have shown much appetite for diminishing the AG consumer protection role. In fact, in 2011 the federal legislation that established the Consumer Financial Protection Bureau encouraged expanded activities by state AGs. Subsequently, the CFPB and state AGs joined forces to address abusive financial products and illegal practices, including short-term loans sold by online lenders.

Modern AGs, on the whole, have defended their fundamental duties as con-sumer protection agents, have embraced their consumer protection responsibilities with enthusiasm, and have garnered widespread public support for their work in the process.

Norman I. Silber, Doug Blanke

See also: Advertising Advocacy; Litigation; Tobacco Activism

Further Reading

Budnitz, Mark E. 2007. "Federalization and Privatization of Public Consumer Protection Law in the United States: Their Effect on Litigation and Enforcement." *Georgia State University Law Review* 24, no. 3: 663–692.

Lynch, Jason. 2001. "Federalism, Separation of Powers, and the Role of State Attorneys General in Multistate Litigation." *Columbia Law Review* 101, no. 8: 1,998–2,032.

National Association of Attorneys General. www.naag.org.

National State Attorneys General Program at Columbia Law School. http://web.law. columbia.edu/attorneys-general.

Totten, Mark. 2013. "Credit Reform and the States: The Vital Role of Attorneys General after Dodd–Frank." *Iowa Law Review* 99: 115–174.

STATE UTILITY ADVOCACY

Because of the importance of electricity, natural gas, water, and communications services in people's lives, it is not surprising that there has been considerable consumer advocacy in these areas. However, because these services have been largely regulated by states, not the federal government, most of this advocacy has been state-based.

Activism on consumer utility issues has expressed itself through initiative petitions in those states permitting measures to be put on the ballot, where they are approved or disapproved by voters. For example, in Ohio in 1976 and in South Dakota in 1978, proposals to establish lifeline (or baseline) utility rates were put on state ballots, where they were voted down. But in Oregon in 1984, a ballot measure to establish a Citizen Utility Board (CUB) was approved, and in Maine in 1986, so was a measure to ban measured phone rates.

Yet, a large majority of all consumer advocacy on utility issues has taken the form of interventions before the state agencies—usually public service (or utility) commissions—that regulate private electric, phone, gas, and sometimes water companies. These interventions have been by nonprofit or government entities that use funding mechanisms approved by their state. These consumer advocacy groups began to be created in the 1970s, when natural gas and electric prices rose significantly during the energy crisis. In that decade and the subsequent one, the main role of the advocates was to challenge proposed rate increases by utilities that, as monopolies, had great pricing power checked only by state regulators.

The challenges faced by these advocates grew during the 1990s and into the twenty-first century as many state legislatures and regulators deregulated utilities, allowing these companies much greater ability to restructure and vary prices. In many states, this deregulation enriched utilities and their executives while raising rates charged to consumers and, in several cases, forcing state bailouts. Today, the main focus of consumer advocates remains consumer protection issues, such as price stability, service reliability, and service quality.

Nearly all influential consumer advocates working on utility issues belong to the National Association of State Utility Consumer Advocates (NASUCA). This organization was established in 1979 by representatives of sixteen state consumer advocate offices, to provide a forum for advocates to exchange ideas, learn from experts, and discuss how to be responsive to consumers of utility services. Today, NASUCA includes forty-four member offices in forty-one states and the District of Columbia. In twelve of these states, state attorneys general provide the consumer representation. In twenty-nine other states, governors appoint consumer advocate office directors. Most of these advocacy offices are funded through state appropriations.

There is one other type of group that intervenes before state public service commissions. These are Citizen Utility Boards (or CUBs) or CUB-like organizations, which were conceived by Ralph Nader and others in the 1970s as independent consumer utility advocates that would be funded through solicitations in utility bill inserts. However, a 1986 U.S. Supreme Court ruling that denied this access forced the groups to find support from other sources—principally, individual contributions and intervenor funding made available by about a dozen states. These two funding sources support most of the work of Wisconsin CUB, Illinois CUB, Oregon CUB, and two California groups—Utility Consumers Action Network (UCAN) and The Utility Reform Network (TURN), which formerly stood for Toward Utility Rate Normalization. UCAN is an affiliate member of NASUCA, and the other four organizations are either members or associate members of the national group, which for many years has been directed by Charlie Acquard.

Over the years, some have criticized these consumer advocates, especially those funded by state appropriations, for being underfunded and subject to political pressure. Although in some states these criticisms have a measure of validity, in general, the advocates have effectively represented the consumer interest, in part because of the training and skills of their professional staff and consulting experts. The typical nonprofit state or local consumer group simply does not have the resources or expertise to challenge hundreds of pages of utility filings in cases on rates or service. Most state advocates do—and have—and in the process have saved utility consumers billions of dollars, helped preserve adequate levels of service quality, and made these needed services more accessible to lower-income consumers.

Stephen Brobeck

See also: Electricity Service Advocacy; Telephone Consumer Advocacy; TURN

Further Reading

Givens, Beth. 1991. *Citizens' Utility Boards: Because Utilities Bear Watching.* San Diego, CA: Center for Public Interest Law.

Gormley, William T. 1981. "Public Advocacy in Public Utility Commission Proceedings." *Journal of Applied Behavioral Science* 17, no. 4: 446–462.

Mayer, Robert N., Cathleen D. Zick, and John R. Burton. 1989. "Consumer Representation and Local Telephone Rates." *Journal of Consumer Affairs* 23, no. 2: 267–284.

SWEDISH CONSUMER MOVEMENT

Sweden is a small country with a tradition of seeking the inclusion of all sectors of society in the discussion of public policy issues. When necessary, government bodies are established to promote the representation of groups that might otherwise be poorly represented. These traditions are clearly visible with respect to consumer issues in Sweden. The government has created and funded the Swedish Consumer Agency (SCA) to represent the interests of consumers, but the SCA's advisory board has representatives of the major private-sector consumer organizations (e.g., the Swedish Consumers Association, the Stockholm Consumer Cooperative Society, the Association for the Municipal Consumer Advisors).

The Swedish Consumer Agency is located within the Ministry of Agriculture, Food and Consumer Affairs, and the SCA's overall tasks are to educate and protect consumers and thereby strengthen the consumer's position in society. As a government body, the SCA's policy objectives are determined by the prime minister and parliament. The SCA is led by a director general, who also serves as the Consumer

Ombudsman (Konsumentombudsman, or KO). The KO can represent consumer interests in relations with businesses and pursue legal action in the courts. The agency does not, however, provide advice to individual consumers: That is the task of local (municipal) consumer advisors. These advisors are trained by the SCA to help consumers budget, use credit responsibly, and solve problems. The advisors also try to prevent consumer problems by meeting with businesses and educating school-age children.

While the SCA is the most important government body that works on consumer issues, it is not the only one. There are four other consumer bureaus in Sweden that represent consumer interests: the Swedish Consumers' Banking and Finance Bureau, the Swedish Consumers Insurance Bureau, the Swedish Consumer Energy Markets Bureau, and the Swedish Telecom Advisors. These bureaus are devoted to providing consumers with information and helping them resolve individual disputes. The bureaus are typically supported by a combination of government and industry funding.

In addition to government bodies, a variety of private-sector consumer organizaitons promote the interests of consumers. The Swedish Consumers' Association is a federation of twenty-eight member organizations. The association attempts to influence political decision makers, business leaders, media outlets, and members of the general public. The association receives half of its funding from the Swedish Consumer Agency and the other half from projects and membership fees. The association publishes the national consumer test magazine, *Advice and Results* (Råd och Rön). The association also has an online project aimed at making young people more aware of consumer rights.

Whereas the Swedish Consumers' Association seeks to educate consumers, the role of Swedish consumer cooperatives is to create direct economic benefits (within a framework of environmental sustainability). Approximately forty of these coops, mostly in the retail grocery trade, collectively own Kooperativa Förbundet, or KF. Among the members of KF, the Stockholm Consumer Cooperative Society is most engaged in policy aspects of consumer and environmental issues; it seeks to influence government bodies, businesses, and other coops. The Stockholm Consumer Cooperative Society has also developed initiatives to reduce food waste and use of bottled water.

Another important organization is the Swedish Society for Nature Conservation, a nonprofit environmental organization that works to strengthen the consumer's power. Financial support is received from membership dues and projects funds. The organization investigates the actions of polluters and attempts to influence politicians and other opinion leaders. The society has also developed a product package symbol that firms may use, after proper testing, to indicate that their product is better for (or less harmful to) the natural environment.

Many organizations are involved in international aspects of consumer policy. At the most immediate level, members of Sweden's government consumer protection bodies cooperate at the Nordic level. For example, members of the Swedish Food Agency participate in Nordic Working Group for Food Safety and Consumer Information. At the level of the European Union, the Swedish

Consumer Agency monitors developments of importance to consumers, and the Swedish Consumers' Association participates in BEUC: The European Consumer Organisation, a coalition consisting of the most important private-sector consumer organizations in Europe. The Swedish Consumers' Association is also a member of Consumers International, the umbrella group for the world's consumer organizations.

Sweden has a strong historical record of focusing on consumer rights, but consumer activism appears to have been stronger some decades ago. Indeed, consumer activism in Sweden was never heavily based on strong grassroots involvement, at least when compared to other countries such as the United States, the United Kingdom, and India. Swedish consumers can directly become members in some organizations, but these organizations tend to focus on single issues, such as food or environmental sustainability, and do not cover a broad range of consumer issues. Furthermore, consumers can become members of the organizations that are part of the Swedish Consumers' Association, but because consumers are not members of the Association itself, their membership in Sweden's most prominent consumer organization is only indirect.

Another possible reason for the continuing lack of grassroots consumer activism in Sweden may be the perception that their interests are being well represented by existing government agencies and consumer organizations. A further reason could be that the forms for consumer activism have changed over time. Instead of being organized collectively in consumer organizations, consumers are today communicating using social media, such as Facebook, blogs, and Twitter. A final reason that consumer activism is weak in Sweden is that it has been partially displaced by environmental activism. Whereas consumer organizations historically prioritized issues dealing with household management and food safety, over time, Swedish citizens have focused more on environmental and ethical issues. Consumer organizations have sought to incorporate environmental issues, but citizen skepticism remains regarding an economic system that relies on growth in consumption, without adequate attention to the environmental limits to growth (Ekström, 2013; Holmberg and Nässén, 2011).

Karin M. Ekström

See also: BEUC: The European Consumer Organisation; Consumers International; Danish Consumer Movement; Finnish Consumer Movement; Norwegian Consumer Movement

Further Reading

Consumers International. 1995. *Balancing the Scales*. Part 1: *Consumer Protection in Sweden and the United Kingdom*. London, UK: Consumers International.

Ekström, Karin M. 2013. "Om behovet av konsumtionskritik i ett konsumtionssamhälle" [The Need for Critique of Consumption in a Consumer Society]. In Lennart Weibull, Henrik Oscarsson and Annika Bergström, eds., *Vägskäl, 43 kapitel om politik, medier och samhälle, SOM-undersökningen 2012* [*Crossroads, 43 Chapters About Politics, Media and Society, The SOM-survey 2012*] (pp. 369–385). SOM-Institute, University of Gothenburg: SOM-report 59.

Holmberg, John, and Jonas Nässén. 2011. "Well-Being: The Path Out of the Consumption–Climate Dilemma?" In Karin M. Ekström and Kay Glans, eds. *Beyond the Consumption Bubble* (pp. 221–235). New York: Routledge.

Micheletti, Michele, and Cindy Isenhour. 2010. "Political Consumerism." In Karin M. Ekström, ed. *Consumer Behaviour: A Nordic Perspective* (pp. 133–152). Lund, Sweden: Studentlitteratur.

Swedish Consumers' Association. www.sverigeskonsumenter.se/Eng/.

T

TELECOMMUNICATIONS RESEARCH AND ACTION CENTER

The Telecommunications Research and Action Center (TRAC) grew out of a movement to establish an independent citizens voice on how the public airwaves are used. During the 1970s, the National Citizens Committee for Broadcasting (NCCB) was especially visible as a leader on broadcasting issues ranging from media concentration to cigarette advertising. In 1980, NCCB changed its name to TRAC.

In May 1967, the National Citizens Committee for Public Television was formed in response to a Carnegie Commission report recommending that an organization of prominent, concerned citizens be established to improve the quality of broadcasting through advancing public television. Thomas P. F. Hoving, then director of the New York Metropolitan Museum of Art, served as chair. The committee's founder–trustees included former Federal Communications Commission (FCC) chair Newton N. Minow, known for labeling commercial television a "vast wasteland," and author Ralph W. Ellison.

The trustees were joined by other prominent figures in public life, the arts, business, education, and television to form the original committee of fifty-two members. Supported by grants from leading foundations such as Carnegie, Danforth, and Ford, the committee became the chief source of information concerning public television as well as its most vocal proponent.

Largely because of the committee's work, including the much-circulated *Citizens Report on the State of Public Television*, Congress appropriated monies as authorized under the Public Broadcasting Act of 1967. These funds included $10.5 million for facilities and $9 million to get the Corporation for Public Broadcasting under way.

In early 1969 the committee's board recognized that reform was needed in many areas of broadcasting, and the name was changed to the National Citizens Committee for Broadcasting. The committee became a catalyst for change in such areas as providing longterm funding for public broadcasting, freeing one hour of prime time television for news reporting and other use by local stations, decentralizing network control of program content, and challenging media cross-ownership, program violence, and overcommercialization.

In January 1971, NCCB moved from New York to Washington, D.C., to work more closely with other public interest groups and have easier access to the FCC, Federal Trade Commission (FTC), and Congress. Warren Braren, the former manager of the New York Television Code Office of the National Association of Broadcasters, became NCCB's executive director. His testimony before Congress, blowing the whistle on the industry's ineffective self-regulation of cigarette commercials, effectively encouraged legislation banning the advertising of cigarettes on radio and television.

The committee conducted the first international study comparing children's television programs and schedules in the United States with those aired in other countries and submitted the findings to the FCC. NCCB also submitted numerous petitions to the FCC from groups and individuals in support of specific children's television guidelines. With more than 16,000 citizen supporters, NCCB became a clearinghouse and resource center for the exchange of information among public interest groups.

When Braren left NCCB to become associate director of Consumers Union, his position was filled by Jane Goodman, who was affiliated with the Office of Communication, United Church of Christ, an activist, public interest group. In 1974, Commissioner Nicholas Johnson left the FCC to lead NCCB. At the FCC, he had defended the rights of listeners and viewers to diverse information sources. Under Johnson's leadership, NCCB expanded its national membership and published a monthly magazine (*Access*) for the public and a newsletter (*Media Watch*) for members.

In this period, NCCB worked closely with public interest law firms in the communications field, mainly the Citizens Communications Center, headed by Albert Kramer, who had served as director of the Bureau of Consumer Protection at the FTC during the Carter administration. The center represented NCCB in administrative and legal proceedings.

NCCB launched several campaigns: One would require the three major networks to air at least three hours of public affairs programming weekly, another would protect the Fairness Doctrine from repeated efforts to repeal it, still another would reduce television violence, and a fourth intended to persuade the FCC to issue rules banning newspaper ownership of television stations in the same markets. The latter two efforts achieved measurable successes.

In the mid-1970s, NCCB, joined by the National PTA, initiated a nationwide effort to inform the public of the potential harm of increasing gratuitous violence on television. A national rating system was created to inform the public about the least and most violent programs, and for several years, the networks reduced the violence in their programming.

NCCB also worked for greater diversity of information sources available to viewers. Drawing from an NCCB petition, the FCC adopted rules that prohibited cross-ownership by newspapers of television outlets in the same community. Furthermore, the rules required the existing cross-ownership be divested. NCCB defended the FCC decision in the courts, and in *NCCB v. FCC* (1978), the Supreme Court ruled that the diversity of ownership sources was a primary purpose of the Communications Act of 1934.

In 1978, Ralph Nader became chair of the organization, with Johnson staying on as head of the organization's lobbying arm, the National Citizens Communications Lobby (NCCL). Samuel A. Simon, a Nader activist and an original member of the 1970 public interest research group, was appointed executive director. Under Simon's leadership, the NCCB broadened its focus to include telephone and telecommunications issues. When the FCC refused to act on NCCB's petition to require AT&T to refund $100 million in "overearnings," the group sued the agency and eventually gained a court of appeals ruling that if the FCC failed to act on a petition, the court would take up the case directly.

NCCB continued working against television violence and promoting the rights of listeners and viewers. It helped launch the National Coalition on Television Violence, which monitored network programming for violent content.

In the meantime, NCCB launched new programs in the telephone and technology fields, in which Simon became a national spokesperson for consumer interests. These initiatives included several books and key meetings on the implications of new information technologies for consumers. This new focus led the organization to change its name to the Telecommunications Research and Action Center (TRAC).

TRAC's program included advocacy, education, and legal intervention. The organization participated before Judge Harold Greene during the supervision of the breakup of AT&T and was the primary consumer witness before Congress in its oversight of the breakup. Later, TRAC led a campaign for legislation to protect consumers against abuses by Alternative Operator Services.

TRAC's legal program not only helped obtain the $100 million refund from AT&T, but also established new rights for consumers as a result of its lawsuit against Allnet, a new long-distance company, for rate discrimination. The U.S. Court of Appeals held for the first time that in some circumstances, associations could represent their members in actions for damages.

TRAC also launched education initiatives with the publication of TeleTips, a rate comparison chart for long-distance services, and "Phonewriting: A Consumer's Guide to the New World of Electronic Information." And it cofounded the Tele-Consumer Hotline with the Consumer Federation of America. From 1984 to the late 1990s, with industry support, the hotline advised individual consumers about telephone services.

When Simon set up his own consulting firm in 1986, he resigned as executive director of TRAC. Though he continued to oversee the organization, without his full-time attention, the organization shifted its focus to consumer education and reduced its level of activity. In 2008, it merged into the National Consumers League.

Samuel A. Simon

See also: Digital Communications Advocacy; Nader, Ralph; Telephone Consumer Advocacy

Further Reading

Cole, Barry and Mal Oettinger. 1978. *Reluctant Regulators: The FCC and the Broadcast Audience*. Reading, MA: Addison-Wesley Publishing Co.
Mayer, Caroline E. 1986. "Simon Says: Enough." *Channels of Communications* 5 (March): 16.

TELEPHONE CONSUMER ADVOCACY

For more than three decades, consumer advocates have sought to ensure that all Americans have access to affordable telephone service and, recently, to Internet broadband service as well. Without being able to communicate with emergency services (police, fire, health care), employers, stores, schools, social services, friends, and especially family members, people cannot participate fully in American life, receiving its benefits and resolving their problems. This principle of universal phone service was articulated well before the emergence of the modern consumer movement in the 1960s, but since then, consumer advocates have made it their priority that all Americans, especially those with low incomes and rural residence, receive this service. Over the past several decades, Consumers Union, AARP, Consumer Federation of America, National Consumer Law Center, and state members of the National Association of State Utility Consumer Advocates have been the consumer advocacy groups that worked the hardest to ensure affordable phone service.

Recognizing the importance of emerging telephone services, in the first decade of the twentieth century, states began authorizing their public utility commissions to oversee the reasonableness of local telephone rates. By 1921, all but three states had established some type of phone rate regulation. In 1910, Congress enacted the Mann–Elkins Act, which asserted that interstate telephone (and telegraph) companies were common carriers with a duty to provide access to service at "just and reasonable rates." It also gave the Interstate Commerce Commission limited authority to enforce this requirement.

In this period, to achieve its vision of "One Policy, One System, Universal Service," AT&T was buying up other companies that offered long-distance telephone services. In the face of antitrust scrutiny following several of these purchases, AT&T proposed to the U.S. Department of Justice (DOJ) that it sell off its telegraph service and be permitted to continue buying independent phone companies and also to allow interconnection with other phone networks, for long-distance calls, for a fee. When DOJ accepted this proposal, AT&T gained the ability to increasingly provide consumers the opportunity to make long-distance calls, not just in a service area served by their small phone company, but also to other parts of the country. As this access grew, the more valuable the phone network became.

By the 1930s, however, only one-third of U.S. households had telephone service. To increase access to this service and ensure that the service was adequately regulated, Congress enacted the Communications Act of 1934, which created a new federal agency, the Federal Communications Commission (FCC). This law charged the FCC to "make available, so far as possible to all the people of the United States, a rapid, efficient, Nation-wide, and world-wide wire and radio communications services with adequate facilities at reasonable charges."

For several decades thereafter, the FCC required AT&T and other phone companies to help ensure universal service through the cross-subsidization of local service by long-distance service. The rationale behind these cross-subsidies was that it was much more important for all Americans to be able to afford local calls than to afford long-distance ones. This same rationale was the basis for state public service commissions requiring the cross-subsidization of local service by service to businesses.

From the mid-1930s to the early 1960s, long-distance rates were established through informal negotiations between AT&T and the FCC. However, partly because of rate increases, in 1965 the FCC established a more formal regulatory system based on cost-of-service ratemaking. In the 1970s, new technologies allowed competitors to offer complementary or similar services to AT&T. After a number of legal challenges to the AT&T monopoly, a 1983 consent decree required the breakup of AT&T into a long-distance company, retaining the name AT&T, and regional "Baby Bell" companies that provided local service.

After this divestiture, while state public service commissions continued to regulate local phone rates, and long-distance and business access charges continued to support local service, consumer advocates and others grew increasingly concerned about the affordability of local phone service, which nearly 10 percent of all U.S. households lacked. These concerns helped persuade the FCC, working with state public service commissions and local phone companies, to create a Lifeline program that promoted universal service by helping low income households afford local service. This program was established in 1984 and enhanced in 1985. Then in 1987, the FCC adopted its Link Up America program, first developed in the states, to help low-income families afford the costs of connection and installation. The Link Up subsidy paid for half the cost of the connection charge (up to $30) and covered the interest for installment payments (to $200) for up to one year.

By the 1990s, new technologies—including cable television, cellular (or wireless) service, and the Internet—had emerged to challenge a phone system that was still dominated by AT&T and the regional Bell companies. When litigation failed to check the monopoly practices of these companies, Congress enacted the Telecommunications Act of 1996. The main purpose of this law was to open communications systems to competition, especially by requiring new competitors' access to the existing phone network. However, it also expanded the concept of universal service to include affordability and new technologies: "Quality services should be available at just, reasonable, and affordable rates." Moreover, these services, including interexchange services and advanced telecommunications and information services, must be available to low-income consumers and rural residents. Thus the Telecommunications Act of 1996 articulated a universal service support mechanism whereby all telecommunications providers contribute equitably to preserve and advance universal services. The law also created universal service support for schools, libraries, and rural health care.

The primary mechanism the Telecommunications Act created to help ensure universal access was a Universal Service Fund to which all telecommunications providers were required to contribute a percentage of their interstate and international end-user telecommunications revenues. In 1997, the FCC established this fund and the Universal Service Administrative Company to manage it. Since then, the fund has been faced with challenges related to funding sources and disbursements. As consumers and organizations reduced their use of traditional long-distance services and expanded their cell phone and Internet communications, support grew for requiring providers of the new services to make contributions to the fund, and, to an extent, that has occurred. At the same time, to gain full access to important communications services, support also grew for providing low-income and rural consumers assistance in purchasing the new services. In 2005, the FCC decided to make available Lifeline discounts to low-income consumers on prepaid wireless service plans while continuing discounts on traditional service plans. In October 2011, the federal agency approved a six-year transfer process that began shifting Universal Service funds to a new $4.5 billion–yearly Connect America Fund that would facilitate greater access among low-income and rural consumers to Internet broadband services.

Over the past two decades, the phone industry has continued to be radically restructured. By 2014, two corporate behemoths remained—AT&T and Verizon. Together, as well as continuing to dominate the traditional landline and cell phone business, the two oligopolies also control about three-quarters of the smartphone market. Yet these companies have been lobbying state governments to free themselves from traditional regulatory oversight. According to a June 2014 report by the National Regulatory Research Institute, thirty-two states have reduced or eliminated public service commission oversight of retail telecommunications service. The erosion of regulatory oversight started with bills that limited basic service and Carrier of Last Resort obligations as well as a state commission's ability to oversee quality of service, customer complaints, and billing matters. Recent iterations of the deregulation legislation focus on prohibiting state commissions from jurisdiction over Voice over Internet Protocol (VOIP) and Internet Protocol-enabled service.

Consumer advocates, especially those working at the state level, have fought this proposed deregulation. To illustrate: Recently, legislation was introduced into the Pennsylvania Assembly that AT&T and Verizon claimed would spur increased competition by ensuring that incumbent phone companies not be at a disadvantage in competing with unregulated wireless and VoIP providers. This legislation was strongly opposed by consumer advocates—including AARP Pennsylvania, the Pennsylvania Utility Law Project, and the Pennsylvania Office of Consumer Advocate—as well as by Local 668 of the Service Employees International Union. The advocates maintained that the bill would lead to higher rates, reduced service quality, loss of affordable basic service in rural areas, and the possibility of loss of wireline service in some areas. A report issued by the Keystone Research Center concluded that the legislation allowed phone companies to raise rates with one day's notice and to eliminate state utility commission oversight over rates, services, and consumer protections. As of July 2014, the state assembly was considering this bill.

At the federal level, AT&T has petitioned the FCC to begin transitioning the telecommunications network to rely entirely on Internet Protocol (IP) for switching communications. Because of the uncertainty regarding whether IP traffic is considered an information service not regulated directly by the FCC, this change would throw into doubt all the public service obligations of communications companies. In response, consumer advocates demanded that the FCC's authority to impose public service obligations be exercised and upheld before any transition is allowed to take place.

Consumers highly dependent on phone service, especially low income and rural households without Internet broadband connections, are threatened by the dismantling of traditional regulatory systems. A 2009 survey by the National Association of State Utility Advocates found that rates rose in seventeen of twenty states that deregulated. An even more serious threat to some consumers is the loss of access to any basic means of communication with other people and with institutions. Consumer advocates will continue to resist deregulation measures that threaten to undermine the progress that has been made towards achieving universal phone service.

Olivia Wein, Stephen Brobeck

See also: Cable Television Regulation; Digital Communications Advocacy; State Utility Advocacy

Further Reading

Lichtenberg, Sherry. 2014. *Telecommunications Legislation 2014: Completing the Process.* Report No. 14-07 by the National Regulatory Research Institute (June).

National Consumer Law Center, Pennsylvania Utility Law Project, and fifteen other groups. 2011. *Response to the Federal Communication Commission's Notice of Proposed Rulemaking on Lifeline and Link Up Reform and Modernization* (April 21).

Rosen, Jeffrey. 2011. "Universal Service Fund Reform: Expanding Broadband Internet Access in the U.S." In Center for Technology Innovation at Brookings, *Issues in Technology and Innovation* 8.

Spulber, Daniel F., and Christopher S. Yoo. 2008. "Toward a Unified Theory of Access to Local Telephone Networks." *Federal Communications Law Journal* 61: 43ff.

TENANT ACTIVISM

Tenant activists believe that tenants in the United States have always been viewed as second-class citizens. They point out that lack of property ownership has profoundly affected citizens in many ways, ranging from disenfranchisement in the nation's early years to lack of access to federal income tax deductions to lack of standing in communities. Tenants have been viewed by homeowners and government officials as transients who have little or no interest in their housing or their community. This perspective was summed up by a letter published in *New York Magazine* in January 1986: "The facts of life are simple: When you rent, you do not own. When you do not own, you do not dictate. It makes no difference whether the rental is a violin, a car, or an apartment. When you rent, you implicitly recognize the right of the owner to control his property. If you don't like it, don't rent."

The relationship between landlord and tenant in the United States is based on English feudal law, dating from the fourteenth century, when land was the most important possession and largely determined one's wealth. Tenants were permitted to live on and farm land in exchange for a portion of the crops grown or monthly rent. Regardless of what happened in the fields—whether there were good or poor crop yields—tenants had to pay rent. Although they were allowed to build a house, they were responsible for its maintenance and repairs.

These English laws were adopted in the United States and were effectively in force throughout the country until the 1960s. Once they moved in, renters were required to pay monthly rent, but this obligation was not reciprocated by an obligation of landlords to make needed repairs to ensure that the housing was habitable. One of the first tenant organizing campaigns to protest rising rents and uninhabitable conditions took place in 1904, when 2,000 Jewish tenants in New York City's Lower East Side began a rent strike. A second tenant uprising in the city occurred in the winter of 1907–1908, when thousands of tenants, mainly women, picketed their tenements and demanded a 25 percent rent reduction. Over the next fifty years, tenant activism and organizing emerged in other cities, including in Philadelphia, Chicago, and San Francisco.

In the 1970s, this organizing and activism spread to other parts of the country, focusing both on public and private housing. In 1969, the National Tenants Organization (NTO) was established to provide a voice for public housing tenants. When tenants of the Stella Wright public housing project—a complex comprising seven high-rise buildings in Newark, New Jersey—held a four-year rent strike to protest habitability and safety issues, it became, at the time, the longest rent strike in U.S. history.

For private tenants, a number of citywide and statewide tenant groups were created to support new legislation and to organize building tenant associations to voice their grievances. Between 1970 and 1985, citywide tenant associations were organized in East Coast cities, such as New York, Philadelphia, Boston, Cambridge, Somerville, Washington, D.C., and several New Jersey cities; throughout the Midwest, including in Cleveland, Columbus, Louisville, Indianapolis, Ann Arbor, Detroit, Chicago, Minneapolis–St. Paul, Milwaukee, Madison, and Topeka; and in the West, including in Dallas, Fort Worth, Austin, Seattle, Portland, Berkeley, Francisco, Los Angeles, Santa Barbara, and Santa Monica. Moreover, statewide tenant organizations were started or grew in New York, Massachusetts, Vermont, Illinois, Texas, California, and New Jersey. In 1980, the National Tenants Union (NTU) was established to bring all these private groups together to support tenant activism.

For all these tenant organizations, four key issues were important—habitability, rents and rent increases, eviction protection, and security deposits. For many tenants, the major concern centered on habitability, heat and hot water, infestations of roaches and rats, and other issues of livability. The warranty of habitability doctrine argument slowly began to gain acceptance, with some courts beginning to reevaluate the relationship in the 1970s. The courts began to agree that tenants have a right to a living space, so that if the housing unit is below the minimum acceptable condition, tenants should pay something less than the actual rent. This warranty of habitability doctrine encouraged tenants to complain and led to the organizing of tenant associations and rent strikes.

Tenants also increasingly advocated eviction protections, rent control, and guarantees of return of security deposits. Through the efforts of local and state tenant associations, a number of states passed laws protecting tenants against arbitrary or retaliatory evictions, and many cities approved ordinances that provided some protection against large rent increases.

From 1979 to 1985, the NTU had its greatest level of success bringing together private tenant activists to protest landlord abuses and support new local, state, and national tenant protections. It succeeded in building and strengthening local tenant organizations, promoting tenants' political and economic rights, and developing a strong national movement.

However, over the last thirty years, a vibrant national tenant movement has ceased to exist, in part because of the improved conditions which resulted from the strengthening of landlord–tenant law. Improved tenant conditions blunted the tenant dissatisfaction that had spurred activism. There are still active state and local groups. For example, in California a coalition of housing and reform-minded groups, Tenants Together, continues to encourage lawsuits against irresponsible landlords and the approval of needed city ordinances and state laws, including protections against "security deposit theft." In New York City, Tenants and Neighbors seeks to organize tenants and support legislative reform. And nationally, the National Alliance of HUD Tenants, made up of several hundred building tenant unions, advocates before HUD and Congress. Yet, these organizations tend to lack the reach and the influence of their forebears. To tenant activists, tenants are still treated as second-class citizens.

Woody Widrow

See also: Community Activism; Mortgage Lending Reform; National Low Income Housing Coalition

Further Reading

Clark, Philip. 1986. "Letter to the Editor." *New York Magazine* (January 6): 6.

Dreier, Peter. 1995. "Organizing the New Tenant's Movement." *Shelterforce* (November/December).

Widrow, Woody. 1994. "Will All Tenants Win?" In John Emmeus David, ed. *The Affordable City*. Philadelphia, PA: Temple University Press.

TOBACCO ACTIVISM

Activism in the United States against tobacco products has been around for more than a century, involving diverse actors having varied motives and targeting a variety of problems. Nevertheless, there has been one overarching achievement: a massive paradigm shift from viewing tobacco as safe or even healthy to recognizing it as an inherently dangerous product that exacts a horrible toll from society. Within that overall story, there have been many subplots, each with its own actors, strategies, and effects on public policy. The subjects of these subplots include warnings on cigarette packages, controls on tobacco advertising and promotion, second-hand smoke exposure and restrictions on smoking in public places, financial liability for the health effects of smoking, regulation of tobacco as a drug, and creation of an international treaty regarding tobacco control.

Emergence of Modern Anti-Smoking Activism

It took decades to establish scientifically that smoking was harmful to health, and it required far longer to shift primary blame for tobacco's ill effects from smokers lacking self-control to tobacco companies seducing young people and creating addicts. In the nineteenth century, an antitobacco movement developed in the United States that paralleled, though on a smaller scale, the alcohol temperance movement. Antitobacco crusaders viewed smoking as an unhealthy habit, attributable to personal weakness. In the early twentieth century, volunteer organizations such as the American Lung Association, American Cancer Society, and American Heart Association ("the health voluntaries") emerged to reduce deaths and illnesses associated with tobacco as part of a broader public health mission. Both the anticigarette leagues and the health voluntaries saw the use of cigarettes and other tobacco products as a moral failure on the part of consumers (many of whom were poor or recent immigrants) whose behavior could be improved by more and better information about the evils of their smoking habit.

During the first half of the nineteenth century, evidence accumulated—despite the efforts of the tobacco industry to suppress and obscure it—that cigarette consumption and cancer, especially lung cancer, were intimately connected. In December 1952, *Reader's Digest*, the most widely circulated magazine at the time, published an article, "Cancer by the Carton," summarizing recent medical research on the relationship between smoking and lung cancer in humans. The article left little doubt that reputable researchers saw smoking as a huge risk factor. Shortly thereafter, a published study showed that cigarette tar caused cancerous tumors in mice. The tobacco industry responded with public relations rather than facts. It ran an advertisement in major U.S. newspapers titled "A Frank Statement to Cigarette Smokers" in which it dismissed the recent study as inconclusive and called attention to the fact that eminent doctors and scientists questioned such experiments. The advertisement included this passage: "For more than 300 years tobacco has given solace, relaxation, and enjoyment to mankind. At one time or another during those years critics have held it responsible for practically every disease of the human body. One by one these charges have been abandoned for lack of evidence." To address the public's concern, however, the advertisement announced the creation of the Tobacco Industry Research Committee to undertake additional research. The real purpose of the new body was revealed in a 1969 memo written by an industry executive: "doubt [with regard to the ill health effects of tobacco] is our product" (Oreskes and Conway, 2010, p. 34).

A pivotal moment in the fight against tobacco occurred in 1964, when U.S. Surgeon General Luther L. Terry released a report of his Advisory Committee on Smoking and Health. The impetus for the report came from the health voluntaries who, in 1961, had urged President John F. Kennedy to act on the problems posed by smoking. As a sign of the cautiousness of the voluntaries, they asked for a solution that would "interfere least with the freedom of industry or the happiness of individuals" (Kluger, p. 222). The report reviewed more than 7,000 research articles and concluded that cigarette smoking was a cause of lung cancer and laryngeal cancer in men and a probable cause of lung cancer among women. The use of the word "cause" was especially notable as the tobacco companies vehemently denied any direct link between smoking and ill health. Although the report did not attribute smoking to tobacco company conduct, the report's conclusions provided the primary justification for passage a year later of the Federal Cigarette Labeling and Advertising Act of 1965. The law required, for the first time in any country, cigarettes to carry a warning, albeit one severely weakened by tobacco industry lobbying. The warning was tame by today's standards: "Caution: Cigarette Smoking May be Hazardous to Your Health." The act was also industry-friendly inasmuch as it prevented states from enacting policies more stringent than those specified in the new law.

The activities of John Banzhaf III, a law professor, and Action on Smoking and Health, an organization he founded, hinted at the more assertive antismoking movement that was to blossom a few decades later. Implicitly blaming the tobacco companies for the thousands of people who became ill and died each year from tobacco, Banzhaf in 1966 successfully petitioned the U.S. Federal Communications Commission, under the Fairness Doctrine governing controversial subjects, to require television and radio broadcasters to provide free air time for antismoking messages. (The production of the ads was paid for by the health voluntaries.) Far removed from older marketing by cigarette companies stressing the health benefits of smoking and the approval of doctors, the new antismoking ads urged smokers to quit and encouraged non-smokers to never start. In 1971, cigarette advertising was banned on radio and TV, so the public service airtime required by the Fairness Doctrine ended as well. The tobacco industry supported the ban as a way to get rid of the pesky and effective antismoking ads.

The dangers of second-hand smoke also mobilized consumer activists. None other than Ralph Nader, the leading consumer protection advocate of the period, petitioned the Federal Aviation Administration (FAA) in 1969 to ban smoking on commercial aircraft. That same year, Banzhaf argued that airlines should be required to have separate smoking and non-smoking sections—a policy rejected by the FAA but adopted in 1972 by the Civil Aeronautics Board (CAB). The CAB also prohibited smoking in aircraft lavatories in 1973 after a tragic fire that caused a crash and killed 124 people. By the 1980s, antismoking activists, the American Lung Association, and the American Medical Association, and other groups gained a major, new ally in their push for a complete ban on smoking on commercial flights—the flight attendants and their labor unions. Whereas passengers might take the occasional flight, flight attendants worked on planes. Self-imposed restrictions by individual airline companies followed, as did laws governing flights departing from or arriving in California. In 1987, almost two decades after Nader's petition, the U.S. Congress banned smoking on domestic flights of two hours or less in duration, and the ban was extended two years later to flights of six hours or less.

During the 1970s, the perils of second-hand smoke also propelled activism at the local level, primarily in the form of campaigns to reduce second-hand smoke exposure. These activists formed groups to promote the right of nonsmokers to be free of environmental tobacco smoke. In California, local and statewide groups used the creative acronym GASP (Group Against Smoking Pollution) to get their point across. These groups began trying to educate the public about the dangers of second-hand smoke, but they quickly progressed to seeking laws limiting smoking in public places such as restaurants and workplaces. In the view of these groups, curbing environmental tobacco smoke was not a matter of asking smokers to be more considerate; it required societal curbs on the behavior of tobacco companies and other businesses that enable smoking.

California, along with New Jersey and Florida, was a hotbed of support for anti-smoking ordinances. In 1977, city of the Berkeley, California, enacted a first-of-its kind law requiring restaurants to have a non-smoking section. In 1978, the health voluntaries, California Medical Association, and other activists placed an initiative statute on the California ballot that would have banned smoking in most indoor environments, but in the face of a multi-million dollar industry campaign against the proposition, voters turned it down. A similar ballot proposition was defeated in California two years later.

Having failed at the state level, California activists concerned about environmental tobacco smoke returned to the local level. In 1981, Californians for Nonsmokers' Rights (renamed Americans for Nonsmokers' Rights in 1988) was established to promote local antismoking ordinances in California and elsewhere. The nonsmokers' rights groups confronted the tobacco companies, often in the form of industry-financed smokers' right groups and front groups. When these efforts were unsuccessful, the tobacco industry often tried local referenda, petition drives, and recall elections of local officials to stymie antismoking ordinances. Facing this resistance but buoyed by a 1986 report of the U.S. Surgeon General on passive smoking, dozens of ordinances requiring smoke-free environments were enacted in California during the mid- and late-1980s. Nationally, more than 400 local antismoking laws were passed by 1990, most of which applied to restaurants or workplaces. In 1990, the town of San Luis Obispo passed the first ordinance in the nation that applied to bars. (The transformation of passive smoking from an impolite act to the release of a deadly pollutant was abetted by two crucial government reports—one by the Surgeon General in 1986 and the second by the U.S. Environmental Protection Agency in 1992—that confirmed the health dangers of, and the deaths attributable to, second-hand smoke.)

Michael Pertschuk, former chairman of the U.S. Federal Trade Commission (FTC) and a mentor of public interest advocates, noted that the national antitobacco movement came of age in 1984 during the campaign to pass the Comprehensive Smoking Education Act of 1984. Looking back from more than thirty years later, it is ironic that Pertschuk praised Matt Myers, leader of the Coalition on Smoking OR Health, as a "Giant Killer" for helping to pass a new but timid cigarette labeling law. The law replaced a single warning with four rotating warnings. But the new warnings weren't especially hard-hitting. One of warnings mentioned that cigarette smoke contains carbon monoxide—not exactly a fearsome message. And another warning almost invited people to continue smoking as long as they quit later: "Quitting Smoking Now Greatly Reduces Serious Risks to Your Health."

The rotating warnings also remained (and remain at the time of this writing) small and inconspicuous. As late as the mid-1980s, "Big Tobacco" was still powerful enough to render even a weak law a major victory for the antitobacco movement.

The Pivotal 1990s

The Comprehensive Smoking Education Act of 1984 was not the final piece of important federal legislation dealing with tobacco issues. In particular, the Family Smoking Prevention and Tobacco Control Act of 2009 was significant for giving the Food and Drug Administration enforcement authority over tobacco products. Nevertheless, by the mid-1980s, activism with respect to tobacco was embarking on three fairly new tracks that were destined to become heavily trafficked in subsequent years. One of these involved the use of mass media to discourage smoking. A second was litigation based on the charge of industry duplicity and, therefore, culpability. The third was an attack on industry efforts to market their products to young people.

As mentioned above, antismoking advertisements appeared briefly in the late-1960s when antismoking groups received free air time as part of the Fairness Doctrine. The use of the mass media to discourage smoking abated until 1984, when the state of Minnesota embarked on an antismoking campaign. In 1988, California voters passed Proposition 99, which increased taxes on cigarettes by $0.25 per package. A substantial portion of the revenue raised through the tax was dedicated to health education, and two years later, an aggressive antismoking campaign began on the airwaves. The states of Massachusetts, Arizona, Oregon, and Florida followed suit during the 1990s. Whereas all these campaigns tried to explain the dangers of smoking, some also hammered on the misdeeds of the tobacco industry. It is difficult to separate cause and effect or know the effectiveness of specific ads, but these mass media campaigns corresponded with a notable decrease in per capita cigarette consumption in the United States. Even more widespread antismoking campaigns via the mass media lay ahead.

At roughly the same time when Minnesota kicked off the use of mass media campaigns to get current smokers to quit and discourage non-smokers from starting the habit, a wave of tobacco litigation was just beginning. When the first reports were published in the 1950s linking cigarette smoking to cancer, lawsuits against cigarette manufacturers began to appear. The tobacco companies prevailed in all these cases based on a combination of three claims: the evidence of tobacco's harmful effects was not definitive, it is impossible to disentangle the multiple causes of cancer, and smokers knowingly assume any health risks when they decide to smoke.

A lawsuit was filed in 1983 by Rose Cipollone that changed the face of antitobacco litigation. Ms. Cipollone was born in 1926. She began smoking as a teenager and continued throughout her adulthood, although she switched from Chesterfields to a variety of other healthier-seeming brands. During the 1960s, Cipollone developed a cough and other symptoms that appeared to be smoking-related. In 1981, doctors found a carcinogenic spot on her lung and removed a section. She continued to smoke, and her lung cancer continued to spread. In 1984, she died from the effects of lung cancer. A year before her death, however, Cipollone filed multiple suits against Liggett and Myers, Philip Morris, and Lorillard. Her essential claim was that that the cigarette manufacturers knew—but did not adequately warn consumers—that cigarettes were addictive and caused lung cancer.

The Cipollone litigation did not result in a massive verdict against the tobacco companies, but it was significant in a number of ways. The evidence-gathering process provided the first look by an outsider into the internal documents of the tobacco companies, and subsequent, more successful litigation was to make extensive use of these and many other internal documents. The district court ruled that Cipollone bore the primary responsibility for her early death because she chose to smoke, but Liggett and Myers bore partial responsibility for failing to properly warn smokers of the health risks of their products. In an attempt to reflect this shared responsibility, the court ordered Liggett and Myers to pay $400,000 to Cipollone's family—the first time a tobacco company had to pay damages to the family of an afflicted smoker. Philip Morris and Lorillard were not held to be liable, because Cipollone had started smoking their brands after the federally mandated health warnings appeared in 1966. Both sides of the case claimed victory. The case wended its way to the U.S. Supreme Court, which ruled in 1992 that the surgeon general's warning shielded the tobacco companies from claims made by people who developed diseases after 1969. The justices did not preclude, however, future claims based on evidence that the industry conspired to hide evidence of the dangers of smoking or lied to the public about these dangers. Subsequent lawsuits would take advantage of this opening.

In October 1994, a class action lawsuit against the tobacco companies was allowed to proceed in Florida. The collective nature of the suit was based on the view that smokers who were both addicted to cigarettes and suffering health damages from smoking had enough in common to be certified as a class. The *Engle* case, named for one of its lead plaintiffs, Howard Engle, initially resulted in a verdict in favor of the smokers, including an eye-popping $145 billion in punitive damages. The decision was reversed on appeal and ended in 2006, when the Florida Supreme Court affirmed the appellate court's decision and also decertified the class. The case was important, however, in providing extensive whistleblower testimony, increasing public awareness of industry misconduct, and promoting greater industry accountability.

In addition to the filing of the *Engle* case, 1994 was a watershed year in the antismoking crusade, as an assortment of members of Congress, federal regulators, state officials, and industry whistleblowers were galvanized to take on the tobacco industry. In April 1994, the chief executives of seven major tobacco companies were called to testify at a hearing held by the House Energy and Commerce Committee and chaired by Representative Henry Waxman (D-CA). Under oath, all seven of the major tobacco company presidents and CEOs who appeared that day testified that they believed that nicotine was not addictive. To most observers, their testimony was laughable and only underscored the intractability of the tobacco companies. It also flew in the face of an investigative news story run two months earlier by Walt Bogdanich of ABC News about the ways in which tobacco manufacturers secretly manipulated nicotine to addict smokers. The exposé, which later received the prestigious George Polk Award in Journalism, featured an interview in silhouette of "Deep Cough," a former employee of RJ Reynolds who had come to tobacco control advocate and attorney Cliff Douglas with her deep misgivings. Her startling testimony gave courage to other industry insiders who had trouble living with their knowledge of industry misdeeds, and it moved FDA Commissioner David Kessler into action. Just one day before the news story was scheduled to air, Kessler, whose investigators had by then interviewed Deep Cough after being introduced to her by Cliff Douglas, sent a letter to the Coalition on Smoking OR Health. In it, he stated that it was his understanding that cigarette manufacturers add nicotine to cigarettes in an effort to deliver specific amounts of the substance and, therefore, the federal government should regulate tobacco products as drugs.

Shortly after the April congressional hearing, other former tobacco industry insiders blew the whistle on their former employers. Victor DeNoble and his former Philip Morris research partner Paul Mele, along with Merrell Williams Jr., who worked as a paralegal for a Kentucky law firm that represented Brown & Williamson Tobacco, provided extensive documentation demonstrating that the tobacco industry knew only too well that its products were addictive and dangerous. Jeffrey Wigand, the most famous whistleblower, emerged in 1996. He appeared on the highly watched news program 60 Minutes and stated that Brown & Williamson had intentionally manipulated its tobacco blend to increase the amount of nicotine in cigarette smoke, in part verifying the earlier ABC News report's findings regarding the industry's manipulation of nicotine. (A 1999 movie, The Insider, was based on Wigand's story; it garnered seven Academy Award nominations.) These whistleblowers backed up their charges with reference to secret industry documents. Additional inside documents from Brown & Williamson were mailed to the San Francisco office of antismoking activist Dr. Stanton Glantz from the anonymous "Mr. Butt" in May 1994. Glantz and his colleagues published the incriminating contents of the documents beginning in 1995 and later released the documents in a 1998 book, The Cigarette Papers.

With the veil that had concealed tobacco industry knowledge and conduct now fluttering in the wind, several state officials were emboldened to take a new legal tack. Beginning in May 1994, Mike Moore of Mississippi, followed within months by the Minnesota, West Virginia, and Massachusetts state attorneys general, brought suit against the tobacco companies for reimbursement of state Medicaid costs incurred in treating smokers. The attorneys generals' argument was again based on industry deceit of the public—and, unlike individual smokers, who might be blamed for their personal choice to smoke, state governments could not shield themselves from financial harm. The suits were high-risk but, if successful, promised high returns.

The Minnesota case, brought by Attorney General Hubert ("Skip") Humphrey III along with Blue Cross and Blue Shield of Minnesota, was particularly important. The case was filed in August 1994 and eventually settled in 1998. The multi-billion-dollar settlement involved one of the largest payouts of all time. But, perhaps more important, 35 million pages of long-secret documents were opened to public scrutiny. These documents revealed industry deceit and influenced the course of tobacco policy both in the United States and elsewhere.

There was only one blemish in 1994 on what was otherwise a spectacular year for antitobacco activists. Three years earlier, in 1991, the health voluntaries had petitioned the Federal Trade Commission to crack down on the use of a cartoon character named Joe Camel in marketing cigarettes. The groups considered Joe Camel to be an egregious example of how the tobacco companies targeted children. In a May 1994 ruling, however, the commissioners of the FTC voted 3–2 to not file a complaint against RJ Reynolds for its Joe Camel advertising campaign. The majority position was that the evidence that Joe Camel led children to smoke was insufficient. (Under pressure from lawsuits, Congress, and health activists, RJ Reynolds decided to take the dromedary on his last ride in 1997.)

Master Settlement Agreement

Up to this point, the diverse antitobacco movement was not necessarily well coordinated, but it had been essentially united by a common enemy—the super-powerful tobacco industry. By 1997, however, there was a growing sense among tobacco activists that they had the industry on the defensive, if not in wholesale retreat. The private lawsuits had uncovered evidence that the tobacco companies had long known their products to be dangerous and additive. The cigarette makers and their trade association suppressed evidence of the former while manipulating the latter to their commercial advantage. The new suits brought by the state attorneys general would strive to hammer home these points with even greater force than private attorneys had and raised the specter of legal awards reaching the billions of dollars.

With public opinion turning against the tobacco companies and lawsuits coming at them from all side, they were ready to bargain. Yet at this critical juncture, cleavages emerged within the antismoking movement between those who would be satisfied weakening the industry and those who wanted to destroy it. The moderates—led by the state attorneys general—believed that they could work with the tobacco companies to arrive at a congressionally sanctioned grand bargain in which the industry would make some significant concessions in exchange for being shielded from legal liability (and financial responsibility) for its past deeds. To represent the health voluntaries and other moderate antismoking groups in negotiations with the tobacco companies, the attorneys general invited Matt Myers, the chief strategist for the Coalition on Smoking OR Health and legal counsel to the recently established Campaign for Tobacco-Free Kids, to join secret negotiations. Myers was conflicted about accepting the invitation. He was suspicious of the tobacco companies, and he knew that any deal worked out in secret with him as the only representative of the public health community would be controversial. But Myers was convinced that only congressional action, not lawsuits, could bring about fundamental reforms, such as giving the FDA jurisdiction over the tobacco industry. He was also aware that without his participation, the public health community would have no representation at the bargaining table, so he agreed to join the negotiations in April 1997.

On June 20, 1997, Mississippi attorney general Mike Moore proudly announced at a massive press conference at the National Press Club in Washington, D.C., that the state attorneys general, representatives of the public health community, and the tobacco industry had hammered out a comprehensive tobacco control deal and would ask the U.S. Congress to enact it. In exchange for a high degree of legal immunity against lawsuits, the tobacco companies would pay $365.5 billion, a third of which would be dedicated to combating teenage smoking. The global settlement also would have given the FDA limited regulatory authority over tobacco, including new restrictions on advertising and stronger package warnings. Senator John McCain (R-AZ) spearheaded the effort to pass a bill, and he managed to get the Senate Commerce Committee, which he chaired, to vote 19–1 in favor of it. Yet, two months later, the carefully crafted compromise died in the Senate. It was the casualty of Republican opposition, industry disaffection with the deal's immunity provisions, and sharp disagreements within the public health community about the settlement's desirability. Even partial immunity for the tobacco companies was too much for the more zealous wing of the antismoking movement.

Whether the failure to enact a global settlement was a major lost opportunity remains a matter of debate. At the time, the same state attorneys general who had negotiated the original legislative deal quickly resorted to Plan B—settlement of their lawsuits without the need for approval by Congress or the support of antitobacco activists. The result was the Master Settlement Agreement (MSA) between the attorneys general of forty-six states, the District of Columbia, and five U.S. territories and the major cigarette companies. Washington Attorney General Christine Gregoire was the lead negotiator for the government side. The deal, reached in November 1998, was narrower in scope than the McCain proposal but nevertheless was a landmark in the fight against tobacco products. Following the basic design of earlier and separate settlements with Mississippi, Florida, Texas, and Minnesota, the MSA required the tobacco companies to pay more than $200 billion to the states over the next twenty-five years (plus additional payments in perpetuity) based on their estimated smoking-related Medicaid costs. The MSA also contained some restrictions on the marketing of tobacco products. In exchange, the attorneys general ended their lawsuits against the tobacco companies. The MSA did not, however, provide any legal immunity against private or federal lawsuits. Finally, the MSA created the American Legacy Foundation—a nonprofit organization dedicated to supporting research on the effectiveness of antismoking programs and to implementing a national antismoking advertising campaign.

Recent Successes and Setbacks

Antitobacco activism continued after the MSA, but it has been less visible, and it has endured some significant defeats. In 1995, FDA Commissioner David Kessler described smoking as, fundamentally, a pediatric disease, because most tobacco addiction begins among teenagers. The next year, he asserted his agency's authority over tobacco products and announced his intention to use its authority to prevent and reduce tobacco use by children. In 2000, after a tortuous legal journey, the U.S. Supreme Court ruled that Congress had not given the FDA authority to regulate tobacco products and that Congress would have to do so by statute before the agency could act.

Almost a decade later, in 2009, Congress passed the Family Smoking and Tobacco Control Act. The act explicitly gives the FDA authority to regulate the manufacture, distribution, and marketing of tobacco products. Many of the law's provisions are directed at discouraging smoking by young people, such as banning sponsorship by tobacco companies of sporting or entertainment events and the use of brand names on clothing and other nontobacco items. Among other intriguing provisions, the statute grants the agency the authority to reduce nicotine to nonaddictive levels if it determines based on rigorous scientific review that doing so will have a net public health benefit.

At least one of the act's high-profile provisions, however, has thus far been blocked—the requirement of bigger, more prominent graphic warnings on cigarette packages and in advertisements. Strong, blunt, pictorial, even gruesome antismoking warnings are the norm throughout the world, having been applied in at least sixty countries. Under the act, the FDA was supposed to put in place nine new and more prominent health warnings. In 2011, the FDA unveiled its proposed warning labels and required them to appear on packages beginning in September 2012. In a victory for the tobacco industry, however, the rule went up in smoke when, in 2013, a federal appellate court affirmed a lower court's decision in striking down the proposed rule on the grounds that warnings violated the First Amendment's protection of free speech. The ruling left open the option for the agency to return to the drawing board and develop more limited graphic warning labels that satisfy the court's concerns, but the agency has not yet unveiled a new proposal.

In private lawsuits, the tobacco companies have been successful in fighting off potentially devastating outcomes. In the final round of the *Engle* case, the Florida Supreme Court threw out a class action lawsuit brought on behalf of 700,000 smokers and their families against tobacco companies. The court agreed that tobacco companies knowingly sold dangerous products and hid the health risks of smoking, but it ruled that the case could not proceed as a class action and that, instead, each case must be proven individually. Additional class action lawsuits have averred that tobacco companies deceptively marketed "light" cigarettes as a safer alternative when the manufacturers knew that smokers would compensate for lower tar and nicotine levels by inhaling more deeply or smoking more frequently. So far, these collective lawsuits have not resulted in judgments against the tobacco companies, but many individual cases have been successful. Plaintiffs' lawyers still face formidable opposition, but under the right conditions, juries are willing to assign culpability to the tobacco companies.

A conspicuous victory for antitobacco activists took place in 2003 when the United Nations adopted the World Health Organization Framework Convention on Tobacco Control (FCTC). The first and still only international public health treaty, the FCTC was quickly ratified by the requisite number of countries and entered into force in 2005. With the conspicuous exception of the United States, the convention is operative in almost all countries, and it governs the production, sale, distribution, marketing, and taxation of tobacco. The agreement sets minimum standards in these areas and encourages countries to enact policies that are stronger than these minimums. The convention has emboldened antitobacco activists around the world to confront the economic and political power of the tobacco companies in the name of advancing public health. Their work has been facilitated by the Framework Convention Alliance, which represents nearly 500 nongovernmental organizations from more than 100 countries.

In 2010, the U.S. Supreme Court passed judgment on the conduct of the cigarette companies. The court declined to hear an appeal by the tobacco industry of a federal district court decision that the major tobacco companies were, officially, racketeers. The companies had violated the Racketeer Influenced and Corrupt Organizations Act (RICO) by conspiring to deceive the public about the dangerous and addictive nature of smoking and to target children to create a new generation of smokers. Coming late in the game, and thanks to a ruling by the appeals court that limited financial remedies, the verdict had little practical effect, but it vindicated decades of antismoking activism. The decision, however, did bar terms such as "light," "mild," and "natural" in cigarette marketing, echoing the similar prohibition contained in the law passed a year earlier granting FDA regulatory authority over tobacco.

Over the course of more than a century, antismoking activists have managed to change both public perception and public policy with respect to cigarettes and other tobacco products. According to a 2014 report of the U.S. Department of Health and Human Services, tobacco control efforts in the United States since 1964 have prevented 8 million premature deaths and contributed to a marked increase in average life expectancy (2.3 years for males and 1.6 years for females). The results of antitobacco activism are hardly confined to the United States, however. Who could have imagined a few decades ago that all pubs in Ireland would be smoke-free by law, that all cigarettes in Australia would be sold in logo-free, drab brown packages, or that the government of New Zealand would set the year 2025 as the date by which tobacco rates would be less than 5 percent? Antitobacco activists still have work to do, especially in addressing increased smoking in low-income, less-educated populations (particularly in the developing world) as well as among females worldwide, but these advocates have truly wrought a sea change in public policy and corporate behavior.

Robert N. Mayer

See also: Front Groups; Initiatives and Referenda

Further Reading

Brandt, Allan M. 2007. *The Cigarette Century*. New York: Basic Books.

Douglas, Clifford E., Ronald M. Davis, and John K. Beasley. 2006. "Epidemiology of the Third Wave of Tobacco Litigation in the United States, 1994–2005." *Tobacco Control* 15, Supplement 4: iv9–iv16.

Glantz, Stanton A., Lisa A. Bero, and John Slade, eds. 1998. *The Cigarette Papers*. Berkeley: University of California Press.

Hilts, Philip J. 1996. *Smokescreen*. Boston: Addison-Wesley.

Ibrahim, Jennifer K., and Stanton A. Glantz. 2007. "The Rise and Fall of Tobacco Control Media Campaigns, 1967–2006." *American Journal of Public Health* 97, no. 8: 1383.

Kluger, Richard. *Ashes to Ashes*. New York: Random House, 2010.

Oreskes, Naomi, and Erik M. Conway. 2010. *Merchants of Doubt*. New York: Bloomsbury Press.

Pertschuk, Michael. 1986. *Giant Killers*. New York: Norton.

Pertschuk, Michael. 2001. *Smoke in their Eyes*. Nashville, TN: Vanderbilt University Press.

Proctor, Robert. 2011. *Golden Holocaust*. Berkeley: University of California Press.

Samuels, Bruce, and Stanton A. Glantz. 1991. "The Politics of Local Tobacco Control." *JAMA* 266, no. 15: 2,110–2,117.

US Department of Health and Human Services. 2014. *The Health Consequences of Smoking—50 Years of Progress: A Report of the Surgeon General*. Atlanta, GA: U.S. Department of Health and Human Services, Centers for Disease Control and Prevention, National Center for Chronic Disease Prevention and Health Promotion, Office on Smoking and Health.

World Health Organization. 2003. *Framework Convention on Tobacco Control*. Geneva, Switzerland.

Zegart, Dan. 2000. *Civil Warriors*. New York: Delacorte Press.

TORT-RELATED CONSUMER ADVOCACY

For almost forty years, insurance companies, manufacturers of potentially dangerous products and chemicals, the tobacco industry, medical lobbies, and other special interests have been engaged in a nationwide campaign to block injured consumers' access to the civil justice system. This movement to restrict the ability of injured consumers to obtain compensation from the companies causing their injuries is commonly known as "tort reform." During this entire period, consumer advocates have fought back to preserve and improve consumers' access to the civil justice system, to increase the accountability of large institutions through the civil justice system, and to support the civil jury system. They have maintained that a weak civil justice system does not protect consumers, especially the most vulnerable, and that a strong system provides large corporations and other institutions with economic incentives to make their products and practices safer.

Before the mid-1970s, consumer rights organizations focused little time or energy on the tort system. Until then, having evolved through the courts for centuries, the common law of torts had generally operated, without much political interference, to afford citizens a means to challenge injustice and negligence. But in the mid-1970s, a liability insurance crisis occurred in which insurance rates for physicians and some businesses started to escalate. Insurers blamed these price hikes on a "litigation explosion." They demanded large rate hikes from state regulators and convinced many lawmakers that the best way to limit these increases was to restrict the legal rights of injured victims through "tort reform." During this period, insurers learned that state regulators would allow rate increases and that state lawmakers would limit the rights of "victims." California, for example, enacted the Medical Injury Compensation Reform Act, which, among other measures, placed a $250,000 cap on non-economic damages for malpractice victims.

After insurers stopped insuring some medical and product manufacturer lines, President Gerald Ford decided to review the situation. He asked an inter-agency working group, which included Federal Insurance Administrator J. Robert Hunter, to examine the insurance crisis and learn whether rising medical malpractice claims were causing the large increases in malpractice coverage rates. When the working group could not find data to answer this question, working with the National Association of Insurance Commissioners (NAIC), it undertook a closed-claim study. This study revealed that there was no "explosion" of claims, and thus no justification for the insurer actions. The group reported back to the White House that insurers had panicked and that the problem seemed related to insurer economics. The group also negotiated with the NAIC to create a new medical malpractice line of data in insurers' annual statements so that rates and losses could be more carefully monitored.

In 1978, a federal inter agency working group on product liability recommended that Congress approve legislation creating a single set of national standards related to product liability. The proposed legislation would preempt product liability laws in all fifty states and include anticonsumer provisions, such as revising strict liability to make it more difficult for injured consumers to sue manufacturers and sellers of defective products. Industry groups had already been calling for such laws, prompting sharp criticism from Ralph Nader, who claimed that no data substantiated a product liability crisis.

In 1981, the first federal product liability bill was introduced in Congress with Senator Robert Kasten (R-WI) as the lead sponsor. This bill became the major civil justice focus for the business community in Congress for many years thereafter. Though it never became law, it was re-introduced every year through the late 1990s and often came close to passage. It did finally pass Congress in 1996 but was vetoed by President Clinton. It was never seriously considered again, in part because of the effectiveness of the consumer opposition.

Insurer efforts at the state and federal levels activated the consumer movement, led by Ralph Nader. Recognizing the need to fight these insurer efforts in a knowledgeable and sustained way, in the early 1980s, Nader offered Hunter, a property-casualty insurance actuary, the opportunity to leave government and establish the nonprofit National Insurance Consumer Organization (NICO). NICO then produced a series of influential critiques of property/casualty insurance industry practices. Also in the early 1980s, three Washington, D.C.–based national consumer organizations united in opposing federal legislation: Public Citizen (Joan Claybrook, Jay Angoff), U.S. PIRG (Pamela Gilbert), and Consumers Union (Linda Lipsen). Throughout the 1980s, Public Citizen also ran a state-based grassroots organizing campaign, led by organizer Craig McDonald, against the bill. Citizen Action also assigned an organizer, Don Weiner, to mobilize its state network against the legislation.

In the early 1980s, insurers began raising rates and reducing or canceling coverage, using these actions as an excuse to start pressing again for tort reform. This "liability insurance crisis" was broader than the last one, affecting municipalities, daycare centers, nonprofit groups, some manufacturers, and nearly all commercial customers, as well as physicians. Studies by the National Association of Attorneys General and several state commissions found that this "crisis" was again self-inflicted—caused by the mismanaged underwriting practices of the industry itself. Before an industry audience, one prominent insurance leader—Maurice Greenberg, chief executive officer of American International Group—complained that the industry's problems resulted from price cuts taken "to the point of absurdity" in the early 1980s.

To the public, however, insurers told a different story. On March 19, 1986, the *Journal of Commerce* reported that the Insurance Information Institute (III) was beginning a $6.5 million nationwide advertising campaign to "change the widely held perception that there is an insurance crisis to a perception of a lawsuit crisis." Around the same time, the American Tort Reform Association (ATRA) was organized. It represented hundreds of U.S. and foreign corporations who supported overhaul of civil liberty laws at the state and national levels. Several dozen ATRA members were insurance companies or insurance-related. Also in this decade, another major tort reform group emerged at the state level—American Legislative Exchange Council (ALEC). ALEC members, which included conservative state legislators and supporting corporations, drafted and pushed model bills. Its Civil Justice Task Force focused on tort reform.

During this period, tort reform proposals typically included the following restrictions on victims' rights: caps on damages (non-economic and punitive), mandatory limits on contingency fees for plaintiff lawyers, modification or elimination of joint and several liability, restrictions on lump sum payments, repeal of the collateral source rule, and relaxed liability standards. Insurers had some success promoting these proposals. During the 1985–1988 legislative sessions, nearly every state passed some sort of tort reform legislation, and a few states enacted across-the-board tort law changes.

However, consumer advocates and attorneys did win a few battles. In 1988, for example, a Florida ballot initiative to cap damages was voted down. More significantly, in the same year, largely in response to rising auto insurance rates, California voters passed Proposition 103. This initiative included a mandatory 20 percent rate rollback and required future rate increases to be approved by an elected insurance commissioner after public hearings. The effort to pass this initiative was spearheaded by Ralph Nader and his colleague in California, Harvey Rosenfield, who formed a new consumer organization dedicated to the passage of the proposition. Since then, this organization—now named Consumer Watchdog—has been one of California's leading consumer groups.

During the 1990s, liability insurance rates changed little and availability of coverage improved, undermining the tort reform movement's principal justification for state tort reform—spiking insurance rates. To keep the federal product liability bill alive, tort reform leaders changed their main rationale for legislation, now arguing that tort reform was needed to keep the United States economically competitive with other nations. In 1991, the White House Council on Competitiveness, under the leadership of Vice President Dan Quayle, embraced tort reform as a priority issue and assigned then U.S. Solicitor General Kenneth Starr the task of developing a plan to overhaul the country's civil liability laws. The "Starr Report," released in 1992, presented fifty recommendations for tort reform, which it said were necessary to "maintain America's competitiveness." Consumer groups argued that this was not the case. Although some of the recommended reforms were included in Newt Gingrich's "Contract with America," broad efforts to enact federal tort restrictions failed.

In the 1990s, though, Congress did enact some industry-specific tort legislation. In 1994, President Clinton signed into law the General Aviation Revitalization Act, which established an eighteen-year statute of repose for general aviation aircraft. In 1996, a Republican Congress passed a product liability bill. President Clinton vetoed it but told Congress to pass something he could sign. They did, and he did. That legislation immunized from liability most suppliers of raw materials and components used in the manufacture of medical implants. Clinton did veto the Private Securities Litigation Reform Act of 1995, which made it more difficult for defrauded investors to file lawsuits for securities fraud, but his veto was overridden, and the bill became law. In 1998, the president signed into law a second bill expanding the first one, the Securities Litigation Uniform Standards Act.

In 1998, new pro- and antitort reform groups were formed. The U.S. Chamber of Commerce created its Institute for Legal Reform to pursue the Chamber's tort reform agenda. In opposition to this agenda, Citizen Action's Dan Lambe organized a civil justice project in Texas and, soon thereafter, a separate organization called Texas Watch. Activists in other states—including Alabama, Kentucky, and Georgia—formed similar groups, though none as long-lasting or influential as Texas Watch. Since 2004, this group has been led by Alex Winslow and has focused on insurance, community safety, patient safety, and tort issues generally.

Also in 1998, Joanne Doroshow organized Citizens for Corporate Accountability & Individual Rights, which later changed it name to the Center for Justice & Democracy (CJ&D). Throughout the last half of the 1980s, Doroshow had been Nader's anti–tort reform and insurance industry staff attorney, then, for nine months, Public Citizen's civil justice lobbyist in Washington, D.C. Since 1998, CJ&D has been the only national consumer organization with an exclusive mission to halt and reverse the momentum for tort reform, especially at the state level.

By 2001, insurance rates, especially for doctors, were again rising. Medical and insurance lobbyists argued that rising tort system costs were largely responsible for these increases. Supported by President George W. Bush, a longtime advocate for tort reform, these lobbyists urged Congress to enact medical malpractice litigation limits. The U.S. Senate rejected related bills at least five times between 2003 and 2006, in part because of the efforts of consumer advocates, especially CJ&D. In January 2003, the group launched a medical rights bus tour, which along the way was joined by malpractice survivors and other consumer rights representatives. The bus, driven by longtime Pennsylvania community activist Gene Stilp, visited a dozen states in the East, South, and Midwest. The next month, CJ&D brought some fifty families from twenty-six states to lobby, hold press conferences, and testify at a "rump" hearing before House Judiciary Committee Democrats. In January 2005, when President Bush traveled to southern Illinois to lay out his tort reform agenda, CJ&D organized a protest, including a news conference with victims who had been denied adequate access to the courts. Despite these protests, several states enacted new tort reform laws, many of which focused on limiting the rights of patients injured by medical negligence. According to the National Conference of State Legislators, by the early teens a majority of states had some kind of limit on compensation; thirty-two states had either modified or eliminated joint and several liability; and thirty states either allowed or required periodic payments. When challenged in court, some of these measures were ruled unconstitutional by state high courts. For example, the supreme courts of Florida, Missouri, Georgia, Illinois, and Wisconsin have struck down their state caps on non-economic damages. However, the Kansas Supreme Court upheld its state cap.

Recently, tort reformers have shifted their focus from traditional tort restrictions to new efforts to restrict tort lawsuits. During President George W. Bush's administration, for instance, federal agencies began inserting language into rule "preambles"—thus avoiding any notice or comment—attempting to preempt state tort law in the event a regulated product caused injury or death. Consumer groups and attorneys fought against these preemption proposals, and in May 2009, the Obama administration stopped the practice. However, several recent U.S. Supreme Court decisions—including *Riegel v. Medtronic* (2008), which dealt with certain dangerous medical devices, and *Pliva v. Mensing* (2011), which concerned generic drugs—have resulted in the preemption of several types of state tort suits. Consumer groups asked Congress and the Food and Drug Administration (FDA) to provide relief from these decisions either through statute or regulation. A Public Citizen petition to the FDA resulted in a rule that, if finally adopted, would restore liability for the generic drug industry.

In other areas, industry has proposed federal and state legislation that would invite invasion of the privacy of asbestos victims while creating delays in compensating them. At the state level, ALEC has promoted this legislation and has helped persuade several states to enact it. ALEC has also focused much attention recently on procedural reforms. For example, its two legislative tort reform priorities in New Jersey in 2013 dealt with appeal bonds and class actions.

CJ&D has continued to lead recent consumer group efforts against these and other tort reforms. During the GM and Chrysler bankruptcies, it worked with automobile crash victims to help persuade both companies to accept liability for certain future product liability claims—relief that both companies had earlier requested from the bankruptcy court. CJ&D has also organized injured patients in opposition to medical malpractice litigation limits.

In the past decade, issues related to class actions and forced arbitration have become a major focus of the business community and, consequently, consumer advocates as well. In 2005, after years of lobbying by the U.S. Chamber of Commerce, Congress passed legislation making it more difficult for consumers to win class action lawsuits against corporations that commit fraud or violations of consumer health, safety, and environmental laws. Then in 2011, in *AT&T Mobility LLC*

v. *Concepcion*, the U.S. Supreme Court upheld class action bans, which are found in arbitration clauses buried in many consumer and employment contracts. By forcing consumers or workers with complaints into private, corporate-controlled systems to resolve disputes, these clauses take away, or severely restrict, the right of people to a trial by jury. The Supreme Court's 2013 decision, in *American Express v. Italian Colors Restaurant*, further limited the ability of groups of individuals to file class action suits.

National and state consumer groups are united in opposition to these court decisions. Their hope is that at some point in the future, Congress will restore these lost consumer remedies.

Joanne Doroshow

See also: Consumer Watchdog; Insurance Advocacy; Litigation; National Insurance Consumer Organization; Public Citizen

Further Reading

Chimerine, Lawrence and Ross Eisenbrey. 2005. *The Frivolous Case for Tort Law Change: Opponents of the Legal System Exaggerate Its Costs, Ignore Its Benefits*. Economic Policy Institute Briefing Paper No. 157 (May).

Doroshow, Joanne, and J. Robert Hunter. 2012. *Repeat Offenders: How the Insurance Industry Manufactures Crises and Harms America*. Report published by the Center for Justice & Democracy.

Haltom, William, and Michael McCann. 2004. *Distorting the Law: Politics, Media and the Litigation Crisis*. Chicago, IL: University of Chicago Press.

Mencimer, Stephanie. 2006. *Blocking the Courthouse Door: How the Republican Party and Its Corporate Allies Are Taking Away Your Right to Sue*. New York: Free Press.

TRADE UNIONS
See Labor Movement

TRANSATLANTIC CONSUMER DIALOGUE

The Transatlantic Consumer Dialogue (TACD) is a forum of more than seventy consumer organizations based in Europe and the United States that promote consumer interests in the government policymaking of the European Union (EU) and United States. The TACD develops and submits policy recommendations to the two governments so that the viewpoints and rights of consumers may be taken into account in transatlantic political and economic negotiations and agreements.

The TACD was launched by the Consumers International's (CI) regional Office for Developed and Transition Economies in September 1998 in Washington, DC. It was set up in response to the US and EU's New Transatlantic Agenda (NTA) and New Economic Partnership (NEP). The governments sought better involvement of civil society groups in transatlantic policymaking through people-to-people dialogues. The TACD, in particular, was a counterbalance to the influential Transatlantic Business Dialogue (TABD, now the Transatlantic Business Council), which was established in 1995. The TACD addresses, within the context of EU–U.S.

trade, economic and regulatory matters that affect safety, health, financial protections, information society issues, food, and intellectual property.

Membership and Governance

TACD membership is generally open to U.S. and European consumer organizations working on the regional, national, and international level that are independent of business and political interests. The TACD started with approximately 60 member organizations in 1998, two-thirds of which were European-based and one-third of which were U.S.-based. Since that time, membership has increased to fifty European and twenty-seven U.S. organizations, with three "observer members" from outside Europe and the United States.

At the time of the TACD's formation, European members agreed that such a forum was desirable, but several U.S. organizations sympathetic to Ralph Nader were opposed. Nader argued that the government sponsorship of the TACD would put the forum in the grip of governments and prevent it from advocating independent consumer viewpoints. After a heated debate and at the end of the inaugural meeting, those organizations close to Nader reluctantly agreed to join and were represented on the TACD Steering Committee. Over time, this organizational divide disappeared, and consumer groups formed under the mantle of Nader have continued to be a part of the TACD leadership.

Several of the TACD's members are national consumer organizations that engage in a variety of consumer issues and publish consumer information that reaches a wide readership. Others members focus on single issues, such as financial services, privacy, digital democracy, food and nutrition, and intellectual property. U.S. members include all the major national organizations, including Consumers Union, the Consumer Federation of America, USPIRG, and Public Citizen. EU members include the European umbrella consumer organization BEUC: The European Consumer Organisation, the European Association for the Coordination of Consumer Representation (ANEC), and a wide range of national consumer organizations from many European Union Member States.

Experts from member organizations participate in the TACD through a number of issue-based policy committees, which can vary according to emerging priorities. In 2014 there were five committees: food, intellectual property, information society, financial services, and nanotechnology. Each committee is co-chaired by one U.S. and one EU member. The committees develop background briefings, consensus policy recommendations, and other advocacy materials.

The TACD's two-decade-long longevity and its continuing ability to advocate for consumers as a unified transatlantic entity are a testament to the profound ability of electronic communication to facilitate the work of civil society groups. All the TACD members easily and inexpensively share information and participate in its iterative and consensus-based policymaking process via listservs, emails, and telephone conferences.

The TACD is governed by a steering committee, which consists of eight members, four delegated by European members and four elected by U.S. member organizations. The steering committee decides on the strategic direction of TACD—a task in which it is supported by the chairs of the policy committees.

The TACD is currently funded by grants from the European Union as well as the Open Society Foundation (an international network of offices created by philanthropist George Soros). The latter specifically funds the intellectual property work with an advocate based in Brussels. Consumers International is the recipient of these grants, and its London office hosts the secretariat of the TACD, which currently consists of a part time coordinator and a senior policy advisor. The U.S. government contributed funds at the outset, but this funding was discontinued after a few years.

Activities

The TACD Policy Committees continuously prepare and update proposed resolutions as policy issues arise and evolve. These proposed resolutions are circulated several times to secure consensus on positions and language among TACD members. When finalized, they are communicated to European and U.S. policymakers. These resolutions form the basis of ongoing TACD advocacy.

Since its founding, the TACD has issued a wide range of recommendations. Issues of privacy and data security for consumers have ranked high on the organization's agenda from the beginning. Over the years, the TACD has urged better protection of privacy and adapted its recommendations to encompass the new security standards after 9/11 and the challenges arising with new technologies such as radio-frequency identification (RFID) and increasingly powerful mobile devices. With respect to the Internet, net neutrality (the principle that Internet service providers and governments should treat all data equally) has been a higher priority for the TACD.

Several additional issues championed by the TACD involve health and safety. TACD has argued constantly for increased access to medicines in developing countries and has promoted trade agreements that take into account the threat posed by HIV to many countries, especially less developed ones. A strong focus has also been on labeling genetically modified organisms (GMOs) to inform and protect consumers. In recent years, the TACD has demonstrated a strong interest in tackling diet-related diseases by calling for limits on food marketing and providing adequate labeling.

In recent years, the TACD has constantly offered its input on issues of intellectual property rights, trade in services, and the provision of public services. Addressing the global financial crisis, the TACD has also called for better consumer protection in financial services. The TACD's current focus is on the Transatlantic Trade and Investment Partnership (TTIP). These ongoing EU–U.S. free trade negotiations are centered on so-called regulatory convergence and will have a major effect on consumer and other protections. At a level that transcends any particular issue, the TACD promotes more transparent and open procedures in international trade negotiations in order to secure and enhance input from consumer organizations and other civil society groups.

The TACD holds an annual meeting attended by member organizations and officials from both governments where policy positions are presented. These meetings are held alternately in Washington, D.C., and Brussels. Throughout the year there are also face-to-face meetings between TACD member organizations and government representatives. Advocacy and face-to-face meetings with the two governments in between annual meetings, the TACD's media activities, and its alliances with other non-governmental organizations have intensified since the initiation of the TTIP negotiations.

Overall Impact

The business interests that enjoy such a powerful role in determining policy in individual nations are equally powerful in transatlantic decision making. While the TACD has sought since its inception to have parity with the Transatlantic Business Dialogue in access and policymaking, the TACD argues that this goal is far from achieved. While governments structure some meetings to equally represent consumer and business interests, structural barriers to parity remain. A case in point is the launch of the U.S.–EU free trade agreement negotiations (TTIP). The U.S. trade negotiation stakeholder input process relies largely on an advisory committee system that provides preferential access to a wide array of business interests with no parallel opportunity within that system for the consumer interest.

An attempt to provide parity occurred when the governments formed the Transatlantic Economic Council (TEC) in 2007. The Business and Consumer Dialogues were both appointed to an Advisory Committee. However, the TACD argues that the TEC was unable to organize itself and operate in an efficient way, and it presently seems to be inactive. The working groups formed by the two governments in connection with the TEC, however, though not transparent, seem to have arrived at various policy positions without the participation of TACD.

Despite disappointment regarding the dominance of business input in transatlantic policy discussions, there have been several positive results from the creation of the TACD. Not surprisingly, it has fostered understanding and cooperation among consumer organizations in the EU and United States. Moreover, it has promoted stronger relations among U.S.-based consumer organizations. Though for many years consumer organizations in the EU have had EU-wide policy coordination and advocacy through BEUC, there had been no parallel development in the United States. The TACD has served to bring together the U.S. organizations within TACD, both in a formal sense and as a result of collegial policy development over the years. In addition, the TACD has also facilitated meaningful transfer of expertise among its members and created a resource for any member seeking more information and support than is available within its own organization.

When the EU reached out to help create a consumer dialogue, it was seeking structured input into the transatlantic policymaking process. That was, without a doubt, a positive decision. What consumers needed from that process was a TACD role with parity with business interests. By that measure, the wheel of progress has turned a bit, but much more needs to be done.

Rhoda H. Karpatkin, Christian Thorun[*]

See also: BEUC: The European Consumer Organisation; Consumers International

Further Reading

Transatlantic Consumer Dialogue. 2014. www.TACD.org.

TRUTH IN SAVINGS ADVOCACY

After passage of the 1968 Truth in Lending Act, which required annual percentage rate (APR) and other standardized loan disclosures, one of its champions, Richard L. D. Morse, worked tirelessly for more than twenty years to pass a companion Truth in Savings Act, finally succeeding in 1991. Morse, a longtime professor and chairman of the Department of Family Economics at Kansas State University, had been appointed a founding member of President John Kennedy's Consumer Advisory Council and chair of its consumer credit committee. He continued to serve on the council under President Lyndon Johnson.

A truth in savings proposal, shaped by Morse, was first introduced by Representative William Roy (D-KS) and Senator Vance Hartke (D-IN) in 1971. As Morse explained in a 1971 paper: "The rationale for standardized disclosure of consumer savings terms is . . . premised on the right of consumers to be supplied the information needed to make informed choices, the need of consumers for a standardized terminology essential for them to comparative shop efficiently for savings services and the responsibility to make performance checks on their savings accounts."

Over the next twenty years, Morse testified before Congress and state legislatures on numerous occasions in favor of the reform. He also published several guides to interest calculation, including "Cents-ible Interest" (1984) and, after passage of the act, "Truth in Savings with Cents-ible Interest and Morse Rate Tables" (1992), a guide to the new law. In 1978, the New York legislature passed truth in savings legislation, and in 1985, the Massachusetts legislature did the same.

Morse had worked with organizations, including the Consumer Federation of America (CFA), to gain support for federal truth in savings legislation. And in the early 1970s, House and Senate bills had been introduced and considered. But it was not until after the mid-1980s phaseout of interest rate restrictions, after passage of the 1980 Depository Institutions Deregulation and Monetary Control Act, that support for a truth in savings act began to grow. After this deregulation, financial institutions began to more aggressively advertise their interest rates and otherwise promote and differentiate their accounts. The 1980 law also expanded nationwide a New England experiment in paying interest on Negotiable Orders of Withdrawal (NOW) checking accounts.

These savings changes drew the attention of consumer advocates, as did new deceptive bank practices on other accounts, such as aggressively marketing

---

[*]We thank Anna Fielder for her thoughtful comments.

checking accounts as free even when an average or minimum balance had to be maintained to avoid a monthly service fee. Yet what galvanized support for truth in savings legislation was the revelation by CFA and U.S. PIRG surveys of the new and widespread banking practice of paying interest on only a portion of savings deposits.

Before deregulation, all banks and savings and loans offered accounts with interest at the highest rates allowed by Federal Reserve Board Regulation Q. But following deregulation, many institutions began not paying interest on the portion of deposits—7 percent—that regulators required to be held in "reserves," while at the same time advertising paying interest on 100 percent of these deposits. Morse's original interest rate tables had pointed out slight differences in total interest paid due to allowable use of several calculation and compounding methods and leap year corrections. But this "7 percent deception" dwarfed the differences caused by use of various calculation methods.

In 1989, Morse contacted Ed Mierzwinski, a new consumer advocate at U.S. PIRG, who agreed to investigate the matter and renew Morse's efforts in Washington. Annual bank fee surveys by U.S. PIRG, as well as by CFA, highlighted the changing bank practices and attracted the attention of consumer reporters. Morse's work on savings disclosures had earlier been featured by leading consumer finance journalist Jane Bryant Quinn, but other reporters and columnists now also began writing about bank savings deceptions.

In the late 1980s, Congress passed legislation to clean up a liquidity and confidence crisis brought on by reckless savings-and-loan (S&L) mortgage loan practices. One way that the S&Ls fueled their need for cash to make risky home loans was by deceptive national advertising to attract small savers to take out certificates of deposit at rates that were higher than the amount actually paid. Congress first enacted the emergency Federal Financial Institutions Reform, Recovery and Enforcement Act of 1989 to bail out the savings and loan sector. The Truth in Savings Act was then incorporated into the Federal Deposit Insurance Corporation Improvement Act of 1991, a follow-up reform to that emergency law.

The Truth in Savings Act established Morse's long-sought annual percentage yield (ASY) disclosure, eliminated the use of "free" on any account subject to a balance requirement, and required that a schedule of all savings and checking account fees be made available to any shopper "on request." The law, however, did permit other fees, such as for ATM card use, for receiving monthly statements, and for overdrafts. On passage of the legislation, Quinn, in her nationally syndicated column, wrote, "On the Washington Mall, savers should erect a statue to Richard L. D. Morse."

Legislation in 1996 sponsored by Senator Richard Shelby (R-AL) established a 2002 sunset provision on the Truth in Savings Act's private right of action—the ability of consumers to sue to enforce the law. Its repeal may have helped lead to the growth of controversial "Overdraft Protection" features on checking accounts. Banks offered not to "bounce" overdrafted checks in return for a "courtesy overdraft fee" usually ranging between $15 to $30.

Banks were encouraged to expand this service by regulator indifference and even a ruling that overdraft protection was, not a loan subject to the more stringent Truth in Lending Act, but a service subject to fee disclosure under the Truth in Savings Act. Consumer problems grew as banks encouraged customers to use debit cards instead of cash for routine small purchases, increasing multiple daily overdrafts. Consumers who purchased a cup of coffee on an overdrawn account were charged a fee that was much larger than the price of the cup. In 2010, regulators addressed this issue with a rule subjecting overdraft protection products to an affirmative opt-in requirement.

Since the passage of the Truth in Savings Act, U.S. PIRG has used regular national bank surveys to monitor compliance with this law. In 2008, the Government Accounting Office used PIRG's secret shopper methodology to confirm PIRG's typical finding that personnel in about 20 percent of bank branches visited failed to provide fee schedules on request. In similar reports, U.S. PIRG and the Pew Charitable Trusts have brought this and other account disclosure problems to the attention of the Consumer Financial Protection Bureau and urged the bureau to require all banks to post all fees and contractual provisions in downloadable machine-readable format so consumer groups, and reporters, can more easily compare these fees and provisions.

Edmund Mierzwinski

See also: Public Interest Research Groups

Further Reading

Morse, Richard L. D. 1997. "Savings Protections." In Stephen Brobeck, ed., *Encyclopedia of the Consumer Movement.* Santa Barbara, CA: ABC-CLIO.

Morse, Richard L. D. 1992. *Truth in Savings.* Manhattan, KS: Family Economics Trust Press.

TURN

Toward Utility Rate Normalization (TURN) was created in 1973 as a 501(c)(3) nonprofit organization to advocate fair rates and high-quality service for residential and small-business customers of California's large investor-owned utilities. For more than four decades, it has been the most active consumer intervenor before the California Public Utilities Commission (CPUC). Known by its acronym, TURN now stands for The Utility Reform Network.

TURN was founded by Sylvia Siegel who initially operated it out of her home with support from volunteers. Siegel's extensive knowledge of utility issues, mastery of legal strategies, sharp tongue, and quick wit helped establish TURN as a highly visible spokesperson for California utility consumers. When she retired in 1989, she was succeeded by Audrie Krause, who had covered utility issues as a reporter for the *Fresno Bee*. In 1995, Krause was succeeded by Nettie Hogue, who had previously worked for Consumers Union and for the California Department of Insurance. Since 2008, Mark Toney, a sociology PhD who has served as an organizer and leader of reform-minded nonprofits, has been executive director. For more than three decades until his appointment to the CPUC in 2011, attorney Michel Florio oversaw the organization's legal advocacy.

TURN is governed by a volunteer board of directors that meets quarterly. For the past two decades, it has operated with an annual budget of around $2 million and a staff of about twelve. Funding comes from membership contributions, attorney fee awards, and foundation grants.

TURN provides information and assistance to consumers through outreach and interventions in individual cases. However, the organization's primary activity has been intervening in hundreds of energy and telecommunications proceedings at the CPUC. In 1975, for example, TURN convinced the CPUC to adopt a conservation rate structure now commonly referred to as baseline rates. In 1982, the organization worked with environmentalists and gas producers to defeat a plan for a $3.9 billion liquefied natural gas receiving terminal. In the mid-1980s, TURN won safeguards for small gas consumers threatened by deregulation. In 1992, the organization convinced the CPUC to adopt consumer privacy safeguards related to caller identification services. The next year, it successfully litigated a complaint against Pacific Bell for imposing late fees on customers who had paid their bills on time. The phone company was required to pay $49 million in customer refunds and fines.

In recent years, TURN has continued its successful advocacy. In 1999, it helped convince the CPUC to disallow ratepayer subsidies for a PG&E nuclear plant. In 2002, it helped persuade the CPUC to require electric utilities to increase their use of renewable fuels. In 2004, it helped convince the commission to provide Family Energy Rate Assistance. In 2007, it successfully challenged unfair utility shutoff policies.

Apart from its interventions at the CPUC, TURN has fought successfully to protect utility consumers in other venues. It helped persuade the state legislature to protect baseline electric wages rates as electric companies were being deregulated. In 2010, it worked with other advocates to persuade a majority of voters to reject PG&E's Proposition 16, which would have restricted municipalities from organizing or expanding publicly owned electric services.

Stephen Brobeck

See also: State and Local Consumer Advocacy Groups; State Utility Advocacy

Further Reading

Escobedo, Duwayne. 1991. "CPUC Gets Mixed Reviews for Intervenor Programs." *Public Utilities Fortnightly* 128 (August 15): 9.
Keppel, Bruce. 1989. "Turning Point." *Los Angeles Times* (July 29): IV, 1.

U

U.S. CONSUMER PROTECTION AGENCY

In 1978, a fierce nine-year battle over the creation of a federal consumer protection agency ended with a victory for business opponents over consumer groups and sympathizers. During this period, the proposed agency was referred to variously as Consumer Protection Agency, Agency for Consumer Protection, Agency for Consumer Advocacy, and Office of Consumer Representation. This article will refer to it as Consumer Protection Agency (CPA).

The effort to establish a federal CPA evolved out of an attempt by Senator Estes Kefauver, a Tennessee Democrat, to create a cabinet-level department of consumer affairs in 1959. Under his proposal the department would be the focal point in the federal government for matters pertaining to and promoting the interest of consumers.

Kefauver was unsuccessful, and after his death, Congressman Benjamin S. Rosenthal, a New York Democrat, took over. Rosenthal also was unsuccessful in creating a cabinet-level department, but the idea evolved into an attempt to create an independent consumer protection agency. Ralph Nader was instrumental in this shift, because he believed strongly in a consumer advocacy agency that would monitor federal consumer protection activities and represent consumer interests before federal regulatory agencies and executive departments.

Nader's views were generally shared by other consumer advocates and organizations, including Esther Peterson, President Lyndon Johnson's first special assistant for consumer affairs; Consumers Union; and the Consumer Federation of America (CFA). As a result, Rosenthal dropped the department idea and, in association with leading consumer advocates, developed a proposal to establish a consumer protection agency.

At the time, consumer advocacy had bipartisan support. Congresswoman Florence P. Dwyer of New Jersey, ranking Republican member of the House Committee on Government Operations, introduced a bill at about the same time Rosenthal did. Her proposal would not create an agency, but rather expand the function of the Office of Consumer Affairs in the executive office of the president. The Nixon administration also introduced a bill providing for consumer advocacy, among other functions, which would assign advocacy functions to a consumer protection division in the U.S. Department of Justice.

From 1969 to 1978 the proposals varied, but several provisions were common to most of the bills. First, a new, independent agency was to be created, headed by a director appointed by the president. This agency would have no regulatory functions and would be independent in the manner of the Federal Trade Commission.

Second, the major proposed function of the agency was to represent consumer interests before federal agencies and courts. In formal hearings the agency would be authorized to intervene as a party, if necessary, to represent the interest of consumers. The agency also was to be authorized to participate in informal proceedings.

Third, the proposed agency would have authority to represent consumer interests in federal civil court proceedings involving review or enforcement of federal agency actions that substantially affected consumer interests. Besides participating in suits brought by others, the proposed agency would be empowered to initiate lawsuits to review agency decisions if a substantial consumer interest were involved.

Fourth, the proposed agency would act as a clearinghouse for complaints of individual consumers against business enterprises. The agency would be authorized not to force businesses to respond to such complaints, but rather to inform the business and relevant federal and state agencies.

The first serious effort to create a federal consumer protection agency began in 1969, at a time when the consumer movement was gaining strength. This effort continued for nearly a decade until early 1978, when supporters became convinced that they could not succeed.

During much of this period, the bill enjoyed substantial bipartisan support with leading proponents coming from both major parties. In the 91st Congress (1969–1970), the Senate passed a CPA bill by a vote of 74–4, and the House Government Operations Committee approved legislation 31–4, but the House Rules Committee failed to clear a bill for House consideration. In the 92nd Congress (1971–1972), the House passed a CPA bill by a vote of 344–14, but the effort in the Senate was thwarted by a filibuster after a cloture motion failed to get sufficient votes. In the 93rd Congress (1973–1974), the House passed a CPA bill by a vote of 239–94, but again a Senate vote was blocked by a filibuster after a cloture motion failed.

In the 94th Congress (1975–1976), the Senate voted 61–28 to create a CPA, and the House voted 208–199 for legislation. However, the latter vote was not a large enough margin to override an expected veto by President Ford, and the effort was abandoned during this session. At the inception of the 95th Congress (1977–1978), in the first year of President Carter's term, the White House sent a strong measure to Congress supporting the creation of a CPA, but for the first time, the House defeated the bill, 227–189, thus ending the nine-year effort.

Until the arrival of Carter, CPA proposals did not receive strong support from the White House. The Nixon administration reflected ambivalence to the agency. Although the Ford administration opposed the most serious congressional proposals, it did direct the seventeen departments and agencies under its control to establish consumer representation offices.

With relatively few exceptions, major U.S. corporations and business associations vigorously opposed the CPA proposal. The legislation was favored by consumer organizations, organized labor, various environmental and other nonprofit organizations, and a few major corporations. Ralph Nader was a leading spokesman in the campaign, and he was joined by Esther Peterson and officials from

CFA and Consumers Union, who built a coalition of senior citizen, religious, and community groups, and state and local officials.

In testimony before Congress, Nader identified ninety-five companies that supported creation of the CPA. Among them were large firms such as Atlantic Richfield, Connecticut General Life Insurance, Gulf and Western, Levi Strauss, Mobil Oil, and Montgomery Ward. However, the U.S. business community was largely united in their opposition to the agency. The three most influential national business organizations—the U.S. Chamber of Commerce, National Association of Manufacturers, and Business Roundtable—as well as the two most powerful small business associations—the National Federation of Independent Business and the National Small Business Association—helped lead this opposition through an ad hoc coalition named the Consumer Issues Working Group (CIWG). This coalition represented the first highly active, broad-based alliance of business groups in the post–World War II period that sought to defeat consumer legislation that it perceived as being threatening.

The success of this coalition in defeating legislation to create a CPA reflected several important factors. In the early 1970s, this group fought hard to keep legislation from being approved by both houses of Congress, at times barely succeeding. But in the post-Watergate era, with increased distrust of the federal government, the CIWG took advantage of the loss of enthusiasm within Congress for creating a new federal agency. This distrust, which President Carter capitalized on in his campaign for president, made it difficult for him to persuade wavering members that they should support the agency.

The defeat of the CPA legislation also reflected, to an extent, the ineffectiveness of the coalition supporting it. One CPA supporter, representative Richard Bolling, a Democrat from Missouri, said that the consumer coalition badly overplayed its hand and tried to bully legislators into voting for poorly written bills. It did not help the coalition that members sometimes disagreed sharply about the bills and legislative tactics.

The business coalition, however, was aided by their effective deployment of superior resources. Not only did this coalition organize broad business opposition to the bill, but it also employed relatively sophisticated lobbying, opinion surveys, and campaign contributions to persuade legislators. What business learned here was later applied to other legislative battles including the successful effort to weaken the Federal Trade Commission in the late 1970s.

George Schwartz

See also: Congressional Consumer Advocacy; Legislative Advocacy

Further Reading

Demkovich, Linda E. 1977. "Even a White House Pep Rally May Not Save the Agency." *National Journal* 9 (June 25): 996+.

Schoenfeld, Andrea F. 1970. "Bill to Create Advocacy Unit Will Be Revived in New Congress." *National Journal* 2 (December 19): 2,771+.

Schwartz, George. 1979. "The Successful Fight against a Federal Consumer Protection Agency." *MSU Business Topics* (summer): 45–56.

U.S. PUBLIC INTEREST RESEARCH GROUP
See Public Interest Research Groups

UNITED KINGDOM CONSUMER MOVEMENT
The story of the consumer movement in the UK is one of both consistency and almost constant organizational change. The consistency—at least in institutional presence, and also in the extent to which it has been a training ground for many British consumer campaigners—has been provided by the product testing organization Which? (originally called Consumers' Association but rebranded with the name of its main magazine in 2004). The repeated organizational change relates to the revolving cast of statutory or government-supported consumer bodies, some focused on individual industry sectors.

Consumers' Association (CA) and *Which?* magazine were established in 1957, closely following the model of Consumers Union (CU) in the United States—a self-funded organization selling its own magazine, purchasing test samples on the open market, and prohibiting manufacturers from using test results or ratings in their marketing, with no government or industry funding. An Anglo-American couple living in London, Dorothy and Ray Goodman, were subscribers to *Consumer Reports* and saw the potential in a British version. Michael Young, later Lord Young of Dartington and perhaps Britain's most prolific twentieth century social entrepreneur, was the driving force behind the new venture and became its first chair. Supported by an initial grant from CU, CA immediately exceeded expectations by attracting 10,000 members in its first week. Critically, the first *Which?* editor, Eirlys Roberts, emphasized that test results should not only be impartial but also communicated simply. This style soon became one of the organization's hallmarks. The "best buy" logo was pioneered in 1958 and soon became part of the national vocabulary.

By 1975 CA member-subscribers rose to 700,000, and by 1990 the number exceeded 1 million. Tougher economic circumstances in the mid-1990s led enrollment to fall back to around 800,000. By then, CA had expanded its range of products to include separate magazines aimed at gardeners, vacation travelers, people interested in health issues, doctors, and children. It also published a wide range of consumer advice books, the most prominent of which was the *Good Food Guide*, which rated the best British restaurants. CA also ran a legal advice service.

From its early days, CA aimed not just to report on the quality of products but to expose business practices that acted against the consumer interest and to drive improvements. The campaigning side of the organization had some notable successes over the years, including influencing key pieces of consumer protection legislation, with legal director David Tench particularly prominent. It also highlighted serious product safety issues. CA increasingly focused on services and shone a spotlight, not only on failures of individual firms or practitioners, but also on entire markets that were acting against the consumer interest (e.g., through a lack of competition), with policy director Stephen Locke as an influential advocate in a range of sectors. Financial services and food policy are two areas where it has had sustained influence.

The appointment of an experienced, energetic campaigner, Sheila McKechnie (later Dame Sheila), as director in the mid-1990s reinforced the organization's campaigning focus and increased its use of techniques more traditionally associated with lobbying by NGOs. Following Dame Sheila's untimely death in 2004, Peter Vicary Smith—much more commercially oriented, albeit with a not-for-profit-sector background—became the new chief executive. Backed by two outstanding senior campaigners in Nick Stace and then Richard Lloyd (both with experience as special advisers to the previous prime minister), Peter Vicary Smith has overseen a sustained period of both strong commercial success and enhanced policy profile. Which? now has 1.4 million subscriptions to its products, a 74 percent increase over ten years and, including 646,000 subscribing to Which? magazine, the highest figure since 1995. The organization has developed a range of new fee-based and free services, including Which? Mortgage Advisers, Which? University and Which? Local. It also established a subscription magazine in India, *Right Choice*, with a small but growing readership.

The past two decades have also been a period in which major changes were made to longstanding business policies at Which? The use of a prize drawing as the primary marketing tool (long disliked by many staff and members) was finally terminated. The *Good Food Guide* was sold to the upscale supermarket chain Waitrose in 2013. Perhaps most significantly of all, in 2002, Which? started to allow recipients of a "best buy" rating to use this designation in their marketing, along with a Which? logo—an action that in previous years would have more likely resulted in a solicitor's letter. It also established the annual Which? Awards and now gives best buy ratings for some manufacturers' entire product line, not just individual products.

Which? has for many years been a lead player in (and funder of) both BEUC: The European Consumer Organisation and its global counterpart, Consumers International. It has also sustained its practical commitment to RICA, the Research Institute for Consumer Affairs, established by Michael Young in 1963. Initially a more academic policy body sitting within CA, RICA quickly adopted a practical focus on the needs of older and disabled consumers. RICA was spun off from CA in 1991 but today still receives a grant from Which? and has a joint work program with it. Its wider impact also included long-term support for the Campaign for Freedom of Information, which after years of lobbying secured the Freedom of Information Act 2000.

Although constituted as a charity for public benefit and justifiably bristling at suggestions that it is only interested in affluent consumers, Which? has, in reality, tended to focus only intermittently on more vulnerable people and has drifted in and out of many subject areas as it has sought to keep the consumer flag flying on a wide range of topics. It has also been focused predominantly on England and Wales, with few resources dedicated to Scotland (although it set up a small office in Edinburgh in 2001) and none to Northern Ireland. As a result, there has been a need for one or more consumer bodies to provide sustained policy input on sometimes low-profile but important topics, and to ensure that consumers in all the nations of the UK are represented.

One such organization was the National Consumer Council (NCC), set up in 1975. Again, Michael Young was a prime mover and its first chair, with the Scottish and Welsh Consumer Councils (SCC and WCC) forming autonomous bodies within the wider organization. Unusually for a taxpayer-funded public body, the NCC was established as a private company rather than by statute, with the result that it enjoyed much greater freedom of action than many other such bodies. Loosely overseen by the business department in central government, with council members appointed by government through an objective and independent process, its role was defined by the constitution of the company. This gave it a particular remit in relation to vulnerable consumers and stated only that it could not get involved in disputes between employees and employers or their representatives. Nor could it handle individual consumer complaints. The NCC had very few powers, as well as more limited resources than CA, so it had to succeed through the quality of its research, the force of its argument, and the strength of its relationships. This proved particularly successful in areas such as consumer protection legislation; public, financial and legal services reform (the latter especially in Scotland); and public utilities, with Dame Deirdre Hutton acting as an especially influential chair of SCC and then NCC at the turn of this century.

There were other NCC successes. One was its strong involvement in the creation and design of the ombudsmen schemes for financial services and support for the Plain English movement. Its articulation of the consumer dimension in public services, including the use of consumer performance indicators to measure delivery to users, was in many ways ahead of its time but is now part of conventional wisdom across the UK political landscape. SCC's mid-1980s work on opening up airline competition between Edinburgh and London was highly influential and arguably led directly to deregulation across Europe.

For a number of years, NCC ran the Consumer Congress, an independent association with a diverse membership of more than 100 organizations and an annual conference that brought them together. These included the National Federation of Consumer Groups (NFCG), which was established in 1963 and in its heyday had more than fifty local groups. NFCG is now called the National Consumer Federation and has a greatly reduced number of local groups, although new leadership has sparked some resurgence in its activities and re-established the Consumer Congress.

In 1985, government established the General Consumer Council for Northern Ireland (CCNI), with a similar economywide policy focus to NCC but also a complaints-handling remit. Over the years, CCNI has gained specific responsibilities in transport, water, energy, and financial sectors. It was scheduled to take on a new responsibility for postal services in April 2014.

There has long been representation of consumers in the utilities. Consumer councils or consultative committees were established by government for coal, electricity, gas, and rail from 1946 to 1948 period, with one for the post office put in place in 1969. The arrangements for gas and electricity changed in the late 1980s when these industries were privatized, with a single energy consumer body, Energywatch, then being established in 2000, with its postal equivalent, Postwatch, being set up in 2001. A single rail consumer body, Passenger Focus, began in 2006. Its role was extended to cover buses and trams in England and Wales (outside London) in 2010. Proposals for it to take on responsibility for air transport were, however, not adopted by government, and the planned merger of Passenger Focus with a similar body, London Travelwatch, was also abandoned.

In October 2008, a new statutory body, Consumer Focus, was created by merging Energywatch, Postwatch, and the National Consumer Council. The new body's structure and funding reflected the history of the predecessor organizations. It covered all consumer policy issues, regardless of sector, was funded by the British government, but also had specific statutory roles relating to energy in Great Britain and postal services in the UK. These latter functions were funded by industry levies collected by the relevant industry regulator. In practice, authority within Consumer Focus were highly devolved, with Consumer Focus Scotland and Consumer Focus Wales being far stronger than the "territorial committees" described in legislation. Alongside policy functions, Consumer Focus provided some casework support for vulnerable consumers of energy and postal services, and it continued the work of Energywatch and Postwatch on small businesses as consumers, which had previously been avoided by NCC.

Although the creation of Consumer Focus was an attempt by the then Department for Trade and Industry to create a well-coordinated approach to consumer representation, the new body did not incorporate the Consumer Council for Water (or its Scottish counterpart) or Passenger Focus, both of which remained independent and continue to be. This arrangement was widely attributed to disputes between the relevant government departments and lobbying by the bodies themselves, particularly the Consumer Council for Water. Consumer Focus did, however, subsequently gain responsibility for water in Scotland.

In October 2010, the Coalition Government under Prime Minister David Cameron proposed to close Consumer Focus as part of its "bonfire" of public bodies. He proposed turning Consumer Focus into a "Regulated Industries Unit" located within Citizens Advice and Citizens Advice Scotland—membership bodies for a network of independent advice agencies that are in part publicly funded and have a strong record on some consumer policy issues, especially around the welfare system, access to justice, and other public services. This restructuring was meant to create more coherence in what was generally accepted to be a complex landscape of consumer protection arrangements, and it also fitted with a "Big Society" narrative in which power moves away from politicians and government and toward local citizens and their voluntary organizations.

At the time of writing, it is unclear how a more centralized UK consumer policy body will be governed by two separate host organizations, one covering England and Wales and the other Scotland, nor the extent to which Consumer Futures (the new name for Consumer Focus) will be wholly absorbed into these bodies. For practical purposes, the staff of Consumer Futures will sit within Citizens Advice, while the Extra Help Unit (which provides casework support for vulnerable consumers) will be part of Citizens Advice Scotland. Consumer Futures will have substantially more research and policy funding for its regulated industries work than the Citizens Advice Service has for all its other policy work put together. Alongside these different consumer bodies sit a variety of consumer panels and other advisory bodies set up by sector-specific regulators—for example, in financial services, legal services, air transport, rail, communications, energy, and food safety. Some but not all of these panels are statutory, and their degree of independence and scope can vary, but, in effect, all act as a "critical friend" to the regulator, and most include members with a Which? or NCC/Consumer Focus background. Some panels have their own secretariat and research budgets. The regulators Ofwat (water and sewage) and Ofgem (gas and electricity) have also acted to require or incentivize regulated monopoly businesses to establish their own effective consumer engagement arrangements, including consumer panels for each water company.

One legal power made available by the UK government to consumer bodies is particularly noteworthy. The 2002 Enterprise Act allows bodies representing consumers to apply for the ability to make "super-complaints" to regulators when they think that a market, or an aspect of a market, is failing consumers. The relevant regulator is required to consider each super-complaint and give a reasoned response within a specified time period. Successful super-complaints have been made by Which?, Citizens Advice, the National Consumer Council, and Consumer Focus, mainly on financial services issues but even including the price of phone calls from prisons.

No description of the consumer movement in the UK would be complete without mention of the remarkable success of the energetic and ubiquitous Martin Lewis and his Money Saving Expert (MSE) website. The numbers are startling. His weekly email offering tips on the best deals is sent to more than 9 million email addresses. The MSE website has advice guides on a wide range of topics as well as Forums for which more than 1 million consumers are registered. The site gets around 11 million visitors a month, and its template letters (for example, to reclaim bank charges) have been downloaded around 13 million times. All this is funded by paid-for "affiliate links" to businesses mentioned in MSE guides, which are added after the guides are written. The success of the MSE service, as well as Martin's Lewis's personal profile, has led to growing policy input, particularly in areas such as financial education and payday loans.

Philip Cullum

See also: BEUC: The European Consumer Organisation; Consumers International

Further Reading

Briggs, Asa. 2001. *Michael Young: Social Entrepreneur.* London, UK: Palgrave Macmillan.
Consumer Focus. 2011. *Through Consumers' Eyes: Meeting Tomorrow's Challenges.* London, UK: Consumer Focus, December. www.consumerfocus.org.uk/publications/through-consumers-eyes-meeting-tomorrows-challenges.
Consumer Futures. 2014. *Building on the Past, Focused on the Future,* March 28. www.consumerfutures.org.uk/reports/building-on-the-past-focused-on-the-future.
Consumers International. 1995. *Balancing the Scales.* Part 1: *Consumer Protection in Sweden and the United Kingdom.* London, UK: Consumers International.

Hilton, Matthew. 2003. *Consumerism in 20th Century Britain: The Search for a Historical Movement.* Cambridge, UK: Cambridge University Press.

Roberts, Eirlys. 1982. *Which? 25: Consumers Association, 1957–82.* London, UK: Consumers Association.

UNITED NATIONS GUIDELINES FOR CONSUMER PROTECTION

In 1985, the UN General Assembly adopted the Guidelines for Consumer Protection. Adoption of the guidelines was the culmination of a campaign by consumer activists from around the world to establish an ambitious and universal set of standards for government consumer policy. The original guidelines were organized into seven areas. Building on the concept of "consumer rights" articulated by U.S. President John F. Kennedy in 1962, activists quickly translated the guidelines into a list of essential consumer rights. The guidelines were revised in 1999 to recognize the importance of the natural environment, and negotiations are currently underway to update the guidelines again by 2015 to keep them relevant to changing technological and economic circumstances.

The campaign by consumer activists for the guidelines emerged from their earlier efforts to protect consumers via the action of the UN and its various international bodies. Consumer groups perceived that the expansion of global commerce was proceeding faster than the ability of consumers to understand new products and services and more speedily than the ability of governments to control commerce in these goods. The result, according to activists, was the sale of dangerous products, including the "dumping" on unsuspecting consumers in less developed nations of products banned or severely restricted in more developed countries. For example, in 1977, the U.S. government banned a carcinogenic flame retardant used on children's sleepwear, but U.S. companies exported their remaining inventory for more than a year. Additional examples that stirred campaigners involved pesticides and pharmaceutical products deemed unsafe in markets such as the United States, the United Kingdom, and Germany. To address the difficulty of one country learning of another's product bans and restrictions, consumer advocates successfully lobbied the United Nations to create a list of products whose consumption or sale had been banned, withdrawn, severely restricted, or not approved by governments. The first such listed was circulated in 1983, and updated versions are created every two or three years.

Another issue that galvanized consumer activists into action at the United Nations was the aggressive marketing of infant milk formula in less developed countries, resulting in 1981 in the World Health Organization (an arm of the UN) adopting the International Code of Marketing of Breast-Milk Substitutes. The code tries to prevent mothers from being discouraged from breastfeeding and ensure that any breast milk substitutes are used safely.

The campaigns waged by consumer activists for UN action revealed how greatly countries varied in the degree of consumer protection provided to their citizens. The International Organization of Consumers Unions (IOCU) therefore made it a priority to convince the UN General Assembly to adopt universal guidelines for consumer protection. At the UN, IOCU had Category I status, which gives it the rights to "sit at the table" and to speak like a national delegation, but not to vote on issues.

The goal of the guidelines was to set out a comprehensive framework for governments in both rich and poor countries to use as a blueprint for protecting their consumers in the global marketplace. The idea immediately triggered fierce opposition. Large transnational corporations and the U.S. delegation charged that guidelines would make the UN a "global nanny" and claimed that a consumer's best protection is a free market. Esther Peterson (former consumer advisor to U.S. presidents Lyndon Johnson and Jimmy Carter) and the IOCU countered that Americans had not depended on unfettered free enterprise "since the days of Teddy Roosevelt" (Peterson, 1984). After much effort and some compromise, the guidelines passed in 1985.

Consumer activists likened the guidelines to an international consumer bill of rights. In a brief document by diplomatic standards, the guidelines cover the fundamentals of consumer protection: Governments should adopt safety regulations, ensure that products are durable and reliable, encourage consumer education and the provision of accurate consumer information, establish mechanisms for redress if consumers experience problems with products, and guarantee freedom for consumers in organizing themselves into groups capable of presenting the views of consumers as part of the policymaking process. Additional paragraphs are devoted to the need for establishing standards that ensure the safety of food, water, and pharmaceuticals.

The Consumer Protection Guidelines were designed to be effectual, so the UN organized two international conferences (in Uruguay and Thailand) to help countries understand and implement them. IOCU also held workshops in Asia and Africa. Gradually, the guidelines were translated into legislation. One of the earliest examples was India's Consumer Protection Act of 1986 (COPRA). Among other features, COPRA promotes the consumer right to redress by creating an Indian version of what is known in the United States as small claims court. In 1993, Japan passed its first product liability law. In Africa, because of the guidelines, a number of countries established departments of consumer affairs. The Consumer Council of Zimbabwe launched a campaign for the establishment of a small claims court that achieved success in 1992. Many countries in Latin America used the guidelines to lobby for broad consumer protection laws or the explicit inclusion of the concept of consumer rights in new constitutions (e.g., Argentina, Brazil, Colombia, and Costa Rica).

As conditions for the world's consumers have changed, the guidelines have been subject to revision. In light of increased environmental awareness, IOCU, which changed its name to Consumers International (CI), urged the UN in the mid-1990s to broaden the scope of the guidelines to address the question of environmentally sustainable consumption. The UN did so in 1999. A more extensive updating of the guidelines is currently underway under the auspices of the United Nations Conference on Trade and Development (UNCTAD), the UN body responsible for consumer protection and competition policy. UNCTAD convened high-level meetings of experts in both 2012 and 2013, and it aims to submit a revised version of the guidelines for a vote by 2015.

So far, there is agreement that the guidelines need to reflect the digital age. A representative of Consumers International points out that when the guidelines were last amended in 1999, "the iPod had not yet been invented, Wikipedia would not exist for another couple of years (nor Facebook for another five), and a new PC had one-eighth as much memory as a modern smartphone" (Malcolm, 2012). Accordingly, CI and other consumer activists would like the guidelines to provide online privacy protections, support consumer access to and fair use of copyrighted works, and protect consumers when engaged in electronic commerce.

In addition to the inclusion of computer-related concerns, most parties to the negotiations regarding revisions to the guidelines also agree that the financial marketplace has become more complex and important since the guidelines were created and last revised. For example, most consumers in Africa, Asia, and Latin America once had little or no access to formal banking institutions. Today, though access to basic banking services is far from assured, many of these consumers are using their mobile phones to perform banking functions. Hence, consumer activists want the guidelines to promote both increased access to financial services and both consumer education and protection for those who are engaged in online banking, including the sending of remittances across national borders.

Revisions to the guidelines that address additional issues are more controversial. For example, many consumer activists from less developed countries want the guidelines to take a stronger stand with respect to the fulfillment of basic consumer needs regarding water, energy, transportation, and housing. Other activists want the guidelines to address collective redress (e.g., through class action lawsuits), not just individual redress. According to Robin Simpson, a representative of CI involved in the negotiations, there is an unspoken divide among the delegations. The richer countries want the revisions confined to financial services and electronic commerce, and the rest of the delegations want a more comprehensive set of revisions. The latter group bristles at the accusation that they have a "laundry list" of relatively unimportant issues (Simpson, 2013).

Still, the disagreements over changes to the guidelines should be placed in context. The debate is over specific issues to be included or excluded. No longer is there any disagreement over whether the guidelines should exist and whether they should be subject to periodic revision. The guidelines have therefore achieved their primary purpose of enshrining the idea that governments around the world have a basic responsibility to their consumers.

Robert N. Mayer

See also: Consumers International; Peterson, Esther

Further Reading

Harland, David. 1987. "The United Nations Guidelines for Consumer Protection." *Journal of Consumer Policy* 10: 245–266.

Malcolm, Jeremy. 2012. "UN's Consumer Protection Guidelines Must Reflect the Digital Age." *Consumers International Blog*, August 1. http://consumersinternational.blogspot.com/2012/08/uns-consumer-protection-guidelines-must.html.

Peterson, Esther. 1984. "U.S. vs. Third-World Consumer Protection." *New York Times*, October 12. www.nytimes.com/1984/10/12/opinion/l-us-vs-third-world-consumer-protection-003930.html.

Simpson, Robin. 2013. "Life and Death Consumer Issues Are Not a 'Laundry List.'" *Consumers International Blog*, July 17. http://consumersinternational.blogspot.com/2013/07/life-and-death-consumer-issues-are-not.html.

UTILITY ADVOCACY

See Electricity Service Advocacy; Energy Advocacy; State Utility Advocacy; Telephone Consumer Advocacy

V

"VICTIM" ACTIVISM

See Product Safety "Victim" Activism

VIRGINIA CITIZENS CONSUMER COUNCIL

Since 1966, the Virginia Citizens Consumer Council (VCCC) has been one of the nation's most effective state and local consumer groups run largely by volunteers. It was founded by Sacha Miller, Jane Rausch, and Doris Behr, northern Virginia housewives who banded together to protest rising meat prices. They picketed supermarkets, demanding an end to unnecessary services, such as trading stamps, that raised food prices. Since then, VCCC has served as the principal voice of Virginia consumers on a broad array of issues.

During the organization's first decade, dozens of volunteers organized chapters in different areas of the state. Legal authority was vested in a board of directors, which included chapter presidents. However, the chapters were given great autonomy to develop initiatives, which included lobbying, regulatory intervention, litigation, complaint handling, and consumer education. The chapters and their volunteers played important roles in enactment of the Virginia Consumer Protection Act (1977), a favorable U.S. Supreme Court decision (1976) allowing the advertising of prescription drugs, passage of a strong new-car "lemon law" (1984), mandated public representation on health regulatory boards, and the establishment of local consumer protection offices.

VCCC never generated a significant stream of income that allowed it to institutionalize itself, but it did attract highly effective volunteer leaders. In its first decade, Lynn Jordan, Judy Kory, Helen Savage, and Barbara Bitters were especially active. By 1986, after most of them had taken government consumer positions or moved on to other challenges, VCCC was revived by Jean Ann Fox, a home economist who had served as a Pennsylvania consumer protection official. Fox established herself as a presence in the statehouse, lobbying successfully for reforms including lower credit life insurance prices, tougher regulation of home contractors, the strengthening of Virginia's consumer protection law, and preservation of the Virginia Office of Consumer Affairs.

During Fox's term, VCCC was also active in utility regulation, participating on behalf of residential ratepayers in Virginia Power rate cases, Verizon telephone cases, and other dockets at the State Corporation Commission. VCCC joined industrial customers and the attorney general in successfully challenging a Virginia Power rate increase at the Virginia Supreme Court. With a budget rarely exceeding $30,000, VCCC also conducted many consumer price surveys, published guides to various services, and held an annual consumer conference that brought together consumer leaders and public officials. In recognition of her capability and contributions, both Consumers Union and Consumer Federation of America (CFA) elected her to leadership positions within their respective organizations.

When Fox joined the staff of CFA as director of consumer protection in 1997, she turned leadership of VCCC over to Irene Leech, a professor of consumer studies at Virginia Tech University. Leech continued the work of Fox with an emphasis on electricity deregulation, telecommunications deregulation, predatory lending, food safety, and general consumer protection. She has maintained working relationships, and communicated frequently, with state administrative, regulatory, and legislative officials. Often involving students in research and education projects, she has worked closely with advocates from AARP and the Virginia Poverty Law Center and, on electric issues, with business and industrial customers. To communicate with the public, VCCC has used email lists, social media, and frequent interviews with news media.

For more than a decade, Virginia advocates have been challenged by an increasingly pro-business, antiregulation state government symbolized by the governor's 2010 slogan: "Virginia: Open for Business." With a general assembly that has been strongly influenced by the Tea Party, the primary mission of VCCC has been to preserve existing protections. Nevertheless, the indefatigable Leech and other volunteers have worked hard to take advantage of any opportunity to advance the consumer interest. For example, their work with AARP to gain mandatory Renewable Portfolio Standards for electricity led to voluntary standards. And their frequent criticism of predatory behavior by utilities and financial institutions has helped restrain the conduct of these businesses. Leech has also been a leader in the Consumer Federation of America, where she has served as president and chair of the policy resolutions committee.

Stephen Brobeck, Jean Ann Fox

See also: State and Local Consumer Advocacy Groups

Further Reading

Anderson, Belinda. 1987. "Consumer Group Fights Never-Ending Battle." *Roanoke Times and World-News* (April 6): B, 2.

Evans, Sandra. 1990. "Volunteers Take Consumer Causes to Richmond." *Washington Post* (March 1).

Martz, Michael, and Paula Squires. 1993. "Fox 'Shatters Stereotype' of a Consumers' Advocate." *Richmond Times-Dispatch* (September 7): B6+.

Nelson, Helen. n.d. *A Guide to Consumer Action.* Report issued by the Office of Education, U.S. Department of Health, Education, and Welfare.

W

WARNE, COLSTON E. (1900–1987)

From the 1930s to the 1960s, Colston Estey Warne was the most influential consumer leader in the country. He helped guide Consumers Union as it grew into the largest and most effective consumer organization in the world, and he was instrumental in the establishment of organizations ranging from the International Organization of Consumers Unions (now Consumers International) to the American Council on Consumer Interests. Moreover, the combination of his ethical commitments and scientific rigor helped ensure that the consumer movement institutionalized itself as an important conscience and monitor of business practices in a free market economy.

Warne was born in 1900 in the Finger Lakes region of central New York State. His father was a farmer, a country store operator, and a pillar of the Presbyterian church. As a college student at nearby Cornell University, Warne was introduced to the writings of Thorstein Veblen as well as to his future wife, Frances Lee Corbett. After his marriage, Warne studied money and banking at the University of Chicago, where his most influential experience was studying with Paul H. Douglas, who introduced him to the field of labor relations and to the international cooperative movement. Illinois cooperatives was the subject of his doctoral dissertation.

Warne's teaching career began at the University of Denver and continued at the University of Pittsburgh (which he left in 1930 after a protest against infringement of academic freedom). He settled at Amherst College, where he worked as an economist for some forty years. He died in 1987.

While at Amherst, Warne did much more than teach and undertake research. In the summer of 1933, for example, he assisted in the training of key organizers of the Congress of Industrial Organizations (CIO). In 1935, when Consumers Union split from Consumers' Research over a labor dispute, Warne became president of the new pro-labor organization.

Warne hoped that Consumers Union would represent a joint effort of consumers and workers to raise consumer living standards, chiefly through product testing, but the labor movement was too occupied with its own challenges to join the effort. Instead, teachers, scientists, engineers, and other professionals recognized the potential importance of a product-testing organization. Warne insisted, however, that Consumers Union not limit its activities to product testing and the publication of testing results in *Consumer Reports*, but that it also serve as an advocate for consumers on a broad range of issues in numerous forums. This vision, as much as anything, strengthened the organization's commitment to communicating with policymakers, publishing books, subsidizing consumer advocacy, and promoting the international consumer movement.

Warne played critically important roles in creating and advancing other consumer institutions. In 1953, he conceived the idea of educators' organizing themselves into a group, which became the American Council on Consumer Interests. In the 1950s and 1960s, Warne actively promoted the spread of grassroots consumer organizations. He persuaded Consumers Union to assess the grassroots consumer movement and then support it. From the late 1980s to the present, Consumers Union contributed funds, through the Consumer Federation of America, to state and local groups. Today, a Consumers Union fund bearing his name helps support other consumer endeavors as well.

Warne was also instrumental in organizing consumer movements in other countries and coordinating their efforts. His travels, communications with advocates outside the United States, and Consumers Union's monitoring of their activities set the stage for the creation, in 1960, of the International Organization of Consumers Unions (now Consumers International). Warne served as the group's president for the next decade, and to this day Consumers Union continues to provide substantial financial support to the international group.

Warne contributed to the public interest in numerous other ways. In the mid-1930s, he was president of the People's Lobby. In the late 1940s, he served on the first Consumer Advisory Committee to the President's Council of Economic Advisers. In 1962, he served a two-year term as a member of the Consumer Advisory Council to the President. Yet more important than any formal position was his effective advocacy of a vision for a more ethical, consumer-friendly society.

Stephen Brobeck

See also: American Council on Consumer Interests; Consumers International; Consumers Union/Consumer Reports

Further Reading

Gordon, Leland J. 1970. "Colston Estey Warne: Mr. Consumer." *Journal of Consumer Affairs* 4 (winter): 89–92.

Morse, Richard L. D., ed. 1993. *The Consumer Movement: Lectures by Colston E. Warne.* Manhattan, KS: Family Economic Trust Press.

Newell, Barbara Warne. 1980. "Tribute to Colston E. Warne." *Journal of Consumer Affairs* 14 (summer): 1–8.

WARRANTY ADVOCACY

Congressional enactment of the Magnuson–Moss Warranty and Federal Trade Improvement Act in 1975 was the culmination of more than a decade of work by Senator Warren Magnuson (D-WA), his staff, regulators, and consumer advocates. It established required disclosures and content standards for warranty clauses in consumer contracts, but, perhaps more significant, it expanded the authority of the Federal Trade Commission (FTC). Since then, Congress has not significantly modified the law's warranty protections.

One would have expected warranty legislation during the 1920s and 1930s, because consumers of that era were aggravated by a flood of shoddy merchandise at bargain prices. However, there was no outcry for legislation regarding warranty protection. The most notable consumer writers at the time, though discussing a myriad of consumer problems, paid scant attention to warranties. Neither *Consumer Reports* nor *Consumers Research*, the primary consumer magazines of that era, editorialized for warranty regulation. The primary consumer problems in this period were health and safety: the specter of children dying from some industry practice overshadowed weak and deceptive warranties.

During the late 1950s and 1960s, the FTC received a deluge of complaints about product warranties from consumers who were particularly upset about those on automobiles. In 1969, the agency commissioned the Task Force on Appliance Warranties and Service to study these problems. In research that included examination of 200 warranties used by fifty manufacturers, the Task Force found that consumers did not understand these warranties, in part because the warranties were deceptive. It concluded that rather than being an assurance of product reliability, as many consumers believed, warranties were used by manufacturers to limit their product liability. Yet warranty issues remained a low priority among those inside and out of government seeking to publicize consumer problems. Not even Senator Warren G. Magnuson (D-WA), whose name would later become synonymous with warranty reform, mentioned warranty problems in his 1968 book *The Dark Side of the Marketplace*.

In the 1960s, consumer groups were not yet well established as a lobbying force, so it fell to congressmen and their staff to serve as consumer advocates by responding to consumer dissatisfaction regarding warranties. In addition to establishing new warranty protections, the staffers saw an opportunity to give the FTC greater authority to make and enforce rules not only related to warranties but other product sales features as well. The key staffer was Michael Pertschuk, who joined Senator Magnuson's staff in 1964 and by the late 1960s was chief counsel for the Senate Commerce Committee that Magnuson chaired. More than anyone else, Pertschuk built early support for legislation within Congress, including the office of Senator Frank Moss (D-UT), who chaired the Commerce Committee's consumer subcommittee. Pertschuk was aided by a sharp critique of the FTC—*The Nader Report on the Federal Trade Commission*, written by several of Nader's Raiders and published in 1969. The report spotlighted the ineffectiveness of the agency, and its findings were echoed a few months later by a commission of the American Bar Association.

In the early 1970s, the Commerce Committee organized hearings that exposed warranty problems and considered specific reforms. In 1971, President Nixon's presidential message to Congress on a "Buyer's Bill of Rights" included a proposed Fair Warranty Disclosure Act and additional authority for the FTC. Newly established national consumer groups joined the campaign for congressional reforms. Joan Claybrook, director and chief lobbyist for Congress Watch (which had been created by Ralph Nader), was particularly active and effective in building congressional support. She was often accompanied by Carol Tucker Foreman, the executive director and chief lobbyist of the Consumer Federation of America. Both worked closely with Pertschuk in this effort to win warranty and FTC reforms.

After years of advocacy, these congressional and consumer reformers were able to persuade Congress to enact legislation, which was signed into law by President Gerald Ford. In 1977, President Jimmy Carter appointed Pertschuk chairman of the FTC. In that role, he aggressively sought to utilize the new authority granted under the Magnuson–Moss Act to the FTC, including issuing rules implementing the warranty provisions of the law.

John R. Burton

See also: Congressional Consumer Advocacy

Further Reading

Federal Trade Commission. 1968. *Staff Report on Automobile Warranties*. Washington, DC: Government Printing Office.
Jones, Mary Gardiner. 1988. "The Federal Trade Commission in 1968: Times of Turmoil and Response," *Journal of Public Policy and Marketing* 7: 1–10.
Pertschuk, Michael. 1982. *Revolt against Regulation*. Berkeley: University of California Press.

WARREN, ELIZABETH (1949–)

Elizabeth Warren is a progressive who, over the past decade, has been the nation's most visible and influential financial services reformer. Since her 2010 election as U.S. senator from Massachusetts, Warren has continued to advocate for reforms in the financial services area but has also spoken out on other progressive issues, including minimum wage increases, net neutrality, and gender equality.

Warren's progressive commitments were shaped by her experience growing up. Born (in 1949) and raised in Oklahoma by parents who struggled financially, Warren was expected to get married and have children at a young age, which she did before finishing school. But her debating skills and accomplishments won her a college scholarship at George Washington University, and after moving back to Houston following her sophomore year, the young mother earned a college degree at the University of Houston.

After moving to northern New Jersey because of her husband's career, she earned a law degree at Rutgers University, then began a career teaching law that took her from the University of Houston, to the University of Texas, to the University of Pennsylvania, and finally in 1992, to Harvard University. In 1995, she was appointed Leo Gottlieb professor of law at Harvard. In 1978, she divorced her husband and, in 1980, married Bruce Mann, a law professor now at Harvard, who has written extensively about financial services issues.

Warren's research interests in bankruptcy provided opportunities that eventually led to her emergence as a consumer leader. Her research in the late 1980s and 1990s made her a national expert on the subject. It also convinced her that efforts by consumer creditors to persuade Congress to restrict consumer access to bankruptcy were unfair. In 1995, she began advising the National Bankruptcy Review Commission, which rejected the industry's proposed restrictions, and joined national consumer groups fighting against "bankruptcy reform" legislation that incorporated these restrictions. These efforts succeeded in modifying the legislation somewhat and delaying its passage (which came in 2005) for nine years.

During this period, Warren continued her research (now with colleagues), which demonstrated, among other findings, that medical bills were responsible for many personal bankruptcies. She also began expanding the scope of her research and writing to the economic plight of the middle class. Her 2001 book *The Fragile Middle Class: Americans in Debt* (with Teresa Sullivan and Jay Westbrook) linked rising consumer indebtedness to other social problems, such as job and family insecurities. Her 2004 book *The Two-Income Trap: Why Middle-Class Parents Are Going Broke* (with daughter Amelia Warren Tyagi) expanded this analysis, arguing that middle-class households were in worse shape financially than they had been decades earlier. This book caught the attention of press and policymakers, greatly increasing Warren's public visibility.

Warren's visibility grew even more after Senate Majority Leader Harry Reid (D-NV) appointed her, in 2008, chair of the Congressional Oversight Panel (COP) that had been created to oversee implementation of congressional legislation in response to the Great Recession of the late 2000s. This panel released a series of reports on diverse financial services topics, including foreclosure mitigation, the AIG bailout, and the Troubled Asset Relief Program (TARP).

Even before her appointment to COP, though, Warren was speaking out about the "tricks and traps" employed by consumer lenders to increase their profits at the expense of borrowers. And in the summer of 2007, she published an article—"Unsafe at Any Rate" in the journal *Democracy*—that proposed creation of a new federal agency with sole responsibility for protecting consumers in the financial services marketplace. This proposal won enthusiastic support not only from national consumer groups, but also from allied community, women's, and labor organizations. It became the top priority of a new financial reform coalition, Americans for Financial Reform, that was initiated at an April 2009 meeting of these groups at which Warren was a featured speaker. Chances for approval of the proposed agency improved considerably when Warren persuaded Congressman Barney Frank, the influential leader of the House Financial Services Committee, to include the agency—now named the Consumer Financial Protection Bureau (CFPB)—in reform legislation.

After that legislation—the Wall Street Reform and Consumer Protection Act—was signed into law by President Obama in July 2010, Warren led creation of the agency as special assistant to the president. While consumer leaders hoped that she would be appointed the bureau's first director, opposition from Republican leaders needed to confirm the appointment persuaded the president to appoint former Ohio attorney general Richard Cordray. Warren then stepped aside but also announced her intention to run for U.S. senator in Massachusetts against Senator Scott Brown, a Republican who had won a special 2010 election after the death of Senator Ted Kennedy.

Warren defeated Brown handily and, after joining the Senate, was appointed to its Banking Committee, where she gained a bully pulpit to criticize banking practices and an advantageous position to propose additional reforms. She then proceeded to regularly fault regulators for failing to criminally prosecute banking leaders whose illegal practices had wrecked the financial services system. She also proposed legislation to reduce the costs of student loans, which now exceed $1 trillion. Warren has spoken out in favor of other progressive reforms—related to the workplace, social welfare, communications, the environment, and gender—and has been discussed frequently as a future presidential candidate.

Stephen Brobeck

See also: Americans for Financial Reform; Credit Card Advocacy

Further Reading

Kirsch, Larry, and Robert N. Mayer. 2013. *Financial Justice: The People's Campaign to Stop Lender Abuse.* Santa Barbara, CA: Praeger.
Warren, Elizabeth. 2014. *A Fighting Chance.* New York: Metropolitan Books.
Warren, Elizabeth. 2004. *The Two-Income Trap: Why Middle-Class Parents Are Going Broke.* New York: Basic Books.
Warren, Elizabeth. 2007. "Unsafe at Any Rate." *Democracy* 5 (summer): 8–19.

WEST AFRICAN CONSUMER MOVEMENTS

West Africa, as defined by the UN, is a region consisting of seventeen countries. Its largest countries in terms of population are Nigeria (the most populous country in Africa), Ghana, and the Ivory Coast. Although west Africa is still one of the poorest regions of the world, growth rates in gross domestic product (GDP) there are the highest in Africa. This translates into a rise in the standard of living for west African consumers, an increase in reliance on imported goods, increased brand consciousness, and a surge in demand for consumer protection. At the same time, huge numbers of people remain poor, and income inequality is high by international standards. These facts, too, have stimulated consumer activism in west Africa.

The most pressing consumer concerns of west Africans center on basic necessities. Access to clean water and sanitation is a major problem in most countries in this region. Whereas three-quarters of the population in Senegal and Ivory Coast have access to safe drinking water, less than half of the populace in Mauritania, Burkina Faso, and Guinea does. Rates of access to sanitation are lower still. Access to electricity is also confined to a minority of the population in most west Africa countries, but ironically, rates of mobile phone subscriptions are often well above 50 percent, even in the poorest west African countries. In many west African countries, less than 10 percent of the population has an account with a financial institution. Making financial transactions via a cell phone is gaining in popularity, but few consumer protections are currently in place.

Literacy—a crucial tool of consumer empowerment—is a scarce commodity in many west African countries, with the literacy rate among males substantially outpacing the rate for females. For example, Mali has the lowest adult literacy rate in the region, with 35 percent of adult males being literate and only 18 percent of adult females. Even for literate consumers, the labels of the products they buy may not be printed in their local language. This is an especially important problem in the case of pharmaceuticals.

Overview

Like other low-income countries, countries in west Africa do not necessarily have well-established governmental institutions of consumer protection, but private consumer organizations are increasingly prominent. Of the seventeen countries in west Africa, nine have at least one organization that belongs to Consumers International (CI), the umbrella organization for the world's consumer groups. All told, west Africa has five full members of CI, eleven affiliate members, and two government supporters. Most of the full members were approved only recently, suggesting that in the future the region will play a more important role in consumer advocacy on an international level. CI has made it a high priority to help build consumer organizations throughout Africa and has established a regional office in South Africa. The office is in the process of cosponsoring a project with the Open Society of West Africa (OSIWA) to improve and strengthen consumer protection within three west African countries: Ghana, Nigeria, and Senegal. Some of the participating consumer organizations include Ghana's Consumer Advocacy Centre (CAC), Nigeria's Consumer Awareness Organization (CAO), and Senegal's Association for the Defense of Consumers and the Environment (ADEC). Under the project, each of these participants is required to create and maintain its own organizational website.

Social media networking has aided consumer activist groups to reach out to local consumers, raise awareness of consumer problems, and offer opportunities for problem resolution. A consumer group in Ghana provides an example. The Consumer Protection Agency of Ghana (CPA) used the social media network Facebook to warn consumers about a massive shutdown of ATMs in the capital city by Ghanaian banks, a potential problem for customers who needed to withdraw money. Advances in communication technology may help consumer activists in west Africa to better promote their objectives, raise awareness of consumer issues, and educate the public.

Activism in the Region's Largest Countries: Ghana and Nigeria

Today, Ghana is a nation of about 26 million people. In 1957, Ghana became the second country in west Africa to gain its independence. (The first, Liberia, was established as an independent nation of former slaves in 1847.) Ghana's GDP per capita is one of the highest among west African countries, as is its ranking in the United Nations Human Development Index. As one of the most rapidly growing and economically influential countries in the region, the status of its consumers as well as efforts to improve consumer protection are closely watched by its neighbors.

In recent years, Ghana's consumers have seen important improvements in access to basic products and services. Accessibility of improved water sources has reached an all-time high, with 80 percent of citizens now having access to clean drinking water. (Only about 13 percent of the population has access to improved sanitation, however.) About two-thirds of Ghanaian households have access to electricity—a high percentage by regional standards. A similar percent of households has access to a mobile phone. Nevertheless, 28 percent of Ghanaians live below the international poverty line of $1.25 per person per day, meaning that many Ghanaians struggle just to have enough to eat. The World Health Organization estimates that 14 percent of children under age 5 in Ghana are underweight. Consumer activism in Ghana occurs against this backdrop of economic improvement combined with continuing challenges.

The most important consumer organization in Ghana, the Consumer Advocacy Centre of Ghana (CAC), was established in 2008 and has recently become a full member of Consumers International. In advocating for consumers, the group seeks to prevent the distribution of banned or expired pharmaceutical products and to ensure that the marketing of legal drugs meets high ethical standards. Similarly, CAC monitors whether the marketing of infant milk formula complies with international ethical standards. The CAC also studies the quality of food in the country's urban areas as well as the introduction of genetically modified foods into the Ghanaian market. Another area of concern for CAC is the exorbitant fees charged to Ghanaian workers living abroad for transferring money (remittances) home to their families. CAC also uses social media to effectively raise awareness of consumer issues without having to worry about governmental interference.

An additional consumer organization addressing the problems of consumers in Ghana is the Consumer Partnership of Ghana (COP). Much of COP's activity is guided by the awareness that consumer education is important in Ghana. Working with government entities and other consumer organizations, COP provides opportunities for consumers to become well educated and informed about the Ghanaian marketplace and to make conscientious choices. COP is also working to make sure that the Ghanaian government lives up to its commitment to put basic elements of consumer protection into place by 2015.

Among African countries, Nigeria has the largest population (169 million). The country gained its independence from Great Britain in 1960. Nigeria's GDP is the highest in west Africa (and second only to the country of South Africa in all Africa). Along with Ghana, GDP per capita is the highest in the west African region. Nigeria differs from Ghana, however, in being far more densely populated (487 versus 267 people per square mile) and urbanized. As of 2010, two-thirds of Nigeria's population lived below the international poverty line, and 27 percent of young children are rated as malnourished, according to the World Health Organization. In terms of the United Nations Human Development Index, Nigeria ranks #153, eighteen places below Ghana. This HDI score places Nigeria in the "low" category compared to Ghana's rating as "medium." Both Nigeria's GDP per capita and HDI rankings are rising, however—an indication of improving consumer well-being.

Access to basic necessities remains a problem in Nigeria. About half of Nigerians enjoy access to electricity, and a similar percentage has mobile phone subscriptions. Sixty-one percent of citizens have access to clean water sources, but improved sanitation is accessible to only 31 percent of the population. Along with

Ghana, Nigeria has emerged as a leading country in the region in terms of its consumer movement. The Consumer Awareness Organization (CAO) has served since 2001 as Nigeria's only full member of Consumers International. CAO focuses on giving consumers a voice in problems that affect products and services, and thereby consumer well-being. CAO also aims to provide a consumer perspective to producer-focused government agencies. CAO's goal is for both producers and consumers to accept their rights and responsibilities in the marketplace. To promote the sovereignty of Nigerian consumers, the organization champions financial education for consumers. CAO believes that financial literacy is as important as reading, writing, and mathematics.

The Consumers Empowerment Organization of Nigeria (CEON), an affiliate member of Consumers International since 2008, was established in 1995. CEON advocates for consumers and works toward achievement of the United Nations' Millennium Development Goals. These goals include eradicating poverty and hunger, reducing child mortality, providing access to clean water and improved sanitation, and improving primary education—all major problems in Nigeria. Improved education, in particular, can empower low-income consumers in making better choices and thereby influence Nigeria's consumer market. Currently, CEON is working on improving the quality of mobile phone service and is demanding multiple mobile companies to compensate subscribers for poor service quality.

Another Nigerian consumer organization addressing the nation's issues is the Foundation for the Defense of Consumer Rights (FODCOR). Established in 2008, FODOR, is an affiliate member of Consumers International. The organization has the ambitious goal of eliminating all forms of exploitation by businesses. FODCOR also focuses on the efficient use of Nigeria's natural resources and prudent environmental management. FODCOR advocates for vulnerable consumers who are often victims of discrimination—women, children, and citizens living with chronic diseases like HIV/AIDS. Recently, FODCOR conducted a project to measure consumer satisfaction with local government agencies. The results were encouraging: 95 percent of complaints were resolved through facilitated dialogue, and only 3 of the 450 cases necessitated a lawsuit. FODCOR continues to seek opportunities for equal treatment of all consumers and fair treatment of consumers by government agencies.

Looking ahead, west African countries will likely experience some of the fastest economic growth rates on the continent and in the world. A major task for consumer organizations in the region is to ensure that economic growth translates into increased well-being for consumers. Whether working separately or cooperatively, consumer activist groups within the region plan to advocate forcefully for consumers.

Robert N. Mayer

See also: Consumers International; East African Consumer Movements

Further Reading

Ijewere, Anthony A., and Stephen O. Obeki. 2011. "Consumerism in Nigeria." *Journal of Research in International Development* 9, no. 2: 186–192.

Nkamnebe, Anayo D., Edwin Idoko, and S. E. Kalu. 2009. "Consumer Protection in Market Transactions in Nigeria." *Innovative Marketing* 5, no. 4: 89–94.

United Nations. 2014. *The Millennium Development Goals Report 2014.* New York: United Nations.

United Nations Development Program. 2014. *Human Development Reports 2014.* New York: United Nations.

WHISTLEBLOWERS

In the Whistleblower Protection Act for federal civil service employees, whistleblowers are defined as those who disclose information evidencing a reasonable belief of illegality, abuse of authority, gross mismanagement, or a substantial and specific danger to public health or safety. Practically, they are individuals who exercise freedom of speech to challenge abuses of power that betray the public trust. Many of these abuses affect consumers.

Whistleblowers cannot be stereotyped by their motives, which range from idealism to vengeance, or by their jobs, which range from maintenance workers to chief executive officers. What they have in common is knowledge they feel compelled to act on to be true to themselves. Deciding whether to blow the whistle means making a choice between valid but conflicting values. The conflict raises issues of personal loyalty and livelihood. Loyalty to one's family involves meeting its income needs, and loyalty to colleagues often discourages whistleblowing.

But whistleblowers often feel another loyalty—a loyalty to their nation as patriots, to the law as citizens, and to the communities where they live as neighbors. That is why 90 percent of scientific whistleblowers in a Research Triangle Institute study said they probably would do it again, even though more than two-thirds reported suffering harassment or serious reprisal. And their actions can make a difference. Studies by PricewaterhouseCoopers and by the Association of Certified Fraud Auditors have confirmed that more corporate fraud is exposed by employee whistleblowers than by compliance departments, audits, and law enforcement combined.

Whether as anonymous informants in the style of "Deep Throat" or as public dissenters, whistleblowers have forced changes. The following examples of whistleblowing represent cases of consumer welfare on which the Government Accountability Project (GAP), a nonprofit, nonpartisan NGO whose mission is helping whistleblowers, has worked since 1982.

During the 1990s, whistleblowers provided the evidence that led to injunctions against two incinerators and the cancellation of three more that released toxic substances such as dioxin, arsenic, chromium, mercury, and other heavy metals into the environment in Arkansas, Indiana, Ohio, and South Carolina. In 1993, whistleblowers helped persuade the Environmental Protection Agency to declare an eighteen-month national moratorium against new incinerators and to institute a combustion policy that established dioxin limits for all hazardous waste incinerators.

Since 1988, whistleblowing disclosures have been the foundation for six campaigns that have succeeded in forcing the Department of Agriculture to cancel deregulation proposals that would have replaced federal meat inspection for the USDA Seal of Approval with an industry honor system. Particularly in the 1990s, whistleblowers working for the tobacco industry—such as Dr. Jeffrey Wigand, made famous by the film *The Insider*—disclosed secret industry additives in cigarettes, creating a political backlash that helped ease political pressures to blunt Food and Drug Administration (FDA) oversight and lessen restrictions on smoking. In the late 1980s and early 1990s, whistleblowing FDA scientists revealed that 80 percent of commercial milk was polluted by antibiotics and other illegal animal drugs, leading to a national testing program for retail milk sales. In the early 2000s, an FDA scientist's disclosures forced withdrawal of over a half-dozen government-approved prescription drugs that were dangerous. The most harmful of these drugs, a pain killer named Vioxx, caused some 50,000 fatal heart attacks. FDA scientists revealed that a similar problem existed with some commonly prescribed animal drugs that caused the death of family pets.

Much GAP-assisted whistleblowing has involved nuclear safety. From 1980 to 1983, at the Zimmer nuclear power plant under construction outside Cincinnati, Ohio, whistleblowers forced conversion to a different energy source by revealing that the nuclear power plant, 97 percent completed, had been built with metal from junkyards passed off as nuclear-grade steel, that many x-rays on safety welds were falsified, and that portions of the plants had never been inspected. In 1983, whistleblowers exposed illegalities that sparked a total overhaul of the post–Three Mile Island nuclear power plant cleanup.

In the financial sector, in the 1990s, whistleblowers warned corporations that financial improprieties and falsification of financial records could lead to bankruptcy for firms such as Enron. Before the recent financial crisis, they warned banks that irresponsible and predatory lending practices would backfire. In both instances, the warnings were ignored but proved prophetic.

Techniques to neutralize dissenters are numerous and can range from smear tactics to legal prosecution. Corporate whistleblowers have been prosecuted for "stealing" evidence of corporate crimes that they disclosed to government investigators. Government whistleblowers can be, and have been, prosecuted under the Espionage Act.

Whistleblowers pay a price to make a difference by "committing the truth," a term coined by Pentagon cost-control expert Ernie Fitzgerald. After his 1968 congressional testimony exposed some $2 billion in cost overruns for the C-5A Galaxy, he was treated as if he had committed a crime. Reprisals are not unique to the United States: A 1999 study from the University of Queensland in Australia found that 94 percent of informants reported direct or indirect harassment after their act of whistle blowing. The phenomenon is so common that NGOs have formed a global solidarity coalition to organize support, Whistleblowers International Network (WIN).

Tom Devine

Further Reading

Devine, Thomas, and Tarek Maassarani. 2010. *The Corporate Whistleblower Survival Guide: A Handbook for Committing the Truth.* San Francisco, CA: Berrett-Koehler Publishers, Inc.

Press, Eyal. 2013. *Beautiful Souls: Saying No, Breaking Ranks, and Heeding the Voice of Conscience in Dark Times.* New York: Farrar, Straus and Giroux.

Soeken, Don. 2014. *Don't Kill the Messenger!* Washington, DC: CreateSpace Independent Publishing Platform.

Vaughn, Robert. 2013. *The Successes and Failures of Whistleblower Laws.* Northampton, MA: Edward Elgar Publishing, Inc.

Vinten, Gerald. 1994. *Whistleblowing: Subversion or Corporate Citizenship?* New York: St. Martin's Press.

WOODSTOCK INSTITUTE

Since 1973, Woodstock Institute has worked locally and nationally for a more just financial system in which lower-wealth persons and communities, and people and communities of color, can achieve economic security and prosperity. Using the tools of applied research, policy development, coalition building, and technical assistance, the institute has built bridges between communities and policymakers in the areas of fair lending, wealth creation, and financial systems reform. Woodstock Institute is a 501(c)(3) nonprofit organization governed by a board of citizen and financial leaders. Its annual budget recently has been a little less than $1 million.

Woodstock Institute was founded in 1973 by Aaron Scheinfeld, an attorney and cofounder of a human resources consulting firm, and his wife Sylvia. Unhappy about Chicago-area redlining, predatory lending, and inequality, they decided to create a conference center in Woodstock, Illinois, where community leaders could meet and tackle issues together. When the need for a permanent presence and programmatic arm became apparent in 1973, the institute was established.

Larry Rosser was appointed the first president of the organization. Under his leadership, the organization was a leader in the successful campaigns to persuade Congress to approve the Home Mortgage Disclosure Act (HMDA) in 1975 and the Community Reinvestment Act (CRA) in 1977. Both HMDA and CRA continue to serve as the cornerstones of Woodstock's research and advocacy to this day.

One of the organization's most influential leaders was Malcolm Bush, who served as president from 1992 to 2008. Having taught at the University of Chicago then having worked for Voices for Illinois Children, Bush brought to the organization a strong policy focus. He was succeeded by Dory Rand, an attorney who had worked for many years at the Sargent Shriver National Center on Poverty Law before joining the institute staff.

One of the institute's greatest accomplishments came in 1985, when the organization and several partners negotiated, with First National Bank of Chicago, the first-ever CRA agreement. The agreement required the bank to provide $200 million in loans for lower-income communities and communities of color. Similar agreements with the Northern Trust Company and Harris Bank in the Chicago area soon followed, and CRA agreements spread to other areas of the country.

Woodstock Institute was also a leader in the movement to support Community Development Financial Institutions (CDFI). The institute formed an exploratory committee that eventually led to the creation of the Chicago Community Loan Fund (CCLF). In 2013, CCLF invested more than $15 million in projects that help revitalize neighborhoods, stabilize families, incorporate sustainable design practices, and leverage additional investments.

Based on this experience, in 1994 Woodstock released a series of publications to document the structure and purpose of these banks, loan funds, credit unions, and other financial institutions created specifically to serve lower-income communities. Later that year, President Clinton signed the Riegle Community Development and Regulatory Improvement Act, which established a federal CDFI loan fund to allocate capital to CDFIs around the country. Since then, the fund has allocated more than $1.7 billion to CDFIs.

In 1999, Woodstock joined and became a leader in the Monsignor John Egan Campaign for Payday Loan Reform. This campaign began after a Chicago parishioner of Egan's tearfully confessed her struggles with two payday loans, which included interest rates of more than 500 percent. The statewide campaign persuaded the Illinois Department of Financial and Professional Regulation to approve consumer protections for the short-term balloon payment loans offered throughout the state. When payday lenders exploited loopholes in the rules, the campaign rallied in 2005 and again in 2010 to push successfully for legislative restrictions on abusive practices.

During the housing crisis of the past decade, Woodstock took a leading role in documenting adverse impacts and shaping policy responses. The institute joined with national partners to successfully advocate for strong new protections in the Dodd–Frank Wall Street Reform and Consumer Protection Act of 2010. After its passage, the institute supported and worked closely with the Consumer Financial Protection Bureau (CFPB), created by the legislation. Woodstock president Dory Rand was appointed to the CFPB's Consumer Advisory Board.

Since 2008, Woodstock has released reports detailing the extent of foreclosures and vacant properties that plagued lower-income communities in the Chicago region. Using this research, both the city of Chicago and the Cook County Board of Commissioners implemented vacant buildings ordinances that hold mortgage servicers, as well as property owners, accountable for registering, securing, and maintaining vacant homes. In 2013, in an effort to stabilize the region's housing market by acquiring, managing, developing, and transferring vacant and distressed properties, Woodstock worked closely with partners and Cook County Commissioner Bridget Gainer to pass a law establishing the Cook County Land Bank Authority as a redevelopment authority.

Dory Rand

See also: Mortgage Lending Reform; State and Local Consumer Advocacy Groups

Further Reading

Storch, Charles. 2008. "New Leader Dory Rand Is No Stranger to Woodstock Institute." *Chicago Tribune* (July 3).

Street, Paul L. 2007. *Racial Oppression in the Global Metropolis: A Living Black Chicago History.* Washington, DC: Rowman & Littlefield Publishers.

Contributors

Ava Alkon
Independent scholar

Erma B. Angevine (deceased)
Past president
National Consumers League

Daniel Okendo Asher
Program officer
Consumer Unity & Trust Society Africa Resource Center

Doug Blanke
Director
Public Health Law Center

David Bollier
Independent journalist

Larry Bostian
Vice president for development
School-Based Health Alliance

Angela Bradbery
Director of communications
Public Citizen

Stephen Brobeck
Executive director
Consumer Federation of America

Mark E. Budnitz
Professor of law emeritus
Georgia State University College of Law

Pedro-José Bueso Guillen
Professor of law
University of Zaragoza

John R. Burton
Professor emeritus of family and consumer studies
University of Utah

Michael Calhoun
President
Center for Responsible Lending

Antonino Serra Cambaceres
Manager of consumer justice and protection program
Consumers International

George Cheriyan
Director
CUTS International

Jeff Chester
Executive director
Center for Digital Democracy

Stephen Clapp
Senior editor
Food Chemical News

Joan Claybrook
Former president
Public Citizen

Judith N. Cohart
President
Personal Finance Employee Education Foundation

Rick Cohen
National correspondent
Nonprofit Quarterly

Mark Cooper
Research director
Consumer Federation of America

Theodore O. Cron (deceased)
Former adjunct professor, National Center for Communication Studies
George Washington University

Jeff Cronin
Director of communications
Center for Science in the Public Interest

Brenda Cude
Professor of family and consumer science
University of Georgia

Philip Cullum
Partner, consumer, and demand-side insight
Great Britain Energy Regulator/Ofgem

Lucy Delgadillo
Associate professor of family, consumer, and human development
Utah State University

Tom Devine
Legal director
Government Accountability Project

Clarence M. Ditlow
Executive director
Center for Auto Safety

Joanne Doroshow
Executive director
Center for Justice & Democracy

Leslie Durham
Graduate student in family and consumer studies
University of Utah

Karin M. Ekström
Professor of marketing
University of Borås

Steven Findlay
Managing editor
Consumer Reports Best Buy Drugs

Albert Foer
President
American Antitrust Institute

Jean Ann Fox
Financial services fellow
Consumer Federation of America

Dan Franklin
Consultant
Consumers Union/Consumer Reports

Monroe Friedman
Professor of psychology
Eastern Michigan University

Jack Gillis
Director of public affairs
Consumer Federation of America

Beth Givens
Director
Privacy Rights Clearinghouse

Linda F. Golodner
Former president
National Consumers League

David Goodfriend
President
Goodfriend Government Affairs

Monique Goyens
Director general
BEUC: The European Consumer Organisation

Susan Grant
Director of consumer protection
Consumer Federation of America

Barbara Gregg
Former director
Montgomery County Office of Consumer Affairs

Visa Heinonen
Professor of economics and management
University of Helsinki

Matthew Hilton
Professor of social history
University of Birmingham

Robert Hobbs
Deputy director
National Consumer Law Center

Thomas Hoffmann
Lecturer in law
University of Tartu (Estonia)

Julia Horwitz
Consumer protection counsel
Electronic Privacy Information Center

Jane Houlihan
Senior vice president for research
Environmental Working Group

J. Robert Hunter
Director of insurance
Consumer Federation of America

Takuya Inoue
Professor of social sciences
Ibaraki University (Japan)

Michael F. Jacobson
Executive director
Center for Science in the Public Interest

Tatjana Jovanic
Assistant professor of law
University of Belgrade

Rhoda H. Karpatkin
Past president
Consumers Union/Consumer Reports

Kathleen Keest
Independent scholar

Robert R. Kerton
Professor emeritus of economics
University of Waterloo (Canada)

Peter Kolba
Head of legal affairs
Austrian Consumers Association

Joop Koopman
Former director of consumer policy
Netherlands Ministry of Economic Affairs

Robert M. Krughoff
President
Center for the Study of Services

Irene Kull
Professor of civil labor
University of Tartu (Estonia)

Breda Kutin
President
Slovenian Consumers' Association

Jim Lardner
Communications director
Americans for Financial Reform

Hans-Peter Lehofer
Judge
Austria Supreme Administrative Court

Madeleine Lottenbach
Student
Georgetown University Law Center

Patty Lovera
Assistant director
Food & Water Watch

Jenni Mack
Chair
Superannuation Consumer Centre (Australia)

Robert N. Mayer
Professor of family and consumer studies
University of Utah

Edmund Mierzwinski
Consumer program director and senior fellow
U.S. Public Interest Research Group

Alan B. Morrison
Lerner family associate dean for public interest and public service law
George Washington University Law School

Aziza Mourassilo
Project assistant
Consumers International Middle East Office

Steven Nadel
Executive director
American Council for an Energy-Efficient Economy

Mark V. Nadel
Adjunct professor
Georgetown University McCourt School of Public Policy

Kimberly Nguyen
Graduate student in family and consumer studies
University of Utah

Gianni Nicolini
Assistant professor of banking and finance
University of Rome/Tor Vergata

Willard Ogburn
Executive director
National Consumer Law Center

Rhea Padilla
Head of media and communications
IBON Foundation (Philippines)

Karel Pavlik
Board member
dTest (Czech Republic)

Ron Pollack
Executive director
Families USA

Sonny Popowsky
Former consumer advocate
Pennsylvania Office of Consumer Advocate

Dory Rand
President
Woodstock Institute

Lucia Reisch
Professor of intercultural communication and management
Copenhagen Business School

Ira Rheingold
Executive director
National Association of Consumer Advocates

Delia Rickard
Deputy chair
Australian Competition and Consumer Commission

Grazyna Rokicka
President
Association of Polish Consumers

Karsten Ronit
Associate professor of political science
University of Copenhagen

Barbara Roper
Director of investor protection
Consumer Federation of America

Herbert Jack Rotfeld
Professor of marketing
Auburn University

Ed Rothschild
Principal
Podesta Group

Manuel-Angel López Sánchez
Professor of law
University of Navarra

George Schwartz (deceased)
Former associate professor, Department of Marketing
University of Massachusetts

Rosemary Shahan
President
Consumers for Auto Reliability and Safety

Jonathan Sheldon
Staff attorney
National Consumer Law Center

Linda Sherry
Director, national priorities
Consumer Action

Norman I. Silber
Professor of law
Hofstra University

Samuel A. Simon
Former president
Telecommunications Research and Action Center

Joshua Slocum
Executive director
Funeral Consumers Alliance

Marcelo Gomes Sodré
Professor of law
Catholic University of São Paulo

Eivind Stø
Director of research
Norwegian Institute for Consumer Research

Judith Stone
President
Safe Highways and Public Education

David A. Swankin
President
Citizen Advocacy Center

Christian Thorun
Director
Institute for Consumer Policy (Germany)

Olivia Wein
Staff attorney
National Consumer Law Center

Rachel Weintraub
Legislative director and senior counsel
Consumer Federation of America

Woody Widrow
Executive director
RAISE Texas

Jung Sung Yeo
Professor of consumer science
Seoul National University

Ying Yu
Research fellow
Wolfson College, University of Oxford

About the Editors

Stephen Brobeck, PhD, has been executive director of the Consumer Federation of America since 1980. His previously published work on social change includes *The Modern Consumer Movement: References and Resources* and ABC-CLIO's *Encyclopedia of the Consumer Movement*. Brobeck holds a doctorate in American studies from the University of Pennsylvania and has taught at several universities.

Robert N. Mayer, PhD, is professor and department chair in the Department of Family and Consumer Studies at the University of Utah. He is associate editor of ABC-CLIO's *Encyclopedia of the Consumer Movement* and coauthor of Praeger's *Financial Justice: The People's Campaign to Stop Lender Abuse*. He is also the author of *The Consumer Movement: Guardians of the Marketplace*. Mayer holds a doctorate in sociology from the University of California at Berkeley.

Index

Note: **Boldfaced** page numbers indicate the location of main entries in the reference guide.

Aaron, Harold, 367

AARP, **1–3**, 18, 71, 118, 121, 124, 159, 199, 218, 221, 230, 232–36, 251, 270, 272, 312–13, 350–51, 360, 393, 452, 454, 494

ACORN, 93–95, 262, 312

Action for a Change, 389

Action for Children's Television, **3–4**, 9

Action on Smoking and Health, 459

Adler, Robert, 242, 244, 401, 405

Advertising Advocacy, **4–11**

Advocates for Highway and Auto Safety, **11–13**, 123–24, 319, 321

Affordable Care Act, 1, 73, 95, 107, 144, 147, 199, 218, 230, 231, 236, 253

African consumer movements. *See* East African consumer movements; Kenyan consumer movement; West African consumer movements

Airline Deregulation Act, 13

Air travel advocacy, **13–15**

All-terrain vehicle advocacy, **15–17**

Alabama Appleseed, 352, 434

Alabama Arise, 352, 434

Alinksy, Saul, 93–94

Alliance for the Prudent Use of Antibiotics, 371

Alliance of Lithuanian Consumer Organizations, 41

Alt, Margie, 390

America Saves, 121, 124–25

American Academy of Pediatrics, 15, 243, 244

American Antitrust Institute, 15, 26, 409

American Civil Liberties Union, 172, 374–75

American Council for an Energy-Efficient Economy, 25

American Council on Consumer Interests, **17–19**, 117, 147, 495–96

American Public Power Association, 195, 395, 397

The American Way of Death, 221

Americans for Financial Reform, **19–20**, 68, 155, 159, 272, 295, 297, 313, 353, 391, 499

Andrus, Ethel Percy, 1

Angevine, Erma, 122

Angoff, Jay, 259, 341, 401, 469

Annunzio, Representative Frank, 167

Antitrust advocacy, **20–24**

Appliance Efficiency advocacy, **24–26**

Arab Federation for Consumers, 309

Arab Forum for Consumer Protection, 310

Ario, Joel, 259, 402

Arizona Consumer Council, 102

Ashton, Betsy, 285

Association of Consumers of Serbia, 414

Association of Massachusetts Consumers, 121, 431

Association of Polish Consumers, 364

Attorneys General. *See* State Attorney General

Aurilio, Anna, 390

Austin, Roni, 382

Australian Communications Consumer Action Network (ACCAN), 30

Australian Competition and Consumer Act, 28

Australian Competition and Consumer Commission (ACCC), 30

Australian consumer movement, **27–32**

Australian Consumers' Association, 27, 137

Austrian consumer movement, **32–36**

Austrian Consumers Association, 33

Ausubel, Lawrence, 152

Authority for Consumers and Markets, 180

Automobile insurance advocacy. *See* Insurance advocacy

Automobile Protection Association in Canada, 65

Automobile Safety Act, 104

Automobile safety advocacy. *See* Motor vehicle safety advocacy

Aviation Consumer Action Project, 13

Aviation safety advocacy. *See* Air travel advocacy

Bach, Amy, 263

Balber, Carmen, 135

Ballot propositions. *See* Initiatives and referenda

Baltic consumer movements, **39–43**

Bankruptcy Reform Act, 151, 332

Bankruptcy reform advocacy. *See* Credit card advocacy

Banzhaf, John III, 459

Baskin, Roberta, 285

Bass, Dennis, 73

Beck, Ted, 120

Becker, Dan, 315–16

Beeson, Jen, 199

Belth, Joseph, 263

Bergengren, Roy F., 112

Berman, Ellen, 195

Berman, Jerry, 374–76

Better Business Bureaus, 10, 98–99

Better Markets, 272

BEUC, 34, 39, 40, 42, **43–45**, 86–87, 161, 165, 176, 213, 226, 275, 346, 365, 416, 418–19, 428, 447, 474, 476, 485

Birnbaum, Birny, 259, 263–64

Bivens, Gordon, 17–18

Blanchard, Larry, 113

Bloom, Ellen, 243

Bogdanich, Walt, 463

Booth, Heather, 19, 196

Bourke, Nick, 360

Boxer, Senator Barbara, 244

Boycotts, **45–47**

Boyle, James, 118

Brandeis, Louis D., 128, 335

Braren, Warren, 449

Brazilian consumer movement, **47–51**

Brazilian Institute of Consumer Defense, 48, 49

Brazilian Institute of Consumer Policy and Rights, 50

Breyault, John, 338

Bridgeland, Brendan, 264

Brill, Julie, 157

British consumer movement. *See* United Kingdom consumer movement

Brobeck, Stephen, 12, 100, 123–25, 152, 259, 341, 400, 433

Brookman, Justin, 376

Brooks, Representative Jack, 258

Brown, Ann, 243, 401

Brown, Jim, 431

Brownlee, Shannon, 234

Bryan, Representative Richard, 157, 315

Budnitz, Mark, 331

Bullard, Mercer, 272

Burkholder, Rebecca, 338

Burnham, David, 374

Burros, Marian, 285

Bush, Malcolm, 506

Bush, President George W., 106, 125, 153, 316, 322, 471, 472

Buyers Up, 266, 325

Cable Television Consumer Protection and Competition Act, 53, 54

Cable television regulation, **53–57**

Calabrese, Chris, 375

Calhoun, Michael, 72

California Public Interest Group (CALPIRG), 133, 136, 158, 390, 392, 393

California Reinvestment Coalition, 352

Call for Action, 99–100, 287

Campaign for Health Security, 230

Campaign for Tobacco-Free Kids, 411, 464

Canadian Association of Consumers, 57, 58

Canadian consumer movement, **57–61**

The Car Book, 67, 124, 285, 319, 320, 404

Caribbean Consumer Council, 63

Caribbean consumer movements, **61–64**

Carter, President Jimmy, 12, 196, 318–9, 340, 490, 498

Catalyst for Payment Reform, 232

Center for Auto Safety, 12, **64–67**, 147, 196, 285, 314–15, 318–20, 322

Center for Democracy and Technology, 172, 376

Center for Digital Democracy, **67–69**, 172, 376

Center for Economic Integrity, 351, 433

Center for Economic Justice, 259

Center for Food Safety, **69–70**, 210, 211, 218
Center for Foodborne Illness, 208, 211, 382
Center for Insurance Research, 264
Center for International Consumer Protection Policy and Law, 91
Center for Justice & Democracy (CJ&D), 471
Center for Media Education, 67, 375
Center for Medicare Advocacy, 234
Center for Responsible Lending, 19, **70–72**, 153, 296, 312, 349, 354, 376, 408
Center for Science in the Public Interest, 9, 70, **72–78**, 208–9, 211, 408
Center for Study of Responsive Law, 324, 327
Center for the Study of Services, **78–83**, 147
Centers for Disease Control and Prevention, 149, 207, 371
Central American consumer movements, **83–85**
Central and Eastern European consumer movements, **85–88**
Central Union of Consumer Cooperatives, 202
Change.org, 236, 267
Charren, Peggy, 3, 9
Chase, Catherine, 12
Chase, Stuart, 141, 283
Chatzky, Jean, 2, 285
Checkbook magazine. *See* Center for the Study of Services/Consumers' Checkbook
Chester, Jeff, 67, 375–76
Chicago Consumer Coalition, 432–33
Child Protection and Toy Safety Act, 241
Children's Online Privacy Protection Act, 375
Children's Television Education Act, 4
Chinese consumer movement, **88–92**
Chinese Consumers' Association, 90
Cipollone, Rose, 461
Citizen Action Illinois, 353
Citizen Action, 19, 94, 196, 206, 229–30, 351, 469, 471
Citizen Advocacy Center, 132

Citizen Utility Boards, 123, 197, 432, 444
Citizen/Labor Energy Coalition, 196, 432
Citizens Communications Center, 450
Citizens for Home Insurance Reform, 433
Civil Aeronautics Board, 13, 302, 459
Clark, Howard, 259, 340
Claybrook, Joan, 12, 144, 197, 259, 318–19, 321, 383–84, 401, 469, 497
Clayman, Jacob, 294
Clayton Act, 21
Clean Air Act, 316, 393
Clean Water Act, 392, 393
Cleveland Consumer Action, 100, 123, 432–33
Clinton, President Bill, 105–6, 151–52, 199, 200, 208, 218, 230, 337, 401, 469, 471, 507
Coalition Against Insurance Fraud, 261
Coalition of Religious Communities in Utah, 352
Coalition on Smoking OR Health, 460, 463–64
Cohart, Judith, 118
Cohen, Stanley E., 284
Cohen, Alys, 331
Colorado PIRG, 392
Common Cause, 172
Communications Act, 3, 6, 55, 450, 452
Communications advocacy. *See* Cable Television Regulation; Digital Communications Advocacy; Internet Activism; Telephone Consumer Advocacy
Communications Policy Act, 53
Community activism, **92–96**
Community Development and Regulatory Improvement Act, 507
Community Nutrition Institute, **96–98**, 397
Complaint resolution, **98–101**
Comprehensive Smoking Education Act, 461
Concerned Consumers League of Milwaukee, 432
Concerned Families for ATV Safety, 16, 381
Conference of Consumer Organizations (COCO), **101–2**, 122
Congressional consumer advocacy, **102–8**

Congress Project, 326, 383–84
Congress Watch, 133, 242, 318, 325–26, 384–85, 391, 401, 497. *See also* Public Citizen
ConnPIRG, 390, 391, 392
Consumentenbond, 137, 173, 175, 177
Consumer Action Handbook, 99
Consumer Action Law Centre (CALC), 28
Consumer Action, 15, 100, **108–11**, 136, 153–54, 272, 296, 316, 354, 376, 408, 432–3
Consumer Advisory Board, 129–30, 507
Consumer Advisory Council, 130, 496
Consumer Advocacy Centre of Ghana, 502
Consumer Advocates in American Real Estate, 401
Consumer Assembly, 101, 121, 125
Consumer Association of Mauritius, 185
Consumer Awareness Organization, 501, 503
Consumer boycotts, 45–47
Consumer cooperatives, 32, 33, **111–17**, 121, 122
Consumer Coordination Council, 246
Consumer Credit Protection Act, 104, 328
Consumer Defense League of Nicaragua, 83
Consumer education, 6, 40, 62, 85–87, 109, 117–21, 185, 223, 225, 238, 245–46, 290, 308–9, 338, 365, 421, 424, 431, 442, 451, 490–91, 493, 502
Consumer education advocacy, **117–21**
Consumer Energy Council of America, 195, 397
Consumer Federation of America, 2, 12, 14–15, 18, 24, 54, 67, 100–101, 104, 114, **121–27**, 133, 147, 149, 151, 158, 172, 195, 208, 211, 215, 242, 253, 258, 261, 270, 286, 296, 313, 315–19, 327, 339, 349, 354, 359–60, 375, 382, 391, 397, 400–401, 403, 406, 408, 431, 451–52, 474, 477, 481, 494, 498
Consumer Federation of California, 294, 433
Consumer Financial Protection Bureau, 10, 19, 72, 99, 120, 147, 155, 167, 260, 268, 287, 296, 313, 353, 355, 356, 391, 401, 408, 433, 443,

479, 499, 507. *See also* Americans for Financial Reform; Legislative advocacy
Consumer Focus, 487, 488
Consumer Information Network, 184, 289
Consumer Insurance Interest Group, 259, 261, 341
Consumer journalism. *See* Journalism
Consumer leagues, **127–29**
Consumer Partnership of Ghana, 502
Consumer Product Safety Commission, 15, 101, 104, 124, 136, 241, 337, 381, 384, 391, 401, 405, 408
Consumer Product Safety Improvements Act, 16
Consumer Protection Agency, 248, 481, 501
Consumer Protection Association of Honduras, 83
Consumer Reports. *See* Consumers Union/Consumer Reports
Consumer representation in government agencies, **129–33**
Consumer Rights Litigation Conference, 333
Consumer Sales Practices Act, 169
Consumer Unity and Trust Society, 246, 289
Consumer Watchdog, **133–35**, 197, 261, 262, 470
Consumers Council of Canada, 60
Consumers Defense Association of the Czech Republic, 161
Consumers Education and Protection Association, 100, 432
Consumers Empowerment Organization of Nigeria, 503
Consumers Federation of Australia, 28
Consumers for Auto Reliability and Safety, 65, **135–37**
Consumers Guidance Society of India, 245
Consumers International, 18, 39, 49, 59–60, 62–63, 82–85, 87, 91, **137–41**, 144, 147, 161, 165, 176, 184, 213, 215, 226, 240, 247, 249, 275, 277–78, 289, 307, 309, 345–46, 359, 363, 371, 411, 412, 414, 416, 420–21, 425, 447, 473, 475, 485, 490, 491, 495–96, 502–3

Consumers Japan, 277–78
Consumers of Costa Rica, 84
Consumers Union of Japan, 278
Consumers Union of Russia, 412
Consumers Union/Consumer Reports, 1,
    7, 15, 17, 18, 23, 26, 57, 59, 64, 104,
    117, 121–22, 125, 136, 137, **141–47**,
    148, 149, 151, 153, 154, 156, 157,
    158–59, 215, 230–31, 234, 242,
    243–44, 251, 258, 260, 267, 271–72,
    278, 283, 293, 315, 317–18, 338,
    354, 367, 371, 375, 382, 391, 393,
    402, 408, 410, 431, 450, 452, 469,
    474, 479, 481, 483–84, 494, 495–96
Consumers' Association of Finland, 205
Consumers' Association of Penang, 305
Consumers' Association, 138, 205, 305,
    306, 417, 447, 484
Consumers' Centre of Serbia, 414
Consumers' Checkbook, 79, 285. *See also*
    Center for the Study of Services
Consumers' Research, 7, 142, 144, 283,
    367, 495
Consumption, Housing, and Environment,
    213
Cooper, Mark, 14, 124, 196, 315,
    409
Cooperative Extension, 118
Cooperative Housing Foundation, 115
Cooperative League of the USA, 112,
    116, 221
Coordination Committee for Consumer
    Organizations, 212
Corbo, Tony, 211
Cordray, Richard, 20, 499
Corporate Average Fuel Economy (CAFE),
    314
Cosmetic safety advocacy, **147–51**
Council of Better Business Bureaus,
    9, 98
Court, Jamie, 134, 197
Cowan, Belita, 368
Cowles, Nancy, 244, 381
Credit CARD Act, 71, 110, 126, 332, 360
Credit card advocacy, **151–55**
Credit report and credit score advocacy,
    155–60
Credit score advocacy. *See* Credit report
    and credit score advocacy

Credit Union National Association,
    112, 121
Credit unions, 111–13
Crenshaw, Elizabeth, 285
Critical Mass Energy Project, 386
Crowley, Sheila, 342
Cruz, Humberto, 286
Cude, Brenda, 264
Czech Association of Consumers, 86, 161
Czech Coalition of Consumers, 86
Czech Consumer Association, 86, 161
Czech consumer movement, **162**

Danish Consumer Council, 163
Danish consumer movement, **163–66**
Dartland, Walter, 437
Davies, Simon, 376
Debt collection advocacy, **166–68**
Deceptive and unfair sales practice
    protections, **168–70**
Delattre, Andre, 390
Denenberg, Herb, 259, 285, 401
Diaz, Arnold, 285
Digital communications advocacy, **170–73**
Dingell, Representative John, 270, 271
Ditlow, Clarence, 12, 64, 315, 318–19
Dixon, Pam, 376
Dodd, Senator Chris, 107, 154, 222, 287,
    297–98
Dodd, Senator Thomas, 104
Dodd–Frank. *See* Wall Street Reform and
    Consumer Protection Act
Dodge, Lowell, 64
Dolbeare, Cushing, 342
Dole, Senator Elizabeth, 320, 353
Domenitz, Janet, 390
Donley, Nancy, 211, 382
Donner, Lisa, 19
Doroshow, Joanne, 471
Douglas, Paul, 104, 122–23, 311
Dreyer, Stan, 116
Drinan, Father Robert, 331
Dubrow, Evelyn, 294
Duguay, Dara, 119
Dutch consumer movement, **173–81**

Eakes, Martin, 70, 72
East African consumer movements,
    183–86

Economic Fairness Oregon, 434
Electricity service advocacy, **186–91**
Electronic Communications Privacy Act, 375
Electronic Frontier Foundation, 172, 375
Electronic Fund Transfers Act, 356
Electronic Privacy Information Center, 172, **191–94**, 375
Ellis, Clyde T., 114
Energy Action, 195, 196
Energy advocacy, **194–97**
Energy Independence and Security Act, 126
Energy Policy and Conservation Act, 27
Energy Policy Task Force, 195
Energy Security and Independence Act, 316
Engler, Robert, 195
Enhancing Consumer Choice, 18
Environmental Action, 73, 314
Environmental Protection Agency, 26, 64, 126, 316, 460, 504
Environmental Working Group, 70, 149
Epstein, Mark S., 397
Eskin, Sandra, 211, 310
Estonian Consumers Union, 39
European Association for the Coordination of Consumer Representation, 474

Fair and Accurate Credit Transactions Act, 120, 158
Fair Credit and Charge Disclosure Act, 151
Fair Credit Reporting Act, 155, 332, 375
Fair Debt Collection Practices Act, 167–68, 332
Fair Housing Act, 311, 399
Fair Packaging and Labeling Act, 104
Families USA, 1, **199–201**, 229–31
Family Smoking Prevention and Tobacco Control Act, 461, 466
Fazal, Anwar, 138, 305
Federal Cigarette Labeling and Advertising Act, 459
Federal Communications Commission, 3, 6, 53, 67, 267, 338, 449, 452
Federal Energy Regulatory Commission, 187, 189
Federal Food, Drug, and Cosmetic Act, 103, 148, 367
Federal Hazardous Substances Act, 241
Federal Housing Administration, 126, 311

Federal Insurance Office, 260, 262
Federal Trade Commission Act, 7, 21, 103, 168–69, 436, 439
Federal Trade Commission, 7, 8, 22, 26, 67, 74, 103, 104, 108, 110, 126, 130, 134, 156, 167–68, 191, 221, 241, 255, 263, 283, 324, 333, 359, 376, 379, 382, 386, 396, 399, 401, 408, 435, 439, 449, 460, 464, 481, 483, 496–97
Federal Union of Consumers, 213
Federation of German Consumer Organizations, 225
Federation of Malaysian Consumer Associations, 306
Federation of New York Housing Cooperatives, 115
Feinstein, Senator Dianne, 243–44
Feltner, Tom, 262
Fennell, Janette, 381
Ferguson, Thomas, 234
Filene, Edward A., 112–13
Financial Counselling Australia, 28
Financial education, 87, 117, 119, 120, 488, 503. *See also* Consumer education
Financial education advocacy. *See* Consumer education advocacy
Financial Literacy and Education Commission, 120
Financial Modernization Act, 375
Finnish consumer movement, **201–6**
FINRA Investor Education Foundation, 120
Fise, Mary Ellen, 124, 242
Flammable Fabrics Act, 241
Florida Consumer Action Network, 434
Florio, Michel, 480
Flug, Jim, 196
FlyersRights, 14
Foer, Albert, 24, 409
Foley, Representative Thomas, 104
Foley, Sheila, 97
Food & Water Watch, 23, **206–7**, 208, 211
Food and Drug Administration, 68–69, 76, 97, 104, 131, 148, 207, 283, 294, 324, 360, 366, 382, 385, 408, 461, 472, 505
Food cooperatives, 115–16
Food Day, 75, 76, 97
Food safety advocacy, **207–11**
Food Safety Modernization Act, 74, 107, 209–10, 360, 405

Ford, President Gerald, 118, 340, 469
Foreman, Carol Tucker, 123, 124, 211,
    401, 497
Foundation for the Defense of Consumer
    Rights, 503
Foundation for the Resolution of
    Consumer Disputes, 174, 177
Fox, Jean Ann, 124, 349, 493
Frank, Representative Barney, 107, 287,
    298, 499
Frankfurter, Felix, 335, 336
Free Press, 172
French consumer movement, **212–15**
Front Groups, **215–20**
*The Frontier of Research in the Consumer
    Interest*, 18
Fund Democracy, 272
Fund for Public Interest Research, 389
Funeral consumer advocacy, **220–22**
Funeral Consumers Alliance, 221–22
Funeral Rule, 221–22
Furness, Betty, 285

Gahdia, Ami, 244
Gardner, Steve, 74
GASP (Group Against Smoking Pollution),
    460
Gelles, Jeff, 286
Gendel, Neil, 108
General Federation of Women's Clubs,
    366, 430
Georgia Watch, 350, 433
German consumer movement, **223–27**
Gilbert, Pamela, 136, 242, 243, 469
Gillan, Jacqueline, 12, 319
Gillis, Jack, 12, 67, 124, 285, 319, 320
Givens, Beth, 375, 378
Glantz, Stanton, 463
Global Trade Watch, 325, 384, 387
Goldfarb v. Virginia State Bar, 302
Goldman, JanLori, 375–76
Goldman, Peter, 137
Golodner, Linda, 337
Gonzalez, Representative Henry B., 157
Good Housekeeping, 282, 283
Gordon, Senator Slade, 315
Government Accountability Project, 504
Grant, Susan, 124, 337, 376
Greenberg, Sally, 243, 338

Guest, Jim, 138, 143, 144
Gurian-Sherman, Doug, 211

Haas, Ellen, 97, 397, 401
Hacker, George, 74
Haddon, William J., Jr., 318
Hall-Crawford, Mel, 125
Halloran, Jean, 211
Hamilton, Alice, 128, 335
Hanni, Kate, 14
Hansen, Michael, 211
Harak, Charlie, 331
Harap, Henry, 17
Harlem Consumer Education Council,
    432–33
Harney, Ken, 286, 400
Hartke, Senator Vance, 477
Hart–Scott–Rodino Act, 21
Hauter, Wenonah, 206, 387
Health Access in California, 229–30
Health Action International, 139, 371–72
Health Care for America Now, 230
Health insurance advocacy, **229–31**
Health Insurance Portability and
    Accountability Act, 375
Health Privacy Project, 376
Health Research Group, 149, 285, 325,
    368–69, 384–85. *See also* Public
    Citizen
Health Security Act, 200, 230
Healthcare advocacy, **231–37**
Heller, Doug, 262
Hendricks, Evan, 374
Herrmann, Robert, 18
Hill, Charles, 331
Hillebrand, Gail, 154
The History of Standard Oil, 194
Hitchcock, Cornish, 14
Hobbs, Robert, 331
Home Mortgage Disclosure Act, 256, 506
Home Ownership Equity Protection Act, 312
Homeowners insurance advocacy. *See*
    Insurance advocacy
Hong Kong Consumer Council, 237
Hong Kong consumer movement, **237–41**
Horner, Blair, 390
Household product safety advocacy, **241–44**
Housing Cooperatives, 114–15. *See also*
    Consumer cooperatives

Howat, John, 331
Hudson, Paul, 14
Hueper, Wilhelm, 367
Humphrey, Hubert ("Skip"), 463
Hunt, James, 259, 263, 340
Hunter, J. Robert, 124, 258–59, 261–63, 339, 402, 469
Hutchinson, Ruby, 27
Hutton, Deirdre, 486

Idaho Consumer Association, 431
Illinois Brick, 22
Illinois CUB, 445
Indian consumer movement, **245–48**
Indonesian consumer movement, **248–50**
Indonesian Consumers Organization, 248
Initiatives and referenda, **250–54**
Inouye, Senator Daniel, 243
Installment credit advocacy, **255–57**
Institute for Consumer Protection, 185
Insurance advocacy, **258–65**
Insurance Consumer Action Network, 261
International Organization of Consumer Unions. *See* Consumers International
Internet activism, **265–68**
Internet governance. *See* Digital communications advocacy
Inter-Republican Confederation of Consumers Societies, 411
Investment Advisers Act, 270
Investment Company Act, 270
Investor protection advocacy, **268–73**
Italian consumer movement, **273–75**

Jacobson, Michael, 9, 73, 211
Jaeger, Arthur, 397
Japan Consumers' Association, 278
Japanese consumer movement, **277–80**
Japan Housewives Association, 278
Jasny, Henry, 12
Javits, Senator Jacob, 298
Jensen, Chris, 286
Johnson, Nicholas, 450
Journalism, **281–87**
Jump$tart Coalition for Personal Financial Literacy, 119–20
The Jungle, 207, 282, 293, 407

Kaiser, Matt and Linda, 382
Kallet, Arthur, 144, 283, 367, 407

Kapor, Mitch, 375
Karpatkin, Rhoda, 18, 138, 144, 318
Karpinski, Gene, 390
Keest, Kathleen, 331
Kefauver, Senator Estes, 368, 481
Kefauver–Harris Drug Amendments, 104
Kelley, Florence, 128, 129, 334, 366, 373
Kennedy, Joseph P., 270
Kennedy, President John F., 117–18, 130, 138, 177, 212, 267, 358, 458, 477, 489
Kennedy, Senator Edward, 144, 148, 152
Kenya Consumer Organization, 289
Kenyan consumer movement, **289–91**
Kessler, David, 74, 463, 465
Kids in Danger, 244, 381
KidsAndCars.org, 381
Kimbrell, Andrew, 70, 211
Kimmelman, Gene, 54, 124
Kirk, Maureen, 390
Klein, Rachel, 199
Knauer, Virginia, 148
Konsument, 33, 34
Koppe, Fritz, 35
Korean consumer movement. *See* South Korean consumer movement
Korean National Council of Consumer Organizations, 424–25
Korn, Alan, 243
Kovack, Kenneth S., 294
Kowalcyk, Barbara, 211, 382
Kramer, Albert, 450
Kristof, Kathy, 286
Krughoff, Robert, 78
Kurtz, Michelle, 262

Labor movement, **293–96**
Latin American consumer movements. *See* Central American consumer movements; South American consumer movements
Latvian National Association for Consumer Protection, 42
Lautenberg, Senator Frank, 4
Lazzarini, Marilena, 49
Leadership Conference on Civil and Human Rights, 19, 71
Leahy, Senator Patrick, 191, 375
Lee, Stewart, 18
Leech, Irene, 494
Lefkowitz, Louis, 439

Legal advocacy. *See* Litigation
Legislative advocacy, **296–99**
Leonard, Rodney E., 97
Levin, Senator Carl, 154, 314
Levine, Laura, 119
Levitt, Arthur, 271
Levy, Stuart, 371
Lewis, Martin, 488
Liebman, Bonnie, 73
Life insurance advocacy. *See* Insurance
    advocacy
Liga del Consumidor, 83, 84
Lightner, Candy, 380
Lipsen, Linda, 258, 469
Lithuanian Consumer Institute, 41
Lithuanian Consumers Association, 41
Litigation, **299–304**
Litigation Group, 299–303, 325, 370,
    384–86, 406. *See also* Public Citizen
Lively, Randy, 119
Lobbying. *See* Legislative advocacy
Locke, Stephen, 484
Loonin, Deanne, 331
Lott, Senator Trent, 322
Lowell, Josephine Shaw, 127
Lower, Ann, 125
Lyons, Paula, 285

MADD, 380
Maffini, Maricel, 211
Maghreb Union for Consumer Protection,
    309
Magnuson, Senator Warren, 104, 122,
    241, 496–97
Magnuson–Moss Warranty Act, 64, 130,
    496, 498
Malaysian consumer movement, **305–7**
Maloney, Representative Carolyn, 107, 154
Mann, Ronald, 152
Manning, Robert, 152
Markey, Senator Edward, 6, 105, 243
Marler, Bill, 211
Maryland Citizens Consumer Council,
    397, 431
Maryland Consumer Rights Coalition, 433
Massachusetts Consumers League, 128
Massachusetts PIRG, 390
Masters, Dexter, 144
Mayer, Arnold, 294
Mayer, Caroline, 285

Mayer, Robert N., 18
Maynes, Scott, 18
Mays, Don, 244
McCain, Senator John, 321, 465
McCarran–Ferguson Act, 258, 339–40
McClure's, 282
McCurry, Dan, 433
McEldowney, Ken, 109, 153, 433
McEwen, Father Robert, 101, 431
McGuire, Andrew, 242
McKechnie, Sheila, 485
Meat Inspection Act, 103, 282
Medicare Rights Center, 234
Mellon, Margaret, 211
Merkley, Senator Jeff, 314
Metcalf, Senator Lee, 104
Metzenbaum, Senator Howard, 105, 125,
    244
Meyer, Louis, 102, 431
Michigan PIRG, 393
Middle Eastern consumer movements,
    307–10
Midwest Academy, 19, 94
Mierzwinski, Edmund, 154, 376,
    390, 478
Military Lending Act, 71, 107, 126,
    353, 409
Miller, Brad, 314
Miller, Douglas R., 401
Miller, Steven, 261
Miller, Arthur, 374
Minnesota PIRG, 393
Mintz, Morton, 284, 368
Mitford, Jessica, 221
Mondale, Senator Walter, 439
Montgomery, Kathryn, 67, 375
Moore, Mike, 463, 465
Moriarity, Erin, 285
Morningstar, Helen, 58
Morrison, Alan, 385–86
Morse, Richard L. D., 477
Mortgage lending reform, **310–14**
Moss, Diana, 24
Moss, Representative John, 241, 242
Motor vehicle fuel economy advocacy,
    314–17
Motor vehicle safety advocacy, **317–22**
Motor Voters, 65, 135, 136
The Multinational Monitor, 327, 371
Myers, Matt, 460, 464

NAACP, 67, 71, 262, 313, 349, 350

Nader, Ralph, 5, **323–28**, 339, 409, 431, 469

Nader's Raiders, 122, 284, 324, 383, 389, 409, 497

National Alliance of HUD Tenants, 457

National Appliance Energy Conservation Act, 25

National Association for Consumer Protection and Promoting Programs and Strategies from Romania, 87

National Association of Attorneys General, 8, 443

National Association of Consumer Advocates, 153, 156, 167, **328–30**, 333, 353–54, 376

National Association of Consumer Agency Administrators, 435

National Association of Federal Credit Unions, 112

National Association of Housing Cooperatives, 115

National Association of Insurance Commissioners, 258–59, 340

National Association of State Utility Consumer Advocates, 197, 432, 444, 452

National Citizens Committee for Broadcasting, 449

National Coalition for Consumer Education, 119

National Consumer Act, 167, 332, 355

National Consumer Council, 485, 487, 488

National Consumer Law Center, 26, 71, 151, 156, 170, 172, 257, 286, 296, 312, 329, **330–34**, 349, 354, 376, 408, 452

National Consumer Organization of Serbia, 414

National Consumers Forum, 185

National Consumers League, 2, 15, 23, 118–19, 121, 124, 208, 215, 243, 265, 293, **334–39**, 358, 366, 451

National Cooperative Bank, 112, 115–16. *See also* Consumer cooperatives

National Cooperative Business Association, 116, 221

National Cooperative Grocers Association, 116

National Council of Consumers and Users, 273–74

National Credit Union Administration, 112

National Endowment for Financial Education, 18, 120

National Energy Conservation and Policy Act, 25

National Environmental Law Center, 393

National Federation of Associations for Consumer Protection in Hungary, 87

National Fraud Information Center, 337

National Highway Traffic Safety Administration, 12, 64, 126, 315, 318, 319, 406, 408

National Insurance Consumer Organization, 124, 258, **339–41**, 410, 469

National Low Income Housing Coalition, **341–43**

National Minimum Drinking Age Act, 380

National Partnership for Women and Families, 232

National People's Action, 94, 262, 349

National Rural Electric Cooperative Association, 114, 121, 195

National Safe Kids Campaign, 243

National Tenants Organization, 456

National Tenants Union, 456

National Women's Health Network, 369

Natural Resources Defense Council, 25, 211, 316

NCPIRG, 392

Neighborhood Economic Development Advocacy Project, 433

Nelson, Helen, 18, 431

Nelson, Senator Bill, 107, 244

Nelson, Senator Gaylord, 104, 369

Neltner, Tom, 211

Netherlands consumer movement. *See* Dutch consumer movement

Network neutrality. *See* Digital communications advocacy

New America Foundation, 172

New Economy Project, 433

New Jersey Citizen Action, 434

New Jersey Consumers League, 128, 335

New York City Consumers League, 127

Newman, Paul, 196

Niagara Frontier Consumer Association, 432

NJPIRG, 393, 394

Nonsmokers' Rights, 460

North American Securities Administrators Association, 271

North Carolina Anti-Predatory Lending Law, 71

North Carolina Citizens Consumer Council, 431

Norwegian Consumer Council, 343, 345–46

Norwegian consumer movement, **343–48**

Nutrition Action Healthletter, 73, 74, 75

Nutrition Labeling and Education Act, 73, 74

NYPIRG, 124, 390, 391, 392, 393, 394

O'Reilly, Kathleen, 123

Obama, President Barack, 14, 20, 92, 107, 154, 211, 230, 316, 322, 338, 388, 390, 401, 499

Ochieng, Samuel, 289

Ogburn, Willard, 331

Ohio Consumers League, 128

Ohio PIRG, 393

Olsson, Erik, 211

Online Privacy Protection Act, 68

Option consommateurs, 60

Oregon Consumers League, 128

Oregon CUB, 445

Oregon PIRG, 259, 390, 392, 393

OSPIRG, 392

Ottinger, Representative Richard, 104

Overtreated: Why Too Much Medicine is Making Us Sicker and Poorer, 234

Pace, Stephen, 114

Pachtner, Kay, 100, 108

Packard, Vance, 5, 374

Parents for Window Blind Safety, 381

Patient Privacy Rights, 376

Patman, Representative Wright, 112

Payday loan advocacy, **349–54**

Payment protection advocacy, **354–58**

Pecora, Ferdinand, 269

Peel, Deborah, 376

Pellegrini, Cindy, 244

Pennsylvania Citizens Consumer Council, 431

Pennsylvania Office of Consumer Advocate, 188, 454

Percy, Senator Frank, 298

Perkins, Frances, 128, 336

Pertschuk, Michael, 10, 241, 242, 401, 460, 497

Peterson, Esther, 18, 101, 121, 130, 139, 259, 294, 341, **358–59**, 402, 481, 482, 490

Pew Charitable Trusts, 153, 154, 349, **359–61**, 382, 408, 479

Phelps, Douglas, 390

Philippine consumer movement, **361–64**

Pills That Don't Work, 370

Pittle, R. David, 242, 401

Pittsburgh Alliance for Consumer Protection, 432

Plunkett, Travis, 124, 152, 262, 360

Poison Prevention Packaging Act, 241

Polish consumer movement, **364–66**

The Politics of Oil, 195

Pollack, Ron, 199

Pollack-Nelson, Carol, 243

Prescription drug advocacy, **366–74**

Prescription Drug User Fee Act, 372

President's Committee on Consumer Interests, 130

Price, Ray, 17

Privacy Act of 1974, 375

Privacy advocacy, **374–77**

Privacy International, 193, 376

Privacy Journal, 374

Privacy Rights Clearinghouse, 375–76, **377–79**

Privacy Times, 374, 376

Product safety advocacy. *See* Household product safety advocacy

Product safety "victim" activism, **380–83**

Proposition 10, 252

Proposition 65, 252

Proposition 103, 11, 133, 134, 259, 261, 327, 341, 470

ProPublica, 287

Protégez-Vous, 60

Proxmire, Senator William, 155, 332, 375

Pryor, Senator Mark, 243
Public Citizen Litigation Group, 14
Public Citizen, 12, 15, 124, 133, 136, 195,
    196–97, 206, 259, 260, 267, 271–72,
    285, 318, 321, 325, 341, 354, 368,
    370, **383–88**, 391, 401, 409, 469,
    471, 472, 474
Public Company Accounting and Reform
    Act, 125
Public Interest Advocacy Centre, 60
Public interest research groups, **389–95**.
    See also U.S. PIRG and related state
    groups
Public Knowledge, 24, 172
Public power, **395–97**
Public Utility Holding Company Act, 187
Public Utility Regulatory Policies Act,
    189
Public Voice for Food and Health Policy,
    97, 191, 193, **397–98**, 401
Pulliam-Weston, Liz, 286
Pure Food and Drug Act, 103, 282, 366

Que Choisir?, 213
Quinn, Jane Bryant, 2, 263, 286, 478

Rand, Dory, 506–7
Rao, John, 331
Reagan, President Ronald, 4, 130, 320
Real estate brokerage advocacy, **399–401**
Real Estate Settlement Procedures Act, 311
Refrigerator Safety Act, 241
Register, Nancy, 125
Regulators, consumer advocates as,
    401–4
Regulatory advocacy, **405–7**
Renuart, Elizabeth, 331, 349
Research, **407–10**
Rhee, Kee-Choon, 423, 425
Rheingold, Ira, 329
Ribicoff, Senator Abraham, 104, 318
Rice, Florence, 433
Richardson, Lee, 431
Rigg, Margaret, 331
Robinson–Patman Act, 21
Roosevelt, Eleanor, 129, 336
Roosevelt, President Franklin, 129, 269,
    336

Roosevelt, President Theodore, 103, 334
Roper, Barbara, 124, 272
Rosenfield, Harvey, 133, 197, 470
Rosenthal, Representative Benjamin,
    104, 481
Ross, Donald K., 389
Rosser, Larry, 506
Rossman, Stuart, 331
Rotenberg, Marc, 191, 375–76
Rotfeld, Herb, 18
Rothschild, Ed, 196
Rowe, Phyllis, 431
Roy, William, 477
Rozova, Ida, 161
Rural electric cooperatives, 111, 113–14,
    121, 196, 397. *See also* Consumer
    cooperatives
Rush, Representative Bobby, 222, 243
Russian consumer movement, **410–12**
Russianoff, Gene, 390

Sable, Robert, 331
Sandbach, Walker, 144
Sarason, Ernest, 331
Sarbanes, Senator Paul, 106, 120
Sarbanes–Oxley Act, 272
Saunders, Lauren, 154, 349
Savings advocacy. *See* Truth in savings
    advocacy
Schakowsky, Representative Jan, 150, 243
Scheinfeld, Aaron, 506
Scheinfeld, Sylvia, 506
Schlink, F.J., 141–42, 144, 283, 367, 407
Schwartz, Ari, 376
Schwartz, Teresa, 382
Seaman, Barbara, 368
Seattle Consumer Action Network, 432
Securities Act, 269
Securities and Exchange Commission, 20,
    126, 405
Securities Exchange Act, 269
Self-Help Credit Union, 70–72, 350
Serbian consumer movement, **413–15**
Service Employees International Union
    (SEIU), 19, 153
Shahan, Rosemary, 65, 135
Shea, Dermot, 431
Sheehan, John J., 294

Sheldon, Jonathan, 331
Shelisch, Peter, 412
Sheppard, Morris, 112
Sherman Act, 21
Sherry, Linda, 110, 153, 376
Shields, Currin, 102, 431
Siegel, Sylvia, 479
Sierra Club, 314–17
Silber, Norm, 18
Silbergeld, Mark, 122
Silverglade, Bruce, 74
Silvers, Damon, 272, 295
Simon, Samuel A., 450
Sinclair, Molly, 285
Sinclair, Upton, 57, 141, 207, 282, 293, 407
Singletary, Michelle, 286
Slocum, Joshua, 221
Slocum, Tyson, 197, 387
Slovene Consumers' Association, 415, 417
Slovenian consumer movement, 415–19
Small claims courts, 99, 392
Smith DeWaal, Caroline, 74, 211
Smith, Neal, 104
Smith, Peter Vicary, 485
Smith, Robert Ellis, 374
Smith, Tom "Smitty," 387
Smoking. See Tobacco activism
Sommer, Henry, 152
Sorkin, Michael, 286
South American consumer movements, 419–23
South Korean consumer movement, 423–26
Spanish consumer movement, 426–30
Staggers, Representative Harley, 104
Stanley, Jay, 375
State and local consumer advocacy groups, 430–34
State and local consumer affairs offices, 435–37
State Attorneys General, 437–43
State utility advocacy, 444–45
Stiftung Warentest, 138, 161, 224, 419
Stilp, Gene, 471
Stone, James, 259
Stone, Judith, 12, 319
STOP Foodborne Illness, 208, 211, 382

Sullivan, Representative Leonor, 104, 123, 148, 155
Susswein, Ruth, 376
Swedish consumer movement, 445–48
Swedish Consumers' Association, 446, 447

Talent, Representative Jim, 107
The Taming of the Giant Corporation, 325
Tanner, Väinö, 202
Tanzania Consumer Advocacy Society, 185
Tarbell, Ida, 194, 282
Telecommunications Act, 53, 55, 375, 453
Telecommunications Research and Action Center, 449–51
Telephone consumer advocacy, 451–55
Telephone Consumer Protection Act, 375
Tellado, Marta L., 144
Tenant activism, 455–57
Tenants and Neighbors, 457
Tenants Together, 457
Tench, David, 484
Tennessee Citizen Action, 434
Tennyson, Sharon, 18
Texas Appleseed, 352, 434
The Therapeutic Nightmare, 368
Thompson, Lea, 285
Tobacco activism, 457–68
Tobias, Andy, 261
Tort-related consumer advocacy, 468–73
Toward Utility Rate Normalization. See TURN
Trade unions. See Labor movement
Transatlantic Consumer Dialogue, 337, 376, 416, 473–77
Truth in Lending Act, 311, 332–33, 477, 479
Truth in savings advocacy, 477–79
Truth in Savings Act, 391, 477–79
TURN, 445, 479–80
Turner, Lynn, 272

U.S. Consumer Protection Agency, 481–83
U.S. Department of Agriculture, 70, 74, 76, 103, 118, 123, 207, 282, 360, 397, 401
U.S. Department of Justice, 21, 136, 257, 267, 332, 338, 400, 452, 481

U.S. PIRG, 15, 19, 124, 154, 156–59, 242–43, 271–72, 296–98, 354, 375–76, 389–95, 408, 469, 478–79

U.S. Public Interest Research Group. *See* Public interest research groups

U.S. Surgeon General, 458, 460

UDAP statutes, 169, 170

Uniform Commercial Code, 169, 354

Uniform Consumer Credit Code, 123, 167, 355

Uniform Deceptive Trade Practices Act, 169

Union des consommateurs, 60

Union for the Interests of Homeowners, 175

Union of Concerned Scientists, 206, 211, 315–16

United Food and Commercial Workers Union, 208, 294

United Kingdom consumer movement, **484–89**

United Nations Guidelines for Consumer Protection, 139, 363, **489–92**

United Policyholders, 263, 433

Unsafe at Any Speed, 8, 27, 284, 318, 323, 383, 407, 409

US Action, 94

Utility advocacy. *See* Electricity Service Advocacy; Energy Advocacy; State Utility Advocacy; Telephone Consumer Advocacy

Utility Consumers Action Network (UCAN), 378, 432, 445

Utility Reform Network, 197, 445, 479

Vacar, Tom, 65, 285

"Victim" activism. *See* Product safety "victim" activism

Video Privacy Protection Act, 375

Virginia Citizens Consumer Council, 124, 431, **493–94**

Virginia Pharmacy Board v. Virginia Citizens Consumer Council, 302

Virginia Poverty Law Center, 434, 494

Vladeck, David, 386

Waldrop, Chris, 124, 211

Wall Street Reform and Consumer Protection Act (Dodd-Frank), 19–20, 72, 107, 110, 113, 120, 126, 147, 155, 159, 260, 272, 295, 298, 313–14, 330, 332, 353, 357, 391, 405, 499, 507

Wallach, Lori, 387

Walsh, Gerri, 120

Ware, Willis, 374

Warne, Clinton, 431

Warne, Colston E., 17–18, 117, 137, **495–96**

Warranty advocacy, **496–98**

Warren, Senator Elizabeth, 19, 152, 153, 158, 391, **498–500**

Washington Community Action Network, 434

Watkins, Clint, 256

Watt, Representative Mel, 314

Waxman, Representative Henry, 105, 243, 462

Wein, Olivia, 331

Weiner, Max, 99, 432, 433

Weinstock, Susan, 360

Weintraub, Rachel, 124, 243

Weisbaum, Herb, 285

Weissman, Robert, 384

Wendlandt, Wendy, 390

West African consumer movements, **500–504**

Western Lithuania Consumer Federation, 41

Westin, Alan, 374

Wheeler–Lea Amendment, 168

Which?, 417, 484–85, 488

Whistleblowers, **504–6**

White, Lee, 195

Who Runs Congress?, 326

Wholesome Poultry Act, 104

Wiesner, Jerome, 374

Wigand, Jeffrey, 463, 505

Wiley, Harvey, 103, 366, 373, 430

Willard, Patrick, 199

Willier, William, 331

Wirth, Senator Timothy, 4

Wisconsin Consumer Act, 167

Wisconsin CUB, 445

Withers, Jan, 380

Witkowski, Chris, 14

Witoelar, Erna, 138, 249

Wolfe, Sidney, 285, 368, 385
Wolfman, Brian, 386
Woodstock Institute, 351, 353, 433, **506–8**
World Privacy Forum, 376
Wu, Chi Chi, 154, 331

Yanin, Dmitry, 411
Young, Michael, 484, 485, 486
Your Money's Worth, 5, 141, 283

Zieve, Allison, 386
Zigas, Barry, 125